The Town School

The Town School

A HISTORY OF THE HIGH SCHOOL OF GLASGOW

Brian R. W. Lockhart

First published in Great Britain in 2010 by
John Donald, an imprint of Birlinn Ltd

West Newington House
10 Newington Road
Edinburgh
EH9 1QS

www.birlinn.co.uk

ISBN: 978 1 906566 22 7

British Library Cataloguing-in-Publication Data
A catalogue record for this book is available
on request from the British Library

Typeset by Mark Blackadder

Printed and bound in Britain by
CPI Antony Rowe, Chippenham, Wiltshire

To those who follow after,
especially Fiona Irene, my first grandchild

CONTENTS

LIST OF ILLUSTRATIONS

Plate section 1

1. Site of the tomb of St Kentigern in the crypt of Glasgow Cathedral.
2. Bishop Elphinstone (1431–1514), Chancellor of Scotland, was a Grammar School pupil.
3. The Old School Building in School Wynd was the site of the Grammar School from 1461 to 1788.
4. The Lintel and Descriptive Stones, of the rebuilding of 1601, became an integral part of the School buildings.
5. Slezer's engraving of College (University) and Blackfriars' Church (1693).
6. The Grammar School building at 294 George Street was the site of the School between 1788 and 1821.
7. Sir John Moore of Corunna (1761–1809) left the Grammar School in 1772 determined on a military career.
8. Prussian Pistols were given to Sir John Moore by the Earl Marischal in 1775.
9. Colin Campbell, Lord Clyde (1792–1863), attended the Grammar School from 1797 until 1803.
10. The Sword of Lord Clyde is now housed in the High School at Anniesland.
11. Statue of General Sir Thomas Munro (1761–1827) in Madras. He was a pupil at the Grammar School from 1769 until 1772.
12. Kirkman Finlay (1773–1842), Merchant, attended the Grammar School in the 1780s.
13. Thomas Campbell (1777–1844), Poet, left the Grammar School in 1791.
14. James Lumsden (1778–1856), Philanthropist, gave over fifty years of public service to Glasgow.

34. Helen Jamieson was the last Principal of the Girls' High between 1969 and 1976.
35. The Girls' High Honours Boards are now situated at Anniesland.
36. The War Memorials are also now to be found at Anniesland.
37. The Memorial Pavilion at Old Anniesland was opened in 1927.
38. Baron Bannerman of Kildonan (1901–69) attended the High School from 1913 until 1920.
39. John Talman was Rector of the High School from 1931 until 1950.

Plate section 3

40. The Science laboratories were opened at Elmbank Street in 1887.
41. The Officers' Training Corps gained official recognition from the War Office in 1909.
42. The Assembly Hall at Elmbank Street opened in 1905.
43. Science laboratory in the Girls' High, 1955.
44. Nina Logan was the legendary Kindergarten Mistress from 1916 until 1953.
45. David Lees was the last Rector of the old High School from 1950 until 1976.
46. Prof. Sir Neil MacCormick (1941–2009) was arguably 'the most distinguished Former Pupil of the High School of the second half of the twentieth century'.
47. Norman S.S. Thomson (1917–81) is regarded as 'Mr High School'.
48. Baron Macfarlane of Bearsden was the influential Chairman of Directors of the High School from 1979 until 1992 and since then has been its Honorary President.
49. Honor Baker was the refounder of Drewsteignton School in 1962 and Principal until 1973. Her husband, Andrew Baker, was Chair of Drewsteignton and then, between 1976 and 1979, of the High School.
50. A Junior School Event with Miss Eileen Robertson and Lord and Lady Macfarlane.
51. Eric Harle was Rector of the High School from 1976 until 1983.
52. Dr Robin Easton was Rector of the High School from 1983 until 2004.
53. The Jimmie Ireland Stand is one of the most recent additions at Old Anniesland.
54. The James Highgate (Art) Building was named after a significant Former Pupil and benefactor.

PREFACE

Following a career of working in distinguished independent schools I found myself well-placed to write histories of George Heriot's School, Edinburgh and Robert Gordon's College, Aberdeen. Both had begun as charitable foundations of the seventeenth and eighteenth centuries respectively. The 'unfinished business' was a history of the High School of Glasgow, where I had spent fifteen years as Deputy Rector (1981–96). I knew it would be the most difficult challenge for, as the burgh school of Glasgow, its origins, long before the founding of the University of Glasgow, lie far back in the twelfth and thirteenth centuries. The first chapter of the book is therefore an attempt to piece together the existing evidence and, in so doing, trace the very early days of the Song and Grammar Schools of Glasgow. However, from the time that the Town Council increasingly involved itself in the running of the Grammar School in the mid-fifteenth century we have more solid documentary evidence for our story.

As Glasgow developed, so too did the Grammar School and the standard of education on offer improved until, in the seventeenth century, its elementary schooling could be claimed to be among the best in Europe. The Town Council in 1600 proclaimed its pride in its burgh school and, whenever it deemed resources to be available, refurbished its buildings. From this time on thousands of Glasgow's most prominent citizens were educated at what came to be regarded as the 'Town School'. Situated first at Grammar School Wynd, then in George Street, and then in John Street, it broadened its curriculum from an emphasis on the Classics by introducing new subjects which enabled its pupils to make their contribution to Glasgow's emerging role as 'second city of the Empire'. The change of name in 1834 to the High School reflected this fundamental change in direction.

The High School faced new competitors for pupils in the nineteenth century: Glasgow Academy, in particular, opened its doors in 1846 as a private school with high fees for almost 400 boys; and many of the first

Academy families had been successful in textiles, brewing, publishing and banking. At about this time the High School had about 650 boys, and a Government report described their parents as 'tradesmen and merchants with a large proportion of clergymen, and members of the medical and legal professions'. Competition for entrants brought home to the Town Council the need to improve the High School. Remarkably, this resulted not in the finding of a new site and the creation of a new building, but instead in the Council buying Glasgow Academy's fine building in Elmbank Street. In 1878 the High School moved there and settled into accommodation fit for the leading school of Glasgow.

The success of the High School led the Town Council to found a similar school for girls at Garnethill in the last years of the nineteenth century. The education on offer at these two selective, fee-paying Corporation schools was much in demand from all sections of the population in the City of Glasgow and beyond. However, this very popularity created significant difficulties when, from 1965 onwards, local authorities throughout Scotland moved to introduce comprehensive education. That policy decision led to the end of fee-paying and selection, the conversion of the Glasgow High School for Girls into Cleveden Secondary, and the closure of The High School of Glasgow after some eight centuries of distinction as 'The Town School'. This book gives the first detailed analysis of the fight to keep selection in Glasgow and to save the High School from extinction.

The events which followed were quite extraordinary, and the final chapters of the book explain how a new independent school was opened, survived and grew up at Old Anniesland. Within a generation it had become one of the leading schools in Scotland. The book ends with comment on recent moves to revive the traditions of Glasgow's Town School.

The contributions of the old and new High Schools to the life of Glasgow are a unique and inspiring story. The rebirth of a great school is a remarkable achievement. All those who have been involved in any way can be proud of what has been accomplished. They have ensured that pupils educated today, and in the future, at The High School of Glasgow – 'The Town School' – will continue to contribute with distinction to the life of the City of Glasgow, Scotland and the wider world.

ACKNOWLEDGEMENTS

Previously, the only person to write a book on The High School of Glasgow was Harry A. Ashmall, and he did so under pressure as the events of the mid-1970s unfolded. Fortunately, he was able to make use of the large collection of papers gathered by Robert H. Small, who for thirty years collected information he thought could be used in any writing of the School's history. I am therefore indebted to these men for their pioneering work.

In his work Ashmall explained in some detail the reasons why he did not produce 'short biographical notes of the School's most famous notabilities'.[1] However nowadays, in an age in which schools usually go to some lengths to publicise their former pupils, I determined to include a selection of those educated at the High Schools.[2] In doing so, I used the 'objective' criterion of an entry in the *Oxford Dictionary of National Biography*, *Who's Who*, *Whose Who in Scotland*, *Who Was Who*, or the *Memoirs and Portraits of a Hundred Glasgow Men*. Those included in these volumes who attended the School[3] have found mention in this work. And what a galaxy of talent there is. There can be few schools anywhere which have seen their like: another reason for including them. Arguably, however, there are many who merit a place but are not included. Perhaps a future history will put this right.

With regard to archival material, I am grateful for the assistance and courtesy shown me by the staff of the Mitchell Library in Glasgow. My thanks also go to other librarians whose archives I consulted: Graeme Wilson of Elgin Heritage Centre; Dr Anne Cameron, Archival Assistant, University of Strathclyde; Mrs J. Murray, Library Assistant, and Mrs Karen Morgan, Archivist, North London Collegiate School (for material on Alice Reid); Tony Jones, Archivist and School Librarian, Emanuel School, Wandsworth (with particular thanks for the photograph from the Emanuel Archive of Shirley Goodwin and his beloved Scottie dog, Bessie); Mrs Rachel Roberts, Archivist, Cheltenham Ladies' College; Elen Wyn Simpson,

Assistant Archivist, Bangor University; Michelle Gait, Librarian, Special Libraries and Archives, University of Aberdeen; Robert MacLean, Senior Library Assistant, Special Collections, Glasgow University Library; and John McKenzie, Librarian, Royal Faculty of Procurators in Glasgow. Others who answered my requests for information included the Rev. William Graham, Scottish Church History Society; Graham MacAllister, and Dr Gary Tiedemann (with material on China missions). Alan and Dr Susan Milligan made certain Latin documents intelligible for me.

Many Former Pupils have been very helpful, especially the following from Elmbank Street who corresponded or communicated with me: Prof. David Walker; Prof. David Flint; Robert Dewar; Dr Ian Maclean Smith; J. Patrick McLaren; Dr Ronald Emslie; Dr Peter Pinkerton; Dr Ken Mills; Prof. John Cowan; Ian Penman; Douglas Boller; Ken Paterson; Prof. Dugald Cameron; Sheriff J. Stuart Forbes; Sir Teddy Taylor; Stuart Shields; Leslie Clark; Prof. John Howie; Richard Orr; Denis A. Nicol; James Cook; Robert Taylor; Murray Hutchison; Alan Thomson; David Herriot; Roddy Kay; Maurice Paterson; Eric Hugh; Brian Miller; and Robin Hagart. I also thank the following Former Pupils from Drewsteignton and the new High School: Melvyn Shanks; Prof. Anton Muscatelli; Neil Dryden; Dr Gillian MacDougall; Dr George Mackie; and Dr Ricky Sharma, as well as former pupils of the Glasgow High School for Girls: Liz Drummond (née Baird); Dr Kathryn Doodson (née Forshaw); Sheila Thomson (née Mills); Dr Elspeth Hepburn; Kathleen Drake (née Caldwell); Katharine Lyall (née Whitehorn); Marion Smith; Elizabeth Thomson (née Highgate); Anne Kermack (née Humphrey); Marjorie Bosomworth; and Gillian Stobo (née Dobson).

Former members of staff have also been generous in their help, and I thank David Mackenzie; Eric Harle; Dr Robin Easton; Eileen Robertson; Jack Bolling; Peter Whyte; Alastair Grant; Joyce Mumford; Sylvia Gardner; Kay Holland; Bill Seaman; and David Williams.

Particular thanks go to Mrs Olive Lees, with whom I spent a sparkling afternoon in April 2009, and Mrs Elizabeth Copland, who shared information with me about her grandmother, Dr Flora Tebb.

Mention also should be made of the directors of the new High School, and especially their chairmen for their interest, support and encouragement. Lord Macfarlane of Bearsden was particularly helpful, and Gordon Anderson, Sir Michael Bond and Brian Adair have all contributed to my understanding of their vision for the School.

A book covering such an extensive period is daunting to write, and thankfully a number of individuals helped me with particular sections. They ensured that many of my mistakes were removed, although I take responsibility for any and all remaining. Thanks go to: Norman Shead, Honorary Research Fellow at the University of Glasgow, for his comments on chapter 1; Rev. John Stevenson for helping with sections of chapters 5 and 6; Henry Philip for reading chapters 7 and 8; Peter Mackay, who was Private Secretary to the Secretaries of State for Scotland in 1973–5, for his insightful suggestions about chapter 9, and Dr Sandy Waugh for his interest, help and contribution to the personal profiles in particular. In order to ensure a balanced overview I turned to Prof. Hugh Begg, who not only spurred me on when I was flagging somewhat, but proved an enthusiastic mentor and friend. And, as ever, Gordon Millar of the Fachhochschule in Lucerne was generous with his time and expertise in the final stages of the writing.

During the last two years I also came to rely on a team of people in the High School itself. The Rector, Colin Mair, was unfailingly welcoming and always found time to support the enterprise. The Bursar, Juliet Simpson, helped smooth the financial side, while behind the scenes Audrey Mackie did a great deal of indispensable research for me, and the School can be very pleased at the way she has reorganised the School Archives. She also persuaded her son Neil to give of his photographic expertise, which he did willingly. Further support in this regard was given by Peter Gilchrist, Head of the Art Department, with excellent quality results. But I owe the biggest debt of gratitude to Katie Keenan (née McLennan), the School's Development Director, who organised my days in Glasgow so efficiently, always ensuring of course that I could partake of the renowned High School lunches, supplied by Allan James and Beta Catering. When I needed help Katie was always on hand. I hope she is pleased with the book, for she can take much credit for its contents.

I would also like to acknowledge the work of all those at Birlinn who have been involved in the production of this book, especially Mairi Sutherland.

NOTE ON STYLE
AND ABBREVIATIONS

Spelling and punctuation are as in the original, where this is quoted in the text and in the endnotes. Reference to 'the School' always refers to The High School of Glasgow and 'Girls' School' to The Glasgow High School for Girls. Normally, other than when indicated otherwise, figures for money are given in sterling. The conversion rate of pounds sterling to Scots pounds was 1:12, while that of pounds sterling to Scots merks was 1:18.

The following abbreviations have also been used in the notes:

Debr.	Debrett's *People of Today*
EA	Education Authority
EIS	Education Institute of Scotland
FCH	First Class Honours
FP	Former Pupil
GA	General Assembly
GCM	Glasgow Corporation Minutes
GHerald	*Glasgow Herald*
GS	Grammar School
GSC	Grammar School Committee
GTCAB	Glasgow Town Council Act Book
HMI	Her (His) Majesty's Inspector
HS	High School
HSC	High School Committee
HSE	High School and Education
HSfG	Glasgow High School for Girls
HSGM	High School of Glasgow Magazine
HSGP	High School of Glasgow Prospectus
MEA	Minutes of the Education Authority
MPHGM	*Memoirs and Portraits of One Hundred Glasgow Men*
MSB	Minutes of the School Board

ODNB	*Oxford Dictionary of National Biography*
PT	Principal Teacher (or Head of Department)
RC	Roman Catholic
SB	School Board
SC	School Captain
SED	Scottish (Scotch) Education Department
SRU	Scottish Rugby Union
TC	Town Council
WW	*Who's Who*
WWBMP	*Who's Who of British Members of Parliament*
WWS	*Who's Who in Scotland*
WWW	*Who Was Who*

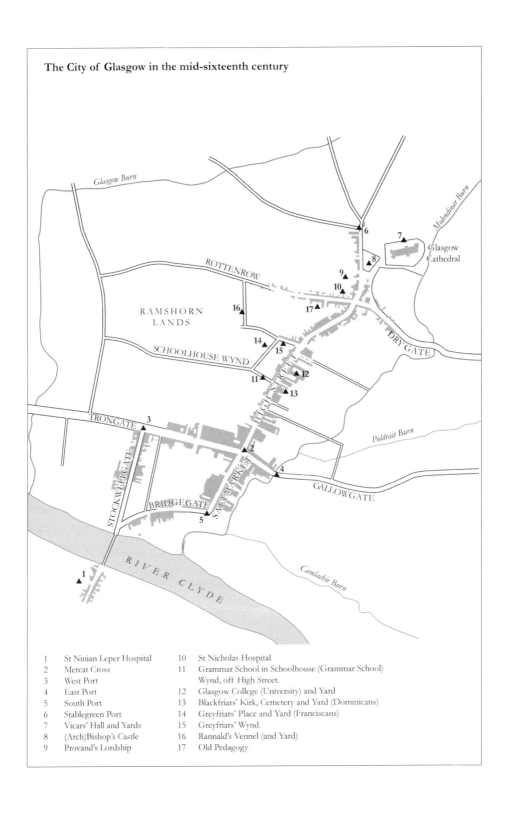

The City of Glasgow in the mid-sixteenth century

1	St Ninian Leper Hospital	10	St Nicholas Hospital
2	Mercat Cross	11	Grammar School in Schoolhouse (Grammar School)
3	West Port		Wynd, off High Street.
4	East Port	12	Glasgow College (University) and Yard
5	South Port	13	Blackfriars' Kirk, Cemetery and Yard (Dominicans)
6	Stablegreen Port	14	Greyfriars' Place and Yard (Franciscans)
7	Vicars' Hall and Yards	15	Greyfriars' Wynd.
8	(Arch)Bishop's Castle	16	Rannald's Vennel (and Yard)
9	Provand's Lordship	17	Old Pedagogy

O N E   Earliest Days to 1600

This chapter describes the evolution of school education from its origins until 1600 in Scotland and, within that general context, in Glasgow. There is attention paid to the curricula followed, the masters who taught and the most distinguished of their pupils. Unfortunately, sources are fragmented and incomplete and it is not possible to be precise on the details of the High School's historic antecedents. Certainly, there is documentary evidence of song and grammar schools providing education in Glasgow in the fifteenth century;[1] and it is probable that the former had been established by the later twelfth century and the latter by the mid-thirteenth century. Assertions that the beginnings of the High School date back even earlier to 1124 are unconvincing and were popularised only in the 1960s and 1970s when the very existence of the High School, the successor of the Song and Grammar Schools, was threatened. It seems likely, then, that the School's foundation will remain 'a matter of conjecture rather than historical proof'.[2]

BEGINNINGS

Although early records on schools are sparse, most standard histories regard the advent of Christianity as the starting point of Scottish education.[3] The first missionaries founded settlements, which were not only places of Christian communion and devotion but also schools for training their successors. The instruction focused on Latin, the language of the Church, thereby enabling future ecclesiastics to read and copy the books of Scripture.

Whithorn has been regarded as 'the cradle of Scottish Christianity', as a consequence of St Ninian[4] founding his church there and his tomb becoming the focus of a healing cult.[5] According to tradition, Ninian dedicated a small cemetery on the bank of the Molendinar Burn in the area which became known as Glasgow,[6] within which St Kentigern[7] is said to have built a cathedral[8] for his own diocese in the later sixth century. Despite the tenuous written evidence for connecting Kentigern with Glasgow, nonetheless he is thought to have become bishop of an area roughly corresponding to the British kingdom of Strathclyde, and on his death around 614 he was buried in Ninian's cemetery. Although, for the next few centuries, there is little information on ecclesiastical use of the Glasgow site, by the early twelfth century its traditions and legends were widely accepted as fact.

From the seventh century onwards the Church, which St Columba represented, established a network of monasteries in Scotland with seminaries attached to a number of them. The schools were conducted by scolocs, young churchmen in training, who assisted rectors (masters) who were in charge of the educational work of a monastery. The rectors were appointed by, and responsible to, the ferleighinn, who was a combination of superintendent and lecturer in the higher branches of learning.[9]

Christian practices brought by Columba did not remain long unchallenged. In 597 St Augustine arrived in Kent as an emissary of the Church of Rome, and a prolonged conflict between the different practices and observances of the two monastic churches began. The result was inevitable. A church relatively poor, small in numbers, and ruled from a remote fringe of Europe could not prevail against the resources and missionary power of the Church of Rome.[10] Thus when England went over to Roman practices a similar movement emerged in Scotland. The marriage in 1070 of the Scottish king, Malcolm III, to Margaret of England helped complete the conversion of Scotland.

It is only in the mid-eleventh century that the historical record becomes more secure and, increasingly, contemporary documents can be relied upon. Bishops can be traced for a number of dioceses, including that of Glasgow, although the earliest there were little more than absentee assistants of the archbishops of York,[11] who claimed authority over the Scottish Church. It was left to David I of Scotland to organise dioceses in a more systematic fashion, both before and after becoming king.[12]

David was a younger son of Malcolm and Margaret and, with little apparent prospect of succeeding to the throne, spent a great deal of his time at the court of his brother-in-law, Henry I of England.[13] There he became aware of how the Church was being reformed and developed in England and Europe. David appreciated that a thorough reorganisation of the Scottish Church would help in strengthening his position. At Glasgow, between 1114 and 1118, he made his ex-tutor, John,[14] the bishop of those parts of Scottish Cumbria[15] over which his elder brother, Alexander I, allowed him authority.

David showed a particular interest in the building of Glasgow Cathedral on the site dictated by the tradition of St Kentigern.[16] Money was being dedicated to its building from as early as *c*.1114. Nonetheless, for all that he was a great supporter of the Church, when he did come to the Scottish throne David determined to establish the integrity of his kingdom. Therefore, a priority for him was to thwart any claims over the Scottish Church, and he charged John of Glasgow with pursuing this objective.[17] Meantime John's new cathedral was ready for dedication in 1136, although this meant it was able to be used for worship rather than being complete.[18]

The organisation of cathedral ruling bodies in Scotland – chapters – tended to be based on English examples, with their increasing emphasis on establishing schools of grammar and music for cathedral cities and the villages nearby. The earliest model was probably Canterbury under Archbishop Lanfranc in 1085–7.[19] This indication of a more public kind of education was paralleled by the formal creation of an office of schoolmaster in some of the English 'secular' cathedrals, i.e., those not staffed by monks.[20]

Scottish church records[21] mention schools and schoolmasters from the early twelfth century onwards: schools appeared at Ellon, Arbuthnott, Dunkeld, St Andrews, Abernethy, Dunblane, Muthill, Perth, Stirling, Linlithgow, Roxburgh and Lanark.[22] Glasgow, however, was not mentioned, despite the expansion in the provision of church schools in many of Scotland's burghs at this time. However, letters of Pope Alexander III in March 1161 and March 1173 confirmed for the Glasgow clergy that Bishop Herbert of Glasgow (1147–64) had adopted the 'reasonable customs and liberties' of the cathedral of Old Sarum.[23] In so doing, Glasgow Cathedral introduced a more precisely defined organisation into its chapter,[24] and produced the earliest cathedral constitution in Scotland.

A SONG SCHOOL

The Glasgow Cathedral chapter, first mentioned in 1161,[25] consisted of a body of ecclesiastics, known as canons, whose four principal members were known as dignitaries: the dean who was the administrative head; the treasurer who was the custodian of the finances and ornaments of the Cathedral;[26] the precentor who regulated the music; and the chancellor who dealt with the charters and documents. As the Glasgow establishment was small, with only seven canons in 1164,[27] the dignitary posts appeared gradually: the dean about 1160/1;[28] and the first recorded treasurer was in office in the 1190s, as probably was Simon, 'styled cantor [precentor] of the church of Glasgow'.[29]

It was not long before the new Cathedral for St Kentigern was being described as small and cramped,[30] leading Bishop Jocelin (1175–99), 'an active promoter of the cult of St. Kentigern',[31] to begin a complete recon- struction of the Cathedral, likely aimed at providing a more appropriate setting for the Saint's tomb at crypt level. Moreover, as a culmination of the struggle with the archbishops of York, Pope Alexander III took the Glasgow diocese under his special care[32] and this encouraged Jocelin to give his Cathedral a more dignified form, with greater space for the high altar and canons' choir at the main level. So a building campaign began around 1181, with need further underpinned by a fire[33] which destroyed Bishop John's original structure.[34] Another dedication of an incomplete church to encourage devotion and donations took place in July 1197.

As the cathedral schools in Scotland were based on Church develop- ments already introduced into England[35] it would have been logical for Jocelin to follow the English secular cathedrals, which from their beginnings had all introduced boy choristers.[36] Furthermore, the completion of his namesake's work on St Kentigern's life formed the principal textual source for a full set of rhymed chants[37] for the latter's feast day (13 January). These chants may have been commissioned for the 1197 dedication, and presumably Simon, the precentor, had to produce a choir of some quality to perform them. A Song School is likely to have been created by Jocelin for this purpose, and the four 'boys of the lord bishop' from about 1208/1214 would therefore be choristers as well as members of his household.[38]

Worship in medieval churches was originally confined to the chancel or choir of the building, where the clergy sang the psalms, antiphons and hymns to plainsong melodies. The vicars' choral[39] was in existence in Glasgow as early as 1201–2. Boy choristers sang, for the most part, what the adults sang. When polyphony[40] was introduced, boy trebles were added and, for the first time, they made a distinctive and essential contribution to church music through singing separate parts. As a result the teaching of music became more complicated, the quality of a boy's voice came to matter more, and polyphonic singing required more rehearsal. With no time to learn reading and plainsong[41] the Song School became more specialised, with fewer boys attending, while others were moved to the Grammar School for their education. The parallel emergence of that School will be described later in this chapter.

Further development of Glasgow Cathedral went on under Bishop

Walter (1207–32), and his successor, Bishop de Bondington (1233–58), with the result that it has come to be regarded as mainly a thirteenth-century building.[42] The bishops of Glasgow became leading ecclesiastics, with no fewer than eleven of them holding the post of Chancellor of Scotland,[43] and Bondington himself was Alexander II's Chancellor from 1231 until 1247.[44] Glasgow became the second most important see in Scotland, after St Andrews, which, around 1250, had become noted for its high standard of singing.[45] Glasgow opened correspondence with it on the issue, which suggests that either it had its own choir capable of adopting polyphonic music comparable to that of St Andrews,[46] or at least the ambition to develop such a choir.

In 1427 bishop John Cameron (1426–46) arranged payment of four merks each to four boys for singing in the Cathedral.[47] By 1432 there were six boy choristers. After Bishop Andrew Muirhead (1455–73) the Song School probably met in the hall on the north side of the Cathedral, which had been built by Muirhead as accommodation for the vicars' choral.[48] Although, in 1508, there remained six boy choristers,[49] by then the School was struggling as boys left for more lucrative posts[50] and it was necessary to divert funds to enable choristers to gain a bursary to the Grammar School when their soprano days were over.[51] After the Reformation in 1560 the need to train boys in elaborate Latin services ended as simple psalm-singing became common. Attempts to arrest the decline of boy choristers failed, and the few song schools that survived became preparatory institutions for grammar schools.[52]

A GRAMMAR SCHOOL

It has been suggested that being enlightened, dutiful, energetic and interested in education, Jocelin may have created a separate Grammar School.[53] Certainly by his time many continental cathedrals had such schools attached to them, and the movement was encouraged by the decree promulgated by the Third Lateran Council of the Western Church in 1179 to the effect that each cathedral had to provide a teacher charged with the gratuitous instruction of not just the clergy of that church but also of the poor scholars.[54] However, it is likely that there was a significant time-lag between the decree being passed and being put into effect. Moreover, the cathedral dignitary responsible for teaching grammar would normally be a chancellor, and Glasgow had no such position until between 1249 and 1258.[55] It seems more likely, then, that the founding of a grammar school was left to Jocelin's successors.

Bondington determined to apply to the chapter of Salisbury for up-to-date information on the customs of that church, including the running of its grammar and song schools. In doing so, he was deliberately reviving the link of the previous century, while knowing that he was communicating with those responsible for a Salisbury which had become the 'model cathedral for the new era'.[56] Under Bishop Richard Poore (1217–37) the cathedral had moved site; a new constitution had been produced, as had a new liturgy: the Use of Sarum, which quickly became the most important summary of the Latin rite in the Middle Ages. Poore had also launched an aggressive fund-raising campaign, sending his cathedral canons round the country – even into Scotland – seeking donations. The migration of scholars from Oxford to Salisbury in 1238[57] and the resulting development of grammar, the arts, theology and law, strengthened its position.[58] Thus when the new Salisbury Cathedral was consecrated on 29 September 1258 by Archbishop Boniface of Savoy it was in the front rank of English cathedrals.

The response to Bondington's inquiry outlined to him that at Salisbury there were two church dignitaries involved in education: the precentor, who was responsible for the cathedral's music and its song school, and the chancellor, who ran the Cathedral's secretariat, drawing up accounts, issuing proclamations and keeping files,[59] while also being responsible for the grammar school attached to the cathedral.[60] Bondington appreciated that schools were being developed in cathedrals[61] to glorify and expand the authority of bishops, who needed to have at their disposal persons of sufficient learning if they were to fulfil their role and functions. Although it is not certain that all of Salisbury's practices were adopted at this time, a few days before his death in November 1258 Bondington granted 'the privileges and customs of Sarum to the cathedral of Glasgow',[62] no doubt interpreted as all liberties and customs expedient and advantageous.[63] It seems probable that this was the point at which a grammar school was formed in Glasgow Cathedral to provide the elementary education in Latin grammar that became necessary as Scotland emerged as a predominantly Christian society. It would enable boys to read the Latin prayer-books and service-books, which were the commonest kinds of books in this period.

Increasingly, literacy proved a useful accomplishment for occupations outside the Church, and Glasgow's Grammar School prepared boys for such careers, 'cleric' and 'clerk' being the same word in Latin. Helping to produce literate people was important for civil administration, and Latin was the written language of the government of a country in which three other languages were still in use: Scots, French and Gaelic. Only Latin was the lingua franca used by the whole clerical class, and some of them went on to master more than the minimum. Both public and private business required record-keeping in Latin, along with a basic understanding of the law professed by notaries, who performed the critical functions of enabling families to handle their property and the various units of the Church to run their affairs.[64]

The Reformation saw the last Roman Catholic archbishop of Glasgow, James Beaton, taking advantage of the terms of the Treaty of Edinburgh of 6 July 1560 and leaving for Paris, never to return. He took with him the original charters and records of the archdiocese from the Cathedral muniment room. In his will he bequeathed the documents to the Carthusian Priory, while to the Scots College in Paris he left his own personal and diplomatic papers and his library of 600 books.[65] Fortunately, the Scots College archivist, Thomas Innes, made a transcript of some of the ancient charters and presented them to Glasgow.[66] However, during the French Revolution, in the late eighteenth century, great damage was inflicted on the College collections when the library was ravaged, although astonishingly some of the early Glasgow material survived, including the fifteenth century Liber Ruber (Red Book).[67]

It is from these remaining incomplete sources that the earliest days of Glasgow's schooling have to be pieced together, and so it is impossible to be precise about the details of the High School's historic predecessors. It is only in the fifteenth century that documentary evidence of song and grammar schools is extant. However, some considerable time before then, probably in the later twelfth century, a song school had been established, while probably in the mid-thirteenth century a grammar school had been created.

FROM CATHEDRAL TO GRAMMAR SCHOOL WYND

The early fifteenth century saw definite advances in learning and literature in the Scotland of James I (1406–37). The foundation of St Andrews University, at the beginning of the fifteenth century,[68] was an event of national importance. In Glasgow, the Cathedral collected a considerable number of books for educational purposes: the cartulary list of 1432 contained 165 books, which covered theological, legal and philosophical topics.[69] However, it included few classical books and not a single book in the Greek language.[70] By this time the Cathedral had begun to take on the work of a college, providing opportunities for acquiring knowledge in a range of subjects, and Bishop William Turnbull of Glasgow focused on starting a course of university status and reputation. In 1451, he succeeded in obtaining a papal bull from Nicholas V to found Scotland's second university.[71] However, Turnbull's early death left the new university without adequate funding. It had no premises of its own, and it was not long before space in the Cathedral was being used for the students, with the young grammar scholars increasingly being squeezed out. The Cathedral library books, too, were soon being used by the students, especially those of use in the philosophical and theological training of young priests. By the 1450s the Cathedral Grammar School was struggling to survive:[72] some of its 'scolaris' (scholars) attended the university as students, and it seems probable that some even shared quarters with the students. A house in Rottenrow, described in 1478 as having formerly been called the Old Pedagogy, may have been used by Grammar School boys for a short time, and the University Pedagogy in the High Street, leased from Sir James Hamilton, may also have been another temporary home.[73] When the university's accommodation problems were eased by a gift, from Lord Hamilton, of a tenement in the High Street in January 1460, it is 'pretty certain that grammar scholars were at first accommodated in the new college'.[74]

Fortunately a generous offer from Simon Dalgleish, precentor in Glasgow Cathedral, came to the rescue of the Grammar scholars. He offered them alternative accommodation to the Cathedral in the form of a tenement, almost directly opposite the university, on the west side of the High Street,[75] leading from the Church to Glasgow Cross,[76] and south of the great vennel of Rannald's Wynd.[77] The donation, dated 20 January 1461, was made in favour of Alexander Galbraith, Rector and Master of the Grammar School, and his successors in office, in return for certain religious services.[78] This re-founding of the Grammar School made a geographical break with the Cathedral and made the secular authority of the Town Council, instead of the Church, responsible for it. The Provost, Bailies and Councillors of the burgh were designated as patrons, governors and defenders of the gift, and as a result were given a new influence and status. Although the diocesan Chancellor was still to have a voice in who was to be appointed, the Town's Provost and citizens were also to have their say. This was a recipe for conflict, especially as the Chancellor continued to resist interference in what he considered his statutory perquisite.

Master David Dunn, a Glaswegian and graduate of 1490, who had become a university official committed to improving the standard of university Latin, was publicly contemptuous of the idea of having to obtain Church permission, and openly began teaching grammar to boys and youths in Town and at the university without obtaining a licence from the Cathedral Chancellor, Master Martin Wan. On 13 September 1494 Wan took his case to the archbishop, Robert Blackadder,[79] declaring that he and his predecessors as Chancellors of Glasgow Cathedral had always had the power not only to choose and depose masters of the Grammar School, but also to care for the School and control its direction.[80] Following judicial inquiry, Blackadder supported Wan, and he prohibited Dunn from keeping a grammar school or instructing scholars in grammar.[81]

However, the issues of jurisdiction and responsibility between church and state had not finally been settled, for in the burghs of Peebles, Dumfries, Brechin and Edinburgh the magistrates and the Council took charge of their schools.[82] So when on 19 June 1508 Chancellor Martin Rede reasserted the claim to control the affairs of Glasgow Grammar School he was opposed by the Provost, Sir John Stewart of Minto, who held that the Town Council had the exclusive right to admit all masters to schools and 'buildings assigned for the instruction of scholars'.[83] On this occasion, Blackadder kept out of the dispute, while Rede did not pursue the matter and appears to have acquiesced in the Provost's claim.[84] Thus, although before the Reformation the Rector of the School remained a priest, from 1508 onwards the Town authorities increasingly asserted their right to have other masters appointed. This, however, was to be more significant in the long term, as for the time being the Church 'continued to watch civic activity with a jealous eye up to the very eve of the Reformation'.[85] Clerical influence remained strong, and in certain respects indeed was strengthened by the foundations of university, churches and hospitals between 1450 and 1525.

The intervention of Dalgleish had been crucial in ensuring the continued existence of the Grammar School. Without it the Bishop's Chancellor would have been left with massive problems with both the School and the university to sustain. Given that heretics were being burned at the stake, it was felt there was an urgency to provide 'proper teaching' and save them. The only way to do this would have been by converting the Grammar School into the arts faculty of the university. Thus it was Dalgleish's offer of a new home and his insistence that the School be given a new lease of life, by being taken over by the Town, which ensured the weakening of the control of the Church in this instance and thus the survival of the School.

The move of the Grammar School, however, from the Cathedral precincts to Grammar School Wynd (as it soon came to be called)[86] did not result in a marked improvement in fortune. Indeed, during the first century at its new site it suffered, like the university, from a lack of funds. It was generally perceived that schools and colleges were 'wholly going to ruin', while the youth of the burgh were becoming inactive through 'ease, sloth and wantonness'. It appeared that lack of financial support had extinguished the pursuit of learning. Eventually the Town Council helped the university in 1566 by diverting funds from the property of local friars for the upkeep of the Principal, two regents and twelve poor students.[87] At the same time it was confirmed that the Rector of the Grammar School would retain the endowment of the chaplaincy of All Saints.[88] A decade later, on 16 November 1577, the Council ordered its master of works to make the School watertight, and the roof was thatched at a cost of £2 8s Scots. The following spring the west end of the building was repaired at a cost of £8 Scots.[89] Unfortunately the Town's limited financial resources restricted the work done. Nonetheless, at least the School was now firmly established and, in December 1600, some funds were found for it from the fines from the Garngadhill crofters, who had been grabbing land, in an unauthorised fashion, from the Town.

EARLY MASTERS

In the period before 1400 in Scotland the office of rector of a school was one of 'high dignity'.[90] As educated men, rectors were liable to be called upon when a document had to be drawn up or a transaction recorded. In October 1477 George Lorne, Rector of the Grammar School, was 'incorporated as a member of the University'.[91] Another Rector, John Reid, followed suit in 1508, while Rector Matthew Reid was Bursar from 1521 to 1525 and chosen as one of the deputies to elect the university's Rector.[92] In the early 1550s Rector Alexander (Archibald) Crawford was also Bursar of the university.[93] These schoolmasters would have been involved in examining those seeking to become graduates of the university. In the later 1550s Robert Maxwell became Rector and, at the time of the Reformation, disputed with the Reformers, in particular John Willock, Superintendent of the west.[94]

After 1400 the post of rector remained relatively high in esteem, and there were several examples of outstanding schoolmasters.[95] In the main, however, the profession of school teaching fell in status. The rise of universities had an adverse effect on schoolmasters, whose limited numbers, geographical isolation and modest direct importance led to a decline relatively and absolutely in wages and conditions of service.

Fortunately at Glasgow the pre-Reformation rectors of the Grammar School were clerics supported by Church endowments. They were chaplains of the leper hospital of St Ninian.[96] Each week they celebrated four masses in the chapel, with commemoration of the dead. They were expected to live in the hospital, which was some distance from the School, and twenty-four scholars lived there too.[97] William Stewart, canon of Glasgow, endowed the chaplaincy[98] in 1494, and the following year the Provost of the collegiate church of Hamilton, David Cunningham, founded the chaplaincy of All Saints.[99] Another was the chaplaincy of St Michael the Archangel.[100] These endowments continued after the Reformation and supplemented the salary of the Rector.

Other sources of income for the rectors before the Reformation were the payments of bleis-silver[101] and bent-silver. The former was a payment made by the pupils toward the cost of lights and candles for the Feast of Purification. Although this ended in 1560 it remained the custom on Candlemas Day in early February for each boy, often accompanied by his parents, to present monetary gifts of esteem.[102] The other fee, bent-silver, was money paid in lieu of giving bent or rushes for the floor of the classroom.

Thomas Jack, 1567–1574

Perhaps financial inducement was a factor in attracting Thomas Jack to the post of Rector between 1567 and 1574.[103] As a Church of Scotland minister, he was presented, in 1570, to the vicarage of Eastwood by James VI, retaining its lucrative income until his death in 1598. Jack was a university graduate, probably of Glasgow, and maintained close links with the university while it was under Andrew Melville's reforming principalship (1574–80), holding office as Bursar, and donating works of St Ambrose and St Gregory to the university library. On Melville's advice, in 1574, he consulted George Buchanan (then in Stirling Castle, acting as tutor to the young James VI and busy preparing his history of Scotland)[104] on a draft classical dictionary in verse.[105] It was a schoolbook of the proper nouns a schoolboy would meet in the stories of Greece and Rome. He dedicated the work to James Hamilton (eldest son of Claud, Commendator of Paisley Abbey), who had been educated under his supervision in the Grammar School. His friendships with Melville and Buchanan led Jack to oppose the Episcopalian government of the Scottish Church and, during Arran's administration of 1583–5, he was imprisoned for his support of Presbyterianism.[106]

Patrick Sharp, 1574–1582

Jack resigned in August 1574 and was succeeded as Rector by another prominent theologian, Patrick Sharp, who arrived just as the Town Council had ordained 'the Sculehouss Wynd and all the vennellis to be simpliciter condampnit and stekit up', in an attempt to arrest the spread of plague.[107] However, it proved to be a minor outbreak, and was over in six months. Sharp was then able to develop friendships, especially with Melville at the university. Soon they were on excellent terms,[108] with Sharp relishing their conversations and acknowledging the debt he owed to Melville in the running of the School. He became 'adept both in the Classics and corporal punishment',[109] yet he exhibited another, more caring and encouraging side to his character in an affectionate letter[110] which he wrote to one of his former pupils, Mark Alexander Boyd of Pinkhill.[111] This was particularly noteworthy given how refractory Boyd had been at school with his constant 'displays of unruliness'. Sharp was also in charge on 24 June 1577 when local merchant Robert Hutchesoun and his wife, Katherine Allansoun, renounced their sasine,[112] title of right and possession of a house and adjacent yard so that it could be joined to the School and 'increase the room thereof'.[113] This was the first extension of the Grammar School since its move in 1461.

While Rector, Sharp displayed his fervent Presbyterianism. In April 1582 he was one of the ringleaders of forty burghers and students who took up arms in an attempt to hold the Cathedral against Robert Montgomery, the newly appointed archbishop of Glasgow.[114] He was called before the Privy Council to explain his actions.[115] He demitted his rectorship soon after and, in January 1586, James VI appointed him Principal of Glasgow University. In this post Sharp ensured stability for the extraordinarily long period of twenty-eight years by keeping the college[116] free from serious political trouble. Finally, in 1615, he resigned, rightly fearing that otherwise he would be deposed by his numerous and increasingly vociferous critics. He left a reputation as a distinguished scholar,[117] but only one of his works, *Doctrinae*

Christianae brevis explicatio (1599), survives.[118] It is a plain textbook of Christian doctrine dedicated, as a token of gratitude, to James VI.[119] In Church matters, too, in which he played an increasingly important part, matters also ended sadly. Sharp inclined more and more to the bishops, until finally he was perceived to be only a King's man.[120]

John Blackburn, 1582–1616

John Blackburn came from a prominent Glasgow family and was chosen Rector in November 1582, following advice from the university.[121] It is likely that he was educated at the School, for he was the son of Archibald Blackburn, merchant burgess of Glasgow. John himself had graduated MA from Glasgow in 1578, before becoming Reader and Exhorter at Cathcart Kirk (1578–80). Like his immediate predecessors, he developed a national profile, and he was appointed a deputy for electing the Rector of Glasgow University[122] and an examiner of its candidates for graduation.[123] The Town Council thought highly of him: he was asked to examine quack doctors in the Town,[124] and in 1600 he was appointed moderator of Glasgow Presbytery. Soon he became an extraordinary beneficiary of pluralism. He became Dean of Faculty at the university (1592–1611), vicar of Cardross (1603–15), moderator of Dumbarton presbytery (1606), archdeacon of Down in Ireland (1606-23) and minister of the Barony in Glasgow (1615–23),[125] which met in the crypt of the Cathedral. As well as the ministry stipends, his salary as Rector of the School included the quarterly fees from the scholars[126] – the main source of his income – supplemented by the rents of its ancient lands,[127] two burgess fees per annum, and various chaplaincies.

Religion played a large part in burgh schools following the Act of 1567 which regulated their teaching. The daily work of the Grammar School began and generally ended with prayer. Before the end of the sixteenth century it was ordained that in addition the scholars should be taught certain forms of prayer – 'formulas precandi' – for use in private, one after rising in the morning and the other before going to bed. Such regulations were enforced by the Town Council in all their schools, especially after 1592 when James VI recognised the liberties of the Reformed Church by the 'Golden Act'. The Glasgow Presbytery took full advantage of its strong position. It ordered, on 15 July 1595, a visitation of ministers and councillors to the Grammar School to monitor the diligence of the pupils. Rector Blackburn was reminded of the need to ensure that all his bairns attended the Kirk regularly, and the Presbytery organised seating for them in the Cathedral in

February 1598.[128] To ensure that the reserved loft area was always available for the School, it was enacted in December 1607 that no Town inhabitants were allowed to use the area on pain of a fine. The Kirk Session also resorted to banning all games indulged in by the boys. Meantime, 'Irish scholars' were to be carefully catechised by Blackburn as a defence against Catholicism, which was considered to be rife among Gaelic speakers.[129]

THE CURRICULUM IN
THE SIXTEENTH CENTURY

The foundation of three universities in fifteenth-century Scotland had important results for education,[130] although at first the standard of learning was little higher than secondary schools, and the only faculty which flourished was that of Arts. Simultaneously, grammar schools spread to more and more burghs throughout the country,[131] but their curriculum was restricted. Pupils were taught to read, write and speak Latin. The highest classes probably studied logic,[132] but this subject came to be concentrated in the universities, leaving only 'disputations' in the school curriculum. These were confined to the more literary of the liberal arts, grammar and rhetoric, in which grammar school boys propounded difficult questions in Latin, and debated and argued them in the same language.

James IV's June parliament of 1496 passed a famous enactment on education. It required the eldest sons of barons and freeholders 'that ar of substance' to be sent to grammar school from the age of eight or nine, and to remain there until they acquired a basic education and had 'perfite latyne'. They would then spend three years 'at the sculis of art and Jure' so that they might gain knowledge and understanding of the law. Unfortunately, in the short term at least, the Act was no more than an expression of 'pious hopes'.[133] Nonetheless it was significant, because it implied the existence of sufficient grammar schools in Scotland to fulfil its provisions[134] and it was the first state legislation aimed at compulsory education. It was also clear evidence that Latin was deemed indispensable for more than the professional classes, and contemplated a class of educated laymen, breaking away from the idea that the educated man was synonymous with a man in holy orders.

Despite the Reformation, the curriculum of grammar schools remained much as it was, with Latin dominant. This ensured that Glasgow University, in particular, could assume that its students would be proficient in Latin, leaving it free to concentrate on mathematics, natural philosophy, moral philosophy and Greek.[135] The Grammar School and university were especially aware of the necessary entrance requirements in the 1570s. The friendship between Patrick Sharp and Andrew Melville made for a close liaison between the institutions.[136] Nor can there be any doubt that for both scholars and students, their respective curricula were demanding in both content and duration.

The Protestant Reformers assumed that Scots children enjoyed great stamina, and the Grammar School timetable in the sixteenth and seventeenth centuries involved nine or ten hours of direct teaching per day, five and a half days a week.[137] It began at five or six in the morning and continued until five or six in the evening, with only two breaks (between 9 and 10 a.m., and 12 and 1 p.m.) during the day. Pupils carried away homework, which would be tested the following morning. Moreover, pagan and Roman Catholic holidays were abolished – including Christmas, in the 1570s – to enable work to continue uninterrupted. Any break from formal schooling was also to be seen as an opportunity to carry on God's work, hence the 'holiday' of eight weeks was taken to coincide with the harvest season to enable children to work in the fields. So the school year lasted forty-four weeks of five and a half days per week from the age of eight and continued for five years. Moreover, learning did not stop on the Sabbath, for the boys met at school at 8 a.m. and had doctrinal teaching and examination until church, to which they were marched in year order. They there took up their places in the 'Scholars' Loft', reserved specifically for them. There pupils listened to the minister for two or three hours and then marched back to school to discuss some aspect of the sermon, talking it over in Latin. In addition, there was usually an afternoon service to attend, and a cross-examination to survive.

On 15 December 1575 the Privy Council of Scotland, under Regent Morton, decided that it would be convenient and profitable if there was only one form of grammar-teaching in all Scottish grammar schools. In January 1576, in order to get agreement among the most learned schoolmasters, George Buchanan was directed to meet with the schoolmasters of Stirling, Edinburgh, Dunbar, Haddington, Glasgow (in the person of Patrick Sharp) and St Andrews.[138] However, the group reported that there was no existing grammar, old or new, which they could recommend as perfect in all parts. The schoolmasters were then instructed to supply the want themselves. To this they responded systematically by a division of labour, which resulted in two books of Latin Etymology, at simple and more advanced levels. They then went further and produced the rest of the Latin grammar in manuscript form. By an Order in Council the printed books were to be used immediately, and the manuscript also once it was available in book form. No schoolmaster or pedagogue in Scotland was to teach grammar publicly or privately from any other textbooks, on the pain of dismissal.

The first two parts of the long-awaited authorised Latin Grammar were published in 1587.[139] By then free competition in grammar books had taken over again and, although this led to progressive improvement, many pupils were still being subjected to poor material. In December 1593 the Scottish Government, led by Chancellor Thirlestane, condemned the inconvenient and injurious multiplicity of grammar books used in schools, and enjoined the use of one authorised grammar only.[140] As before, however, this proved difficult to enforce.

The failure to establish a common or universal Latin grammar for schools led to a renewed attempt by a Parliamentary Commission in 1607, but that was also unsuccessful. Nonetheless, David Wedderburn,[141] master of Aberdeen Grammar School, published a grammar[142] in 1632 which, partly through its own merits and partly through the support it received from the Convention of Royal Burghs, attained a large measure of popularity. In time, others were produced. In practice, grammar schools almost invariably followed similar courses and made few adjustments to their teaching methods and content, which remained unchanged throughout the sixteenth and seventeenth centuries.

THE GRAMMAR SCHOOL IN 1600

Despite the growing power of the burghs and the Reformation of 1560, ecclesiastical influence in education continued. The burgh appointed the Rector – a churchman – but it did not attempt any innovations in the traditional curriculum, and the notion of a purely secular education was unknown. Although the place of religious instruction in schools was taken for granted, bibles were expensive and little used in schools before the 1630s. The main religious texts were Calvin's catechism and a psalm book.[143]

According to one commentator the standard of medieval school education in Scotland was, as compared with England and France, decidedly low – even 'backward'.[144] Unlike in France, there was no provision for the supervision or inspection of schools. The curriculum, even in the reputable Grammar School of Glasgow, was narrow. Boys went on to university at an early age; much that was studied there was later provided in schools. The schoolmaster had much the same status as that of the most poorly paid and indifferently educated of the clergy.[145] Many only made ends meet by also being chaplains, and many gave up teaching for more lucrative clerical posts if they had the opportunity.

As schoolmasters received no particular training, and usually had neither the inclination nor the aptitude for it, the grammar schools of Scotland were often staffed with men incompetent at schoolmastering and unable to keep good discipline. But who else would take on the post or remain for such poor remuneration?[146] The only hope usually was to allow larger and larger classes, with the result that 'the usefulness of a Scottish schoolmaster declined as his popularity increased'.[147]

Moreover, schools were fee-paying institutions. Whilst recognising that 'the children of the poore must be supported and sustained of the charge of the Kirk', the Protestant Reformers in 1560 had insisted that the sons of the 'rich and potent' should be educated at 'their own expense because they are able [to pay fees]'.[148] Education was prohibitive for the less well-off, and even expensive for the better-off. Effectively this meant that the Grammar School was 'reserved to burgesses' sons',[149] although some families were helped by Council bursaries and benefices: Henry Gibson, son of the Commissary Clerk of Glasgow, had his education at the Grammar School supported by the latter means between 1584 and 1591.[150]

Notwithstanding all of these difficulties, there is plenty of evidence suggesting a widespread provision of a basic education in reading, if not in writing. As far as the grammar schools were concerned, provision was extensive and increasingly sophisticated, with Scotland having what amounted to a national curriculum. This was the result of the use of standard textbooks and the interest taken by both the General Assembly of the Reformed Church and parliament[151] in what was taught. Moreover, the impact of the printing press, which from 1507 created a much wider reading public, and the extensive presence of schoolbooks in the inventories of booksellers, both also point to a growing level of literacy and put into context the tactics of ministers and schoolmasters who sought to paint as black a picture as possible of educational provision. In 1539 well over a hundred boys from grammar schools attended university which, given the country's small population, was a creditable number.[152] By 1600, Scotland was already exhibiting the 'signs of a new self-confident literate society',[153] and its educational record was 'something of an achievement and a boast'.[154]

There had been advances, too, in the Grammar School of Glasgow, which was now run by an increasingly interested magistracy aware of the issues which needed their attention in order to secure its future. Fortunately there was almost never any complaint against the Rector[155] except, as there was no superannuation fund, when he might remain in post too long. Among the scholars, there might be individuals who caused problems, but there was never any concerted rebellion. The brighter pupils, perhaps teaching themselves in their large classes, were sometimes forgiving in later days and wrote of their masters with gratitude and affection, while the bulk of involuntary pupils wasted their time and learned little or no Latin. The consolation for them was the fact that lack of Latin did not seem to hold them back in the Trades' House or the Merchants' Hall.

PUPILS

Around 1438 William Elphinstone, who had just been appointed rector of Ashkirk and a prebendary canon of Glasgow, sent his son, William (1431–1514) to the Grammar School, the Cathedral being near their home. William junior became the outstanding Scottish lawyer and administrator of the fifteenth century. Ordained a priest in 1455, he studied for an MA at Glasgow University, proceeding to study canon law at Glasgow and Paris, then in 1470 civil law at Orleans. He became Rector of Glasgow University in 1474–5 and Chancellor of Scotland (1488).[156] He lost office following James III's murder after the defeat at Sauchieburn and turned to his bishopric of Aberdeen, which he strove to reform. His lasting contribution was the foundation of Scotland's third university, King's College, in Aberdeen, in 1495.[157]

It has been claimed that George Buchanan (1506–1582) attended the School. Robert Baillie, Principal of Glasgow University, referred to him being 'bred in our Grammar School',[158] but this was written a century and a half after Buchanan's birth and the statement is unsupported. Buchanan was born in the Killearn parish, Stirlingshire, and 'left local schooling' aged fourteen.[159] He was then a student in Paris before briefly being a soldier. He graduated at St Andrews University and Paris University and taught at the latter, returning to Scotland about 1537. He was active in political affairs as Moderator of the General Assembly and in opposing Mary, Queen of Scots. In addition, he tutored the young James VI, was a public servant, political theorist, historian and administrator. Although his early schooling 'remains rather mysterious',[160] nonetheless, the claim of Glasgow Grammar School appears at least as strong as the claims of Killearn, Dumbarton or Stirling.

John Spottiswoode (1510–1585)[161] was orphaned when four years old, so 'his friends put him to [Grammar] School in Glasgow',[162] and he went on to Glasgow University in 1534. He became a Scottish Protestant Reformer and Superintendent of Lothian. By the time of the Reformation he had been moving in reforming and anglophile circles for a generation. He contributed to the First Book of Discipline and the Confession of Faith. He officiated at James VI's Protestant coronation at Stirling in July 1567.

Perhaps another scholar at the School in this period was John Graham, fourth Earl of Montrose (1573–1626). His family maintained an interest in Mugdock in Lennox and his father became Keeper of Glasgow Castle in 1583. He was a nobleman who became involved in national politics from the later 1590s. He was admitted to James VI's Privy Council in March 1604, the king noting that 'it is expedient that men of his rank and qualitie sould in thair youth be trayned up in imployment in our affairis, that, being of rype age, they may be the mair capable'.[163] In March 1625, shortly before his death, he was appointed to the post of President of the Privy Council under Charles I.[164]

One significant historian has claimed that Montrose's famous son, James Graham, first Marquess of Montrose, (1612–1650), royalist army officer, had part of his early education at the Grammar School.[165] However, although he was sent to Glasgow in 1624 to study under William Forrett,[166] there is no documentary evidence confirming that Montrose was a pupil there.[167] Nonetheless, the confidence in local schools did result in a number of young nobles attending the School, for there was in this period little social pressure to separate them from their social inferiors. In 1595, the Maxwell kindred held a conference to discuss the education of the young ninth Lord Maxwell and his brothers. It recommended to the boys' tutor, Lord Hamilton, that the 'youngest twa sons be putt to the schools in Glasgow quhair it is thocht your lordships kynnisfolks may be friends to thame'.[168]

The most striking difference between the education of Scottish and English nobles in this period was the lack of increasingly exclusive schools available to the former in Scotland, where there was nothing comparable to the great endowed schools of Eton and Westminster (or indeed the new boarding schools in France or Spain, often run by Jesuits). What Scotland had instead were some schools, especially in the larger royal burghs, which were of a higher standard than the others. The Grammar School of Glasgow was one of these. By the next century it could claim its elementary schooling to be among the best in Europe, producing high levels of literacy.

TWO The Grammar School
in the Seventeenth Century

This chapter describes the work on the School buildings in the seventeenth century. The lintel and descriptive stones of 1601 were an integral part of the Grammar School buildings as their site changed in the centuries following. They moved to George Street in 1788, then John Street in 1820; then, with a change of name to High School, to the north wall of the central building in Elmbank Street in 1878, before finally being placed in the interior of the new School at Old Anniesland in 1977. There is also discussion of the high esteem in which rectors of the School were held in comparison to the low status of their assistants, and teachers generally in Scotland. Again, attention is paid to the curriculum and its continued domination by Latin, and further details given on the most distinguished pupils of the School.

BUILDINGS

The Town Council claimed to be proud of its burgh School, stating on 23 August 1600 that its members 'think na thing mair profitabill, first to the glory of God, nixt the weill of the towne, to have ane Grammer schole'.[1] However, its building in Grammar School Wynd was in a ruinous state and clearly concerned the Council. Rector Blackburn was instructed to raise the matter at every Council meeting until refurbishment was undertaken and completed, while meantime the best stones of the back almhouse, adjoining St Nicholas Hospital, were to be used to repair and enlarge the schoolhouse. By 22 December a building contract had been authorised and the masons, wrights and slaters were to complete the work 'as gud chaipe as thai can'.[2] To finance the work the Council directed Blackburn, in January 1601, to use the 400 merks which Harry, the porter to Glasgow University, had left to that institution. The final bill for the work authorised was paid on 14 March 1601,[3] but further work was needed as early as 1607.

During the work of 1600–1 the pupils were housed across the street in the Blackfriars' Kirk,[4] and the Wednesday and Friday services held there were transferred to the 'Hie Kirk'. When the School building was reopened there was mounted over the doorway a stone containing the city arms and the Latin inscription: 'Schola Grammaticor. A Senatu Civibusque Glasguanis Bonar. Literar. Patronis Condita'.[5] The lintel and descriptive stones were to move with the Grammar School as it moved to different parts of Glasgow in the centuries following.

As the years passed, the accommodation deteriorated again and by mid-century it had become positively dangerous. Eventually, on 25 February 1656, the Council determined to demolish the building as soon as practicable. Within six weeks the 'maner and forme' of the new School was agreed, and by the summer the mason, John Clerk, had been chosen and the work of rebuilding begun.[6] On 9 August the Council agreed that 'some littill thing' should be raised on the west gable for hanging a bell.[7] This extravagance, however, was only carried by a majority of votes, and it took until 1663 before any progress was made on the matter. Meantime, the steeple was completed in late October and the mason's bill of £36 Scots for thirty-six days' work was paid before the end of the year.[8] The resulting improvements were, for the most part, sustained as the Council paid increasing attention to the state of the School building and attempted to maintain a School worthy of the city.

RECTORS AND THEIR ASSISTANTS

With an increasing roll John Blackburn was given a chaplaincy to augment his emoluments, and the fees paid by the boys were also increased.[9] As he had been Rector since 1582, he found it increasingly difficult to cope with the more than 300 boys in the School. On 14 April 1610 he complained to the Council of 'grit and commoun abuse' from the scholars who absented themselves from classes and services, and caused damage to the property of neighbouring gardens when indulging in their pastimes and rivalry with local apprentices. Although games did not occupy a very prominent place in school life, archery, bowls, golf, handball and wrestling were practised, but without definite system or rules. The Council determined to fine any further transgressors £10 Scots for any and every offence, and the scholars, and apprentices, were banned on Sundays from frequenting the yards, where they had been indulging in 'alie-bowlis, Frenche kylis and glaikis'.[10] The boys were encouraged to use their leisure time in preparing their bows for archery.[11] For the most part, however, they were cooped up in the School the whole day long. No one was allowed to go out even for a short time without taking with him a baton, which had to be brought back before another boy was allowed to leave.

Punishment was meted out for minor and major infringement of the School rules by means of birch rods or a tawse: a leather strap with split ends, often hardened in a fire, and a broad thong, or with divided ends, attached to a wooden handle. The Rector was expected to punish misdeeds both in and out of School.[12]

As discipline deteriorated, the Council appointed Robert Blair (1593–1666) as Blackburn's assistant in 1614. A merchant's son who had just completed his university course in philosophy, Blair took on the 'very laborious task'[13] of controlling half of the boys. His memory of this was 'being outwearied with the tail of the day, I oft went to bed without supper, not for want but for weariness'.[14] Within two years Blair had moved on. He became a regent at Glasgow University and, in time, emerged as a significant politician and churchman.[15] He left his mark, according to Robert Baillie, as 'greater than any man I know living, to insinuate the fear of God in the hearts of young scholars'.[16] Certainly Blackburn knew how much he had come to rely on Blair, and the latter's departure hastened his own resignation. Blackburn had proved industrious and competent, and he was a man of influence who was highly regarded. He had been a good servant to the School and the university. One of his later acts as Rector was to present to the university library his copy of Onuphrius Panvinius's *Fasti et Triumphi Romanorum*, an illustrated quarto volume which had been published in Venice in 1557. He wrote on the fly-leaf the inscription 'Communis bibliotheca Collegii Glasguensis. Ex dono Johannus Blackburnii. Anno Dom. 1615', and added his signature.[17]

William Wallace, 1617–42

The practice of appointing assistants (or doctors, as they came to be called) continued and was extended in the seventeenth century as a result of the large number of boys enrolled in the Grammar School. There was no salary provision until 1649, and this meant dependence on a small part of the scholars' fees. Under William Wallace, Rector from 1617 to 1642, two were introduced: John Hammiltoun and James Alderstoun.[18] The former was a Glasgow graduate, who fell on hard times after he left the School;[19] the latter was also a Glasgow graduate as well as a disappointed, kirkless 'expectant' minister.[20]

Wallace had proved a diligent schoolmaster for more than a decade at Irvine Grammar School, with a salary of £40 Scots per annum and an allowance of £5 Scots for house-rent. He took over from the aged incumbent as master of Stirling Grammar School in October 1612 and clashed with one of its doctors, James Bradye, who was banished from the burgh in November 1614. Wallace produced 'The Muses Welcome to the Kings Majestie At His Happie Returne' when James VI and I visited Stirling in June 1617 after fourteen years' absence from Scotland.[21] Rev. John Livingston[22] was one of his pupils, and he described Wallace as 'an good man and a learned humanist'.[23] He thrashed the First Year and gained a reputation as a strict disciplinarian, but exhibited some charm to the fourth and fifth years.[24]

Soon after Wallace arrived in Glasgow, probably in October 1617, the Privy Council had returned to the topic of producing the perfect Latin grammar which would be taught throughout the land. Alexander Hume, Rector of the newly founded Prestonpans Grammar School, composed a work he thought worthy of this accolade, but the committee set up by the Privy Council heard testimony especially from John Ray, Master of the High School of Edinburgh, who was very critical of the text. In July 1623 the Privy Council decided to summon the rectors of grammar schools from Aberdeen (David Wedderburn), Dundee (James Gleg), St Andrews (Henry Danskene), Perth (John Durward) and Glasgow (William Wallace), as well as Hume and Ray, each with two or three of their pupils 'for peruseing and conferring upoun the said grammer and for putting of their scollaris to ane tryall'.[25] However, no consensus resulted and seven years later Wallace appears still to have been employed on the same investigation.[26]

It was under Wallace's stewardship that the Town Council returned to the lapsed policy of inspection.[27] The first one for some time took place in the Grammar School in May 1636.[28] The format followed was an announcement made by the Provost and bailies that they would visit the School the next week and then report back to the Council on their findings. As such inspections became more regular and the Town authority was now unassailable, it was agreed to allow the city ministers to become involved in the process. Classes were examined on the work done, while the two highest classes were dictated themes in English which were translated into Latin for the examiners. After the examination the boys who disappointed were reproved, those who did badly were not promoted, and those who did well received prizes and rewards.

As Rector of the Grammar School, Wallace engaged in university business, helping to install a professor of Greek and acting as the (university) rector's assessor. He received as salary the sum of £20 16s 8d Scots yearly, to which was added the chaplaincy rent of St Michael the Archangel and £12 Scots for the annual ground rent of the correction house.[29]

Traditionally the Council appointed staff for definite periods ranging from three months to eleven years (plus two years for the process of replacement), although on some occasions appointments were made at the pleasure of the Council,[30] which left teachers very insecure.[31] On 16 October 1630, after thirteen years in post, William Wallace's initial contract expired. He was summoned to appear before the Council, which decided that as he had carried out his duties as Rector 'faithfullie and truelie' he should be allowed to continue in post.[32] The Council then allowed him to retain his post for as long as he did his duty. He died still in office in early 1642.

David Will, 1642–1649

Wallace was replaced as Rector by David Will. He had graduated from Edinburgh University in July 1619 and immediately thereafter became a doctor in Edinburgh's High School. He became a candidate for the chair of Humanity at Edinburgh in 1623 but, despite pleasing the regents most at interview with his experience and knowledge,[33] the post was given to Samuel Rutherford.[34] In 1625 Will became Rector of Stirling Grammar School, where he remained in post until moving to Glasgow in 1642.[35] While at Glasgow he underwent inspections in September 1644 and April 1646. The School was also forced to close down during the outbreak of pestilence which spread to Glasgow in 1645–6. It reopened in early May 1647 but was closed again during the summer, finally resuming in November of that year. Announcements about the School were read from the pulpits of city churches.[36] Given the long breaks, the doctors found themselves in financial difficulties, and the Council alleviated the situation on 27 November 1647 by allocating £55 Scots to be divided between them 'for thair straits'.[37] However, the lack of a secure and settled salary created constant problems for doctors, and every so often resulted in desertion. To avoid this, the Council determined on 14 April 1649 that the first doctor would be paid £100 Scots annually and the second doctor paid 100 merks.[38] Despite this, on 23 July 1659, John Wingate, who had become second doctor in November 1657, complained of great hardship and his salary was increased to 150 merks annually.[39] In the meantime, on 4 December 1649, after only seven years in post, Will gave up his Glasgow appointment, being tempted back by Stirling on improved conditions of service.[40]

Francis Kincaid, 1649–1681

Francis Kincaid, son of a maltman, graduated from Glasgow University in 1632, became schoolmaster at Hamilton around 1635 and was Rector of the Grammar School between 1649 and 1681. He soon found himself with staff difficulties. On 17 August 1652 the Town Council set up a Committee of Four to meet with Kincaid and Robert Speir, one of the doctors, to discuss 'the contraversie fallin out betuixt thame'.[41] Following the meeting the Committee reported back to the Council, which decided on 24 August to remove Speir from his post.

Kincaid grew old and infirm in his post until the Council met with him to see if he would be willing to give up his office because of his age and failing health. He was encouraged to do so with the offer of retaining part of his salary during his lifetime. Kincaid agreed. His reputation was sound, and one of his distinguished pupils, James Wodrow, spoke highly of him 'for his gravity, piety and exact discipline among the scholars'.[42]

George Glen, 1681–1689

In September 1681, when Kincaid was replaced, the Council held his successor, George Glen,[43] to be fit academically but 'wold say nothing to his uther qualificatiounes'.[44] Eventually he was appointed, but he was soon dismissed because his control of the pupils was so weak. Robert Wodrow[45] told of an occasion when his Presbyterian father had to go to Glen to complain about bullying by Episcopalian Archbishop Paterson's second son. 'Mr Glen was an easy well-natured man, and very frankly said the bishop's son was a very rambling youth, and brought him much uneasiness, and indeed he durst scarce make any complaints of him, nor check him for anything he did'. Wodrow's father was unimpressed and reckoned that Glen 'was very unfit to have the government of a school'. As a result he took Robert away from the School.[46]

On 21 May 1688 Hugh Muir[47] was accused of a line of 'crimes', including verbal abuse against Bailie Gilhagie and striking some scholars 'too sevearlie'. He was suspended and ordered to be put in prison during the Council's pleasure. The Provost and four others formed a Committee to hear the grievances against him.[48] It received a letter from the archbishop of

Glasgow reporting complaints against Muir by another doctor, who held that Muir deserted his charge for a day or two without permission. He also alleged that Muir exercised 'too rigide and cruell methods of discipline', and not only was he insolent to Gilhagie in public, he was also rude and disrespectful to the Rector. Following the archbishop's recommendation[49] the Council dismissed Muir on 26 June 1688.[50] Although on the face of it this appears to be a case of Church influence and involvement, it should be noted that the Council had already decided, almost a month before the archbishop's intervention, to dismiss Muir. Giving the impression, then, of going along with the archbishop was probably a way for the Council to underline its loyalty at a time when political and religious conditions were very sensitive.[51]

George Skirven, 1689–1715

During the 1688–9 Glorious Revolution and the restoration of the Protestant succession, education became a prominent issue of debate amongst those running schools in Scotland. An Act of Parliament in 1690 laid down that rectors had to subscribe to the Westminster Confession[52] and take the oath of allegiance. On 30 July 1690 the Glasgow magistrates were directed to lay the testimonials of Rector George Skirven[53] and the doctors of the Grammar School before the Visitation Committee. Exactly a month later these were produced and signed by Skirven and his assistants, who also swore allegiance to King William and Queen Mary before signing the Confession of Faith. The schoolmasters had to be judged to be sound politically as well as spiritually before exercising their authority.

On 20 August 1694 a third doctor was appointed to take office on 1 October, as there were 'so many scholars in the Grammar School'.[54] He was given a salary of £100 Scots and was expected to fulfil the role of precentor in one of the Town's churches as well as his teaching post. Rev. John Walker[55] took on this post in May 1695, but within two years he was dismissed for disrespectful conduct towards the Rector.[56] However, the ministers protested and on 1 October 1698 were able to reappoint him as a doctor on his previous terms of employment and with his income enhanced with ex-gratia payments.[57] However, complaints continued to be made against him and his appointment was finally terminated on 18 December 1707.[58] With the Protestant succession secured, it was clearly no longer necessary to take religious issues into account as long as appointees were Protestants and decisions on staffing could again be determined by local considerations. The dismissal of schoolmasters was therefore possible even if they were ministers. This was underlined on 25 September 1707 when a petition, supported by a considerable number of burgh inhabitants, was received which complained about Rev. William Marshall.[59] An investigation found he was unfit for, and incapable of, teaching and as a result of that 'prejudice children were receiving' Marshall was dismissed.[60]

Rev. Archibald Marshall was a doctor in the Grammar School from 1692 until 1697, moving on to become minister of Kirkmaiden, Wigtownshire. In his new position he developed a reputation for being a zealous persecutor of witches.[61] He moved to nearby Kirkcolm in 1700, and in his new charge Marshall turned his attention to ghosts. His years of teaching 100 boys at a time helped him challenge the ghost of Galdenoch Castle, situated north-west of Stranraer. Several of the neighbouring clergymen had tried to lay this ghost, but all in vain. Marshall proved more successful by the somewhat unclerical method of roaring and shouting it down.[62]

On 7 March 1711 the ministers and magistrates reported on a recent visit to the Grammar School,[63] where they had taken trial of the educational standards. They had asked the Rector, Skirven, to give over in writing a 'Scheme of his manner of teaching'. Although he did this, the Council found it too general and he was asked to give a more detailed report. When this was not forthcoming, the university's Principal, John Stirling, and Glasgow Presbytery representative, Andrew Tait, were asked to press for more progress. When none was made they moved to replace Skirven, but this was interrupted by the 1715 Rebellion.

The social position of the rector of grammar schools in general and Glasgow Grammar School in particular, and the relatively high estimation in which the office was held, was generally maintained throughout the seventeenth century.[64] This partly explains the decision of John Ray in 1606 and Thomas Crauford in 1630, both Professors of Humanity at the University of Edinburgh, to give up their respective chairs in favour of taking up, in turn, the post of Rector of the High School in Edinburgh. They believed that to do so was promotion.[65] In salary terms, their university successor, William Skene[66] (1680–1717) was paid 500 merks annually, while Rector Skirven in Glasgow received a comparable 460 merks in 1697.

The situation, however, was somewhat different for teachers generally, and their status remained low. Indeed their emoluments were depressed further in a period of inflation at the beginning of the century. In 1627 the average stipend of ministers in twenty-four parishes making returns for the

Plantation of Kirks[67] was 485 merks, while the average burgh school salary was no more than 150 merks.[68] There were no significant improvements in the course of the century. One doctor, however, found a way of supplementing his income. John Anderson was a master in the Grammar School from 1649 to 1679 and the author of a number of poems. On 22 March 1662 he received payment from the Council Treasurer for dedicating a book to the magistrates of Glasgow. In this case, at least, political awareness and flattery did reap financial benefit.[69] Generally, however, a teacher's lot was not a happy one. His income usually depended mainly on the quarterly fees the scholars brought him, and plague, dearth or civil war could empty his classroom for months at a time, leaving him near destitution. In December 1600 the fees were raised to 6s 8d Scots, 5s of which went to Rector Blackburn and a mere 20d to his assistant. To increase income the teacher had to encourage huge classes. The hours, too, were long and demanding. Fortunately, Glasgow was strongly Presbyterian, and this probably helped ensure that the Grammar School did not follow the example of the burgh schools of Aberdeen and Edinburgh, where there were repeated disturbances and even, on occasion, serious rioting.[70]

THE CURRICULUM

During the seventeenth century each rector managed the Grammar School in the way he thought best without thinking it necessary to consult the Town Council or keep a record of happenings and transactions. As late as 1696, Rector Skirven, when asked to give an account of his method of teaching, stated that the work in the School was carried on 'according to a standard formula, observed these hundred years and upwards in the said School'.[71] However, the university authorities were insistent on interfering in methods of teaching and the content of the curriculum.

It seems probable that Glasgow, like other grammar schools, insisted that their Latin scholars were not allowed to speak English within, or even outside, the School, publicly whipping them if they transgressed.[72] Thus by the time they left the School, it was expected that Former Pupils would be able to write trade correspondence in perfect and precise Latin; and, if they were so inclined, they could continue reading the ancient Roman authors, whose texts abounded with adages and homilies thought to be of use to members of the emerging urban middle class. As a result, entrants to Scottish universities lived in a culture in which Latin was to remain the language of lectures and tutorials into the eighteenth century. In addition, they were expected to have mastered the text of the authorised version of the Bible.[73] Yet some who arrived at university were found unfit for the first class. A Professor of Humanity was appointed at Glasgow between 1637 and 1660 to give Latin instruction. This was an open criticism of the standards of the Grammar School, and as such was viewed by the latter as an encroachment on its prerogatives.[74]

However, in April 1643, the university authorities determined to go further[75] and set out what the Faculty of Arts expected in 'Method and Principles of Instruction in the Grammar School'. It suggested that before pupils entered on a five-year course in Latin at the School, they should have completed a preparatory course in reading, writing, and in 'committing some [Latin] words to memory'.[76] It then proceeded to detail the ideal programme of study to be followed.

In the first year, during the first six months, the rudiments of etymology would be taught; in the second six months pupils would learn syntax, and short sentences were to be committed to memory, so 'inculcating piety, good morals, and conduct, to be rendered into the vernacular in the best style possible'. In the second year pupils were to be introduced to Despauter[77] and the colloquies of Corderius,[78] and later to the select epistles of Cicero,[79] the minor colloquies of Erasmus,[80] and the sacred dialogues of Castellion.[81] So for the first two years the aim was to produce fluency in reading and writing Latin, through understanding grammar and undertaking months of exercises. By the end of this time pupils were expected to talk about various Latin dialogues and epistles.

The third and fourth years would be altogether much more exciting. In the third year Terence[82] and Ovid[83] were to be studied, together with the psalms of Buchanan, and the scholars would do exercises in Latin composition. Horace[84] was to be studied in the fourth year, along with more of Buchanan's psalms; those who were able were expected to compose heroic, elegiac or lyric verse, while those who did not have such ability would work on converting loose sentences into grammatical language and the writing of themes. All was designed to achieve a thorough grounding in History and Literature. Finally, in the fifth year, the pupil would listen to lectures on Rhetoric, read further from the Classical poets, enter on the study of the elements of Greek grammar and translate themes into Latin 'following as closely as possible the style of Cicero, Caesar or Terence', and again, if competent to do so, continue with verse writing.[85] Pupils unable to meet the demands of the course, through sickness or failure to keep up academically, could expect to repeat a year, so it might take a scholar more than five years to complete the curriculum.

Such detailed prescription was followed by the university's expectations in the area of *Communia*.[86] Revision classes and oral assessments should be held towards the end of every week, while after mid-day on Saturdays instruction on the current teaching of the Presbyterian Church should be given in the vernacular to those in first year and in Latin to the others. As well as communal prayers the pupils should be taught private prayers for morning and evening. They should learn how to take on character roles and speak out dramatically, in a circle of spectators, the dialogues, speeches and comedies they had learned. This was intended to help them to acquire the faculty of clear expression and good acting. They were to be inspected in late April and late October by 'grave and learned men' from Town and university. During this, vernacular topics were to be dictated to the two higher classes, for them to turn into Latin immediately and hand over to the inspectors for examination. When the process was complete, all of the pupils of each class were to be formally named at a public meeting and were to go to that place and ranking which each deserved.

There is no document existing which details the reaction of the Town Council to this programme, but it seems likely that the magistrates would wish assurances that the Rector had such matters very much in hand. It is probably no coincidence that one document has survived from about the year 1660,[87] signed by Rector Kincaid, in which he set out clearly the work to be done in the School. It seems to have been forwarded to the magistrates so that they could formally approve.

During the morning from 6 a.m. to 7 a.m. the five classes of scholars learned 'their repetitions out of the Grammer [sic]' on which they were examined before 8 a.m. All classes then worked on expositions until 9 a.m. After breakfast another hour was spent learning more grammar, and on Mondays and Wednesdays an hour was spent on the theme of the day, which was corrected for an hour (and this theme was revisited the following day).[88] In the afternoon the pupils spent one and a half hours preparing and learning certain lessons, followed by another hour and a half hearing the prepared lessons. On a Friday the timetable was modified: repetition of grammar took place from 6 a.m. until 8 a.m. and was examined during the following hour; after breakfast pupils worked on their theme and verse;[89] while in the afternoon from 1 p.m. until 3 p.m. repetition of the set work was followed by two hours in which the scholars had to repeat perfectly what they had just learned. The day ended with a final hour between 5 p.m.

and 6 p.m. with the pupils preparing themselves for Saturday's disputations. On a Saturday morning there were disputes until 9 a.m., and after breakfast, between 10 a.m. and 12 noon, writing. In the afternoon it was regulated that 'pairt of Ursine's Catechise be taucht . . . to the thrie superor Classes: and a pairt of the Inglish Catechise to the laichest classes'. On the Sabbath the catechism was to be explained in the morning and examined in the afternoon. All in all, it was a regime of 'overstrained application'[90] and as such unlikely to be maintained for any length of time.

Indeed it seems that matters deteriorated quite soon after the departure of Kincaid, for between 1683 and 1708 the university again had to appoint another Professor of Humanity who had the teaching of Latin as part of his job description. This led to further discussion on the fitness of Grammar School boys for university and the decision to set up a committee, on 6 August 1685, to report on the 'state of the Grammar School'. After a visitation and due deliberation, Principal Fall wrote a courteous letter disclosing his committee's findings to the Town on 12 October. He accepted that grammar scholars, having completed their five years' study at the School, would be received into the Humanity class but could not bypass it and join a higher class at the university. He went on to spell out suggested refinements in the Latin curriculum for the School, which included even more emphasis on perfecting grammar. There was no mention of Rhetoric or Greek, which were seen as university subjects. Special care was to be taken by scholars and masters to ensure that even amongst themselves they spoke nothing but Latin. Finally, the doctors should be assigned to particular classes and be answerable for their efficiency.[91]

The Council reacted, finding unacceptable 'that article in the proposallis anent the humanitie class' and determined not to have their burgesses restricted in the manner suggested. Nonetheless, it was willing to accept the Principal's curriculum suggestions and also appreciated the need to improve standards, including the quality of the Rector himself. It was no coincidence, therefore, that the Council acted decisively when faced with complaints against Muir in 1688 and Glen in 1689.

In the seventeenth century, Glasgow's Town Council showed considerable zeal in promoting education and maintaining standards. It also ensured a satisfactory modus vivendi with the Church,[92] which co-operated in the appointment of staff and the general management of the Grammar School. However, the curriculum remained static, and although the earliest notice of Mathematics in Scotland appeared in Glasgow in 1660,[93] no further mention was made of the subject until the next century.

Nonetheless, in two areas Glasgow led the way. Firstly, the earliest visitations of the School were in the later sixteenth century and were more searching than elsewhere because they included the powerful combination of ecclesiastical, municipal and academic elements. Secondly, as a result of such visitations the Grammar School was the first school in Scotland to introduce competition for prizes and the use of rewards, a feature which some burgh schools introduced only in the nineteenth century. Such an enlightened approach played some part in Glasgow's commercial success.[94]

Given that a small part of the patrimony of the Church was secured for education, the Council's support of the School is commendable. Throughout the seventeenth century, and indeed up until 1872, its burgh contributions were entirely voluntary, and were produced even when there was little in the way of readily available funds. It is clear, then, that care for the management of the Grammar School and anxiety for its success generally characterised the actions of its managers in this period. This was particularly creditable given the proliferation of other kinds of schools, including writing schools and fencing schools. By 1663 Glasgow had no fewer than seventeen authorised teachers, including Huguenots hired to teach French.

In Scotland generally the programme of the *Book of Discipline* of 1560 was implemented in the seventeenth century: the state in 1633, 1646 and 1696 gave parliamentary backing for the funding of a parochial school system, supplementing the burgh grammar schools, with the Church acting as managers for the whole enterprise, locally and nationally. The 1696 Act was of particular importance, not as a beginning to national schooling in Scotland – for Scotland already had an extensive network of schools – but as a reminder of the educational duties of hard-pressed localities in a period of famine and distress. In 1700 a Presbytery inquiry into Glasgow and Ayr schooling found no concern about lack of school provision but instead concentrated on the issues of widening the curriculum and the effectiveness of teaching.[95]

This was to lead directly, within a generation, to the first burgh school, Dumfries, adding a range of 'commercial' subjects to its traditional classical curriculum.[96] However, the Grammar School in Glasgow remained loyal to a curriculum devoted to the *ars grammatical*, which it held to be the most constant and fundamental subject of instruction; the only instrument, indeed, fitted for educating everyone, irrespective of his circumstances, capacity and inclination, without taking into consideration the age at which he was to leave School, or the occupation which he intended to follow. In a period when Latin was not viewed as a dead language, when it was the vehicle for transmitting learning and carrying on correspondence among European countries, when the literature of no other country could be compared with the richness of that of ancient Rome, it seemed natural to continue the study of Latin. For at least another century the Grammar School retained its conviction that a Classical training was a powerful, even indispensable, instrument for disciplining the mind.[97]

PUPILS

Although Glasgow had developed a broad manufacturing base by the seventeenth century, a small group of merchant families working particularly in clothing, textiles and food processing already controlled civic offices, overseas trade, and commercial ventures. Their growing prosperity was reflected in the buildings constructed for the Town and themselves. They and a small but increasing professional class sent their sons to the Grammar School.

Early in the seventeenth century (Sir) Robert Spottiswood (1596–1646), judge and politician, second son of the archbishop of St Andrews, attended the School. He went on to Glasgow University and Oxford, becoming a Fellow there. Spottiswood's abilities and his father's position brought him speedy advancement. He became a judge in the Court of Session, and as Lord Dunipace was elected its president in October 1633. In 1636 he was appointed Secretary for Scotland. As a supporter of Charles I in the Wars of the Three Kingdoms he fought with Montrose. Following the latter's defeat in 1645, Spottiswood was found guilty of high treason by the Scottish Parliament and beheaded on 20 January 1646 at the Mercat Cross in St Andrews.[98]

Robert Baillie (1602–1662) was born in the Saltmarket, Glasgow, son of a merchant. He attended the School, and between 1617 and 1620 the University of Glasgow. At both school and university he was taught by Robert Blair,[99] whom he later acknowledged as having been, after his parents, 'the first and principall instrument of whatever piety, good letters, and moral virtue that he had'.[100] In 1631 he was appointed minister of Kilwinning in Ayrshire.[101] He reluctantly conformed to the religious policies of Charles I in Scotland, but by 1639–40 he accepted the need for armed resistance to the King. He preached Presbyterianism, and was in the delegation which failed to agree on terms with Charles II to bring him to

Scotland in 1649 following the execution of his father. In July 1650, he retreated to his duties at Glasgow University.[102] With the Restoration of the monarchy in 1660, Baillie was appointed Principal of the university and is remembered as a scholar.[103]

William Montgomery (1633–1707) was raised by his maternal grandparents in Tyrone, Ireland, and was sent hurriedly to Scotland via Derry in October 1641 following the outbreak of rebellion in Ireland. He returned to Derry after spending a short time studying Latin at the Grammar School and Glasgow University. A good student, he became fluent in Latin, Greek, French and Dutch. Montgomery was an ardent supporter of the Royalists in the Wars of the Three Kingdoms, a zealous Anglican,[104] and a member of the Irish Parliament, 1661–67.

From 1643 to 1657 the Marquess and Marchioness of Douglas, as Roman Catholics, were constantly harried by the Lanark Presbytery, which gained control of the education of their children. After the Marquess supported Montrose, in January 1648, he was forced to agree to send his son, Lord William Douglas (1634–94), to the Grammar School. However, on 22 November 1649 the Marquess was allowed to move his son to Lanark school, provided he continued with James Veitch, the tutor appointed by the Presbytery.[105] When Charles II returned to the throne in 1660 the family fortunes improved dramatically, and Douglas[106] played a prominent part in public affairs in Scotland and England until his death in 1694.[107]

Another pupil at the School was James Wodrow (1637–1707), Church of Scotland minister and university teacher, son of the Chamberlain to the Earl of Eglinton. He attended Glasgow University, where he was a distinguished student, graduating first in his class. He was much influenced by his Divinity Professor, Robert Baillie.[108] He also became acquainted with Covenanting ministers, including Robert Blair. When Episcopacy was dominant Wodrow was a proscribed field preacher. Later in 1692 he became Professor of Divinity at Glasgow, and in the following sixteen years he taught about 700 students.[109]

Robert Wodrow (1679–1734) was a victim of bullying at the School and was withdrawn in 1688. His father set up a private school for Presbyterians, which Robert attended. He went on to Glasgow University and secured the charge of Eastwood, where he was ordained in 1703. 'He remained there for the rest of his life as a popular and active parish minister, resisting all attempts at moving him to higher-profile charges such as Stirling or Glasgow.'[110] Nonetheless, he was active in opposition to the Treaty of Union (1707) which he saw as offering insufficient security for the Presbyterian

Church of Scotland. He is best remembered for his *History of the Sufferings of the Church of Scotland* (1721–2), which, although written from a pro-Presbyterian stance, relied on primary sources.

William, third Duke of Hamilton, had ambitious plans which centred on his heir and eldest son, James, Earl of Arran (1658–1712). Following the accepted practice of the Scottish peerage, he sent James to the local school in Hamilton when he was about six, and then at about eleven to the Grammar School in Glasgow. Arran attended for two years before going on to university for four further years. He retained his singing master, attended dancing school and learned to handle a pike and musket. His tutors and family complained that he was high-spirited, thoroughly spoilt, and that he wasted his time, spent too much money and lied to cover up his misdemeanours.[111]

Clearly the Duke of Hamilton did not blame the Grammar School for how Arran appeared to be turning out, for he sent his sister's two surviving sons, William Johnstone, second Earl[112] of Annandale (born February 1664) and John (born September 1665) to the Grammar School in October 1674, following the deaths of their parents. George Glen, later master in Glasgow, became the Earl's private tutor.[113] Soon after joining the School, and again in 1677, the Earl had the distinction of becoming Candlemas 'victor', and his younger brother also gained this honour in 1678. Both participated enthusiastically in the School sports of golf and football. In the latter game, as 'victor', both had to buy a football for their classmates. Although they lodged in Glasgow, the brothers made occasional excursions to the family home in Hamilton. When they left for the ducal palace, crowds of citizens turned out to see them leave and share in the freely distributed money. The young Earl left in October 1677 to attend Glasgow University and went on to have a colourful and significant political career,[114] while John continued at the School until 1681.

THREE

The Grammar School in the
Eighteenth Century

This chapter follows the history of the Grammar School in the eighteenth
century through the leadership of successive rectors. It discusses the
pressures on them and their responses according to their varying characters
and abilities. It explains why the Town Council decided to abolish the office
of rector in 1782 and the repercussions of that radical move. Other issues
covered include the move of the School to George Street in 1788, the careers
of significant masters and the growing number of distinguished Former
Pupils as Glasgow emerged from 'dear green place' to second city of the
Empire.

RECTORS

William Hamilton, 1715–1731

George Skirven finally resigned from his post as Rector as a result of old age
and infirmity on 12 December 1715. He was replaced in the following month
by William Hamilton, governor to Lord Boyd, son of the Earl of
Kilmarnock. During this process the Town Council reasserted its authority
in the matter of appointments and resignations. It examined the 'literature,
qualifications and good education' of Hamilton,[1] before making him Rector.
As for Skirven, the Council showed compassion by awarding him a
quarterly allowance of 50 merks, as he was 'nocht able to do anything for
himself'.[2]

   Hamilton found that the Glasgow Presbytery was determined to inspect
the Grammar School at every opportunity. On 5 January 1721 its Moderator
and a group of ministers arrived to monitor the class examinations of the
Rector and doctors. This was followed by questioning on discipline, which
Hamilton claimed was sound. The schoolmasters were encouraged to take

special care to teach the scholars the principles of the Christian religion, to restrain them from vice and immorality and to ensure that they attended church regularly, listened to the sermon preached and observed the Sabbath. The scholars were exhorted to be diligent and painstaking in their learning and to obey their teachers. Following the failure to obtain a scheme of learning from Skirven, the Presbytery was determined that Hamilton would not have the same freedom. It requested that Hamilton's written scheme detailing the manner of his teaching be presented at their next meeting.[3]

Under Hamilton the number of pupils fluctuated. In consequence the teaching complement was reduced from four to three in 1723, but in June 1727 a fourth was employed once more. However, the Council appreciated how poorly paid the teachers were, deeming their salaries 'mean'[4] and, to compensate, the school fees were increased to 2s 6d a quarter,[5] while the salary of the doctors was raised to £15 per annum.

The use of public buildings and their grounds for events was common in the early eighteenth century. In the case of the Grammar School, public balls, shows, comedies and plays took place on their premises, but the magistrates were concerned as, on at least one occasion, the evening had ended in a 'great disturbance in the citie'.[6] A party of students had decided to produce *Tamarlane* in the university, but this was opposed by the university authorities, unsympathetic to play-acting in general and objecting, in particular, to the wearing of women's clothes by male students. In the event the play went ahead in the School on 30 December 1720 and a *Prologue and Epilogue* were specially written for the occasion by two of the students taking part. The opportunity to satirise the university dignitaries was not missed.[7] This led, on 20 January 1721, to the Council ruling that only activities by the scholars related to their learning could, in future, be performed in School buildings, and the audience for such events was to be restricted to the teachers and their pupils.

James Purdie: 1731–1756

When Hamilton died, aged forty-three, in early September 1731, the Council examined the qualifications and literature of James Purdie, who had graduated from Edinburgh University in 1705 and since 1717 had been Rector of North Berwick Grammar School.[8] Being a noted grammarian, he was appointed Grammar School Rector. He was soon involved in appointing staff replacements, as some of the doctors did not stay long in post. With three doctors the School appeared to be fully staffed, but Purdie persuaded the Council to add a 'supernumerary',[9] Robert Maltman. This was a radical move, especially as he was charged with teaching and carrying forward 'the boys of slow genius in every class'.[10] Maltman was given £100 Scots a year, and his appointment was clearly seen as something of an experiment for, unlike other teaching staff, he had temporary tenure and faced re-election annually.[11] Nonetheless, the appointment was an early indication that the Council was taking increasingly seriously the problems regarding standards of learning in the School.

Purdie was clearly pleased to follow the Council's more interventionist stance by exerting his authority over his staff. By December 1734 he was authorised to determine the books to be used by doctors with scholars. He was permitted to examine classes as often as possible, thereby monitoring also the standards of teaching of his colleagues. In order to widen reading generally, in March 1735 £10 was made available to develop a library in the School but, like a previous effort in July 1682 when an inventory of books was carried out and a cupboard made in which to keep them, this made little progress.

Such developments, however, caused friction between Purdie and the staff, especially the recently appointed Thomas Harvie.[12] The Council was quick to deal with these 'disorders and jarrs'[13] and supported Purdie. On 11 October 1738 it went a step further: in future the 'whole government of the School shall be lodged in the Rector', who alone would prescribe the method of teaching and the direction and superintendence of the doctors. The Rector would determine discipline in all classes and do what was necessary to establish and maintain order and promote the learning of the scholars. In all of this, the Rector was to be accountable only to the magistrates and Council as patrons of the School. At the same time the doctors were given fair warning 'to submit to the Rector as their superior in the school' or they would 'furthwith amitt, forfeit, and lose their office as under master'.[14] To underline this point Harvie's contract was modified and was to be reviewed annually. He seems to have taken heed of the warning, for he was re-elected every year until he demitted his post in May 1756.[15]

The firm approach by the Council went some way to ending internal strife in the School for half a century. Progress was also made in several other areas. In November 1738 John Murdoch, the Writing master, successfully petitioned to be allowed to teach boys of the School from the age of seven or eight,[16] and although the emphasis was still on writing in Latin, his teaching encompassed Arithmetic, Book-keeping and Navigation.[17] Such subjects were not within the School curriculum but were becoming increasingly popular out of school hours.[18] In December 1738 the school fees were raised to 3s 6d a quarter, and they were raised again in October 1742 to 4s, with the doctors having their salaries augmented. However, any goodwill engendered was dissipated by the doctors having to give over to the Rector a quarter of the fee from the class they taught. Purdie astutely offered to waive his right to these fees provided his salary was increased from £25 11s 1d to £40. 'For the good of the school' the Council agreed unanimously to this.[19] And prize books for the best scholars were introduced in May 1740 for the first time. The Rector was given £5 annually to buy the books, which were to have the Town's arms imprinted on them.[20]

Purdie was a member of a dining club frequented in the 1740s by a number of prominent university professors and academics. Alexander Carlyle joined the group while attending classes at the university from November 1743[21] and wrote about the members in his *Autobiography*.[22] He said of Purdie that he had 'not much to recommend him but his being an adept in grammar'.[23] Carlyle also related the 'comet story'. The group were very interested in comets – the age saw the beginning of the mass production of telescopes – and when Purdie had viewed such a great and uncommon phenomenon of nature his only interest was to settle the gender of the Latin 'cometa'.[24] Sadly Purdie developed another unfortunate habit, that of 'dram drinking', usually for a few days at a time. In order to live comfortably Purdie took in six to eight boarders, with his eldest daughter, Nelly, keeping house. One Saturday in April 1745 Nelly contacted Carlyle pleading for his help. Apparently, Purdie had been very drunk the previous weekend and had not been completely sober since, missing School all week. Carlyle found Purdie in a terrible state: Purdie had determined to resign his post because of his drink problem, although he had few savings because of his idle and wasteful sons. According to Carlyle's optimistic account, he helped Purdie to break his habit and Purdie returned to School the following Tuesday 'in perfect health'.[25]

By this time visitations had become major occasions and included the Provost, magistrates, ministers and professors of the university. The Rector had an elegant Latin oration ready, after which he, 'at great length and with great exactness, examined the first class in Virgil, Caesar, Buchanan's Psalms and all parts of Grammar'.[26] The expected result was usually achieved: 'The skill and diligence of the master, as well as the proficiency of the scholars, was so visible to everyone present, that it gave general satisfaction.' Such visits normally ended with the Provost ordering that book prizes be distributed by the Rector to those whom he deemed particularly diligent as an encouragement to others to follow the good example set by the winners.

Purdie continued in office until 9 April 1756, when he resigned, in consideration of his advanced years and 'bodily frailtys and infirmitys'. Considering the 'extraordinary assiduity and care' with which he had discharged his rectorship, as a mark of respect and reward the Council believed that Purdie merited 'for his past faithful and laborious services' an annuity of £40 during his lifetime.[27] He died in August 1757. Although one of his daughters married well and lived in Edinburgh, two others (Nelly and Margaret) were indigent and petitioned the Council for assistance to relieve their condition. They were given £21 in September 1757 provided that they made no further claim.[28]

James Barr, 1756–1782

On the same day that Purdie resigned, the Council elected Rev. James Barr[29] as the new Rector. The following day Patrick Holmes was elected under-master, given both his experience as precentor in the Blackfriars' Church and because he had already taught his scholars Writing in a large room in Castlepen's Land near the School. He was soon to prove 'one of the most popular teachers of his day',[30] but unfortunately he died prematurely in February 1767. Up to this time doctors had come and gone on a regular basis.[31] Most found the job too demanding and the salary too low. In the case of Thomas Irvine, previously schoolmaster in Port Glasgow, a number of complaints were made against him in his six years as doctor. He was frequently guilty of gross drunkenness and was finally dismissed in 1767 as unfit to be in charge of youth.[32] However, from the 1760s a period of stability ensued, presumably as a result of improved salaries.[33] William Bald, previously schoolmaster in Paisley, held the office of doctor from 1761 until his death in 1783.[34] Alexander Bradfute and John Dow were both appointed in 1767; Bradfute remaining until 1787[35] and receiving an annuity of £30 for life, and Dow until his death in 1794.[36]

ASPECTS OF EDUCATION

Rector Barr was left to a considerable extent to get on without interference or supervision. Being a good Latin grammarian he produced two textbooks, the first of which in 1763 was intended for 'the young scholar, especially those of a slower capacity'.[37] His work of 1770, which is still extant, was entitled *A*

Practical Grammar of the Latin Tongue, Adapted to the Rules of Mr. Ruddiman's Rudiments. One can assume he did this precisely because there was no committee of the Council involved in drawing up any plan of education or taking charge of the general interests of the School.[38] Nor were there any arrangements made for examinations at stated regular times, nor for the marking of places. Magistrates were hardly ever seen in the School except at the annual examination and distribution of prizes, which only involved the last few weeks of every session. So Barr was left with the entire superintendence of the business of the School and he was expected to deal with this by using a degree of authority over the other three teachers. This continued to cause friction and discontent, leading to discord and strife. As a mark of his precedence the Rector wore a gown in the School, which the other masters were not allowed to do. In the Common Hall, there was one large pulpit and three small pulpits; at the morning meeting, when the School was convened and the masters seated in their places, one boy read a chapter of the Bible, and then the Rector gave a prayer, at the conclusion of which the classes went to their respective rooms. The three doctors began a rudiment class in rotation, and handed over the scholars to the Rector, who taught them in their fourth year, and who, in addition to instruction in Latin, explained the elements of the newly emerging discipline of Geography.

The textbooks used were much concerned with facts, especially vocabulary lists and grammatical rules in Latin. However, as the century progressed, the method of instruction and the imparting of facts were modified to take account of the scholars' youth, and some attempts were made to suit the tastes of children. One of the earliest textbooks on learning to read English and Latin was published by John Porterfield.[39] He had taught in Glasgow for some time before opening a school in the High Street in Edinburgh. He favoured rote-learning, but included an analytical approach to language, the method of syllabication,[40] which was developed as the century wore on. Few of the writing books have survived, but many writing masters produced their own copy-books. The most popular textbook in Arithmetic was *Cocker's Arithmetic* which, published in 1678, remained a standard text for at least a century. In Latin, Despauter's text remained a standard grammar in Scotland, although there were a number of revisions. James Kirkwood, schoolmaster at Linlithgow, produced a revision in 1695 for Lord Stair, and advocated the use of pictures, maps and wall diagrams. Thomas Watt offered another revision in 1704, in *Grammar made Easie*, and included an English translation of the Latin. Then in 1714 the popular *Rudiments of the Latin Tongue,* produced by Thomas Ruddiman, Keeper of the Advocates' Library, appeared. This was an entirely new work which supplanted all previous texts and became the standard grammar for the rest of the century.[41]

Early each February the scholars convened in the Common Hall and gave their customary Candlemas Offering. The doctors sat in their pulpits, while the boys in each class were expected to walk up one after another to the Rector and give him an 'offering'; having done so, they then went to their own master and gave him an offering too. When the sum given was under 5s, no notice was taken, but when it amounted to that sum, the Rector said 'Vivat' (let him live) and all the boys responded with a stamp of feet. Given 10s, the Rector responded 'Floreat' (let him flourish) and the boys gave two stamps. For 15s, the Rector's response was 'Floreat bis' (let him flourish twice) and three stamps resulted. Given 20s, the Rector said, 'Floreat ter' (let him flourish thrice) and four stamps followed. For a guinea or more, the Rector responded 'Gloriat' (let him be glorious), when six stamps were given. When all had finished the Rector stood up and in a loud voice declared the 'Victor', announcing who had given the largest sum. On this, the Victor was hailed by the whole assembly of scholars with thunderous applause.

Discipline was severe and all boys feared their masters. In August 1824 Sir Thomas Munro, who was at the School in the 1770s and was himself a strong and fit youth, wrote to a one-time fellow pupil:[42] 'I never think of you without looking back half a century, when we were in Glasgow and went to School in fear and trembling to meet Bald.' Munro's biographer noted that Bald was 'a tyrannical teacher, whose chief pleasure consisted in punishing his pupils'.[43] Perhaps it was this reputation which led the managers of Hamilton Grammar School to offer Bald its rectorship in 1765, which he turned down. Bald was not alone in his methods. Robert Reid[44] has written how 'severe and rigorous' Dow was at punishing wrong-doers. Both inflicted their cruelty without fear of reproach, for they were deemed 'good fellows'. The Council approved of such methods, and on Dow's death the magistrates gave £10 to his family. The boys remembered him less kindly.

THE CHANGES OF 1782

Without a Rector, 1782–1815

General concerns about the state of several schools in Glasgow led to the formation of a Council committee to look into the situation on 25 October

1775. However, as little seemed to improve, the committee was strengthened in March 1782.[45] Its six distinguished members included three future Lord Provosts: John Campbell, John Campbell jnr and Gilbert Hamilton; two successful merchants, Alexander Brown (Convenor) and William Coats; and Walter Stirling, a magistrate.[46] They immediately consulted Church and university representatives and, wasting no time, on 13 May unanimously proposed a line of radical recommendations for the Grammar School. The Council accepted them on 26 June.

The central change was to be the abolition of the office of Rector, which was deemed surplus to requirements and indeed a hindrance to sound administration. Instead, the business of education was to be placed under the direction of all four masters, who would be of equal rank and have equal authority and salaries. To symbolise the new situation the masters were all expected to wear gowns in their classes. Moreover, each master would, in turn, begin a rudiment class on 10 October and carry it forward for four years.[47] As the work of the Rector consisted 'only'[48] of presiding in the Common Hall, directing the discipline of the School and regulating the method of study, it was the belief of the committee that all three of these functions could 'be effectively carried on without a Rector'. The master of the oldest class[49] would preside in the Common Hall and take prayers; he was to ensure that the persons who put on the fires and cleaned the rooms did their duties properly. The rules and acts of School discipline were to be agreed upon and carried out by the four masters consulting together, with a casting vote given to the master of the oldest class. A standard curriculum would be approved by the Town Council which, after consulting with the masters and other persons of education, should 'easily' establish a general plan to be addressed in all classes and observed by every master 'with very few discretionary deviations'.[50]

The introduction of this new system meant more direct involvement in running the School by the Town Council, which decided to elect annually a committee to superintend its operation. This Grammar School Committee (GSC) would visit the School once a month and would include not only councillors but also 'some gentlemen of learning'. They would hear the boys read or repeat their lessons, inquire into the state of the School and have the power to bestow small rewards upon those boys who impressed them with their ability and diligence. From the first the GSC stressed the need to concentrate on the less able so that the poorer performers could be brought up to the level of the others.

At the same time certain regulations were confirmed while others were updated. Fees remained at 5s a quarter and the Candlemas Offering was continued, although the use of the words 'Vivat', 'Floreat' and 'Gloriat' were no longer to be used. Each boy was now expected to pay 6d a quarter for coals. The hours of attendance were to be, in winter, from nine to eleven and from twelve noon until two in the afternoon; in summer, from seven to nine, from ten to twelve noon, and from one to three in the afternoon. But the vacation was to be only four weeks commencing on 1 July, augmented by a number of 'play-days' throughout the year: at the time of the spring and winter sacraments (from Wednesday afternoon until Tuesday morning); Christmas day; New Year's day; the last Friday in January and Candlemas day;[51] May day;[52] the King's birthday;[53] the Deacons' choosing day;[54] and two or three days after the annual examinations as the Provost determined. There was to be only one meeting on a Saturday in winter and none in summer, but there would be no holiday on Wednesday afternoons as formerly.

In Glasgow a curious custom grew up around the keeping of the Candlemas holiday by both Grammar School and university, the Town's two oldest educational institutions. About the middle of January each year one student from each of the four nations in the Natural Philosophy class of the university, dressed in their scarlet gowns, repaired to the School and requested a play-day for all of its classes; this deputation was met with much approbation and applause. In way of response, four of the boys from the oldest class in the School visited the university and having first pronounced a memorised Latin oration to the Principal, they proceeded to enter several lecture rooms and requested in Latin that the Professors give their students a holiday on Candlemas day. The schoolboys were always well received and their wish granted.[55]

While allowing this traditional practice to continue, the Council turned to more worrying problems. It appreciated that the existing schoolhouse had neither 'free air nor good light' nor even a playground for the 'innocent diversions of the boys'. Thus it accepted the GSC's recommendation that a new School be built not too remotely for the general population, with a requirement that it be spacious, well lit and well-ventilated. It was also important for the health and the morals of the boys that they had an enclosed courtyard adjacent to the School, extensive enough for all of them to use at leisure times. Although not stressed at the time, the Council must also have had in mind the 'bickering' that went on in the city streets. In the late eighteenth century snowball fights in the High Street between university students and Grammar School boys were common, and by tradition the

ABOVE. Site of the tomb of St Kentigern in the crypt of Glasgow Cathedral. (© Crown Copyright: RCAHMS. Licensor www.rcahms.gov.uk)

LEFT. Bishop Elphinstone (1431–1514), Chancellor of Scotland, was a Grammar School pupil.

The Old School Building in School Wynd was the site of the Grammar School from 1461 to 1788.

The Lintel and Descriptive Stones, of the rebuilding of 1601, became an integral part of the School buildings.

Slezer's engraving of College (University) and Blackfriars' Church (1693). (Reproduced by permission of the Trustees of the National Library of Scotland)

The Grammar School building at 294 George Street was the site of the School between 1788 and 1821.

RIGHT. Sir John Moore of
Corunna (1761–1809) left the
Grammar School in 1772
determined on a military
career. (Reproduced by
permission of the National
Portrait Gallery, London)

BELOW. Prussian Pistols were
given to Sir John Moore by
the Earl Marischal in 1775.

LEFT. Colin Campbell, Lord
Clyde (1792–1863), attended
the Grammar School from
1797 until 1803.

BELOW. The Sword of Lord
Clyde is now housed in the
High School at Anniesland.

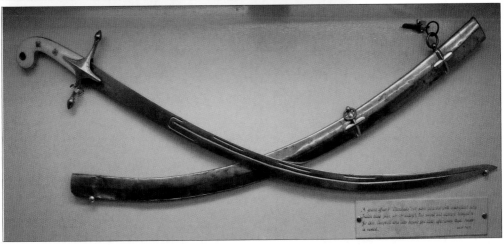

Statue of General Sir Thomas Munro (1761–1827) in Madras. He was a pupil at the Grammar School from 1769 until 1772.

Kirkman Finlay (1773–1842), Merchant, attended the Grammar School in the 1780s. (Reproduced by permission of Merchants' House, Glasgow)

Thomas Campbell (1777–1844), Poet, left the Grammar School in 1791.

James Lumsden (1778–1856), Philanthropist, gave over fifty years of public service to Glasgow. (Courtesy of RCAHMS. Photograph by M. Turnbull. Licensor www.rcahms.gov.uk)

The Grammar/High School building in John Street from 1821 until 1878.

William Chrystal was Rector of the Grammar School from 1815 until 1830.

Sir Henry Campbell-Bannerman, Liberal Prime Minister, 1905–08, had been a pupil at the High School from 1845 until 1850.

schoolboys would 'order' older men to take off their hats and 'order' women to curtsy. Stone-throwing occurred in better weather, and the situation deteriorated after the founding of Wilson's Charity School in 1778.[56]

Taken together the proposed changes were a radical departure from previous structures and procedures. As Barr did not seem to have been a particularly ineffectual Rector, at first glance it is difficult to understand why the abolition of his office was unanimously supported. Financial considerations do not seem to have been important. On retirement, Rector Barr was to be given an annuity of £60. On his death, three years later in 1785, when this sum could have been saved, the Council agreed to increase the salaries of the masters by £5 to £25 per annum, and further to augment the salary of the master teaching the oldest class (which they all did in rotation) to £30.[57] However, it is the suggested administrative changes which give some hint of the real cause of the disappearance of the office of Rector.

The emphasis on equality for all schoolmasters and the end of distinctions between them, even to the extent of their all wearing black gowns to demonstrate that they were all university graduates, implies that differentiation of status was the source of the problems. This is borne out by a report of the GSC in 1830 in which its members 'understood that the jealousies and dissensions to which the distinction then gave rise'[58] had been the cause of the rectorship's abolition. Certainly there had been a history of discord, as in 1734 and 1738 the Council felt obliged to define the Rector's powers, stressing his authority and threatening any master who did not fall into line with loss of office. This was a reiteration of previous practice and was only needed because of the personality clashes between masters. Despite the change in personnel, the problem seems to have continued simmering, and by 1782 the Council was unwilling to go on defending the Rector and his office. Unfortunately the new arrangement did not solve the issue, as, with no master in charge, the School was to be even more fragmented than it had been before. This, however, was the system until 1815.

Later in 1830 the GSC suggested, somewhat unconvincingly, their educational reasons for the demise of the Rector's office. The object of learning Latin could be accomplished in four years of diligent study. Indeed, it argued that to take longer would hold back the cultivation of other branches of knowledge likely to be of more practical use in future life. Moreover, if the courses did prove too short and a Rector *was* needed, it would be easier to add a year and appoint a Rector than to dispose of one, although such an appointment would only be possible when a vacancy occurred.[59] Yet the School had operated in its earliest days with one master and, throughout the sixteenth century, with a master and one doctor. So, in 1782, it would surely have been possible to carry on with a Rector and three masters for a four-year course. Again, it appears that the real reason for not doing so was that harmony amongst the staff was deemed more likely when no one member held authority and power for a prolonged period.

THE NEW GRAMMAR SCHOOL IN GEORGE STREET, 1788–1821

Once the central decision on the rectorship had been made the other arrangements were advanced. At the end of June 1782 the Council began to search for a 'proper piece of ground fit for building thereon a new Grammar School',[60] which was to contain rooms for teaching French, Arithmetic and Book-keeping out of hours. Following the resignation of Barr, advertisements were placed in the Glasgow and Edinburgh papers and 'by a great majority of votes' Daniel Macarthur, schoolmaster in Glasgow, was appointed to complete the complement of four masters.[61]

In November 1782 the new GSC was formed with Bailie Alexander Brown (Convener), William Coats and Gilbert Hamilton. They were joined by six university professors, and together they visited the School for four consecutive months and reported back to the Council on 26 March 1783. The masters appeared 'faithful, careful and diligent' and the boys were proficient, but two classes were found to be very large. It was agreed that if in future a class went above fifty in number the master would teach the poorest-performing third for an extra hour each day.[62]

By 1784 the GSC was expanded in size and the convenership taken over by Gilbert Hamilton. It remained conscientious in its visitations to the School, and with favourable reports the Committee turned its attention to the building of a new School. On 4 December 1786 it reported, recommending that the Council allot a piece of ground without cost to the project and that the old building be sold to defray the costs of providing the new accommodation. On 25 April 1787 the Committee was authorised to agree with subscribers and tradesmen the contract for the new School. However, the Council would accept no responsibility for any expense, limiting its contribution to the land and the monies raised by the selling of the old building.[63] Only when the new building was complete would the Council accept responsibility for its upkeep and maintenance.[64]

The foundations of the new School in George Street[65] were dug during June 1787 and the foundation stone laid on Monday 16 July.[66] The architect John Craig[67] produced an 'elegant'[68] even 'handsome'[69] building in the popular Adam style. The main frontage was of two storeys, with slightly projecting wings of three storeys on each side. There was a ground-floor Common Hall in the central part of the building and six classrooms in each of the wings.[70] The playground behind the School was enclosed with dwarf stone walls surmounted by iron palisades. The accommodation was considerably more than was immediately needed for the School, which explains why as late as 1792 it remained unfinished.[71] William Craig and Sons were paid £219 19s for the work on 5 June 1793.[72] All in all it looked as if the School would remain a considerable time in its new site on the north side of George Street.

MASTERS AND THEIR CLASSES

The improved accommodation helped bring stability to the staff. After the appointment of James Gibson[73] in January 1794 there were to be no further changes for a decade.[74] Daniel Macarthur taught in the School from 1782 to 1808; David Allison[75] from 1783 to 1809, while John Wilson taught from 1787 to 1805.

Macarthur had been a firebrand in his younger days, preaching virulent anti-Catholicism in his sermons.[76] However, this did not prevent the Town Council from electing him, for he had built up a good reputation for his private classes in the rudiments of the Latin language, French and English grammar. One of his private pupils for Latin was Thomas Muir (1765–1799), the political reformer, who then went on to study law at Glasgow and Edinburgh universities before being tried for sedition in 1793. Macarthur appeared as a witness for the defence in the famous trial of Muir.[77]

Macarthur is remembered for keeping his classes in very good order, without being a harsh disciplinarian. He affected to speak 'the English language with an English accent, which made him appear a stiff and formal dominie; but he pronounced the Latin tongue in good broad Scotch idiom'.[78] His first class of 1782–6, consisting of 110 boys, included some of exceptional ability: the lawyers Alexander McGregor (1772–1839) and George Morrison (d. 1844); Alexander Brown, surgeon in India, (1773–1798), dux of class in 1783 and 1786 and Snell Exhibitioner[79] in 1790; Alexander McAslan (d. 1841), dux of class in 1784 and 1785; Hugh Houston, who gave a gold guinea at a Candlemas Offering and was declared 'Victor';[80] John Rae, advocate in Edinburgh; Thomas Watson, of the private banking family; (Sir) James Barns (d. 1850) who became a Lieutenant-General, fighting throughout the French Revolutionary and Napoleonic Wars; Thomas Brown (1774–1853), surgeon to Glasgow Royal Infirmary and Professor of Botany at Glasgow University, who made money in India and inherited wealth, building Langside House and dying the wealthiest man of the class; Thomas Christie (1774–1829) who was head of the Smallpox Hospitals in Ceylon before becoming a GP in Cheltenham; Matthew Gardiner (1776–1865) who became Moderator of the General Assembly in 1837 and was minister of Bothwell Church between 1802 and 1865, dying 'Father of the Church'; and Archibald Monteith (d. 1842) who was the 'recognised arbiter of beauty in Glasgow' and had an elaborate mausoleum built in the Glasgow Necropolis.[81]

His class of 1795–9 was made up of 115 boys, whose average age was eight to nine years old. A son of the then Provost was in the class,[82] which was a 'fair representation of the respectable and industrious classes of the community' at that time.[83] In 1802 the *Glasgow Courier* carried details of Macarthur's curriculum. In addition to his Classical lessons, he offered instruction in English grammar, composition and spelling, as well as in Writing, which was especially useful, he claimed, for 'those who are afterwards to be employed in commercial transactions'.[84] His publicity had the desired effect, for among the boys he enrolled that year was William Weir (1794–1876), who was dux in his final year (1806).

When Macarthur died in early February 1808 four prominent newspapers carried the intimation. The *Glasgow Courier* summarised the man and his contribution to education:

> Though distinguished as a Preacher, for fidelity and usefulness, he was particularly eminent in his profession as a Teacher, which he exercised for ten years in a private Academy, and twenty-five in the Grammar School. His diligence and success in teaching, joined with mildness of disposition and gentleness of manners, gained the affections of his pupils and the approbation of the public, while integrity of character, benevolence of heart and unaffected piety secured him the esteem of all who had the pleasure of his acquaintance'.[85]

Contemporaneous with Macarthur on the School staff was David Allison, who proved to be a highly respected teacher whose classes remembered him years after they had left. His popularity resulted in the largest class in the School's history in 1806–7 – 174 scholars – claimed at the time by the *Glasgow Courier* to be the largest class under one schoolmaster in Scotland. It held this circumstance to be gratifying to Allison as a teacher, bringing honour to him as an individual, and a strong mark of public approval of the School.[86]

In a tribute to Allison in May 1809, his 'constant and indefatigable attention' to his profession and his pupils was praised and his excellent personal qualities commented on.[87] It should perhaps also be mentioned that he 'was a rigid disciplinarian of the good old type, who seems to have whipped the dead languages into his pupils'.[88] On his death a marble tablet, suitably inscribed, was erected to his memory in the choir of Glasgow Cathedral. 'It deserves to be generally known, that this monument was both suggested by, and executed at the expense of, the boys who were under the tuition of this valuable teacher.'[89]

CLASS MEETINGS[90]

The number of Former Pupils known to distinguish themselves in later years increased substantially in this period. It was also at this time that the practice began of those who were educated in the Grammar School dining together on 10 October, the anniversary of the day they entered the institution. The first meeting was generally held within five years of the pupils leaving. Class meetings were aimed at cherishing early friendships and remembering schooldays, and where possible their master was invited as a guest. One of the oldest was the class of Patrick Holmes, who commenced with a group of 107 in 1762. Its first Class Meeting was in 1769, and a number of members continued to meet regularly for fifty years. In 1775 Robert Gray jnr gifted an elegant silver medal, which was worn regularly at its meetings. In the later 1770s the class contributed £11 10s 6d for the relief of Jean, the daughter of their late teacher, who was in straightened circumstances. Another daughter, Giles, was given a pension from Hutchesons' Hospital following the intervention of two of the class. In 1789 Tin Smith, a classmate who needed capital to develop his business, was given £70 as start-up money. These were examples of the many instances where the benevolence of a class sought out and assisted early associates who needed help. The last meeting of this particular class was in 1818, when there were five members present.

PUPILS

During the eighteenth century Glasgow became an international entrepôt with strong commercial connections. The city was transformed primarily as a result of the growth of the tobacco trade with the American colony of Virginia. The dominance of the 'tobacco lords' ended with American independence in 1776, and they were replaced by an equally powerful cadre of West India merchants trading in sugar and rum, and later by the East India merchants. They brought unprecedented wealth and stimulated a range of manufacturing, banking and associated activities.

These developments ensured that Glasgow's merchants strengthened their economic and political ascendancy and confirmed their position as the most prestigious group socially. Yet within the urban elite there were gradations, with those involved in overseas trade the wealthiest sector providing the majority of Glasgow's Lord Provosts.[91] However, the customary educational route for their sons was the Grammar School, which remained 'a popular institution,'[92] followed by a year or two at Glasgow University.[93] In the 1740s around a quarter of matriculated students at the university recorded their father's occupation as 'industry and commerce' and this rose to the remarkable figure of one half by the 1790s.[94] However, only 12 per cent of them appear to have entered merchant careers: between 1765 and 1774, 48 per cent opted for the Church; 9 per cent for medicine; 8 per cent for law; 5 per cent for the military; 5 per cent for teaching and 4 per cent for administration.[95]

Categorising Grammar School pupils suggests somewhat different results, but the first two Former Pupils underline the difficulties involved in this process: the first exemplifies the varied career of a wealthy man, and the second the varied career of a polymath.

Robert Reid (1773–1865) was born in the Candleriggs, the son of a Glasgow cabinet-maker. He was educated in Macarthur's class (1782–6), and at the University of Glasgow. At 17 he was apprenticed to muslin manufacturing; at 19 he became a partner in the firm; at 20 he set up own muslin business. In his twenties he joined a shipping partnership trading with Jamaica, then a mahogany importers, then a pottery company and finally an upholsterer. In his thirties he became a partner in a commission agency and in his forties he began cabinet-making. He retired at 59 in 1832, and contributed, under the pseudonym of Senex, articles on local memorabilia, collected and published as *Glasgow Past and Present* in three volumes between 1851 and 1856. He also published *Old Glasgow and Its Environs* in 1864.[96]

(Prof. Sir) William Hamilton (1788–1856) was born in Glasgow, the son of William Hamilton, Professor of Anatomy and Botany. He attended Gibson's class from 1796, going on to study Medicine at Edinburgh before being awarded a Snell Exhibition. He achieved an outstanding First, his examiners being 'astonished' at his erudition. He abandoned Medicine and in 1813 was admitted as an advocate at the Edinburgh bar. He was elected to a professorship of Civil History at Edinburgh University and carried out anatomical research which discredited phrenology.[97] He turned to Philosophy, in 1829, writing influential articles which resulted in his election to the chair of Logic and Metaphysics at Edinburgh University in 1836. He produced philosophic tracts, but his reputation suffered much from John Stuart Mill's *Examination of Sir William Hamilton's Philosophy* (1865).[98]

Merchants

Gilbert Hamilton (1744–1808)[99] was a Glasgow merchant and agent for the Carron Iron Company. He was the founder and first secretary of the Chamber of Commerce in 1783: the first in Britain. He was Convener of the GSC, 1783–98 and 1806–8, and Lord Provost of Glasgow, 1792–93.

James McGill (1744–1813) was the eldest son of an ironsmith, who attended the School (1749–56) before matriculating at Glasgow University. He emigrated to Canada and became a fur trader.[100] He was elected to the Legislative Assembly of Lower Canada. He was nominated to join the Governor-General's Executive Council, and as a brigadier-general helped defeat an invading American army in October 1813. He bequeathed his farm, Burnside, and £10,000 for the founding of McGill College in Montreal.[101] The college became a university in 1821.

John Hamilton (1754–1829) became a wealthy merchant trading with the West Indies. He was appointed Lord Provost of Glasgow in 1801, 1802, 1803, 1810 and 1811. His son, William Hamilton of Northpark, also went on to become Lord Provost of Glasgow in 1829.

James McKenzie (1760–1838) was in Bald's 1769–72 class. He became a wealthy merchant, serving as Lord Provost of Glasgow, 1806–8. He built the opulent Craigpark House and grounds, which were sold in 1850 to Alexander Dennistoun.

John Buchanan (1761–1839) was also a member of Bald's 1769–72 class. He became a successful Glasgow merchant and was a governor of Wilson's School. He served as Tory MP for Dunbartonshire between 1821 and 1826.

Kirkman Finlay (1773–1842) was the son of a textile merchant and attended Glasgow University. He traded with the Americas and sent ships to India and the Far East, breaking the East India Company's monopoly. He was Lord Provost, 1812–14 and 1818; elected Free Trade Tory MP for Glasgow Burghs in 1812–18 and Malmesbury in 1818–20; and Rector of Glasgow University, 1819–20. He was buried in the Blackadder Aisle in Glasgow Cathedral. His statue[102] can be found in Glasgow's Merchants' House commemorating his contribution to furthering Glasgow's trade.[103]

James Ewing (1775–1853) left the School in 1787 and became a member of the 'sugar aristocracy' which dominated Glasgow's institutions. He became Convener of the GSC 1817–18; Lord Provost, 1832–3; and Whig/Radical MP for Glasgow from 1832 until 1835. His popularity waned with the growing antipathy towards the reliance of the sugar industry on slave-labour in the Caribbean, but he left significant bequests to many public institutions.

James Smith (1782–1867)[104] attended Glasgow University before joining his family's West Indian trading business. He served in the Renfrewshire militia during the Napoleonic Wars, was 'father' of yachting on the Clyde and made contributions to geology.

James Burns (1789–1871)[105] was the son of a minister. In 1818 he went into business with his younger brother, George. He ran steamers to Liverpool and Ireland; from 1839 he ran mail ships to Halifax and Boston,[106] later adding New York and Mediterranean trade routes. The brothers ultimately owned 107 Clyde-built steamers. He was a Town Councillor, 1836–45.

Michael Scott (1789–1835) was the son of a Glasgow merchant. He attended Allison's class between 1797 and 1801 and then graduated from Glasgow University. He went to Jamaica, where he learned to manage estates. He published *Tom Cringle's Log*, and later began to produce stories based on his Jamaican experiences. He was buried in the Necropolis.[107]

Alexander Dennistoun (1790–1874)[108] was in Wilson's 1799–1801 classes before attending Glasgow University. He joined the family cotton-trade business, working in the New Orleans, Liverpool and Le Havre branches. He became a director of the Union Bank of Scotland and Whig MP for Dunbartonshire, 1835–7. He founded the suburb of Dennistoun in 1861.

William Hamilton (1790–1866) was dux of Wilson's class in 1801, 1802 and 1803. He became a West India merchant and Lord Provost of Glasgow, 1826–8.

Manufacturers (Industrialists)

Charles Macintosh (1766–1843) was the son of a well-known dyer. About 1820, he found a method of sealing a layer of rubber between layers of cloth. The resulting waterproof material was commercially successful for making garments and other products.[109] The Macintosh name became a household word (soon modified to Mackintosh). He proved an innovative chemist and was elected in 1824 as a Fellow, Royal Society (FRS). A stone at the north wall of Glasgow Cathedral graveyard marks his burial place.

William Murray (1790–1858)[110] was the son of a city merchant. He was in Macarthur's 1798–1802 class, being dux in his rudiments year. He became the coal- and iron-master of Monkland Iron and Steel Company. He was President of Anderson's College, 1844–58 and a Town Councillor, 1850–8.

John Smith (youngest) (1784–1849) was born in Glasgow and attended Glasgow University before joining the family bookselling business in 1803. He was responsible for extending and diversifying its publications, and by the 1820s he was in sole charge. In 1835 the bookshop moved to 70 St Vincent Street. In public life he was secretary of the committee for the relief of the industrious poor and a Glasgow merchant Bailie (1827–34).[111]

Churchmen

(Rev.) David Ure (1749–1798) studied Divinity at Glasgow University and became parish minister at Uphall. His *History of Rutherglen and East Kilbride* (1793) contained the earliest illustrations of Scottish fossils and led to Ure's reputation as the 'father' of palaeontology in Scotland.[112] His collection is still preserved in the Hunterian and Kelvingrove museums.

(Rev.) John Jamieson (1759–1838) attended the School in 1765–6 and entered Glasgow University to study Theology at the age of nine. He took on the charge of Forfar before being called to Nicolson Street, Edinburgh in 1793. He was largely responsible for the 1820 Reunion of the secessionist Anti-burghers (of which he was one) and Burghers.[113] Almost single-handedly he completed the *Etymological Dictionary of the Scottish Language*, which was published in two volumes in 1808.[114]

(Prof.) Ralph Wardlaw (1779–1853) was the son of a Glasgow merchant and attended Allison's class from 1787–91, before matriculating at Glasgow University. He was ordained into the Congregational Church on North Albion Street in 1803. He became Professor of Systematic Theology at the Glasgow Theological Academy while keeping on his busy urban pastorate, and he was active in the British and Foreign Bible Society. He worked to establish schools for the children of the labouring poor of Glasgow and was instrumental in the formation of the Glasgow Anti-Slavery Society (1823). This stance was unpopular, given Glasgow's West Indian connections, and led to a decline in attendance at his church as well as press attacks on him. It also led to a split in his family as his cousin, James Ewing, was a dominant figure in the Merchants' House. His memorial is a colossal marble portrait bust (by John Mossman, 1853).[115]

Military

(Sir) John Moore (1761–1809)[116] was born into a medical family and attended the School,[117] leaving in early 1772. He determined on a military career and was presented with a pair of Prussian pistols and a pocket edition of Horace[118] by George Keith, Earl Marischal in May 1775. He saw action in the American Revolutionary War and was wounded in the French Revolutionary Wars. He served in Ireland during the insurrection of 1798, was wounded attempting to free the Netherlands from French control in the following year, and wounded again in 1801 trying to oust the French from Egypt. His participation in the capture of Cairo and the successful siege of Alexandria resulted in Moore receiving the thanks of parliament on his return home. Between 1802 and 1807 he established a celebrated training camp for light infantry at Shorncliffe.[119] In 1808 Moore was sent to northern Spain and, facing overwhelming French forces in the Peninsular War, he was killed at Corunna. (One of the burial party may have been Colin Campbell, another pupil of the Grammar School.) Glasgow raised nearly £4,000 for a statue in George Square, which was completed by John Flaxman in 1819.[120] Throughout the nineteenth century Moore was famous and much admired, and Rev. Charles Wolfe's 'Funeral of Sir John Moore' (1817) remained a popular and powerful elegy.[121]

(Admiral Sir) Graham Moore (1764–1843), a brother of Sir John, also attended the School and befriended Thomas Munro. He entered the navy in 1777, serving in the West Indies, North America, and in the English Channel. When war broke out in 1793 he was active in the North Sea and on the coast of France, achieving conspicuous success against French privateers and intercepting Spanish treasure ships. By 1819 he was commander-in-chief in the Mediterranean. In his final years he became an admiral and commander-in-chief at Plymouth. Although a brave and resourceful naval officer, he missed all the great fleet actions of his time but benefited from the patronage of the Duke of Hamilton.[122]

James Hamilton (1777–1815) was in Allison's 1785–9 class. He was a professional soldier, and by the time of Waterloo in June 1815 he was a lieutenant-colonel, commanding the Scots Greys. He was killed in the battle while leading a charge on horseback.

(Sir) Neil Douglas (1780–1853) was the son of a Glasgow merchant. He joined the Cameron Highlanders, serving with Sir John Moore at Corunna. As lieutenant-colonel he commanded, in 1812, in the battles of the Pyrenees. His battalion fought at Quatre Bras and Waterloo, where he was wounded. He became Lieutenant-General (1846) and was Governor of Edinburgh Castle (1842–7).[123]

Thomas Hamilton (1789–1842) was born in Glasgow, the son of William Hamilton, Professor of Anatomy and Botany, and younger brother of William. He attended Allison's class from 1798–1801 and Glasgow University. Following failure in business, he embarked on a military career, serving in the Peninsular War, Canada and the occupation army in France following Napoleon's defeat. On his retirement, he published the novel *Cyril Thornton*, which contained fictionalised accounts of his early life in Glasgow and his military experiences, followed by *Annals of the Peninsular War*. After a visit to America he produced the popular *Men and Manners in America* in 1833.[124]

Medical

(Dr) John Moore (1729–1802), son of a Presbyterian minister, attended the School, 1737–41, before going on to university. He developed an extensive practice as a surgeon in Glasgow. In middle age he moved to London, where as a writer he achieved celebrity as a social observer and amateur historian. His most famous work[125] was published in 1789. After extensive travel in France he followed this, in 1793, with a narrative journal on his experiences. Later he published an assessment of the financial conditions which led to the French Revolution.[126] He sent his sons to the Grammar School.

(Prof.) William Hamilton (1758–1790) left the School in 1770 and went on to Glasgow University, before studying Medicine in Edinburgh and London. In 1781 he was appointed to his father's chair of Anatomy and Botany[127] at Glasgow, and the following year, on the latter's death, he inherited a large surgical practice, to which he added Obstetrics.[128]

(Dr) James Moore (1762–1860), a younger brother of Sir John, studied Medicine at Edinburgh and London, and served as an army medical officer. By 1784 he had set up a practice in London and published on a variety of

medical and surgical topics. He was an early defender of Jenner's new vacci-
nation and became director of the National Vaccine Establishment. His
fame, however, owed more to his narrative defending his brother's actions in
Spain (1809) and his two-volume life of Sir John Moore (1834).[129]

(Dr) James Watson (1787–1871) was in Gibson's class from 1796, being
its dux in 1797 and 1798. He was President of the Glasgow Faculty of
Physicians and Surgeons, 1838–41, 1849–52 and 1857–60. As 'father of the
faculty', he ensured it gained the same privileges in medical licensing and
education as other Royal Colleges under the 1858 Medical Act.

Legal

David Boyle, Lord Shewalton (1772–1853), joined Bald's rudiments class in
1781–2[130] and went on to study at St Andrews and Glasgow Universities.[131]
He was called to the bar in 1793 and became Solicitor-General for Scotland
(May 1807) in Portland's administration. He was Tory MP for Ayrshire from
1807–11, going on to be a Lord of Session and then Lord Justice Clerk, a post
he held for nearly thirty years. His final posts were Lord Justice-General and
President of the Court of Session.[132]

Colin Dunlop (1775–1837) attended Bradfute's 1783–7 class and was its
dux in the rudiments year. He became an advocate and Whig/Radical MP
for Glasgow, 1835–6. He extended the Clyde Iron Works. He was buried
under a large monument in the Necropolis.

Colin Donald (1777–1859) was the dux of Dow's class in 1785, 1786 and
1788 (losing out in 1787 to Thomas Wallace, from Halifax, Nova Scotia). He
became a solicitor and served as Commissary Clerk of Lanarkshire (1817–58).

George Dunlop (1777–1852) attended Allison's 1785–9 class and was its
dux in 1787–8. He became a Writer to the Signet.

John Jardine (1777–1850) also attended Allison's 1785–9 class, being its
dux in 1785–6. He was a Snell Exhibitioner, 1795–7. He became an advocate
and was Sheriff of Ross and Cromarty, 1833–50.

George Baillie (1784–1873) was in Gibson's class between 1793 and 1796.
He trained to be a solicitor and was admitted to the Faculty of Procurators
in 1811. He founded Baillie's Institute with £18,000 (the savings of his
lifetime). He was buried near the south door of Glasgow Cathedral.

John Fleming (1790–1869)[133] attended Glasgow and Edinburgh
Universities. He joined the Faculty of Procurators (1812). He, and his
partners, purchased the lands of Kelvinside (1839) and Gartnavel (1845) to
produce the most prestigious residential district in Glasgow.

John Dunlop (d. 1842) was dux of Daniel Macarthur's fourth class (1794–8) in 1796 before going on to attend Edinburgh University. He was called to the bar in 1807 but concentrated on publishing his *History of Fiction* in three volumes in Edinburgh. He became Sheriff-Depute of Renfrewshire in 1816, an office he retained until his death. In 1823 he produced the first two volumes of a *History of Roman Literature*, and his final works in the 1830s were *Memoirs of Spain* and *Poems* (of his father).[134]

Academic

(Prof.) John Robison (1739–1805) left the School in 1750 to study at Glasgow University. He was appointed to chairs of Chemistry at Edinburgh and Glasgow, and in 1772 secured a professorship in Mathematics at Kronstadt. He later accepted the chair of Natural Philosophy at Edinburgh and became General Secretary to the Royal Society of Edinburgh between 1783 and 1798. Robison researched and published on electricity, optics, astronomy, dynamics and practical mechanics.[135]

Duncan Macfarlan (1769–1844) was the son of a farmer at Aberfoyle. At the School he was dux of Bradfute's fourth (and final) class in 1782–3. He became the parish schoolmaster at Stewarton, a post he retained for over fifty years.

(Prof.) John Maclean (1771–1814) became the first Professor of Chemistry at Princeton University in 1795 and then two years later Professor of Mathematics and Natural Philosophy there. In 1812 he was appointed Professor of Natural Philosophy and Chemistry at the William and Mary College in Virginia.

(Prof.) William Meikleham (1771–1846) attended Bradfute's 1783–7 class. He was the first Rector of the newly created Ayr Academy. In 1799 he became Professor of Astronomy at Glasgow University, and in 1803 Professor of Natural Philosophy, a post he retained until 1846.

(Prof.) John Burns (1775–1850) became visiting surgeon to the Royal Infirmary (1797). He was appointed Professor of Anatomy and Theory at Anderson's College in 1799 and held the post of Regius Professor of Surgery at Glasgow University between 1817 and 1850. He gained an international reputation on abortion and midwifery.

Financial

James Lumsden (1778–1856)[136] was the son of a printer and engraver. On leaving the School he entered his father's wholesale stationery firm, which he ran after his father's death. A reforming Whig, he gave over fifty years of public service to Glasgow and became Lord Provost, 1843–6. He was a successful fund-raiser for the Royal Infirmary, provided homes and night refuges for the homeless and was behind the formation of the Glasgow Savings Bank in 1836. He was the moving spirit in 1838 in the formation of the Clydesdale Bank, and was its first chairman. He also helped found the City of Glasgow Life Assurance Company, the City and Suburban Gas Company and the Caledonian Railway Company. He endowed a Gold Medal at the School for Mathematics, which he saw as of paramount importance in a commercial city.[137] He was involved in many local causes or public events,[138] being Provost when the foundation of the new Glasgow University building on Gilmorehill was laid. He was honorary treasurer of Glasgow Royal Infirmary for over twenty years, and it is fitting that 'his memory and services should be perpetuated in bronze, by [John] Mossman, in front of an institution so noble'.[139]

Donald Cuthbertson (1784–1864) attended Dow's class, 1792–4, then Gibson's class, 1794–6, being dux in 1795. He graduated from Glasgow University in 1801 and was the first Scottish chartered accountant to earn a university degree.[140] He joined his father's firm, becoming a partner in 1810. He was first secretary and treasurer, Royal Asylum for Lunatics at Gartnavel, 1814–64; and Convener of the High School Committee, 1827–33.

Allan Cuthbertson (1786–1864) trained with his father (William), the 'first professional accountant in Glasgow'.[141] He joined with his elder brother, Donald, to form D. & A. Cuthbertson in West George Street. He was a council member of the Institute of Insurance and Actuaries, 1854–64.

William Ewing (1788–1874)[142] attended the School and the university before establishing a marine underwriting business. From 1825 until 1859 he managed the Association of Underwriters. He founded a chair of Music at Anderson's College, and was a philanthropist to humane and educational institutions.

Administrators (Politicians)

(General Sir) Thomas Munro (1761–1827), was born into a comfortable merchant family and joined Bald's 1769–72 class. While at the School he surpassed all his schoolfellows in athletic exercises and was particularly eminent as a boxer. He attended Glasgow University before, in 1779, becoming a cadet in the East India Company. Promotion was slow, but in

1820 he was appointed Governor of Madras, an honour usually reserved for British politicians rather than company officials. His period of office was a time of significant accord, as he was one of the few British administrators who sought to put Indians in high office.[143] He was created a baronet of Lindertis (in Forfarshire). The administrative framework he set up in southern and western India was to last till the end of British rule.[144] His statue, on horseback, is to be found in the middle of Chennai's famed island, Madras.[145]

James Cleland (1770–1840) joined his father's firm as a cabinet-maker. He proved a successful businessman and urban property developer. In 1807 his plan for the building of a new Grammar School was adopted.[146] Between 1814 and 1834 he held the post of Superintendent of Public Works, being responsible for extensive town improvements. He published *The Annals of Glasgow* (1816), and *The Rise and Progress of the City of Glasgow* (1820).[147] To mark his retirement, in 1834, as a result of £4,600 being raised by public subscription, a tenement was erected at the top of Buchanan Street (No. 249) which bore the inscription 'The Cleland Testimonial'. He occupied this building until his death.[148]

Writers (Artists, Architects, Poets, Journalists).

James Graham(e) (1765–1811) went on from the School to Glasgow University. He became an advocate, writing verse as a means of recreation. In 1804 Graham published a descriptive and meditative poem entitled 'The Sabbath'. Within a year it had gone into three new editions, which included a sequel, 'Sabbath Walks'. In 1806 he published *Birds of Scotland* and a pamphlet advocating trial by jury in civil cases. A collection of his poems appeared in two volumes in 1808, followed by *British Georgics* (1809) and *Poems on the Abolition of the Slave Trade* (1810).[149]

Thomas Campbell (1777–1844) was the son of a tobacco importer. He proved an exemplary pupil in Allison's class at the School and was popular with his fellow scholars, participating in all their pastimes.[150] He left in 1791 to enter Glasgow University, where he won prizes for writing verse and acquired a reputation as a debater and translator. The publication of *The Pleasures of Hope* in 1799 proved an immediate success. Successive editions of his poems supplemented his income and his *Gertrude of Wyoming* (1809) was well received. He gave a series of successful lectures which helped contribute to the good reception of his *Specimens of the British Poets* (1819). Then he entered on his most successful venture, the editing of the *New*

Monthly Magazine. Publically he was much involved in establishing a university in London and was elected Rector of Glasgow University (1826–9).[151] In his later years he produced biographies of Sarah Siddons and Petrarch, remaining much admired in Scotland, where he was given the Freedom of the City of Edinburgh, with Glasgow students establishing a Campbell Club in his honour. He was buried in Westminster Abbey.[152] He was the most famous of Glasgow poets, having produced several stirring patriotic war songs. A statue of Campbell, sculpted by John Mossman, was erected on the south side of George Square in 1877.[153]

FOUR

From Grammar School to High School

In this chapter the reasons behind the brief revival of the post of Rector between 1815 and 1830 are examined, and the further move of the School – to John Street in 1821 – is explained. Included are a discussion of how the curriculum of the Grammar School became the centre of public attention in the 1820s and the role of Henry Paul in transforming the School into the High School in 1834. As in previous chapters there is emphasis on the teaching staff and their methods, and the ever-increasing number of distinguished Former Pupils and their growing contribution to Glasgow and beyond.

THE MOVE TO JOHN STREET

For a time, at least, the accommodation in George Street seemed more than adequate. Three rooms were let in August 1799: one room to ironmongers for use as an Episcopalian chapel;[1] a second room to a French teacher, and the third to Wilson's Charity School. All were charged £12 per annum.[2] However, by the beginning of session 1804–5, class sizes had risen again,[3] and the Hall was found to be too small for ordinary morning meetings and the annual examinations. Temporary solutions failed to solve the problem so, on 30 September 1807, Gilbert Hamilton moved that a larger and more commodious School be built. The Council agreed and, assuming that there was no public burden on the town, authorised the Grammar School Committee to consider an appropriate site and procure plans and estimates. As a result a plain building, on the ground immediately behind the George Street site with entry from Montrose Street, was decided upon. John Cleland produced three different designs, and the Committee chose one estimated to cost less than £2,000 sterling.

At this stage, however, matters stalled, because for the next four sessions the School roll went down.[4] It was June 1814 before the matter came before the Council again. By then the numbers had recovered and after 1815, with the addition of a fifth class, they were not to fall below 500 again until 1824.[5] It was remitted to Bailie Rodger to procure plans and estimates and report back.[6] His committee reported in August that the plans would cost under £2,500, and it wished to go ahead and put the old schoolhouse up for auction, with an upset of £2,500 and entry of July 1815. However, the Council dragged its feet.[7]

There was no further progress until Thomas Alston, Convener of the GSC, raised the matter again in January 1820, by which time the roll had increased to 570. He stressed that the accommodation situation had become acute and, with more teachers and pupils than ever, it was now worse than it had been in 1807 when the matter had first been proposed. The Council agreed that the Committee should bring forward proposals.[8]

On 29 May 1820, the GSC produced detailed plans to build on the north side of the existing playground with fronting to the south, and entry from Upper Montrose Street. The playground was to be enclosed with a wall and would include an arcade for play and shelter during bad weather, and water closets for the scholars. Both of the planned two storeys contained a larger hall (35 feet by 30 feet) and two smaller halls (33 feet by 30 feet);[9] the larger rooms were to accommodate 140 boys and the smaller rooms 130 boys. It was planned to include small anterooms or libraries attached to each for the use of masters, and meetings of the Committee would also be accommodated. As a Common Hall would be used only at annual prize distributions, it was decided that provision would be an extravagant use of scarce funds.[10]

The Committee recommended an immediate start to building because the costs of labour and materials were much reduced – it suggested that these were 20 per cent lower than in 1819 – at 'this season of great mercantile depression'.[11] Although there was no offer for the existing buildings, the Committee recommended that the Council should wait until trade revived to sell or let the property.[12] This argument persuaded the Council to go ahead with the contracts, which came in at £1,814.[13]

On 14 August 1820 the foundation stone of the new School building was laid by Convener Alston, and the ceremony was attended by Provost Henry Monteith MP and his Council. Although the proceedings appear to have been marked with much self-congratulation there was also a genuine appreciation of the importance of this great undertaking. After all, the Grammar School already had an illustrious history and it was expected that its future would be no less successful. On Tuesday 17 July 1821 the new site of the School in John Street was opened.[14] Dr Chrystal, in thanking the magistrates for their attention to the interests of the School, held that the new accommodation 'was not surpassed by any in the Kingdom'.[15] It was to remain the premises of the School for over half a century.

MASTERS

The French Revolutionary and Napoleonic Wars (1793–1815) were a period of rising prices in Scotland. From November 1795 the salary of the master of the oldest class was £30 and the others £20 each: the fees charged to the boys were increased from 5s to 6s a quarter. However, following a petition from the masters in September 1799 regarding the need for increases in both salaries and fees, on 7 November, the GSC agreed that the quarterly fee should be raised to 7s 6d, but that there would be no salary increase.[16] Given this decision, salaries remained a major issue as masters struggled to provide for their families and maintain their position in society.[17] Understandably they continued to complain how unfavourably their situation compared with ministers, whose stipends were raised from £300 to £400 per annum.[18]

John Wilson's resignation in June 1805 on the grounds of advancing age and infirmity was the first staff change for a decade. He requested an annuity. The GSC met him and recommended £60 per annum for life, given his 'assiduity, fidelity and success in discharging his duties'.[19] There were fourteen candidates for the vacancy and William Chrystal was appointed in September 1805. Born at Fordhead, Kippen in 1776, the son of a local farmer, Chrystal was educated locally, entering Glasgow University in 1791 and graduating MA in 1795. He went on successfully to study Divinity, although he did not enter the Church. Instead he became a private teacher of Classics in Glasgow before, in 1800, being appointed Rector of Stirling Grammar School.

In August 1807 the Grammar School masters petitioned for fees to be raised from 7s 6d to 10s 6d per quarter.[20] The GSC, aware that fees in other schools had just been raised, agreed to the increase provided a number of conditions were also met.[21] When classes exceeded 70–80 the master would be obliged, at his own expense, to provide an 'usher' to assist with the education of the boys and to enable the master to progress the 'duller' boys so as not to impede the rest.[22] Masters could continue to give private classes, but these could not contain any of their own public pupils, following complaints from parents about the expense and suspicions of partiality.[23] The Committee also had a clear opinion on the length of the course. It believed that the existing four years was not long enough for the boys to come to terms properly with the Latin language. To do this a fifth year was necessary. The Town Council, however, remained unconvinced and, as a result, the GSC report was left to lie on the table, ostensibly to allow further consideration.

Daniel Macarthur died in 1808 and, following advertisements in the Glasgow and Edinburgh newspapers, eighteen candidates applied for his vacant post. The Council was pleased with the number and their quality, which it felt reflected well on the state of teaching in Scotland. The GSC chose a shortlist of five which, after interview, was reduced to two, its thinking being coloured by the growing consensus in its ranks that the Council would soon agree to move to five classes. John Dymock,[24] Rector of Kelso Grammar School, was appointed to the vacancy, but Gilbert Hamilton again failed in his efforts to establish a fifth class at this time. When David Allison died, the Committee re-examined the details of those who had applied earlier and appointed Robert Douie, Rector of St Ninian's, Stirling, to take Allison's place.[25]

CLASS MEETINGS

Old record books are still extant for some class meetings. Daniel Macarthur's fourth class met between 1802 and 1851 as an 'association for the purpose of calling to remembrance and celebrating the days spent in their youth'. Macarthur's fifth class met for the first time in the Nile Tavern in 1806, and the last recorded meeting was in 1857.[26] David Allison's sixth class met from 1808 until 1846. The meetings were held annually on 10 October (the first day of the School session). The classes were known by the master's name; the number used indicated the number of classes taken by that master since he began teaching in the Grammar School (the masters remaining with the same class throughout the four-year course).[27]

WILLIAM CHRYSTAL: RECTOR, 1815–1830

On 2 March 1813 a petition, which had been drawn up by thirteen 'respectable inhabitants', was forwarded to the GSC. It held that during the summer months the hours of the Grammar School were 'unnecessarily numerous'. Six hours were deemed to be 'too large a portion of the day for the study of the Latin language', there being many branches of learning perhaps equally important, at least to those intending to follow a mercantile profession. The boys were fatigued by the length of time involved, and the confinement of over 100 boys in one room for six hours was even injurious to health. Moreover, many boys travelled a distance to the School and it was difficult for them to arrive for a 7 a.m. start. The School would do well to follow the example of schools in England, where morning classes had been abandoned and the hours taught were the same in summer as in winter.[28]

On 30 April the Council accepted that four hours (instead of six) was the maximum time for boys to concentrate effectively. With immediate effect the summer-month lessons were changed to 10 a.m.–12 noon and 1–3 p.m., in the expectation that this would lead to increased proficiency. Classes were to begin promptly and be dismissed on time to ensure that other classes were not disrupted.[29]

On 4 November 1814 Samuel Hunter moved that a Committee be set up to reconsider the issue of establishing a fifth year in the School. The Council remitted the matter to the GSC, which was to investigate.[30] Three weeks later, having discussed the issue with ministers who backed the proposals, the Committee supported a fifth year on the grounds that boys were leaving the School for university at too young an age, and before being properly prepared for university work. Further, it recommended that although the four masters should continue to teach, in rotation, the same set of scholars for four successive years, at the beginning of the fifth year the class should be placed under the tuition of a fifth master or Rector. However, 'to prevent all disputes or contests for power among the masters',[31] the fifth master or Rector was merely to precede the others in rank and degree, and should have no authority or control over the other masters.

The Committee also detailed its recommended curriculum. In the fifth class the boys should be instructed in the higher branches of Roman literature, and also in the correct and scientific use of their own language. Moreover, the boys should also be taught Geography, ancient and modern, and the Rector should give a class on the elements of Greek to those who intended to pursue that subject. It held that by this scheme the boys who were destined for university would carry with them all the previous attainments requisite to enable them to prosecute their future studies with success, while those boys who were destined to go into business would take with them valuable lessons liable to be of the greatest use to them in future life.[32]

The GSC appreciated that the fifth class would be smaller than the others, so it recommended that the Rector's salary be paid partly from Corporation funds. It suggested £100 a year and a fee of 15s a quarter (instead of the 10s 6d which the other masters would continue to collect).[33] Although the Council stalled again, by 4 April 1815 there was a majority to proceed with the proposals[34] and, on 30 May, it agreed to follow the GSC's recommendations. The Council then proceeded to elect unanimously one of the existing masters, William Chrystal,[35] as Rector, and at its meeting in August, faced with seventeen applications, it elected William Lorrain,[36] Rector of Jedburgh Grammar School, as Chrystal's replacement.

Chrystal carried into effect the plan of education spelled out the previous year by the GSC, and on 5 April 1816 approval was given to spend £30 on globes, maps and books for teaching Geography and Antiquities.[37] However, the new arrangement of a fifth class necessitated accommodation changes. The GSC pressed for the removal of the boys of Wilson's Charity and Jamieson's Scottish Episcopalian congregation, to enable three classes to be taught in the west end and two in the east end of the School. This had the advantage of needing only two entrances, allowing order to be improved and maintained more easily. It also suggested putting down paving in the east courtyard and levelling the playground, and also appointing a janitor, to help with discipline and cleanliness. To house him, an apartment was to be created at a cost of £200 and maintained by quarterly payments of 3d from each scholar. Further, to keep friction to a minimum, the Committee wanted each master and class to have separate supplies of coals and storage areas.[38]

The Council generally accepted these recommendations, although took its time with their implementation. In late September the appointment of a janitor was sanctioned by the Town's finance committee, with a limit of £262 of expenditure on his house,[39] which was built in a corner of the courtyard.[40] Despite the demanding job description[41] numerous candidates came forward, with John Allison appointed janitor and taking up employment in September 1817.[42]

At this time the GSC proposed appointing a Writing and Arithmetic master, who would offer lessons after school hours.[43] It seems likely that its members had been impressed by the more wide-ranging curriculum promoted by the Rector of the High School in Edinburgh, Dr Alexander Adam. This persuaded the Glasgow Council to elect Adam Stevenson, a local teacher, on 27 December 1816, to the post. He was to fit up his own room in the east wing, and his wages, although regulated by the Council, were to be paid directly by the parents of pupils.[44]

In August 1820 James Gibson resigned after twenty-seven years service, and the Council granted him an allowance of £100 per annum, which was to be paid for by his successor.[45] The scholars of his last class, 'after an address expressive of the unfeigned regard and affection which they entertain for him as their teacher, presented him with an elegant Silver Cup'.[46] The Council also expressed its high regard of his 'fidelity, zeal, abilities, and great success during a long period of service'. He was replaced by William Pyper of Maybole, who was appointed from among twenty-one applicants.[47] However, by March 1821, Pyper, surprised by the low numbers in his class, appealed for further financial support, which the Council gave in the form of an additional allowance of £75, which was to be reviewed annually.[48] In February of the following year the Council raised this to £95, but by then Pyper, probably concerned by continuing financial insecurity, was looking for employment elsewhere. Later, in 1822, he moved to the High School in Edinburgh[49] and his place at the Grammar School was taken by William Cowan, Rector of Darlington Academy.[50]

Although Chrystal was deemed to be the equal of the other masters, he appears to have taken the lead on a number of educational matters.[51] He was prominent in the discussions to set up a library[52] in October 1822, when James Ewing[53] gifted 20 guineas. The scholars were to contribute 1s a year, producing £25 for the purchase of books. As in Edinburgh, the library would open for an hour every Saturday morning, and Chrystal and the other masters agreed to attend in rotation.[54] Chrystal then approached the Council asking for recompense for the masters who had bought new gowns on the occasion of George IV's visit to Scotland. This was agreed, the total bill coming to £36.[55]

Chrystal was also much involved in the controversial issue of Candlemas gratuities. By the 1820s the system was being increasingly criticised as degrading to the masters and opening up the temptation of dishonesty to the boys. The traditional defence that it resulted in poorer parents being subsidised or supported by wealthier parents did not seem to be borne out by the facts, for frequently it appeared that poorer households gave more through pride, while those deemed wealthy tended to give less so as not to be accused of ostentation. Following correspondence between the GSC and the masters in January 1822 an agreement was reached.[56] However, the Council was again slow to ratify, although such gratuities were being generally abandoned elsewhere. Eventually, on 14 February 1826, following a further petition from the masters in which Lorrain graphically underlined his dire situation by threatening to pitch a tent in the school playground to house his family,[57] the Candlemas gratuities were abolished, and the fees were raised to 13s 6d for masters and 19s for Chrystal.[58]

The differential in fees and salary between Chrystal and the other masters became an increasing problem, especially as salaries continued to erode. In December 1826 the four masters – Dymock, Douie, Lorrain and Cowan – petitioned the Council detailing their plight. With inflation and a decrease in class numbers their salary emoluments were not adequate, and only an increase in salaries to £50 each per annum (from £35) could relieve the immediate problem. The Council agreed to this request on 16 January 1827, and indeed backdated the increase to the previous November.[59] With the financial issues temporarily put to rest attention now focused on the curriculum.

THE ORGANISATION OF THE GRAMMAR SCHOOL AFTER 1815

At a meeting of the GSC in October 1786 the textbooks had been settled. For the first year, they were Ruddiman's Rudiments and some Cordery; in second year more of Cordery, Nepos, part of Grammatical Exercises, and Mair's Introduction; in third year more of Mair, with Caesar and Ovid; in fourth year, Sallust, Virgil, and part of Horace were to be used. Prosody[60] was more prominent than formerly, while one class a week was generally devoted to reading the Scriptures, and another to some abridged history of Scotland, England, Rome or Greece. In the afternoon in the fourth year, Moor's Greek grammar and a little of the Greek Testament would be taught.

The hours of School attendance were confirmed as two hours in the morning and two hours in the afternoon, except on Saturday when there was no afternoon class. Prayers continued to be said by each of the masters in their respective classrooms at the beginning of the morning. The boys continued to be examined eight times a year by a committee of the Town Council, clergy and professors. As there were no particular days fixed for these examinations, the masters and scholars were always required to be prepared.

With the appointment of a Rector, and the introduction of a fifth year, in 1815, some modifications were made in the curriculum. The Rector devoted one class a day to the Latin Classics – Virgil, Livy and Horace – and the other to the Greek grammar and language exercises. If boys were young they were retained in the Rector's class for more than a year, and if their numbers warranted it a separate class was formed, allowing the study of Cicero, Tacitus, Terence, Homer and Xenophon. In some years, during the summer months, the Rector found it necessary to hold an extra class daily before breakfast to study Geography, Antiquities and Mythology.

At the close of session, usually the last week in September or the first week in October, prizes were distributed for merit and good attendance by the Lord Provost. This event had become a dignified and formal occasion, and a local church was used to accommodate the numbers. Traditionally, class prizes for merit were given to a quarter of the boys who ranked highest on the average of the eight examinations, while prizes for good attendance were awarded to those who had not missed any school class. This involved significant numbers: on 3 October 1825, 138 prizes were given for scholarship, and 255 were given for attendance.[61] Besides books from the Corporation, gold and silver medals were also awarded. In 1817 Convener Ewing gave a silver medal, converted into a gold medal in 1823, for the best scheme of a Greek verb; in 1820 Convener Alston introduced a silver medal for ranking dux on an average of five years; and also in 1820 the Corporation offered a silver medal for the best specimen of penmanship.

Between 1782 and 1825 some 111 boys received dux prizes, one of whom, Andrew Tennent, gained the dux prize in all five of his years at the school (1821–5), while six others – David Paterson (Dow's class, 1789–92); John Nimmo[62] (Allison, 1790–3); William Cowan (Wilson, 1791–4); John James (Macarthur, 1796–9); James Muir (Gibson, 1809–12); and Robert Paisley (Gibson/Chrystal, 1818–21) – received the dux prize in four of their School years.[63] In 1800, in Gibson's class, Hugh Stewart and Patrick Gordon, 'being of equal standing', drew lots and Stewart won the dux prize. John Davie, in the twenty-four examinations he sat in Dymock's class during the three years he was at the School (1823–5), lost only one place. The story of James Halley, dux of Douie's 1825 class, can be found in a contemporary memoir.[64]

CURRICULUM DEVELOPMENTS

In April 1823 the curriculum of the Grammar School became the centre of attention following a series of articles written by J. Sheridan Knowles,[65] published in the Glasgow *Free Press*.[66] He wrote of large classes, averaging around 100, being taught all at the same time, and all with the same material and at the same pace, with no differentiation. As good pupils were held back and there were long 'tails' of less able pupils in each class, Knowles argued for increased salaries for masters to enable them to employ at least two ushers to help with each class.

It took time for these criticisms to hit home, but as School numbers declined towards the end of 1824[67] the GSC began an inquiry into the reasons behind this development. It asked for staff comments and Rector Chrystal responded as spokesman of the masters. He held that 'the present system of education in our School is too limited to meet the views and wishes of the community; and that a public seminary, in order to be popular, must include within itself the means of affording those branches of education which are considered necessary, not only for entering the University with advantage, but which may be requisite to qualify for the various kinds of business, which young men may have occasion to pursue in a large commercial city'.[68] Chrystal suggested including in the curriculum Arithmetic, Mathematics, English, Modern Languages, Geography and Drawing, each requiring one or more able masters with a suitable number of ushers.

The Council was not keen to make extensive, and hence expensive, changes, and the matter did not progress until the intervention of Rev. Patrick McFarlan[69] of St John's, who wrote to Robert Dalglish, the Dean of Guild.[70] He claimed that parents were keeping their sons away from the School because its classes of 90–100 meant the neglect of a number of scholars, and because of the inordinate time spent on classical instruction 'to the exclusion, as they allege, of other branches of education of at least equal importance'.[71] McFarlan suggested starting School at 9 a.m. instead of 10 a.m., and introducing a wider curriculum. This time each master responded individually to the GSC, offering different insights into the issues, but generally they were defensive, their contributions seeking to justify the status quo.[72]

Nonetheless, in spite of the lack of enthusiasm from the masters for change, by October 1825 they had added British and Ancient History, Modern and Ancient Geography, exercises on the Scriptures, English Composition,[73] and some Mathematics to the curriculum, while retaining the dominance of Latin. It was also agreed that classes should begin half an hour earlier to fit in the 'extras' without increasing the fees. Only Mathematics was treated differently and was taught from 5 p.m. to 7 p.m. in the evening, at a very moderate fee.

How significant was the new scheme of work now adopted? A valid comparison would be with the High School in Edinburgh, which was being rebuilt, between 1825 and 1829, on a new site on Calton Hill. 'Firmly classical in style, the building encapsulated both the architectural thinking of the day as well as the largely classical thrust of the school curriculum.'[74] Changes in Edinburgh were restricted to the introduction of a general knowledge class in 1827, taught by the classical masters and embracing the study of English Literature, History and Geography, while the first Arithmetic and Mathematics master was not appointed till the following year. Given this context the changes in Glasgow compared well with those being contemplated elsewhere. However, the *Scots Times* of 6 October 1827 thought differently, claiming that education in Glasgow had not seen 'the slightest improvement' in the first quarter of the century and 'pre-eminent in this race of dullness has been the Grammar School'. This led to a bitter and bruising battle in the press, which raged for three months and covered the system of teaching, the numbers in classes, the lack of differentiation, the institution of prizes and the content of the curriculum in the School.

Public criticism led to increasingly strained relationships between the masters and the GSC,[75] reaching a peak in May 1829 when the masters were accused of following no regular course of instruction and increasing fees despite the Committee's specific order not to do so.[76] Chrystal and the masters quickly and strenuously rejected these allegations. They had fulfilled agreements reached, taught the subsidiary subjects and charged no additional fees. Pupils had been informed that extra attendance and the extra fee were optional. However, the Town Council weighed in, reiterating the prescribed course of education to be followed and the rate of fees to be charged. The Committee was told to repeat the instructions already given and to report if it met with 'any further opposition' from masters so that the necessary measures could be adopted to enforce compliance.[77]

Dymock, Douie, Lorrain and Cowan claimed that at their appointments they had been given control over the course of education to be followed and would only accept the Committee's enactments if they concurred with them.[78] They also defended the right to charge extra fees for additional instruction. William Cowan, the most recent addition, determined to resign with effect from 22 October 1829 and, given the general turmoil, it was decided not to fill the vacancy but instead to give his class temporarily to the Rector, who was to be assisted by Gavin Lochore.[79] The system was clearly not working well, and all the arguments of 1782 and 1815 again resurfaced. The Council asked the GSC whether the Rector's fifth class should be discontinued and the curriculum for Latin and Greek reduced to four years, as formerly.[80]

NO RECTOR AGAIN FROM 1830

A decision had not been made when, on 7 June 1830, a tragic accident, which was to have significant consequences, occurred. On that day two young men hired a boat, crewed by two experienced sailors, from Helensburgh on a pleasure trip. When they were going aboard from the beach they met Rector William Chrystal, who was looking for transport to Dunoon, and kindly offered to take him across the Clyde. They set off in a moderate breeze, but it is thought that a sudden squall arose and the boat sank suddenly. Two fishermen who were near the scene of the tragedy rowed immediately to the spot only to find Chrystal's body floating lifeless. It was later reported that a schooner nearby had also found herself in difficulties, losing her main and fore topmasts in the sudden change in conditions.[81]

The manner and shock of Chrystal's early death was all the greater because he was held in such high esteem. 'He was beloved and respected by all who enjoyed the benefit of his instructions; his bland and kindly manner and his benignity of disposition, secured to him their love and affection, while his varied Classical knowledge, and his happy method of communicating it, gained him their respect and esteem.'[82] As a result a group of his friends and former pupils raised funds to place a bust[83] and memorial stone in Glasgow Cathedral.[84] It was inscribed in Latin which, translated, read: 'Sacred to the memory of William Chrystal, LLD, Rector of the Grammar School of Glasgow, whom a premature death carried off by Drowning in the Firth of Clyde. This Monument of Affection his sorely disconsolate Pupils and Friends have Erected.'[85]

Chrystal was also well regarded in the wider community, and as early as April 1816 the degree of Doctor of Laws (LLD) had been conferred on him by the Senate of Glasgow University. His death deprived the School of a highly respected Rector, and there was no obvious successor.

On 30 July 1830 the GSC decided that a four-year course was preferable to one of five years and that the title of Rector should be abolished.[86] It recommended that all four classes be taught by one master for four years, all masters being equal and independent. If there was a demand, the teacher who had completed the fourth class could offer an additional class after normal hours. The Council accepted these recommendations on 2 September 1830, and John Clarke Rowlatt,[87] Classical master at Ayr Academy, was appointed in place of Cowan.[88] The care of the School was thus given over to Dymock, Douie, Lorrain and Rowlatt.

THE 1834 REPORT

Putting the clock back did not appeal to Henry Paul, Convener of the GSC. At a meeting on 22 November 1833 he spelled out his desire to make the School a more general teaching establishment, with all the branches of a liberal education included in its curriculum. He held that a Classical education was no longer adequate for a commercial city such as Glasgow, where an increasing number of pupils did not take up the learned professions. His Committee approved of his suggestion that a correspondence should be opened up with the managers and teachers of similar schools.

Information was gathered in the next six months which was to form the basis of an important report presented to the Council in September 1834 as Dymock's and Douie's retirements approached. Paul submitted the correspondence received from the patrons of the new academies in Edinburgh and Belfast – Edinburgh Academy[89] (opened 1824) and the Royal Belfast Academical Institution[90] (opened 1814) – and a number of public documents relating to those schools. They operated a modern system of education which embraced 'a wider compass of instruction' and incorporated into language classes 'the most valuable practical branches of scientific and mercantile knowledge'. The recently introduced plans for education, which included specifically English grammar and composition, Arithmetic, Mathematics, French and Spanish, had been operated successfully and brought the schools into line with the educational requirements of the time. Importantly, their Classical instruction had not suffered as a result. Moreover, Paul held that teaching subjects in smaller blocks of time 'exhilarated' and concentrated the mind of the scholar; 'quietens his zeal, and enables him to acquire a greater extent and variety of knowledge'.

Paul therefore recommended introducing those changes which seemed particularly relevant for Glasgow, where a significant proportion of the young were destined for a life in commerce and studied Classical literature as a branch of a liberal education, rather than as an object of professional necessity. To ensure that Glasgow became an efficient scientific and mercantile, as well as Classical, seminary, he proposed that the disciplines be taught by different staff in separate departments: Classics, English, Mathematics and Modern Languages. Instead of filling up the forthcoming teaching vacancies with Classical teachers, he proposed to appoint an English teacher, who could teach grammar, composition and the popular parts of Rhetoric and Logic; a teacher to give instruction in the higher branches of Arithmetic, Mathematics and Geography; and a third teacher qualified to teach Modern Languages.[91]

The report was accepted. Paul's vision of making the Grammar School a more general teaching establishment[92] was deemed so significant that it warranted a change in the name of the School – from Grammar School to High School. The new arrangements again moved Glasgow ahead of the other prestigious Scottish grammar schools in its curricular arrangements. At the same time, two highly esteemed members of the 'old guard' on its teaching staff – Dymock and Douie – retired.[93]

John Dymock had been an excellent teacher and a scholar of some note, having edited, or shared in the writing of, fourteen books.[94] He typified the scope of the work undertaken by the best of the Classical masters before 1834. His Fourth Form in 1825–6 read *Cataline's Conspiracy*, forty chapters of *Jugurthine War*, forty-one chapters of *Livy* Book 1, 'almost all' of Virgil's *Eclogues*, two books of the *Aeneid*, and all those *Odes* of Horace in Sapphic metre, with a few in other metres. The class also studied Geography, Mythology and Antiquities, and 'committed to memory the whole Rules of Prosody'. The lessons were regularly parsed, those in verse scanned, and the rules given for the quantity of each syllable. 'A portion of the Scriptures was read every day, and the boys frequently questioned on the meaning of the verses.'[95] For such drive and teaching commitment he was awarded the degree of LLD from Glasgow University in 1829.

Robert Douie's second class, which was enrolled on 10 October 1813, produced its own *Sketch and Catalogue*. It was printed in 1834 by a member of the class, George Richardson (and reprinted in 1852). On its first day 104 scholars enrolled.[96] The class was still reuniting nearly forty years later, and Douie himself, by this time an octogenarian, attended the 30th Reunion Meeting in 1849.[97] His third class, 'retaining after the expiry of eleven years since the completion of their studies under him a sincere respect for his upright and honourable character',[98] presented him with a silver salver.

In retrospect it was not the introduction of the radical curriculum changes of 1834 which was surprising but the fact that the Council had taken so long to implement them. Certainly they had a long gestation. As early as 1700 the Synod of Glasgow and Ayr – comprising presbyteries across west-central Scotland – set up an inquiry into schooling within its bounds, and the replies concentrated entirely on the curriculum and on the effectiveness of teaching. Presbyteries wanted to offer, at the higher stages, alternatives or additions to Latin, with more practical Mathematics, Modern Languages, Geography, and commercial History for those whose careers did not depend on their going to university. This interest in Scotland in broadening the curriculum and providing 'modern' subjects of instruction – the better to serve the needs of a city emerging as a commercial and industrial centre – continued throughout the nineteenth century.[99]

In the burghs the new movement towards a more practical education took the form of Writing or Commercial Schools, in which Book-keeping, Arithmetic and sometimes Mathematics were taught. Schools of this type were established in Dumfries in 1723, in Stirling in 1747, and in Banff in 1762. In other places the reaction to the exclusively classical curriculum expressed itself in a reorganisation of the course of study in the grammar school itself, as in Ayr, where the Council in 1746 greatly broadened the scheme of education by adding a scientific element, consisting of Mathematics, Navigation, Surveying, Natural Philosophy and Book-keeping, to the existing curriculum of Latin and Greek.

However, by far the most powerful influence was the complete rejection of the Classical curriculum at Perth in 1760, where a petition to its Council presented a powerful case for the advantages of science as opposed to the 'grammatical knowledge of dead languages and skill in metaphysical subtleties which had hitherto constituted the whole of higher education in Scotland'.[100] As a result of this memorial Perth Council resolved to establish an entirely new type of school to which the name 'Academy' was given, and it was opened in due course in 1761. Not only were all the teaching and exercises to be in English, but no provision at all was made for instruction in languages, and the scheme of study was confined entirely to modern subjects such as Mathematics, Natural Science, Astronomy, Physics, English, Civil History, the principles of Religion, and later Chemistry, Drawing and Painting. This remarkable precedent[101] was rapidly emulated elsewhere, and similar academies were established in Dundee in 1786, Inverness in 1788, Elgin and Fortrose in 1791, Ayr in 1794 and Dumfries in 1802. Their curricula were not entirely uniform, as they occasionally included additional subjects such as Geography and French, but their influence introduced variety into Scottish education.

PUPILS

When Sir Archibald Alison came to Glasgow on his appointment as Sheriff of Lanarkshire in 1834, he sent his son, Archibald, to the newly renamed High School. He found that the West Indian 'sugar aristocracy' came first in rank, followed closely by cotton magnates, with whom they occasionally mixed; next in the social hierarchy came calico printers, and then the iron- and coal-masters.[102]

Politically, the merchant class remained dominant too and, in particular, two individuals – both educated at the Grammar School – stand out in this period. Kirkman Finlay, having chaired the first Glasgow Chamber of Commerce and Manufactures, went on to hold the office eight times, and also became Lord Provost and Tory MP.[103] His close personal associate, James Ewing, dominated the Town Council and was elected as a moderate Conservative MP in the period before burgh reform in 1833.

The careers of the former boys of the 1820–4 class of William Pyper and William Cowan bear out the numerical significance of the merchants. Of the 65 known, some 26 became merchants, 23 were traders, 7 entered medicine, 6 the law and 3 the church. A high proportion went abroad, the destinations being: Canada 7, Australia 5, West Indies 4, USA 4, India 3, Egypt 3 and South America 1.[104]

Merchants

Peter Neilson (1795–1861) was the son of a cloth manufacturer. After university he joined his father in exporting cambric and cotton goods to America. As an inventor he proposed improvements to the lifebuoy and had his suggestion for iron-plated ships adopted by the Admiralty. He was interred in the burial ground near the north-west corner of Glasgow Cathedral.[105]

(Sir) George Burns (1795–1890) was a son of the ministry and joined Allison's last class in 1805. He went into trade with one of his brothers, James, and in 1830 they joined with others to form the Glasgow Steam Packet Company of steamer services between Glasgow, Liverpool, Belfast and Londonderry. By 1839 he had joined with David MacIver and Samuel Cunard, forming the British and North American Royal Mail Steam Packet Company. Their ships developed a reputation for technical innovation and quality of service.[106]

Walter Buchanan (1797–1877)[107] was the son of a Baltic merchant trader. He took over the family business and developed the East India market when the East India Company's monopoly had been broken. Adept at languages, he became Whig/Liberal MP for Glasgow, 1857–65.

William Ewing (1798–1866)[108] boarded with Dr Chrystal in order to attend the Grammar School after the death of his father. Although a popular pupil, lack of means led him to leave the School early, but by 1815, he was partner in a tobacco and sugar trading company. He was one of first directors of the Union Bank and instituted the Scottish Amicable Life Assurance Society. He also took a leading part in the formation of the Forth and Clyde Railway.

(Sir) John Pender (1816–1896) was the son of a textile merchant. He received a gold medal for Design at the Grammar School. He followed his father's trade, managing a textile firm, before embarking as a textile trader on his own account. He developed an extensive trade to India and the Far East. He successfully laid a transatlantic cable in 1866 and a link to India in 1870. Pender then formed the largest submarine telegraph company in the world. His next venture was the electric lighting of London. He was Liberal MP for Totnes (1862–6) and Wick Burghs (1872–85) and sat as a Liberal Unionist for the latter (1892–6).[109]

(Sir) Michael Connal (1817–1893) attended Rowlatt's class in 1826–7. He headed a merchant and shipping company. He was chairman of the School Board, 1876–82, and was knighted for services to education. He was buried in the Cathedral grounds.

Manufacturers (Industrialists)

Henry Dunlop (1799–1867)[110] attended Glasgow University before joining the family cotton-spinning business.[111] He was a councillor (1833–43); Lord Provost (1837–40); Chairman, Glasgow Chamber of Commerce 1841, 1850 and 1862; and Deputy Chairman, Edinburgh and Glasgow Railway Company.

John Blackie jnr (1805–1873)[112] attended Gibson's class. In 1826 he became a partner in his father's publishing firm, which published particularly educational texts and children's books, taking advantage of compulsory education. He was a councillor, and as Lord Provost (1863–66) brought forward a city improvement scheme.

James Merry (1805–1877) was the son of a coal-master and attended the School from 1815, before going on to the university. In 1835 he became sole proprietor of the firm and over the next twenty years, in partnership with Alexander Cunninghame, he built a large business empire which operated three ironworks, twelve collieries, and numerous iron mines and was the second largest producer of pig-iron, and was third in rank as a colliery operator in Scotland.[113] He became Liberal MP for Falkirk Burghs (1857–8 and 1859–74). His highly successful stable won the Derby, St Leger and Two

Thousand Guineas twice, and the Gold Cup and Oaks. He was buried in the Glasgow Necropolis under a bronze-headed tombstone.

Robert Dalglish (1808–1880)[114] headed Dalglish, Falconer & Son, a family firm of calico printers in Lennoxtown. He lived in Kilmardinny House from 1853 and was Radical MP for Glasgow, 1857–74. He was regarded as a great orator and the 'most popular member of the House of Commons' (*Vanity Fair*, 1873).

(Sir) James Lumsden (1808–1879)[115] attended Arts classes at Glasgow University before becoming a partner in the family wholesale stationery firm (1852). He was Dean of Guild (1860–2); Lord Provost (1866–9) and chair of the Glasgow and South-Western Railway Company and Clydesdale Bank.

(Rev.) William Wingate (1808–1899) was the son of a silk merchant. He was dux of Dr Chrystal's fifth class in 1821–2, and was also awarded the Findlay Silver Medal.[116] He became a partner in his father's business but determined to become a Christian missionary to the Jews. He studied German and Hebrew in Berlin in 1841–2 before joining the mission in Pest. He worked there and in Moldavia until all Scottish missionaries had been expelled (1852). Throughout the rest of his long life, Wingate continued to work for Jewish conversion without pay or position.

Charles Randolph (formerly Randall) (1809–1878)[117] was the son of a bookseller, printer and stationer. He was taught by Lorrain and attended classes at Glasgow University and Anderson's College. He opened a millwright's business in Glasgow in 1834. The firm won fame for the accuracy of its gear-cutting and machining. In 1839 John Elder[118] joined with Randolph and they extended their activities to England, Ireland and mainland Europe. The firm prospered and during the American Civil War in 1864 equipped five blockade runners with high-speed naval compound engines. By then their firm – the Fairfield shipyard – was the most successful shipbuilding and marine engineering business on the Clyde, employing some 4,000 people. Randolph retired in 1868 and Elder died soon after. Elder and Randolph, 'by pioneering the compound engine, ensured the Clyde's continuing technical domination of the world shipbuilding industry in the second half of the nineteenth century'.[119] In 1883 Elder's widow, Isabella, gifted the 37-acre park in Govan as a memorial to her husband. The Fairfield workers responded by contributing to a statue of John Elder, which was unveiled in the park in July 1888.[120]

James Scott (1810–1884)[121] joined a company of calico printers, becoming a partner in 1830. He established Scotland's largest cotton-spinning firm and erected oil-works at Clippens, Renfrewshire. He was

Glasgow City Treasurer (1851–5) and founded Kelvingrove Park.

James White (1812–1884)[122] was in the Pyper and Cowan class, reunions of which he attended annually. He attended Glasgow and Edinburgh Universities and became a solicitor. He joined the family firm in the chemical business, which after 1830 began manufacture of bichromate of potash, and took over the commercial aspects of the business (1851). He was president of the Chamber of Commerce; chair of the Glasgow Deaf and Dumb Institution and chair of the National Bible Society. His memorial statue was erected to the left of the entrance to the Necropolis, 1890.[123]

Walter Blackie (1816–1906)[124] attended Glasgow, Leipzig and Jena Universities before joining the family publishing firm. He specialised in topographical and educational publications. He was clerk of Glasgow University's Council.

(Sir) James Bain (1817–1898)[125] rose to become general manager of coal- and iron-masters, William Baird & Son. He became a partner in colliery and ironworks at Whitehaven, Cumberland. He was a member of Glasgow Town Council (1863–77), becoming Lord Provost (1874–7). He was an early President of the High School Club, 1876–7, and Conservative MP for Whitehaven, 1891–2.

(Sir) William Collins (1817–1895)[126] left the School in 1829 and was apprenticed to the family publishing business, becoming a partner in 1843. Under him the business printed and published dictionaries and other reference books, and standard editions of household classics. The company developed a strong export market and the firm set up offices round the world. It employed 2,000 workers and produced 2 million books a year. In 1881 it began to publish diaries. In practice the company gained a virtual monopoly, through economies of scale, in printing the Bible in part or in whole. Collins was a Glasgow City councillor, representing the Liberal Party (1868–83), and closely scrutinising the city's public expenditure. From 1877–80 Collins was Lord Provost of Glasgow, the first avowed teetotaller to hold the post, and served on the School Board, 1888–94.[127] He was buried in Glasgow Necropolis. A memorial fountain, sculpted by John Mossman, was erected in 1881 in recognition of his work in the temperance movement.[128]

William Rae Arthur (1818–1897)[129] worked in the drapery and then the calico printing business. He was a councillor (1857–71); Convener of the High School Committee; Town Treasurer, (1866–9) and Lord Provost (1869–71). He was a Conservative in politics and the first President of the High School Club, 1870–2.

Churchmen

James Halley (1814–1841)[130] was son of a grocer. He entered the School in 1821 and was dux of Douie's fourth class in 1825 and Rector Chrystal's class in 1826. At Glasgow University he won prizes in Latin, Greek, Logic, Physics, Philosophy and Botany. In Theology, which he began in 1832, he won the highest prizes in Hebrew, Church History and Systematic Theology. He was an exceptionally promising Church of Scotland minister, but his life was cut short by tuberculosis.

(Dr) Robert Kalley (1809–88)[131] was the son of a wealthy merchant. He proved a controversial medical missionary and Protestant proselytiser in Madeira and Brazil, being deemed 'the wolf from Scotland'.

Military

(Field Marshal Sir) Colin Campbell (formerly Macliver) (Baron Clyde) (1792–1863) was the son of a carpenter.[132] He attended Gibson's class between 1797 and 1803[133] and Gosport Military Academy. He was involved in the Peninsular War with Sir John Moore at Salamanca and Corunna.[134] He served in the colonies and China, and was prominent in the Second Anglo-Sikh War. At the outbreak of the Crimean War he accepted command of one of the two armies in the field with the rank of Major-General and had success against the Russians at the Alma. He was in charge of defending Balaklava with a force which was attacked by a much larger Russian force. His Highland infantry – the 'thin red line' – stood firm and drove off the Russians: 'Amid the Crimean failures Campbell's own reputation was enhanced.'[135] He received the Freedom of the City of Glasgow and a sword of honour 'in the presence of a crowded assembly'.[136] On the outbreak of the Indian Mutiny in July 1857 Campbell accepted the post of Commander-in-Chief in India. He relieved Lucknow and pacified the north of India.[137] In July 1858 he was made Baron Clyde of Clydesdale, and in 1862 became a Field Marshal. A statue of him was erected in Glasgow.[138] Competent and successful rather than brilliant, 'to his contemporaries he was a great soldier, who had saved the British Empire in India'.[139]

Medical

William Mackenzie (1791–1868)[140] was the son of a muslin manufacturer. He was in Wilson's class before matriculating at Glasgow University, becoming a surgeon in 1815. He co-founded the Glasgow Eye Infirmary in

1824. His *Practical Treatise on the Diseases of the Eye* (1830) was the standard textbook for a generation.[141]

(Prof.) John Towers (1791–1833) was dux of Allison's class in 1802, 1804 and 1805. He became a surgeon at the Royal Infirmary, 1815–16, and succeeded his father, James, to the Regius Chair of Midwifery.

William Weir (1794–1876) was in Macarthur's 1802–6 class, becoming its dux in 1806. He became a surgeon and physician in the Royal Infirmary, and President of the Faculty of Physicians and Surgeons, Glasgow, 1847–9.

Robert Hunter (1795–1864) was the eldest of four brothers (John, James and William) who were all educated at the School. Robert had a distinguished medical career and was elected President of the Royal College of Physicians and Surgeons, Glasgow.

(Prof.) Andrew Buchanan (1798–1882)[142] was the brother of Walter. He was Professor of Materia Medica, Anderson's College, 1828–39. He founded the *Glasgow Medical Journal* (1828). He was Professor of the Institute of Medicine (Physiology), Glasgow University, 1839–76 and President, Faculty of Physicians and Surgeons, Glasgow.

John Fleming (1809–1879)[143] ensured the continuation of Glasgow Royal Infirmary as a teaching hospital with its own medical school when Glasgow University moved to Gilmorehill and had the Western Infirmary as an integral teaching hospital in 1874. He had been President of the Glasgow Faculty of Physicians and Surgeons, 1865–8 and 1870–2.

(Prof.) Thomas Thomson (1817–1878) was born in Glasgow, son of the Professor of Chemistry at Glasgow University. He attended Douie's classes between 1825 and 1828, and the university. He joined the East India Company as an assistant surgeon, serving in Afghanistan and India, and published an account of his explorations. He worked with Joseph Hooker in India and Nepal and helped Hooker produce his 1855 work on the flora of India. He superintended the botanical garden in Calcutta, was promoted to surgeon-major in 1859 and became Professor of Botany at Calcutta Medical College.[144]

Legal

Henry Bell (1803–1874)[145] was the son of an advocate. He was educated at the School and at the University of Edinburgh. In 1828 he founded the *Edinburgh Literary Journal* and produced a defence of Mary, Queen of Scots, which became a best-seller. He became an advocate in 1831 and sheriff-depute for Lanarkshire in 1839, gaining a reputation as the best judge on the circuit.[146] He was appointed sheriff-principal in 1867, and on his death in office he was the first person in the nineteenth century to be buried in the nave of the Cathedral.

(Sir) James Parker (1803–1852) attended Chrystal's 1811 and 1812 classes. He then went to Glasgow University and to Trinity College, Cambridge, in 1821. He was called to the bar in 1829 and took silk in 1844. The Whig ministry made him Vice-Chancellor in 1851, the year he was knighted.[147] His career was cut short by an early death.

William Towers-Clark (1805–1870)[148] was always near the top of Dymock's class, being dux in 1818. He attended Glasgow University, completed his law apprenticeship and joined the Faculty of Procurators (1829). He represented the Whigs in the Registration Courts after the 1832 Reform Act.[149] He was expert in conveyancing and mercantile law.

John Russell[150] (1816–1899) became a barrister (1841); Recorder of Bolton (1865); and judge of the county court of Manchester (1869).

Academic

(Prof.) Granville Pattison (1791–1851) was the son of a muslin manufacturer. Between 1802 and 1804 he attended Allison's sixth class,[151] and proved a 'very poor student' according to class records.[152] He went on to take medical courses at Glasgow University and became a lecturer in Anatomy, Physiology, and the principles of operative Surgery. He was accused of illegal exhumation – he was ultimately found 'not proven'[153] – and later of professional incompetence. In the event, he was censured for not following agreed procedures. In 1819 he moved to America and became chair of Surgery in Baltimore, helping to establish the first modern residential teaching hospital in America. In 1827 Pattison obtained the chair of Anatomy at the new University of London and also became Professor of Surgery three years later. However, he was asked to retire in 1831 as his old-fashioned, conservative approach was not in tune with that of the new institution.[154] Nonetheless, he became Professor of Anatomy first at Philadelphia (1832–41) and then New York (1841–51).[155]

(Prof.) John Couper (1794–1855) attended the Wilson/Chrystal class, 1803–7, being its dux in 1805. He was appointed Regius Professor of Materia Medica at Glasgow University, 1833–65.

(Prof.) Thomas Graham (1805–1869) was the son of a prosperous Glasgow merchant and manufacturer of light woven fabrics for the West Indies. From 1814 to 1818 he attended the class of Dymock and Chrystal. He became Professor of Chemistry at Anderson's College in 1830.[156] He discovered Graham's Law[157] in 1831 and by the mid-1830s 'he was recognised as a chemist of European stature',[158] often referred to as 'the father of colloid chemistry'.[159] He became a Fellow, Royal Society and in 1837 Professor of Chemistry at University College, London. He produced an influential textbook, *Elements of Chemistry*. He was buried at Glasgow Cathedral and his statue is in the south-east corner of George Square.[160]

John Stenhouse (1809–1880) was the son of a calico printer. He attended Dymock's classes from 1819 and went on to study Chemistry at Glasgow University, Anderson's College and at Giessen (1837–9). He was elected Fellow, Royal Society and lectured in Chemistry at London's St Bartholomew's Hospital (1851–7). He wrote more than 100 papers on chemical subjects and patented a number of inventions. He was buried in the Cathedral cemetery.[161]

George Gardner (1812–1849) was the son of the gardener to the Earl of Dunmore. He attended the School from 1822 and acquired a good knowledge of Latin.[162] He studied Medicine at Glasgow University and gained his MD in 1835. He determined on botanical travel, and his trip to Brazil (1836–40) brought home 60,000 specimens, representing 3,000 species of plants. He was working on a manual of Indian Botany when he died early.[163]

(Sir) Joseph Hooker (1817–1911) was the son of the Professor of Botany at Glasgow University. He attended Douie's classes (1825–8) and University, graduating MD in 1839. He was assistant surgeon on the HMS *Erebus* and spent four years exploring the southern oceans. He produced six large volumes of plates on the flora encountered on his voyage. He began a lifelong correspondence with Darwin and was the first to share his ideas on natural selection.[164] Meantime, Hooker concentrated on the geographical distribution of plants, the mapping of which was crucial, given that the wealth of Britain's Empire was largely based on plants.[165] He visited India and Nepal, producing a volume on its flora and the *Himalayan Journals* (dedicated to Darwin) in 1854–5. This period also saw the publication of several of his important taxonomic publications, where he classified, named and reclassified species. He succeeded his father as director at Kew Gardens, remaining in charge until 1885. He kept the gardens for scientific and utilitarian purposes and resisted attempts to extend the opening hours for the general public.[166] He was elected President of the Royal Society in 1873 and received the OM in 1907.[167]

(Dr) (Robert) Angus Smith (1817–1884) was the son of a manufacturer. He attended Douie's classes from 1826, and at university studied Chemistry in Giessen. He became assistant to Lyon Playfair, Professor of Chemistry at

Manchester. He carried out research for the Royal Commissions on mines (1864), on cattle plague (1865) and for the Local Government Board (1879). He was elected a Fellow, Royal Society in 1857.[168]

(Prof.) (William John) Macquorn Rankine (1820–1872)[169] was the son of a civil engineer. He studied at the School in 1829–30, first with Chrystal and Lochore and then Rowlatt.[170] Widely read and talented he became an engineer, winning prizes for essays and papers. In the 1840s he began work on thermodynamics and became a Fellow, Royal Society (1853).[171] At Glasgow in 1855 he became Professor of Civil Engineering and Mechanics and was elected President of a new and dynamic Institution of Engineers in Scotland. He raised funds for the new buildings – a cathedral of science – at Gilmorehill. Rankine was responsible for Glasgow University offering a degree of BSc for science subjects which included Engineering.[172]

John Murdoch (1819–1904) excelled in Douie's 1829–33 classes at Classics and Drawing, and decided to become a teacher.[173] In 1842 he was appointed Headmaster of a teacher training school in Kandy, Ceylon. When school fees were raised he resigned and became a Christian missionary, supported by his home church in Scotland, simultaneously working to improve conditions for Tamil workers in the coffee plantations. He founded a Christian book society, publishing and distributing school books and tracts. He continued his work after the Indian Mutiny of 1857 and he produced *The Indian Missionary Manual* (1864) which became the standard work. In 1904 he was awarded the Kaiser-i-Hind medal by the Indian government.

Thomas Harvey (1823–1901) was a Snell Exhibitioner, 1842. He went into teaching, becoming class master, Edinburgh Academy 1847–56; Head, Merchiston Castle School, 1856–63; and then Rector, Edinburgh Academy, 1869–88, when he instituted a Preparatory Department for boys under ten and provided a mid-day meal for the boys.

Financial

(Sir) Andrew MacEwan (1812–1866)[174] was apprentice to the leading accountant in Glasgow.[175] He was involved in the establishment of Glasgow Stock Exchange (1844), becoming its first secretary.

Administration (Politicians)

John Strang (1795–1863)[176] inherited his father's wine business, selling out by 1834. Then a man of independent means, he translated stories from French and German for British periodicals. He pressed for the creation of a 'garden cemetery' to adorn Glasgow, and his pamphlet, *Necropolis Glasguensis*, of 1831, led the Merchants' House to lay out the Necropolis, modelled on the graveyard of Père Lachaise in Paris, in the Fir Park (which it owned), near Glasgow Cathedral. He served as City Chamberlain for twenty-nine years, much respected for his sound management of the municipal finances. His most popular book was *Glasgow and its Clubs* (1855). He was buried in the Necropolis that had been inspired by his vision.[177]

John Dennistoun (1803–1870) went into the family dyeing and bleaching business and became Whig MP for the City of Glasgow (1837–47).

(Sir) William Milne (1822–1895) was the son of a merchant. He trained in commerce and emigrated to Australia in 1839. He became a member of the House of Assembly and was elected, in 1869, to the Legislative Council. He served as chief secretary (1870–2), and then as its president (1873–81), contributing to the construction of overland telegraph, waterworks, light-houses and railways.[178]

Writers (Artists, Architects, Poets, Journalists)

John G. Lockhart (1794–1854) was born the son of a minister. He attended Macarthur's sixth class (1802–5), in which he was deemed clever rather than industrious, often being absent sick but still retaining his position in the class. He was full of fun and humour but was averse to rough sports and the 'stane-bickers'.[179] During his third year he took pulmonary consumption but made such progress in his studies that on his recovery he was advised by Macarthur not to complete the curriculum but instead to go straight to university,[180] where he excelled as a Classical scholar. He was awarded a Snell Exhibition and gained a First Class degree in Classics at Oxford in 1813. He learned German, Italian, Spanish, Portuguese and French. In 1815 he attended Edinburgh University to read Law and became an advocate in the following year. He connected with Tory literati, including Walter Scott, whose elder daughter, (Charlotte) Sophia, he married in 1820. He contributed to *Blackwood's Edinburgh Magazine* and wrote four novels. Meantime he had become editor of the (Tory) *Quarterly Review*, a post he held for twenty-eight years. His best known work was his biography of Sir Walter Scott, which, although inaccurate in details and generally idealised, was an attempt to capture 'the near heroic regard in which Scott was held in his time'.[181]

John Graham-Gilbert (1794–1866)[182] was the son of a West India merchant. He trained as an artist in London and established himself as a portrait painter. He was elected an academician of the Scottish Academy. He narrowly lost the election to the presidency of the Royal Scottish Academy in 1864. He was buried at the Glasgow Necropolis,[183] and his monument is a marble portrait medallion by William Brodie.[184]

James Dennistoun (1803–1855)[185] attended Glasgow University in 1815. He became a member of the Faculty of Advocates but never practised. He collected early Italian and Dutch paintings and illuminated miniatures from manuscripts. He belonged to several societies formed to collect materials for illustrating the history of Scotland. However, his most significant work was *Memoirs of the Dukes of Urbino, Illustrating the Arms, Arts, and Literature of Italy from 1440 to 1630* (3 volumes, 1851).[186]

Patric Park (1811–1855) was the son of a mason and builder. He attended the 1820–4 class of William Pyper and William Cowan.[187] He was apprenticed to the builder of Hamilton Palace in 1825 and then worked at Murthly Castle. He spent two years in Rome studying under the sculptor, Bertel Thorvaldsen. Back in Scotland he produced large marble works including the larger than life-size statue of the industrialist Charles Tennant (1838) in the Glasgow Necropolis. He was best known as a portrait sculptor, being considered the best in Scotland.[188] His busts can be found in Edinburgh, Glasgow and London galleries and museums.

Peter Macliver (1822–1891),[189] cousin of Lord Clyde, went on to Glasgow University and became a journalist, founding the *Daily Press* of Bristol. A magistrate in Somerset, he was Liberal MP for Plymouth from 1880 to 1885.

Given the large number of successful Former Pupils, it is not surprising that in this period at least one became notorious rather than distinguished. Walter Blair was the son of a vintner in the Candleriggs and probably attended James Gibson's 1804–8 class[190] before going on to university. 'He was remarkable for his close application and general good conduct. He studied Medicine, and was for some time assistant surgeon on board one of His Majesty's vessels.'[191] He and William Baird appeared at the Circuit Court on 8 April, where they were found guilty of six different sets of assaults and robberies, and were executed in front of the New Jail on 3 June 1818. According to a contemporary report Blair addressed the large crowd, saying: 'May this be a warning to others not to fall into the scenes of vice into which we have plunged. This is all I have to say; and I hope our case will be the last example which it will be necessary to make in this city.'[192]

FIVE

The High School in the
Mid-Nineteenth Century (1834–1872)

This chapter explains the success of the 1834 changes and looks in detail at
the subject departments and their leaders. It also focuses on external criticisms of the School and the growing competition from other schools: in
particular, the Glasgow Academy. The chapter ends with the renewal of the
debate on leadership, and the founding of the High School Club to cater for
the extraordinary wave of distinguished Former Pupils, details of a number
being highlighted.

THE REMODELLED HIGH SCHOOL

The remodelling of the Grammar School into the High School in 1834 was
carried out quickly. By 30 October the three new staff envisaged in Paul's
report had been appointed: Alexander D'Orsey[1] to head the English
department; James Connell[2] of Irvine to teach Mathematics, Geography
and the higher parts of Arithmetic[3]; and Dr John Gerlach[4] of Dollar
Institution to take Modern Languages. They joined the Classical masters,
Dr William Lorrain, who had been awarded an LLD from Marischal
College in 1824, and the recently arrived John Rowlatt.

The High School was an immediate success: the number of pupils
attending increased markedly, and even the Latin classes had sixty more than
during the previous session.[5] In total there were 343 pupils to be instructed
in the new branches of study. Such a result was gratifying to the High School
Committee (HSC, formerly GSC): and Councillor Lumsden's gift of £25 at
the beginning of the session, to found a gold medal to be given annually to
the most proficient in the Mathematics class, was followed at the end of
session by the introduction of three similar medals: the first from Hugh
Tennent[6] of Well Park to the most proficient pupil in each of the departments in rotation; the second from James Hutchison[7] to the best Greek

scholar; and the third from Henry Paul[8] to the outstanding pupil in the Fourth Latin Class.

The HSC made three more decisions which also advanced the school curriculum. First, towards the end of 1834 the use of a room for an hour in the afternoon or evening was granted to H.L. van den Houten to teach Drawing, a subject not offered before. This arrangement continued until September 1842 when Houten resigned. Second, in 1836 the teaching of Chemistry by Hugo Reid[9] was promoted by allowing the use of a room on Saturdays in the School. This move proved successful and in 1837 Reid's work was extended to include the elementary branches of Natural Philosophy, Chemistry and Natural History. When Reid left in 1840 for a post in Liverpool his successor, W.M. Buchanan, was appointed to a new department of Experimental Science.[10] And third, in September 1837, the HSC agreed that Veechiarelli start classes for Spanish and Italian. However, with little demand for them, these were soon discontinued.[11]

In late 1836 Dr Lorrain, who was approaching sixty-five years of age, wrote to the Convener of the HSC, Henry Paul, informing him that he was now experiencing severe pain while undertaking his duties. He was awarded a retiring allowance of £100 per annum[12] and, befitting a popular teacher, he received a silver jug and dressing case from his students. In April 1837 John McMillan, Rector of Dumfries Grammar School, was appointed as replacement.

AN OUTSIDER'S VIEW

The first educational commentary on the School by an outsider was made by Alex Dallas Bache,[13] an American educator and scientist, who was sent by the Board of Trustees so that Girard College of Orphans in Philadelphia could obtain information and report back on good practice abroad. He visited Europe between September 1836 and October 1838, and his 666-page report relating to practice in 278 schools was produced on 1 May 1839;[14] six pages were devoted to the High School.

In his general comments Bache observed how closely the School was involved with the university, more so than its equivalent in Edinburgh. He saw a major defect in a lack of uniformity in teaching methods, and a major strength in a system which enabled pupils who were intended for different pursuits in life to follow the studies most appropriate to them. The curricular structure was geared to the needs of a manufacturing and commercial city, although Bache thought that two separate schools, each with a fixed course of instruction, 'would answer the end proposed much better'.[15] Here Bache was influenced by the German model of the Gymnasium and the Realschule.

Bache commented on all the departments. The Classical department prepared boys for the university, but as the pupils went there at an early age and had no need of an advanced attainment level for entry the studies were 'comparatively elementary'. The English department prepared very young boys for their other classes and offered an 'admirable' course, beginning with the alphabet; then spelling, meaning and derivative of words (using the Bible to develop moral and religious knowledge and introducing readings in History and Elementary Science); then dictation, composition and letter writing (introducing Natural History and Manufactures with specimens and experiments); then recitation (from History and the British Classics); then pronunciation, punctuation and analysis of narrative and descriptive pieces; finally reaching the higher levels of Grammar, Logic and Rhetoric. Bache made particular mention of the English master, Alexander D'Orsey, who had travelled on the continent and at home seeking out improvements. The result was his adoption of teaching methods 'which produced excellent results'. D'Orsey had especially studied the secret of success in the more modern German schools, and had been influenced by their methods. His techniques were deemed 'among the best which I saw abroad' and those adopted to teach spelling were praised as 'very remarkable'.[16]

In the Mathematical (and Commercial) department Bache commented on the special teaching given to potential clerks, book-keepers, surveyors and navigators. He mentioned Physical Geography; the elements of Astronomy; Arithmetic; Geometry; Trigonometry; Algebra and Logarithms; in Higher Mathematics, Differential and Integral Calculus; and the elements of Natural Philosophy.

He made only passing mention of foreign languages (French and German), Writing, Drawing and the Chemistry course. Interestingly, he also noted the existence of a school library and a growing collection in Natural History. Pupil walks stimulated the study of Mineralogy and Geology, which were also supported by a cabinet of specimens. He also commended the teaching about local trades and the visits organised to various firms in Glasgow.

Bache also approved of the schoolroom arrangement, with benches and raised platforms and the securing of attention by moving the pupils to different places in the classroom. He had also been told that 'corporal punishment is not at all resorted to'. He liked, too, the break of ten minutes between classes for recreation when the classes were two hours long.

For Bache the freedom of choice of courses at the High School had advantages but he would have preferred a simpler arrangement, with parallel courses in different schools being regulated so that the choices of branches of study would not be left to parents, who were generally unwilling, or even unable, to judge in such matters. Having decided on their career destination a pupil should enter a regulated course, with a system of transfer from school to school to remedy any mistakes or to allow a change of direction.

There is no evidence that the Town Council paid any attention to Bache's comments and suggestions. However, he exerted a major influence on the course of American secondary education by his introduction of a four-year course which did not require the study of Classical languages and was designed to prepare pupils for life in the professions. He also recommended a clerical course for those so inclined, and an elementary course for those who were going into the trades or could not spend a full four years in high school. He made the then radical proposal that schools should have a playground to ensure that pupils had both physical exercise and a means of amusement during the school day.[17] Although it seems that Bache himself was most influenced by German models, one can see some signs that certain features of Glasgow High School were helpful in designing his curricular model and school system after he became first Principal of Philadelphia Central High School in 1839.

THE DEPARTMENTS

The Classical department and its place in the School had been weakened by the changes of 1834, especially as other subjects increased their popularity. Fortunately a partnership of two teachers came together to give the department, and indeed the School, quality and stability at a time of transition. John Rowlatt[18] resigned in November 1838 and Fletcher Low,[19] Rector of Linlithgow Grammar School, was appointed early the following year. John Macmillan[20] left in November 1844 to join the staff of the High School in Edinburgh and was replaced by Patrick (Peter) McKindlay LLD.[21] Low and McKindlay were to prove a loyal and distinguished team for over twenty years.

Low was an excellent teacher and strict disciplinarian, which proved a successful combination with large classes. Admission to his elementary class was not difficult to attain. In a newspaper advertisement Low held that 'boys about nine years of age, who can read a chapter of the Bible with tolerable accuracy, are perfectly qualified for this class'.[22] Some 140 boys took his classes in 1845. When he decided to retire in 1866, aged sixty-six, the Council awarded him an annuity of £150[23] and sent him an effusive letter of thanks. On his retirement a public dinner was held, and his former pupils presented him with a number of gifts, including a pair of gold spectacles bearing a Latin inscription. When he died in 1881 the *Glasgow Herald* contained a fulsome obituary.

McKindlay, Low's colleague, was ten years younger than him. A genial, kindly gentleman whose patience and enthusiasm encouraged the boys to learn, he had two initial advantages: his father, John, was a teacher – proprietor of Laurieston Academy – and he had attended the Grammar School, winning the Ewing Gold Medal in Greek in 1824.[24] He had ninety-eight pupils in 1845 just after his arrival,[25] and the numbers increased as he built his reputation as a knowledgeable and well-prepared teacher. He proved himself an accomplished scholar and was recognised as such by the pupils.

McKindlay's health broke down in March 1866,[26] and with Low's retirement, an era ended and stock could be taken of the changes which had been introduced into the School since 1834. Measured in terms of enrolment these had been successful,[27] but the six subject departments acted independently, and even within departments there was no systematic sharing of good practice. Some councillors wanted to strengthen the position of Classics, others bemoaned the lack of course regulation, which frequently meant a pupil leaving the School without a rounded education. It was in this situation that Provost Arthur recommended, on 25 July 1866, that the complement of Classical teachers should be increased from two to three and that they be graded head master, master and assistant master. Further, he made a plea that, when circumstances permitted, the head master in the Classical department should become Rector of the School. However, his job description would not include the academic departments, where the masters would remain autonomous but would be restricted to taking 'such general oversight of the whole School, as to enable him to advise the parents and guardians of the pupils, and qualify him to be the medium of communication with the Town Council and its committee, in all matters affecting the interests of the Institution'.[28]

Arthur's recommendations were accepted by the HSC, but it was a different story when they went before the Council in August 1866. Many

councillors did not agree with the Committee on the subject of the reintroduction of the position of Rector. Some opposed on principle, others on the
grounds of present inexpediency. Ultimately the motion was agreed but only
'on the understanding that the question of the appointment of a Rector, and
who, if any one of the teachers, should be Rector, is reserved'.[29]

A month later, on 5 September 1866, the new masters were appointed.
William Kemp, Classical master of Greenock Academy, was made head
master of the Classical department; D.H. Paton, Rector of Stirling High
School, became the new second master; and John Hutchison was appointed
assistant master. The HSC confirmed that the appointments of Kemp and
Paton were dependent on them working as a team, and they both indicated
that they were prepared 'to work cordially together and in harmony with the
Council.'[30]

The English department had opened in October 1834 under D'Orsey[31]
with a mere 11 pupils, but this number increased every year, reaching 327
only eight years later in October 1842. Such numbers not only confirmed
that the previous curriculum had been too narrow but also reflected the
dedication[32] and ability of D'Orsey. He went on to launch a series of initiatives which brought him into conflict with the Town Council and with his
colleagues at the School. His radical proposals to introduce an infant class
to be taught the alphabet, and a ladies' class for instruction in general
History and Literature, were dismissed as going beyond the constitution of
a secondary school and diverting attention from the subjects already laid
down for his department. Nonetheless, D'Orsey persevered and had to be
reprimanded for disobeying instructions. The janitor had to be given strict
orders to open the school building to D'Orsey only for the classes outlined
in the prospectus.[33]

Understandably D'Orsey's actions and self-conceit made him
unpopular with the staff. He gave evidence before the Earl of Kerry's Select
Committee on Education in England and Wales in 1835.[34] The following
year his teaching colleagues protested to the HSC about D'Orsey's habit of
going on lecturing tours in England. They felt it was 'quite derogatory to the
character and interests of the seminary that any of their number should
itinerate the country . . . most especially as they might be held as agreeing
in peculiar opinions entertained by Mr. D'Orsey, which they assuredly did
not'. The Council, however, could not end the lecture tours altogether, and
they continued in vacation time.

In 1839, Convener Paul charged D'Orsey with interfering with other
departments by teaching aspects of Geography, Chemistry and

Phrenology.[35] Matters grew worse when, in 1841, without reference to anyone, D'Orsey wrote about the English department as though it were a school in its own right. His interest was in spoken English rather than grammar and this bias was clear in the work of the department. It was clear that 'he had no intention from the very first day of making the English department of the High School a mere ABC establishment'.[36] By 1844 D'Orsey had opened a private preparatory school in Sauchiehall Road, producing a prospectus deemed by the HSC as 'objectionable' as it identified the School too closely with D'Orsey's own enterprise.[37]

Often keen to help his pupils, and always to promote himself, D'Orsey rather overdid it. By the early 1850s he had written extensively on aspects of English composition, spelling, reading and grammar;[38] he had been ordained and was the incumbent of St John's Espiscopal Church at Anderston;[39] he ran the Queen's College for Ladies in West George Street; he boarded pupils in his home, and he lectured on an extensive number of topics. He suffered a slight haemoptysis[40] and he began having haemorrhages, which occurred even when he was teaching. As a result he asked for leave of absence from his teaching in March 1851.[41] The Committee would probably have been more sympathetic if the request had not come at a time when parents had been complaining that his classes had not been instructed often enough and after a number had taken away their sons. It therefore insisted on substitute teachers during his absence. Then D'Orsey submitted a letter from Madeira with an accompanying medical certificate which held that his health would not permit him to return to Glasgow.[42] However, the Committee knew that he had started a school in Madeira and insisted that he either return for the beginning of the 1854 session or resign. After much haggling D'Orsey resigned having gained a commitment of £50 per annum from the Council and £100 per annum out of fees paid by pupils from his successor.[43]

D'Orsey's time at the School underlined the freedom which masters still had in their contractual arrangements, although his was the extreme case. D'Orsey continued his colourful career after his departure.[44] He lived on until his eighties and collected £6,000 in total from a commitment which ended in 1854, some forty years before his death.

Colin Pearson, who acted as substitute in D'Orsey's absence, was certified insane in September 1853, and removed to Gartnavel Asylum.[45] His successor, James Simpson, was chosen from twenty-six applicants and taught in the School for five years.[46] Following him, James Bell, who had been Head of Glasgow Academy's English department for ten years, was chosen from twenty-two candidates and remained on the School's staff from 1859 until 1879, building up his reputation as a good teacher. Some 702 boys took English in 1873.

The Mathematics department was led first by James Connell, from 1834 until his 'lamented'[47] death in 1846, and then by James Bryce until 1874. Both of them made an outstanding contribution to the development of their subject and department. The result was a deserved reputation in university circles that the School had, by the 1870s, the best Mathematics department in any school in Scotland. This did not happen overnight; indeed in 1835 the Convener of the HSC, Henry Paul, was praising Connell[48] while at the same time complaining about the small number of boys studying Mathematical Science. In May 1836, there were 74 studying Arithmetic, 13 studying Mathematics and 27 in Geography, while in 1841 the corresponding numbers were 191, 48 and 112 respectively. This increase masked a real problem: in 1844 Connell informed the Town Council that over his ten years in post, only around 40 pupils had studied Higher Mathematics. As all his other classes were very popular the Council approved his suggestion that he teach more Arithmetic and reduce the Mathematics course to one year.[49] He also extended his Geography syllabus to include current affairs. He produced a textbook on Differential and Integral Calculus, which was highly valued by teachers and used in the High School until 1870.

James Bryce (1806–1877) was born in Ireland to Scottish parents and graduated MA from Glasgow University in 1828, having won the Blackstone prize for Classics. He taught Mathematics at Belfast Academy, producing a *Treatise on Algebra* in 1837. He became Head of the Mathematics department at the High School in 1846,[50] with a special interest in Natural History. He was an enthusiastic geologist and researched and published extensively. It was this work which led Glasgow University to bestow on him an honorary LLD degree in 1858.[51] He was instrumental in founding the Glasgow University Graduates Association and became a President of the Educational Institute of Scotland (EIS).[52] He was a stimulating father to his sons who attended the School, and he proved to be a brilliant and successful Mathematics and Geography teacher to a generation of High School pupils. In a memorial to him it was claimed that 'Paddy' Bryce had four gifts as a teacher: lucidity, ingenuity, vivacity and geniality.[53] He retired in 1874 when 46 boys were studying Mathematics, 286 Arithmetic and 162 Geography. His departure ensured that Geography was 'restored to its more natural connection with English'.[54]

The Modern Language department proved a disappointment under Gerlach, who was the subject of a number of complaints in his first year. His attendance was so irregular that parents wishing to enrol their sons could rarely meet him. His disciplinary methods were also controversial, and he resorted to using a stick to beat the boys. Matters were brought to a head when Convener Paul visited the School on 13 October 1835 to find Gerlach's pupils disturbing other classes. Paul warned Gerlach so firmly that he protested in writing at Paul's language.[55] However, in the light of Gerlach's conduct, and the revelations that he had been charged with rioting in the streets and involved in fraud, the Committee decided that he should go. He was replaced in October 1836 by Felician Wolski,[56] of Polish descent, who remained as principal master in Modern Languages – French and German – until 1872. French was the dominant language[57] until the 1860s when the Committee, anxious to make German more widely available, appointed John Koerner as Wolski's assistant, to concentrate on that language.[58] Koerner died in 1874 and was replaced by Clemens Schlomka, a graduate of Rostock University, who inherited twenty-two boys taking German.

The other departments had only one teacher. Adam Stevenson died in 1841 and Allan Macnab became teacher of Writing and Book-keeping, but without a salary, depending totally on fees. Some 309 pupils took the subject in June 1845, its continuing popularity enabling Macnab to remain on the staff until 1868.[59] The Art department was run by James A. Hutchison from 1843[60] to 1874. He had 78 studying the subject in June 1845, a reasonable number given the emphases on University and commerce, although Hutchison himself confided to an HMI in the 1860s that he was 'disappointed with the little importance attached to his department'.[61] However, the Schools' Inquiry Commission reported that he was 'perhaps the best teacher of his subject in Scotland in spite of the difficulties of his position in the High School'.[62] On his retirement in 1874 some 130 boys were taking Drawing and Painting. Botany and Natural Philosophy under Keddie attracted 16 boys in 1872, but he gave up due to 'unsatisfactory arrangements'. He agreed to remain in the prospectus in the hope that the School Board would improve matters.

Parental demand in 1838 for accommodation for Gymnastics led to the furnishing of a shed and the provision of some basic equipment. Francois Foucart, who a decade before had been organising fencing lessons in Greenock[63] and a fencing academy in the former School buildings in George Street,[64] agreed to take the pupils for 21s a quarter. He failed, however, to persuade the Council to create a gymnasium, which was deemed too costly.[65]

When finally it was constructed in 1868, Francois Foucart's successor, Charles Long, fell out with the HSC, which authorised the completion of the interior and roof of the gymnasium[66] but claimed that all purchases of apparatus and the maintenance of equipment were Long's responsibility. Unsurprisingly, Long left, to be replaced in 1870 by Captain Walter Roland who was to teach the boys Drill and Gymnastics.[67] Attempts to introduce Vocal Music in 1850 and Elocution in 1861 both failed.[68]

COMPETITION

Although there were many private teachers in Glasgow, they tended to follow trends set by the High School, as was seen in the 'great vacation debate'.[69] The summer vacation lasted six to seven weeks, and private teachers wished to resume classes on the first or second Tuesday in August, which meant beginning the holiday in late June. Despite this, early in 1835, the HSC decided to resume classes on the fourth Tuesday in August, which meant beginning the vacation in early July. A heated debate ensued, which ended with the private teachers falling into line, despite their misgivings.

However, as the nineteenth century progressed the School faced more serious competition for pupils from a number of other schools in the city. These included the private 'English' schools which taught English, Geography, Writing and Arithmetic[70] to boys and girls, and which no longer needed a licence from the Town Council to operate, as had been the case in the seventeenth century. The most celebrated of these were the schools run by William Angus and William Munsie. Commercial academies also emerged, in which Writing, Arithmetic and Book-keeping were taught. The most successful of these was run by John McCall, with William Leiper aiming his schooling at older boys. Then in October 1846 the Glasgow Academy opened, and from spring 1847 it was situated in a splendid new building in Elmbank Street. Originally it was to be an academic institution 'for the children of the better classes', but these words were later deleted. Its staff salaries were attractive: James Cumming,[71] the first Head, had a salary of £500 guaranteed for three years, and the fees were set at 3 guineas a year in the younger classes, rising to 15 guineas in the final fifth class of the Classical department. A three-year elementary class was introduced for boys aged six to prepare them for the work of the Classical department, to which they would progress at about the age of nine. However, it was only three years after opening that the curriculum was made more flexible to cater for those who wanted their sons to have an education for entry to commerce rather than a classical background. By that time the roll had risen to 357, not far short of the maximum goal of 400.

The Academy's directors had chosen a site for their school at the western edge of the city's built-up area. The middle classes had been moving steadily westwards, away from the industrial and working-class areas of the city centre. Many of the families of the first Academy pupils were those successful in the textile industry, and they included merchants and a number involved in the banking sector, brewing and publishing. It seemed as if the High School had a significant competitor. This perception was intensified when the Academy followed the High School and did away with the post of Rector in 1851.[72] Certainly the Academy was a concern, while parish schools, despite being strengthened by the legacies of James Maxwell and Andrew Bell, and Hutchesons' Hospital, which had grown in resources with the development of its lands on the south side of the river, were not seen as a threat, as they catered for a different clientele.

By the time of the Argyll Commission in the mid-1860s, the educational sector had expanded further. The Blythswood district – the fashionable residential quarter – housed twenty-two 'private adventure' schools. Moreover, one secondary school in Glasgow was connected with Anderson's College, which specialised in modern subjects, and Scotland's leading Roman Catholic school, the Jesuits' St Aloysius College, which was founded in 1859, moved to Garnethill in 1866.

DIVISION

In February 1867 the HSC returned to its discussions on the future constitution and government of the School, and in particular reconsidered that part of its recent report which had met with opposition. Its resulting recommendations were for the most part uncontroversial, and these encompassed staffing, prizes and accommodation. On staffing, the Committee wished to appoint three additional teachers, one in each of German, Natural Science, and Gymnastics and Fencing. On prizes, the Committee suggested that 'Institutional Prizes'[73] should be presented to boys who had attended a certain number of years in *all* departments, in an attempt to discourage the custom followed by parents of choosing some subjects to the exclusion of others.[74] On accommodation, the Committee wished to investigate how the School could be enlarged and improved and, in particular, given that so little of the playground was protected from the weather and there was such limited scope for any physical exercise in the School, pressed for a gymnasium to be an immediate priority.

The HSC then revisited the controversial issue of reviving the post of Rector. There seemed very good reasons to do so. During the previous thirty years there had been occasions when a Modern Language master, or a Dancing master, had been 'president' of the School for three months, yet such teachers were only in attendance for three hours each day. The remainder of the time, the School had been without an official or representative Head. The appointment of a permanent Rector would overcome this and would bring the School into line with every other school of comparative status in Scotland. He would act as a permanent president at all meetings of the masters and could be the 'medium of communication on the affairs of the School with the Committee'. He would also be the point of contact for parents and guardians regarding the progress of pupils, and would advise on the classes which scholars should enter. However, the Committee appreciated the need to appease critics, and recommended that the powers of the proposed Rector be circumscribed. He would have no control over, or direction of, departments other than his own. There would be no supervisory function over other teachers' methods, course content or departmental discipline.

As the HSC members believed they were proposing a neat solution, they were taken aback by the strength and virulence of opposition to their proposals. They had completely misjudged the situation. It would appear that some members of the Council, having made up their minds when the issue had previously been discussed and, thinking that the subject had been dropped, were now annoyed at its reappearance. However, it was the outspoken resistance from other quarters which so surprised the Committee.

The School's masters argued that the change would alter for the worse their contract arrangements and also their status by, in effect, demoting them to subordinates.[75] Moreover, they argued that a Rector with a pecuniary interest in one department could not be entrusted with directing pupils into subjects and classes. Their case was supported by a group of self-styled 'old High School boys' who attacked the whole idea in the newspapers of the day, arguing that the absence of a Rector had made no difference at all to the education they had received.

A war of words was waged in the press throughout the early months of 1867. A number of articles were intemperate in their language, arguing in no uncertain terms that no good would come of a rectorship under any circumstances. Yet even the more moderate were not convinced and bemoaned the fact that such sensitive matters had been brought forward without any staff consultation. Moreover, the qualifications which were desired in a Rector – general culture, breadth of educational views, business capacity and seniority of age – were not necessarily to be found in the head of the Classical department, rather than elsewhere in the School. In April, even the merchants of the City brought forward a memorial against the recommendation.

By the time the Council voted on the proposals at its May meeting it was clear what the result would be. By 30 votes to 7 it decided that the recommendation to appoint a Rector would not be acted upon.[76] There was to be no central administrative figure and the School would continue to be administered by each master in rotation.

The issue of bringing back the post of Rector in 1867 was only one of a number in which the HSC proved unrepresentative of the views of the majority of the Town Council. Probably this is not altogether surprising for interested parties were often appointed to the Committee, and others tended 'to go native' and support what seemed best for the School rather than reflect Council policy, which was guided by the imperative of keeping public expenditure as low as possible. Indeed, some councillors viewed the High School as a School for better-off citizens, who were perfectly able to pay for the education of their children. From their perspective, any expenditure upon the School of any portion of funds drawn from the whole community was both unjust and unnecessary.[77] This view became widespread when public attention was drawn to the seemingly large incomes being made by the masters from fees. This had led the Council, as early as April 1845, to decide that High School teachers would receive no salaries from funds which they administered.

THE ARGYLL COMMISSION

In the mid-nineteenth century two fifths of the children in Scotland, especially in Glasgow, were not receiving any education, and unsuccessful attempts were made to devise a national educational system. Simultaneously, the Privy Council system common to Scotland and England was developing along its own lines, with the priority on curbing rising costs to be borne out of general taxation. By 1862 the Revised Code with 'payment by results' was introduced in England, but it was another two years before it was applied in Scotland. Even then, the protests of Scottish MPs led to its suspension, and in August 1864 the Government conceded a Royal Commission on Scottish Education headed by the 8th Duke of Argyll.[78]

The extensive remit of the Argyll Commission extended to all types of public and private foundations as well as teacher-training institutions. It appointed assistant commissioners to survey education on the ground, and they published three reports in four volumes and three special reports between 1865 and 1868. The most significant were those on Elementary Schools (1867), which included Glasgow, and the Burgh and Middle-Class Schools (1868).[79] Thomas Harvey[80] was involved with James Greig in producing the report on the High School in the former, while Harvey, along with Alexander Sellar, an advocate who later became a Liberal MP, produced the report on the School in the latter. Generally the commissioners found the general state of the burgh schools satisfactory, and the commission did not propose major changes. However, Harvey's reports on the High School, after his visit in 1865, were critical in a number of areas and influential in decision-making in the future.[81]

The Report on the State of Education in Glasgow[82] held that altogether the buildings and arrangements 'scarcely befit the sole burgh or grammar school of a city like Glasgow'.[83] Although its site was convenient for the mass of pupils, it was far from areas where higher education was established and from where a high school might be expected to draw its catchment. Its position probably explained the founding of Glasgow Academy in the West End. The School was a 'collection of six schools loosely strung together'[84] and had no restriction for entry.[85] Despite, or because of, the rotation of masters as president, there was still confusion, with the Mathematics and the highest Classics classes meeting at the same time. Harvey also commented on the small numbers of pupils who finished the five-year course: most left for business and university after three or four years. Nonetheless, given their results, the School 'in spite of its want of system, will bear comparison with any school in the City',[86] with only Glasgow Academy as a serious rival as a Classical school. Harvey ended with a balanced judgment: the High School was an 'excellent' school, but he recommended a more systematic course, more equipment and more status for the Classical masters, and a move to a more favourable site.

The Report on the State of Education in the Burgh and Middle-Class Schools of Scotland[87] assessed the School within the Scottish context of similar schools. Harvey found it strange to find Glasgow among the ranks of the unendowed schools[88] and wondered where the former patrimony from the Roman Catholic Church had gone after 1560. There was no trace of such revenue, which must have been mixed into the general funds of Glasgow as time passed. With few endowments the School was fortunate that the Town Council supported it with voluntary funds. In terms of fees the commissioners produced a table of average rates per scholar, which suggested that Glasgow was offering a very competitive product:[89]

Edinburgh Academy (private)	£12 7s 3d
Edinburgh High School (Council)	£10 3s 0d
Glasgow Academy (private)	£ 8 13s 9d
Glasgow High School (Council)	£ 5 11s 10d
Aberdeen Grammar School (Council)	£ 4 3s 9d

However, the playground 'of very moderate dimensions' was laid with gravel and was not adapted for football, cricket or any other games. The buildings were 'only moderately good'. The rooms were 'scantily furnished' with the necessary equipment, and were scarcely large enough for the classes. With no fixed curriculum, one department could be thronged while another was nearly empty.[90]

Although the wealthier classes had homes in the newly built up areas of the city to the west, the site was probably still the best available for the majority of the parents of prospective pupils. The 650 boys on the School roll belonged 'to the middle classes', their parents being described as 'tradesmen and merchants with a large proportion of clergymen, and members of the medical and legal professions'.[91] They came from all parts of Glasgow and by railway from neighbouring towns, in some cases travelling over 12 miles. On average they took three to five classes in the School[92] and in some cases attended other schools for particular subjects. There was a public examination or exhibition of the scholars once a year, to which the professors of the university, the local ministers and the Town Councillors were invited. In addition the masters had periodic examinations of their higher classes in Writing. At the end of each session there was a 'profuse' distribution of prizes, chiefly books, with a few medals. The total number of prizes given in September 1867 was 412.

The staff was composed of 'thoroughly efficient teachers'.[93] Generally, 'the teaching in all the departments was excellent'. No time was wasted; the teaching was direct and thorough, and was aimed at making the boys sound scholars. These positive comments were overlaid with the highly satisfactory personal relationships between teachers and pupils which were a marked feature of such schools.

Harvey made some telling overall remarks.[94] He questioned the practice of having boys whose ages ranged from eleven to fifteen studying together in the same large class. Without a Rector he 'doubted if the organisation of the school can be perfectly satisfactory'. Despite the view of the patrons that the absence of a prescribed curriculum was an advantage, it seemed to Harvey to add to the expense of education and he suggested a reduction in fees for those boys following a complete course. He also recommended a readjustment of the subjects taught in the several departments and the need for more regular examinations. Finally, Harvey highlighted the fact that the Classical masters had a lower income than not only the teachers of new subjects, but also the teacher of the mere mechanical art of Writing. Taken together these were powerful arguments for change. Moreover, the commissioners found only 'six schools in Scotland to which the designation of secondary school is applicable',[95] and the Council must have been concerned that these did not include the High School, which was categorised as 'mixed elementary and secondary'.[96]

Harvey saw the School at a particularly unfavourable time, when the roll was high. Nonetheless, the Town Council had little defence from the criticisms, particularly as some of the defects had existed for a considerable period.[97] It appreciated that although some improvements could be made, what was necessary was not just tinkering with existing practices. The remedy, if Glasgow was to have a school to be proud of, was to find a new site and build a new school. This realisation was the result of the revelations of the reports of the Argyll Commission. It dispelled 'illusions associated with a complacent contemplation of the past and drew attention to the needs of the present'.[98]

CLASS MEETINGS

The tradition had grown up of the Latin classes holding annual dinners, beginning usually five years after leaving school and continuing until only a few members were left. Rowlett's class of 1832–6 certainly did so, and according to Dr Paton[99] the Latin class entering the Grammar School in 1795 invited the 115 boys of the class to a dinner in Mrs Porteous's in the Trongate on Monday 11 October 1802. Fourteen attended.

Dr McKindlay's Latin class of 1847–52 had a roll of 121 names and had its first dinner in the Star Hotel, Buchanan Street in October 1857, with 22 attending. In 1860 the addresses of 86 were ascertained, and of these some 27 were already abroad. By 1868 numbers had dropped away, and only 6 appeared, but the dinner was revived in 1882 and continued until 1896. Viscount James Bryce was the most distinguished of the class, but worthy of mention were John Cameron, editor of the *Straits Times*, Singapore; David Leslie, merchant in Natal; Roger Duke, Post-Master of Malta; James Lindsay, City Accountant of Ottawa; Capt Wallace Gilmour RA, combatant in the Indian Mutiny; George Paterson, Principal Collector of Customs, Ceylon; Rev. John McSwaine, Moderator of the Presbyterian Churches of Australia; Hugh Lusk, Premier of Auckland Province (1870); and Robert McLean, who went on to Glasgow and Cambridge Universities before becoming an advocate and being involved in a number of well-publicised court cases.[100] The class records were last in the hands of Sir William Copland, civil engineer, whose son presented them to the School.[101]

The class meetings of Dr Low's Latin class of 1854–9 began in October 1866, chaired by George Buchanan, deemed the best scholar of the class and dux of the Third and Fourth Years. The roll contained 94 names. Low attended some of the early meetings. In 1872 it was decided that a class album would be compiled, and in time this became the property of the last survivor, Thomas Holt, who died in January 1924.[102]

McKindlay's class of 1855–60 had a class roll of 128, and at its dinner on 10 October 1913 some 8 Old Boys answered 'adsum' of the 23 reported as still alive.[103]

McKindlay's class of 1861–6 had 113 names on its roll at its first dinner in 1871 and included 4 clergy; 4 lawyers; 5 chemists; 6 doctors; and 36 merchants. Already 15 lived in England; 5 in Australia; 5 in New Zealand; 2 in China; 2 in America; 2 in India; 3 in Canada; 2 in South America; 1 in South Africa; and 1 in Singapore. It held its nineteenth annual dinner in the St Enoch Station hotel in October 1889,[104] with 9 members present, under the presidency of W.T. Geddes.[105]

McKindlay's Latin class of 1865–70 was the last he enrolled, because within a few months he took ill. John Hutchison, later Rector, and Alexander Murdoch, later lecturer in Greek at Glasgow University, took over his classes until the end of session. The class had 137 names on the roll, and in the First Year was divided into senior, middle and junior divisions. By Fourth Year this was down to one division, and only 20 boys remained for Fifth Year. In 1895 it was found that 29 of the original class were dead, and of the callings 7 had entered the church; 1 the army; 8 were in law; 10 in medicine; 16 followed other professions; and 68 had business careers. The Jubilee dinner of the class, with 12 classmates present, took place on 5 November 1925.[106]

The Latin class of 1867–72 had 146 on the roll and held its first annual dinner in the Atholl Arms Hotel, with 29 attending in 1876. It had a remarkable record holding its 50th annual dinner in the North British Hotel on 28 October 1925, when 15 attended. The dinners continued until October 1937 (the 62nd), when 8 classmates dined with Talman, the Rector of the day.

It was the formation of the Glasgow High School Former Pupils' Club in 1870 and its gradual rise in importance[107] which ensured that class meetings and societies declined in significance. A few survived,[108] but generally the energies which previously had been dissipated into a diversity of channels were absorbed into the new, single stream.

THE HIGH SCHOOL FORMER PUPILS CLUB

It was in keeping with the ideas prevalent at the time that the Club's original interest in the School was confined to encouraging scholarship by the foundation of prizes for annual competition. Indeed, for some years after 1870 the relationship between Club and School was not close. Although this was partly due to the introduction of the School Board in 1872, it was more the result of the low numbers who joined the Club, which led to a level of Club indifference in the development of sport. This only changed with the purchase of the playing fields and the erection of the War Memorial Clubhouse and Pavilion. It was the acquisition of Old Anniesland which resulted in the Club becoming a separate legal entity in 1919. Paradoxically, this strengthened the relationship between the bodies, which was secured by the arrangement whereby every schoolboy on leaving the High School automatically became a member of the Club. Increasingly, the future of the School seemed dependent on its alumni, who by the late 1920s were beginning to claim a share in the government of the school.

PUPILS

In the mid-nineteenth century Glasgow experienced the fastest urban growth in Europe, but despite the resulting social problems its citizens took great pride in the City's industrial and economic success. The transition from textiles to metalwork revealed the adaptability of its merchants and manufacturers. There was a variety and flexibility in Glasgow's economic base, and the challenges of urban development led the city's growing middle class into social reform.

The citizens also loyally supported their Town School. Indeed, the dominance of the High School in this period is illustrated by the extensive profiles which follow. Whatever external reports might indicate, Glasgow had faith in its burgh school, and the mid-nineteenth century was a 'golden age' in terms of the achievements of its former pupils. Henry Campbell arrived in 1845 and was soon followed by James Bryce.[109] Less than a generation later Bonar Law attended. Only the High School, other than Eton and Harrow, can claim to have educated two modern prime ministers. It produced others, like Bryce, who played a part on the national stage, but as important was its contribution to the production of a Glasgow elite imbued with a powerful civic pride.

The Taunton Report of 1868 confirmed the middle-class nature of the School. Landed proprietors and the professional classes accounted for 8.8 per cent; 43.8 per cent came from first-class merchants and large farmers; 42.5 per cent from second-class merchants and superior traders; and only 5 per cent from small traders, clerks, artisans and labourers. Fortunately, the diversity and extent of the middle class meant that poorer classes were represented in its ranks.[110]

Merchants

James Campbell (1825–1908) attended Rowlett's Latin class in 1834–8 and 1840–1 before joining his father's wholesale merchant firm. He was influential in creating the new University of Glasgow buildings at Gilmorehill. He was Deputy Chairman of Glasgow School Board, Convener of the HSC, 1873–6, and served on national education commissions. He was Conservative MP for Glasgow and Aberdeen Universities, 1880–1906 and the older brother of the prime minister, Henry Campbell-Bannerman.

(Sir) John Muir (1828–1903) (Baron Muir) was the son of a Glasgow cotton trader. After university he joined the textile exporting business of Finlay & Co., and revitalised the firm, becoming sole proprietor. He diversified from the competitive cotton market, developing into the infant tea industry. By the 1890s Muir was the world's major stakeholder in the growing and marketing of tea, employing over 90,000 in Britain and India. He became Lord Provost of Glasgow (1889–92). He was largely responsible for the Glasgow International Exhibition of 1888. Its surplus was the basis of the Kelvingrove Art Galleries Fund. His four sons all attended the High School.[111]

Sir James King (1830–1911)[112] attended university, becoming a manufacturing chemist merchant. He was Chairman of the Caledonian Railway Co., the Clydesdale Bank Ltd, and the Chamber of Commerce. He was President of the High School Club, 1877–9, Dean of Faculties at Glasgow University, 1879–82 and 1904–10, and Lord Provost, 1886–9.

James Cleland Burns (1832–1908) was the grandson of James Cleland (author of the 1825 *History*). As younger son of Sir George Burns, he became a partner in the family shipping line. He produced the 1878 School *History* and was President of the High School Club, 1880–2.

William Strang Steel (1832–1911) was the businessman founder of W. Strang Steel & Co., merchants in Burma. He was a landowner in Selkirkshire and Roxburghshire.

(John) Annan Bryce (1841–1923) was the younger brother of Viscount Bryce. He studied at Glasgow, Edinburgh and Oxford, being President of the Oxford Union in 1871. He took employment with East India merchants, specialising in forestry work. While in Rangoon he sat on the Legislative Council of Burma. He was elected in 1906 as the Liberal MP for the Inverness Burghs (until 1918).[113]

(Sir) David Richmond (1843–1908)[114] attended the School between 1857 and 1859. He became an iron tube manufacturer and merchant; a councillor, 1879–99; Lord Provost, 1896–9 and President of the High School Club, 1899–1902. He launched the successful campaign for reconstruction of the Royal Infirmary.

Patrick Dunn (1848–1932) was senior partner in a firm of merchants and steamship agents in Glasgow. He was Chairman of Glasgow School of Art, 1914–30.

David Clark (1849–1926) attended Aberdeen and Glasgow Universities before joining his father's grain merchant and ship-owning business. He secured Maxwell Park and the Burgh Hall for Pollokshields.

(Sir) James Bell (1850–1929),[115] son of a successful city merchant, became a partner in a firm of steamship owners. He was a director of the Clydesdale Bank, and of the Midland Bank. He was a councillor, 1890–6, and Lord Provost, 1892–6, advocating electricity for lighting, suggesting purification of Clyde, acquiring Bellahouston Park for the citizens, and taking the tramways into municipal ownership. He was President of the High School Club, 1895–9 and Dean of Guild 1898–1900.

(Sir) Joseph Maclay, first baron, (1857–1951)[116] was the son of a Glasgow master upholsterer. By 1885 he was partner in a tramp-ship firm which became one of the largest shipping concerns on the Clyde. He served on Glasgow Town Council (1899–1906), and as a Liberal he advocated temperance and was active in evangelical and philanthropic causes. His contemporary at school, Bonar Law, was responsible for Maclay becoming minister of Shipping in Lloyd George's Government in December 1916. He increased the building of merchant ships and supported a trial for convoys despite Admiralty opposition. His organisation for the transport of American troops to Europe, largely in British ships in the later stages of World War I, was 'a remarkable logistical feat'.[117] After the war, Maclay obtained the early decontrol of shipping. He received the Freedom of the City of Glasgow in 1922.

Manufacturers (Industrialists)

James Stevenson (1825–1905) was the son of a Glasgow cotton-broker. After Glasgow University he followed his father as partner of the Jarrow Chemical Company in South Shields, which became the largest chemical company in England in the 1870s, employing 1400. He became the Radical Liberal MP for South Shields (1868–95).[118]

George Goyder (1826–1898) worked for firms making precision and surveying instruments. He migrated to Australia, and by 1861 he had become Surveyor-General of South Australia, a post he held for thirty-three years. He was involved in the development of mining, railways, forestry and water regulation.[119]

John Crosfield (1832–1901) went into the family soap business and took over the firm completely in 1875. He invested in the Brunner, Mond Company when it went public and became its first chairman. With a Quaker background, Crosfield proved an enlightened employer and campaigned against intemperance and vice.[120]

Sir William Copland (1838–1907) became a civil engineer (1856). He was Deacon Convener of Glasgow Trades (1891–3) and chair of the Governors of Glasgow and West of Scotland Technical College (1897–1907).[121]

Michael Simons (1842–1925) joined the fruit firm founded by his father, Benjamin, in the Candleriggs. He developed agencies in fruit importing and fruit distribution in the USA and Canada, and contributed to the success of the 1888 and 1901 Exhibitions.

(Colonel) William Clark (1843–1930)[122] was a sewing-cotton manufacturer. He became a director of Glasgow Chamber of Commerce and Merchants' House; a councillor, 1873–9; Chairman of the Glasgow Liberal Unionist Association (1880–5); supporter of the Volunteer Movement and President of the High School Club, 1889–91.

George McCulloch (1848–1907) was educated at Anderson's College. He emigrated to Australia, and large deposits of silver were discovered on his land at Broken Hill in 1883. He became a multi-millionaire and developed a remarkable art collection.[123]

Robert Duncan (1850–1924) won engineering prizes at Glasgow University and went on to be a manufacturer of marine engines and boilers. He was elected Conservative MP for Govan (1906).

William Chrystal (1854–1921), the grandson of Rector Chrystal, studied Chemistry and became a technical partner in the Shawfield Chemical Works, the largest and oldest of their kind in the world.

(Sir) William Beardmore (Lord Invernairn of Strathnairn) (1856–1936) was the son of a partner in the Parkhead Forge, where he was apprenticed. He attended Anderson's College and the Royal School of Mines in South Kensington. By 1886 he had become sole partner in the business, and he diversified and expanded the works, adding shipbuilding in 1900. He went into the motor car building business in 1902, adding steel making in 1905. By 1913 he began aircraft manufacture and supplied much war material. With the peace, he assumed that trade would expand, but this miscalculation led to the collapse of many of his activities and forced him into retirement. The Beardmore Glacier in Antarctica, the largest glacier in the world, was named after him by Ernest Shackleton, whose Antarctic expedition of 1907–9 he had heavily funded.[124]

(Sir) Walter Menzies (1856–1913) joined his father's tube-making business. He became the Liberal MP for South Lanark (1906–13).

(Sir) James Macfarlane (1857–1944) was Chairman of Macfarlane Lang & Co. Ltd, the bread and biscuit manufacturers. He became Deacon Convener of Glasgow Trades House (1899) and was Chairman of the Managers of Glasgow Royal Infirmary from 1914 until 1939.

(Sir) Frederick Macleod (1858–1936) was sole partner of Macleod & Co., Bilboa (Spain) and Glasgow, and proprietor of the Grangemouth Iron Company.

Churchmen

(Very Rev.) Thomas Leishman (1825–1904) was the son of a Glasgow manse.

He left the School in 1838 and became a distinguished Classical scholar and bibliophile at Glasgow University. A minister from 1847 to 1895, he was Moderator of the General Assembly in 1898.[125]

(Rev.) Alexander McLaren (1826–1910) was the son of a manufacturer. An able student, he attended Rowlatt's Latin class (1835) before studying Latin and Greek at Glasgow University. Influenced by his father's lay preaching he trained for the Baptist ministry at London University, winning prizes in Scripture, Hebrew and Greek. He became a minister in Southampton then, in 1858, in Manchester. Many of his sermons were published, as were over forty volumes of Bible exposition. He was Baptist Union President in 1875 and 1901. 'Commentators ranked him as one of the greatest preachers of the nineteenth century.'[126]

(Rev. Principal) Robert Rainy (1826–1906) was the son of the Professor of Medical Jurisprudence at Glasgow University. He attended the School from 1835 to 1838, going on to Glasgow University and graduating MA. He studied Divinity under Thomas Chalmers and became minister of Huntly Free Church (1851) and the Free High Church, Edinburgh (1854). He was made Professor of Church History in New College, becoming its Principal in 1874, and retaining this post until his death. He was considered the 'ecclesiastical statesman' of his church, being Moderator of the original Free Church in 1887, and Moderator of the original United Free Church in 1900 and 1905. He gradually updated Free Church theology and aimed at a union of the various Free Churches, succeeding in uniting the Reformed Presbyterian (1876) and United Presbyterian (1900) churches with his United Free Church.[127]

(Very Rev.) John Lang (1834–1909) was born a son of the manse. He spent a year under Low and Bryce, followed by studies at Glasgow University. He proceeded to study Divinity and was minister in the historic Barony Church in Glasgow from 1873 until 1900. He was Moderator of the General Assembly in 1893. He was active especially in education[128] and housing, and supported trade unions and efforts to bring about a fairer society. In 1900 he was appointed Principal of Aberdeen University, bringing to fruition the opening of the new buildings at Marischal College. His third son, (William) Cosmo Gordon Lang (1864–1945), was archbishop of Canterbury from 1928 until 1942.[129]

(Rev.) Archibald Scott (1837–1909) was the son of a Lanarkshire farmer. He was in McKindlay's 1847–52 class, and after university he became a minister. His main charges were Maxwell Church in Glasgow and the prestigious charge of St George's, Edinburgh. He became a church leader, and at his death he was a member of twenty-seven committees, four of them as convener. It was his overture in 1907 which began the process of reunion with the United Free Church of Scotland.[130]

(Dr) George Robson (1842–1911) did well academically in Low's 1852–7 class. He attended Glasgow University and became a minister in Inverness, then Perth. He was editor of the Missionary Record of the United Free Church of Scotland, and Moderator of the United Free Church, 1903.[131]

James Gilmour (1843–91) became a missionary for the London Missionary Society. Using Peking (Beijing) as a base, for twenty years he made annual trips into Mongolia. He succeeded David Livingstone 'as the missionary icon who laboured in an extremely remote and difficult field with no converts'. His book *Among the Mongols* became a classic work.[132]

(Very Rev.) Michael Hutchison (1844–1921) developed an early taste for Classical literature at the School before attending Oxford. He was ordained in 1867 and was Rector of St Ninian's, Glasgow, 1870–1920 and, after 1903, Dean of Glasgow and Galloway.

(Rt Rev.) Pearson Muir (1846–1924) became minister of Glasgow Cathedral, 1896–1915. He was Moderator of the General Assembly of Church of Scotland, 1910–11, and Chaplain in Ordinary to George V in Scotland, 1910.

(Rev.) John Struthers (1851–1915) was in McKindlay's 1861–6 Latin class, being first in Latin and Greek, and becoming Paul Medallist in his final year. He also did well academically at Glasgow University before becoming minister of the Reformed Presbyterian Church, Greenock. From 1888 he produced the *Morning Watch*, a national Sunday School magazine, judged 'one of the hundred best books in the world'.[133]

(Rev.) Thomas Burns (1853–1938) was minister of Lady Glenorchy's Parish Church, Edinburgh, 1882–1930. He was Chairman of the Royal Blind Asylum and School, 1894, and a senior chaplain during World War I.

(Very Rev.) John Smith (1854–1927) studied Divinity at Glasgow University. He was minister of the Old Partick Parish (1886–1927), Chairman of Govan School Board, Convenor of the Business Committee of Glasgow University, and Moderator of the General Assembly, 1922.

Military

(General Sir) Archibald Alison (1826–1907)[134] was the son of first baronet and historian, Sir Archibald, and was brought up from 1835 in Possil House. Following attendance at Glasgow and Edinburgh Universities, he entered the army in 1846. During the Crimean War Sir Colin Campbell appointed Alison his military secretary. He was active in suppressing the Indian Mutiny, distinguished himself during the Ashanti expedition of 1873–4, and covered himself with glory in the Egyptian campaign of 1882. He was presented with a sword of honour from the citizens of Glasgow.[135]

(Surgeon-General) James Jameson (1837–1904) became an army surgeon, being promoted for highly meritorious service rendered during an epidemic of yellow fever in Trinidad. He was Director-General of the Army Medical Service.

Medical

(Dr) Norman Kerr (1834–1899) was the son of a Glasgow ship-owner. He graduated from Glasgow University and spent most of his working life as Medical Officer for St Marylebone. From his late teens he promoted temperance, supporting legislation for the compulsory treatment of drunkenness, which he believed was a disease. The Habitual Drunkards Act (1878) and the Inebriates Act (1898) resulted in great measure from his campaigning.[136]

(Dr) Asher Asher (1837–1889) was the son of a stationer and a good scholar at the School and the university. His medical degree in 1856 was the first achieved by a Glasgow-born Jew.[137] He worked locally before moving to London in 1862 and there provided medical care for the Jewish poor. He gave advice on ameliorating the situation of Jewish immigrants in Galicia, USA and Russia. A memorial plaque to him was erected at the entrance of the Garnethill synagogue.[138]

(Dr) James Russell (1837–1904) was the son of a Glasgow grain merchant. He did well academically and completed a medical degree. He took charge of Glasgow's fever hospital in 1865, before serving as the City's first full-time Medical Officer (MO) from 1872 till 1898. He was also MO of the Local Government Board for Scotland, where he rigorously applied the provisions of Public Health Acts. He received the memorial medal of the Royal College of Physicians of London for his promotion of public health.[139]

(Prof.) James Finlayson (1840–1906) was a member of Low's 1852–7 class.[140] He graduated with honours in Medicine. In 1875 he was appointed physician in charge of wards, and lecturer in clinical medicine, at the newly built Western Infirmary. He held this post until his death, forging a reputation as an outstanding clinical teacher. He was also physician to the

Royal Hospital for Sick Children in Glasgow, with a large consulting practice. He was President of the High School Club, 1892–5.[141]

(Dr) Samuel Sloan (1843–1920) was greatly influenced by Low and Bryce when at the High School, and was first in Greek and Mathematics and second in Latin. He went on to study Medicine at Glasgow and became a physician and lecturer in Clinical Obstetrics at Glasgow Maternity Hospital.

(Prof.) Samson Gemmell (1848–1913) attended McKindlay's class between 1861 and 1864 and graduated in Medicine from Glasgow University. He was resident physician at Glasgow Fever Hospital, the Royal Infirmary and then the Western Infirmary. He was chair of Medical Practice at Anderson's, before becoming Professor of Clinical Medicine, Glasgow 1900 and Regius Professor of the Practice of Medicine, 1908.

(Dr) John Wilson (1855–1930) was Medical Officer for Lanark County between 1894 and 1924.

Legal

Alexander McGrigor (1827–1891) became a solicitor and took over the family firm of McGrigor, Murray and McGrigor in 1853. He was Glasgow University Dean of Faculties, 1876–9, and Rector's Assessor, 1884–7. As Honorary Secretary of the Glasgow International Exhibition of 1888, he was instrumental in cataloguing Glasgow University Library.

Joseph Taylor (1828–1904) was the son of a merchant. After attending Glasgow and Edinburgh Universities he became Dean of the Glasgow Royal Faculty of Procurators (1898– 1903).

Hamilton Maxwell (1830–1923) became Sheriff of Bombay and Chairman of the Bank of Bombay (1878). Later he was a professional artist with a Paris studio, 1893–1908.[142]

David Balfour (1836–1912) was a lawyer and member of Faculty of Procurators. He became Sheriff-Substitute of Lanarkshire, 1876, then Glasgow, 1880–1910.

(Sir) Archibald Lawrie (1837–1914) was the son of the Professor of Surgery at Glasgow University, from which he graduated in 1856, before being admitted to the Faculty of Advocates (1860). After judging in Scottish sheriff courts and district courts in Ceylon, Lawrie became, in 1892, the senior judge on the Supreme Court in Ceylon.[143]

Richard Campbell (1840–1901) became Advocate-Depute in Gladstone's 1880 Liberal Government, resigning over Irish Home Rule. He was Sheriff of Dumfries and Galloway, 1890, and of the Border counties, 1896.

William Miller (1848–1904) was the son of a Glasgow warehouseman and pawnbroker. After three years at the School he studied Mathematics and then Law at Glasgow University. He joined the Faculty of Advocates and moved to Edinburgh, although he continued a teaching commitment at Glasgow University. He is seen as a 'pioneer in the systematic study of Jurisprudence on its scientific side'.[144]

James Millar (1855–1917) studied at Glasgow University then graduated in Law from Edinburgh University. He became an advocate and legal secretary to the Lord Advocate (1905). He was Sheriff-Substitute, Lothians and Peebles, 1906–8; and Sheriff of Lanarkshire (1908).

Academic

(Rev.) John McSwaine (1835–1909) was in McKindlay's 1847–52 class. He then attended Glasgow and Edinburgh Universities before becoming Classical master at Stirling Grammar School. He was made a Fellow of the EIS, 1873, Moderator of the Presbyterian Church of Australia, and chaplain to the military forces of Australia.

(Prof.) John Hales (1836–1914) became an assistant master at Marlborough College, 1860–3. He went on to become Professor of English Literature, King's College, London, retiring in 1903.

(Prof.) John Ferguson (1838–1916) was the son of a merchant from Alloa. He attended McKindlay's 1847–52 class and Glasgow University, where he won several prizes. He found employment with Professor William Thomson (later Lord Kelvin) in the field of Electrometrics. In 1863 he matriculated in Medicine to pursue his studies in Chemistry: by 1869 he had the responsibility for running the Chemistry department, and in 1874 he was appointed Regius Professor. He was President of the Glasgow Archaeological Society (1891–4) and President of the High School Club, 1910–12.[145]

(Prof.) David Finlay (1840–1923) was in Low's 1852–7 class. He became Professor of Practice of Medicine, Aberdeen University, 1891–1912, and was senior physician to Aberdeen Royal Infirmary. He was a member of the General Medical Council, 1901–11, and Hon. Physician-in-Ordinary to the King in Scotland.

(Prof.) Alexander Buchanan (1844–1915) won the Latin and Greek Gold Medals at the School. He studied Arts and Medicine at Glasgow before becoming senior Demonstrator of Anatomy, 1868. Between 1873 and 1915 he was Professor of Anatomy at Anderson's College Medical School.

John Buchanan (1844–1925) was the son of a Glasgow merchant. He graduated from Glasgow University and studied Chemistry at Marburg, Leipzig, Bonn and Paris, before becoming assistant to the Professor of Chemistry at Edinburgh. He joined the scientific team sailing round the world on HMS *Challenger* (1872–6), contributing to the development of Oceanography. He went on to publish over 100 scientific papers. He became a Fellow, Royal Society in 1887. He was awarded the Gold Medal from the Royal Scottish Geographical Society in 1911.[146]

(Prof.) John Clark (1844–1907) was in Low's 1852–7 class and studied at Anderson's College, Goettingen, Heidelberg (under Bunsen) and Paris. He was appointed Professor of Chemistry at Anderson's (1869–70), formed a firm of analytical and consulting chemists, and became Public Analyst for Glasgow, Lanark and Renfrew counties.

John Horne (1848–1928) was the son of a Stirlingshire farmer. He attended Glasgow University, leaving to work with a geological survey. He studied the rocks of the north-west Highlands of Scotland and the southern uplands, and his field work resulted in two large volumes published in 1899 and 1907. Between 1901 and 1911 he was assistant Director of the Geological survey with responsibility for Scotland and completed much work on the Scottish coalfields. He was elected Fellow, Royal Society (1900) and was its President, 1915–9.

(Prof.) John Thomson (1849–1933) was Professor of Chemistry, Queen's College, London, 1880–7; Emeritus Professor of Chemistry, King's College, University of London, 1887–1914, and Vice-Principal, 1905–14. He was also President of Institute of Chemistry of Britain and Ireland, 1900–3.

(Prof. Sir) James Dobbie (1852–1924) became Professor of Chemistry, Bangor, 1884–1903; director, Royal Scottish Museum, 1903–9; and Principal, Government Laboratories London, 1909–20. He was President of the Institute of Chemistry, 1915–18 and President of the Chemical Society, 1919–21.

Thomas Miller (1852–1936) attended Glasgow and Cambridge Universities, winning various fellowships. He taught Mathematics at the Wesley College, Sheffield. He became Principal of the Borough Road Training College, London.

William Rutherford (1853–1907) was the son of a Glasgow minister. He attended the School, St Andrews University and Balliol College, Oxford. He became a Classical master at St Paul's School, London. After three major publications he was elected a Fellow and Tutor of University College, Oxford. However, he took up the headmastership of Westminster School in 1883. There he proved a reformer, introducing a modern side and a termly personal interview with each boy, and also began regular morning services. His abolition of rowing was opposed by the boys and Old Boys, but his reforms were influential in Westminster's development.[147]

(Prof.) William Smart (1853–1915) was the son of the manager of a Barrhead threadworks. He became a partner in his family firm before it was sold. He completed a degree in Philosophy, being influenced by Edward Caird, the Professor of Moral Philosophy and leading Idealist thinker in Scotland. In 1892 he became the first specialised lecturer in Political Economy in Glasgow University and its first Professor in 1896. He was a member of the Royal Commission on the Poor Law in 1905, helping to draft large parts of the majority report.[148]

(Prof. Sir) Mungo MacCallum (1854–1942) was Professor of English Literature and History, University College, Wales. He became Professor of Modern Literature at Sydney University 1887–1920; then Warden, 1924; Vice-Chancellor, 1925–7; and Chancellor.

(Prof.) James Mavor (1854–1925) was the son of a minister and teacher. As the eldest of a large family he left the School early, but in his autobiography[149] he commented on the good teachers and scholars at the School. He became one of Scotland's leading economists, lecturing at St Mungo's College before in 1892 being appointed Professor of Political Economy at the University of Toronto, a post he held for thirty years. He travelled worldwide as an adviser to governments. His seminal work, *Economic History of Russia*, was written in two volumes in 1914. His nephew, O.H. Mavor (James Bridie), also attended the School.[150]

(Very Rev. Prof.) Sir John Herkless (1855–1920) became Regius Professor of Ecclesiastical History, St Andrews University, 1894–1915; and Vice-Chancellor and Principal of St Andrews University, 1915–20.

(Prof.) Hugh Walker (1855–1939) was a Snell Exhibitioner at Oxford. He became Professor of English Literature, St David's College, Lampeter, and Mayor of Lampeter, South Wales from 1900 to 1902.

(Prof.) William McCormick (1858–1930) did well academically at the School and studied at Glasgow, Gottingen and Marburg Universities. He was Professor of English at University College, Dundee; Secretary of the Carnegie Trust for Universities of Scotland; and Chairman of the Advisory Council on Scientific and Industrial Research.

(Rev. Prof.) William Alexander (1859–1929) was a highly qualified scholar. He became Professor of Biology and Chemistry, Bombay, 1885; a lecturer in Free Church College, Glasgow, 1899–1900 and United Free College, Aberdeen 1901–2; Professor of Apologetics and Pastoral Theology in Free Church College, Edinburgh 1904; and Moderator of the General Assembly of the United Free Church, 1911.

(Prof.) James Watson (1859–1923) studied at Glasgow, Tuebingen, Geneva and Berlin. He became Professor of Chemistry at Anderson's College (1889).

Financial

John Graham (1828–1904) trained as an accountant, and with his uncle formed the partnership of Lang and Graham. He was President of the Institute of Insurance and Actuaries (1881–4).[151]

Sir John Cuthbertson[152] (1829–1905) studied under McMillan, 1839–44. He became a chemical and produce broker in Glasgow. He was chairman of the School Board of Glasgow for eighteen years, Convener of the HSC from 1882 to 1885, a member of the University Court, and a governor of the Glasgow and West of Scotland Technical College.

William Graham[153] (1838–1909) attended Glasgow University before joining his brother's CA firm. He was chairman, Glasgow School Board, and was President of the High School Club, 1905–8.

Robert Gourlay (1841–1916)[154] was in Low's 1852–7 class. He attended Glasgow University before joining the Bank of Scotland. He worked in its head office in Edinburgh (1861–5) before becoming manager of the Glasgow main branch (1879–1905). He was President of the High School Club (1886–8) and Dean of Guild.

(Lt-Col.) Easton Aitken (1842–1923) was in Low's 1852–7 class. He was a member of the Institute of Chartered Accountants and Actuaries. He chaired the Glasgow Stock Exchange in 1889, 1890, 1891, 1898 and 1903.

James Hedderwick (1845–1926) attended Glasgow University before becoming a stockbroker. He was chairman of the Glasgow Stock Exchange (1894–6), President of the Glasgow Chamber of Commerce, Chairman of the Glasgow Royal Infirmary, and a director of the Merchants' House.

Adam Rodger (1855–1946) was an investment adviser who became chairman of investment trusts and assurance companies. He was four times Provost of Rutherglen and was the Coalition Liberal MP for Rutherglen, 1918–22. He was granted the Freedom of Rutherglen in 1940.

Administrators (Politicians)

(Sir) Francis Sandford (Baron) (1824–1893) was the son of the Professor of

Greek at Glasgow University, which he attended before winning a Snell Exhibition. Following Oxford and a short spell in teaching he joined the Education Department, being promoted to Assistant Under-Secretary (1854) and Permanent Secretary (1870). There he remained until 1884, becoming a Charity Commissioner and first Permanent Under-Secretary to the newly created Scottish Office. He proved a meticulous, highly competent and politically neutral administrator.[155]

(Sir) James Dickson (1832–1901) worked in the City of Glasgow Bank. In 1854 he emigrated to Australia, opening his own firm, which did well in the building boom in Brisbane in the early 1880s. He was elected to the Queensland Legislative Assembly in 1873 and held various ministerial offices. In 1898 when Premier Barnes died suddenly, as a stopgap measure Dickson was chosen as Premier, Chief Secretary and Home Secretary. He held these posts for fourteen months. During this time he played a crucial role in bringing Queensland into the federation of the Australian colonies. He proved a keen advocate of the Imperial cause and readily committed Queensland troops to the Boer War. He was chosen to be the first Minister of Defence in the new Australian Federal administration but died suddenly after attending the first cabinet meeting.[156]

Duncan Gillies (1834–1903) was the son of a Glasgow market-gardener. He worked as a clerk in the Post Office until 1852, when he emigrated to Australia. He became a miner in Victoria and successfully won a seat in Parliament in 1861, becaming a minister with different portfolios under different administrations. He became Premier and Treasurer of Victoria in February 1886. His government over-extended the finances of the state through large borrowings and public works, and the resulting economic expansion turned into a severe depression. He was forced out of office in November 1890 and led the Opposition for four years. In 1902 he was voted Speaker of the House of Assembly, a post he retained until his death.[157]

(Sir) Henry Campbell-Bannerman (1836–1908)[158] was born as Henry Campbell[159] at Kelvinside House, Glasgow, into a wealthy, commercially successful family. His father, James Campbell, was leader of Glasgow's Conservatives and served as Lord Provost (1840–3). Other than summers, Henry was brought up in the family town house at 129 Bath Street and attended the High School between 1845 and 1850, taking Classics with McKindlay. He did well academically and took first place in the junior division of his class in the prizegivings of 1846, 1847 and 1848. In this last year he was also winner of the Tennent (Well Park) Medal for the best Latin Scholar in the Third Year, and did particularly well in Greek and Writing.[160]

After a European tour he attended Glasgow University (1851–3) and then Trinity College, Cambridge (1854–8), where he studied Mathematics and Classics, but his results were 'disappointingly modest'.[161] After university he joined the family firm and became a partner in 1860. He moved away from his Conservative background and entered parliament in 1868 as a Liberal for Stirling Burghs, a seat he was to retain until his death. He was made Financial Secretary at the War Office in 1871 but made little impact there, and in Opposition he remained spokesman on defence. However, he impressed while at the Admiralty and made his reputation in the difficult job of Chief Secretary for Ireland (1884–5). In Gladstone's final governments he was Secretary of State for War. In 1899, at the age of sixty-two, rather reluctantly, and in the absence of a determined challenge from Asquith, Campbell-Bannerman was chosen to be the Liberal leader in the Commons. Given Liberal divisions over the South African War, C-B (as he was commonly known) did better than most expectations in the 1900 election.[162] When the war ended and Balfour took over both Conservative leadership and the premiership from Salisbury, Liberal fortunes rose and C-B managed to achieve a coalition of Liberals. With the slogan 'peace, retrenchment and reform' the Liberals won a landslide victory in the election of January 1906.[163] C-B's assured and effective performances in the Commons brought him respect and affection. His Government was successful in accepting the 'suspensory veto' to deal with the Lords and laid the basis for self-government for South Africa. He was genuinely concerned with the plight of the poor but was a Gladstonian Liberal, wishing to reduce public expenditure. He nonetheless passed legislation on factories, workshops, mines and workmen's compensation, and laid the groundwork for further reforms. Ill health forced him to resign in April 1908 and he died two weeks later. He was buried in Meigle parish churchyard. He had received the Freedom of Glasgow in January 1907, and many throughout the country mourned his loss.[164] The *Times* held that no PM had inspired more affection.[165]

(Sir) James Bryce (Viscount) (1838–1922), in 1846 followed his father, who had been appointed Head of the Mathematics department, to the School. Between 1847 and 1852 he was in McKindlay's class. In 1854 he entered Glasgow University and won a scholarship to Trinity College, Oxford, where he gained an FCH in Moderations (1859), the best first of the year in Greats (1861), and graduated BA (1862), before becoming President of the Union (1863). He then went on to achieve a fellowship at Oriel. He became an accomplished walker and mountaineer; Mount Bryce, in the

Rockies, was named after him, and he was President of the Alpine Club (1899–1901). He was called to the English Bar in 1867. His interest in educational reform led to him becoming a member of the Taunton Commission looking into endowed schools. He became a Law professor at Manchester's Owens College, joined the agitation for women's legal equality and higher education, and supported the cause of the North in the American Civil War. His history book, *The Holy Roman Empire* (1864), proved a great success. In 1870 Gladstone appointed him Regius Professor of Civil Law at Oxford, and the following year he was active in the abolition of the University Tests. His political career developed further with the leading part he played in the Bulgarian agitation (1876) and he became Liberal MP for the packed-slum constituency of Tower Hamlets in 1880, moving to the loyal and less demanding South Aberdeen seat in 1885. In the Liberal Administration of 1886 he was Under-Secretary for Foreign Affairs and supported Gladstone's Irish Home Rule measures. Out of office, Bryce wrote his 'greatest work' *The American Commonwealth* (1888). In 1892 Bryce joined Gladstone's Cabinet as Chancellor of the Duchy of Lancaster, and was promoted by Rosebery in 1894 to President of the Board of Trade. He was an influential chair of the Royal Commission on Secondary Education (1894–6). Under C-B, Bryce had a brief and unsuccessful tenure as Chief Secretary for Ireland, and in 1907 he was sent as Ambassador to Washington, where he remained until 1913, carrying through a limited treaty of arbitration with USA. On the formation of the British Academy (1912) Bryce was one of its first forty-nine members. He was created Viscount Bryce of Dechmont in Lanarkshire in January 1914. He chaired the committee which investigated German conduct in occupied Belgium, and was chair of a joint conference of both houses reporting on the future of the House of Lords. He supported informal bodies pressing for the creation of a League of Nations and was influential in producing schemes, with his 1917 memorandum becoming a key document in the Versailles negotiations.[166] The ceremony to give him the Freedom of the City of Glasgow was postponed when war broke out; it was rearranged for February 1922, but he died two weeks before the new date.

(Rt Hon.) Thomas Buchanan (1846–1911), brother of John, was educated at the School,[167] Sherborne School and Balliol College, Oxford. He was elected a Fellow of All Souls College, Oxford and was called to the English Bar. He was elected to parliament unopposed as a Liberal for Edinburgh City in 1881, and although elected as a Liberal Unionist in 1886 he returned two years later to his Gladstonian allegiance. He represented

Aberdeenshire East (1892–1900) then Perthshire East (1903–10). Late in life he became Financial Secretary to R.B. Haldane at the War Office in C-B's Government (December 1905) and contributed to the reorganisation of the army and territorial forces. In 1908–9 he was Parliamentary Under-Secretary to Lord Morley at the India Office and was Government spokesman in the Commons.[168]

(Rt Hon. Sir) Henry Craik (1846–1927) was the son of a Glasgow minister and between 1857 and 1860 attended the School,[169] which he left aged fourteen to attend Glasgow University. A Snell Exhibition took him in 1865 to Oxford. In 1870 he joined the Education Department, being chosen Secretary of the Scotch (sic) Education Department in the new Scottish Office in 1885, a post he held until 1904. Craik ended the discredited 'payment of results', and also abolished fees, in elementary schools. He raised standards by creating a Leaving Certificate linked to university entrance (1888) and extending state grants to secondary schools in 1892. He became Conservative MP for the Universities of Glasgow and Aberdeen from 1906 to 1918 and for the Combined Scottish Universities from 1918 to 1927. He was the first President of the High School London Club (1922–7).[170]

Hugh Smith (1846–1907) was a director of a number of companies and was Liberal Unionist MP for Tyneside, Northumberland, 1900–6.

(Sir) Henry Robson (1848–1911) was a member of London Stock Exchange, 1872, Liberal candidate in the elections of 1895, 1906 and 1910, and Mayor of Kensington 1905–6.

(Rt Hon.) Lord Dickson ((Charles) Scott Dickson) (1850–1922) became an advocate (1877) then QC (1896). He was Solicitor-General for Scotland 1896–1903; Dean of the Faculty of Advocates, 1896–1915; Unionist MP for Bridgeton 1900–6 and Glasgow Central 1909–15; Lord Advocate 1903–5 and Lord Justice-Clerk 1915–22. He was President of the High School Club, 1908–9.

(Rt Hon.) John Macdonald (1854–1939) was a Liberal MP: for Bow and Bromley, 1892–95; Falkirk Burghs, 1906–18; and Stirling and Falkirk Burghs, 1918–22.

John Rutherford (1857–1923) trained as a veterinary surgeon. He became a member of the Canadian House of Commons and a Canadian delegate at international conferences. He was Commissioner for Railways, Veterinary Director-General, 1902–12, and Live Stock Commissioner, 1906–12, for Canada.

Andrew Bonar Law (1858–1923) was brought up in New Brunswick,

Canada, the son of a Presbyterian minister. Following the death of his mother he lived with his aunt's wealthy relatives, the Kidstons. He attended the School between 1873 and 1875, where he showed some academic promise.[171] However, he ended his formal education at sixteen in 1874[172] and joined Kidston's banking business. Thanks to Kidston funding he gained a partnership in Jacks & Co. and, following the Kidston political leanings, he won a Glasgow seat[173] for the Conservatives in the 'khaki' election of 1900. He became Parliamentary Secretary to the Board of Trade in 1902 and, as a tariff reformer, stressed the need for Imperial Preference and Industrial Protection. It was this issue that took him to the top of the Conservative Party. He gained a safe seat in Dulwich in May 1906, and in Opposition his good parliamentary performances stood out in the depleted Conservative ranks. He was the standard-bearer on the Tariff issue in the key battleground of Lancashire in December 1910, but lost. Nonetheless his campaign had made him a national figure, and he returned to parliament after a victory in Bootle in March 1911. When fierce criticism led his leader, Balfour, to resign, Bonar Law was elected unopposed by unanimous vote. He had a difficult first three years in post when he attempted to modify the Tariff programme, and had difficulties uniting the Conservative party over Ireland. His support of resistance to Home Rule for Ulster was tantamount to offering support for armed resistance to the authority of an elected Government. The war transformed matters. In May 1915, to avoid open criticism on the conduct of the war, prime minister Asquith reconstructed the Government and included Bonar Law as Colonial Secretary and a member of the War Committee. Conscription and the situation in Ireland led to Conservative attacks on Asquith, and the failure on the Somme confirmed the need to review the focus of the war effort. This led to the resignation of Asquith and his replacement by Lloyd George, supported by Bonar Law. The Liberals were now dominated by the Conservatives in the coalition, with Bonar Law as Chancellor of the Exchequer, leader of the House of Commons and, in effect, the deputy prime minister. As Chancellor he was responsible for raising the funds necessary to prosecute the war effort. Although he played little part in the strategy for conducting the war, he maintained the Government's credit-worthiness against considerable odds. Bonar Law supported the coalition in the election of December 1918. When the Conservatives emerged as the largest party, Bonar Law was MP for Glasgow Central. He tended to run domestic affairs for Lloyd George with a style that preferred conciliation rather than confrontation. He was able to secure Ulster's exclusion from Ireland in 1920, keeping it in the UK. Ill health forced him to resign in March 1921, but he remained politically active. When in October 1922 the Conservatives left the coalition and the Conservative leader, Austen Chamberlain, resigned, he returned to became leader of his party and prime minister. The Conservatives won a comfortable majority in the following General Election. Bonar Law success-fully concluded an Irish treaty, but reparations led to problems with France, and the level of repayment to America of war debts meant unpopular increases in taxes. Bonar Law's health deteriorated again and he resigned in May 1923. As the first Conservative leader not from the aristocracy, he was their first modern leader.[174] He was President of the High School Club, 1902–5, and was given the Freedom of the City of Glasgow in 1922. He wanted to be buried in Helensburgh cemetery beside his wife, who had died in 1910, and two sons who had been killed in the war, but his family agreed to his burial in Westminster Abbey.

Writers (Artists, Architects, Poets, Journalists)

Oswald Mitchell (1826–1904) was a historical writer whose books included *Burns and His Times: As Gathered from His Poems* (1897) and *Old Glasgow Essays* (1905). He co-wrote *The Old Country Houses of the Old Glasgow Gentry* (1878) and *The Glasgow Story* (1878). He was President of the High School Club, 1883–5.

John Stevenson (1831–1908) attended Glasgow University. He worked in the architectural offices of David Bryce in Edinburgh and Gilbert Scott in London. He had a period in Glasgow before joining E.R. Robson, the chief architect for the School Board in London. His 'Queen Anne' style was used for redbrick houses in London's Kensington, Hampstead and Belgravia. His commissions included university buildings at both Oxford and Cambridge.[175]

William Leiper (1839–1916) designed prominent Glasgow and West of Scotland public buildings. He decorated the Banqueting Hall of the Glasgow Municipal Buildings. He is considered to be one of the greatest architects of his era.

Robert Buchanan (1841–1901) attended both Glasgow Academy and the High School while his father was working in Glasgow as editor of the *Glasgow Sentinel*, a socialist newspaper. He attended Dr Low's 1854–9 Class[176] and enrolled in Greek and Latin classes at Glasgow University, leaving to go to London in 1860, where he enjoyed some success writing for the stage. His book of poems, *Undertones* (1863), was awarded a medal by the Society of Fine Arts. He proved a prolific writer, publishing forty-seven more plays and a further twenty-five novels.[177]

Michael Barrie (1842–1909) was the son of a Glasgow shoemaker. In 1864 he became a journalist on the *London Standard*. Entering radical circles he became a friend of Karl Marx and in 1871 was chairman of the federal council of the International Working Men's Association. However, as the decade progressed he supported Disraeli's foreign policy during the Eastern Crisis of 1875–8. Back in Scotland he failed in his attempt to launch an anti-Liberal alliance of labour based in Aberdeen, and also was unsuccessful as a Conservative candidate.[178]

Wellwood Rattray (1849–1902) was a landscape painter and a regular exhibitor at the RSA and throughout Europe.

Edwin Hedderwick (1850–1935) headed newspapers founded by his father, including the Glasgow *Weekly Citizen* and *Evening Citizen*. His low profile was deliberate, so as not to interfere with his impartiality.

George Watson (1851–1904) was apprenticed to Napier shipbuilders, qualifying as a naval architect in Glasgow, 1872. He was a designer of racing, cruising and steam yachts.

Malcolm Watson (1853–1929) was a journalist who joined the *St James's Gazette* (1887) and the *Daily Telegraph* (1889). He was the author of many plays.

Samuel Fulton (1855–1941) was a regular exhibitor in Scottish art exhibitions, specialising in sentimental compositions of animal studies (notably lap dogs).

Temple Moore (1856–1920) had his early education at the School. In 1875 he was articled to George Gilbert Scott jnr. From about 1890 he designed over forty churches and became a leading ecclesiastical architect in England. He also worked on schools, parsonages and parish halls. He continued the Gothic revival style popularised by Pugin and the Scott father and son.[179]

(Sir) James Guthrie (1859–1930) was the son of an Evangelical Union minister. He was sent in 1869 to the School, where he took the Classical side. He matriculated at Glasgow University in 1874[180] but abandoned his Law course. 'Chiefly self-taught', Guthrie was active in Scotland in the early 1880s, 'developing rapidly as an innovative and experimental painter'.[181] After 1885 he turned to portraiture and flourished professionally. He became President of the Royal Scottish Academy (1902–19).[182]

Thomas Morton (1859–1928) studied Art in Glasgow, London and Paris. He exhibited in Britain, Europe and the Americas. He was Curator of the

Kirkcaldy Museum and Art Gallery, and Keeper at the National Galleries of Scotland from 1908.

John Thomson (1859–1933) was the son of Alexander 'Greek' Thomson. He became a partner in the architectural firm that designed Gartcosh Asylum, Stobhill Hospital, Glasgow Parish Council Offices, Govan Municipal Buildings, Royal Insurance Buildings, and St James's School.

six   The High School under the School Board, 1872–1918

This chapter describes how the High School fared under the Glasgow School Board, the reasons behind the move to Elmbank Street in 1878 and the leadership of a number of Rectors, especially H.J. Spenser (1901–3), who was 'the first of the modern Rectors'. It continues the history of subject departments and shows how rugby football became increasingly an important part of school life. It ends with the effect of the Great War on the School and, as in the other chapters, with the pupil profiles of a period which proved rich in the production of talented individuals.

NATIONAL DEVELOPMENTS

During the nineteenth century a dual system of education developed in Scotland. It was composed of the statutory parish schools, still limited to rural parishes, and a very diverse sector of denominational and voluntary schools.[1] Attempts to merge the two systems and achieve a more rational use of resources were unsuccessful. Nonetheless, the Government was determined that its greatly increased expenditure on schools required much greater and more rigorous supervision. It held that Scottish education needed an inclusive, nationwide, centrally controlled state system, despite the fact that the educational inquiries of the 1860s and 1870s seemed to confirm that the existing varied provision of local schooling was generally satisfactory in terms of range and quality.[2]

   The Education (Scotland) Act of 1872 created a 'state' system by giving control of most schools to an elected School Board in each burgh and parish, with the Presbyterian churches being persuaded to begin handing over their schools to these Boards.[3] They did so to safeguard the position of religious education in the new schools and to relieve the financial burden on their members, who could not have been expected to contribute to the upkeep of two sets of schools. Also created was the Scotch Education Department (SED),[4] which its early secretaries, Henry Craik and John Struthers,[5] turned into a powerful bureaucracy, giving Scotland a more centralised and uniform system than England. It supported the expansion of post-elementary provision without, however, creating a system of secondary education for all. Their preferred route for the majority of children was through supplementary courses in elementary schools, extending their studies until they were about fourteen years of age, when they would leave to enter work. The curriculum for these children was narrowly centred on vocational skills rather than the breadth which characterised the Leaving Certificate, introduced in 1888, as the main route to university.[6]

The 1872 Act made education compulsory from ages five to thirteen, revised to fourteen in 1901. But this was theoretical, as children could leave earlier, from the age of ten, if they had mastered the 'three Rs'. The Act did little for secondary schools other than transfer burgh schools – unhappily termed 'higher class' schools – to the Boards.[7] Resources came instead from endowments, and between 1870 and 1886 a number of residential 'hospitals' were turned into secondary day schools. Additionally 'higher grade' public schools were founded by the new Boards as extensions of elementary schools, aimed especially at educating the skilled working class. In 1892 the first state grants for secondary education appeared,[8] and although schools differed significantly they formed an increasingly effective national network able to prepare pupils for universities and for business careers.[9]

The special category of 'higher class' schools created under the 1872 Act was defined as those mainly giving 'instructions in Latin, Greek, Modern Languages, Mathematics, Natural Science, and generally in the higher branches of knowledge'. Such schools, which included the High School, were free of the irksome restrictions of the Revised Code, including not being examined by Her Majesty's Inspectors, but they could neither receive government grants nor be supported out of the Board's rate income. They might be fortunate to have endowments, but these were limited, or aid from the Town Council, but this was hard to come by, and so mainly depended on the fees fixed by the teachers with the approval of the Boards.[10]

Generally, it was believed that it was a parent's duty to provide for his own children so far as he was able; that it was a parent's right to send his child to the school of his choice; and, moreover, that a private school also had a right to exist so long as it was efficient. Boards did not aim for a monopoly of education, and held back from secondary education largely for fear of injuring private schools.[11] Perhaps, however, this should not be overemphasised. The main factor which deterred local burghs from extending beyond elementary education was finance, as the state funded only the lower level of schooling.

THE HIGH SCHOOL UNDER THE SCHOOL BOARD, 1872–1878

Following the election of the first School Board in Glasgow in March 1873, the most pressing and immediate task was to build the schools needed for the Town's many illiterate children. The Board undertook a census of all existing schools. The High School was included in this exercise, for its former manager, the Council, had handed it over to the new authority. On 14 July 1873 a sub-committee, under the convenership of J.A. Campbell, was appointed to report on the 'circumstances of the High School'.

The sub-committee spelled out the financial implications of the 1872 Act to the Board: section 46 committed the Town Council to pay to the Board the sum which had previously been spent on the High School annually;[12] the Board could use the General School Fund monies raised by the School Rate for the enlargement of the School buildings only; expenditure on salaries and other current charges had to be financed from the Council contribution and the School fees; previously each member of a teaching department had retained the fees paid to that department, but fees were now to be paid to the Treasurer of the Board, who was to redistribute to the teachers in whatever proportion the Board saw fit.[13] In 1873, 712 boys matriculated at the School in a total enrolment of 2,408 courses, averaging over three courses each. The total fees collected were £4,522 at an average payment of just over £6 by each pupil.

The sub-committee then went on to detail the serious problems inherited by the Board, especially as 'the premises were considered far from suitable for the Grammar School [sic] of so great a city'.[14] The issue was not new[15] but the Board was clearly not in a position to contemplate building a new High School when all its efforts were concentrated on providing schools for those who had none. So the old quarters in John Street were patched up and enlarged a little.[16] A new School would have to wait.

The Campbell sub-committee laid down a programme of improvement for the Board to follow. Fundamental would be a reintroduction of the post of Rector, who should be the head Classics teacher, and he alone would be solely responsible for leading the School. However, it was appreciated that funds were not immediately available for this change to be introduced. Other priorities included not admitting pupils who were too young to start Latin, and the reorganisation of the curriculum: it should be regulated and uniform for all pupils up to the stage where Classical and Modern sides would be offered.

Every year, usually for three weekdays in June, two university examiners visited the School and reported to the Board on the work of the departments. Between 1874 and 1879 they praised the progress of the Classical department, singled out the leadership of Thomas Muir in Mathematics, and commented with regret on the death of the 'experienced and successful' James Bell of the English department in 1879. The curriculum developed: Singing was introduced by William M. Millar in 1874, and Music was being taken by forty pupils three years later; Gymnastics, begun under Captain Walter Roland in 1870, was soon attracting ninety participants, and a further eight took fencing.[17] Natural History grew in popularity to thirty-six pupils in the 1876–7 session and its teacher, William Keddie, introduced Saturday excursions. Only occasionally were the examiners critical: sometimes of parents, who placed family arrangements ahead of school attendance and took their children away on vacation during term-time;[18] sometimes of Board and staff, for the lack of a systematic and well-organised Science teaching course, and in particular the absence of laboratory work.

There was soon an appreciation within the Board that the ever-widening curriculum – essentially a feature begun in 1834 but now growing – needed coherence and structure. For a generation there had been no composite course. Pupils had enrolled for the subjects of their choice, with none being compulsory. The School prospectus of 1874–5 introduced a new concept: boys could still enrol for individual subjects, but it was now advised that a specific course should be followed. As an incentive to parents it was made more expensive if the entire new curriculum was not studied as a whole.[19]

The Optional or New Curriculum of 1874[20] followed a three-year common course of Latin, English, Arithmetic (Mathematics in Fourth Form) and Writing, with additional subjects as follows:

In First Form: Singing, Drill and Gymnastics
In Second Form: Drawing, Drill and Gymnastics
In Third Form: Greek and/or French, and Drawing
In Fourth Form: pupils could opt for a Classical or a Modern
    course; the former continued Greek and French, while the

latter took French, German and Natural Science
In Fifth Form: Classical pupils added German, while Modern
pupils added Drawing and Book-keeping.

The success of this major change can be seen in the rise of numbers taking certain subjects in the next decade. By 1884–5 the school population had reached 807 and subject take-up was: English 642; Arithmetic 586; Writing 508; Latin 417; Drawing 361; Mathematics 264; French 257; Science 226; Fencing, Drill & Gymnastics 178; Singing and Theory of Music 146; Greek 110; German 108; Book-Keeping 63; Phonography 39.

THE COLEBROOKE REPORT OF 1875

The positive reports of the examiners on the School, however, were not borne out during the next national inquiry in 1875. Shortly after passing the 1872 Act, a Royal Commission, under Sir Thomas E. Colebrooke, had been set up to inquire into all educational endowments in Scotland. Although these were few compared with England and involved relatively small sums of money, there had been no previous attempt to assess Scottish educational endowments collectively, and consequently the task proved considerable. The Assistant Commissioner who looked into the Glasgow situation, John Meiklejohn, visited the School on 14 January 1874 and wrote a critical section on it for the 1875 Third Report.[21] By then some of his comments had already been overtaken by the introduction of the New Curriculum, but that did not negate his pointed remarks on relations with the Town, organisation, the School's buildings and teaching.

Meiklejohn held that 'the relation of the School to the Town is not very close, and has not lately been of very great benefit to the School. Considered as an endowed School, it is by far the most poorly endowed School in Glasgow in proportion to its size and importance'. Moving to organisation, Meiklejohn commented on the timetable, in which Writing[22] commanded the same amount of time as Latin, and more years in the average pupil curriculum.[23] He accepted that the Board was likely to tackle the 'unworthy' buildings but stressed how intolerable the situation was. The School was bounded on the north by a tinsmith's shop; on the west by a packing-box maker; and on the east by a weaving shop. Hammering was sometimes very loud and persistent, preventing the School windows from being opened, while smoke sometimes blew thick from the packing-box factory.

Meiklejohn judged the playground as far too small, while its loose gravel surface discouraged most games. The rooms themselves were much too small for the size of classes, ninety-eight being fitted into a room with a capacity of fifty; sixty-four in a room for twenty-five, and twenty in a room fit only to be a lumber-room. The Geography class was being taught in an outbuilding intended for Gymnastics. There was no shelter for the boys, nor an area for homework or private study to take place.[24]

With little help from the Town, the School depended on its fees for salaries, and the schoolmasters were forced to crowd in as many pupils as possible, taking on as few assistants as possible. Good teaching methods and lofty expectations and aims were discarded. Want of endowment also led to inadequate retiring pensions for teachers, and this encouraged them to stay on beyond the time when they were able to do their job efficiently.

Meiklejohn examined the two highest classes in each department.[25] The Mathematical department was deemed 'by far the most successful and best worked in the School'.[26] On the other hand, the English department achieved 'an extremely low standard' and training in 'parsing', 'composition' and 'History' was as meagre as he had found anywhere.[27] Latin and Greek suffered from too little time being devoted to them.[28] Pupils taking French varied greatly in standard, but all needed an extra year studying the subject.[29] The German department lacked 'both life and numbers' and was in a poor condition.[30] The Writing department was the most greatly savaged, for it cultivated and enforced one style when boys would benefit more by developing their own style more easily and more quickly. The boys produced a few lines in beautiful copperplate in the Writing class, but elsewhere they produced bad and careless writing. Meiklejohn believed that three-quarters of the time in this class was entirely wasted.[31]

Although the School sub-committee presented the Board with information[32] which in some cases removed, and in others modified, the unfavourable impression given by Meiklejohn, in the meantime newspapers such as the *Bailie* had a field day at the School's expense.[33] There was no recognition of the fact that changes were already underway. Indeed, by the time of the Report's publication the School had been enlarged and improved, its teaching staff had been increased with a consequent decline in class sizes, and the HSC held that it had never been in a more efficient state. Most informed observers probably believed that Meiklejohn had been too critical, but damage had been done to the School's reputation and only the speedy introduction of significant measures would alleviate the situation.

THE MOVE TO ELMBANK STREET 1878

Fortunately it was not too long before the opportunity came along to improve matters dramatically. Glasgow Academy's building in Elmbank Street had been designed by Charles Wilson and opened officially on 5 May 1847. Despite the growing scholastic reputation of the Academy, financial issues loomed large in its early days and there was pessimism in some quarters over the future effects of the 1872 Education Act. The concern – a mistaken one, as it turned out – was that there soon would be little need or demand for privately run schools such as the Academy.

It was in this climate that on 23 March 1877 the Academy directors offered to sell their 'handsome and substantial' buildings at Elmbank Street with two frontages[34] to provide a new home for the High School.[35] On 6 April the Board responded by offering the asked-for price of £32,000,[36] and possession was taken in June 1878, when at long last the High School acquired buildings that it and Glasgow could be proud of: sixteen class-rooms and a gymnasium.

Wilson's original Italian palazzo design for Elmbank Street had included four statues of famous men of learning to grace the front of the building. These, however, were never executed, presumably for financial reasons, but the inspiration which had thus been denied the scholars of the Academy was now provided for the High School boys, who entered their new home under the gaze of Homer, Cicero, Galileo and James Watt.[37] The sculpting by John Mossman,[38] and erection of these eight-feet high statues[39] was paid for by several of the Board members.[40] According to one opinion the statues added grace, lighting up the whole elevation, 'which previously was wanting somewhat in expression'.[41] Also set into the wall of the building at this time was the lintel stone of the old Grammar School. It had originally been rescued by Michael Connal,[42] who had then presented it to the School when it was still located in John Street.

The *Glasgow Herald*[43] claimed that the new site was more likely to suit the convenience of the general public and 'in course of time . . . pupils from the country, from the anticipated changes in the railway termini'. The university examiners, in their report of August 1879, deemed the new premises 'much superior to those formerly occupied by the School, in the amount of accommodation, in the fresher and healthier air, and in the size of the playground'.[44]

The move to Elmbank Street prompted the Board to reinstate the post of Rector. On 10 June 1878 the HSC recommended the appointment of Dr

David Paton, head of the Classical department, from the opening of the new school session in September.[45] His appointment as Rector was to be seen as a way of affording a means of communication with the Board and the parents on matters pertaining to the welfare of the School. Without fuss or argument this change was accepted.

During its first decade in its new site the High School consisted of the 'Centre block', a gymnasium, and janitor Robert Hardie's house on the north side of the main building.[46] However, by 1881–2, the annual inspection criticised the unsatisfactory nature of the Science classroom: 'Gloomy, and, as far as we could judge, badly ventilated, with a disagreeable smell.' With Science now on a more systematic footing, it was deemed desirable to have less 'makeshift' accommodation.[47] By June 1884–5, criticism was becoming more trenchant: the Inspectors did not see how even the most conscientious teachers could do better without laboratories,[48] and the delay in acting on this was short-sighted.[49] This galvanised the Board into action, and by the time of the next round of inspections in June 1886 plans drawn up by Glasgow architect, James L. Cowan, were available for perusal. Professor Chrystal of Edinburgh University held that when the science buildings were complete the School would be 'one of the best equipped secondary schools in Scotland'.[50] The new north wing (later 'B' block) was quite well matched on the west front and linked to Wilson's facade by an archway. During its construction a tablet celebrating the Golden Jubilee of the reign of Queen Victoria was erected,[51] and it was officially opened by Rt Hon. Lord Balfour of Burleigh, Chairman of the Educational Endowments Commission, on 30 September 1887.[52]

The School roll, which was 798 when the 1887 north wing was opened, rose significantly in the mid-1890s, reaching a new record of 940 in session 1894–5. Because of the large year forms, classes were divided for teaching purposes into a significant number of sections, and for the first time two Junior School specialists were appointed. The Board determined to add a further wing, providing much needed classrooms and allowing the establishment of a junior department, which would be a distinct and separate part of the School. Meantime, the Junior School met at 27 India Street under the superintendence of David S. Henderson, seconded from the English department. Cowan was re-employed as architect, and again the south wing was linked to the main building by a triumphal arch screen. The new wing[53] was opened by distinguished Former Pupil Sir Henry Craik on 21 September 1897, and the occasion was also attended by Rt Hon. Charles Dickson, who presented £100 to be divided among the five School boys highest in the Glasgow University Bursary Competition. There was accommodation for the Junior School, English, Manual Instruction by means of a workshop, and a new gymnasium.

Subsequent annual inspections continued to highlight the need for improved accommodation. In 1900 the departmental libraries were praised, but a school library was encouraged: at the end of session 1901–2 the Rector could report that the formation of such a library had 'supplied a long-felt want.'[54] The Inspectors turned their attention to the lack of provision for supplying lunch within the school during the mid-day break, and the fact that the half-hour provided was too short to allow many pupils to go home.[55] During 1904 the Board determined to build a large hall capable of holding 1,050 boys, a kitchen, dining accommodation, a lunch buffet, and a large common room for masters. The new building fronted Holland Street and was used for the first time at the annual distribution of prizes on 28 June 1906. The Board now held the School to be 'fully equipped'. It also meant that the whole of the Upper School could now assemble in the Hall for prayers every morning, and all boys, except those going home for lunch, were kept on the premises throughout the school day.

The pattern of secondary education established by the Board in the 1890s continued largely unchanged throughout its period of control until 1918.[56] It was conscious of the need to keep fees low to ensure that its schools were open to a wide spectrum of pupils, which was behind its support for the reform of educational endowments.[57] However, it decided that it would 'not meantime be advisable' to support Cameron's Parliamentary Bill of March 1881 in favour of free education,[58] the introduction of which was estimated to result in a threefold increase in the School Rate. Nonetheless, the increase in funds for secondary education enabled the High School to reduce its fees in September 1893.[59] Previously virtually without free places, the School now received each year bursaries from an Endowments Board, twenty from the Burgh Committee, and a further twenty-two through the Board.[60]

The School flourished, helped by the fees being kept at pre-1900 levels. By 1916 its roll was over 1,000 pupils for the first time[61] and many other pupils were turned away for lack of space. Of the higher grade Schools, however, only Whitehill prospered, as Glasgow had more secondary school places than there were candidates to fill them. Nonetheless, the introduction of a Group Leaving Certificate in 1902[62] acted as an incentive particularly to the pupils in higher grade schools to remain at school in order to gain this hallmark of success. Academically, they competed for pupils with the High School, which still suffered from the 'general apathy towards education among the better-off classes'.[63] In Glasgow, commercial firms habitually recruited boys for their offices as soon as they reached fourteen.

RECTORS

David Paton, 1878–1901

When Dr 'Daddy' Paton assumed the responsibilities of Rector in September 1878, his powers were not as extensive as those of the Grammar School rectors in the mid-eighteenth century. This probably suited Paton, who was of retiring disposition.[64] He had been educated at Madras College, St Andrews, and between 1847 and 1851 at St Andrews University, where he was the outstanding Classical scholar of his day. He returned to Madras as assistant classical master for two years before becoming Rector of Banff Academy, where in two years he increased numbers from 50 to 150. In October 1856 he was appointed Classical master at Stirling High School, where hitherto each department had retained complete autonomy. However, in 1863 Stirling Council decided that a Rector was needed to take 'general superintendence' of its school and appointed Paton to a post with modest duties and commensurately modest additional salary.[65]

In September 1866 Paton accepted the position of second master in the Classical department at the High School in Glasgow, and in June 1873 he took over the department, which he continued to run even after becoming Rector. Indeed, he inherited five autonomous departments which were allowed to continue without undue interference. Nonetheless, School inspections praised his 'sagacity, tact and unremitting care'[66] and his light touch was rewarded in session 1892–3 when Horace F. Wallace became First Bursar in the Glasgow University Bursary Competition and the school took five of the first nine places. In Paton's penultimate year, Robert Harvie came first (out of 179 candidates) and, in his last year, Thomas David King-Murray equalled that achievement. If on his retirement in 1901 Paton handed on to his successor an almost unchanged system, it was academically a very successful School.

H.J. Spenser, 1901–1903

Harry Spenser was born in 1866 in Nottingham and achieved a First Class degree in Classics at St John's, Cambridge.[67] He was chosen as Rector by the

School Board, which was impressed by his ideas for change. He was introduced to the School by its chair, Sir John Cuthbertson, who stated prophet-
ically: 'Boys of the High School, this is your new Rector, and if he does half
the things he says he is going to do, you are for it.'[68] Spenser offered a radical
departure from the past and in particular wished to create 'a thoroughly
healthy public spirit in the School'.[69] He believed in nurturing the talents of
his pupils and was interested in all their activities. Indeed, his essential aim
was to build a community where every boy would secure an all-round
education. In the mould of other 'muscular Christian' headmasters of the
time, Spenser was enthusiastic about fresh air and physical activity – rowing
and cricket being his passions – and this led to direct and forceful encouragement to improve sporting standards. The results were nothing short of
dramatic. Almost as soon as he arrived on 1 March 1901, the rugby[70] and
cricket[71] teams started winning, while golf[72] and swimming[73] were added to
cycling[74] as other sports on offer.

Spenser understood how desirable it was for a boy to acquire interests
beyond the academic curriculum. For him school was not just about preparation for work in life, but also about teaching the proper use of leisure. In
his first year Spenser added photography, botanical excursions and an
Orchestral Society[75] to the already existing Literary[76] and Musical[77]
societies. He introduced monthly lectures on subjects 'beyond the ordinary
school curriculum', which were delivered by prominent citizens in the
Writing room.[78] In early 1902 he produced persuasive arguments for the
establishment of a School Cadet Corps: it would improve physique;
inculcate habits of obedience, discipline and self-control; help the boys
realise their responsibilities and duties as British citizens; and develop a
unifying ethos. However, he disabused the Board and parents of the idea
that membership of the Corps was intended to be a preparation or introduction to a military career. Within a few months, over 200 boys, aged
twelve and over, joined the School Corps, which was attached to the 1st
Lanarkshire Rifle Volunteer Corps. Drill was held on Monday and Thursday
afternoons for an hour: the War Office supplied the carbines, bayonets,
slings and belts; the boys supplied their own uniforms, consisting of neutral
green jacket, Douglas tartan kilt and hose, Glengarry cap, sporran, spats,
and badges for cap and sporran.

Spenser also brought with him strong views on the need for the boys to
identify with, and be proud of, their school. He brought in the first uniform
regulations. All boys had to wear one or other of the authorised caps or
hats:[79] a maroon cap with badge worked in yellow (Motto: virtus sola

nobilitas); a straw hat with school colours on the band; or a Glengarry with school badge in silver (recommended as a dress bonnet). It was a bonus if a boy wore a school tie, school belt or school blazer. To promote School activities Spenser allowed the silver badge to be worn on any cap by members of the Cycling Club, while members of the First XV were allowed to wear the School Football cap, and the School colours on jersey, shirt and stockings. Members of the First Cricket XI alone were allowed to wear School colours on silk cap and sash.

Neat, formal, dignified, almost a dandy in his dress, with a clear voice and piercing glance, Spenser rarely relaxed his bearing. With a great grasp of detail, he took firm decisions rapidly and, it was said, 'was rather prone to ride roughshod over opposition – in short, his personality was of the most uncompromising kind'.[80] A kinder assessment saw him as 'generous, impulsive, full of ardour and ideas'.[81] He was an exciting teacher, particularly for the older pupils, and encouraged an intellectual open-mindedness and a respect for the opinions of others. His apparent remoteness and his tendency towards brief fits of violent anger were balanced by his personal kindnesses to staff and pupils alike and by his strong sense of justice. He was a strict disciplinarian but appears to have detested corporal punishment. In addition, he expected boys to settle their own differences and adjust their own behaviour as far as possible without the intervention of the staff. This was to be done by means of the Ephorate, which consisted of two representative members of each form elected each session, one by the form master and one by the boys.[82] Five senior boys (from Forms IV, V and VI) elected from this body, together with the editors of the magazine and captains of the first XV and first XI, formed the School Council, which had sole moral authority to report to the Rector on matters deemed important.

To a great degree Spenser was the first of the modern rectors, and with only a limited teaching commitment, having given over the Classics department to Hutchison, he was focused on his agenda of change. However, he had to tread warily and take the Board and the staff with him. He was the only graduate from an English university at the School. Excluding the modern linguists, who qualified abroad, of the eighteen other graduates twelve had graduated from Glasgow, three from Edinburgh, two from Aberdeen and one from St Andrews. However, within a year three English graduates were appointed: Frank Beaumont (London), Cecil Willson (Cambridge) and W.J. Wray (Oxford and LSE). Soon it was not uncommon for English graduates to apply and be appointed to all levels of post in the School. He also appointed the first ladies to the teaching staff –

five in 1902–3. They thoroughly identified themselves with the life of their respective classes and of the School, to the great advantage of both. To Miss Home Morton was due the credit of interesting the school in the Eastpark Homes[83] and of founding in February 1903 the School cot, which was supported by voluntary contributions from the boys for years to come. As Spenser said: 'No education can be called complete which does not include practical and systematic philanthropy.'

Having seen the curriculum in operation Spenser introduced for session 1902–3 a complete reorganisation,[84] which took a number of years to work through the School. He introduced the 'form system' which insisted on a fixed curriculum and a certain degree of proficiency in all subjects before promotion was allowed. Spenser was aiming at the all-round development of the individual boy, with specialisation only in the senior years. Spenser thought it 'folly' to allow or encourage young boys to excel in one or two favourite subjects to the detriment of the rest of his curriculum,[85] for they would have problems with any preliminary examinations for university entry, which insisted on general proficiency. The form teacher would not just be the 'guide, philosopher, and friend' but also the 'focus for the collective knowledge of the staff with regard to the individual boy'. A system of termly reports would communicate the information gleaned to the parents, and so any boys drifting or going astray would be noticed and checked. For Spenser the possibility of immediate co-operation between parents and form masters was one factor in the superiority of day schools. The essentials of the system which Spenser thus laid down were to last until the introduction of specialist guidance staff in Scotland in 1971.[86]

From 1902 the Junior School was divided into a preparatory department, consisting of three classes taught by mistresses, commencing with the Froebel system,[87] and a junior department of three classes taught by masters. Boys joined Prep I at six years of age and could be promoted in special circumstances. Great stress was laid on the need for a thorough grounding in primary subjects before moving on, and only after achievement of the old Sixth Standard were boys allowed into the Senior School, where in the first two years in Forms I and II most boys were expected to take a common course[88] which included Latin.[89] Promotion now was possible at the end of each term throughout the secondary. In Form III the 'non-Latin' course continued without Latin and Greek, while the other boys were offered a 'Modern and Scientific' course (with Latin, German and French) or a 'Classical' course (with Latin, Greek and French). In Forms IV and V further specialisation was allowed in the four courses offered: the 'non-Latin', the 'Modern' and the 'Classical' continuing unchanged, while the 'Scientific' involved Science in place of Latin. In Form VI the school under Spenser offered a 'Higher Commercial' course (in place of non-Latin) on the lines established by his friend, John Lewis Paton, at University College School (UCS) in London.

Spenser was at pains to stress that the courses on offer all provided a liberal education and were an excellent preparation for professional, mercantile or business careers. Whatever course was decided upon, Spenser strongly promoted the Leaving Certificate examinations, believing that those who did not take them would suffer from a serious handicap throughout their working life.

If Spenser was full of advice to parents on curricular matters, at least it was clearly set out in a logical and detailed manner in the annual prospectus. He also codified the School rules and in another relatively modern practice set down the School homework policy and introduced the practice of putting boys on a monthly report, which the Rector himself checked regularly. This was backed up by the provision of homework supervision for boys who needed help in this area. Even holidays were not to be fallow. 'Holiday reading' was given out with the term reports, and parents were expected to 'give every opportunity and encouragement to their boys to read the books suggested'. Such co-operation was demanded in the contentious matter of attendance. Spenser told his parents that absence should only be for serious reasons. Education was an asset, and an individual and a country would not succeed if it was not valued.

Fatefully, however, Spenser's friend at UCS, Paton, moved on to take over Manchester Grammar School,[90] and Spenser was offered and accepted the vacant headship in London. He left the School on 11 September 1903.[91] He had succeeded in his aims of quickening the pace of School life and changing its tone. In less than three years Spenser had raised the School roll from 859 to 944 and left an enduring mark, establishing some enduring traditions and making it an organic unity for the first time.[92]

Frederic Spencer, 1903–1904

The Board was keen to build on Spenser's achievements and make the School the premier school in Scotland. However, it split over the choice of who should succeed Spenser. Twenty-four candidates applied for the post and after interviewing nine of them, on 16 September 1903 the vote stood deadlocked at seven votes each for John Hutchison, head of the Classical

department, and A.J. Pressland of the Edinburgh Academy. The Chairman
of the Board, Robert Allan, had supported Pressland but decided not to cast
another vote. This resulted in a decision to readvertise the post. This time a
further twenty-two candidates applied, and on 13 October Frederic Spencer
was elected by nine votes to the six for Hutchison. The salary of £750 was
agreed upon and the new Rector took up his post on 2 November 1903.[93]

Frederic Spencer was arguably the most outstanding scholar the School
had ever had as Rector. Born in 1860 he had been schooled at Kingswood
School in Bath, and between 1878 and 1882 he taught Modern Languages at
Hull Grammar School, obtaining a degree of BA from London in 1881. After
a year at the University of Paris he became an assistant master at the Leys
School in Cambridge; after graduating in 1886 in Medieval and Modern
Languages, he was able to become chief master of the Modern side at Leys.
He took a PhD from the University of Leipzig in 1889 and was recognised
as an authority on Anglo-Norman Literature in the thirteenth century. In
the same year he accepted the chair of Modern Languages at University
College of North Wales.[94] In 1894 he became the Professor of the French
Language and Literature, and of the German Language and Literature, and
while in Bangor in 1897 he edited a book entitled *Chapters on the Aims and
Practice of Teaching.*[95]

However, Spencer was totally inexperienced in the complexities of
running a school, and to have to face such a challenge in a country with a
different educational system made the task virtually impossible. He later
admitted to facing 'initial difficulties', but his brief tenure and departure
within a calendar year suggests he underestimated the demands of the post,
and suggests also that the Board had underestimated how far the School had
developed in a very short time under Harry Spenser.

Nonetheless, there were some positive advances across a number of
curriculum areas in 1903–4. In particular the Junior School, increasingly
seen as crucial to the future welfare of the School, improved its staffing,[96]
and this led to a decrease in the over-large class sizes. Spencer requested a
further appointment in the form of a fully trained and efficient
Kindergarten teacher to relieve Miss Downie. He believed that she was
overburdened in her role, which involved being responsible for three
separate classes. One advance already achieved was bringing all the junior
department classes together in one wing of the school building.

Spencer was pleased with the success being achieved in French and
German and the sustained quality of the work in English and Classics. The
Classical Sixth had rarely, if ever, left the School better prepared for

university work. He also defended the Mathematics department; it suffered greatly, as the best mathematical talent was usually found in the Classical forms, which concentrated the boys' efforts on Latin and Greek to the detriment of their other subjects. Indeed, he persuaded the Board to give extra time to the subject.[97] Moreover, he went out of his way to emphasise the quality and relevance of the Commercial courses, rightly believing that the boys and their parents needed some convincing to break away from the more traditional areas.

Like his predecessor, Spencer understood that flourishing clubs and societies meant a great deal for the corporate life of the School. The Cadet Corps remained popular and was now fully staffed, and Spencer made an appeal for financial help to organise a full Pipe Band. Spencer welcomed the new School Song written by A.L. Taylor and set to music by Dr A. H. Mann of King's College, Cambridge,[98] and announced the imminent publication of a School Song Book as another way to bind together the School community. A Boxing Club was added to the ever growing, and highly impressive, list of activities on offer. Spencer also changed the School's colours, which became the Cameronian colours of green, blue and white. Caps were unchanged, but the badge was changed to silver, which was deemed better suited to the 'bumbee tartan', as the colours were irreverently called.[99]

Spencer continued the policy of appointing from without the Scottish educational system. In 1903–4 George W. Humphries, a Classics graduate from Queen's College, Cambridge; Thomas Keen, an Honours English and French graduate from London; Hulbert C. Normand, a Modern History graduate from Oriel College, Oxford; and N.A. Saunders, formerly a scholar of Pembroke College, Oxford and a Classics and History graduate, all joined the staff.

When Spencer determined to accept Lord Londonderry's nomination to be Staff Inspector of Secondary Schools in England,[100] the Board was in a quandary. After two long meetings[101] it decided to advertise the post of Rector at a salary of £750 per annum, and a shortlist of four candidates was drawn up on 6 June. They were all external candidates. Then at the last minute two internal candidates were asked to join those being interviewed: both were seen as safe. The first was A.J. Gunion Barclay, a graduate of Edinburgh University, and a founder member and third President of the Edinburgh Mathematical Society, who had been appointed head of the Mathematics department at the School in 1892. The HSC had recommended the appointment of a 'vice-rector' in February 1894 and had pressed Barclay's claim for this new post. In the event the Board remitted the issue

Viscount James Bryce (1838–1922), Jurist, was a pupil at the High School between 1847 and 1852.

Andrew Bonar Law, Conservative Prime Minister, 1922-23, had been a pupil at the High School from 1873 until 1875.

The School building in Elmbank Street was sold by the Glasgow Academy Directors to the Town Council in 1878.

David Paton was the High School Rector between 1878 and 1901. He was the first Rector since 1830.

Harry Spenser was High School Rector from 1901 to 1903. He was 'the first of the modern Rectors'.

The academic Frederic Spencer was High School Rector in session 1903–04.

John Hutchison was the only Former Pupil to become Rector, a post he held from 1904 to 1909.

Shirley Goodwin, Rector from 1909 until 1913, with his beloved dog, Bessie. (Reproduced by permission of Emanuel School Archive)

Peter Pinkerton was Rector of the High School from 1914 until 1930.

The statues adorning the front of Elmbank Street were added for High School entry in 1878. (© Crown Copyright: RCAHMS. Licensor www.rcahms.gov.uk)

Garnethill School became the Glasgow High School for Girls from 1894.

James Milligan, the first Rector of the Girls' High between 1894 and 1905, pictured with his staff.

ABOVE LEFT. Alice Reid was the first Principal of the Girls' High from 1905 until 1926.

ABOVE RIGHT. The popular Dr Flora Tebb was Principal of the Girls' High from 1926 until 1947.

LEFT. Frances Barker was Principal of the Girls' High from 1947 until 1969.

ABOVE. The long-awaited new build for the girls in Cleveden Road in 1968.

RIGHT. Helen Jamieson was the last Principal of the Girls' High between 1969 and 1976.

CLASSICAL

Year	Name
1914	DOROTHEA A. PATON
1915	ELIZABETH S. SCOTT
1916	MARY P. EWING
1917	EMMIE C. GIBB
1918	ANNIE SCOTT
1919	HELEN R. MOODIE
1920	ELIZABETH C. CALDER
1921	JESSIE H. MACLEHOSE
1922	GRACE M^cC. ROBERTSON
1923	JEAN G. HURLL
1924	MARJORIE F. POMPHREY
1925	MARY S. CRUICKSHANK
1926	MOIRA F.A. MORE
1927	ANNIE S. ROBERTSON
1928	ELIZABETH Y. NISBET
1929	ELISABETH M. BRUCE
1930	AVRIL M.K. READING
1931	NO AWARD
1932	MARY M. INNES
1933	JANET G. HOLMES
1934	ELSIE M. STEWART
1935	HELEN G. MACDONALD
1936	DORIS M. YOUNG
1937	DORIS J. NEILSON
1938	ADELINE O.M. COOK
1939	ANNIE H. M^cNICOL
1940	MARGARET R. BOSOMWORTH
1941	SHEILA M^cALISTER
1942	NANETTE H. NISBET
1943	DORIS J.H. BRECHIN
1944	ELLA J.W. SCOTT

	Name	Year
	MARGARET M. CAMPBELL	1893
	AGNES HOOD HUTTON	1894
	ISABELLA THOMSON MILLER	1895
	MARGARET THOMSON ROBERTSON	1896
	JEANIE CHESNEY	1897

CLASSICAL · MODERN

CLASSICAL	Year	MODERN
CATHERINE BENNIE	1898	MAY THERESA ALEXANDER
ANNIE MURRAY MACGREGOR	1899	MARY COPLAND
HELEN MUIR	1900	ELSIE FRAME MACDONALD
ELSIE FRAME MACDONALD	1901	AGNES M^cCRAE MARSHALL
AGNES M^cCRAE MARSHALL	1902	MARGARET BARR MOIR
MARION WILSON RANKIN	1903	NETTIE HUNTER STEIN
MARGARET STIRLING M^cLEOD	1904	ELIZABETH PITCAIRN HOGG
BETHIA MACFARLANE COWAN	1905	ELIZABETH FULLERTON
JEANIE BIRKNYRE TRENCH / FRANCES MARGARET MARTIN	1906	JANET EUNICE COPELAND
MARGARET CAMPBELL M^cMILLAN	1907	CATHERINE MORRISON MACKINNON
ELEANOR JANET MORRISON DONALDSON	1908	MARJORIE MAY FERGUSON
HELEN YOUNG MURDOCH	1909	CHRISTINA DALRYMPLE AITKEN
ETHEL MARY M^cADAM	1910	EDITH HILL WILSON
JESSIE R. HAGART	1911	DOROTHY M. MICHAEL
ANNIE G. KIDD	1912	CATHERINE F. DAVIDSON
GEORGINA MURDOCH	1913	ISABELLA M^cLAREN

GOLD MEDALLISTS

MODERN

Year	Name
1914	JESSIE S. M^cLEOD
1915	ELIZABETH S. COOK
1916	EVA M. STURROCK
1917	MURIEL H. CALDER
1918	MATILDA T. TENNENT
1919	AGNES K. STIRLING
1920	ELIZABETH S. YOUNG
1921	BARBARA M. CUTHBERTSON
1922	VIOLET M. PURVES
1923	MARY C. ROBERTSON
1924	BETHIA ROBERTSON
1925	ROSA F. M^cLAREN
1926	JEAN M^cI. SHAW
1927	MARY M^cC. LANGWELL
1928	GRACE C. PRENTICE
1929	CHRISTINA S. CRUICKSHANK
1930	JANET S. MILTON
1931	BETTY R. REID
1932	MARGARET M. LAPSLEY
1933	ABBIE E. CHISHOLM
1934	JEAN S.N. MIDGLEY
1935	M. WINIFRED ROBERTSON
1936	CATHERINE H. FOREMAN
1937	SHEENAH J. M^cK. RUSSELL
1938	CISSIE M. HEMPHILL
1939	MARY I.C. RUSSELL
1940	ANNE S. M^cNAUGHTON
1941	MARY B. NEILSON
1942	GILLIAN B.B. RODGER
1943	ELSPETH J.A. BAIRD
1944	MARGARET H. NEILSON

The Girls' High Honours Boards are now situated at Anniesland.

The War Memorials are also now to be found at Anniesland.

The Memorial Pavilion at Old Anniesland was opened in 1927.

Baron Bannerman of Kildonan (1901–69) attended the High School from 1913 until 1920.

John Talman was Rector of the High School from 1931 until 1950.

back for further consideration by nine votes to five.[102] The other was John Hutchison, the head of the Classical department and founder member of the High School Club, who had been an unsuccessful candidate when Spencer was appointed.

John Hutchison, 1904–1909

On 9 June the Board decided on a straight vote between Hutchison and A.C. McDonnell, headmaster of Armagh Royal School. Hutchison won by eight votes to six (with one abstention), although Chairman Allan again did not support him. Nonetheless, he was offered and accepted the post of Rector effective 1 September 1904, but at the reduced salary of £650. His appointment pleased the Old Boys in particular,[103] for he was after all 'the product and pride of the school'.[104]

Hutchison ('Hutchie') was born in Glasgow in 1842, and at age seven he entered Hutchesons' School in Crown Street. As medallist there he followed the then custom of attending the High School for four years as a reward. He went to Glasgow University in 1859 on a bursary, and on his passage through the arts course he did some teaching in the Mathematics department of the School, assisting his former master, Bryce. He joined the Classical department of the School in 1866, becoming its head in 1901. As well as his Classics he devoted much time to History and Theology and had a particular interest in the development and working of higher schools and universities. In 1885 he published a translation of a work on German universities by Professor Conrad of Halle University. He was an examiner in Classics at Glasgow University and gained an honorary LLD from that university. He was Convener of the University Business Committee, and from April 1904 Assessor of the General Council on the University Court.

As expected and hoped, Hutchison's period as Rector was a time of steady progress and consolidation. Under Miss Macintosh the Kindergarten experienced 'marked success'[105] and reached its capacity within three years. The Junior School also flourished under Mr Watson and it provided a solid grounding, with two full classes being promoted, after passing the Qualifying standard in class 6, to Senior School every session.[106] This was regarded as a particular success as about one third of the boys were new to the School at class 5/6 stage. This was in fact a matter of contention and concern, for it highlighted the issue of parents sending boys to the School only for a term or two to make up specific deficiencies, rather than sending them there for their complete education.

In the Senior School the issue took a different form: many boys still left the School early and went on to work without completing courses or taking qualifications. This did mean that much more individual learning could be supported in the smaller classes at the top of the School, but the Sixth Form numbers could have been increased markedly. While Latin had thirty-three boys and Greek a mere thirteen, the Commercial courses were poorly supported. Hutchison welcomed the new Intermediate Certificate and Group Leaving Certificate (substitute for passes in separate subjects) introduced by the SED in 1905–6 as helping with this problem. By 1907–8, to meet the curricular requirements involved, Hutchison announced the 'New Curriculum'.

The work of the first three forms of the Senior School would henceforth consist of continuous courses in English, Science, Mathematics, Drawing, and either Latin or French. At the end of the Third Form the Intermediate (Group) Certificate Examination would be attempted. The work of Forms IV, V and VI would be geared towards the Leaving Certificate on either the Classical or Modern side. The beginning of Greek would be postponed until the Fourth Form, but Hutchison hoped that the greater maturity of boys when they began Greek would result in the accomplishment of as much in three years as had formerly been achieved in four. He advised parents to allow their boys to take the full school curriculum, either Classical or Modern.

Hutchison's curriculum changes did little to solve the problems facing the School. Certainly Science was now being taught to a growing number of boys,[107] but Greek's decline continued. Only one third of the boys who attended the lower half of the Senior School in 1908 sat the Intermediate Certificate and took their studies further. In his final year in office, Hutchison introduced four periods of Latin or French to class 6 as a way of strengthening their grammatical drill in the Senior School.[108] Otherwise he defended the curriculum and was particularly proud that every boy had two periods of Drill in the timetable, which he believed was crucial for health and physical development.[109] He had no answers to the criticisms of parents about too much homework and claims that the School exerted too much academic pressure on the boys. Yet, as the inquiry into the matter suggested in December 1908, this was more about lack of communication and co-ordination between the departments.[110] Traditional Rectors still saw their academic staff as headmasters in their own right, and a challenge to their autonomy was unthinkable. However, Hutchison did use the form system to monitor and deal with indiscipline. He inspected the form punishment books regularly, introduced after-school detention in February 1905, interviewed boys who did badly in examinations, and generally pressed all staff to maintain standards.[111]

When Hutchison reached the age of sixty-seven, he and the Board agreed a generous retiring allowance of £400 per annum.[112] He left in September 1909 after fifty-four years of connection with the School as pupil and teacher, and proudly admitted to feeling gratified in handing over to his successor an efficient institution.[113] This assessment was formally confirmed when, following a bequest in the will of J.B. Douglas, former Secretary of the High School Club, the sculptor Barr produced the Dr John Hutchison Memorial Plaque, which was dedicated in October 1954.[114]

F. Shirley Goodwin, 1909–1913

Thirty-eight candidates applied for the post of Rector, and the Board interviewed a shortlist of six drawn up by the HSC. They included the Senior School Classical master, William King Gillies; (Fritz) Shirley Goodwin, second Classical and House master in Perse School, Cambridge; and Peter Pinkerton, head of the Mathematics department at George Watson's College. On 3 June 1909[115] Goodwin won ten votes against four for Gillies and he took up the post of Rector on 1 September 1909 at a salary of £650 per annum.

Shirley Goodwin was born in February 1880, the second son of Professor Alfred Goodwin, Fellow of Balliol College, Oxford, and Professor of Greek and Latin at University College, London. He was educated at University College School from 1892 to 1899, going on to Balliol College, Oxford. However, he did not complete his finals in 1904, because of an illness which eventually was to cut his life tragically short. He was awarded both BA and MA in 1906 when he had already begun his teaching career. He taught Classics and Modern Languages for a short time in 1905 at Malvern Link Preparatory School before joining the staff of Loretto in Musselburgh as Head of Classics and Modern Languages. He remained there for two years before briefly teaching at Manchester Grammar School in 1907, and then spent two years as second Classical master at the Perse School, Cambridge.

On 2 September 1909, when introduced to the High School, he set out his aims as being to send boys to Oxford and Cambridge and to the army and navy; and to ensure that the School came top in everything, and in particular became champions at cricket and rugby football. He impressed others as being a pious and dignified young man with a forceful personality and a seemingly limitless capacity for hard work. Although not a distinguished scholar he was an outstanding teacher, with a talent for encouraging the boys with his warmth and enthusiasm.

In his short spell in Glasgow, Goodwin left his mark by his deep commitment to the extra-curricular life of the school.[116] For him, school societies militated against carelessness and selfishness and more than any other aspect of School life engendered and developed espirit de corps. School was not merely for teaching a boy to work hard, but also to play hard as well. Goodwin himself was involved in an array of activities, taking a special interest in the Officers' Training Corps, of which he was the Commanding Officer. Although in December 1909 it gained official recognition from the War Office, Goodwin saw its principal purpose as educational: it was 'training in obedience, in self-reliance, co-operation and alertness'; it opened eyes to the possibility of war and produced sober citizens who, realising the destructiveness of war, did their best to prevent it.[117]

He worked to achieve a playing field for the School, a cause taken on by his successor. It was he who instituted, in 1910, the House system and, given the importance he placed on the recently developed form system, Goodwin took the logical step of naming the Houses after the form teachers:[118] Keen, Gillies, Taylor and Barclay.[119] Although originally instituted to encourage the apathetic to support relays at Sports Day, it gave a fillip to School life generally out of the classroom and, as such, was crucial in contributing to the special ethos that was developing within the School. It was left to his successor, Pinkerton, in 1917 to change the House names to commemorate distinguished Former Pupils.[120]

Goodwin also changed the School Council and Ephorate into a prefect system. There were to be two classes of prefect: Form and School. The Form prefects were two from each form, one chosen by the form master and the other by the form (subject to the form master's veto). They were to include boys 'who have distinguished themselves for public spirit'. Their duties were confined to form matters and they were under the School prefects, whose duty was the welfare of the School and 'police duty'. The School Captain[121] was to be head of games, and he was to have a lieutenant, six sergeants and four privates chosen by the Rector, while the other prefects were co-opted by the body of office-bearers.

Towards the end of 1913 Goodwin was successful in his application for the headship of Emanuel College, Wandsworth. Plagued with ill health, he had the added burden of a wife who also did not keep well and who did not take to the Scottish climate. Surviving photographs show a man sitting hunched in his chair as if in discomfort. In 1916 he was to suffer a severe head injury in an accident. With high blood pressure and heart disease, he gradually wore himself out in the service of Emanuel. Having been seriously ill twice he was warned that he could die at any time, and he gave instructions that, whatever happened, school life should not be disrupted. He died in June 1927 at the age of forty-seven.[122] At the High School he was remembered fondly for his 'endearing ways': lecturing the pupils after prayers on the virtues of cold baths, or the duty of raising caps to masters encountered in the street; his passion for fire drills; and demonstrating wrestling grips upon 'Jumbo' Steel's portly person.[123]

Peter Pinkerton, 1914–1930

Peter Pinkerton was born in June 1870 in Kilmarnock, the son of an engineer on the local railway and a grandson of his namesake, who was a small farmer in Ayrshire. He was educated at the local academy, where he was medallist in Classics and Mathematics. In 1890 he gained an MA from Glasgow University, graduating with distinction in Classics, with First Class honours in Mathematics and Natural Philosophy, and winning the Breadalbane and John Clark scholarships. He then went as Royal Exhibitioner to Dublin, where he spent two years attending the Royal College of Science, taking first place in Mathematics, Mechanics, Physics and Chemistry, and second place in Botany.

After this rigorous preparation Pinkerton began his teaching career in Allan Glen's School where, from 1893 to 1899, he taught Mathematics, Physics, Classics and German. He applied unsuccessfully for headships at Wallacehall Academy, Dumfriesshire (1896) and Dunfermline High School (1898) but was thereafter appointed to the post of Head of the Mathematics department at the Royal Academical Institution, Belfast. Three years later, in 1902, he took up the same post at George Watson's College,[124] acting as Deputy Head there from October 1911. The editor and author of a number of academic papers, he became secretary (1904–8), then president (1908–9), of the Edinburgh Mathematical Society. He was chosen as Rector of the High School from a large number of candidates at a special meeting of the Board on 3 December 1913, and was formally installed on 5 January 1914.[125] He got down to business immediately and his first achievement was the opening of a shooting range in June 1915. It was constructed substantially of red fire-clay brick and was erected along the Holland Street wall of the playground (109 feet long by 15 feet wide), with a Salerno battle practice target fitted.

Meantime, the War had called away almost all men physically fit for the trenches, but Dr Pinkerton was able to persuade the authorities to advertise stop-gap assistants in most departments. Thus, although teaching appointments were permanent elsewhere in Glasgow, in the High School they remained temporary.

The Departments[126]

Even after becoming Rector, Paton continued to run the Classical department. He was the 'most thoroughly human of all the teachers'.[127] His team of Hutchison and Purdie (until 1882) was joined by Andrew Anderson, from Stirling High School, in 1878. Anderson was elected first president of the Literary and Debating Society on its formation in 1888, founded the Golf Club, and was censor of the Magazine.[128] Alexander L. Taylor (A.L.T.) joined them in 1895 from Ayr Academy, where he had been the trusted assistant, in Classical teaching, of the distinguished Rector, William Maybin. However, he was promoted to the headship of the English department in 1905, soon proving that his mastery of English language and literature was as profound as his knowledge of the Classics. 'The changes that he made in the methods and practice of our English studies were an education to his staff as well as to his boys. To listen to his teaching was a treat, it was so alert, so incisive, so inspiring and, above all, so thorough.'[129] His time in control of the English department was very successful and happy, but when the Classical headship fell vacant in 1913, his earlier predilections led him to seek, and be successful in, a move to that department.[130] He was much involved in the wider life of the School: he contributed at various times to golf, rugby and cricket, the annual Sports, the OTC, the Musical Society, the 'Lit' and the Magazine. He wrote the Old Boys' Song and when he was the guest of honour at the School dinner on his retirement in 1923, he saw it as the proudest moment of his life.

Although A.L.T. stayed on at the School, other classicists who served on the staff went on to become leaders in other Scottish schools. William Montgomerie (1901–11) became headmaster of Jordanhill College School; Alexander R. Cumming (1905–9) was described by an HMI as 'the best rector in Ayrshire';[131] William King Gillies (1904–13) became Rector of Hutchesons' GS (1913–19)[132] and then Rector of the Royal High in Edinburgh (1919–40);[133] William R. Merry[134] (1905–23) became headmaster of Strathbungo Secondary; and Hugh F. Martin (1913–19) served successively as headmaster at Madras College, Dollar Academy and Stewart's College. Robert M. Allardyce (1905–12) produced a number of textbooks[135] and became Director of Education for Glasgow in 1929. The strength of the department was confirmed when Israel Levine[136] came first in 1910 in the Glasgow Bursary Competition (out of 334 candidates) – the fourth time a High School boy had achieved that distinction in a decade.[137]

The English department had been run for two decades by James Bell until his death in 1879. During this time David S. Henderson was appointed as assistant Writing master, and in 1895, after twenty-four years' service, he was made head master of the Junior School under Paton. However, following a serious illness in 1903 he was transferred back to his original department, where he remained until retirement in 1912. Bell was succeeded by Henry Barker, known as 'Daddy' by the boys. He had been a pupil at the School (1841–3) before going on to Glasgow University, where he gained a First in Classics and Philosophy. Before coming back to Glasgow in 1879 he had been Rector of the Chanonry School in Old Aberdeen for seventeen years.[138] Annually, the HM Inspectors congratulated him on his work and that of his departmental staff,[139] and he retired to Banchory in 1895. William Law moved from the Classical to the English department, becoming its head before leaving to be head of the Pupil Teacher Institute. Dr James H. Steel was promoted from his post as Principal Teacher of English to become headmaster of Allan Glen's School in 1917 (he retired in 1943).[140] John Clark went on to become Director of Education for Glasgow (1919–29) and in 1925 was awarded an Honorary Fellowship by the EIS.[141] James A. Wotherspoon (1905–23) began teaching English but was transferred to Mathematics, and James Pollock (1910–12; 1914–25) transferred in the opposite direction.

Leadership of the Mathematics department had been given over to Thomas Muir[142] in 1874. He proved not only to have a real talent for teaching his subject but was also acknowledged as one of the greatest mathematicians of his time. It was noted[143] that he kindled an intellectual interest in Mathematics in his pupils, and 'in almost every civilised country in this world . . . the name of Dr. Muir is respected'. He encouraged individual initiative, not instructing a class until all the pupils had exhausted their own resources. He conceived the ambitious project of writing a history of determinants, which he completed in stages throughout his life. By the mid-1880s the High School and Glasgow Academy 'stood alone'[144] in the quality of their mathematical work in Scotland. Thus Muir's departure in 1892 was a great loss to the School when he moved to South Africa, where he reorganised the whole public education service from elementary school to university.[145] Of his assistants, William Thomson (1874–8) became Rector of Dunfermline High School (1878–85) and then headmaster of Hutchesons' Girls' School for thirty years; William Reid served from 1874 to 1913 and played an important part in the growing extra-curricular life of the school;[146] Robert S. Wishart also joined John Street, in 1877, proving to be a good teacher and an enthusiast for Natural History; while Farquhar Macdonald became successively Rector of the Miller Institute, Thurso, then of Dingwall Academy, where he served for twenty-three years. Robert A. Nicolson (1865– 1923) was educated in the School at John Street and returned to teach Mathematics and Science in 1887. Owing to his tireless efforts, the work in Science advanced and when, in 1910, the Science department was separated from Mathematics he became its first head. Outside School he was an examiner in Physics for St Andrews and Glasgow Universities. A.J. Gunion Barclay replaced Muir as head of Mathematics:[147] he came originally from Hawick and had been head of Mathematics at George Watson's College.[148] On his retirement George D.C. Stokes[149] ran the department from 1914 till 1922 and was contemporaneous with Dougald McQuistan (1914–19), who went on to become Professor of Natural Philosophy at the Royal Technical College.

In 1884 Francis Joseph Amours was appointed head of the French department. He was a native of Normandy who came over to Britain in 1864 and stayed on. He taught in Gloucestershire before spending two years teaching in Edinburgh and, thereafter, joined the staff of Glasgow Academy in 1869.[150] He understood the problem of turning out linguists in a limited time. His 'French Primer' and 'Study of French Verbs' formed the basis of his teaching, which emphasised accuracy in reading and writing. As a scholar he wrote books in English on Scottish Literature and History; he retired in 1904. His assistant, James Moyes, died, after almost thirty years' service in French, in 1912, aged 59. Amours was succeeded by Thomas Keen,[151] who was head of the department until 1925 when he became Rector of Bellahouston Academy. He was also conductor of the School's orchestra for a decade. Richard Kaiser served eighteen years in Modern Languages: he had been born in Hamburg but became a naturalised British subject in 1909. He worked alongside George W. Humphreys (1904–19)[152] and George T. Ford (1909–14) who was killed, after enlisting, at Gallipoli in 1915. The department proved innovative and, following an agreement between the SED and the French Government, the School took foreign language students who gave conversation classes and, in the case of Monsieur Dodanthun, 'entered with considerable spirit into the general and social life of the school'.[153] In German, following the retirement of Schlomka[154] in 1903, Dr William Chalmers took over, but during the Great War the department was dissolved.[155]

In Science, William Douglas (1908–23)[156] set high standards, ably assisted by John Cuthbertson (1900–42) and Hugh Smith (1907–33) who, running parallel with his interest in the Boys' Brigade, was captain of the OTC. In Drawing, James Campbell (1874–1902) was succeeded as PT by Paddock; he in turn was succeeded by John Young, who served seventeen years, dying aged only 51 in December 1921. He introduced handicrafts – pottery, metal work and etching – to the mainly academic curriculum. In Drill and Gymnastics, Captain Walter Roland died in 1883 and his brothers, George and Henry, took on his work. They were aided by Sergeant McNeil, and the result was that the 'physique of boys developed admirably.'[157] From 1897 until 1902 the department was headed by William Henry Lewis, who left to become an inspector of Gymnastics. Skill and success in Writing and Book-keeping continued under J. Dalziel Maclean until 1903. He was to be the last Writing master. Music was introduced comparatively late to the School, and its development owed much to William H. Miller from 1875. He also organised Music teaching in all the Board schools of Glasgow. He was succeeded in 1894 by R.L. Reid.[158]

The Junior School had opened with 116 boys in 1895 with David ('Beastie') Watson in charge (following Henderson) from 1903 to 1910. James Mitchell played an important part, teaching Primary 7 classes from 1912 to 1933, but this section of the School owed most to the ladies. Mrs Marquis (1896–1911) and Miss Morton (1896–1903) taught in the Bath Street church hall until the new building was ready. Another early staff member was Miss Barrowman (1903–20), who proved an enthusiastic suffragette. It was, however, the sisters Logan who made 'an unforgettable contribution'.[159] Miss Sarah Logan taught in the Junior School from 1902 to 1939, and her interest in every facet of the whole school's life made its mark on all she encountered.[160]

RUGBY FOOTBALL

The arrival of Peter Pinkerton as Rector gave an impetus to the plans for a new athletic ground. Rugby football had become an increasingly important part of school life after 1870, although organised games did not appear in School records until after 1878. The boys organised the sport themselves and used 'Jennings' Track': a grass-covered space in the middle of a cycle-racing cinder track located on the opposite side of Crow Road from the present Anniesland pitches.[161] On leaving the School a number of boys joined rugby clubs in Glasgow, particularly West of Scotland. Four who played for West won international caps between 1874 and 1893.[162] Meantime, an FP Football Club had been formed in 1884, but needed reviving in 1889–90 and again in 1895–6 when Charles W. Stewart became Secretary.[163] Pitches close to Crow Road were used until 1900, when the move was made to Scotstoun agricultural ground.

Rugby at FP and School level saw a significant upsurge, with John M. Dykes[164] gaining ten caps between 1898 and 1902 and Gordon C. Kerr (Old Dunelmians) gaining eight caps between 1898 and 1900, while the then Rector, Harry Spenser, as Honorary President of the FP Club, gave much encouragement. The overall result was tying for second place in the Unofficial Championship in 1901–2. Spenser's successors as Rector also played their part in the advancement of the Club. Dr Hutchison, Rector and Honorary President, had five rugby-playing sons. Rector Goodwin, as Honorary President, at the beginning of season 1909–10, provided twenty-four rugby balls and presented two challenge cups for School form matches. Also, he allowed kicking practice in the Elmbank Street playground, which led to an improvement. However, being mere tenants on their ground meant a lack of investment in its state and facilities, so Goodwin went on to spearhead the plan for a new ground – one full-size pitch, three smaller pitches, a stand, a pavilion and a cricket square – off Great Western Road. However, George M. Frew[165] and a line of players were to become internationalists before that became a reality.

Given that comparable day schools such as Glasgow Academy and George Watson's both possessed well-equipped playing fields, Pinkerton was determined that the School should be on an equal footing with its competitors. The Board agreed to commute the annual payment of £100 which it made towards the cost of the grounds into a capital sum of £2,500. This enabled the Club to make a conditional arrangement to buy thirteen acres stretching south-west of Anniesland Cross[166] for £6,500 and, expecting equipment to cost another £3,500, a financial appeal was launched in June 1914. Unfortunately the war intervened, but Pinkerton persevered and, supported by the High School Club and its officers, especially Hugh R. Buchanan, the land at Anniesland was eventually bought in 1919. Coupled with the work of the first groundsman, Arthur Taylor (1920–41), the coaching of staff members Herbert Ellicott and William Barclay, and the talent of a number of younger players, a 'golden age' in rugby began in the post-1918 period.

PUPILS

By the early twentieth century 'Greater Glasgow' had been created and its position as 'Second City' in the Empire was unchallenged. The Clyde was still producing nearly half the nation's shipping, and the related industries boomed. The 1911 Exhibition revealed much confidence and growing prosperity. However, the focus on the local community solving its own problems was weakening, and there were growing signs that Glasgow's social cohesion was crumbling. The High School emphatically continued to reinforce the harmonious integration of society through philanthropic endeavour and the promotion of the public good, as can be seen by the profiles below.

However, the dominance of the School's middle-class clientele can be seen in the occupations of parents recorded in the 1902 Register. Some 75 were designated merchants, 55 clergymen, 49 physicians/surgeons, 40 lawyers, 37 engineers, 36 company managers, 32 manufacturers, 29 teachers, 28 accountants, 17 bankers, 13 stockbrokers, 10 dentists, 9 professors, 9 architects, 8 farmers, 6 ship-owners and 4 veterinary surgeons. Amongst their number were the Medical Officer of Health, the Glasgow City Registrar, the Treasurer of the Corporation, an HMI[167] and the Spanish Consul.[168] The boys of the artisan class were represented by 33 clothiers, 24 builders, 23 iron and steel workers; 21 house factors, 12 butchers, 12 grocers, 11 bakers, 8 slaters and 7 printers, but they were outnumbered considerably, despite 77 bursaries being awarded that year.

Merchants

Harry Watt (1863–1929) attended Glasgow University and was a successful athlete, specialising in the 100 yards hurdles. He became a cotton-yard merchant. He was elected Liberal MP for Glasgow College in 1906 and re-elected in January and December 1910.

James Couper (1870–1946)[169] was a ship-owner and member of the Baltic Shipping Exchange, Trades' House, Merchants' House, and the

Chamber of Commerce. He was Glasgow Maryhill Conservative MP, 1924–9 and a member of the British Delegation attending the Conference of the Inter-Allied Parliamentary Union at Washington and Ottawa in 1925.

Andrew Crawford (1871–1936) was chairman and managing director of Andrew Crawford & Co. Ltd, steamship owners and brokers.

(Sir) John Loudon (1881–1948) was a provision and produce importer who became Commissioner of Income Tax, 1935–48.

John Gammie (1900–1968)[170] [1912–15; commercial traveller][171] was manager, Liner Department, British Ministry of Shipping, 1915–18; Cunard Steam Ship Co., 1919–39; British Ministry of War Transport, New York, 1939–45; and Vice-President of States Marine Corporation, 1945–66.

(Sir) John Burns (1903–91) [1913–18; manufacturer's agent; 'good conduct, industry and ability'] was Director, James Finlay & Co. Ltd, 1957–74.

Manufacturers (Industrialists)

Sir Hugh Reid (1860–1935) (Baronet) attended Glasgow University. He was an engineer with Neilson & Co. in Springburn, becoming its senior partner in 1894, when it became part of the North British Locomotive Co. Ltd.[172] He was made a Freeman of Glasgow (1917), was Dean of Guild (1917–18) and President of the Royal Glasgow Institute of Fine Arts, 1925–9. He was President of the High School Club, 1922–4.

Roland Muirhead (1868–1964) was the son of the Gryffe tannery owner in Bridge of Weir. He attended the School (1880–3) but left early to begin an apprenticeship at the factory, the running of which he took over. In 1897 he reorganised the tannery to give the workers a share in its ownership. He supported 'progressive' movements and the radical wing of the Scottish National Party.[173]

(Colonel) Sir Frederick Stewart (1870–1950) was chairman of numerous engineering and locomotive companies in Britain and the Empire, serving on the boards of banks and businesses.

(Sir) William Weir (Viscount) (1877–1959) was the son of a successful Glasgow engineer. He took up an apprenticeship in the family business, in time becoming managing director and chairman of G. and J. Weir.[174] His work on warships led to his appointment by Lloyd George in 1915 as Director of Munitions in Scotland during World War I. He was instrumental in the decision to form the RAF, becoming President of the Air Council in 1918. He was adviser to governments on civil aviation, the armed forces, electricity supply, trade and employment. He was President of the High School Club, 1924–6. He received the Freedom of the City of London (1957).

Alexander Quig (1892–1962) was the son of a Glasgow engine-driver. He attended the School from 1905, leaving to work with an explosives company. He rose to chairman by 1936, and became commercial director of Imperial Chemical Industries (ICI) and one of its deputy chairmen (1948–56). He promoted a staff college to train incoming managerial staff. He was a founder member of the British Institute of Management. He chaired the government committee which reviewed the structure and management of the Air Ministry.[175]

(Sir) James Douglas (1893–1964) became a farmer (like his father), a land valuer and chairman of the Scottish Milk Board, 1950–62.

Churchmen

(Dr) John Graham (1861–1943) was the son of a customs officer and attended the HS between 1875 and 1877. After ordination into the ministry in 1889 he, and his wife Katie, became foreign missionaries in Kalimpong in the eastern Himalayas. They established the St Andrew's Colonial Homes, a model village, which grew to house more than 600 children who were rescued from tea plantations and the slums of Calcutta. In 1931, he was the first missionary to become Moderator of the General Assembly of the Church of Scotland.[176]

(Rev.) John Hutton (1868–1947) became minister of Westminster Chapel (1923) and editor of the *British Weekly*, 1925–46.

(Very Rev.) Donald Fraser (1870–1933) was the son of a Free Church minister. He went to the School and Glasgow University before attending the Free Church College to train for the ministry. After ordination in 1896 he went as a missionary to British Central Africa. For thirty years he worked among the Ngoni people of northern Malawi, supported by his wife Agnes, a medical doctor. He became Moderator of the United Free Church in 1922–3. In his final years he returned home and played a prominent role in national and international church affairs.[177] He was President of the High School Club, 1930–2.

(Rev.) Nicol MacNicol (1870–1952) was a missionary of the Church of Scotland in Bombay 1895–1901 and Poona 1901–31. He became a lecturer in Natural and Comparative Religion at Oxford University, 1932–5.

(Rev.) William Gardiner (1874–1959) was minister of Cambusnethen

Old and Quarter, and for over thirty years a missionary in Calabar, where he worked with Mary Slessor.

(Rev.) Horace Wallace (*c.*1876–*c.*1947) was the son of a Hamilton clergyman. He was First Bursar in 1893 and qualified in Divinity, becoming a member of the English Presbyterian Mission in Shantou (formerly known as Swatow) in Guangdong province in China. He worked there from 1903 until 1947.

(Very Rev.) Matthew Stewart (1881–1952) was a parish minister in Hamilton, 1926–48 and Moderator of the General Assembly of Church of Scotland, 1947–8.

(Rev. Prof.) William Manson (1882–1958) had charges at Oban and Pollokshields. He was Professor of the New Testament, Toronto, 1919–25 and Edinburgh, 1925–46, and Professor of Biblical Criticism, Edinburgh University, 1946–52.

(Rev.) John Lamb (1886–1974) [1902–3; clergyman] was parish minister of Fyvie (1912), Hyndland, Glasgow (1923) and Crathie (1937–63). He became Domestic Chaplain to the Queen in Scotland, 1952–64.

Military

(Brigadier-General) James Wylie (1862–1937) was a solicitor then advocate in Natal (1889). He was a member of its Legislative Assembly and Executive Council. He commanded the Durban Light Infantry in the Boer War, in the Natal Rebellion (1906), and in the campaign in German South-West Africa, 1914–16.

(Major-General) Alistair McNeill (1884–1971) was a professional soldier in the Indian Medical Service, reaching the rank of Major-General in 1941.

(Major-General) Archibald Munro (1886–1961) [1902–3; Medical Officer] joined the Indian medical service in 1908. He was mentioned in despatches in World Wars I and II. He was promoted to Major-General in 1940 and was Director of Medical Services, India 1941–3.

(Major-General) John Macfie (1891–1985) entered the School in 1907. He was the most distinguished medical graduate at Glasgow in 1915. He joined the RAMC in World War I. He became Deputy Assistant Director-General of Army Medical Service, War Office, 1932–6; Deputy DGAMS, War Office, 1943–6; DDMS, East Africa Command (1946–8), Scottish Command (1949), Western Command, UK (1950–1) and Colonel Commandant, RAMC, 1951–6. He was Honorary President of the High School Club.

(Major-General) John MacQueen (1893–1980) was a member of the Canadian Commission in World War I. He was Director of Ordinance Service, Canada, 1938–9; Dep. Quartermaster General, Canadian military HQ, London, 1941–5; Master General of the Ordinance, 1945 and President, Canadian Arsenals Ltd, 1947–61.

(Major-General Dr) William Hamilton (1895–1969) was the son of a banker. He was active in the two world wars. He became Director of Medicine and Consulting Physician to the Army, 1951–5.

Medical

(Dr) Joshua Ferguson (1870–1951) became President of Glasgow University Union, 1893–5, and was the most distinguished medical student of his year in 1895. He was Medical Referee for Renfrewshire under the Workmen's Compensation Act, and to the Ministry of Pensions. Between 1928 and 1930 he was President of the Royal Medico-Chirurgical Society of Glasgow.

(Dr) Hamilton Marr (1870–1936) studied Medicine at Glasgow University. He became Medical Superintendent, Glasgow District Asylum, (1901–10) and Senior Commissioner in Lunacy for Scotland (until 1935).

(Dr) Joseph Christie (1871–1936) became a surgeon in New Zealand at New Plymouth, then Wanganui. He was the New Zealand representative on the League of Red Cross Societies.

(Dr) Alexander Maclennan (1872–1953) was the most distinguished medical student of his year at Glasgow. He became Consulting Surgeon in Dunoon, the Royal Hospital for Sick Children (Glasgow), Stirling and Falkirk hospitals.

(Sir) Malcolm Watson (1873–1955) was the son of a Renfrewshire commercial traveller and clothier. He graduated from Glasgow University with commendations in arts then Medicine. He entered the Malayan medical service, where his success in a programme of mosquito control 'was a landmark in preventive medicine'.[178] He became adviser on malaria to governments across the world. He was President of the High School London Club, 1935–6.

(Prof.) Archibald Young (1873–1939) studied at Glasgow, Berlin, Breslau and Heidelberg Universities and was a surgeon during the Boer War. He was Regius Professor of Surgery, Glasgow University (1924–39) and President of the Faculty of Physicians and Surgeons, Glasgow. He was a pioneer in operative treatment of fractures and pain relief. He was President of the High School Club, 1938–9.

(Prof.) John Henderson (1876–1949) was consulting physician to the Royal Infirmary, Glasgow; Professor of Medicine, St Mungo's College, Glasgow, 1913–47; and President of the Faculty of Physicians and Surgeons, Glasgow.

(Colonel) James McPherson (1876–1963) studied Medicine at Glasgow, Edinburgh, London and Vienna before joining the Indian civil service, where he worked in the Political Medical Department between 1908 and 1933.

(Dr) Halliday Sutherland (1882–1960) was the son of the Deputy Commissioner for Lunacy in Scotland. He attended the School between 1892 and 1896, gaining first prize in English.[179] He studied Medicine at Edinburgh and opened a tuberculosis dispensary in London in 1911. As a Roman Catholic he waged a campaign against birth control. He became Deputy Medical Officer for Coventry in 1941 and started the mass radiography centre in Birmingham between 1943 and 1951. He published a volume of reminiscences, *The Arches of the Years*.[180]

(Dr) Charles Duguid (1884–1986) left the School in 1902 and after graduating in Medicine from Glasgow emigrated to Australia. He was Moderator of the Presbyterian Church in South Australia in 1935. He led a crusade on behalf of Australian aborigines and succeeded in having a Federal Government minister appointed for the Territories in 1951 and achieving state agreement to the Pitjantjatjara land rights bill of 1980.[181]

(Prof.) Ralph Picken (1884–1955) was Medical Officer in Cardiff between 1921 and 1933. He held the posts of Professor of Preventative Medicine (1933–49) and Provost of the Welsh National School of Medicine (1945–55).

(Dr) John Kinloch (1885–1932) was the son of a grocer and farmer. He graduated in Medicine from Glasgow University. In 1923 he became reader in Public Health at the University of Aberdeen and then succeeded as head of the University's Public Health Department and Medical Officer for Aberdeen. He applied advances in Bacteriology and Immunology to Public Health.[182] In 1928 Kinloch was appointed to the newly created post of Chief Medical Officer at the Department of Health in Scotland.

(Prof.) Gilbert Strachan (1888–1963) attended the School on a bursary 1902–5. He became Professor of Obstetrics and Gynaecology, University of Wales, and Consulting Obstetrician and Gynaecologist, United Cardiff Hospitals.

(Prof.) Robert Lennie (1889–1961) [1902–5; oil manufacturer] became Regius Professor of Midwifery at Glasgow University, 1946–54, and Clinical Examiner in Gynaecology, Edinburgh University.

(Dr) John Knox (1891–1964) [joined 1905; headmaster of Kent Road School] was Administrative Medical Officer and Medical Superintendent, Aberdeen Royal Infirmary.

(Prof.) James Mackintosh (1891–1966) [joined 1904; solicitor] became Chief Medical Officer, Department of Health, Scotland, 1937–41; and Professor of Public Health, Glasgow University, 1941–4, and University of London, 1944–56.

(Prof.) John Glaister (1892–1971) [joined 1902; Professor of Medical Jurisprudence] became a barrister in the Inner Temple (1925); Assistant and Lecturer in Forensic Medicine, Glasgow University, 1919–28; Professor of Forensic Medicine, Cairo University, 1928–31; and Professor in Forensic Medicine, Glasgow University, 1931–62.

(Dr) William Lightbody (1893–1962) [joined 1906; manager] – was senior Medical Officer, Palestine, 1920–37 and Sierra Leone, 1938–49. He became senior lecturer in Tropical Medicine at Liverpool, 1949–59.

(Prof.) Noah Morris (1893–1947) [joined 1904; jeweller] became Regius Professor of Material Medica and Therapeutics, Glasgow University (1937–47). He was the father-figure of the Glasgow medical faculty and, as an early believer in 'holistic' medicine, encouraged the development of geriatric medicine.

(Prof.) Thomas Read (1893–1974) became Professor Emeritus of Clinical Dental Surgery and Warden of the Dental School and Hospital, Leeds University.

(Dr) Herbert H. Pinkerton (1901–1982) [1914–20; Rector of High School; he arrived from Watson's College with his father] was the best medical graduate of 1926 at Glasgow University. He trained in Anaesthetics and became head of department in the Western Infirmary. He became a Fellow of the Faculty of Anaesthetics (1948) and Fellow of the Royal College of Physicians, Glasgow (1964). He was President of the High School Club, 1966–7, a director of the new School, and a member of its Educational Trust.

(Dr) James Imrie (1903–1974) [1917–19; butcher] became a police surgeon and was father-figure to the Glasgow police until 1970. He was 'the foremost forensic pathologist in Britain'.[183]

Legal

(Sir) Thomson Wilson (1862–1929) was a partner in a law firm and became Clerk of the Peace for Glasgow and Liberal MP for North-East Lanarkshire, 1910–11.

(Hon.) John Nicholson (1868–1941) was a lawyer in Australia and Mayor of Perth, 1914. He was a member of the Legislative Council of Western Australia, 1918–41.

William Henderson (1873–1959) became President of Glasgow and Cambridge Unions and was private secretary to Lord Kelvin. He was elevated to the Bar, 1900, becoming Leader of the Parliamentary Bar, 1938–49, Leader of the Midland Circuit, 1940–50 and a QC in 1952.

(Sir) Robert Walker (1873–1956) became a solicitor, 1896, Town Clerk of the Burgh of Pollokshaws, 1902–12 and County Clerk of Lanarkshire, 1923–38.

(Sir) Edward Wallace (1873–1943) joined the Indian Civil Service, serving in Madras from 1895. He became a judge in the Madras High Court, 1924–33.

(Lord) John Wark (1877–1943) attended Glasgow and Berlin Universities before entering the Scottish Bar, 1901. He was Advocate-Depute, 1913–20, Sheriff of Argyll, 1920–33 and a Senator of the College of Justice in Scotland from 1933. He was President of the High School Club, 1941–2.

Lord Birnam (Sir David King Murray) (1884–1955) was First Bursar in Glasgow 1901. He entered the Bar, 1910, becoming Solicitor-General for Scotland, 1941–5, Senator of the College of Justice in Scotland and Lord of Session (1941–5). He was Conservative MP for North Midlothian, 1943–5.

William Murray (1889–1935) [1902–6; contractor] became an advocate at the Scottish Bar in 1919.

(Rt Hon.) Lord Patrick (William) (1889–1967) [1903–6; lawyer] became an advocate, 1913; QC 1933; Dean of Faculty of Advocates, 1937–9; and a Senator of HM College of Justice in Scotland, 1939–63.

(Sir) George Honeyman (1898–1972) [1912–15; widow; Dux of class 6] became a barrister at the Inner Temple, 1924; QC, 1955; and the chairman of various government inquiries at home and abroad.

William Munro (1900–1992) [1916–18, preserve manufacturer; 'attainment and conduct were very good'] was called to the Scottish bar, 1925. He practised in Singapore and Malaya, 1927–57, and he became a QC (Scotland), 1959.

(Sir) William McLean (1901–1965) [1910–19; manager, Clyde Shipping Co.; 'confident, resourceful and humorous'] became a QC (Scotland); Sheriff in the Borders (1952–5), Renfrew and Argyll (1955–60), Lothians and Peebles; and Sheriff of Chancery in Scotland (1960).

(Sir) Roy Wilson (1903–1982) [1916–20; clergyman] was called to the

Bar, Gray's Inn, 1931. He became a QC. He served in India as a brigadier in World War Two. He was President of the Industrial Court, 1961–71, and of the Industrial Arbitration Board, 1971–6.

(Sir) Archibald Craig (d. 1927) became a solicitor and clerk of the General Council of Glasgow University. He was a member of the Merchants' House, Glasgow, chairman of the Glasgow Unionist Association, and a Freeman of London.

Academic

(Prof.) John Mackenzie (1860–1935) was the son of a Glasgow cloth-worker. Between 1870 and 1876 he attended the School, where he was inspired by Thomas Muir, becoming First Bursar then going on to a brilliant career first at Glasgow and Edinburgh Universities, then Cambridge, where he was elected to a Fellowship at Trinity. In 1895 he was appointed Professor of Logic and Philosophy at University College, Cardiff. He was elected a Fellow, British Academy in 1934. He is held to be a representative of the later phase of the neo-Hegelian school of British Idealistic philosophy.[184]

Robert Buchanan (1861–1931) attended Glasgow University, gaining scholarships for original research. He studied under Weigert at Frankfurt-am-Main and Koch at Berlin. He was the bacteriologist for Glasgow Corporation (1899–1930) and President of the Faculty of Physicians and Surgeons, Glasgow (1925–7).

(Prof.) Robert Wenley (1861–1929) was a lecturer in Philosophy at Glasgow University from 1886, then Professor of Philosophy in the University of Michigan (1896–1929).

(Prof.) Lawrence Crawford (1867–1951) was Professor of Pure Mathematics at Cape Town University (1918–38), and for a time Vice-Chancellor and Acting Principal of that University. He became President of the Royal Society of South Africa (1936–41) and a member of the City Council of Cape Town.

(Sir) John Cumming (1868–1958) attended Glasgow Academy and High School, both in Elmbank Street, before going on to be an Exhibitioner at Balliol. He joined the Indian Civil Service, working in Bengal, 1889–1921. He was Vice-Chancellor, School of Oriental Studies, London, 1926–46, and President of the London High School Club, 1928–32.

(Rev. Prof.) William Fulton (1876–1952) attended the School (1888–93), where he was Classical Dux and medallist in Mathematics and English. He came third in the Glasgow Bursary Competition and studied at the

Universities of Glasgow, Marburg and Berlin. He became minister of Paisley Abbey, 1909; Professor of Systematic Theology, Aberdeen University, 1915–27; Professor of Divinity, Glasgow University, 1928–47; and Principal of Trinity College, Glasgow, 1938.

(Prof.) John Dunn (1883–1944) was Professor of Pathology at Birmingham (1919–22), Manchester (1922–31) and Glasgow Universities (1936).

(Prof.) Alexander Ross (1883–1966) was chair of Mathematics and Physics (1912–29) then Professor of Physics, University of Western Australia (1929–52).

(Prof.) Daniel Dougal (1884–1948) became Professor of Obstetrics and Gynaecology at the University of Manchester.

(Prof. Sir) Ian Heilbron (1886–1959) was the son of a Glasgow wine merchant. He was educated at the Royal Technical College and Leipzig University. He became Professor of Organic Chemistry at the Royal Technical College. Subsequently, from 1920 on, he held chairs in the same field at Liverpool, Manchester and then Imperial London, which he left in 1949 to become Director of the Brewing Industry Research Foundation. He made important contributions to the chemistry of penicillin. He received the Fellowship (1931) and the Davy (1943) and Royal (1951) medals of the Royal Society, and the American Medal of Freedom in 1947.[185]

(Prof.) Herbert Paton (1887–1969) [1902–4; clergyman] studied at Glasgow and won a Snell Exhibition. He was a Fellow and Lecturer in Philosophy, Queen's College, Oxford. During World War I he worked for Admiralty Intelligence. He was the British representative on Polish Affairs at the Paris Peace Conference of 1919; and was a member of the Committee for Intellectual Co-operation of the League of Nations. He was Professor of Logic and Rhetoric, Glasgow University, 1927–37, and Emeritus Professor of Moral Philosophy, Oxford University, 1937–52.

(Prof.) John Burton (1888–1962) [1902–4; clergyman] became Professor of Surgery, Glasgow University, 1935–53.

David Anderson (1889–1980) attended the School (1902–6), being Modern Dux in 1904–5. After teaching at Queen's Park Secondary, Madras College and Daniel Stewart's, he became HM Chief Inspector of Schools.

(Prof.) William MacInnes (1892–1977) [joined 1906; water inspector] was appointed Head of the Modern Language Department, Senior War Office School of Education. After posts at Manchester and Glasgow Universities he became Professor of French at Hull University, 1932–57.

(Ian) Graham Andrew (1893–1962) [joined 1908; minister] was Rector of

Elgin Academy, 1922–33; headmaster, Robert Gordon's College, Aberdeen, 1933–43; and headmaster, George Watson's College, Edinburgh, 1943–53.

(Sir) James J. Robertson (1893–1970)[186] was the son of a buildings super-intendent and attended the School in 1906. He was headmaster, Fort William Secondary 1926; Rector, Falkirk High School, 1931; Rector, Royal High School, Edinburgh, 1940; and Rector, Aberdeen Grammar School, 1942–59. He was President, Scottish Secondary Headmasters' Association, 1944–6, and influential on the Advisory Council on Education in Scotland.

(Prof.) Alec Macfie (1898–1980) [1908–16; widow; an 'admirable character' whose 'work was always distinguished'; School Captain 1915–16] was a lecturer (1930–45) then Professor (1946–58) of Political Economy, Glasgow University.

(Rev. Prof.) William Tindal (1899–1965) [1906–17; writer] became Chaplain to HM Forces; a lecturer in Christian Sociology, New College, 1936–45; and Professor of Christian Ethics and Practical Theology, New College, Edinburgh University, 1945.

(Prof.) George Wyburn (1902–85) [1914–20; lawyer] took a medical degree and became lecturer (1930), senior lecturer (1935) and Regius Professor (1948–72) of Anatomy, Glasgow University.

Financial

(Sir) John Mann (1863–1955)[187] attended Glasgow University and became a Chartered Accountant. He was Financial Adviser in the Ministry of Munitions of War, 1915; Assistant Financial Secretary in Ministry, 1917; and Controller of Munitions Contracts, Ministry of Munitions, 1917–19.

(Sir) William McLintock (1873–1947) (first Baronet) was the son of a Glasgow Chartered Accountant, entering his father's business. He created a number of companies, including Cable and Wireless Ltd in 1929, and was financial adviser to the Government in the creation of the London Passenger Transport Board in 1933. He urged that an ethical responsibility be developed by companies, to ensure that shareholders were properly informed. He overhauled the Royal finances.[188] He was President of the High School London Club, 1936–7.

Douglas Porteous (1891–1974) [joined 1904 from Glasgow Academy; tea-merchant] became the Principal Actuary, Government Acturial Department, 1936, and Deputy Government Actuary, 1946–53.

Alexander McBain (1896–1990) became a CA and taxation corre-spondent of the *Glasgow Herald*. He was chairman of the Scottish Special

Housing Association. He was awarded a papal knighthood for his fifty years as financial adviser to the Roman Catholic Church (1978), only the second non-Catholic to be so honoured.

(Prof.) Robert Browning (1902–1974) [1912–20; property agent; 'first class ability'] became a partner in a firm of Chartered Accountants, Glasgow, 1927–69. He was Professor of Accountancy, Glasgow University, 1950–64; Director, Clydesdale Bank, 1957–69; and President of the Institute of Chartered Accountants of Scotland, 1965–6.

(Prof.) William Kennedy (1903–1979) was the son of the headmaster of the Bridge of Weir Orphan School. He was educated from 1914–20 at the School, where the register described him as a 'quiet, well-behaved boy of average ability.' He entered Glasgow University in 1921 to study agriculture. Having graduated, he took a further degree in geology in 1927. He won a scholarship and studied in Zurich. He worked on geological mapping in the West Highlands of Scotland. In 1945 he became Professor of Geology at Leeds University. He gained many honours including Fellow, Royal Society (1949).[189]

Administrators (Politicians)

(Sir) William Barton (1862–1957), son of a mining engineer, was elected Liberal MP for Oldham, 1910–18 and Coalition Liberal MP for Oldham, 1918–22.

James Stewart (1867–1943) was elected a Glasgow councillor and became Treasurer of City of Glasgow and Convener of Finance. He was Deputy Chair of the Corporation, 1930–2.

(Sir) William Reid (1871–1939) attended the School, 1886–8, then Cambridge, 1889–91. He joined the Indian Civil Service in 1891, becoming Chief Secretary of Assam in 1912 and Acting Governor in 1925.

James Davidson (1872–1939) was Commissioner for Railways, Queensland, Australia, 1918–38, and Chairman of its Transport Board.

James Cleland (1874–1914) had a successful School career before further study at Glasgow and Balliol. He was Liberal MP for Bridgeton, 1906–10.

(Lord) David Fleming (1877–1944) was the son of a prominent lawyer. He was educated at the Universities of Glasgow and Edinburgh. He was admitted to the Faculty of Advocates in 1902 and, after the war, was Advocate-Depute. In 1921 he took silk, and in the following year he was appointed Solicitor-General for Scotland in Bonar Law's government. He won the seat of Dunbartonshire in the election of 1924 and was reappointed

Solicitor-General under Baldwin. In December 1925 he was elevated to the Scottish Bench. He received the freedom of Rutherglen in 1926. He was President of the Boys' Brigade and chaired the committee (1942) which outlined a plan to open the doors of English public schools to children from local authority schools. He chaired the London Appellate Tribunal for conscientious objectors.[190] He was President of the High School Club, 1943–4.

Alexander Montgomerie (1879–1958) was founder and first editor of the School magazine. He went on to Balliol College, becoming an English barrister before joining the Indian Civil Service in 1903. He was Home Secretary to the Bombay government, 1923–26.

James Dyer (1880–1940) joined the Indian Civil Service and became President of Council, Bhopal, Central India, 1932–4.

(Sir) William Sutherland (1880–1949) won the Ewing Medal at Glasgow University for the most distinguished graduate of his year. He was Secretary for the Cabinet Committee on Munitions, 1915; Private Secretary to Lloyd George 1915–18; Liberal MP for Argyll, 1918–24; Parliamentary Secretary to Lloyd George, 1918–20; and Chancellor of the Duchy of Lancaster, 1922. He owned a colliery business. He was the first of the modern spin doctors.[191]

(Sir) Gilbert Hogg (1884–1950) joined the Indian Civil Service in 1907 and became the Chief Secretary to Government in Bengal (1933).

William Carse (1899–1987) [1914–17; baker] joined the Indian army, 1918–20; and served in HM Consular Service in Americas, Africa, Europe and Asia, 1923–56.

William Smith (d. 1948) was a City councillor in Glasgow, 1906–36, the force behind the building of the Kelvin Hall. He was one of founders of the Smoke Abatement League, and an opponent of air pollution.

Writers (Artists, Architects, Poets, Journalists)

George Eyre-Todd (1862–1937) was a Scottish patriot who became the editor of *Scottish Country Life,* 1908–13. He wrote the *Book of the Cathedral* (1898); *Story of Glasgow* (1911); and produced *History of Glasgow*, volume II (1931) for Glasgow Corporation (and volume III in 1934).

(Sir) Maitland Park (1862–1921) became chief editor of the *Cape Times* in South Africa (1902).

(William) Kennedy Jones (1865–1921) was sub-editor of the *Glasgow Evening News* before becoming editor of the London *Evening News* (1894–1900). He reduced its political coverage and, with more sport, competitions and serialised fiction, circulation increased. His vision of a halfpenny newspaper printed in London but wired to provincial cities for printing, distribution and early morning sale led to the foundation (with Lord Northcliffe) of the *Daily Mail* in March 1896, which transformed the newspaper business. He became the Unionist MP for Hornsey.[192]

Alexander Paterson (1865–1944) was editor of the *Yorkshire Evening Post* and *Daily Despatch* before becoming managing editor of Allied Newspapers in Manchester from 1924 until 1939.

John Downie (1871–1945) was a portrait, genre, and landscape painter.

Andrew (Hamish) Blair (1872–1935) became editor, managing director and founder of Calcutta newspapers.

William Wells (1872–1923) became a landscape painter, who exhibited in the most prestigious British and continental galleries.

(Prof.) Alfred Stewart (1880–1947) was the son of the Professor of Divinity at Glasgow University. He attended Glasgow and Marburg Universities, and University College, London. He became Professor of Chemistry at Queen's University, Belfast, in 1919. He was 'essentially a chemist of the classical pre-quantum mechanics tradition'.[193] In later life, under the pseudonym J.J. Connington, he wrote twenty-seven novels, all but two of which were detective stories. His reputation as a novelist overshadowed his reputation as a scientist.

William McWhirter (1888–1955) [1902–6; electrical engineer] was Managing Director, Associated Newspapers Ltd and Northcliffe Newspapers Group Ltd. He was father of the McWhirter twins, founder of the *Guinness Book of Records* and a President of the London High School Club, 1937–8.

(Prof.) Osborne Mavor (James Bridie), (1888–1951) was the son of a Glasgow engineer. His 'first real school' was the High School, which proved a 'sad-coloured place of enormous size through which bearded men, gowned like clergymen, walked solemnly'. However, he only attended it for one session, for 'family fortunes must have improved' and he was sent the following year to Glasgow Academy 'for the sons of gentlemen'.[194] When at Glasgow University, the Old Boys of the Academy told him that he might associate with the better sort of HS boy, but he would do himself no good 'by mixing with the riff-raff and bobtail who had been unfortunate in their early education'.[195] He eventually became a GP and then Professor of Medicine in Anderson's College of Glasgow. He began writing plays in 1928, penning forty in total, and was prominent in the establishment of Glasgow Citizens' Theatre (1943) and the founding of a College of Drama in Glasgow (1950).[196]

George Sandilands (1889–1961) [1903–4; warehouseman] became a painter, writer and art critic. He was Secretary, Faculty of Arts, French Institute, 1921–39, and Registrar of the Royal College of Art, South Kensington, 1939–49.

(Sir) James Gunn (1893–1964) was the son of a Glasgow clothier. He attended the School (1906–8) and then the Glasgow College of Art, the Edinburgh College of Art and the Academie Julian in Paris. He served in the Great War, in which he lost two brothers. In 1929 he decided to devote himself to portraiture, following Velazquez. Portraits of prime ministers, field marshals, judges, academics, bankers and even the singer Gracie Fields were executed. He painted George VI in 1944 and his wife, Elizabeth, in 1946. His portrait of Elizabeth II was voted 'painting of the year' at the Royal Academy in 1953.[197]

Sport, Culture and Entertainment

Walter Arnott (1861–1931) was the son of a Glasgow grain merchant. He played football, joining Queen's Park in 1882 and becoming 'the first Scottish player to enjoy cult status'.[198] He made ten consecutive appearances for Scotland against England (1884–1893) and won five Scottish cup medals with Queen's Park, but remained firmly amateur. He was said to be the first full-back who passed judiciously out of defence instead of just clearing his lines.

(Prof. Sir) John McEwen (1868–1948), son of a minister, proved a good Classical scholar, leaving the School in 1884. After graduating from Glasgow University he attended the Royal Academy of Music (RAM) in London. Following time as a choirmaster and teacher, he became Professor of Harmony and Composition at the RAM, Glasgow, in 1898. He produced a sizeable body of varied work, the best known of which, *The Solway Symphony*, was composed in 1911.[199] Between 1924 and 1936 McEwen was Principal of the RAM, Glasgow.

John Dykes (1877–1955) attended the School (1885–94) and was the first Former Pupil to play rugby for Scotland. He gained ten caps, 1898–1902, and was President of the Scottish Rugby Union (SRU), 1920–2. He was President of the High School Club, 1919–22.

Sidney Smith (1900–1931) [1914–17; timber measurer] came from Glasgow Academy. He gained a number of hockey caps, playing at outside right, between 1925 and 1930.

John Bannerman (Baron Bannerman of Kildonan) (1901–1969) [1913–

20; post office official; School Captain and captain of rugby] attended Glasgow University, graduating in agriculture. He then spent three years on a scholarship at Oxford and Cornell. Between 1921 and 1929 he won thirty-seven consecutive Scottish rugby caps, being on the winning side on twenty-five occasions, including winning the 'triple crown' in 1925. He later became President of the SRU (1954–5). In 1930 he became farm manager, then factor, to the Duke of Montrose. He was active in the creation of the Scottish National Party in 1934 but became disillusioned with the widespread in-fighting. As a Liberal he fought elections in Argyll, then Inverness and finally Paisley in 1964. Between 1956 and 1965 he was chairman of the Scottish Liberal Party (SLP), which became distinctive as a home rule party promoting rural interests. He became joint president of the SLP in 1965. He helped promote the creation of a Highlands and Islands Development Board and the Gaelic language and culture.[200] He was President of An Comunn Gaidhealach. He was President of the High School Club in 1962–3.

Fyfe (formerly James) Robertson (1902–1987) grew up in poverty in Garnethill [1914–20, minister; good at English but 'lacking in application']. He began working in Glasgow and London for national daily and Sunday newspapers. He proved a serious investigative writer, becoming well-known for campaigning for 'good' causes. He moved to the BBC TV programme *Tonight*, soon becoming a household name. He later worked on *Twenty-Four Hours* and *Nationwide*. He was recognised by 'his Scottish accent, his slow, over-emphatic voice, his deerstalker hat and his goatee beard'.[201]

James Ireland (1903–1998) [1916–21; wine merchant] worked with William Younger and Co. Ltd as its Dundee manager, then as London manager of Scottish and Newcastle Breweries, retiring in 1968. He was a Scottish rugby internationalist, gaining eleven caps, 1925–7 (being part of a triple crown winning team), and was later an international rugby referee. During World War II he was a lieutenant-colonel in the Royal Marines. He was President of the SRU, 1950–1; President, High School London Club, 1962–3; and President, High School Club, 1964–5.[202]

SEVEN

The Glasgow High School for Girls

This chapter traces the evolution of Garnethill Public School under James Milligan and the creation of the Glasgow High School for Girls. It examines the leadership of the Principals – Alice Reid, Flora Tebb, Frances Barker and Helen Jamieson – and their achievements. The chapter ends with an analysis of the background to the School's transformation into Cleveden Secondary.

JAMES MILLIGAN AND THE GENESIS OF THE GLASGOW HIGH SCHOOL FOR GIRLS

Although the Glasgow School Board concentrated on elementary education, it was still determined to provide secondary education facilities for all who could and would take advantage of them. However, for the sake of efficiency there was an early realisation that higher subjects would have to be concentrated in a limited number of schools. Five were selected: the City School, which inherited the old building of the High School; John Street; Kent Road; Whitehill; and Woodside. Each was carefully placed in an area likely to provide an ample supply of higher pupils.[1] The other two secondary schools were the High School, set apart as a 'higher class school', and Garnethill, a school which 'had won for itself a quite unique reputation in Scotland'.[2]

Garnethill Public School was built in Buccleuch Street in the district of Milton to the north of Sauchiehall Street. Its catchment area included the university and the mansions of Park Circus in the west, as well as respectable lower-middle and upper working-class parents in the east.[3] They were ambitious for their children and willing to make sacrifices to provide them with a good schooling. The Board responded by choosing an experienced and successful headmaster, James Milligan, to lead such a promising school.[4] He was destined to make Garnethill 'the most outstanding public school in Scotland'.[5] From 1880 onwards its annual inspection reports were full of superlatives. In 1883, in the Glasgow University examinations, Garnethill took 21 per cent of the prizes, including four of the six open bursaries, three of which were won with the highest marks ever recorded.

The School's success led Milligan to begin a campaign for more generous staffing and higher salaries. He further proposed that the Board recognise Garnethill's uniqueness by conferring a special title – Intermediate Public School – so recognising that it went further and beyond a mere elementary school. Milligan rightly saw Garnethill as the first satisfactory solution to the urgent educational problem of the day: the supply of a genuine secondary education to the children of Glasgow.[6] It was the 'prototype of public secondary schools in Scotland'.[7]

Garnethill parents desired advanced classes for their children and the Board delivered them. The school building had unusually good facilities, such as physics and chemistry laboratories, an art studio and a dining room. A better staff–pupil ratio was enjoyed – 1:93 compared with 1:120 in the other local public schools in 1882 – and the quality of individual teachers appears to have been exceptionally good, with both Milligan and his deputy having degrees. Milligan was also given a special payment of £100 over and above his normal salary entitlement.

The outstanding achievements of Garnethill, and similar schools to a lesser degree, seriously affected even the best of private schools. The rolls of both Glasgow and Kelvinside Academies slumped,[8] especially after 1885 and the opening of Hillhead Public School by the then Govan Board. It was established on the Garnethill model: a well-staffed and well-equipped school situated in a prosperous and supportive community.[9] By Christmas 1885 the numbers in Glasgow Academy had fallen to 343 from a level of 405 a year earlier.[10]

Garnethill continued to flourish academically. In the university examinations in 1890 it provided a quarter of all successful candidates and a third of those on the 'Distinguished Candidates' list. A boy was accepted into the Indian Civil Service – the highest of accolades – while one girl won an Entrance Scholarship to the Royal Holloway College and another to Girton College, Cambridge. These successes in England were extraordinary, particularly as girls were not accepted by Glasgow University until 1892. Mary Miller Allan[11] became Head of Leeds Higher Grade School for Girls in 1895, and eight years later she was appointed the first woman principal of Homerton College, Cambridge.[12]

The School was composed of two buildings: the Old School and its tower (1878), housing the elementary pupils, and the New School (1884) which housed the secondary classes. Milligan introduced informal French into the curriculum of the former, and those in the latter who were willing and able were taught German. Garnethill pupils were allowed to sit the new Leaving Certificate Examinations for the first time in 1892. Its results were good but were somewhat below that achieved by the High School.

	Honours	Higher	Lower[13]
Garnethill	17 (20)	44 (103)	189 (287)
(High School in brackets)			

However, the following year in 1893, its results were every bit as good as the High School:

	Honours	Higher	Lower
Garnethill	12 (11)	86 (88)	288 (255)

These excellent results, together with the fact that many of Garnethill's most successful pupils were girls, opened the way for the Board to realise its ambition,[14] which it had spelled out as early as 1883 in reply to the SED's Circular 55 on Higher Education. 'In public higher class schools the provision for girls is very restricted compared with that for boys, while in the private higher class it is the reverse. The Board hope to see higher class inspected schools for girls erected in different parts of the district.' Although it was normal in industrial Scotland for schools to be mixed gender it was not unusual in public schools to see division into girls' and boys' sections usually from the second or third standard upwards.[15] Moreover, the Board had instructed its architects to build schools in such a way as to separate girls and boys everywhere except in the classroom, which resulted in separate stairs, entrances and exits for the sexes.[16] Moving to separate but equal schools for girls and boys was also a way of attracting middle-class girls who would not have been sent to a mixed-gender public school.[17]

In 1894 with the aid of the Secondary Education Grant the Board turned the upper department of Garnethill into the Glasgow High School for Girls (GHSG). A Lady Superintendent, Miss Lawson, was appointed to oversee the morals, manners and behaviour of the girls, not just in the classroom but also in the neighbourhood. Girls' education was clearly subject not just to the pressures of gender, but also of social class.[18] The following year the Junior School was reserved for girls, except for boys under the age of eight years.[19] Its excellent Leaving Certificate results continued:

	Honours	*Higher*	*Lower*
1896	23 (11)	100 (118)	175 (345)[20]
1897	10 (33)	137 (123)	284 (238)

Although the School became the Girls' High, male staff continued in post, and one photograph of this time shows fourteen male and fourteen female teachers.[21] New rooms were provided for the Rector (as the Head began to be called) and his secretary, while two classrooms and an extra cloakroom were created, to be followed later by the hall,[22] kitchen, luncheon room and fully equipped gymnasium. Then the music department, headed by David Lamond, elder brother of the well-known pianist, opened in the house in Hill Street, which later accommodated the three infant classes.[23] The girls were drawn from a wide geographical area.

It was in 1899 that Garnethill was declared a higher class school for girls. As far as the girls were concerned its creation came about with 'the minimum of fuss and ceremony'. However, it was a real achievement for Milligan personally, who had struggled to combat 'ignorance, prejudice and . . . pettiness'.[24] As well as gaining parity of status with the High School, the School now operated outwith the regulations of the Code, which entailed the loss of grants. Although this meant that fees had to be raised, this, if anything, encouraged enrolment.[25] It also enabled an integrated curriculum to be adopted throughout the whole school. It was the only Board school to teach the girls both Latin and Greek[26] and Milligan tried to persuade the girls to take one or more science classes.[27] This met with only limited success, given parental disapproval, but he remained confident of an increase as girls looked more towards medicine as a career.[28] Meantime, it was no surprise when the first two women to be awarded MA degrees at Glasgow University, in April 1895, were Isabella Blacklock and Sarah Blair, both from Garnethill.

Milligan continued as headmaster, 'widely recognised as the outstanding public school teacher of his day'.[29] Glasgow University acknowledged his educational work in June 1901 by conferring on him the degree of Doctor of Law,[30] a distinction given to no other teacher throughout the period of the Board. He retired in 1905 as a result of ill health and was awarded a retiring allowance of £325 per annum.[31] The HMI Report for 1905–6 praised his 'sagacious guidance', and commented on the high esteem in which all in education held him as well as 'the admiring affection of many thousands of old pupils'.[32]

MISS ALICE REID: PRINCIPAL, 1905–1926

The Board interviewed ten candidates for Milligan's post in September 1905.[33] Miss Alice Reid was unanimously elected[34] and was introduced to the School on 23 October. She appeared to have the perfect curriculum vitae for the first woman Principal of the Girls' High.[35] Born in London in February 1865, the daughter of a licensed victualler, she spent three years attending the City of London College before becoming a pupil at North London Collegiate School.[36] This was headed by the legendary Miss Buss,[37] who saw the primary function of a school as character training. Miss Reid did well at English and Botany at school and went on to Bedford College, London University, taking a BA in English. Her first teaching post was at Darlington Training College before a spell at Cheltenham Ladies' College between 1897 and 1905 under the famous Miss Beale.[38] She was, therefore, well-equipped to take on a headship herself given her personal experience of Frances Mary Buss and Dorothea Beale, both pioneers and reformers of girls' education in England. She immediately set to work. In her first year, 1905–6, she introduced a more definite curriculum, in many respects similar to that of the boys of Elmbank Street, and followed its lead over the Form System and the extension of lunches.[39]

Miss Reid soon came to value particular members of Staff who pre-dated her on the staff. Miss Helen Lawson was a member of staff for forty years from 1886, with a reputation for being 'full of fun'. She was also a very good teacher, who gave her pupils a thorough English grounding and an appreciation of the value of simplicity and sincerity of expression. As founder of the Old Girls' Club[40] and the donor of numerous prizes she enriched the heritage of the School she served so long and so well.[41] As for new appointments, Miss Reid was present at interviews conducted by the Board when women from far and wide were appointed to be her colleagues. An early appointment was that of Miss Georgina Wishart (a friend of hers from Cheltenham)[42] as Principal's Assistant[43] and Principal Teacher of Classics. Miss Wishart had a genuine love of the Classics and a rare gift for imparting knowledge. Her interest in the junior girls and their teachers helped to bring the whole school together. Like Miss Reid she also was a pioneer in education, being one of the early women students of the University of London. Another appointment of 1906 was that of Miss Annie J. Arnott.[44] She proved a distinguished scholar, gaining a First Class Honours in Modern Languages from Glasgow University, and exhibited a deep knowledge and love of French language and culture, and the gift of poetic expression in her own tongue. Miss Margaret Robertson had been one of James Milligan's pupils from the age of ten, leaving the school in 1896 as the School Gold medallist[45] and becoming the first woman to achieve a First Class Honours in History at Glasgow, before returning to the Girls' High in 1908 as a teacher of History. She was an outstanding teacher, of whom countless Old Girls had fond memories. Mention 'Significances' and 'One, five, six and nothing for the Pope' (Miss Robertson's unique summing up of the Scottish Reformation) and they waxed eloquent about this wonderful woman who enlivened every History lesson with her enthusiasm and the ability to capture the interest of all her pupils.[46] One member of staff who taught History went on to make it. Mrs Helena Normanton,[47] barrister and feminist campaigner, was a member of staff from October 1913 to October 1915. She was one of the very first women called to the English Bar in November 1922, and also one of the very first females to be made a KC in 1949.

Ostensibly the Girls' High had a strict discipline regime but actual punishment was unusual, with no sanction beyond the hated 'Report to your Form Mistress'. A pupil of this time has written: 'The most lasting impression my schooldays have made on me was that we were disciplined. It may have been irksome at first, but latterly it troubled few of us, and I do not doubt now that we are all the better citizens because if it.' The Prospectus of 1914–15 deemed the experiment of 'self-government' a success,[48] with Form Captains the 'custodians of the honour of the Form' and prefects and monitors also elected.

Under Miss Reid the prospectus proclaimed the Girls' High a high-class secondary school preparing girls for home life and branches of work then open to women. With a teaching staff of thirty-five (twenty-six of whom were in the Senior School) it offered Classical, Modern or Scientific courses which met the requirements of Intermediate and Leaving Certificates. It was divided into three departments: a Prep, for girls aged five to seven, based on Froebel principles; a Junior School, where a timetable was introduced for girls from eight to twelve, taking them to the standard of the Qualifying Examination; and then Senior School, with girls leaving at sixteen to go into business, or eighteen if they were going on to university.

There were two Prep classes, and their curriculum included Scripture Reading, Writing, Arithmetic, Drawing, Nature Knowledge, Singing, Needlework, Drill and Games. In the Junior School under Miss Wishart, French was added in the lower stages[49] and Experimental Geometry and Physical Measurements at the higher stages. In the Senior School the curriculum was composed of English Language and Literature, Classics (Latin and Greek), Modern Languages (French and German), Mathematics (which included Geometry, Algebra, Trigonometry and Dynamics), Science (with Botany, Physics, Chemistry and Hygiene), Music (with Singing, Piano and Violin Instruction) and Commercial Subjects. Physical Education, given to all classes in the School, was based on calisthenics,[50] and each PE teacher had received training from Martina Bergman-Oesterberg.[51]

Gold medals were awarded for the Classical and Modern sides from 1898, but five years earlier Margaret Campbell gained the first school Gold Medal and also won a scholarship to Newnham College, Cambridge. Milligan had reacted to the latter by parading her round every room in the school so that all could share in, and be inspired by, her success. It was not long before Reid had another triumph to add to the growing list, for the achievement of boys from the High School coming first in the Glasgow University Bursary Competition was emulated in 1908 when Eleanor Donaldson[52] became the first woman (from 224 candidates) to do so. Despite this academic background Reid, however, placed emphasis on producing all-rounders, with hockey,[53] golf[54] and tennis the school sports, and basketball being taken by the younger girls. A Literary and Debating Club followed in 1909, and the first inter-school debate with the High School took place.[55] An increase in numbers, with the school roll hovering just under 1,000, may have been attributable to these achievements.

In the first year of World War I (1914–15) 1,000 articles, mainly khaki scarves and helmets, were knitted by the girls out of school hours. They decided they did not want prizes, and these were replaced by certificates: the money saved was given over to maintain a bed in the Scottish Military Hospital in Glasgow, while the staff maintained a bed in the Scottish Hospital at Rouen.

The first edition of the School magazine was produced in January 1920. It was a slim, grey-covered volume of twelve pages and had no photographs, illustrations or advertisements. However, it gave a snapshot of school life, mentioning the existence of an Art Club, the Literary and Dramatic Society, Hockey and Tennis Clubs, and the possibility of a dramatic society.

ALICE REID IN PERSPECTIVE

Alice Reid's appointment, as the first woman Principal, had been a significant event. In Scotland in the later nineteenth century the growth of secondary education offered more attractive careers to graduates, but Scottish universities were slower than some universities south of border with regard to the admission of women.[56] The path of women was further hindered by the predominance of mixed schools and, as there appeared no objection to girls being taught by men, the prestige of the graduate meant that men normally monopolised secondary headship posts.[57] Miss Reid, however, had graduated in England and came with unrivalled teacher training and experience. By the time she retired in March 1926, after twenty-one years in post, her influence had pervaded all aspects of School life.[58]

She had dealt well with the two considerable tasks which faced her on appointment. These were, first, to bring the curriculum of the Preparatory and Junior schools into more vital connection with the work of the Senior School; and, second, to make adjustments to the curriculum of Senior classes 1, 2 and 3, so as to meet more effectively the needs of those pupils who did not proceed beyond the Intermediate Certificate without prejudicing the claims of the pupils who went on to the full Leaving Certificate. Her introduction of a Form system and weekly Form Staff meetings ensured that she and her staff knew all the pupils well.[59] She set classroom standards by continuing to teach pupils in all Senior School years, and she visited classes each week for mark reading, in an uncanny way detecting the slackers and encouraging the workers. For the first time pupils were involved in the selection of prefects and monitors, giving them a share in school responsibilities. A Kindergarten was opened, while at the senior end a steady increase in Leaving Certificates was achieved. Following two fairs held in the School in June 1922 and June 1924, which raised £1,060 (toward the purchase of land) and £1,279 (for levelling, fencing and drainage of the land) respectively, the playing fields were opened at Kirklee.[60] And so a distinctive School developed, with strict discipline and the beginnings of a School uniform.

The only disappointment was that hopes for a new building were not to be realised in her time.[61] This, however, was not her fault, for she constantly stressed the inadequacies of the School's accommodation, a theme also taken up by HMI from 1911 onwards.[62] She also convinced the Education Authority, which began looking at every possible site for a new School; in January 1925 Shamrock Street and the Garnetbank School site were those being discussed.[63]

When Miss Reid intimated her forthcoming retirement, the Committee on Secondary Education decided by a 9–3 vote to invite applications for her post from women only.[64] Applicants were also to be below forty-five years of age and would be offered a salary of £1,000 per annum (less a 3 per cent deduction given the state of national public finances). Miss Georgina Wishart would carry on at the School until the end of session, which she did, and retired to Cheltenham[65] with Miss Reid.

Three non-teaching staff made their mark in the School at this time. Mr Grindlay went about his janitorial duties in a maroon long coat, while the groundsman at Kirklee, Mr Bain, was also a favourite. Miss Jessie Goodfellow joined the lunch room staff in 1912, and as corridor maid looked after the needs of the Principal and her staff until her retirement in 1946.

MRS FLORA TEBB: PRINCIPAL, 1926–1947

Following a good response to the adverts, some nine ladies were interviewed. All nine had degrees with First Class Honours. Five were employed in schools in England, while two were internal candidates: Annie Arnott, and Flora Tebb (née Ritchie),[66] who had only left the Girls' High after thirteen years' service a few months earlier to became Principal Teacher of Modern Languages in Bellahouston Academy. On 3 June 1926 a shortlist of three was interviewed by the EA, with thirty-four present, under Sir Charles Cleland. Flora Tebb was chosen unanimously over ladies from Manchester High School for Girls and North Kelvinside Secondary School.[67]

Flora Ritchie was born in June 1883 in Greenock. Her father was a minister so she was brought up in the manse in Greenock, then in Gourock. She was the eldest of four, with two sisters and a brother (who died of measles aged twelve), and was taught at home by her father, helped by girls from both France and Germany. She graduated with her First Class degree in French and German in April 1905 and seemingly had no immediate ambitions to become a teacher. She fell in love with and went out to the Far East to marry an accountant working for Jardine Matheson. They lived in Yokohama in Japan and then Tientsin in China; they had a young son and expected another addition in July 1912. However, in March of that year her husband was sent on business to Shanghai where he became unwell with typhoid fever. Although admitted to the European hospital he deteriorated and died; he was in his early thirties. This was a life-changing tragedy for Flora Tebb, who struggled home by boat in a journey which took over six weeks. In order to support her two small children, Dewar and Marion, she went into teaching. She always said she knew she would never remarry, as she would never find such happiness again, and so it was necessary for her to do as well as possible in her career so that she could pay to educate her children.[68]

To a great extent Mrs Tebb took up where Miss Reid left off. The HMI Report on her first full session held that 'under the tactful and kindly management of the new principal (Mrs Tebb) the work of the session has proceeded smoothly and steadily and has been attended with a gratifying amount of success. This A1 School is unhappily housed in C3 premises.'[69] Further reports praised her further: in 1928–9 'the supervision exercised by Mrs Tebb is characterised by marked ability, sympathy and discretion', and in 1932–3 'the Principal brings to bear on all school activities the influence of a gracious and cultured personality'.[70]

Mrs Tebb introduced a number of significant innovations in her time as Head. In session 1935–6 she founded the Parent–Teacher Association, which proved active and enthusiastic, and was one of the first to be formed in Glasgow.[71] The School Sports were started on 15 June 1928 at Old Anniesland. The fair held in April 1934 in the Gainsborough Halls, near Charing Cross, raised £2,251, which bought an additional hockey pitch and two more tennis courts at Kirklee,[72] also enabling the Pavilion to be extended and electric light and hot water to be installed. The School Song came into being, both words and music composed by Miss Annie Scott Gow, a member of the Mathematics department from 1913 till 1939, when she left pending her marriage to Dr King-Gillies of Edinburgh. A new School crest, whose four symbols – the lamp, the tree, Pegasus and Glasgow Cathedral[73] – combine to represent 'enlightenment through knowledge, culture and religion, to fit us for any enterprise', was designed by a former pupil, Miss Marguerite Benson. The Tower, a real crow's nest unsuitable as a classroom, was converted into a study for prefects. And after the war in 1945 she introduced the House system: four houses – Atholl, Douglas, Lochiel and Montrose – were formed, each with a House Mistress and a House Captain, and a distinguishing coloured badge. Inter-House rivalry gave a new impetus to school sports in particular.

A rich and varied school experience was offered to the girls. The school regularly fielded six Hockey XIs,[74] tennis, badminton[75] and swimming teams,[76] while country dancing and an outdoor club gained support at times. Other clubs operating more consistently over the years were debating,[77] literary and dramatic, music, United Nations[78] and Scripture Union. 'Special Efforts Weeks' raised money for many charities, while a number of girls regularly helped on a Saturday morning in the YWCA Play Centre. School trips took Senior girls to Paris, Geneva and Canada; visits to film shows, concerts and lectures, such as that given by 'Grey Owl' in the Lyric Theatre, were not infrequent, as were interesting visitors to the School, who widened horizons and stimulated interest in many and varied topics, thus bearing out the truth of the school motto, 'Non schola, sed vitae discimus'.[79]

Certain characteristics stand out as far as the teaching staff was concerned during this period, namely the number of Former Pupils who were appointed to its complement, the loyalty of so many who spent a large part of their career at the School, and the close relationship that existed between the staff individually and collectively with Mrs Tebb. Miss Christina Aitken had been the Modern Medallist at the School in 1909, and after taking a brilliant First in French and German she joined the staff before her promotion to Head of Modern Languages at Jordanhill School (then Hillhead HS).[80] She was also secretary of the Old Girls' Club. Miss Hope Primrose, also a Former Pupil, joined the Classics department and was important in the development of the library before going on to Laurel Bank. Indicative of a different age is the fact that at least seventeen members of staff each gave over twenty years' service to the School, and of that number eight remained for thirty or more years.[81] In June 1938 Miss Muir retired, having worked under Milligan, Reid and Tebb. She was followed by Margaret Gorrie of Mathematics, who spent thirty-two years on the staff, and Elizabeth McNabb, who joined as Miss Wishart's replacement as Head of Classics in 1926, and then by Miss Bertha Murray, who left after twenty-three years' service to become Head of English at Hamilton Crescent Junior Secondary.

The achievements of the Old Girls multiplied in this period. In 1923, Isobel Guthrie became the first woman CA in Scotland; in 1924, at the Art School, the Newberry Medal for highest distinction in the diploma examination was won by Nancy McCrechie. In 1925, Muriel Jeffrey was elected the only woman member of the Faculty of Procurators; in 1926, the Brunton medal prize for the most distinguished medic at Glasgow University was won, for the first time, by a female – Janet Niven – and in 1934 it was won by Margaret Green. In the Faculty of Arts, the Herkness Prize for the most distinguished graduate was won by Grace Robertson[82] in 1928, May Flint in 1929, Annie Robertson and Mary Langwell[83] (shared) in 1933 and Margaret McArthur in 1934. Mary Langwell went on to join the Inland Revenue department after taking first place in the Higher Civil Service Examinations.

WORLD WAR II

At the beginning of World War II the Girls' High suffered greatly through the withdrawal of pupils to attend schools outside Glasgow and nearer their homes. To combat this, the school introduced home education for classes 4 and 5, and this idea became so widespread and popular that the Senior School was opened for full-time instruction on 14 November 1939, following the completion of air raid shelters. Two girls, who were visiting Canada that summer, had to wait till the development of a convoy system before they could start for home in November. Meantime, with girls evacuated by their parents throughout Scotland, a number of staff were attached to schools in Reception Areas. Largely because of the black-out school clubs, with the exception of hockey,[84] did not function in session 1939–40.

By 1940 a degree of normality had returned and some clubs resumed, but the annual Sports Day and Parents' Day did not take place. In May, the staff entertained a detachment of Chasseurs Alpins then billeted in the McLellan Galleries. Hospitality included a meal and a concert with music by both visitors and the visited. Prizegiving was held as usual at the end of June in the High School hall, but the School stayed open during the summer months. Although attendance was low, some girls and staff helped the Red Cross by patiently picking sphagnum moss for use in wound dressings. Gas mask drill took place in the classroom, girls finding amusement in producing a terrible noise by laughing into the mask. Air raids during school hours required girls to grab coats and gas masks and hurry down to the sand-bagged cloakroom to await the 'All Clear'. Raids at night were on the whole longer and more frequent – the longer the better for the schoolgirl, as a delayed 'All Clear' legitimately postponed the time of her arrival at school next morning. These interruptions, along with changes in school hours and, later, in staff, who were required to spend time away, inevitably brought added burdens to Mrs Tebb and senior staff, but they appeared to cope with remarkable calm and a noticeable esprit de corps.

The bombing raids on Clydeside touched the school very closely, as the 'Blitz' in March 1941 claimed the lives of two High School girls. Kathleen Blake, of Fifth Year, died with her mother and two brothers while her father was out doing his duties as an Air Raid Warden, and Shirley Cameron of Primary 7 was killed along with her mother and father. These deaths occurred on the same night under the one roof. Following these events arrangements were made for a school country section. On Saturday 3 May

1941, at Buchanan Street Railway Station, eighty-one girls with staff boarded the train for Pitlochry en route for Bonskeid House, home of the Barbour family. December saw the departure of thirty juniors to their temporary home at Faskally. It was only when they had all returned in early 1944 that the school became busier and livelier again.

The girls contributed in a number of ways to the war effort. Two joint concerts with the High School raised money for the Red Cross: £100 in 1942 and £150 the following year. On a regular basis money was raised through the War Savings Association which in total, by May 1945, had produced £17,000 for war savings. Weekly contributions to a Wool Fund were used to buy wool for the busy band of knitters. As well as woollen comforts, books and magazines were sent to merchant seamen, while Christmas parcels went to the Merchant Navy and to the men in trawlers. The girls adopted a ship, the tanker *British Courage*. Sphagnum moss was brought in and silver paper collected. It was also in wartime that the decision was made that Glasgow schools should change their holiday dates to suit the fruit-picking and harvesting seasons. This meant the session beginning in early August with a month's break from mid-September to mid-October.[85] Berry-picking camps took place in 1942 at Essendy, near Blairgowrie, and in 1944 near Alyth. At one farm the berries were unfit for eating, and instead they were to be used to make dye for Forces' uniforms, which made the girls feel they were really helping the war effort.

During the war, from 1942 to 1945, Katharine Lyall (Whitehorn) was a pupil. She recently gave the Girls' High a glowing tribute in her autobiography.[86] Before coming to Glasgow she had experienced very unhappy schooling, but it only took two days before she made friends and began three 'super' years at Glasgow. Miss Ethel Barlow, her Form Mistress, who taught English and History, was 'a woman of elegance and a fantastic teacher'. Miss Barlow had herself been a pupil in the School, and after teaching experience in Cambridge and St Leonard's she joined the Girls' High staff in 1929.[87] Miss Margaret Robertson, who also taught History, was 'a formidable lady with a grey bun' who, being ambidextrous, 'used to amaze her class by starting a sentence on the blackboard with her left hand and continuing the other half with her right'. She was Head of the Department and had also been a pupil at the School (from the age of ten). She retired in 1945. Other members of staff recalled by Miss Whitehorn were 'a loopy eccentric called Miss Meldrum' who taught Art and the 'appalling Miss Morrison' who taught Mathematics. Although claiming not to be good at academic subjects, Whitehorn gained a creditable Leaving Certificate with

Higher English and Art, and Lower Mathematics, French and History. After a previously unhappy educational experience, 'Scottish kindness, Scottish good sense and a sound, traditional uncompromising untrendy Scottish education were dead right for me and I spent three happy years there.'[88]

The School celebrated its 50th Anniversary in 1944, and on 16 June a Commemoration Service was held in Glasgow Cathedral. The Right Rev. Dr E.J. Hagan, Moderator of the General Assembly of the Church of Scotland, conducted the service, assisted by Rev. Dr Neville Davidson of the Cathedral, the Rev. Professor J.G. Riddell of Glasgow University, and the Rev. William J. Baxter of Dowanhill Church. Mrs Tebb and the School Captain, Mary Kellock, also participated. In the evening a reunion of the Old Girls' Club was held in the school. A Jubilee Fund was set up by staff, parents, and past and present pupils combined in order to fund a University Bursary, and the target of £1,050 was raised by June 1945.[89]

After two days' holiday to celebrate the end of the war in Europe, the two High Schools held a joint service of thanksgiving in Wellington Church on 10 May 1945.[90] The service was conducted by Professor Riddell, the lessons were read by the Captains of the two schools, and Dr Jarvis, School Chaplain, gave the address. There was no doubt an even more special bond between those pupils who lived together through 'the war years of strain, anxiety and difficulty'.[91] It probably explains the remarkable fact that twenty-one of those who left school in 1946 were reunited in 1996 to celebrate their own Jubilee.

In 1944 Miss M.P. Ewing left to become headmistress at Morrison's, Crieff.[92] She had been Classical Medallist at the school in 1917 before going on to gain a First Class Honours in Classics at university, then teaching at Manchester High School for Girls (1921–4) and subsequently at the Girls' High as Assistant (1924–41) then Principal Teacher (1941–4). The end of the war saw a number of retirements, including Miss M.E. Thomson, who had been teaching since 1907, and Miss Elaine Macdonald,[93] who had spent fifteen years in the English department. She had been a double Gold Medallist at the Girls' High, being Modern Dux in 1900 and Classical Dux in 1901, and gained four class prizes at Glasgow University before gaining First Class Honours in English in 1907. She had been highly successful in preparing her pupils for the Glasgow Bursary competition.

The following year, in 1946, they were followed into retirement by Vice-Principal Annie Arnott; Miss Renwick, who had been head of the English Department for twenty years; and another former pupil, Miss Mina Walker, who had joined the Latin staff in 1916. Also in 1946 Mrs Muriel (Tully)

Calder, another ex-pupil who had been Dux and Modern Medallist and who had been a member of staff since 1923,[94] was promoted to Head of Science, while in 1947 Elizabeth MacDougall, another past pupil, who had been on the staff for twenty years, was promoted to PT Science at Pollokshields Secondary School.

According to the HMI Mrs Tebb had proved 'sympathetic, gracious and discriminating' and 'had guided the School with conspicuous success'. With the demand for places high – with an average roll in Kindergarten and Junior School of 514, and 566 in the Senior School – Mrs Tebb determined to retire at the end of the 1946–7 school session. The HMI continued the plaudits: 'The admirable tone and sound attainment of the school during her period of office were in no small measure due to her fine personality and to her wise and sympathetic direction.'[95] She was popular, helped by a legendary memory for names. She was warm and sincere, unassuming and approachable, and her teaching was scholarly and effective. She was given respect and won admiration and affection. Throughout her long retirement many old girls and staff communicated with her regularly. She was often accosted in the street by Former Pupils, who would always make complimentary comments about their time in school. All in all she proved a truly remarkable leader. She was elected Fellow of the Educational Institute of Scotland in 1946. Her achievements were noted by Glasgow University which, in 1949, awarded her an honorary LLD degree. Between 1946 and 1948 she was a member of the University Court.[96] She remained interested in education and the School until her death, aged 93, in a nursing home in London in February 1976.[97]

The only blot on her record was the continuing scandal of accommodation. When Mrs Tebb was appointed she was probably heartened by the then Education Authority's attempts to deal with the problem. In 1930, when the local government structure changed, it seemed that the newly created Glasgow Corporation understood the urgency, and early on it placed the issue on its agenda.[98] A Corporation Committee was set up to find suitable accommodation; it met on 9 December 1930, and on 27 and 30 January, 24 April and 5 June 1931, but no progress was made. Only when a special committee was set up in April 1933, and following visits to further possible sites, was a recommendation forthcoming on 7 March 1934 that a new Girls' High be built at Cleveden Road. This was accepted by the Education Committee on 12 April 1934. Matters seemed to be gathering pace, for on 15 February 1935 it was agreed that Bailies Biggar and Symington and education officials should visit schools in Scotland and England to obtain information on the latest accommodation and equipment needed. Almost as an afterthought the Property Sub-Committee of the Corporation agreed by four votes to three to allow Mrs Tebb to visit Bolton to do likewise.[99] By February 1936 the plans for a new School had been agreed at sub-committee level, and land adjacent to the site had been bought by the Corporation.[100] But the immediate result was that the girls had to soldier on in an unsavoury part of town.

When Mrs Tebb informed the Corporation's Education Committee that she would be retiring, it set up a sub-committee, chaired by Councillor Hood, which determined that applications for her post would be sought from members of the Corporation's teaching staff, not over fifty-five years of age, who possessed First or Second Class Honours degrees. As there were thirteen applications it was decided that all should be interviewed, and on 16 June 1947 Frances Barker, PT Modern Languages at Jordanhill School, was recommended to the Education Committee, which accepted the decision by 20–2 on 27 June.[101]

FRANCES BARKER: PRINCIPAL, 1947–1969

Frances Barker was Dux of Hyndland Secondary School in 1919 and won prizes in French and German at Glasgow University. She studied abroad at Heidelberg, the Sorbonne, Grenoble and Strasbourg and completed a First Class Honours degree in French and German. Her postgraduate teacher training took place in Glasgow and she taught Modern Languages at Bellahouston Secondary (1924–43) and then at Hutchesons' Girls' School.

Despite her strong academic record, things did not go well from the very beginning. She did not hit it off with a number of the older, more conservative staff, who were steeped in the traditions of the Girls' High and would rather leave or retire than accept changes they felt were not wanted nor needed, introduced by someone they did not like nor respect. Deputy Head Miss Elizabeth Morrison, who had been an outstanding student, gaining a First Class Honours in Mathematics and Natural Philosophy and the Ewing Scholarship, retired after twenty-one years as Head of Mathematics but only one as Deputy. Miss Jessie Robertson, a Former Pupil, in charge of the Kindergarten, left for Laurel Bank. They were followed by the retirement of Miss Adeline Bate, who had joined the staff in 1910 and served for fourteen years as Head of Science; Dorothy Ritchie, after twenty years in the French department; and Miss Liston of Art.

Within eighteen months of Miss Barker's appointment, following press reports of disharmony on the staff of the School, and following consultations between the Director of Education,[102] Miss Barker and some staff, the matter was given over to the standing sub-committee of Teachers and Teaching for consideration and recommendation.[103] It met on 12 January 1949 and examined the relations between the Principal and staff since her appointment on 1 September 1947, which had reached a nadir on 3 December 1948 when senior pupils had been assembled by the Principal in an investigation into the alleged loss of a purse. The sub-committee decided to interview the Principal and certain members of staff in an attempt to pinpoint the reasons for the strained relationships, in the belief that the exercise of common-sense and goodwill on both sides would clear up matters.[104] This was done on 28 February at the School, with the pupils being given a half-holiday.[105]

On 19 March 1949 the sub-committee asked the Director, Treasurer Hood and Councillor Scanlan to see what they could do to reconcile the parties, and asked for a report on progress by the end of session. This decision was remitted to the full Education Committee for approval and this was forthcoming, but only by twenty-four votes to twenty, as a significant group wanted a special committee of enquiry with a legal assessor to deal with the impasse.[106] By this time the parents had determined to discuss the situation, and 500 attended a meeting on 30 March, passing a resolution calling for an immediate independent enquiry into the state of tension in the School and the detrimental effects this was having on pupils' education. Parents alleged that discipline had suffered and that all the prefects except one had resigned. Parents of Sixth Formers expressed dissatisfaction with pupil reports, some of which had no good conduct marks. The meeting appointed a committee of twelve to continue to watch over the interests of parents, and if necessary to call another meeting. The Education Committee agreed to hear three representatives from this parents' committee at the city chambers on 6 April.[107] Unfortunately, this private meeting seemed to get nowhere.[108]

Appreciating the growing impatience of councillors the Director and Scanlan reported that they had begun weekly visits to the School to discuss ongoing management matters. If anything, however, things seemed to be worsening rather than improving. Since December, there had been further incidents, resulting in staff protests over measures being taken by a seemingly unrepentant Principal. It seemed to Councillor Warren at least that, with the unrest among staff, pupils and parents the reputation of the School was being seriously harmed and the corporate life of the School was at a standstill.[109]

Nonetheless, it was decided to go ahead with these regular visits.

Faced with this situation, after a three-hour meeting on 22 June, the sub-committee on Teachers and Teaching, supported by Bailie Donaldson, chair of the Education Committee, pressed for an advocate to be appointed to begin a formal inquiry into events at the School. This motion was agreed 7–5. However, two days later, this was reversed by the full Education Committee by 23 to 21, in favour of a motion allowing the Director to continue his lower key efforts at reconciliation[110] and giving him until the end of the year to improve matters. The parents were totally dissatisfied with this 'incomprehensible' decision, pressing instead for 'decisive action'.[111] Within a week 300 parents had attended a special meeting and, with only three dissenting, decided on a direct approach to the Secretary of State with a request for an immediate local enquiry under the Education (Scotland) Act, 1936. They demanded the end of 'procrastination'. However, Secretary of State Woodburn declined their request, believing it was better to leave the matter in the hands of the educational authority.[112] The parents had no alternative than to continue to monitor matters.

Between June and December 1949 fortnightly visits to the School were made, and on all these occasions Miss Barker was interviewed. The heads of department were seen as a group twice and the assistant teachers were seen once. It was reported that during this time that a School Captain, Vice-Captain and fourteen prefects had been appointed, and that the School Finance Committee had been reconstituted and was operating. Such improvements were welcomed, although the situation was deemed not yet wholly satisfactory. The Education Committee agreed to continue the visiting arrangement until Easter 1950, with more meetings with staff involvement.[113]

On 31 March, although 'it could not be claimed that harmony had been restored', it was agreed that as sufficient progress had been made the regular visits of the Director could now be scaled down, with a view to ending at the close of the school session.[114] By then Dr Mackintosh had visited another five times, reporting that despite improvements, and the efforts of staff, the School still did not have 'the same atmosphere which you would expect to find at other secondary schools in the city'.[115] Nonetheless, on 3 July 1950 he recommended that 'the stage had been reached that special regular visitations . . . could be discontinued'. The Education Committee agreed.[116] By this time Miss Margaret Fraser, the longest-serving member of staff, had retired, and Miss Mary McLean, after twenty-three years service, had gone to Govan High School.

It is clear that the relationship between Miss Barker and her staff never fully recovered from the disputes of her early years in office. The continuing open criticism of the Principal by a section of staff continued to affect the views of parents and even the girls themselves, who saw her as a distant, strict authority figure to be feared rather than approached. Even Head Girls in their one-to-one meetings with Miss Barker, and those involved in School Council or prefect meetings, viewed her as someone who commanded respect rather than affection. She resided in an inner office that seemed to keep the rest of the world out with a plush velvet curtain draped over the door. Her aloofness was the more obvious to the whole School community, because her predecessor had proved such a remarkable and humane leader. Fortunately, in Miss Jean McCulloch, the Deputy Head and Head of Classics, the girls had someone to turn to. She had had a glittering career at Glasgow University, winning the Blackstone Gold Medal and Herkless Prize for the most distinguished woman graduate of her year. Tiny, with hair pulled back in a bun, her spectacles on the end of her nose, and often wearing spats, she came to be loved. She retired in June 1963 and was succeeded by Miss Jane Crawford, Head of English, as Vice-Principal.

Over time, changes in the staff complement became fewer. In 1951 Agnes W. Thomson, who had joined the Music staff in 1925, retired, along with Elizabeth Stewart, who had been a member of the English department since 1930; while the following year Miss Margaret I. Cranston, after spending thirty-five years teaching Mathematics, followed suit. There then followed a hiatus until 1955, when Miss Margaret W. Sime retired after a lifetime of service teaching Biology, as did Miss Helen S. Ross, who had been Head of the English department since 1946. Then in 1956 Miss Elizabeth Marshall did likewise: she joined the Mathematics department as a temporary appointment in 1919 but had so impressed that she was transferred to the Junior School, where she spent her working life. Two years later, in 1958, Miss Lilias ('Gubby') McGregor retired. She had gained a First Class Honours in Mathematics and Natural Philosophy, and taught at the Girls' High between 1921 and 1945 as an Assistant and between 1948 until 1958 as Principal Teacher of Mathematics. She was also talented musically. A Former Pupil, Miss Mary G. Kerr joined the Mathematics staff in 1945, was Housemistress of Lochiel (1948–57), and left in 1958 to become PT at Strathbungo Secondary School. In 1959 Miss Muriel Calder, Head of Science, retired,[117] to be followed the next year by Miss Anne C. Cameron, who had been appointed to take charge of the Commercial department in

1923 (and had been seconded by the Corporation between 1940–3 to found and develop the Youth Service Panels).

Jeanie Russell had been appointed the first Infant mistress in the history of the School in August 1948, but as a result of a change in Glasgow's educational policy, she was also destined to be the last. She had overseen the expansion of the Kindergarten, but it was closed at the end of session 1963–4 and Miss Russell was redeployed in the Music department. The upside of this helped increase musical activity in the School, which Miss Barker was very keen to achieve but, worryingly, the loss of the Kindergarten saw the beginnings of change in the nature and composition of the School.

The curriculum of the Primary School remained very traditional, with an emphasis on English and Mathematics. There was no sport, only PE, and no foreign languages.[118] Teaching methods were also traditional, with few outings, and all homework written into a homework diary, which was expected to be checked and signed every evening by a parent. There was a definite division between primary and secondary, and a closed door in the corridor emphasised the differentiation.

The curriculum in the Senior School became somewhat rigid, with a second language (Latin or German) offered to about half the year group, with the other half taking Home Economics in a separate building in Renfrew Street. Generally girls would study English, Mathematics, French, History (or Geography) and Science.[119] Careers advice was limited, as it was assumed that most girls, if able, would attend Glasgow University, it being left to the individual to work out what was required for which course. Some girls left after attaining a Third Year certificate to go to secretarial college (Skerry's), and a number after Fifth Year to university or college if they had the entry grades. However, many girls completed a Sixth Year to top up their Higher group. A few of these attended an advanced Mathematics class with Peter Whyte at Elmbank Street, but most of them struggled, perhaps because they hitherto had been taught to satisfy the examination syllabus and were not used to being stretched academically.

By session 1960–1 the School was affected by the national shortage of teachers, especially in the areas of Mathematics, Science and Physical Education. The Corporation agreed that the School could, in the short term at least, end the voluntary games programmes for girls in Senior 4, 5 and 6, and this was replaced by instruction in academic subjects and in hygiene. The disappointment and seeming downgrading of physical activity in the curriculum helped persuade Miss Joanna Loudon to retire. She had arrived in 1926 as an assistant in Gym, having graduated from Dartmouth College, then under the direction of Madame Bergman Osterberg, whose leadership and inspiration marked the beginnings of all later Colleges of Physical Training for women in Britain. She was on the staff from 1926 till 1933, returning in 1945 as the formidable Principal Teacher, feared by many of the girls. It was only at the beginning of session 1962–3, with the arrival of two new PE staff, that all physical activities were resumed.

The senior girls made their own way to Kirklee on Games afternoons. However, if it was wet there was no practice. Even on Saturdays games seemed to have been cancelled at the first sign of bad weather. Perhaps this was because there were no showers in the wooden Pavilion and only two toilets, and the fact that girls had to go home on public transport, some a considerable distance. No alternative arrangements were made, and girls would often be found in Coplands or Dalys having afternoon tea if hockey practice was cancelled. In summer, tennis was the main sport but there was a limited amount of coaching. A little athletics took place thanks to the younger staff who took an interest. Some girls did participate in Glasgow schools' competitions, but the successful ones were usually members of an outside athletics club. Meantime, the funds of the school's own athletic club (dating from the mid-1920s) ran out about 1960 and it was left to the EA to maintain the fields.

Girls took part in a limited number of trips for music, hockey and art camps at Castle Toward. Miss Barker introduced fencing, but as all the equipment and coaching was expensive, it was a sport for the minority rather than the whole school. Nonetheless, the standard reached was high and several girls went on to become Scottish internationalists.[120] Her other great success was progress on the long-promised new accommodation. No one had a good word for the buildings, which had nothing to commend them. The basement classrooms in Junior School were very dark and in some cases through-going, which meant constant disruption to classwork. Milk deliveries were left at the Buccleuch Street entrance and empty bottles were stored there until the uplift the following day. With no fridges, in warm weather milk often went 'off' and the area had a terrible aroma. There were only a few places which could be described as bright and cheery. The classrooms had high ceilings and were gloomy as were the corridors. As the building had been erected on a hill and faced north, there was no sense of light. At least Miss Barker had the backing of the whole school in a campaign for an improved environment. After January 1960 the support of the Parent–Teacher Association was particularly helpful on the issue, as it formed a sub-committee which twice met the Director of Education, Dr H.

Stewart Mackintosh, to impress on him the urgency of the buildings problem. Ultimately, the decision was made in 1965 to go ahead with the accommodation at Cleveden, and this led to work being started on the new School.

The building cost £521,000 and accommodated 670 girls. During the last week of June 1968 there was an exodus to the new site at 42 Cleveden Road, which was officially opened on 26 August. For the girls who moved from the dark, rambling buildings of Garnethill overlooking the Beatson Hospital to the leafy West End suburbs with town houses and Westbourne as neighbours, there was a tangible feel-good factor. The facilities were first class, with a new gym, games hall and swimming pool. The eight science labs were well-equipped and very roomy. The assembly hall, dining hall and cafeteria were modern, and all were designed to have an impact on the curriculum that could be offered, including a language laboratory of a standard that allowed oral examinations in modern languages. Moreover, all facilities were on site, so there was no longer the need to go halfway down Garnethill for Home Economics or lunch. And the layout of the buildings seemed logical, ensuring departments were to be found easily, unlike the complex intertwining staircases of the old building which had led to different places. Even the playing fields were more easily accessed.

Miss Barker lived with her unmarried sister, Dorothy, in Bearsden. Dorothy Barker attended many school events, always immaculately dressed and in a position of importance at her sister's side. Her support must have been important, for the general impression remains of a Principal who communicated little with her staff, a number of whom seemed to have scant respect for her and indeed in some cases seemed positively antagonistic towards her. Despite this many girls found School a very positive experience, and they were happy and enjoyed their time at Garnethill. Yet the School was narrow in outlook, and the girls followed instructions and learned what they were told to learn and little more. Many of them found university a shock, as they realised how ill-prepared they were for a world in which they had to think for themselves.

The move to the new School had been keenly awaited by generations of girls, and for those involved in 1968 it seemed a dream come true. Miss Barker, too, could now think of retiring. However, before she left, debate had turned to the topics of fee-paying and selection.

MISS HELEN JAMIESON:
THE LAST PRINCIPAL, 1970–1976

Helen Jamieson joined the staff of the Girls' High in 1947 as a non-graduate teacher in the Primary department. She had qualified from Jordanhill Training College but was in the process of studying as an external student for a degree from London University. Nursing an ill mother and having a full-time job meant long hours of study well into the night. However, much to her credit, Miss Jamieson successfully gained an Honours degree in Geography and subsequently she was appointed to the Geography department of the School, where she spent three years. She then moved to become first a lecturer at Jordanhill College and then Head of the Geography department there. In 1963 she became Principal of the Women's Teaching Centre in Aden, returning home in 1969 to become Principal Teacher of Geography at Allan Glen's School, the first woman to hold this post. The following year in October 1970 she was appointed the fifth Principal of the Girls' High.

Her Vice-Principal, Katherine M. Black, who had joined the staff in October 1962 as Head of Classics, was known for her administrative ability, which included preparation for examinations and prizegiving. Mrs Joyce Lindsay, wife of Maurice Lindsay, poet, broadcaster and cultural historian, joined the English department in 1968. Together with Miss Morven Cameron, who was Head of Department, a very effective and inspiring teaching duo was formed. Both were talented and moved in academic circles that included Norman McCaig, and this brought richness to the whole experience of being taught by them. An anthology, *The Scottish Dog*, was edited by the Lindsays and contained a number of detailed drawings by Morven Cameron, demonstrating the range of interest of these remarkable women.

Miss Elizabeth Bennett was a member of the Modern Languages department; she left in 1967 to get married at Glasgow University Chapel. A number of her pupils, especially her form class, went along and took photographs. It was not until 1994, on the death of John Smith, leader of the Labour Party, that a number of them realised he had been the groom at that wedding and that their former French teacher was Baroness Smith of Gilmorehill.

The decision of the Education Committee to abolish selection led to uproar. In the case of the Girls' High the change meant the removal of the First and Second-Year pupils to their local schools in September 1972, the existing Third-Year pupils were not to be allowed to complete a Sixth Year in the School, and the intake of local children was to begin in session 1972–3. The School joined other selective schools in presenting their views to the Committee on 28 February 1972. The Old Girls' Club, led by Mrs Nancy Davidson and Mrs Isa Cowan, vigorously attacked, in particular, the proposal to transfer the First and Second Year pupils elsewhere in the middle of their school careers.

On 21 March, 1973 the School's name was changed to Cleveden Secondary, and a year at a time it became a co-educational school, the last High girls leaving five years later. However, although diminishing each year they stamped their traditions on the new comprehensive. Miss Jamieson paid tribute to them, saying that much was demanded from them, for not only were they learners they were also educators. It has been noted elsewhere the ironic circumstance that in 1894, when Dr Milligan started to withdraw the boys from his hoped-for Girls' High, many of his boys were sent to Albany Academy, whose headmaster was a Mr Jamieson. It was to be his grand-daughter who received young boys into her Girls' School in the 1970s.

Miss Jamieson is remembered fondly. She proved a sociable person and worked hard to maintain staff morale in the new and challenging circumstances. As the last selective cohort of girls moved through the school, it was followed by a mixed comprehensive year group. The school motto was no more, but the new school badge for Cleveden bore a very close resemblance to that of the Girls' High. A new technical department had to be created in the playground, boys' sports had to be catered for, and other adjustments had to be made around the School both in facilities and staffing. Having completed the process of change Miss Jamieson retired in 1980 to live with her sister in Killearn.

PUPILS

Mary Agnes Hamilton (1882–1966) gained an open entrance scholarship to Newnham College, Cambridge; became Labour MP for Blackburn, 1929–31; British delegate to the League of Nations Assembly 1929 and 1930; Parliamentary Secretary to the Postmaster General; Governor of the BBC, 1933–7; an alderman of London CC, 1937–40; and a civil servant, 1940–52. She wrote biographies, including *Sidney and Beatrice Webb* (1933) and *Arthur Henderson* (1938).

Catherine Roy (1883–1976) was a nurse in World War I. She was Matron-in-Chief, Queen Alexandra's Nursing Service, 1938–40.

Mary Sturrock (1892–1985) was the daughter of the director of the Glasgow School of Art in Garnethill. She was influenced by her family's friendship with Charles Rennie Mackintosh. She was a member of the Edinburgh Group of painters which exhibited before and after the First World War.

Annie Dunlop (1897–1973) was a historical researcher who worked in the Scottish Record Office, 1934–8 and taught History at Edinburgh University, 1942–8.

Lady (Dr) (May Deans Tennant) Baird (1901–1983) was Gold Medallist at the School in 1918. She was involved with social and local government work, 1938–54. She chaired the North-East Regional Hospital Board (Scotland) 1947–66. She was given the Freedom of the City of Aberdeen, 1966 and was a National Governor of the BBC in Scotland, 1967–70.

Mary Carson (1902–1993) took a degree at Glasgow in 1925, then became editor of the *Scots Observer*. She was women's feature editor of the *Glasgow Herald* (under the pen name Jean Kelvin), 1931–62.

Bessie Johnston (née Hourston) (1905–1998) was an honorary life member of the Glasgow branch of the British Red Cross. She gained an MBE and the title 'Scotswoman of Year'. She was President of the Old Girls' in 1970.

Margaret Brodie (1907–1996) attended the Glasgow School of Architecture. She was the site architect for the Glasgow Empire Exhibition in 1938 in Bellahouston Park. She had a teaching post at the School of Architecture.

Helen Highet (née McInnes) (1907–1985) was the daughter of a Glasgow foreman joiner. She attended for a year at the Girls' High and gained a degree in French and German in 1928 and a diploma in librarianship from London in 1931. She moved to Oxford when her husband became a don there and to New York permanently in 1938 when he became Professor of Classics at Columbia University. Her first novel, *Above Suspicion*, was published in 1941 and made into a film starring Joan Crawford and Fred MacMurray in 1943. In total, 'the Queen of Spy Writers' wrote twenty-one novels, which had sold 23 million copies by 1985.[121] Several more of her books were made into films and she won a number of awards.

(Prof.) Anne Robertson (1910–1997) left the High School in 1928 and gained First Class degrees at Glasgow and London. She became a lecturer and reader in Archaeology, 1939–74, and titular Professor of Roman Archaeology, Glasgow University, 1974–5.

Isa Cowan (née McGhie) (1912–1996) gained an Honours degree in

Classics. She proved a remarkable and loyal Secretary of the Old Girls' Club from 1957 until 1992, when she became Honorary President.

(Lt-Col.) Muriel Gibson (1912–2005) was commissioned in the WRAC and served in Africa, Germany and Italy, being mentioned in despatches. A nationalist since 1932, she served as administrative Secretary of the SNP and stood as a candidate in 1970. She was also secretary of the Royal Scottish Country Dance Society and Russian Ballet Society.

(Dr) Eileen Wybar (1915–1989) graduated in medicine from Glasgow and gained an MD for her work on bone marrow. She became Assistant MO for Jordanhill College, and Principal MO for Hamilton College. She was active in the Girl Guide Movement, was President of the Old Girls' Club in 1983 and a Trustee of the new High School.

Martha Arnott (née Grant) (1916–1997) was a dancer, therapist and teacher in the Margaret Morris movement.

Jean Walker (1917–2006) was a teacher of speech and drama. She was appointed to teach young offenders (aged seventeen to twenty-one) in Barlinnie prison.

Agnes Thomson (1918–2008) was a trained physiotherapist. She was responsible for setting up the Philemon Housing Association in her campaign against homelessness and poverty.

 (Dr) Sheenah Russell (1920–2007) was Modern Dux at School in 1937 and went on to win the class medal in clinical medicine at Glasgow. She was the first full-time consultant paediatrician in Dumfries and Galloway Royal Infirmary, and was a fellow of the Royal College of Physicians, Edinburgh.

Anne Smallwood (1922–2002) joined the Inland Revenue in 1943, becoming Under-Secretary, Inland Revenue, 1971–3 and Commissioner of the Board of Inland Revenue, 1973–81.

(Dr) Elizabeth McHarg (1923–1999) gained a First Class Honours in Mathematics and Natural Philosphy at Glasgow University and a PhD from Cambridge University. She held the posts of lecturer and senior lecturer in Mathematics at Glasgow University.

Mary Sherrard (née Stiven)[122] (b. 1923) was a journalist, involved with the WRNS. From 1942 she worked on cracking German codes at Bletchley Park.[123] She was National President, Women's Guild, Church of Scotland, 1993–6 and Representative on the Women's National Commission, 1993–8.

Marion Smith (b. 1923) trained as a nurse in Edinburgh during World War II. She completed her midwifery training in London and remained at Queen Charlotte's hospital as a staff midwife. Following a time as theatre sister in Edinburgh she returned to Glasgow in 1952 and spent thirty-two years at Canniesburn Hospital. Active in the Women's Guild, she was a Trustee of the National Trust, President of the Old Girls' Club in 1975 and a Director of the High School (1979–93).

Nancy Davidson (née Morrison) (1924–1988) attended the High School 1929–42 before completing a degree and teacher training. She taught speech training and joined the Jordanhill College staff as lecturer and adviser. She was President of the High School Old Girls' in 1972 and a Director of the High School.

(Dr) Margaret Kerr (1924–2010) graduated in medicine from Glasgow University in 1948. She became a pioneer in neonatology and spent most of her career in the west of Scotland. She was elected a Fellow of the Royal College of Physicians and Surgeons of Glasgow in 1981, and her achievements gained wider recognition when she was elected Scotswoman of the Year in 1982.

Rena Watt (1924–2007) had a series of appointments as a Mathematics teacher before becoming Head Teacher of Kingsridge Secondary School in Drumchapel in 1974. She was the first female Head Teacher of a comprehensive school in Scotland. She later became Head Teacher of Bannerman High School.

Marjorie Bosomworth (b. 1928) was Dux of the School in 1945. She taught in Glasgow and Hamilton and was Warden of the Girls' Hostel in Golspie before becoming the headmistress of St Margaret's School, Aberdeen in 1970. She was in the first group of female burgesses appointed by Aberdeen City in 1983.

Katharine Lyall (née Whitehorn) (b. 1929) was a columnist on the *Observer*, 1960–96 (being Associate Editor 1980–8). She became the agony aunt of *Saga Magazine*, 1997 and wrote her autobiography, *Selective Memory* (2007).

Margaret Auld (b. 1932) was a hospital staff midwife, sister, assistant matron, and matron, 1955–73. She became Chief Nursing Officer, Borders, 1973–6; then Chief Nursing Officer, Scottish Home and Health Department, 1977–88.

Judith Tankel (née Wolfson) (1934–2006)[124] was honorary social worker to the Glasgow Jewish Welfare Board. She became a marriage guidance counsellor and was a member of the Children's Panel. She became the first woman president of the Jewish Representative Council and founder member of the Glasgow Jewish Choral Society.

Moira Ferguson (b. 1935) was chair of the Scottish Pre-School Play Association (SPPA) 1982–4; chair, Scope in Scotland, 1984–5; and the

National Executive Officer, SSPA from 1988.

(Prof.) Joyce Tait (née Graham)[125] (b. 1938) attended the Girls' High 1945–55 before completing degrees in Glasgow and at Cambridge universities. She was Professor, Environmental and Technology Management, Strathclyde University; Director, Scottish Universities Policy Research and Advice Centre, Edinburgh University; Director 2002–7, and since 1997 Scientific Adviser, ESRC Innogen Centre, Edinburgh University.

Marion Dodd[126] (b. 1941) joined the Foreign Office, 1962–4; was with the Iron and Steel Institute, 1964–7; BBC Singers, 1967–84; and has been Musical Director, Roxburgh Singers since 1996. She became an ordained minister, 1988, and has been a minister in Kelso since 1989.

Anna McCurley (née Gemmell)[127] (b. 1943) was a freelance communications consultant; a secondary history teacher, 1966–72 (teaching at the Girls' High from 1967–9); and a Jordanhill College tutor, 1972–4 before becoming a Strathclyde regional councillor, 1978–82 and Conservative MP, Renfrew West and Inverclyde, 1983–7. She defected to the Liberal Democrats in 1998.

Lesley Barrie[128] (b. 1944) was in hospital management, 1966–77, being District General manager, Inverclyde District, 1977–81 and Glasgow SE, 1981–3; a hospital administrator, Glasgow 1983–7, Stirling, 1987–91, Forth Valley, 1991–3; and General Manager and member, Tayside Health Board, 1993–7; as well as senior lecturer, Public Health department, Dundee University, 1994–7.

(Rev.) Janet MacMahon (née Gallacher)[129] was a Chief Speech Therapist, Greater Glasgow Health Board; assistant minister, Cairns Church, Milngavie and Govan Old, 1989–90; Chaplaincy Co-ordinator, Southern General Hospital, Glasgow, 1992–2002; and minister of Castlemilk West, 2002–6 and Kilmaronock Gartocharn, 2006–9.

(Rt Hon). Lady (Hazel Aronson) Cosgrove[130] (b. 1946) attended the High School 1953–63. She became an advocate at the Scottish Bar, 1968–79; Sheriff, Glasgow and Strathkelvin, 1979–83, and Lothian and Borders, 1983–6; QC (Scotland), 1991; temporary judge, Court of Session and High Court, 1992–6; and a Senator of the College of Justice, Scotland, 1996–2006. She was Scotland's first female High Court judge.

Alison Spurway (née Middleton) (b. 1946) graduated in History from Glasgow University, 1968. She became Senior Administrative Officer to the Senate Office at Glasgow University. She has been a Trustee of the HS Educational Trust since 1993. Active in the Girl Guide movement, she was awarded the Laurel Award by Girlguiding UK in 2005.

Maren Caldwell (née Hunter)[131] (b. 1947) was Appeal Director, Strathcarron Hospice, 1989–92; Director of Fundraising, Scottish Medical Research Fund, 1992–4; and Head of Regional Fundraising and Communications, RNLI.

(Dr) Dorothy Anderson (née Mitchell)[132] (b. 1950) trained in Radiology, Western Infirmary, Glasgow. She was Registrar, Senior Registrar, then Consultant Radiologist, Glasgow Royal Infirmary from 1981. She was clinical lecturer, then senior lecturer, Glasgow University from 1982.

(Prof.) Jean Beggs[133] (née Lancaster) (b. 1950) was a post-doctoral Fellow, Edinburgh 1974–7 and Cambridge 1977–9; lecturer, Biochemistry, Imperial College, London, 1979–85; Research Fellow, Edinburgh University, 1985–99. She is a distinguished British geneticist and Professor of Cell Biology at Edinburgh University. She was elected a fellow of the RS in 1998 and was awarded its Gabor Medal (2003).

(Prof.) Sheila McLean[134] (b. 1951) was area reporter, Children's Panel, 1972–5; lecturer 1975–85 and senior lecturer 1985–90, School of Law, Glasgow University; International Bar Association Professor of Law and Ethics in Medicine since 1990, and Director, Institute of Law and Ethics in Medicine since 1985, Glasgow University. She has served on a number of national medical and ethical committees.

(Prof.) Caroline MacDonald[135] (b. 1951) was lecturer and senior lecturer, Strathclyde University, 1983–92; Chairman, European Society for Animal Cell Technology, 1994–7; Professor and Head of Department, Biological Sciences, Paisley University, 1992–7; Assistant Principal, Paisley University, 1997–2004; and Pro-Vice Chancellor, Glasgow Caledonian University since 2004.

Caro Fraser (b. 1953) followed her father, George Macdonald Fraser, author of the *Flashman* books, into professional writing in 1991 having been a advertising copywriter and commercial lawyer. Her first novel, *The Pupil*, became the foundation of a series of further legal novels, and she has also written a number of romantic fiction works.

Gillian Stobo (née Dobson) (b. 1953), Chemistry graduate, returned to teach at Girls' High/Cleveden for six years as selection was ending and co-education introduced. She joined the staff of the new High School in 1993. She was appointed President of the Ladies' Section, 1997–8 and the first female President of the High School Club, 2004–5. She became Principal of Craigholme School in 2004.

Lynda Keith (née Hewitt) (b. 1954) taught in a variety of primary and nursery schools in Scotland and England before returning to Jordanhill

College of Education in 1990. She became senior lecturer and course director of the PGDE (Primary) at Strathclyde University. She is a director of the High School and recently became an educational consultant.

Anne Fyfe Pringle[136] (b. 1955) joined the Foreign and Commonwealth Office in 1977, serving in Moscow, San Francisco, Brussels and Equatorial Africa. She was made Head, Eastern Department, 1998–2001; Ambassador to Czech Republic 2001–4; Director, Strategy and Information (FCO) 2004–7; and presented her credentials as Ambassador to Russia to President Medvedev in January 2009. She was awarded a DCMG in the 2010 New Year Honours List.

(Dr) Hilary Hansell (née Dobson) (b. 1956) became School Dux, 1974. She followed a career in medicine as a Consultant Radiologist, being Clinical Director of the West of Scotland Breast Screening Programme.

Muriel Barbour (née Gray)[137] (b. 1958) graduated from Glasgow School of Art and became a professional illustrator; a presenter and broadcaster from 1982; a newspaper and magazine columnist; Rector, Edinburgh University, 1988–91; also producing numerous publications and doing extensive charity work.

Dorothy Gillies (d. 1981) graduated from Edinburgh in Classics. She became headmistress of Grantham and Kesteven Grammar School for Girls, and in 1942 was accused by her most famous pupil, Margaret Roberts (later Thatcher), of 'frustrating her ambition' by not teaching her personally the Latin necessary for University entrance.[138]

Sheila Alexandra Kerr graduated from Glasgow in 1926 and went on to Oxford University. She became headmistress of Surbiton High School, Kingston upon Thames in 1949.

Janice Forsyth,[139] press officer, Glasgow Mayfest 1983; public relations for arts events 1983–89; broadcaster in radio and TV; columnist, the *Scotsman* and *Scotland on Sunday*.

OLD GIRLS

With Mrs Tebb taking on the Presidency of the Old Girls' between 1931 and 1947, the secretaryship was shared by Miss Ewing and Sheila McLennan (1931–3); Miss Ewing and Mary Johnston (1934–40); Miss Ewing and Marguerite Benson (1941); Marguerite Benson and Miss Rigg (1942–3); Miss Rigg and Miss Adeline Cook (1944–5); and Miss Rigg and Miss Doris Dunlop (1947).

Miss Barker was President of the Old Girls' in 1948–9, with Miss Doris Dunlop as Secretary. They were followed by the team of Mrs E.M. Currie and Mrs D.C. Taylor (1950), Mrs Currie and Miss W.Y. McTaggart (1951), and Miss M.T. Robertson and Mrs G. Waddell (1952). While Miss M.W. Leckie was Secretary from 1953–6, her presidents included Dr D.M. Forsyth and Miss Jessie R.M. Robertson.

Then followed the remarkable tenure of Mrs Isa W. Cowan. Her presidents included Mrs N.H. Fleming (1957), Dr Margaret Leckie (1959), Miss R.K. Bisset (1960), Mrs Margaret MacKinnon (1961), Mrs Doris Taylor (née Dunlop) (1962), Mrs Esther Sellar (1963), Miss Alexa Taylor (1964), Mrs Laurie Brechin (née McCulloch) (1965), Dr Doris McWalter (1966), Mrs Mary Taylor (1967), Mrs Margaret Murray (1968), Mrs Queenie McPherson (1969), Mrs Margaret Wood (1971), Mrs Margot McCutcheon (1973), Miss Christina Keachie (1974), Mrs Muriel Scott (née Malcolm) (1976), Mrs Dorothy Donald (née McKinnon) (1977), Mrs Eleanor Dunlop (née Jackson) (1978), Mrs Mary Downie (née Webb) (1979),[140] Miss Caroline Stevenson (1980),[141] Miss Helen Lind (1981); Miss Sheena Coburn (1982), Mrs Elizabeth Thomson (née Highgate) (1984), Mrs Sheila Thomson (née Mills) (1985),[142] Mrs Angela Schnéeberger (née Burt) (1986), Mrs Elizabeth Drummond (née Baird) (1987), Miss Barbara Webb (1988), Mrs Anne Tietjen (née Greig) (1989), Mrs Heather McMillan (née Kelly) (1990), Miss Moira Young (1991) and Mrs Katie Keenan (née McLennan) (1992).[143]

Mrs Heather Smith was Secretary of the Ladies' Section in 1993–5, and since 1996 Miss Una Syme has remained in post. Presidents in this period included Mrs Gillian Mackay (née Burt) (1993), Mrs Margaret Norman (née Love) (1994), Mrs Sheila McIntyre (née McVey) (1995), Mrs Marcella McLennan (née Mackay) (1996), Dr Elspeth Carrick (née Higgins) (1997), Mrs Margaret Scott (née Yorston) (1999) and Mrs Aileen Lamont (née Currie) (2000).

EIGHT

The High School between the Wars

This chapter deals with changes in the School in the inter-war period, giving particular prominence to building improvements; the tenure of two towering heads, Peter Pinkerton and John Talman; the subject departments, including Kindergarten and Primary; and detailing again the distinguished Former Pupils of the time.

THE LEGACY OF THE SCHOOL BOARD

The School Board of Glasgow had proved efficient, enlightened and forward-looking, and it ensured that the development of education was continuous and progressive.[1] However, contrary to the general practice of Boards to set one common fee for all schools in their jurisdiction, the Glasgow Board introduced a great range of charges between schools, and within each school the fee went up according to the seniority of the class. This system worked on the principle that, while all Glasgow schools provided an equally good education, within every district of the city, schools should be available at fees which were adjusted to suit the different parental income groups. This led to a degree of social selection between schools, reflecting what parents wanted. Meantime, the Board worked hard to ensure that the reorganisation of endowments helped the children from poorer households with both elementary and secondary education by means of a considerable number of bursaries and scholarships.[2]

In the mid-1880s the Liberal Party committed itself to the abolition of school fees. In Scotland there was a strong reaction. Sir Francis Sandford, Under-Secretary of State for Scotland and a School Former Pupil, defended fees on the occasion of the opening of Gorbals School in 1885. Both the *Scotsman* and the *Glasgow Herald* joined arguably the foremost educationist of the day, Professor S.S. Laurie, in holding that the abolition of fees made certain that 'the child became more and more the child of the state, and less and less the child of its own father and mother'.[3] The Glasgow Board appeared to be in good company on the issue. Its members feared that free education meant education free from parental control, free from religious instruction, and free from economical management.

Parliament deemed otherwise and, by the mid-1890s, all fees had been ended in Glasgow's elementary schools.[4] Those, however, who aspired to secondary education paid fees. Fortunately, these were lowered by the direct subsidies from the Burgh Committee on Secondary Education, and the extensive number of bursaries available meant that in practice only one pupil in every two had to pay the small sums involved.

By 1918 fees had gone in all but a few state secondary schools. The High Schools retained higher fees from £1 10s to £2 per quarter, while Whitehill and Woodside paid 7s 6d a quarter. For the Board, and many citizens, maintaining the difference was for reasons of prestige, or snobbery, but it was fully justified by the high quality of the education on offer. This policy of low fees in a very few schools was retained well into the modern period.

NATIONAL DEVELOPMENTS

The SED had shaped secondary education before 1918 'partly through strict control and partly by benign pressure'.[5] Although much progress had been achieved, it had proved difficult to co-ordinate educational policy given the multiplicity of Boards and Secondary Education Committees. In England the administration of education was transferred to the county and borough councils in 1902, but Boards continued in Scotland until the end of the 1914–18 war. Their demise was postponed by a national faith in the Scottish educational tradition.[6]

In early 1918 Robert Munro, Liberal Secretary of State for Scotland, introduced a bill simplifying educational administration. The Education (Scotland) Act replaced the 947 School Boards with ad hoc Education Authorities, elected every three years by proportional representation, in each of the thirty-five counties and in the five burghs of Glasgow, Edinburgh, Aberdeen, Dundee and Leith.[7] These new authorities took over all the functions of the Boards, and their position was enhanced by the recommendation that they appoint professional directors of education to manage the service locally. Unfortunately, the EIS opposed the ad hoc system, believing it inevitable that, as in England, sooner or later education would be transferred to the county councils.[8] Thus, from the beginning, the new authorities were not regarded as a permanent unit of administration.

Their existence, however, was threatened earlier than expected by a dispute over where responsibility lay for the feeding of needy school children. This led to overlap and confusion, which was a major factor in the publication by the Conservative Government, in June 1928, of a White Paper outlining proposals for a wholesale reconstruction and simplification of local government in Scotland. The main thrust of these reforms was to reduce the burden of rates on the country's productive industries, and since this would deprive local authorities of much of their revenue and render their functioning impossible, the Government would make good the loss by means of a block grant. The necessary corollary, for maximum efficiency, was the co-ordination of local services under enlarged town and county councils, so that all other local bodies, including Educational Authorities, would be abolished.

The Government's bill became law in spring 1929. Thereafter, school education was controlled by the thirty-five county and city councils, each with its own Education Committee, to which educational matters had to be referred.[9] This remained the system of local government in Scotland until the introduction of districts and regions under the Local Government (Scotland) Act 1973.

If the administrative arrangements of the 1918 Act did not last, more important was the principle it established of free and universal secondary schooling, although financial crises[10] and resistance from the SED[11] delayed its implementation for a couple of decades. Thus fee-paying was retained in designated schools, the school-leaving age remained fourteen,[12] and access to secondary education was restricted in the belief that only a small, relatively gifted minority could profit from a full secondary course.[13]

By the 1930s the SED accepted a division in secondary courses between 'senior' (lasting five years) and 'junior' (lasting three years) courses. Senior secondary students followed a predominantly academic line of study and took examinations at age 17–18 that enabled access to higher education. The rest – nearing 90 per cent, who were designated junior secondary students – took no national examinations.[14] However, the SED insisted that these two routes had 'parity of esteem',[15] although in the towns the two kinds of courses tended to end up being taught in different types of schools. Thus, generally, Scotland had a selective system based on the 'twelve plus' examination, which was given new authority by the development of intelligence testing. Even for the political left, selection was accepted as an expression of equality of opportunity. It was only after the Second World War, and with the breaking down of the old industrial economy of Scotland, that the traditional assumption, that academic education and examination qualifications could be restricted to the few in society, began to be undermined.[16]

The framework of secondary provision remained stable from the 1930s until the 1960s; nonetheless, the political atmosphere of progressive social reform in the post-Second World War period helped create an expectation that mass schooling was a complement to mass democracy, and from this hope came the next wave of radical ideas. The Advisory Council's Report of 1947, mainly the work of a former High School pupil, J.J. Robertson, recommended a system of undifferentiated secondary schools, based on what it presented as the traditional model of the rural omnibus school. Although not accepted by the SED, this was the centrepiece for reform campaigners in the following decade.[17]

The selective system did change slowly and, by the end of the 1950s, the proportion of children attending senior secondaries had risen to close to 30 per cent. The new Ordinary Grade examination, introduced in 1962, was soon being used in many junior secondaries as a way of proving their academic credentials. Increasingly the dual system was not only resented for its seeming unfairness – middle-class children finding it much easier than working-class children to enter senior courses – but for being contrary to the Scottish tradition of meritocracy. It was also seen as wasteful of talent. The way was open for the ending of selection.

LOCAL DEVELOPMENTS

The immediate post-First World War issue for both High Schools was the question of fees and fee levels. Various attempts were made to ensure fees were in line with costs.[18] It was at this juncture that James Maxton, one of the very few Labour politicians to be elected onto the Glasgow Educational Authority,[19] pressed for the complete abolition of fees, but lost the vote 19–13 in June 1920.[20] As further fee schemes were suggested, there was no consensus and the status quo, of comparatively low fees fixed in 1919–20, was retained, and the rolls of both schools remained above 1,000 each in the immediate post-war period.

The High School community was proud of the School's Roll of Honour, which numbered 2,706, of whom 1,714 were officers. In total they amassed thirty-four DSOs, three with bar; 174 MCs, nine with bar; and 111 other decorations.[21] The 478 Old Boys who fell in action or died on service were commemorated in the beautiful Book of Remembrance, lovingly edited by Frank Beaumont, senior English master of the School. Sadly, it included the four sons of the Very Rev. John Brown, minister of Bellahouston parish and Moderator of the General Assembly of the Church of Scotland (1916–17): the eldest, John, had been Dux of the Classical side and had gained a First Class Honours at Balliol, Oxford, at the age of nineteen, before being killed in Egypt in April 1917; the second son, Sandilands, was sports champion and was killed on the Western Front in October 1918; the third, George, died in Mesopotamia in May 1917; and the youngest, Harold, was killed on the Western Front, aged twenty, in July 1916.

In June 1920 the Town Council agreed to the construction of a School War Memorial,[22] and the committee set up to supervise its construction thought that the work should, if possible, be entrusted to a Former Pupil. There was a pleasing response to a request for design suggestions, and John Keppie, acting as assessor in the competition, chose the plans of architect William Wright. The Memorial was to be in two sections, on either side of the vestibule, at the principal entrance to the School. On the south side there was envisaged a dedicatory inscription on a marble panel; on the north side a panel with the names of Former Pupils who had fallen in action or died in service. The lower part would be in the form of a sarcophagus, with the names of the principal battles carved on the shields placed in the frieze. The Memorial was planned to be of Seaton stone, a close-grained stone from Devon.

On Tuesday 14 February 1922, in the afternoon, the Memorial at Elmbank Street was unveiled by an FP: the Rt Hon. Andrew Bonar Law. In the yard, within a greater outer crescent composed of boys of the School, a large gathering of Old Boys, parents, and relations of the fallen, and round them the members of the OTC, were grouped. The Rector, Dr Pinkerton, presided, and after Bonar Law's address a number of wreaths were laid. The Educational Authority took responsibility for the Memorial's upkeep,[23] but it was agreed that the organisation of the fund owed everything to Rector Pinkerton, as convener of the Fund Committee, and Hugh Buchanan.[24]

The success in raising funds by means of personal appeal and a bazaar suggested that other ventures were possible. On 10 March 1924 another fourteen acres of playing fields at Old Anniesland were bought. In the competition for designs for a memorial clubhouse and pavilion, fourteen plans were submitted. The assessor, again John Keppie, awarded first place to Alex Cullen of Hamilton. The site for the building was chosen at the south-east corner of the main rugby pitch, and the front commanded an uninterrupted view over all the playing fields. Approached by a flight of steps, the central feature on the main floor was an entrance hall, while on the upper floor there was to be a large assembly room. The dressing room accommodation was to be placed in the two-storey back wing. The opening ceremony was performed by General Sir Ian Hamilton on 1 October 1927.[25]

While the Educational Authority continued to discuss the best way to improve accommodation at the Girls' High, its Property Committee recommended, in March 1927, the consideration of an extension to the buildings of the School at Elmbank Street. The architects, Watson, Salmond and Gray, were asked to draw up plans.[26] By September 1928 these had been forwarded to the SED for consideration. With progress made in acquiring adjoining property in Elmbank and Holland Streets, the contrast with the lack of progress at Garnethill was stark. The authority responded by setting up a Special Committee on the High Schools under convener Hugh R. Buchanan in March 1929.[27] It did not take long for the committee to suggest various accommodation solutions. The possibility of converting the playing fields at Kirklee was rejected after a visit there and to the new facilities at Anniesland, and instead a radical proposal was suggested, namely that the girls should move to Elmbank Street and the boys to Old Anniesland.[28] This, however, was remitted for further consideration, while another plan to acquire more land around Elmbank Street to site both schools was blocked by the authority in May 1930. This was the situation when Glasgow Council took over matters, and the result was a return to the original 1928 plans for an extension to the School at Elmbank Street.[29]

The 'New Building' – 'A' Block – was occupied during the summer term of 1934 and formally opened by Sir Charles Cleland on 26 October.[30] In the basement were situated the school boilers and electrics, the OTC room and the armoury. On the ground floor there was a good-sized examination hall, a large gymnasium with modern equipment,[31] the carpentry and engineering workshops, two Physics laboratories and a dark-room. The first floor housed three Physics and three Chemistry laboratories. On the second floor were positioned a lecture theatre, which seated 150 and was provided with every facility for cinema and lantern projection, three Art rooms, one room for arts and crafts, one for Engineering Drawing and one for Biology. The Mathematics department was temporarily housed in the new building, while the old north building (opened in 1887) was gutted and rebuilt to house Modern Languages, Classics and Mathematics. Given such splendid accommodation, it was not long before it was being argued that the old centre block ('C' block), which had been the nucleus of the school's development since before the war, was in need of renovation. A Council Property Sub-committee approved plans as early as October 1936,[32] and the contract was agreed in February 1938.[33] However, the main masonry contractors, John Kirkwood and Smith, went into liquidation[34] and it was not until 1957 that this block was finally brought back into full use.

On his appointment in 1919, groundsman Arthur Taylor, from Yorkshire, began the process of levelling, draining, turfing and preparing eleven pitches at Old Anniesland. In 1923 Willie Woods, a miner from Cumberland, was taken on as assistant. It took until 1931 for them to complete the work started in 1919 on the 27 acres. A decade of fruitful association between the men developed until, in 1940, on Taylor's death, Woods took upon himself the care and maintenance of the ground he had helped so much to create.[35]

Herbert Ellicott had come from Merchiston in 1904. At the School he taught Modern Languages and was rugby master until 1920. He spent almost as much time with the FPs as with the School and forged an important link between them.[36] With an improved ground and better coaching the School began to produce more rugby internationalists, and the 1920s was a 'golden age' for FP rugby, when eight players won sixty-seven caps.[37] William Barclay took over from Ellicott as rugby master and continued his efficient work with the School and the FP Club until 1938. At his farewell dinner at the Grosvenor Restaurant in Gordon Street in June 1952, he was toasted by R. Wilson Shaw,[38] one of his most successful pupils, who had led Scotland to a famous victory over England at Twickenham in 1938. Barclay had proved an inspiring coach. He was replaced in this position by Colin Mackenzie, a Watsonian,[39] who joined the staff in 1936 and took over rugby two years later. He proved an enthusiastic, competent and devoted master-in-charge. He was followed in this by J. Kenneth Clark, a Hillhead High School FP and Classics teacher, under whom the game continued to flourish.

RECTORS

Peter Pinkerton: Continued

Pinkerton was intimately involved in the day-to-day activities of the School, frequently emerging from his office sanctum to teach a range of classes in a variety of subjects. This served two related purposes: he could assess the effectiveness of the teachers by their progress through the curriculum; and he could also assess the talents and achievements of individual boys. A powerful presence in the classroom, he was full of energy and life, and his methods were thorough and rigorous. In his teaching, as in his thought, he hated the slipshod.[40] As Rector he was a conspicuous success, being fair, sympathetic and just, qualities which endeared him to the boys. They knew they were expected to work hard but most did so willingly for someone who knew every boy individually. Although at times his knowledge of the boys seemed uncanny, this was the result of his determination to know the names and location in the classroom of each pupil in order that he could address them personally. He took a great interest in the career prospects of the pupils, encouraging their efforts and steering them in directions appropriate to their abilities. His leadership qualities also endeared him to his staff, who supported him loyally. One of them saw him as 'a god to the boys and . . . revered by their parents'.[41] The result was a School ethos permeated with a spirit of confidence in Pinkerton. His wife, Margaret, had died the day after the birth of her only child, Herbert, in 1901. Rector Pinkerton remained a widower and 'lived, ate and breathed High School'.[42]

It was during Pinkerton's tenure that the School motto 'Sursum Semper'[43] was applied to the School crest, and on 8 February 1919 the School was granted its arms by the Lord Lyon King of Arms. The upper third of its shield is red and carries an open book, with the edges of the pages gilded, between two laurel wreaths. The book and wreaths are symbols of learning and reward. The lower part of the shield is identical to the Arms of the City of Glasgow: the tree represents a bough kindled by a word from Kentigern into flame to relight the lights in his church extinguished by his enemies; the robin was restored to life by Kentigern; the bell represents the Church and See of Glasgow, and had been consecrated and brought by Kentigern from Rome; and the salmon with the ring in its mouth is a reminder of an ancient legend.

At the High School Club Dinner in February 1929, Pinkerton spoke of the changes in the management of the School. It had been run by the Church, the Council, the Board, the Education Authority, and now appeared to be going back under Council control again. Despite all these changes it had survived because its ethos inspired affection in the people of Glasgow. Looking to the future Pinkerton believed that its best safeguard would be management by a governing body whose sole interest was in the School. Such an arrangement would help overcome Pinkerton's chief complaint: his inability to keep staff. The constant changes upset the balance and stability of the School, and something had to be done to overcome this difficulty. Unfortunately, it was to take another half-century before Pinkerton's prophetic words were to be acted on.

Dr Pinkerton died in office in November 1930 from colon cancer. His most recent HMI report (of 1928–9) had praised his 'vigorous and skilled direction' of the School.[44] He had also been responsible for the procurement of the playing fields and carrying out the War Memorial scheme. On Saturday 11 March 1933 a bronze medallion of Dr Pinkerton, the work of Benno Schotz, was placed on the wall of the Pavilion at Anniesland in his memory. He is remembered for much else: his powers of organisation, of memory, of concentration, and of tenacity, which were devoted to the improvement of the School on its teaching side with conspicuous success.

John Talman, 1931–1950

On Pinkerton's death twenty-four candidates applied for the Rector's post, and of these eight were interviewed. The strongest appeared to be the School's own William Kerr[45] and James Munro, but John Talman was chosen, partly because he seemed the natural successor to Pinkerton. He was also from Ayrshire, and also a neat-minded Christian scholar whose similar style was genial yet authoritative, heavy handed against wrong, and with a preference for the occasional committee of one.

Talman was born about 1888, the son of the manager of the Dalmellington Iron Mine Company store in Lethanhill.[46] He was educated at Ayr Academy under Maybin and became a pupil–teacher in the mining village of Benwhat before attending Glasgow University, graduating in 1907 with a First Class Honours in History and Constitutional Law. After a spell at Heidelberg studying school organisation in Germany, he taught at Provanside and Hutchesons' Boys. He was outstandingly versatile, being responsible for discoveries in colour photography, experiments in wireless telegraphy and inventing model examination papers, which led to an interest in educational theory and innovation. Between 1910 and 1912 he was assistant to Dr William McKechnie, Professor of Constitutional Law and History, before taking over the post of Principal Teacher of English at Allan Glen's School, which he held for seventeen years, latterly being Deputy Headmaster as well.

Talman ('The John') settled quickly into his new School and new role. His first HMI Report of 1932–3 concluded that 'the School and its interests are in the hands of capable and well qualified staff who are guided by the Rector with singular understanding'. The School's success was seen again in 1934 when the School Dux, John W. Evans,[47] came first in the Bursary Competition. By 1935–6 it was held that 'the Rector brings to his task a refreshing vigour and acuteness of mind and a flair for devising new solutions to old problems'. Glowing reports on Talman's leadership were contained in the 1938–9 report, while in 1944–5 it was deemed that 'the School owes much to him; he has ably guided it through a very difficult period'.

Although a renowned teacher himself, Talman decided not to visit class-rooms, believing that teachers had the right to work without interference in their own domain and to develop their own methods. He trusted his staff completely, but made it known that he was always accessible and ready with counsel and sympathy should difficulties arise. As for control, Talman exercised a constant, impersonal and dispassionate scrutiny over work and results. Although apparently rather remote, in fact he took a keen personal interest in staff and pupils alike. He could name every boy, and knew his strengths and weaknesses. He did not praise often, but high standards of discipline, duty and conduct were maintained.

Education was an early casualty of the Second World War. During the early days of September 1939 schools throughout the country were compul-sorily closed, and in Glasgow the education machine of the City was hurriedly dismantled. Pupils whose parents had chosen evacuation were sent away to places of greater safety. School staff were used to help with the large exodus.

Schools like the High School had worked hard at creating a special ethos, and generally pupils were reluctant to lose their identity. Fortunately, in mid-October 1939, the Government relaxed its ban on the opening of schools in Glasgow, at least to the extent of allowing senior forms to assemble at a limited number of schools on approved sites, with the proviso that adequate air-raid shelter was available. Immediately, High School boys and masters jumped at the chance to assist. Their offer was promptly accepted. In four days the sandbag protection was so far advanced that the three highest Forms could safely return to Elmbank Street. With a judicious mixture of labour and lessons, the fortification was completed. By December the School accommodated Forms III to VI in the mornings, while Forms I and II were restricted to the afternoons, with the Junior School classes not involved in the arrangement. For those juniors who were not evacuated, and for whose education no provision had been made, an organisation of cells was set up under committees of parents who assumed financial responsibility for their upkeep.[48] High School teachers whose services were not otherwise required by the Education Committee provided the instruction. Miss Nina, for example, and the Kindergarten were located on the top floor of the Herbert Pinkerton family home at 11 Lilybank Gardens, while Junior 4 and 5 were moved to space in the Commercial College on Pitt Street.

The School garden flourished during the war, with fresh vegetables changing hands at moderate prices. High School pupils often left the School with schoolbag, gas mask and a string bag of sprouts, carrots and turnips. The garden was in Maryhill, next to a girls' Borstal, and the boys were discouraged from climbing its walls and throwing potatoes at the girls.

In this period the first lesson of the day was a religious prayer, including the Lord's Prayer, and it was accepted as normal that Jewish pupils would wait in the corridor until the short religious period ended. This situation evolved, and on Friday mornings at prayers, following the singing of a psalm and a paraphrase, the Jewish boys joined before the Rector exhorted the school with well-chosen words on the subject of the day. One of the few times when Talman did not take morning prayers was in September 1941, when he explained that he was saying goodbye to his son, James,[49] who was leaving to join his RAF squadron. Cruelly, Talman suffered the loss of James, who was killed while serving in the RAF in July 1944; courageously, on the day of the announcement of his son's death, Talman gave the Assembly reading himself. He read the moving story of David's misery on the death of his son, Absalom. Unforgettable to all present was his finish, almost in a whisper and in deep passion, with the words: 'Oh, Absalom, Absalom, my son, my son!'

Some 1,563 Former Pupils served their country in the Second World War. The casualties were grievous. The Book of Service and Remembrance, published in 1948, detailed 147 who paid the ultimate price.

The views of the staff towards the Rector were coloured by sympathy and admiration as he bravely struggled on, also coping with an operation for throat cancer in May 1946, which entailed an absence of two months. When he returned, he had a microphone and speakers installed so that he could speak to the boys in the croak he had been taught to manage. During Talman's absence, James Paterson was made Acting Rector. He had an outstanding academic record. He was Classical Dux of Dumfries Academy and had come first in the Bursary Competition. He graduated in 1923 with First Class Honours in Classics, teaching and lecturing before joining the

High School, and teaching Latin from his own textbook.

The curriculum remained focused on subjects for university entrance: English, Mathematics, Classics, Modern Languages, Physics and Chemistry, with a nod to History. In retrospect a serious deficiency was the Biological sciences. A range of extra-curricular activities was available besides the traditional rugby, cricket and OTC. One interesting innovation of Talman's was a compulsory athletics course with graduated standards for size and performance, held annually for several years to encourage all, especially the lethargic, to undertake physical activity.

Talman retired in 1950, remembered for his ready wit, his encyclopaedic knowledge, his powers of good conversation and his excellence as a public speaker.[50] According to Small, he was 'a mental giant, a genius'.[51]

DEPARTMENTS[52]

In the Classics department, William Lobban[53] served from 1907 until 1928, while Percy Gent, an Oxford graduate, taught between 1918 and 1937. Dugald M.S. ('Pa') Duff, who gained a First Class Honours (FCH) in 1914, served for the first time between 1924 and 1940 before taking up the post of PT[54] Classics at Whitehill School in 1940. R. Gordon ('Greasy Mac') McCallum, another FCH, also had a break in his Elmbank Street career,[55] his first stint being from 1928 till 1949. The same course was followed by J. Kenneth ('Nobby') Clark, who was an assistant in the department 1943–51. The PT from 1930 to 1946 was James ('Monkey Pat') Paterson,[56] and others who made important contributions were John B. Craig (1928–43), Robert H. Small and J. Roy ('Beaky') Leitch. Craig also had a FCH degree.[57] Small taught in the High School from 1932 to 1951 before promotion to PT Classics at his old school, Whitehill. He carried his learning lightly, and even after his departure he retained a consuming interest in the history of the School. Leitch was a Former Pupil of the School who taught there between 1935 and 1955, and later returned to complete his teaching career at Elmbank Street. He did an outstanding job in organising the annual School Prizegiving and was a prime mover in the Literary and Debating Society. John A. ('The Grunt') Muir had a slow and ponderous way of speaking, and as PT Classics from 1946 to 1950 he taught in the small attic classroom beside the staff room at the top of 'B' Block; he went on to become headmaster of the City Public School.

In the English department, Frank Beaumont was appointed in 1902 and worked under, successively, Struthers, Law, Taylor and James H. Steel[58] before himself becoming PT in 1918. He proved a gifted teacher and left in 1925 to become headmaster of North Kelvinside.[59] He was replaced as PT by William Kerr, whose textbook on grammar and composition remained popular for a generation. Another inspiring teacher, Robert McEwan, took over the reins from 1934 until 1943, before becoming headmaster of Whitehill Secondary. William Dewar also was praised for his time as PT (1943–7), and he went on later to the headship of Knightswood Secondary. He was followed by Alexander B. Tawns (1947–51) who retired from King's Park Secondary. Noteworthy English assistants included Joseph Compton, who became Director of Education for Ealing 1937–57; Parry Gunn, who taught English and Elocution between 1926 and 1945, as well producing pageants; William ('Wee Bill') Barclay (1914–52), a much liked and respected teacher of English and History who produced effective rugby teams; I. Graham Andrew, a Former Pupil, who taught briefly (1920–2) before a career of headships;[60] another FP, George Mills, who taught successfully (1923–41) before illness led him to resign from his post as PT in Jordanhill College School; Gilbert K. Dunlop (1928–43) who went on to be Second Master at Milton; Alexander C. ('Pa') Gillespie[61] (1932–48); Philip Hutton (1935–47) who edited the Second World War Book of Service and Remembrance; and William M. Brown (1933–52), who contributed much to the OTC, running the unit with a rod of iron.

In Mathematics, James Munro (1919–1932) became Rector of Rothesay Academy, then Director of Education for Bute (1947–53); Malcolm ('Popeye') Muir (1922–40) was a stern and fatherly figure who founded the Angling Club and became headmaster of Dinard Street; David Cameron (1925–8) was a natural sportsman who became Rector of Montrose Academy; George Wilson Blair (1927–36 and PT 1938–46) married Miss Jean Smillie, the School's Assistant Registrar from 1926 till 1940, and was successively headmaster of Knightswood and Govan secondary schools; David McCulloch (1929–39) was much involved in school sport; Andrew B. Cameron (1932–46), an FCH, went on to become Director of Education in Dunbarton (1959–73); PT Andrew Hutchison (1932–8) became headmaster of Hyndland School; William Wright (1932–47), an FCH, became PT at Victoria Drive; Alexander Goldie (1933–46), another FCH, became headmaster of the Central School in Aberdeen in 1954 in time for its name to be changed to Aberdeen Academy, and also 'masterminded the revolutionary move from the heart of town to the sylvan west end, where it became known as Hazlehead Academy';[62] Archibald Bell (1936–40), another FCH graduate, gained promotion to PT Mathematics at Jordanhill College School; Thomas W. Glen (1940–54) was an enthusiast for 'Moral Rearmament'; Thomas Henderson (1940–6) became Director of Education, Midlothian (1957–75); and Kenneth F. Kerr (1941–53) proved a strict but effective dominie. Robert D. McIlroy, following twenty years at Hillhead, took on the post of PT of Mathematics in 1946; he resigned also as Depute Rector in December 1953.

In Modern Languages, Keen was succeeded as PT in 1926 by Herbert Ellicott,[63] whose tenure lasted until 1931, and who served as interim Rector between the illness of Pinkerton and the arrival of Talman. John MacPhee was PT from 1931 to 1937[64] and he, along with R.M. Jack, produced a number of French textbooks. (Rev.) Samuel L. Weir taught in the department from 1922 until 1944, being PT 1937–44 and going on to become Head of Hillhead School.[65] He was replaced by James W. Chadwin (1940–7), who revitalised the department and was also Depute Rector for a short time before going on to the headship of Greenock Academy. Internal promotions continued with Stewart G.L. Simmie, an FCH graduate in French and German, who joined the department in 1936, becoming PT 1947–60.[66] Assistants included James M. Milne, who went on to become Rector of Nairn Academy, retiring in 1947; John 'Bunnylugs' Hutchison (1927–36) who became Rector of Hutchesons' Grammar School; Ernest T. Abbott (1930–54), noted for his problem-solving; John Scrimgeour (1930–50), who became PT at Dunfermline High School; James 'Beaky' Walker (1930–40), remembered for his devotion to the League of Nations Union, which at one stage had virtually the whole school as members, became PT at Shawlands; William Black (1934–46), another FCH graduate in French and German; and Charles M. ('Chick') Anderson (1934–57), with French and Spanish, was a popular international hockey player. The tradition of having foreign language assistants, which began as early as 1907, continued and was a factor in the success of the department.

A number of staff in Science had over a decade's service, including PT William Douglas (1927–42), W. Macdonald Gregory (1915–35), Wilfred Whalley (1918–35), John W. Cuthbertson, David Mowatt (1927–43), Neil Ferguson (1933–45) – replaced by Murdo J. MacDonald (1945–57) who also taught Mathematics – William Garland (1935–45), Kenneth Macrae (1935–46), Norman L. Nicol (1935–47) and Arthur J. Drummond (1937–45), who became PT at Queen's Park. John D. ('Narky') Robertson was PT between 1943 and his death in 1954, and his assistants included James ('Mono') Crawford (1938–55) and William ('Jake') Harkness (1946–55), who were close friends and tea makers. William ('Spike') Gillespie (1945–56) is also remembered kindly. In 1935 a new Botany class was formed with David S. Cuthbertson, and thirty-two boys were chosen to study the subject in place of Physics.

In Music, Archibald M. Ross was sole Music master from 1936 to 1943. He became full-time in September 1937 and then left to become Superintendent of Music from September 1943. He was replaced by James Gilmour Barr, who left to become PT Music at Jordanhill Training College. His post was in turn taken by Harry McGill in January 1946.

Dr Robert M.W. Cowan gained an FCH in English, being awarded the Ewing Scholarship. He taught briefly in Hamilton, and three years at Hutchesons' GS before joining the English Department of the School in 1926. He also gained an Honours LLB from the University of London (1937) and produced a DLitt thesis on 'The Newspaper in Scotland' in 1944. The first PT at the School in History was Douglas Herd, who held the post briefly in 1944–5 but, as was common at the time, successful English teachers were promoted into these posts. So after nineteen years service in the English department, Cowan was made PT History (1945–6) before going on to become Director of Education in West Lothian (1946–58). The post of PT in Geography was created at the same time as History, and Mary ('Ma') Calder took over this role between 1944 and 1970; she was full-time from 1966, and up till then had worked between the girls' and boys' schools.

In Physical Training, PT Alexander Brison (1924–37) became Supervisor of the subject in Dunbartonshire. He was replaced by Thomas C. Croll (1937–46). Assistants included Dan McBride (1922–26); Richard Hughes (1926–45); James Jackson (1934–8); and Keir Hardie (1938–49).

In Art (Drawing), the PT was Hugh Wilson (1936–50), and as well as Leslie ('Minty') Millar (1933–73), assistants included Robert A. Gowans (1934–9) and James S. Burgess (1939–45).

Piping was taught by Pipe Major Robert Reid. Once a week, the OTC Pipe Band led a parade of sixty cadets from the School to the drill hall of the HLI on West Princes Street. The Commander of the OTC was Captain Thomas (Bouncer) Brown of English.

The High School Masters' Golf Club was formed in May 1914. Its first committee consisted of Messrs Douglas, Chalmers, Ellicott and Taylor, and its first secretary was Mr Rae. The first stroke competition was played over Troon in June 1914. The club was in abeyance during the two world wars but has continued until today. At its AGM in 1922 it was agreed to elect a captain from the staff each year. The first captain was the Rector, Dr

Pinkerton. The Ramshorn trophy, a snuff mull, gifted by Rector Talman, was first competed for in 1938, and the Core Cup was added in 1962 to reward the best scratch score. The first dinner was held in the Grand Hotel on 25 December 1931 and, as of 2008, there were still twenty-nine members on Honorary President Alastair Grant's mailing list.

The Kindergarten and Primary School were housed in 'D' Block[67] on the south end of the Elmbank Street site. The building had some ten class-rooms and a gymnasium, as well as toilet and cloakroom facilities. Class sizes were typically between thirty and thirty-five. There was a separate playground on the southern edge of the campus. For most boys the junior school was a positive formative experience – the High School at its best. However, for others the strong discipline of the time led to fear of the belt, which was a well-used instrument.

It was in the Lower Kindergarten of Miss (Agnes) Nina Logan that the real foundations were laid of what was called 'The High School Boy'. Miss Nina was the most charming and incomparable Kindergarten mistress, devoting thirty-seven years of her life, from 1916 to 1953, not only to guiding the first steps of her boys into education and independent existence, but also to helping them share in the widest corporate life of the School in every aspect. All who came under her spell remained for always her appreciative and devoted admirers, and throughout his life none of her pupils ever lost his pride in having been one of 'Miss Nina's boys'. While it remained her constant achievement to lay a solid foundation for future education, her methods were pupil-directed rather than subject-related. Above all, Miss Logan bred into each and every one of these boys the essentials of good behaviour and equally good manners.[68] By her presence and personality she graced the School. 'No one present at the Complimentary Dinner and presentation to mark her retirement in 1953 can forget the enthusiasm and affection demonstrated by several hundred colleagues, former pupils and parents who filled the Ballroom of the Grosvenor Restaurant.'[69]

Nina Logan was one of many spinsters who dedicated their lives to the education of primary pupils and formed the basis of the high reputation that Scottish schooling then enjoyed.[70] They all had pianos in their classrooms, which were used to some effect when accompanying the boys in 'Onward Christian Soldiers' and the National Anthem – repeatedly! Religious belief was assumed if largely unnoticed, while those of the Jewish faith had their own arrangements. The annual Sports Days at Old Anniesland saw all the boys in their whites, and even those who did not win anything were provided with a memento by Miss Nina. From the beginning, the idea of caring for the less fortunate was gently expressed. Each boy supplied a toy for the disabled children of the East Park Home and, in the final years of the war, collections of waste paper were made, with cardboard medals issued by army ranks according to how much one collected.

Boys progressed to the Upper Kindergarten with Mrs Nancy Moore (1942–6) and Miss Jackson, and on to Junior 1 with Miss Peggy R. Young (1931–65) and her radiant smile, and then to Miss Doris Barrie (1942–59), whose classroom was just inside the left-hand door of 'D' block on the ground floor. She was a rather different character, remembered as a diminutive woman who had a very caring attitude towards her pupils. They then went on to Junior 3 and the delightful Miss C. Eileen Stewart (1946–71).[71] Mr William (Bill) Ewing arrived at the school in August 1949 to take Junior 4, while the youthful Miss Lindsay C. Montgomery (1949–67)[72] took Junior 5 before the boys spent two years in Primary 6 with the memorable Miss Isobel Ralston (1933–69),[73] who taught one of the two Qualifying classes, or Miss Mary Hilary Pate (1937–50), a rather elegant lady, tall, slim and statuesque, but also a disciplinarian and very severe.[74] Both Miss Ralston and Miss Pate maintained the idea of excellence, of giving 100 per cent; they set standards, and the boys were expected to meet them. 'Rally' was quite a martinet, although in the best way, and very effective at getting her class through the 'Qually' (eleven plus). In 1950–1 her class had the temerity to present her with a round-robin seeking less homework; nothing more was heard of it! She had an affinity with the sea and took her class on outside visits to the Fairfield Engineering and Shipbuilding Company. Towards the end of her long life she still maintained a disciplinary 'hold' over her boys, and displayed a remarkable financial acumen. Miss Pate was also held in high regard, and when she died her funeral was attended by a number of her Former Pupils.

The general assistant – the title 'matron' would not be quite right – 'Violet' Farrell looked after the cloakroom and helped with combs, coats, cuts and awkward shoe laces. She had a little cubby hole near Miss Nina's classroom, from which, from time to time, she dispensed assistance and comfort to her young charges.

Fred Luke (1895–1983) was a farm worker from Hampshire before enlisting in 1913. At the battle of Le Cateau on 25 August 1914, while he was serving as a driver for the 37th (Howitzer) Battery of the Royal Field Artillery, he volunteered to retrieve their heavy guns to avoid them falling into the hands of the Germans. With German forces closing on three sides, he and two others only completed their mission by returning through a curtain of shrapnel thrown up by British artillery covering the general retreat. Observers were astounded at the speed and audacity of the operation. For their heroic madness the three comrades were awarded the Victoria Cross; as Fred was only eighteen he was one of the youngest VC recipients.[75] After the war Luke married and moved to Glasgow, where he joined the High School staff as a janitor.[75] He served again in World War Two as a ground gunner with the RAF. A remarkable and modest man, his funeral took place at the Linn Crematorium.

CLUBS: AT HOME[76]

The inaugural meeting of the London Club was chaired by Sir Henry Craik in 1922. Its Secretary, Cecil Denham, worked tirelessly in that post for over twenty years, before becoming the first Honorary President in 1961. Its membership reached 240 in 1973. Meantime, an Edinburgh Club was formed in 1959, while the mother Club in Glasgow held its Centenary Dinner in 1970 and played a significant role in the efforts to save the School in the 1970s.

CLUBS: OVERSEAS

Following an abortive effort to found a Club in New York in 1922, the first successful overseas clubs were formed in Calcutta in 1925 and Montreal in 1929. A Ceylon Club in Columbo appeared in 1932, a South African Club met in Johannesburg from 1935 and a Burma Club flourished for a time in the 1930s. Less successful were the efforts in Manila (1932), Nairobi (1935) and Malaya (1940). However, by the 1950s most clubs had been replaced by 'consular service' in the form of a local representative. By 1976 there were High School consuls in Canada, USA, Holland, Australia, Penang and Kenya.

PUPILS

During the inter-war period the key sectors of the Scottish economy experienced major difficulties on a scale unprecedented in her post-Union history. Economic depression jolted the hitherto unshakeable sense of civic pride.

William Beardmore had successfully extended his industrial empire, and in 1919 took the lead in a number of innovative enterprises. By 1926 his company was on the brink of bankruptcy, and in the following year he was ousted from executive control. Such was the fate of the leader of Scotland's foremost engineering and ship-building business. Such failures made others sceptical of abandoning old ways, so strengthening ideas of retrenchment and the inevitability of decline. Funding for schooling was cut, and children continued to receive an education dictated by their social background. For its part, the High School pursued a strictly academic curriculum, enabling most of its boys to go on to university and a professional career.

Merchants

Samuel Dow (1908–1976) [1917–21; spirit merchant][77] was Chairman, Scottish Wholesalers Wine Merchants Assoc., 1953–7, and President, Wine and Spirit Association of Great Britain (Int.), 1964–5.

Alister McCrae (1909–1996) [1920–7; timber merchant] joined a shipping company. He completed war service in Middle East and Burma. He became senior partner and Managing Director, British and Burmese Steam Navigation Co. Ltd (1963); a Freeman of the City of London, (1959); and Chairman, Clyde Port Authority, 1966–77.

Manufacturers (Industrialists)

(Sir) Robert Maclean (1908–1999) [1920–25; tea merchant; an individualist who showed maturity of mind] became Vice-Chairman, Scottish Board for Industry, 1952–60; President, Glasgow Chamber of Commerce, 1956–8; Chairman, Council of Scottish Chambers of Commerce, 1960–2; and Honorary President, Stoddard Holdings Ltd. He was chair of the High School Educational Trust until 1982.

William Fraser (1911–1990) [1923–26; electrical engineer; first in his class two years running] became a production engineer, 1935; Managing Director, Scottish Cables Ltd, 1948–62 and its Chairman, 1958–76; and Chairman BICC Ltd,[78] 1973–6.

(Dr) (Benjamin) Arthur Hems (1912–1995) [1918–30; tool furnisher] attended Glasgow and Edinburgh Universities. He joined Glaxo, 1937 and became Chairman, Glaxo Research, 1965–75 and Managing Director, Glaxo Research, 1967–77.

James Fyfe (1919–2007) attended the School 1925–37, becoming a quantity surveyor, Deacon of Incorporation of Masons (1974) and Deacon Convener of Trades' House (1980).

Angus Murray (1919–1982) [1924–36; doctor; exhibited a 'buoyant personality' and was much involved in sport] trained to be a mechanical engineer, serving with the Royal Engineers, 1940–6. He became Chairman, Redman Heenan International plc, 1972–82 (Chief Executive, 1971–6), and Cardover Investments Ltd.

Gabe Bryce (b. 1921) [1932–35; electrical engineer] was in the RAF, 1939–46. He was Chief Test Pilot with Vickers-Armstrong (Aircraft) Ltd. (1951–60) and the British Aircraft Co. (1960–4).

Colin Hope[79] (b. 1924) [1929–35; manufacturing confectioner] went on to Glasgow Academy. He became Managing Director, Stenhouse International; and Director, Merchants' House of Glasgow, 1981–7, 1988–94, 1995–2001 and 2002–5.

Alexander (Alastair) Paterson (b. 1924) [1935–41; commercial traveller] took a First Class degree in Engineering from Glasgow in 1947. He was President, Institution of Structural Engineers, 1984–5; and President, Institution of Civil Engineers, 1988–9.

Baron Macfarlane of Bearsden[80] (b. 1926) (Norman) [1941–45; company director] founded N.S. Macfarlane & Co. Ltd, 1949, which became Macfarlane Group (Clansman) plc, 1973, where he was Chairman (1973–98) and Managing Director (1973–90). He became Chairman of United Distillers plc. (1987–96); Hon. Life President of Macfarlane Group plc (1999). He was created Baron 1991 (Life Peer). A selection of the offices he has held include: Hon. President, Scottish Ballet (from 2001); Hon. President, High School of Glasgow from 1992 (Chairman of Governors 1979–92); President, Royal Glasgow Institute of Fine Arts (1976–87); Member of University of Glasgow Court (1979–87); President of the High School Club, 1971–2; Lord High Commissioner of the General Assembly of the Church of Scotland (1992, 1993 and 1997). He was awarded the Freedom of the City of Glasgow, 2007.

Robert Gemmill (b. 1930)[81] [1944–7; petroleum rationing officer; Classical Dux, 1946–7] was fourth in the Bursary Competition and achieved a First Class degree in Economics at Glasgow. He worked in manufacturing management, becoming a management consultant. He was a member of Glasgow University Court, 1990–2001. He played rugby for Glasgow High FPs, helping to secure the Unofficial Championship in 1951 and 1962, and won seven caps for Scotland.

(Dr) Alastair Ramsay (b. 1930) [1944–8; chemist; arrived from Chicago] went on to graduate from Glasgow University. He became an important benefactor of the new High School and is a member of its Educational Trust.

Gordon Anderson (b. 1931)[82] [1937–49; engineer] became a CA (1955). He was chairman of Arthur Young 1987–9; Ernst and Young (Dep. Sen. Partner 1989–90); Chairman, Bitmac Ltd, 1990–6; Lloyds TSB, 1994–9; President of Institute of CAs of Scotland, 1986–7; President of the High School Club, 1978–9; and Chairman of Governors of the School, 1992–2001.

Charles Burgess (b. 1933) [1943–51; chartered surveyor] became a partner in a surveying practice from 1965. He was Chairman, Royal Institution of Chartered Surveyors (Scotland), 1990–1.

James Mowat (b. 1936) [1945–54; mining engineer] had various technical and managerial appointments. He was Managing Director, Anderson Strathclyde, 1980–9; and Chairman, Inverere Investment Ltd, 1990.

Ian Docherty (b. 1939) [1950–7; manufacturer's agent] joined the family clothing agency and manufacturing business. He captained the High School FP side which won the 1961–2 Unofficial Championship. He became a Director and Trustee of the High School. He took over the chairmanship of the Appeal Committee in 1981, remains a member of the Educational Trust and was President of the High School Club, 1994–5.

Churchmen

(Rev. Canon) Malcolm Clark (1905–2002) [1917–22; doctor] became a deacon, 1934; priest, 1935; Dean, Collegiate Church of St Vincent, 1982; and Dean of Edinburgh, 1983–5.

(Rev.) Anderson Nicol (1906–1972) [1920–2; chemist; a 'good scholar of exemplary character'] became minister of West Kirk (St Nicholas), Aberdeen, 1948–67; chaplain to the Queen in Scotland, 1964–72; and minister, Dundurn, St Fillans, Perthshire, 1967–72.

(Rev.) Ellis Shaw (1908–1983) [1919–26; CA] went on to Glasgow, Tubingen and Marburg Universities. He gave a lifetime of service to the Church in South India.

(Very Rev.) John Gray (1913–1984) [1927–30; butcher; gaining the Buchanan scholarship] became President, Glasgow University Union, 1934–5; minister, St Stephen's, Glasgow 1946–66, and Dunblane Cathedral 1966–84. He became Moderator of the General Assembly, 1977–8.

(Rev. Canon) Arthur Hodgkinson (1913–1995) [1924–31; traveller] became deacon, 1939; priest, 1940 and priest-in-charge, St Ebba's, Eyemouth. He was Provost of St Andrew's Cathedral, Aberdeen, 1965–78, and in charge of the diocese of Edinburgh, 1982–6.

(Rt Rev.) Robert Halliday (b. 1932)[83] [1941–51; leather goods agent] was a deacon, 1957; priest, 1958; assistant curate, 1957–63; Rector, Church of the Holy Cross, Edinburgh, 1963–83; Rector, St Andrew's Church, St Andrews, 1983–90; and Bishop of Brechin, 1990–6.

(Rev.) John Russell[84] (b. 1933) [1945–51; docks manager, Bombay] became a minister, 1957. He held charges in Ontario, Motherwell, Rotterdam and Kintyre, 1958–78; and was minister of Tillicoultry parish, 1978–2000.

Military

(Air Vice-Marshal) Thomas Macdonald (1913–1996) [1923–7; costumier] joined the RAF Medical Brigade, 1933; and became PMO, Bomber Command, 1956–8; PMO Middle East Air Force, 1958–61; and PMO Technical Training Council, RAF 1961–5.

(Major-General) John (Jack) Irvine (1914–1998) [1922–33; teacher; deemed 'intelligent' and 'industrious'] graduated from Glasgow and joined the RAMC, 1940. After war service in Africa and the Mediterranean, he served post-war in Austria, Korea, Malaya, Germany, and Ghana. He was director, Medical Services, British Army of the Rhine, 1973–5.

(Colonel) J. Neilson Lapraik (1915–1984) [1927–34; sales manager] studied law. He did service in the western Desert, Abyssinia, Eritrea, Sicily and the Aegean islands. He was mentioned in dispatches six times and became known as 'The Black Spot'. In June 1952 he took command of the 21st SAS regiment. He was President of the London High School Club, 1955–6.

(Air Marshal Sir) Harry Burton (1919–1993) [1932–4; engineer; noted for his perseverance] joined the RAF, 1937 and saw war service in Europe, India and the Pacific. He was CO RAF Scampton, 1960–2; and C-in-C Air Support Command, 1970–3.

(Major-General) Charles Dunbar (1919–1981) [1927–37; doctor; 'industrious'] saw war service with the Royal Artillery and the Parachute regiments, and post-war service in Palestine, Malta, Egypt, Cyprus, Suez, Jordan, Aden, Libya and Germany. He was Director of Infantry at the War Office, 1970–3.

Medical

(Prof.) David Anderson (1904–1988) [1918–21; draper; winning the Smart Prize and becoming Modern Dux] became Professor of Midwifery and

Diseases of Women at Anderson College of Medicine, 1934–7; Freeman of the City of Glasgow; and Muirhead Professor of Obstetrics and Gynaecology, University of Glasgow, 1946–70.

(Prof.) Thomas Anderson (1904–1990) [1917–23; commercial traveller] became a hospital physician in Glasgow; Professor of Infectious Diseases, University of Glasgow, 1959–64; and the Henry Mechan Professor of Public Health, University of Glasgow, 1964–71.

(Sir) Hector MacLennan (1905–1978) [1918–23; journalist; he had mature opinions and was seen as a natural leader] became an eminent gynaecologist, working at the Glasgow Royal Maternity and Women's Hospital, 1934–71. He was Chair, Scottish Tourist Board, 1969–74, and Lord High Commissioner to the General Assembly, 1975 and 1976.

(Dr) Archibald Kerr (1907–1990) [1916–23; lawyer; with 'great ability and sunny temperament'] became a lecturer in Clinical Surgery, Glasgow University, 1946–72; surgeon, Western Infirmary, 1954–72; and President, Royal College of Physicians and Surgeons, Glasgow, 1964–6.

(Dr) Kenneth Hutchin (1908–1993) [1922–5; engineer] left the School at sixteen to become an engineer, but later studied Medicine. He spent three years in a prisoner-of-war camp in South-East Asia. He became medical correspondent of the *Sunday Telegraph* then the *Daily Telegraph*. He wrote an international best-seller, *How Not to Kill Your Husband* (1962), and a series of sequels.

(Sir) Ralph Southward (1908–1997) [1919–25; sailor; judged a 'very intel-ligent, earnest worker'] won the Paterson Bursary for Medicine at Glasgow University and became a physician, Western Infirmary and Royal Hospital for Sick Children, Glasgow; apothecary to the household of Queen Elizabeth, Queen Mother, 1966–86, to the household of Duke of Gloucester, 1966–75, to Her Majesty's household, 1964–74, and to the Queen, 1972–4.

(Dr) James Liston (1909–1996) [1921–26; river pilot; a 'clever, self–assured boy'] became Medical Officer, Kenya, 1935; Director of Medical and Health Services in Sarawak, Hong Kong, and Tanganyika, 1947–59; Medical Adviser, Ministry of Overseas Development, 1964–70, and Chief Medical Adviser, Foreign and Commonwealth Office, 1970–1.

(Prof.) Joseph Knox (1911–1984) [1923–9; chemistry lecturer; did well in the Bursary Competition] became a surgeon, Glasgow Royal Infirmary, 1935–6; lecturer in Physiology, University of Glasgow, 1940–4, and King's College, London, 1944–54; and Professor of Physiology in University of London at Queen Elizabeth College, 1954–74.

(Prof.) James Hutchison (1912–1988) [1927–9; engineer; proved a 'very sound' pupil] held Glasgow hospital posts, 1934–61; Professor of Child Health, University of Glasgow, 1961–77; Dean of Faculty of Medicine at Glasgow, 1970–3; President, Royal College of Physicians and Surgeons, Glasgow, 1966–8; and Professor of Paediatrics, University of Hong Kong, 1977–80.

(Prof.) Hugh McLaren (1913–1986) [1922–31; slater; excelled at sport] joined the RAMC, 1940–6. He was Professor of Obstetrics and Gynaecology, University of Birmingham, 1951–78.

(Dr) John Smith (b. 1913) [1921–7; restaurateur] went on to Sedburgh before joining the RAMC, 1940. He did hospital work in Glasgow, joining the Department of Health for Scotland, 1947, and becoming deputy chief MO, Scottish Home and Health Department, 1963–75.

(Dr) Archibald Young (1913–1996) [1920–32; surgeon] studied at Cambridge and qualified in Medicine at Glasgow (1936). He was with the RAMC in North Africa and Italy during the war. He became a teacher of Anatomy.

(Dr) Thomas Semple (1915–2008) [1921–32; writer] was a pioneer in cardiological techniques in Scotland. In 1963 he was the first in the UK to promote successful cardiac resuscitation.

(Prof.) George Edington (1916–1981) [1926–34; warehouseman] gave a lifetime of service to medicine in West Africa.

(Dr) Martin Whittet (1918–2009) was the son of the Head of the School's Art department. Following experience at Glasgow Royal and Gartnavel in 1951, he became physician superintendent and consultant psychiatrist at Craig Dunain in Inverness, which he transformed over thirty years from a closed asylum to an open hospital. He researched and published on alcoholism and depression.[85]

(Dr) Robert Brittain (1919–1972) [1931–6; canvas merchant], had a distinguished university career, graduating MA, BL, BSc, MBChB, LLB, DPA. He was Forensic Medicine Lecturer at Leeds University and London Hospital Medical College; Consultant Psychiatrist, State Hospital, Carstairs; and Senior Registrar, Broadmoor Hospital.

(Dr) James Anderson (1923–2002) [1934–40; bank accountant] was appointed Medical Superintendent, 1957; District MO, Eastern District, Greater Glasgow Health Board, 1974; and Unit East 1 MO, Glasgow Royal Infirmary and Royal Maternity Hospital, 1984.

(Prof.) Crawford McAslan (1923–1983) [1931–40; boot factor] studied Medicine at Glasgow. He became a GP in Dunoon, emigrating to the USA in 1962. He became a lecturer, then Professor (1971) of the Department of Anaesthesiology at the University of Maryland. In 1978 he was made chairman of the department at Baltimore city hospitals.

(Prof.) John Brocklehurst (b. 1924) [1934–9; managing director] held medical posts, 1952–70. He became Professor of Geriatric Medicine, University of Manchester, 1970–89; and Associate Director, Research Unit, Royal College of Physicians, 1989–98.

(Prof.) James Lawrie (b. 1925) [1937–41; clergyman] was the Professor of Surgery in Ahmadu Bello University Hospital, Zaria, Nigeria.

(Prof.) Calbert Phillips (b. 1925) [1933–8; minister] became Professor of Ophthalmology, University of Manchester, 1965–72; Professor of Ophthalmology, University of Edinburgh; and Ophthalmic Surgeon, Royal Infirmary, Edinburgh, 1972–90.

(Dr) Henry Tankel[86] (1926–2010) [1933–43; wholesale jeweller] was a Fulbright Scholar 1954–5; President, Glasgow Jewish Representative Council 1974–7; President, United Synagogues of Scotland, 1978–85; Chairman, Glasgow Jewish Housing Association, 1996–2001; and a surgeon, Southern General Hospital, Glasgow, 1962–91.

(Dr) Archibald Wallace[87] (b. 1926) [1937–43; commercial traveller] became a medical practitioner, Campbeltown from 1950. He was Hon. Sheriff of North Strathclyde, 1950.

(Prof.) William Cranston (1928–2007) [1933–6; inspector of taxes; deemed 'exceptionally promising'] held hospital posts in Aberdeen and London. He became first assistant in the department of Medicine, Radcliffe Infirmary, Oxford, 1961–4; and Professor of Medicine, United Medical and Dental Schools of Guy's and St Thomas's Hospital, 1964–93.

(Dr) Kenneth Mills (b. 1929) [1941–7; insurance] became Medical Officer, RAF, and was Senior Lecturer, Orthopedic Surgery, Dundee University, from 1968.

(Prof.) Malcolm Cameron (1930–2003) [1942–8; clerk; qualities of leadership were deemed 'high'] became a lecturer in Pathology, University of Glasgow, 1962; senior lecturer/Reader in Pathology, London Hospital Medical College, 1965–72; and Professor of Forensic Medicine, University of London at the London Hospital Medical College, 1973–92.

(Dr) John Dagg (b. 1933) [1943–51; seed merchant] held junior hospital posts, 1958–65. He was a Fellow, Washington Medical School, 1965–7, and Western Infirmary, Glasgow, 1968–72; and consultant physician, Western Infirmary from 1972.

(Prof.) Peter H. Pinkerton (b. 1934) [1939–52; anaesthetist] trained in

Glasgow, Oxford and Buffalo, NY. He became Professor of Pathology at Toronto University and Head of Haemotology at Sunnybank Health Sciences Centre, retiring in 1999.

Charles Gillis (b. 1937) [1943–55; pharmacist] was lecturer/senior lecturer in Epidemiology and Preventative Medicine, Glasgow University, 1965–73; and Director, West of Scotland Cancer Surveillance Unit from 1973.

(Prof.) John Howie (b. 1937)[88] [1951–5; Professor of Bacteriology; School Captain 1954–55] was involved with laboratory medicine, 1962–6. He was a GP, Glasgow, 1966–70; lecturer/senior lecturer, General Practice, University of Aberdeen, 1970–80; and Professor of General Practice, Edinburgh University, 1980–2000.

(Prof.) A. Ross Lorimer (b. 1937)[89] [1953–4; teacher] was Registrar in Medicine, Royal Infirmary, Glasgow, 1963–6; lecturer, Cardiology, University of Glasgow, 1966–71; Consultant Cardiologist, Royal Infirmary, Glasgow, 1971–91; Hon. Professor of Medicine, Glasgow, 1991–2001; and President, Royal College of Physicians and Surgeons, Glasgow, 2000–3.

(Prof.) Charles Forbes[90] (b. 1938) [1948–55; manufacturer's agent] was assistant lecturer in Materia Medica, Glasgow University; lecturer in Medicine, Makerere, Uganda; Registrar in Medicine, Glasgow Royal Infirmary; and Professor of Medicine, Dundee University.

(Dr) Gordon MacBain (1938–2005) [1943–56; accountant] became senior surgeon in the Southern General Hospital.

(Prof.) Peter Howie[91] (b. 1939) [1951–7; Professor of Bacteriology] trained in obstetrics and gynaecology in Glasgow. He became lecturer/senior lecturer, Glasgow, 1971–8; clinical consultant, MRC Reproductive Unit, Edinburgh University, 1978–81; Professor of Obstetrics and Gynaecology, Dundee University, 1981–2002; and Deputy Principal, Dundee University, 1996–2001.

(Prof.) David Lawson (b. 1939) [1950–6; civil engineer] held junior medical posts, Glasgow. He became physician in Boston, 1970–2; consultant physician, Glasgow Royal Infirmary, 1973–2003; Chairman, Committee on Safety of Medicines, 1987–93; and Professor of Medicine, Glasgow University, since 1993.

Legal

(Sir) Harald Leslie, Lord Birsay (1905–1982) [1918–23; master mariner; 'keen and most trustworthy'] graduated in Law at Glasgow University and was called to the Scottish bar in 1937. Between 1947 and 1951 he served as Advocate Depute. He took silk in 1949.[92] He became Sheriff in the Scottish Borders in 1956, and in northern Scotland in 1961. As chairman of the Scottish Land Court from 1965 he took the title Lord Birsay, He became Lord High Commissioner to the General Assembly of the Church of Scotland in 1965 and 1966. He was made an Honorary Fellow of the EIS and, in 1973, a Knight of the Order of the Thistle. He was President of the High School Club, 1968–9.

(Hon. Lord) James Leechman (1906–1986) [1915–24; writer; exhibited 'very fair ability and good character'] joined the Faculty of Advocates, 1932 and became Advocate-Depute, 1947–9; Clerk of Justiciary, 1949–64; Solicitor-General for Scotland, 1964–5; and Senator of College of Justices for Scotland, 1965–76.

(Prof.) John Halliday (1909–1988) [1925–8; timber merchant; a 'very good student'] graduated from Glasgow with an MA and LLB (with distinction). After qualifying as a solicitor, he became a partner in a law firm in Glasgow. From 1955 until 1979 he also held the part-time post of chair of Conveyancing at Glasgow University. In 1965 he became a part-time Scottish Law Commissioner and was influential in reforming the law on personal bankruptcy and land tenure. He was awarded the first honorary membership of the Law Society of Scotland.[93]

Edward Hendry (1911–1965) [1923–9; lawyer] was admitted to the Faculty of Advocates, 1940; and was Sheriff Substitute of Dumfries and Galloway, 1952–65.

John Buchanan (1912–1985) [1919–31; writer; School Captain, 1930–1] was a solicitor. He founded the Milngavie pipe band, became SNP Provost of Milngavie and founded Milngavie Civic Trust. He served on the School's Board of Governors until 1983, and was President of the High School Club, 1976–7.

Arthur McIlwraith (1914–1994) [1925–32; valuator] became a solicitor, 1945–72. He was Sheriff, South Strathclyde, Dumfries and Galloway, 1972–85.

Stanley Gimson (1915–2003)[94] [1928–31; manufacturer's agent] joined the RA, 1941 and was a prisoner-of-war, River Kwai. He became an advocate, 1949; QC (Scotland), 1961; Sheriff Principal, Aberdeen, Kincardine and Banff, 1972–4; Chairman, Pensions Appeals Tribunals, Scotland, 1971–95; and Sheriff Principal of Grampian, Highland and Islands, 1975–82.

(Prof. Sir) Thomas Smith (1915–1988) [1923–9; restaurateur; left from class 1A as a 'promising, original pupil'[95]] went on to Sedbergh, then Christ Church, Oxford, as Boulter Exhibitioner, graduating with First Class Honours in jurisprudence in 1937. He was called to the Bar in England in 1938 and in Scotland in 1947, and became Professor of Scots Law at Aberdeen University in 1949. He became a QC (Scotland) and moved to the chair of Civil (Roman) Law at Edinburgh University in 1958. A decade later he transferred to the chair of Scots Law at Edinburgh, which he held until 1972. He was a Commissioner on the Scottish Law Commission.[96] He was knighted on his retirement in 1981. He then became general editor of the new *The Laws of Scotland: Stair Memorial Encyclopaedia.*

Lex Watson (1915–2008) [1930–3; solicitor] was a solicitor who worked tirelessly for the Scottish Scout movement, and was Commissioner for handicapped Scouts.

Baron Wilson of Langside (1916–1997) (Harry) [1924–33; solicitor] was called to the Scottish Bar, 1946. He became Advocate-Depute, 1948–51; Sheriff Substitute, Greenock, 1955–6, Glasgow 1956–65; QC (Scotland), 1965; Solicitor-General, Scotland, 1965–7; Lord Advocate, 1967–70; and Sheriff Principal, Glasgow and Strathkelvin, 1975–7.

(Hon.) Judge (John) Finlay (1917–1989) [1929–35; minister; 'worked well in spite of indifferent health'] was called to the Bar, Middle Temple, 1946; became a QC, 1973; and was a Circuit Judge, 1976–89.

A. Leonard Aitkenhead (1918–2004) [1928–35; teacher] graduated from Glasgow in Arts (1938) and Law (1939). He completed his Law apprenticeship after the war, and in 1950 became a partner in A.J. and A. Graham. He was Honorary Secretary, (1952–65) and President (1974–5) of the High School Club.

Baron Emslie of Potterton (1919–2002) (George) [1930–7; insurance company manager; deemed 'a very good scholar'] went on to Glasgow University, where he graduated MA in 1940. He was mentioned in dispatches and appointed MBE (military division) for his war service. After the war he was admitted to the Scottish Bar in 1948, specialising in personal injury cases. He took silk in 1957. Emslie was appointed Sheriff of Perth and Angus in 1965, and two years later he was elected Dean of the Faculty of Advocates. Following his appointment to the Court of Session in March 1972, he was appointed Lord President of the Court of Session and Lord Justice General of Scotland, posts he held until his retirement in 1989. He was made a life peer in 1980. He was Vice-Chair of the Trustees of the National Library of Scotland and FRSE (from 1987).[97]

Robert Taylor (1919–1993) [1931–7; rep.] was called to the Scottish Bar,

1944 and Middle Temple, 1948. He became a lecturer in International Private Law, University of Edinburgh, 1947–69; Sheriff Principal, Stirling, Dunbarton and Clackmannan, 1971–5; and Sheriff Principal, Tayside, Central and Fife, 1975–90.

(Sir) James Highgate (1920–1997) [1931–8; engineer; contributed to the school orchestra] became a solicitor; President, Scottish Conservative and Unionist Association, 1987–9; and a Governor of the High School, 1981–90. He was the brother-in-law of Norrie Thomson.

Marcus Stone (b. 1921) [1932–7; furniture dealer] became a solicitor 1949; advocate 1965; Sheriff, Stirling, Dumbarton and Clackmannan, 1971–6; Glasgow and Strathkelvin, 1976–84; and Lothian and Borders, 1984–93.

Norman Irvine (1922–2005) [1933–8; civil engineer; 'self-reliant' and 'quick-witted'] became a solicitor, 1943. He was called to the Bar, Gray's Inn, 1955; became a QC, 1973; and Recorder of the Crown Court, 1974–86.

John Mowat (1923–2001) [1927–34; surgeon; an 'excellent pupil'] was a journalist, 1947–52. He was an advocate, 1952; Sheriff Substitute/Sheriff, Fife and Kinross, 1960–74, Lanark and Glasgow (later Strathkelvin), 1974–88; a QC (Scotland), 1988; and Sheriff Principal, South Strathclyde, Dumfries and Galloway, 1988–93. He presided over the fatal accident inquiry following the Lockerbie disaster.

David Cunningham (1924–1995) [1929–42; garage proprietor; showed 'considerable powers of leadership'] became a solicitor, 1951. He was legal assistant, senior legal assistant, assistant, deputy, in the Office of Solicitor to the Secretary of State, 1954–80; and Solicitor to the Secretary of State, 1980–4.

Thomas Boyd (1925–2006) [1939–43; widow] graduated MA and LLB from Glasgow and became senior partner in his firm in 1971. He specialised in commercial conveyancing.

William Haggarty[98] (b. 1926) [1937–43; motor hirer and contractor] became a solicitor, 1950. He was Honorary Sheriff, South Strathclyde, Dumfries and Galloway and a Governor, Craigie College of Education, Ayr, 1983–91.

James Chadwin (1930–2006) [1940–7; teacher; Modern Dux (1946–7)] gained a scholarship to Oxford University. He appeared as QC in several high-profile murder cases, the most famous being as counsel for Peter Sutcliffe in the Yorkshire Ripper trial in 1981.

Iain Baillie (b. 1931)[99] [1945–9; railway engineer] became an international lawyer. He was senior European partner in Ladas and Parry (of New York, Chicago, Los Angeles, London and Munich); and was admitted to the New York Bar and federal courts, including the Supreme Court.

Hector Maclean (b. 1931) [1940–9; factory foreman] became an advocate, 1959. He was Sheriff, North Strathclyde, 1968–88; and Sheriff, Lothian and Borders, 1988–2003.

Leonard Turpie (1934–2008) [1940–52; doctor] was President of the Glasgow University Conservative Club and University Dialectic (Debating) Society. A lawyer, he became a Conservative councillor for Kelvinside in 1968 and leader of the Conservative group until 1982. He was Secretary of the FP Club and took a leading part in the fight to save the High Schools.

J. Stuart Forbes (b. 1936) [1945–53; manufacturer's agent] became a solicitor, 1959; advocate, 1962; Sheriff, Lothian and Borders, 1976–80; and Sheriff, Tayside, Central and Fife, 1980–2002.

Alexander Forbes[100] (b. 1937) [1948–54; lawyer] became a solicitor, 1961. He was Chairman, Scottish Friendly Assurance Society Ltd., 1996–2006; and partner in Robertson Paul (Solicitors) Glasgow.

James Fraser (b. 1937) [1946–55; commercial traveller; Classical Dux] became a solicitor, 1961; partner, Bird Son & Semple, 1967–84; and Sheriff, Grampian, Highland and Islands, 1984–2002.

Alexander Douglas Forbes (1938–1994) [1948–56; cashier] became a lawyer. He was Secretary of the High School FP Rugby Club for eighteen years, and a Governor of the new School.

Academic

(Prof.) Alan Lendrum (1906–1994) [1917–22; minister; noted for his 'very good conduct and excellent capacity'] became Professor of Pathology, St Andrews University, 1947–67; Professor of Pathology, University of Dundee, 1967–72; and was chairman of the Governors of Duncan of Jordanstone College of Art, 1975–7.

(Prof.) James Hyslop (1908–1984) [1919–26; science inspector; deemed an 'all round first-class boy' who was School Dux, 1925–6] took a First Class degree in Mathematics at Glasgow University and studied at Christ's College, Cambridge. He became a lecturer at Glasgow University 1933–41; Professor of Mathematics, Witwatersrand University; and between 1963–75 was Principal and Vice-Chancellor, Rhodes University.

(Prof.) John Aitken (1913–1992) [1923–5; inspector of ships' provisions; 'earnest and painstaking'] became Professor of Anatomy, University of London at University College, 1965–80.

(Prof.) Lionel Stones (1914–1987) [1926–32; gas engineer; 'eminent in social subjects'] studied at Glasgow and Oxford. He became a lecturer in

History, University of Glasgow, 1945–56. He was Professor of Medieval History, Glasgow, 1956–78; President, Glasgow Archaeological Society, 1969–72; and Chairman, Ancient Monuments Board of Scotland, 1968–73.

Daniel Martin (1915–2006) [1927–32; widow] was a lecturer in Mathematics, Royal Technical College, Glasgow, 1938–47 and lecturer/senior lecturer, Mathematics, Glasgow University, 1947–80. He became a Fellow of the RSE.

(Prof.) William Watson (1917–2007) [1926–30; assistant secretary; proved 'excellent' in every way] was a member of the Intelligence Corps, 1940–6. He became Assistant Keeper, British Museum, 1947–66; Professor of Chinese Art and Archaeology in the University of London, at the School of Oriental and African Studies, 1966–83; and Head of Percival David Foundation of Chinese Art, 1966–83.

(Prof.) David Flint (b. 1919)[101] [1929–36; grocer] became a CA. He was appointed lecturer in Accountancy, University of Glasgow, 1950; Professor of Accountancy, 1964–85; Dean of the Faculty of Law, 1971–3, and Vice-Principal, 1981–5, Glasgow University. He was also President, Institute of CA of Scotland, 1975–6.

Louis de Banzie (1920–2007) [1925–38; yarn manager] became the Keeper of the School's archives and produced the High School of Glasgow Scrapbook.

(Prof.) Hugh Clegg (1920–1995) [1927–30; minister] went on to Oxford University and became a protégé of G.D.H. Cole. He was a fellow of Nuffield College and Professor of Industrial Relations at Warwick University (1967). He became an influential academic voice on the industrial relations practices of the Wilson and Callaghan governments.

David Stewart (1920–2006) [1935–7; school teacher; a 'good worker'] was a schoolmaster, 1947–65, at Kelvinside Academy and Galashields Academy. He was appointed Rector, Selkirk High School, 1965–81. He was a member, Selkirk Town Council, 1967–75 and Borders Regional Council, 1982–6.

(Prof.) David Walker (b. 1920)[102] [1929–38; banker; won the Mackindlay Prizeman in Classics] became an advocate (Scotland) 1948, a barrister, Middle Temple (1957) and a QC in Scotland (1958). He was founding Professor of Jurisprudence, Glasgow University, 1954–8; Regius Professor of Law, Glasgow University, 1958–90; Fellow of the British Academy (1976); and a Fellow of the Royal Society of Edinburgh (1980). He was Chairman, High School of Glasgow Educational Trust, 1982–2002.

(Prof. Sir) Alastair Currie (1921–1994) [1935–8; master baker] became lecturer/senior lecturer, Pathology, University of Glasgow, 1947–59; Professor of Pathology at Aberdeen University, 1962–72 and at Edinburgh University, 1972–86; pathologist, Royal Infirmary, Edinburgh; and consultant pathologist for Lothian Health Board. He was President, Royal Society of Edinburgh, 1991; and Chairman, Governors of Beatson Institute for Cancer Research, 1984–91.

(Prof.) John Hawthorn (1921–1993) [1933–8; printer and publisher] became Professor of Food Science at the Royal College, Glasgow (later Strathclyde University) in 1958, the first such appointment in the UK.

(Prof.) Donald MacRae (1921–1998) [1934–8; engineer] graduated from Glasgow University in History in 1942. After taking another year of Economics he attended Balliol College, Oxford, gaining a First Class degree in PPE. He became a lecturer in Sociology at the London School of Economics (LSE) in 1945, reader in 1954 and professor in 1961. He was the founding editor of the *British Journal of Sociology* (1950–64) and played a major part in developing the subject.[103]

George Riddell (1925–1988) [1931–43; clergyman] became Vice-Principal of Jordanhill College of Education. He was a member of the Consultative Committee on the Curriculum, 1976–83 and was first chair of its Secondary Committee.

(Prof.) Thomas Douglas (1926–2009) [1935–43; mechanical engineer] became a veterinary surgeon, 1948–50; lecturer, University of Glasgow, 1954–77; Professor of Veterinary Biochemistry and Head of Department of Veterinary Biochemistry (Clinical), Glasgow University, 1977–90; and Dean of the Faculty of Veterinary Medicine, 1982–5.

(Prof.) Robert Jack (b. 1928)[104] [1942–5; bank agent] became a solicitor (Scotland), 1951. He was Professor, Mercantile Law, University of Glasgow, 1978–93; partner, McGrigor Donald & Co., solicitors, 1957–93; Convener, Company Law Committee of Law Society, 1978–85; and Chair, Hutchesons' Educational Trust, 1978–87.

(Prof.) Duncan Murchison[105] (b. 1928) [1933; railways] was a lecturer at Durham University, 1960–4; lecturer, reader in Geochemistry, Newcastle University, 1964–76; and Professor of Geology, Newcastle University, 1976–9.

(Prof.) Ioan Lewis (b. 1930) [1941–7; widow (typist)] was a lecturer, African Studies, University College of Rhodesia and Nyasaland, 1957–60; lecturer in Social Anthropology, University of Glasgow, 1960–3; lecturer, reader in Anthropology, UCL, 1963–9; and Professor of Anthropology, LSE, 1969–93.

(Prof.) John Cowan (b. 1932) [1942–9; lecturer in Technical College] became a design engineer, 1954–64. He was a lecturer, Heriot-Watt College, 1964; Professor of Engineering Education, Heriot-Watt University, 1982–7; and Director, Open University in Scotland, 1987.

(Prof.) Robert Downie (b. 1933)[106] [1942–51; chartered secretary] was lecturer, 1959, senior lecturer, 1968, and Professor of Moral Philosophy, 1969–2002, University of Glasgow.

John Mauchline (b. 1933) [1941–51; University Professor] became a research biologist UKAEA, 1958; research biologist, Scottish Association for Marine Science, 1962; and UK Editor *Marine Biology*, 1977–95.

(Prof.) Alan Smith[107] (b. 1936) [1949–55; traveller] was assistant in History, lecturer, senior lecturer and reader, Glasgow University, 1962–92; Professor in Modern History 1992–5; and Professor of Early Modern History, 1995–2002.

(Prof.) James Whitelaw (1936–2006) was a Fulbright scholar who became Professor of convective heat transfer (1974) at Imperial College, London. He published more than 300 research papers and successfully supervised 86 PhD students.[108]

(Prof.) Dugald Cameron (b. 1939)[109] [1944–56; aero engineer] was an industrial designer, 1962–5; lecturer, 1963–70, Head of Product Design/Design, 1970–91, Director, 1991–9, Glasgow School of Art; Professor, Glasgow University, 1993–9; Visiting Professor, Strathclyde University since 1999; and visiting Professor, Aerospace Engineering, Glasgow University since 2000.

Walter Sneader (b. 1939) [1952–7; masseur] became a leading world authority on the history of dogs. He was President, Glasgow Jewish Representative Council, 1986–9; and Senior Lecturer and Head of the School of Pharmacy, Strathclyde University.

Financial

(George) Roy MacGill (1905–2001) [1917–22; manufacturer's agent] became a CA, 1928; Town Chamberlain, Airdrie, 1932; Burgh Chamberlain, Dunfermline, 1947; general manager, Cumbernauld Development Corporation, 1956–70; and deputy chairman, Scottish Special Housing Association, 1971–6.

Ian Bowie (1913–2002) [1920–31; actuary] was a successful CA, becoming senior partner in Peat, Marwick, Mitchell and Co. in London. He was President of the London High School Club, 1958–60, and he and his wife Jean, who attended the Girls' High from 1928–33, became important benefactors of the new High School. His older brother, William (1909–1996) attended 1920–6; his younger brother, George (1920–1997), who attended 1927–38 and was considered 'academically brilliant', was School Dux in 1938, and took first place in the Glasgow Bursary Competition.

Gordon Allan (1914–1994) [1928–31 after Glasgow Academy] became a CA; a director, George Outram & Co. Ltd, 1960–75; Holmes McDougall Ltd, 1966–72; President, Scottish Daily Newspaper Society, 1971–3 and a director, Glasgow Chamber of Commerce, 1971–75.

George Dewar (1916–1998) [1924–34; bank accountant] came first in CA examinations. He became senior partner in Scotland of Peat, Marwick, Mitchell & Co., 1958. He was President of the Institute of CA (Scotland), 1970–1, and Treasurer of the High School Club, 1951–66.

Maxwell Thornton (1916–2008) [1927–34; rep.] became an actuary and reached a senior level in Scottish Amicable. He was Secretary of the Scottish Chess Association, 1959–74, and President of the Faculty of Actuaries in Scotland, 1975–7.

Norman S.S. Thomson (1917–1981) [1922–35; manufacturer's agent; School Captain 1935–6], President of the High School Club, 1972–3. Deemed 'Mr High School', he worked tirelessly to ensure the successful rebirth of the School at Old Anniesland. His bust by James Barclay was unveiled there in April 1983. His sons, Christopher and Alan, were School Captains in 1965 and 1970 respectively and his grand-daughter, Rebecca Mackintosh, was School Captain in 2008.

A.D. (Sandy) Maclaurin (1926–2006) [1931–9; textile manufacturer] took a Law degree at Glasgow and went on to be a CA, becoming senior partner in his firm. He was a Governor of Drewsteignton (from 1971) and, after the merger, of the new High School for over twenty-five years. He was Honorary Treasurer of the High School Educational Trust.

David Bruce (b. 1927) [1939–44] became a CA, 1955. He was partner, Deloitte Haskins and Sells, 1974–87; and President, Institute of CA (Scotland), 1980–1.

(Dr) Duncan Cameron (1927–2006) [1936–44; linen merchant] qualified in law and as a CA. He was assistant accountant, Edinburgh University, 1952–65; Secretary, Heriot-Watt University, 1965–90; and Chairman of Council, Royal Scottish Geographical Society, 1983–8.

W. Stewart McFarlane[110] (b. 1933) [1943–51; CA] became a CA and was President, Glasgow Chamber of Commerce, 1990–2.

Administrators (Politicians)

William Paterson (1911–1976) [1920–30; boot and shoe merchant] became a solicitor (Scotland), 1936; and served in the Foreign Service as Secretary, Counsellor and High Commissioner. He was British Consul-General, Sao Paulo, 1965–8 and Secretary, Government Hospitality Board, 1968–76.

(Sir) Norman Graham (1913–2010)[III] [1925–31; engineer; Joint Dux of School, 1930–1] went on to gain a First Class degree at Glasgow in History. He entered the Department of Health, Scotland, 1936, becoming Private Secretary, Principal Private Secretary, Assistant Secretary and Under-Secretary of various Scottish Government departments, 1939–63, and Secretary, Scottish Education Department, 1964–73. He was a Fellow of the RSE.

(Sir) Gilmour Anderson (1914–1977) [1929–32; solicitor] became the youngest Progressive Glasgow Town councillor, 1938, and a solicitor, 1939. He was President, Scottish Unionist Association, 1960–1; and Chairman, Conservative Party in Scotland, 1967–71.

(Sir) James (Duncan) Jones (1914–1995) [1923–30; widow; 'bright and intelligent'] gained a First Class degree from Glasgow before going to Oxford. He joined the Admiralty, 1941, and the Ministry of Town and Country Planning, 1946. He became Principal Private Secretary, Under-Secretary, Deputy Secretary, and Secretary of Government departments, 1947–72; and Permanent Secretary of the Department of the Environment, 1972–5.

Douglas Smith (1915–1988) [1926–32; buyer; an 'excellent worker'] joined the Inland Revenue, 1938. He became Assistant Secretary, Inland Revenue, 1952–9; Under-Secretary, Medical Research Council, 1964–7; and Commissioner of Inland Revenue, 1968–75.

(William) George Pottinger (1916–1998) [1928–33; clergyman] became Assistant Principal, Principal, Private Secretary, Assistant Secretary, and Under-Secretary of (Scottish) Government departments from 1939. He was Secretary, Department of Agriculture and Fisheries, Scotland, 1971. He was jailed for five years in 1974, following his conviction for corruptly receiving gifts from the architect John Poulson.

Colin Campbell (b. 1919) [1924–36; goods manager; had 'outstanding linguistic gifts' which won him the Modern Dux] studied at Glasgow, Rennes and Heidelberg. He was employed in the UN Language section, and was a member of the UN Commission supervising Korean elections (1948) and the Commission on Eritrea (1950).

(Sir) (John) Ian Thomson (1920–2008) [1928–36; company director; 'exemplary'] served in the Colonial Service in the Pacific before and after Japan's attack on Pearl Harbour. His work in Fiji from 1946 made an 'outstanding and abiding contribution to Fiji and the Fijian people'. He was Administrator in the British Virgin Islands, 1967–71.

Robert Dewar (b. 1923) [1929–41; surgeon; SC, 1940–1] took a degree in Forestry at St Andrews University. He was Conservator of Forests, Nigeria and Nyasaland, 1944–64; Permanent Secretary, Minister of Natural Resources, Malawi, 1964–8; and World Bank Agriculturalist, 1969–84.

(Sir) George Moseley (b. 1925) [1936–9; Post Office] was Assistant Principal, Assistant Private Secretary, Private Secretary, Principal Private Secretary, Assistant Secretary, Under-Secretary, and Depute Secretary, of various Government departments, 1950–81. He was Permanent Secretary, Department of the Environment, 1981–5; and chairman, British Cement Association, 1987–96.

Charles Boxer (b. 1926) [1931–42; clergyman] took on a Church of England ministry, 1950–4; was apprentice to a solicitor, 1954–8; joined the Dominican Order (RC), 1958–67; became a Senior Community Relations Officer, Wandsworth, 1967–77; and Director, Community Affairs and Liaison Divisional Commissioner for Racial Equality, 1977–81.

(Sir) Ian Sinclair (1926–2008) [1934–9; managing director; gained a scholarship to Merchiston] read law at Cambridge. He spent thirty-four years in the Diplomatic Service, the last eight (1975–84) as Legal Adviser to the Foreign and Commonwealth Office. He became a QC in 1979.

(Sir) Teddy (Edward) Taylor (b. 1937)[112] [1943–54; cashier] became a journalist with the *Glasgow Herald*, 1958–9; an industrial relations officer, 1959–64; Conservative MP for Glasgow Cathcart, 1964–79; ; Parliamentary Under-Secretary, Scottish Office, 1970–1 and 1974; Opposition spokesman on Trade, 1977 and on Scottish Affairs 1977–9; Conservative MP for Southend East 1980–97 and for Rochford and Southend East, 1997–2005.

Iain MacCormick (b. 1939) [1944–57; solicitor] was captain in the Yeomanry, 1957–67; and Scottish Nationalist MP for Argyll, 1974–9. He became one of the original members of the Social Democratic Party, founded in 1981.

Writers (Artists, Architects, Poets, Journalists)

Alastair Borthwick (1913–2003) [1924–9; electrical engineer; left school at sixteen to become a copytaker on the *Evening Times*] moved upwards to the

Glasgow Weekly Herald and wrote about rock-climbing for its open-air page. His first book, *Always a Little Further*, in 1939, became a classic. He began a broadcasting career, which continued until 1995. 'On air he was prolific as he was catholic in subject matter.'[113]

Robert Rogerson (1917–2007) [1929–36; joiner] went into private practice as an architect until 1982.

(Prof.) Edwin Morgan (b. 1920)[114] [1934–7; iron merchant; did excellent work for the School magazine] had posts in the English department, University of Glasgow, 1947–75, before becoming Professor of English, 1975–80. He became Poet Laureate for Glasgow, 1999–2005 and has been the National Poet for Scotland since 2004.

John Dickie (b. 1923) [1935–41; stockbroker] worked on the *Sheffield Telegraph*, Reuters and the *News Chronicle*. He became diplomatic correspondent of the *Daily Mail* in 1960, becoming known as 'Scoop Dickie'.

Iain M. Lindsay-Smith (b. 1934) [1939–51; superintendent in remand home] became a reporter on national newspapers, 1951–71; deputy editor, *Yorkshire Post*, 1971–4; editor, *Glasgow Herald*, 1974–7; executive editor, *Observer*, 1977–84. He was Chief Executive and Managing Director, Lloyds of London Press Ltd, 1991–7.

Sport (Entertainment)

Andrew Jamieson (1905–1978) attended the School between 1917 and 1921 and was deemed 'a fine golfer'. He beat the great Bobby Jones 4 and 3 in 1926 at Muirfield in the quarter-finals of the British Open Amateur Championship. He defeated the American captain, Bob Gardner, 5 and 4 in the Walker Cup at the Old Course later the same year. He went on to win the Scottish Amateur Championship at Western Gailes in 1927.

Thomas Riddell (1905–1998) [1917–23; cashier] was Scottish mile champion eight times between 1925 and 1935 and set three Scottish native mile records, clocking 4 minutes and 15 seconds in 1933. He was selected for the 1930 Empire and the 1932 Olympic Games but rejected the invitations because of work commitments.

James McKechnie (1911–1964) [1919–22; chemical merchant; conduct and work proved excellent] joined the oil industry, 1928; H.J. Heinz in 1930; and became a professional actor, 1934, who specialised in radio, 1941.

Howard Lockhart (1912–1987) [1927–30; solicitor] became Scotland's first 'disc jockey', broadcasting from 1923. He pioneered radio greetings programmes, and was an announcer and producer for BBC Scotland in

Glasgow and Aberdeen. He published his autobiography, *On My Wavelength* (1973).

Thomas Mackinnon (1912–1981) [1921–9; chemist] gained an apprenticeship in climbing on rock and snow in Scotland, Norway and the Alps. He was an automatic choice for the Scottish Himalayan Expedition (1950), which conquered seven peaks. Although he missed out on the 1953 Everest climb, 'Big Tom' took part in the 1955 Kangchenjunga Expedition. He was a pharmacist in Glasgow.

(Prof.) Cedric Thorpe Davie (1913–1983) [1921–9; teacher of singing; regarded as 'brilliant' and 'exemplary'] became a composer (film, theatre and radio). He included in his twenty film scores four for Walt Disney. He was Master of Music, 1945–78 and Professor of Music, 1973–8, University of St Andrews.

(Dr) Hugh Kennedy (1913–2005) [1925–32; spirit merchant; School Captain 1931–2, captain of rugby and CSM of the Cadet Corps] played in the Championship winning 1st FP XV in 1935–6. He was President of the High School FP Rugby Club. He worked as a well-respected GP in Strathbungo on the south side of Glasgow.

(Robert) Wilson Shaw (1913–1979) [1920–32; manufacturer; good sportsman] completed a Chemistry degree in 1936 and became an analytical chemist at ICI, 1936–55. He gained nineteen successive caps for Scotland at rugby and had the distinction of captaining the successful Triple Crown winners in 1938.[115] He was President of the Scottish Rugby Union, 1971 and Trustee of the High School Educational Trust, 1976.

Walter McLeod (1915–2008) [1924–32; auctioneer] was capped at ice hockey in 1934 and 1935. He also set a Scottish record for winning eight caps at golf for Scotland in home internationals.

Harold Sheppard (1917–1997) [1928–35; stationer; school cricket captain and a fine batsman] gained twenty-two Scottish caps for cricket between 1938 and 1952. He became a lawyer in Singapore.

Tom Pettigrew (1925–2006) [1936–42; Director, Earl Haig Poppy Fund] spent a lifetime promoting the sport of badminton. He was President of the Scottish Badminton Union, 1985–7, and was instrumental in establishing a home for badminton in Glasgow at the Cockburn Centre.

(Dr) Frank Deighton (b. 1927) [1938–44; clergyman], physician in Glasgow, won twenty-three golf caps between 1950 and 1960. He was Scottish Amateur Golf Champion in 1956 (Troon) and 1959 (Old Course). He played on the British side in the Walker Cup against America in 1957.

Angus Cameron (1929–1991) [1939–47; grocer] was Captain of the FP

XV for six seasons (and played in the 1950–1 and 1953–4 teams, which won the Scottish Unofficial Championship) and captained Scotland on nine occasions (1951–6).[116] He was Vice-Captain of British Lions on their 1955 tour of South Africa.[117]

James Mactaggart (1928–1974) [1937–46; SC 1945–6] has been labelled 'the most brilliant television director and producer that Scotland ever bred'.

Ian Foote (1930–1996) [1941–6; tea and coffee merchant] became a first-class football referee who officiated at three Scottish Cup finals in 1975, 1979 and 1981.

Colin Baxter (b. 1931) [1936–49; rep.] won thirty-three caps in tennis home internationals. He was Scottish Singles Tennis Champion in 1956, 1958 and 1959, and Scottish Hard Courts Champion, also in 1959. He played at Wimbledon, 1953–63.

John Fraser (b. 1931) [1942–7; stock taker; 'very keen on acting'] became a BAFTA-nominated actor of cinema, television and theatre. One of his earliest roles was as Inigo Jollifant in the second film version of J.B. Priestley's *The Good Companions*. He went on to have starring roles in *El Cid*, *The Trials of Oscar Wilde* (playing Lord Alfred Douglas) and Roman Polanski's *Repulsion*.

William (Bill) Tennant (1933–1993) [1942–50; depute manager] trained as an actor at RSAMD. In 1957 he successfully auditioned for the newly launched STV and became an announcer, and an anchorman on the news and current affairs programme *Here and Now*. He was the first recipient of the Scottish Television Personality of the Year.

Andrew Little (b. 1939) [1944–58; manufacturer's agent;] was School Captain (1957–8) and Captain of School rugby and cricket. He was a talented sportsman and formed a classic half-back rugby partnership with Gillie Greig in the 1960s. Son of the Anniesland stalwart John Little, Andy was President of the Scottish Cricket Union in 1991 and a long-serving member of Glasgow District Rugby Committee and the Scottish Rugby Union Committee. He was President of the High School Club, 2002–3.

NINE   The High School under Lees,
        1950–1976

This chapter deals with the rectorship of David Lees (1950–76) and the subject departments of the School. It examines the ethos of Elmbank Street and discusses the School's shortcomings in its final days. A detailed critique of the issues of fee-paying and selection follows, and leads into the sad story of the closure of The High School of Glasgow and the conversion of the Glasgow High School for Girls into a local comprehensive.

DAVID LEES: RECTOR 1950–1976

David Lees was born in Airdrie in August 1910. His father was schoolmaster in Glenmavis. He was educated at Airdrie Academy and gained a First Class Honours degree in Classics at Glasgow University in 1930. His career at Jordanhill College of Education was also outstanding and gained him a further year of postgraduate study at McGill University (in Canada), from where he graduated with an MA in Education in 1932.[1] Returning to Scotland, he embarked on a teaching career, becoming PT Classics at Campbeltown Grammar School (1933–46). During the Second World War Lees joined the Intelligence Corps and, thanks to his ability with foreign languages, he became expert in Japanese.

Lees was one of sixty-five applicants for the post of Rector at Elgin Academy in July 1946 and was appointed when he gained 'a clear majority over the other three short-listed candidates'.[2] He resigned on 2 November 1949 and spent a short time in administration as Director of Education in Roxburghshire (1949–50). Although he enjoyed the new challenge, he was separated from his family,[3] who stayed in Elgin as he vainly sought suitable, affordable accommodation for them in the Borders.[4] He also missed school life, and so he applied for the post of Rector of the High School when it became available in 1950.

The Glasgow Corporation Education Committee had advertised for a male under the age of fifty with an Honours degree, and received sixty-four applications.[5] A sub-committee drew up a shortlist of ten to be interviewed. It included the rectors of Greenock Academy, Hawick and Falkirk High School, two Heads from England and a PT from Winchester College, as well as David Lees. At the age of thirty-nine, Lees was chosen; although some Councillors wished to interview others, this was defeated 25–6.[6] He was welcomed to the School on 28 August by Major Donaldson, chair of the Education Committee and Former Pupil of the School. In his address Lees paid a warm tribute to Robert McIlroy for his work in the interregnum, and confirmed him as Depute Rector. He promised no sweeping changes, but undertook to maintain the standards and uphold the name of the School.

David Lees inherited a school of 868 boys (527 secondary and 341 primary), which by session 1958–9 had grown to 1,207 (807 and 400). However, it was then that the Corporation ended the Primary 1 intake. Secondary numbers grew to 919 (1962–3), while primary figures fell to 168 (1967–8). With the future of the School in doubt, secondary numbers began to decline too, reaching 674 (1972–3), with the primary by then only 127. In the intervening years Lees' main contributions were threefold: seeking to maintain a competent quality of staff who would teach within a framework recognised as standard in Scotland; maintaining a strict discipline within the School that would enable adequate teaching to take place; and working, with considerable success, to improve the buildings within which pupils and staff were accommodated.

Under Lees' leadership, the curriculum both in the Junior and Senior Schools was academic, thus fulfilling the wishes of the vast majority of parents that their sons be conducted to the gateway, at least, of higher education. In his early years Lees had been identified as a teacher of talent. In 1931 his Jordanhill tutor commented on 'his interesting and stimulating teaching which shows the mark and ease of scholarship' and on his resourcefulness in situations which were not straightforward and easy. At the High School he did spend some time teaching Latin to the Prep class (Primary 7 going into First Year in the Senior School), but his period as Rector was not marked by innovation in either curriculum development or teaching methods. Nevertheless, despite losing many able teachers to promotion elsewhere, Lees and his staff managed to increase Certificate presentations, and cohorts of well-qualified boys were sent to universities and colleges, business and industry.

The 1950s and 1960s were not periods of major reform in Scottish schools, and Lees was happy to continue offering a broad-based curriculum[7] with a considerable amount of freedom for individual choice in academic subjects. In Primary 7 of the Junior School there was a narrow focus on achievement in the eleven plus qualifying exam. Thereafter, streamed classes in the Senior School from First Year upwards had about thirty pupils in each. The general approach and the class sizes proved particularly successful with the academically able and those others who applied themselves diligently. The assumption made by the School, pupils and their parents was that, typically, most of the academically able boys would go to Glasgow University, perhaps after sitting the Bursary exam, and study traditional subjects there. And many boys did that, with 1965 the annus mirabilis: ten boys were placed in the top 100 in the Bursary competition, with five in the top ten, of whom Philip Chalmers (Dux) was first, David Stirling second and Malcolm Livingstone third. Despite a temptation to follow that by tightening the educational screw, Lees courageously continued to give boys a remarkable degree of freedom to develop their talents within a school education broadly conceived[8] – an enlightened approach which has considerable resonance today.

Though Lees was never actively involved in any extra-curricular activity, throughout his time as Rector the School continued the tradition of providing an impressive array of after-school activities, all supervised by teachers who gave generously of their free time to ensure that those with vision beyond their school books could develop their interests and increase their abilities in the company of their fellow pupils. The results were remarkable. Horizons were broadened by the Scottish Schoolboys' Club, Scripture Union, choirs, Stamp Club, Ship Society, Science Club, Railway Club, Aero-Modelling Club, Photographic Club, Chess Club, Literary and Debating Society, and the Combined Cadet Force (CCF). Highlights of the year included the inter-school debates organised by the Literary and Debating Society; voluntary participation in the CCF, with its twice weekly parades, pipe band and annual camp; and the School choir and orchestra, with their splendid annual concert.

With assistance from staff, pupils excelled in individual and team sports, including rugby, cricket, golf, tennis, swimming, rowing, athletics, basketball and curling. Many brought distinction to the School by representing Glasgow Schools and then Scottish Schools. The rugby XV of 1962–3 went through the season without defeat for the first time since 1929–30.[9] There was no stigma, although a little regret, attached to those who did not choose to play their games at Old Anniesland. For instance, in 1959–60 there were schoolboy internationalists in rugby and as well as in soccer and hockey, although the latter two games were not then played at the School. All of these activities, and more, complemented the academic offering so that pupils had every opportunity to develop their talents within a school environment which recognised that education must be underpinned by scholastic endeavour but consist of more than simply academic achievements.

The culture of Elmbank Street placed a significant emphasis on discipline. By the 1950s the School Rule Book issued to every new entrant ran to some sixteen pages; and the behaviour of each pupil was expected to conform to its content. David Lees condoned, and personally used, the belt for shortcomings not only in behaviour but also in academic work. Although a tradition of physical punishment had been established by his predecessors – and it should be remembered that a harsh regime was the norm in the years before the introduction of guidance systems[10] – there is no doubt that Lees and many of his staff took this approach to a new level. For that minority whose unruly behaviour might otherwise have gone unchecked, corporal punishment was a useful weapon used in the interest of the majority. However, some pupils recall that it was used over-enthusiastically by some of the less talented members of the teaching staff. For those pupils who were less academically able rather than simply disruptive, the threat of belting could add nothing to their progress or to 'the happiest days of their lives'.

Outside the classroom, Lees and his staff relied heavily for maintenance of the established order on the twelve prefects who made up the School Council. The Rector appointed the School Captain, but that boy then had freedom to choose a Vice-Captain and the others from among the fifth and sixth years. Academic ability was not a prerequisite, but the Captains of rugby and cricket, together with the Sergeant Major of the CCF, could expect to be appointed ex-officio, with others chosen to represent sports and major extra-curricular activities of the School. In appointing the School Captain, Lees did not restrict his choice to those who excelled in sports, nor did he rule out anyone who had repeated a year,[11] placing more emphasis on commitment and attainment in some aspects of school life allied to maturity and level-headedness.

The prefects had their own Council Room from which to operate and were expected to act as role models for the Junior and Senior Schools, setting standards of dress and behaviour for others to follow. For those who deliberately stepped out of line, prefects had the power, underpinned by the authority of the Rector, to require miscreants to write lines. However, all significant breaches of the School rules were dealt with by members of the teaching staff as they saw fit.

As in similar selective schools, there were some pupils who, for various reasons, rebelled against the prevailing ethos. That small minority saw themselves as outsiders. Critics of the system, despising what was available and those who benefitted from it, they were consequently unwilling to take part fully in the scholastic, sporting and other offerings of the School.[12]

Lees and his staff depended not only on the acquiescence of parents towards his methods of discipline, but also on their active assistance in maintaining the academic standards to which the School and its fee-paying parents aspired. Considerable emphasis was placed on homework, and specially formatted diaries, complete with the School crest, were introduced in Primary 5, which parents were required to sign at the end of each week guaranteeing that the pupil had at least attempted to complete the set tasks. These diaries were continued into the Senior School, but only as aides-memoires of what had to be completed. A further check, and record of performance, was provided by the termly report cards, which also had to be signed by a parent or guardian and included a record of attendance. The report card recorded for each subject the mark obtained by written exami-nation, the class average, and the relevant teacher's estimate of the pupil's attitude and application.

While Lees and his staff depended on parental support, they did not always welcome parental intervention or even dialogue. For instance, it is unlikely nowadays that any Head would be able to resist the establishment of a Parent–Teacher Association, as Lees did in 1960, on the grounds that individual and informal approaches to a Head meant there was no need for parents to be involved on general matters affecting the affairs of the School which their children were attending and to which they were paying fees.

In the issue of accommodation Lees was persistent in his requests to the Corporation, and it paid off. He had inherited the boarded-up Centre Block which had been awaiting refurbishment since before the Second World War because, understandably, the construction of new-build public sector housing had been given higher priority. Before the war, architects had been chosen – Messrs McCaig, Watson, Salmond and Gray, 111 Union Street – and contracts had been placed with trades in May 1938. The work was to involve the provision of additional classrooms, and a library and a gym, in the existing Centre Block. The monumental position of the old Centre Block was to be retained, but there was to be considerable internal alter-ation, as well as replacement of the east half of the block by several entresol

242 The Town School

floors. The contract also included a new entrance from Holland Street, two janitors' houses, and alterations to form an improved entrance to the cloakroom and refectory in the Assembly Hall block. Any hope of advancing the work ended in 1940, partly due to the wartime exigencies and partly as a consequence of the main contractor going into liquidation. The Centre Block was made wind- and water-tight and was used as a store by the Education Authority, while the janitors' houses were occupied.

When, in 1954, the School was deemed a priority again, Lees recognised that the current accommodation requirements were rather different from those of 1938. In October 1955 new contracts were issued. Cloakrooms were decentralised, and the large area they formerly occupied was joined to the existing refectory to provide a large dining hall with increased kitchen and catering facilities. The plans for the Assembly Hall were modified to provide a stage and retiring rooms. When the reconstructed Centre Block and Assembly Hall were completed, they were formally opened on Thursday 4 June 1959.[13]

This resulted in a change in the quantity and quality of classrooms. 'C' Block accommodated English, History, Geography and Music, with some additional rooms for Classics and French. The gymnasium added greatly to the facilities, and at last a library had been created on the top floor. The building also included the Rector's study, the Prefects' (Council) room, and the School office, which was run with great efficiency by the formidable Miss Catherine McLaren, Registrar from 1940 until 1968. Moreover, the refurbishment of the School hall and the dining hall greatly improved the quality of school life in general and lunches in particular. The classrooms in 'B' block – which housed Classics, Modern Languages and Mathematics – were mostly large and airy, with high ceilings and large windows, but the desks were still of considerable vintage and etched with the various comments of pupils from yesteryear. 'A' Block, built around a central well, housed the Science laboratories, the Art department studios, an exam hall, a lecture theatre, cloakrooms, toilets and some Mathematics classrooms.

Every department in the School benefited from Lees' thoroughness in the provision of accommodation, and all who worked with him appreciated his aim to produce the optimum conditions for teaching and learning. However, by 1972 it was clear that the outcomes were not as successful as he had wished. An HMI Report[14] produced in that year suggested that the newly introduced Business Studies 'compared favourably with anything to be seen in other schools in the West of Scotland', and that Mathematics was 'among the best'. The departments of English, Social Subjects and Classics were 'in good shape' and the Arts were 'well catered for', but the teaching of Science was 'a little better than average' and Modern Languages were 'disappointing'. Although exam results were creditable and the School generally effective and largely successful, HMI clearly expected more and regretted that many of their visits coincided with the Rector's absence.[15] The result was that inspectors were not reassured, and contrasted their findings with their conclusion following a recent inspection at Notre Dame. It was doing its 'creditable best', thanks to the leadership of its headmistress, who was 'single-minded and clear-sighted' and whose staff was 'in no doubt as to her values, policy, and aims'.[16] The implication was clear: the High School was judged as falling behind the standard of similar schools and falling short of the high expectations of the HMI, and Lees had not been able to 'clear their minds through direct discussion with him'. Both Lees' reputation and that of the High School suffered, as its case was not properly put. The HMI assessment of 1972 was a factual snapshot from the 'experts' and was important in influencing views and decisions in the future. It had no room for mitigating explanations. Lees' incapacity at a crucial time was compounded by ever-increasing apprehension in the School about the threat to its future, and the declining staff morale which was increasingly taking hold as the evolving system in Glasgow moved toward neighbourhood, non-selective education.

Taking an overall view of the two decades when David Lees was Rector, it is clear that his administration of the resources made available to him was outstanding. For that he was respected by members of staff who responded well to his style of leadership. His widow still regularly receives cards from some a third of a century on from his death.[17] They remember the Rector's support for them in any conflict with parents or outside bodies, his willingness to take on the education officers at Bath Street, the considerable autonomy given to staff in their classrooms, where teaching was carried on with the minimum of interference, and his compassion for boys and their families when they experienced hard times. On the whole, his pupils, at least those who kept the rules and were in tune with his approach to their education, also respected him. He became proud of the School and its traditions, and he was dedicated, particularly in his later years of office, to ensuring that its history was known and that its position in Glasgow and Scotland should not be undermined.

On his appointment to follow Rector Talman, David Lees had promised no sweeping changes, undertaking to maintain the standards and uphold the name of the School. Unlike Dr Pinkerton, Lees had wider educational and other interests to which he devoted his time outside of school hours. However, throughout his period as Rector he had, with changing emphases, remained true to his promise. It was his considerable misfortune that, in his later years as Rector, the same Glasgow Corporation which had appointed him made the achievement of his objectives for the School and its pupils such an uphill struggle.

When the School in Elmbank Street was closed by the Corporation in June 1976 Dr David Lees retired, with Sir Henry Wood noting 'his high intelligence, his sound scholarship and his steadfastness and determination'.[18] During his time in Glasgow Lees had also made a considerable contribution to education nationally. He was Chairman of the Board of Governors of Jordanhill Teacher Training College (1959–71),[19] Chair of the Scottish Council for Training of Teachers (1961–6)[20] and founding Chairman of the General Teaching Council of Scotland (1966–71). He was awarded a CBE in 1963. He was active in the Educational Institute of Scotland, being awarded a Fellowship, and he received an honorary degree of Doctor of Laws from the University of Glasgow in 1970. He was Chairman of the Business Committee of Glasgow University and a member of the Convocation of Strathclyde University. In retirement he joined the Board of the new High School, and took pleasure in its early development and success. He remained an avid supporter of Airdrieonians Football Club, becoming a Director and then Vice-Chairman of its Board (1980–5). He died in June 1986.

DEPARTMENTS[21]

Lees was fortunate to take over a High School staff of well-established teachers, who for the most part remained for lengthy periods. During the 1950s it was usual for new appointments to come from among experienced teachers in other Glasgow schools. It was also customary that most teachers of academic subjects were Honours graduates with a Chapter V qualification which allowed them to teach all stages of the secondary curriculum from First to Sixth Year.[22] Moreover, the School had a large Sixth Year, with a significant number of pupils following the syllabus for the Glasgow University Bursary Examination. However, by the 1960s there was a shortage of well-qualified Mathematics teachers, and as a result some new staff only held an Article 39 teaching qualification, which restricted teaching up to Third Year level; at this time these teachers were paid less than

Honours graduates. In the 1970s, with the future of the School under threat, many staff changes took place as teachers understandably took opportunities to move to more secure positions.[23] In this situation Lees fought hard in the interests of the School. Although it was widely felt that he was treated badly in his final years as Rector, he was allowed to remain in post after retirement age to oversee the closure of the School.

With the opening of 'C' Block, the staff room at the top of the administration block declined in use as most departments gained their own staff room areas. The loss was palpable, as the old staff room had been for many years an important focal point for staff. During the short break of forty minutes for lunchtime, it was a centre of activity: some marking, some last-minute preparations, discussions, a game of bridge, and the famous 'keepie uppie game' with a shuttlecock[24] all took place.

In the Junior School, most of the staff of the 1940s remained. Robert E. Rankin, who had left the staff in 1946 after eight years, returned between 1951 and 1958. His didactic approach encouraged independence in learning and initiative in studying. He lived up to his strict disciplinarian reputation, but this advanced rather than held back his career, for he was to go on to become Primary Adviser in Glasgow. When Miss Nina Logan retired, she was succeeded briefly by Miss Ethel Williamson in 1953[25] and then by Miss Peggy Young, who had originally joined the High School in 1932 from St James's School and had in her charge Primary 3, until she took over the Kindergarten in 1954. She built up a reputation as a fine teacher.[26] However, four years later the decision was made by the Corporation to end the teaching of the very young. Miss Young progressed with her then Primary 1 class through the subsequent stages until they reached the Primary 5 stage together.[27] It was this last stage that Miss Young was teaching at the time of her retirement after thirty-four years' service in December 1965. There was also the redoubtable Miss Newton, who looked after the welfare needs of the boys. Arthur Maciver (1947–55), Bill Ewing (1949–60), Mia Scott (1954–7 and 1959–65), Margaret Hobson (1957–67) and Janet Core (1966–73) are also remembered with a mixture of respect and affection.

In Classics, Gordon McCallum returned for his second spell between 1950 and 1953 and was Depute Rector before becoming headmaster of Queen's Park Secondary. Dugald ('Pa') Duff also returned in 1951 and taught until 1962, retiring finally in his mid-seventies. A scholar and a gentleman, he taught with patience and skill and was a Burns enthusiast who could quote at length. He was replaced by ('Ratty') Joe Hamilton (1962–76).[28] J. Kenneth ('JK') Clark also returned to become PT between 1956 and 1963 and proved a genial, kindly man with a great sense of humour.[29] George Chalmers joined in 1951 and took over as PT in 1963 and Depute Rector in 1966.[30] Kenneth Dyer (1972–5) took over as the last PT Classics in the School. Ian ('The Pit') Pitkeathly (1955–65) was a genuine, kind teacher with a slightly donnish manner,[31] while Jim Picken[32] (1959–66) coached rugby and went on to become number two at the Scottish Schools Inspectorate in Dalkeith. Bob ('Shiny Bub') Grassom (1963–70) had a rosy complexion affected by the sun which shone through his classroom window on the first floor of 'B' block; he went on to become Deputy in Girvan Academy. Roy Leitch, who returned to the School between 1960 and 1972, was also a memorable character and began a tradition of Burns Night celebrations. Mention should also be made of (Big) John Henderson (1957–66),[33] Richard Orr (1965–9)[34] and Raymond Taylor (1966–70), who became PTs at North Kelvinside, Hillpark and Bellshill respectively. Katherine J.V. Thomson (1971–74) went on to an illustrious career at the new High School.

In English Jack ('Daddy')[35] Orr was PT from 1951 until 1962, becoming headmaster of Crookston Secondary, and he was replaced by the respected Islay Shanks, PT from 1962 until 1972, and also rowing coach. Duncan Walker (1953–7) went on to become Rector of Blairgowrie High School, while Hector Macmillan (1949–62), who 'moonlighted' as a well-informed rugby correspondent, became PT at Adelphi Terrace, and Norman Macaulay (1954–63) became PT in Riverside.[36] Captain Bob ('Flash') Morton (1951–63) edited the School's Magazine, and was seen as a fine role model as well as being Commanding Officer of the OTC.[37] Slightly iconoclastic, Donald ('Cowboy') McCormick (1962–8)[38] instilled in his pupils a love of English literature, and he and David Menzies (1959–67)[39] were in charge of the Dramatic Society. Auditions were hotly contested, and public performances were always well-attended and often led to rave reviews. The Art department pupils, under the guidance of the punctilious Leslie Millar, produced the scenery, while others undertook the stage management, make-up, lighting and sound teams. The School was fortunate in that the new Assembly Hall had a fully functioning stage with proscenium arch and curtains, which allowed productions to be presented in a very professional manner. Tony Paterson (1957–67) also had a great interest in dramatics, and he went on to become Adviser to the Citizens' Theatre. More recently Alexander Gillies (1964–76) was appointed the last PT of the department in 1972, and he was aided by David Strachan (1965–75) and W.W. Bond (1972–6).

When Talman retired, the PT of Mathematics, Robert McIlroy, was made Acting Rector in 1950 for six months, during which time the strain took its toll. He retired in January 1954 with heart trouble, leaving a strong department of well-qualified and experienced teachers, including Tom Glen, strict disciplinarian Murdo MacDonald (1945–57), Sandy ('Chooky') Robertson, and Captain Jim Cowper, who took a considerable interest in the running of the OTC. The department was soon reinforced by the colossally patient Bill Pennycott (1956–62), Donald McNab (1958–65), Alistair Innes (1959–70), John Smith (1960–72) and David Moyes (1962–70). In January 1954 Peter ('Piggy') Whyte was appointed Principal Teacher of Mathematics, and he soon proved a competent successor to the line of his able predecessors. He had been educated at Shawlands Academy, where he was School Captain in 1930–1, and at Glasgow University. He taught at Jordanhill College School and Kelvinside Academy and, during the war, he reached the rank of Squadron Leader in the RAF. At the High School he was responsible for the steady increase in the number of Certificate Examination presentations, and the SED invited him to become a member of the Mathematics Syllabus Review Committee, while the Exam Board appointed him a member of the Mathematics Subject Panel. He also acted as Chair of the Scottish Mathematics Group responsible for the production of new textbooks. When in 1961 Deputy Rector Ure died suddenly, Whyte was an obvious choice for the vacant post, and for five years he proved his worth as an administrator and teacher. He left in 1966 to take up the post of Rector at Hutchesons' Grammar School. His successor, Robert Finlayson (1966–8) was also a member of the group producing textbooks, and went on to become headmaster of Allan Glen's School.[40] In 1968 he was followed by William Wilson, who returned to the High School[41] to be PT from Jordanhill College School, and he remained until 1973, when he moved to Hillpark Secondary as Assistant Head. He was succeeded by Peter Macmillan (1973–4), and in 1974 by the last PT Samuel Graham (1972–6),[42] his APT being R.J. Hart (1973–6). Andrew Livingstone (1968–70) was to become a successful Head of St Columba's School, Kilmacolm, and Douglas Smith gained a headship in Dumfries.

In Modern Languages, Stewart Simmie ran the department with long-serving teachers including Charlie ('Chick') Anderson; Ian 'Piff' Crerar (1935–55), who was qualified in French and Latin but taught German and was also known for his cricketing endeavours;[43] Ernest ('Ernie') Abbott (1930–54); James Maxwell (1948–60), who was replaced by Alexander Fitzgerald (1960–70); Duncan Clark (1954–64), who left to become PT at Hutchesons'; and Angus ('Zombie') McInnes (1955–65).[44] Arthur ('Paddy') O'Neill joined the staff in 1946 and succeeded Simmie as PT in 1960. He proved a ruthless disciplinarian, which was probably important in his promotion to Depute Rector in 1966. He shared the running of the School with Chalmers in 1971–2 during Lees' illness. With the future of the High School in jeopardy, he left in 1973 to become PT at Lossiemouth. He was succeeded by Leslie ('Corky') McCorkindale, who was on the staff from 1957 unitl 1967, returning[45] as PT in 1972–3. Meantime, David ('Fats') Young (1960–4) took over cricket before he joined HM Inspectorate; Hugh M. Campbell (1960–8) went on to Craigbank Secondary; while John Cummings (1966–76) was transferred, when the High School closed, to Victoria Drive; and PT Iain Macdonald (1968–76) moved to Hyndland.

The Science department under John ('Narky') Robertson included John McBride (1950–9),[46] who gave generously of his time to assist in the running of the junior rugby teams, and the talented and infinitely patient biologist, Dr James ('Doc') Low (1950–64).[47] William ('Jake') Harkness (1946–55) and James ('Mono') Crawford (1938–55) were a formidable double act. They were great friends and serial tea drinkers who inhabited neighbouring labs and taught and belted in tandem. When, in 1952 Willie Wright (1945–52) left to become PT at Dumfries Academy he was replaced by David C. ('Bandit') Mackenzie (1952–63), who ran the Cricket Club and regularly took School parties abroad. He went on to be Depute Head at George Heriot's and Rector of Falkirk High School (1971–89),[48] as well as serving for ten years as Chairman of Governors of Moray House College. Mackenzie was followed onto the staff by Bill Lilly (1956–63), Kenny McDonald (1959–72) and Bob Miller (1963–8). Robertson was replaced as PT by John Ure,[49] who joined from Jordanhill College School. He arrived with great plans and was Depute Rector from March 1955, but his health deteriorated. He took ill at school on 23 February 1961 and died within a few hours. The Science department was split in 1962, with Frank Dorward (1961–71) taking charge in Chemistry, while Vince Grant (1962–73) became PT in Physics. He made Physics fun and, inadvertently, dangerous. His lisp meant that he was the most imitated teacher on the staff. They were succeeded by George Younger (1971–4) and William Hamilton (1971–4 and PT from 1973), who were both promoted before the School's closure, to be replaced by Niharendu Banerjee (Chemistry 1975–76) and Robert Wright (Physics 1968–76 and PT from 1974). There were frequent changes in Science staffing. Those who served longer spells included Alastair Grant (1955–65), who was promoted to PT Physics at Bellahouston Academy; Stanley Brown (1956–62), who went on to Dunoon Grammar School; James Hamilton (1963–72), who became PT at Westbourne; Hugh Blackwood (1966–71); and John McBride. PT

Guidance Stanley Mumford (Physics 1970–6) and Joyce Mumford (Chemistry 1972–6) were both transferred to Shawlands Academy when the High School closed. Frank Bates (1969–75) was an exception in that he joined the staff of Drewsteignton and became a member of the staff of the new High School.

Harry McGill was a very important figure, being PT in Music from 1946 to 1964 and laying the foundations for a very strong department. He had an assistant, Douglas Gillies, who left to take up the post of Assistant Controller of Music, BBC Scotland, being succeeded by James Paisley (1955–9), who became PT Music at Coatbridge HS. Jack Bolling (1959–76) succeeded Paisley and became PT in 1964. He was to prove inspirational musically. Including classroom and instrumental staff, there were fourteen staff in total, with excellent assistants in Ian Milligan (who became PT at McLaren High School) and Bill Ritchie (who became PT at Glasgow Academy). The music in the Primary School was looked after largely by Cameron McNicol and Pearl Bolling.

The Senior Orchestra played at Assembly every Friday morning, and the pupils had a platform to display their talents at the end-of-session concerts in the St Andrew's Hall,[50] which held about 2,000 and was filled for two nights. In all, some 400 to 500 pupils participated. A significant number went on to a career in music. David Kent (1953–67) and Cameron Merriweather (1947–60) went into teaching; Willie Muir (1945–58) became principal viola in the Johannesburg Symphony Orchestra; Donald Goskirk (1947–60) joined the string section of the RSNO; Ian McPhail (1955–64) won a scholarship to study with Andre Gertler in Belgium and now plays in the Stuttgart Chamber Orchestra; Alan Hazeldine (1965–6) won a scholarship to study conducting in Varna with Celibidache, and conducted at the Guildhall School of Music in London;[51] the Boyd brothers both took up music, Eric (1964–73) as head of strings and orchestral organiser for schools in Ireland, and Douglas (1968–76) studied oboe at the Royal Academy in London and won a scholarship to study with Maurice Bourgue in Paris. He went on to a recording contract with Deutsche Gramophone and an international career as an orchestral conductor and oboe soloist. Bill Eddie (William Alexander) (1956–65) became a piano recitalist who lectures, teaches and writes on music. Alexander Bruce was the last PT of Music from 1972 to 1976. Bolling himself was PT until 1971, when he was appointed Assistant Rector. On the closure of the High School in 1976, he became Assistant Head at Hillpark.

In Physical Education William ('Sponge') Core (1937–63), became PT in 1945. He had been a pupil at the High School and, back on the staff, insisted on the highest standards. He was distinctive in his later years for refereeing junior rugby matches from a static position on the half-way line by way of a megaphone. He was succeeded by William Taylor, who had been on the staff from 1947 to 1956 and then returned as PT between 1963 and 1976. George Maclachlan (1949–61), an ex-paratrooper and himself a useful scrum half for Whitehill FP, was a gifted rugby coach under whose watchful eyes the senior rugby teams prospered and a succession of pupils were selected to play for Glasgow Schools and Scottish Schools.[52] The outstanding success of the FP side in the 1960s was a continuing tribute to his skills. Mike Hunter, for example, went on to play for Scotland. Bobby Dunlop, a pupil in the school in the 1930s, returned to the staff in the early 1950s.[53] Charlie Forsyth (1967–76) was to become a stalwart in rugby coaching at the new High School. All PE masters taught in the junior as well as senior departments.

The Art department was under PT William Hunter (1950–61), who had his watercolours exhibited at the Glasgow Institute of Fine Arts. His staff included Robert McLellan (1957–67). George Macdougall was PT between 1961 and 1976, and his staff included Lindsay Aitkenhead (1964–74) and Mark Gray (1967–74). A character memorable to the pupils was James Robson (1949–65), and Leslie 'Dusty' Millar[54] deserves a special mention for all he did for extra-curricular activities, including the Annual Sports at Old Anniesland during his long association with the School between 1933 and 1973.

Miss Mary ('Ma') Calder was the only lady on the secondary staff, but she taught only part-time,[55] as she was PT Geography at both Boys' and Girls' High Schools. Gordon Monteith (1957–65) taught Geography, as did Bernard ('Bernie') Partridge (1957–76), who also ran the Rowing Club. He was a kindly man who fired a number of boys with enthusiasm for chess, ensuring that the School was well represented in Scottish national competitions. The last PTs in Geography were Donald Hall (1970–4) and Alastair Stewart (1974–6).

John Morison (1946–68) was quietly efficient as PT History, full-time from 1961, and he was joined by Ian Gillies (1955–61) and Harry Ashmall (1961–5), who appeared a complete teacher – highly disciplined, motivating and amusing – and went on at an early age to headship.[56] Major Alastair Mack (1966–9), who had held a commission in the Highland Light Infantry, also taught History. He was very much the British army officer, and conducted himself as such within the School. He proved a very effective CO of the School CCF, ensuring its survival at a time when, following the demise of National Service, the boys were less inclined to participate in military activities. CCF camps were routinely held at Cultybraggan in Perthshire, but in the 1960s Mack took the summer camp to Osnabruck in Germany. The scout campsite at Auchengillan continued to be used for outdoor training, and field exercises following the Annual Inspection were always held there.[57] The last PTs of History were Gordon Monteith, who returned from 1971 to 1974, and Michael Grant (1974–6).

When Commerce (Business Studies) was added to the curriculum, it was led by the highly successful Barry Finlayson (1967–73),[58] who took over as PT in 1970. His presentation figures for Economics and Accounting were amongst the highest in the country. He was followed by Norman Wilson and G.D. Mackenzie (PT 1975–6), with J.J. Curnyn as assistant (1973–6).

Most staff appreciated the special character of Elmbank Street, which was solid, imposing and, in a way, grand. On the move from Elmbank Street, they saw themselves as 'exiles' forced to move elsewhere.[59] A few thought of joining the new High School. However, the vast majority feared that its ethos would be nearer to that of an English public school rather than the Scottish tradition with which they felt comfortable. Consequently, they were not too disappointed when Drewsteignton did not make strenuous efforts to employ them. Understandably they preferred to transfer to a 'good' local comprehensive, and the result was few staffing continuities with the new High School.[60] Indeed, with new buildings, new staff and new pupils (with a few exceptions), it is not surprising that not everyone connected with the old School welcomed the new School. In taking the name of High School, the new School was making a statement of intent.

FEE-PAYING AND SELECTION

In August 1927, those schools under the Glasgow Education Authority whose designations contained the title 'High School' or 'Academy' were, with five exceptions, renamed simply 'Secondary'. A year later fees, which were 'nominal' in the main, were abolished in eight of the Authority's fifteen fee-paying schools[61] but retained in some five exceptions.[62] Fearing that this might be extended further, the High School Club pressed the SED for legislation to allow the High School to have its own Board of Governors, while still being funded by the Education Authority. As the SED opposed this, nothing came of it.[63]

On 27 May 1943 the full Corporation decided by 47 votes to 41 (with 7 abstentions) that the Director of Education, R.M. Allardyce, draw up proposals ensuring the end of fee-paying in these remaining schools by the beginning of school session 1944–5. While so doing, Allardyce calculated that the annual cost to the ratepayers would be £50,545. He recommended, for practical reasons, discontinuing the High School.[64] He held that to continue to operate the School as a non-territorial school for pupils of very high intelligence with the necessary provision of a different secondary curriculum would threaten the status and usefulness of the existing territorial secondary schools. In coming to this view, Allardyce was influenced by Glasgow's efforts since 1939 to create a secondary school tradition equal to that of the fee-paying schools.[65]

In October 1943 the Corporation's Education Committee decided that a reshuffling of territorial areas was a more acceptable political solution than the closure of the High School. However, it pressed for the ending of fees in the primaries of the five schools. Such plans, however, ran counter to the policy of the Scottish Secretary of State in the National Government at Westminster, Tom Johnston.[66] He was concerned about the already overcrowded primary classes and the effect of distributing significantly more children into these schools.[67] With an overriding priority to avoid controversy, in February 1944, advised by the Secretary of the SED,[68] Johnston rejected the Corporation's plans. These received a further blow in September 1949 when the Progressive (anti-Labour) majority on the Council, in control of Glasgow for the first time since the war, rescinded the previous resolution to abolish fees in the five schools which still had them by 25 votes to 20.

Although the immediate threat to the High School had passed, there was no complacency in the School community. The appreciation was widespread that, when the SED was satisfied that the congestion in Glasgow schools would not be aggravated, then the High School would become a territorial school with a catchment area stretching from St George's Cross to the Clyde and from Central Station to Finnieston Ferry.[69] Those residing in the city but outwith that area, as well as those living beyond the city boundary, would have to attend the nearest school in their locality. The lack of continuing support for the School was also seen when, in 1945, land at Anniesland was purchased compulsorily for housing. The High School Club protested that the land might be needed for a school building. The response from the SED held that 'the new school, if and when erected, would constitute not a public school under Glasgow Educational Authority, but an independent fee-paying school conducted by a body of voluntary managers'.[70] Concerns about future intentions led Rector Talman to speak out in June 1945, defending the

School's heritage and its continuing unique and indispensable contribution to the social and cultural life of Glasgow and beyond.[71]

Realising what would be lost if the School perished, the Club determined to raise an endowment of £250,000 to save it, and it advertised the endowment fund in the June 1949 edition of the School Magazine. It believed in the right of parents to retain responsibility for the upbringing of their children and, by preserving the mixed geographical and social base of the School, the aim was to develop good citizenship and avoid a narrow parochialism of outlook. Severance of the link with Glasgow burgh was to be regretted, but the Club rejected the view that the existence of a non-territorial School would be detrimental to the best social order. Instead it planned for an independent governing body to run the School, continuing the highest traditions of service and scholarship.[72] Moreover, given an adequate endowment, the School would keep the fees at existing levels and offer free places to those who could not afford to pay. Given a co-operative and complementary relationship with the local authority, it was also hoped that it would be able to extend the practice it already operated of supporting pupils from primary schools with scholarships to the School.

However, despite the generosity of a number of individuals,[73] the target was not nearly reached. An article in the Magazine speculated: 'Probably the uncertainty about what would happen to the monies pledged if the target was not reached, or if the immediate need passed off, inhibited many potential donors and even more must have suspected or hoped that the Glasgow Corporation would have more urgent things to do after the War than to end the role of the School as THE City school.'[74]

Such resolve weakened the campaign against the School, especially as loyalties to the selective system and senior secondary schools remained strong in Scotland in the post-war period. Labour politicians in local government in Glasgow and elsewhere believed that the system embodied 'equal opportunity' in a classically meritocratic form: it provided equality of opportunity for children of equal ability irrespective of their social origins.[75] Belief in an egalitarian system pervaded the assumptions of Scottish policy-makers and ensured that there was little pressure from the Scottish Labour Party to support comprehensive reform,[76] and this despite the abolition of selection for secondary schools becoming Labour Party policy south of the border in 1951.[77]

Although the specific threat to the High School diminished meantime, generally in Scotland local authorities followed the advice[78] of Circular 206 of 1951 supporting 'omnibus' or 'comprehensive' schools as the best form of secondary education. Glasgow opened its first purpose-built comprehensive school, Crookston Castle School, in the south-west of the city in 1954, and in the country at large in the twenty years after the end of the Second World War the number of local authority fee-paying schools halved in number – falling from fifty-six to twenty-eight.[79]

Whatever reasons the 1945 Labour Government had for allowing local authority fee-paying schools to continue in Scotland,[80] its successor elected in October 1964 under Harold Wilson took a different view. It moved to abolish what it saw as an educationally undesirable system of subsidised privilege; local authorities charging fees in any of their schools anywhere in Britain now had to stop, and absorb them into a neighbourhood comprehensive system.[81] On 27 October 1965 Circular 600 was issued by the Labour Secretary of State, William Ross,[82] giving guidance to authorities on how to reorganise secondary education in Scotland on comprehensive lines. In line with the then Labour Government's intentions announced the previous February, the all-through comprehensive school was to be found in all but three areas of Scotland: Aberdeen City, Clackmannanshire and Shetland. By the end of that year, the only significant groups of Education Authority schools not covered by comprehensive reorganisation were the fee-paying schools in Glasgow and Edinburgh, about whose future no agreement had been reached. Of the 3,200 public schools in Scotland, only 26[83] were fee-paying local authority schools and, of these, 6 were in Glasgow and 7 in Edinburgh, making up less than 2 per cent of the total school population. In the Glasgow total of 5,177 pupils, some 3,798 were in secondary and 1,379 in primary: the High School (boys) was the largest school, with a total population in 1965 of 967 (including 185 primary pupils). The imbalance between the sectors in the Glasgow figures was the result of the Glasgow Education Committee's policy of closing the Kindergarten department of the Girls' High in 1962, and reducing the primary intake into the High School. Session 1957–8 was the last year of intake at age five into the latter; such a strategy was adopted to meet the criticism that it was easier to enter the High School secondary from its own primary than from other primary schools. By the late 1960s, the earliest stage to which boys were admitted was Primary 5 (age nine).

Demand for places in fee-paying schools appears to have remained strong, and generally increased. The roll of the High School secondary (went up from 499 (1948–9) to 919 (1962–3) before falling somewhat to 870 (1964–5) and 782 (1967–8); after some fluctuations, the roll of the Girls' High, which was 566 in 1947–8 had grown by another 20 by 1967–8. The main factors in this trend were the perceived quality of education on offer and the low level of fees charged.[84] Remarkably, the fee levels of 1912 remained unchanged for forty years, and even by the 1960s the 'smallness of the sums involved is, indeed, almost literally unbelievable'.[85] It was thus argued that very few parents were prevented from sending their children to fee-paying schools for financial reasons.[86] Choice seemed to be available without divisiveness. The most expensive fees were those of the Boys' School, set at £23 2s per annum for secondary and £18 9s for primary. The Girls' High fees were £16 4s for all classes. In all cases there had been no change since April 1952.[87] The proportion of pupils attending the High Schools from outside their own area was very high: 1 in 3 for the boys, and 1 in 5 for the girls. With these figures, there was a concern that if these Schools were forced to become territorial, both the quality and number of their pupils would decline.

In June 1966 the SED issued Circular 614, which asked local authorities to modify their schemes of transfer from primary to secondary education, on the lines of the advice given in Circular 600. John Bain, Glasgow's newly appointed Director of Education, recommended to the Corporation Education Committee on 7 September that 'as and when practical' over the next five to seven years, Glasgow's transfer scheme be modified, while in the meantime the existing arrangements should continue. Such a response was unacceptable to the SED,[88] whose Scottish Secretary of State, Willie Ross, a former primary school teacher, who had worked in a number of inner-city Glasgow schools, viewed the continuance of fee-paying schools as inconsistent with the comprehensive system of education.[89] Bain and the Education Committee were told to think again.

On 23 February 1967 Bain produced another cautious report, setting out the pros and cons of charging fees and stressing the need for consultation with the representatives of individual schools, which he gave over to a special sub-committee for further discussion. Only on the casting vote of its convener, George Moore, was the decision made to recommend ending selectivity and the payment of fees. A week later the Education Committee accepted this recommendation, although Councillor Moore was quoted as being 'anxious to retain as far as possible all that is good' in the selective schools.[90] Although concerned, High School defenders remained 'reasonably confident',[91] primarily because a few Roman Catholic schools were 'protected by law'.[92] In particular, St Mungo's Academy had made an agreement with the Corporation in 1955 that enabled the school to revert to the control of the Marist Brothers as a selective non fee-paying school. This had been concluded to give a better educational deal to Catholic pupils by allowing the Catholic working classes to rise to middle-class status. To tamper with this by making the school comprehensive would be politically risky for the Labour party, which had only a wafer-thin majority of three in the Council.[93] Leaving such difficulties aside, at least in the meantime, Glasgow decided that thirty-four of its schools would be formally recognised as comprehensive schools, and the transfer from primary schools to these comprehensives would follow Circular 614.

The municipal election results of May 1968 brought further succour to High School supporters. For the first time since 1949, Labour lost control of Glasgow to the Progressives and Conservatives, who formed a minority administration with Scottish National Party support. So, when Ross pressed ahead with Government plans to end fee-paying in local authority schools, on 27 September 1968 the Glasgow Education Committee reasserted its determination to retain fee-paying and selective Corporation schools. Shortly thereafter this became the policy of the full Town Council.[94] However, this clash between local and central government only slowed down rather than diverted the latter from pursuing its ultimate ends, given the majority that Labour had at Westminster.[95] On 25 November 1968 the Education (Scotland) Bill was introduced into the Commons by Ross and it passed its Second Reading 182 votes to 132 in January 1969. Despite attempts by the House of Lords to amend the legislation, the Government had its law placed on the statute book, and school education was to be provided by authorities without payment of fees.[96]

The struggle was not over, however. The 1969 Act had mentioned some exceptional additional facilities which an authority could provide and charge for, and these included 'social, cultural and recreative activities' as well as 'physical education and training'. A special sub-committee of Glasgow's Education Committee recommended that fees of £15 per annum for secondary pupils and £9 per annum for primary pupils should be charged from the beginning of session 1970–1 for the use of such facilities by pupils in the High Schools (Boys' and Girls'), Hillhead HS, Allan Glen's School and Notre Dame. The lawyers on the sub-committee had found a loophole – but it was legal.[97] The selective nature of these schools and of the non fee-paying St Mungo's Academy was also to be retained. The full Education Committee approved these recommendations on 28 November 1969.[98]

Secretary of State Ross increased the pressure in a letter, dated 23 January 1970, intimating that in terms of Sections 7 and 30 of the Education (Scotland) Act of 1962, as amended by the Education (Scotland) Act of

1969, he required Glasgow to submit for his approval, by 31 March, its arrangements for admitting children to the secondary departments of the city's fee-paying schools in the form of revisions of, or modifications to, the existing transfer and educational provision scheme.[99] This was given over to the special sub-committee, whose detailed response was accepted by the Education Committee on 20 March 1970. There was to be no climb-down. Indeed, with Labour ranks split,[100] the Corporation held that continuing selective schools was not incompatible with developing comprehensive schools,[101] that other priorities were more pressing than the selective schools and, with no funds being made available by Central Government for school building in any case, it would not be practical for many years to contemplate any changes.[102] The Corporation therefore stood by the transfer scheme of February 1968.

This was the situation when matters took another twist, this time at Central Government level. The prime minister, Harold Wilson, decided to call a General Election in June 1970, and during the campaign the Conservative Party reaffirmed its commitment to giving local authorities freedom to choose the form of educational organisation for their area.[103] This seemingly reasonable and responsible position was soon to prove a tragic hostage to fortune. Meanwhile, however, to the surprise of many pundits, the Conservatives under Edward Heath gained a majority of thirty. Heath appointed Gordon Campbell as his Secretary of State.[104]

Matters began well for the supporters of the fee-paying local authority schools. Responding to its new political masters, the SED issued Circular 760 withdrawing previous instructions dealing with the reorganisation of secondary education on comprehensive lines, and in July 1970 Campbell brought forward his first Scottish bill, restoring to education authorities the power to charge fees in a limited number of schools.[105] This was welcomed by Glasgow's Corporation on 26 November 1970, but the fragile majority supporting these moves locally was exposed as ratification was passed by only fifty-two votes to forty-seven. However, the results of the municipal elections of May 1971 dramatically changed the arithmetic, for the Labour party was returned to power in Glasgow with a majority of twenty-one. Fee-paying was immediately ended in the city's Corporation schools, and attention turned to the issue of selectivity.

Faced with this renewed threat, the Former Pupils of the School revived their plans of 1945–6, which involved establishing an independent school to carry on its traditions. By June 1971, however, a new stumbling-block had appeared. This took the form of the plans of the Glasgow Education

Committee, which favoured using the Elmbank Street buildings as a replacement for the Dundas Vale Teachers' Centre, scheduled for demolition in a proposed road programme. With this scenario prominent it seemed likely that any continuation of the School would mean building a new school, estimated to cost in the region of £1 million. At least land was available for building, as the High School Club owned the Anniesland playing fields, which had been bought, and ownership retained, by the FPs presciently to ensure that they could never be taken over by the Corporation. However, even assuming that planning permission could be obtained to build, the total costs involved in the venture made the prospect of retaining low fees bleak. If the result was a completely independent fee-paying establishment along the lines of Glasgow Academy,[106] then many argued that the particular ethos of the old School would be lost. Nonetheless, with what seemed a popular cause, hopes remained high because of good leadership at Council level with lawyer Leonard Turpie, Conservative councillor for Kelvinside and de facto leader of the Tory group as well as Secretary of the FP Club of 3,800 members, and because of support from experienced people such as Former Pupil Teddy Taylor, Conservative MP for Cathcart.

Glasgow's new Education Convener, Dr Daniel Docherty,[107] was appointed chair of a special sub-committee to consider the future of the corporation's selective schools. The existing arrangements were immediately rejected, and Director of Education Bain was instructed to produce a new paper on 'Future Arrangements for Selective Schools'. However, when it recommended retaining elements of selectivity with the former fee-paying schools becoming city-wide comprehensives, it was rejected out of hand[108] and Bain was instructed to produce a revised version. In this, discussed on 22 December 1971, Bain still advised a cautious approach, arguing that 'a complete reorganisation in August 1972 rather than a phased change-over will do untold harm to the educational prospects of most of those secondary pupils who have to change schools'. He further suggested that immediate changes could lead to some teaching staff leaving the profession, which would mean inadequate staffing at the schools in their new forms, or in local secondaries, whose rolls were bound to increase.[109] But such recommendations did not weaken what was now Labour's clear and united resolve to end further selective intakes.[110] Nor did they gain much sympathy from SED officials, who were critical of Bain's proposals, which seemed already to be dead in the water.[111]

The early months of 1972 saw an intense public debate.[112] Supporters of the selective schools mobilised and an umbrella organisation, the Freedom of Choice Committee, representing parents' groups from all the selective schools, co-ordinated the campaign. Representations from pupils,[113] parents and Former Pupils were heard by the special sub-committee of Glasgow's Education Committee in early March.[114] Ten days later, the Glasgow Presbytery opposed the end of selectivity in city schools by a 'massive majority'.[115] Of the 5,692 separate letters and telegrams to the Scottish Office on the issue, only twenty-one favoured Glasgow's proposals. A petition of 45,000 signatures was amassed. In the House of Commons, Teddy Taylor demanded the need for 'proper consultation'.[116]

On 6 March 1972 Glasgow's Town Clerk informed the SED that the city's Education Committee had approved proposals for reorganisation to take effect in August. There would be no further selective intake, and S1 and S2 classes would be transferred to local comprehensives.[117] The former selective schools would become local comprehensives, but both the High School primary and secondary would be discontinued,[118] the Elmbank Street building being used as a teachers' centre. Faced with these decisions, on 13 March Sir Norman Graham of the SED advised his political masters of the recent memorandum he had received from his Glasgow inspectors, HMCI Chirnside and HMI Johnston.[119] They had been asked to assess the educational contribution of selective schools in Glasgow to the school system.[120] Their report did not help the selective cause:[121] indeed it was a devastating indictment of these favoured schools. Although the selective schools had a favourable pupil–teacher ratio and a significant number of Honours graduates on their staffs, their achievements were not 'commensurate with this fact'. Perhaps this was because the schools had to rely increasingly on older teachers who had not sought (or achieved) promotion elsewhere; indeed, the selective schools no longer seemed to be attracting young, able, ambitious teachers. The result was a limited contribution to curriculum development[122] and educational thinking compared with that being made by staff in (formerly selective) now comprehensive schools such as King's Park, Shawlands and Hillpark. Even when reviewing examination results, the Inspectorate praised the creditable performance by selective schools; but there was evidence that some of their pupils were being insufficiently challenged, and pupils at the lower end of the ability range performed less well than what could reasonably be expected. Importantly, the results of 'creaming' away many talented children had a markedly adverse effect on certain comprehensive schools,[123] while the curriculum in many primary schools was distorted, as it was shaped to meet the needs of pupils seeking entry into the selective schools. Although all this suggested that the selective schools were generally efficient and successful on the whole, they were far from outstanding academically.[124] Indeed their disappointing performance overall meant that they could expect little support from the SED.

The Secretary of State and Hector Monro MP met SED officials on 16 March and, after consulting the Lord Advocate, the SED wrote to the Corporation a week later saying that until the Secretary of State had approved (or not) their proposals, on which he wanted further information, Glasgow should continue the primary schools and plan for a selective intake in August 1972. It was further expected that it would carry out detailed consultations with staff and parents.

There followed an inconclusive meeting on 14 April, at Glasgow's request, between the Secretary of State and Monro and Docherty,[125] at which the minister repeated the message of the letter. Although he clarified that he would judge the Glasgow proposals on their merits, he said that needed time to do so, while the Corporation needed to consult those most affected. Docherty held that consultations had taken place in 1967 and 1968, and the views of the parents were already well known. It was therefore unreasonable to expect further consultation. The Corporation were intent on pressing ahead with implementation for 1972–3. On hearing this, leaders of the affected schools became directly involved, resulting in Rector David Lees being severely censured[126] and the headmistress of the Girls' High, Helen Jamieson, cautioned by the Education Committee for writing directly to the Secretary of State challenging the policies being pursued by their local authority employers.[127]

The date on which the SED wrote to Glasgow, saying that the Secretary of State would not be able to reach a decision in time to take effect before school year 1973–4, and in effect asking for the organisation of a selective intake in August 1972, was an unfortunate one. It was 3 May, the day after Labour swept home with a huge block of seventy-nine councillors in Glasgow's local elections. With a large and confident majority behind him, Docherty, still Convener of the Education Committee, was in no mood to compromise; he is reported to have told the Secretary of State to 'go to Hell!'[128] Within the week his committee had confirmed by 22 to 15 votes that the Corporation would not be arranging any selective intake, despite the legal advice of its officers.

With an imminent Conservative Conference due at Perth and public interest high, the Secretary of State, Gordon Campbell, privately detailed his proposals for handling the issue on 12 May and asked Edward Heath for his backing.[129] Based on SED advice, Campbell intended to consider Glasgow's proposals on their merits, but he would ask for further information and adequate time to examine them. He had already pointed out to the authority the need for wider consultations on their plans with affected parents and teachers. He deemed the timescale of ending selective intake by autumn 1972 unrealistic, and if Glasgow refused, as it was threatening, to arrange any selective intake for next session, Campbell intended that the Lord Advocate[130] would apply to the Court of Session for an order requiring the authority to fulfil its statutory obligations.[131] Although Campbell's proposals were aimed at the 'high-handed manner' and 'breakneck speed' with which Glasgow's Labour majority were pressing ahead, he, significantly, held that his actions would not be prejudicial to his eventual decision on the scheme.[132] Campbell met up with Heath at Perth, and the prime minister agreed with the strategy.

On 16 May, Campbell went to law to force the authority to comply with its legal obligations. The First Division of the Court of Session[133] responded, on 14 June, by unanimously making an Order requiring the Corporation to discharge its responsibilities: according to the Court, the end of fee-paying the previous August had not affected its requirement for making selective arrangements.[134] The Corporation still refused to back down, and by 69 votes to 25 decided to appeal to the House of Lords. In the event, however, the Lords had a backlog of work which precluded an early decision. As a result, the Lord Advocate obtained a further Order from the Court of Session, which kept decision-making in Scotland and prevented further delay.[135] At last, on 5 July 1972, the Corporation caved in: headteachers were authorised to make arrangements for selective entry for 1972–3, but to underline the fact that its policy was unchanged, the Corporation also wrote to all parents informing them that no guarantee would be given that any child beginning education in a selective school would complete their education in that system.[136]

Nonetheless Campbell's tactics seemed to be working, and on being updated on 12 July 1972 Heath minuted 'well handled' in the margin of the briefing report.[137] Although the end of selection might only have been postponed for a year, expectations were high that a Conservative Secretary of State would find a way to save the situation. However, he was genuinely caught between the two conflicting policies of supporting educational authorities' freedom of choice on the one hand and parental choice within the sector on the other. He and Monro were very conscious of the degree of heat that the issue generated in Tory circles especially. So the SED was asked to seek legal advice on the issue of parental rights in schooling. However, there was no comfort here either for those wishing a more interventionist stance. It was found that there was indeed a 'general principle', but this could be discarded when balancing an authority's duties against the wishes of the parents. In the Lord Advocate's view, arguing the right of choice between different methods of education, as well as between different schools, made it impossible to quote any statutory provision or case law. In practice, it had not been customary to offer parents any say in the methods of education for their children.

In a parliamentary reply on 8 August to Teddy Taylor, Campbell stated that he had agreed to there being no intake later that month into the High School primary,[138] and two days later it was reported that Campbell had agreed to the Corporation's plans to end the selective intakes at Hillhead and Notre Dame primaries, which in future would be territorial.[139] In the High School case this decision was 'without prejudice to its long-term future'.[140] However, as Rector Lees knew only too well, this would prove problematic for staff, pupils and parents. The delay in the decision on selection by the SED, albeit caused by the Corporation's inadequate consultation and provision of information, was bad enough for those committed to the School, but a decision which seemed to prepare the way for the end of selection was unsettling also for prospective parents considering such a commitment.[141]

By early October Glasgow had informed Campbell of the details of its consultation with teachers and parents[142] at the schools affected, and reiterated its plea for a prompt ministerial decision. The SED saw these developments and the educational arguments as being of less importance than the political argument. This was now heavily weighted in favour of the end of selection, and even Turpie's eighty-four page memorandum calling for a public inquiry did not shift the official viewpoint.[143] A relatively senior SED official preparing the papers for a ministerial decision was moved to write: 'I am very conscious that our comments are almost completely one-sided. I have searched through all our files and we have noted very little in favour of the schools.'[144]

On 4 January 1973 SED Secretary Graham recommended the approval of Glasgow's proposals subject to certain safeguards. His argument for doing so was couched in terms applicable to all affected schools, and the High School case was considered only in the context of managing the closure with the least harm to the existing pupils. He reminded the Government that the official line was that all proposals should be aimed at adequate and efficient schooling. He held that it appeared the Corporation was in the process of doing this by incorporating the selective schools into their programme of moving towards a completely comprehensive system of schools in Glasgow. Despite his own background Graham could not support the continuation of selective schools, partly given the critique produced by the HMI six months earlier, and partly on the grounds that they undermined the authority's comprehensive policy towards which it had been working for over twenty-five years.[145] He repeated the argument that the schools generally had underachieved,[146] and concluded with the argument, surprising to a minister in a Conservative Cabinet trying to reduce the power of the trade unions, that a decision to reject the Glasgow proposals 'would be very badly received by the teaching profession who are committed to the principle of comprehensive education'.[147]

There is no reason to suppose that Campbell ever contemplated overruling his officials. Indeed, his reasonable and non-partisan style was a pleasant change and welcome contrast to the often difficult Willie Ross. Unfortunately for the School its ardent supporter, Teddy Taylor, who was originally the Under-Secretary for Education and Health, had resigned his post in 1971 over Heath's determination to join the European Community. His continued presence at that level might have made a significant difference, although Campbell's record suggested he was a minister content to ignore his own party and ministerial colleagues[148] and instead to judge issues on the merits as he saw them.

To those who argued that Campbell had no option than to go along with the end of selection in Glasgow, it should be remembered that the system which confronted him at this time in Scotland was still far from the comprehensive system envisaged by its proponents.[149] It took until 1982 before all selection in the non-fee-paying sector was ended.[150] Had the decision on the form of school organisation been one for central government alone, or had Campbell had a more 'Tory' view of the issue, it perhaps would have been reversible. However, it should be noted that Hector Monro, not a natural compromiser or follower of the civil service line, said in January 1973 that 'if we are to implement Circular 760 our only grounds for disagreement with Glasgow are those of adequate consultations . . . but it would be a difficult question to debate'.[151]

Some commentators have suggested that Campbell should have considered following a parallel course with his education counterpart in England, Margaret Thatcher,[152] who, against her will as she claimed, approved local schemes for comprehensive reorganisation but wherever possible preserved in them some degree of selective education.[153] In fact, the SED consulted the DES and reported to ministers that she only rejected or modified local Education Authority proposals on the grounds of inadequate accommodation or other operational reasons. Of more than 2,600 proposals, she rejected or amended a mere 115. Campbell, of course, kept her in the picture on what he proposed to do in Glasgow and Edinburgh, and she did not object.

With such straws in the wind, Campbell's written answer to Teddy Taylor in the House of Commons on 9 March 1973,[154] accepting Glasgow Education Committee's plan to end selectivity in Corporation schools, was not a total surprise. He did so to allow each educational authority 'as much freedom as possible to decide for themselves the form of secondary education best for their areas'.[155] It marked the death-knell for the existing High School, however. With no further selective entry the School would decline in numbers, and when it ceased to be a viable unit[156] Campbell would accept its closure. Although Campbell ensured that existing pupils at the School would not be dispersed until they had completed either their primary (by 1974)[157] or secondary education, such a lingering death seemed small consolation. The four other selective schools – Allan Glen's, Hillhead, Notre Dame and the Girls' High – were to be phased into the city's comprehensive system.

Glasgow's Conservative councillors passed a unanimous vote of no confidence in the Secretary of State. For Rector Lees, Campbell's decision was a bitter blow: understandably, he could not forgive him for his 'betrayal of election promises'[158] and failure to deliver meaningful consultation between the Corporation and School staff and parents.[159] But although Campbell infuriated not just natural Conservative voters by declining to intervene to save the School, for him the most important issue was being consistent with accepted party policy.[160] And, no doubt, he was fortified in this by the consistent advice from the SED professionals, both that the selective schools had not recently distinguished themselves and that their survival would be at odds with Glasgow's comprehensive plans for the city as a whole.[161] He had also to reckon with the difficulty of how he could force an authority to run a few selective schools, which it might simply run down by denying them the resources they needed.

On 5 April 1973 the Corporation decided that the Girls' High would be renamed Cleveden Secondary School from the beginning of session 1973–4. Conservative demands for Campbell to delay Glasgow's education reorganisation until after local government reforms, which were planned for 1975, were rejected.[162] But, given the inevitable Labour control of Strathclyde,[163] it seems highly unlikely that this would have made any difference. He also held that the parents of the High School pupils had no right to a public inquiry. He agreed, as was obvious, that the School had no viable local catchment as a non-selective secondary school, particularly since the opening of Woodside Secondary[164] in March 1973. It was left to Dr Docherty to claim that Glasgow was now entirely covered by all-through, six-year comprehensives, and that 'no other city in Britain enjoys such equality and adequacy of provision'.[165]

What was, and perhaps still is, difficult to understand was why the closure of the School was accepted without at least a trial period of some compromise 'solution', such as a city-wide catchment, or as a school for older secondary pupils post-Ordinary Grade, or indeed movement elsewhere. Director of Education Bain, despite his commitment to the comprehensive principle, was known to have been astonished at the decision to close the School.[166] It seems likely that he believed, with some justification, that Glasgow schools were being used as 'test-beds for unproven political theories'.[167]

Would an attempt to have created one beacon of academic excellence in a Glasgow school have harmed the comprehensive model that much? Why had the High School's venerable tradition and unique position not counted for more? Why was it so unloved that no alternative to closure was seriously considered? Answers to such questions are complicated by the fact that most of the discussions in the SED and Glasgow were not just about the High Schools on their own, but about all five[168] selective schools. Was there a conscious policy on the part of the Labour-controlled Council to ensure that the debate was not just about the High School? Bain had tried to devise a role for the School, but this was shot down quickly by his political masters. This and the unwillingness of the Corporation to allow the Elmbank Street buildings to be used by any successor school suggest that a degree of culpability can be laid at the door of Labour politicians and their allies. Yet supporters of the School also failed to produce the creative thinking needed to deal with the financial and logistical problems.[169] Although the *Glasgow Herald* promoted the idea of a grant-aided[170] solution, there is no evidence that this was pursued as a viable option. No formal approach was made to Campbell to take this forward or make the case for an investment of public money.

As 'an honest man' with a 'strictly constitutional view of the duties of his office'[171] Campbell had done precisely what his party had promised when in Opposition, namely, to reverse the Labour Government's policy, which had deprived local authorities of the discretion to choose the form of education they thought best. But it was precisely this freedom that, once local government was also controlled by the Labour Party, meant the end of fee-paying and then selectivity. It meant that the Conservative Party, in an extraordinary political move, allowed the character of some great schools, which had contributed significantly to Scottish education, to be changed but not, in the minds of many, improved. However, in allowing the High School to be closed, Campbell ensured that any 'rescue' attempt would be left to its parents, Former Pupils and a number of Glasgow citizens who had come to realise what had been lost. Little did anyone expect how dramatic and successful that rescue was to be.

PUPILS

There is fragmentary evidence that the High School was now no longer the dominant force it once was, and with a weakening of its reputation it seemed no longer the automatic choice for parents ambitious for their sons. Competition had intensified, and in 1955 there were almost 500 candidates for the 93 places at Glasgow Academy,[172] whose reputation was heightened when the *Sunday Times* judged it the best school in Britain for awards to Oxford and Cambridge in 1964.[173] Nonetheless, the High School continued to produce talented individuals who went on to very successful careers.

Businessmen

Ian Ferguson[174] (b. 1943) [1952–61; draughtsman] joined Unilever, then IBM. He became Executive Chairman, Data Connection Ltd, 1981; and served on a number of Government committees on apprenticeships, training, qualifications and skills.

Stuart Shields (b. 1944) [1950–63; sales officer; School Captain, 1962–3] followed Glasgow University with Unilever training, 1967–8. He had a long career with ICI in all its metamorphoses, holding senior management positions, mostly in sales, marketing and business strategy in UK and USA.

Stanley Stewart (b. 1944) [1957–63; electrical engineer] was a senior pilot, flying Boeing 747 for British Airways, and an aviation author.

(Prof.) Gordon Hewitt (b. 1945) [1952–63; journalist] graduated from

Glasgow and became a lecturer in Political Economy, chair at Manchester Business School, and Professor of Business and Corporate Strategy at the University of Michigan. He chaired the Court of Abertay University; was presenter of BBCTV Sportscene and became a member of the High School Educational Trust.

Allistair McDicken (b. 1945) [1957–63; estimator] worked as a test pilot for British Aerospace.

Derek Halden (b. 1960)[175] [1969–72; teacher] specialised in transport planning. He was Director of a Transport Planning Consultancy; Honorary Research Fellow, Aberdeen University, 2003; Editor, Scottish Transport Review, 2004; and Chair, Scottish Transport Studies Group, 2007.

Churchmen

(Rev.) Johnston McKay (b. 1942)[176] [1947–60; minister] attended Glasgow and Cambridge Universities. After becoming assistant minister, St Giles' Cathedral, he held ministries at Bellahouston Steven and Paisley Abbey. He was senior producer, then editor of religious programmes for BBC Scotland, 1987–2002; and minister, Barony St John's, Ardrossan.

(Rev.) Michael Mair (b. 1942) [1947–60; minister] was a community worker in Coventry before being inducted into Aberdeen Holburn West in 1980. Translated in 1999 to Dundee Craigiebank, he retired in 2007.

(Very Rev.) David Lunan (b. 1944)[177] [1949–62; CA] held charges at Calton New Parish, St Andrews Lhanbryd, Moray, and Renfield St Stephen's, Glasgow. He was Clerk to the Presbytery of Glasgow, 2002–8, and Moderator of the General Assembly of the Church of Scotland, 2008–9.

(Rev.) David Doyle (b. 1948)[178] [1960–6; minister] attended Cambridge University. He had charges at East Kilbride Old; Tulliallan and Kincardine; and St Mary's, Motherwell.

(Very Rev.) David Lacy (b. 1952)[179] [1965–9; senior rep.] was minister, St George's West, Edinburgh; Knightswood St Margaret's, Glasgow; and Henderson Parish Church, Kilmarnock. He was Moderator of the General Assembly of the Church of Scotland, 2005–6.

Military

(Major-General) Robin Short (b. 1942)[180] [1954–61; manager in ICI] was RMO Black Watch, 1967–72; RAMC, 1972–6 and 1981–8; Director, Medical Operations and Logistics, 1991–4; Director-General of Medical

Services, 1996–9; and Operations Director PHC Ltd, 1999–2007.

(Colonel) Donald Ross (b. 1946)[181] [1951–5; builder's manager] became a professional soldier with the Argyll and Sutherland Highlanders, 1965–96; and was Lord Lieutenant of Dunbartonshire, 2007–8.

(Commodore) Angus Ross (b. 1956) [1968–74] joined the RN prior to gaining a degree from Strathclyde University. He served in the Falklands campaign and became Head of Veteran Services before retirement. A former President of the London Club, he is currently a Trustee of its Bursary Fund.

Medical

(Prof.) John Boyd (b. 1940) [1950–57; cashier] was clinical Professor of Obstetrics and Gynaecology at the University of Alberta.

(Dr) Burnett Lunan (b. 1941) [1950–9; CA] became lecturer, Aberdeen University; senior lecturer at Nairobi University in obstetrics and gynae-cology; Consultant Obstetrician, Princess Royal Maternity, Glasgow, 1977–2005; Consultant Gynaecologist, Royal Infirmary, Glasgow, 1977–2005; President, Royal Medico-Chirurgical Society of Glasgow, 1991–2; and President, Glasgow Obstetrical and Gynaecological Society, 2002–4.

(Dr) John Calder[182] (b. 1942) [1951–60; accountant] became MO, Malawi; Senior Registrar in Radiology, Glasgow University, Nairobi University and Aberdeen University; and Consultant Radiologist, Victoria Infirmary, Glasgow, 1986–2007.

(Prof.) (Duncan) Angus McGrouther (b. 1946)[183] [1958–63; GP] became Registrar then Senior Registrar, Plastic Surgery, Canniesburn Hospital, Glasgow; Plastic Surgeon, Sunderland and Canniesburn; and Professor of Plastic and Reconstructive Surgery (first established British chair) UCL, 1989–2001, and Manchester University, 2001.

(Prof.) Archie Young (b. 1946)[184] [1951–64; surgeon] became consultant with the Rehabilitation Research Unit, University of Oxford, and the Royal Free Hospital and Medical School, London. He was Professor of Geriatric Medicine, Royal Free Hospital Medical School; and Professor of Geriatric Medicine, University of Edinburgh, 1998.

(Dr) Kenneth Collins (b. 1947)[185] [1956–64; doctor] was MO for Newark Lodge; Research Fellow, Centre for the History of Medicine, Glasgow University; and Chairman, Scottish Council of Jewish Communities, 1999–2003.

(Dr) Roger Hughes (b. 1947)[186] [1956–64; teacher] became Registrar in Anaesthesia, Glasgow Royal Infirmary; Senior Registrar/Lecturer in

Anaesthesia, University of Glasgow; and Consultant in Anaesthesia and Intensive Care, 1980.

Hew Mathewson (b. 1949)[187] [1962–67; doctor] became Principal Dental Surgeon, Edinburgh University; Assistant Director, Dental Studies, Edinburgh University 1987–99; Chairman, Scottish General Dental Services Committee, 1991–7; President, General Dental Council 2003.

(Dr) Peter Kyle (b. 1951)[188] [1956–68; company secretary] became a lecturer, Ophthalmology, Glasgow University; Senior Clinical Lecturer; and Consultant Ophthalmologist, Southern General Hospital NHS Trust, 1982.

(Dr) Alastair Scotland (b. 1951)[189] [1956–61; lecturer in education] specialised in plastic surgery, and became Consultant in Public Health Medicine; Director of Medical Education and Research, Chelsea and Westminster Hospital, 1996–2001; Chief Executive 2001–5, and Medical Director of the National Clinical Assessment Service, 2005

(Dr) Mark Hamilton (b. 1955)[190] [1964–73; minister] became a lecturer, National University of Singapore; Senior Registrar, Glasgow Royal Infirmary, 1987–90; and Consultant Gynaecologist, Aberdeen Maternity Hospital.

(Dr) Douglas McLellan (b. 1955)[191] [1967–72; electrical engineer] became Registrar in Pathology, Southern General Hospital, Glasgow; Honorary Senior Registrar in Neuropathology, Institute of Neurological Sciences, Glasgow; Senior Registrar in Pathology, Western Infirmary, Glasgow; and Consultant Pathologist, Victoria Infirmary/Southern General.

Legal

Frederick Kennedy (b. 1940) [1949–58; superintendent] carried on private, industrial and local government legal practice. He was Reporter to Children's Panel, Glasgow; Director of Administration, Fife Regional Council; and Regional Reporter, Strathclyde.

Lord Hamilton (Arthur)[192] (b. 1942) [1949–60; wholesale chemist; Classical Dux] attended Glasgow, Edinburgh and Oxford Universities. He became an advocate, 1968; QC (Scotland), 1982; President, Pensions Appeal Tribunal for Scotland, 1992–5; Senator of the College of Justice, 1995–2005; Lord Justice General of Scotland and Lord President of the Court of Session, 2005.

Terence Macnair (b. 1942)[193] [1952–60; civil engineer] became Town Clerk, Lochgilphead; senior partner, MacArthur Stewart (and Orr) 1970–2003; and Hon. Sheriff, North Strathclyde, 1988.

Rt Hon. Lord (Alexander) Philip (b. 1942)[194] [1954–60; railway official] attended St Andrews and Glasgow universities. He became an advocate 1973; QC (Scotland), 1984; Chairman, Medical Appeal Tribunals, 1988–92; Chairman, Scottish Land Court, 1993–6; President, Lands Tribunal for Scotland, 1993–6; and Senator of the College of Justice 1996–2007. He was President of the High School Club, 2007–8.

Raymond Williamson (b. 1942)[195] [1948–60; insurance manager] became a partner, MacRoberts Solicitors, Glasgow and Edinburgh, 1971–2006; Chairman, RSNO, 1985–91; Governor, RSAMD, 1990–2002; Dean, Royal Faculty of Procurators in Glasgow, 2001–4; High School Club Secretary, 1972–88 and President, 2003–4. He remains a School Governor and a member of the High School Educational Trust.

William Dunlop (b. 1944)[196] [1949–62; journalist; School Captain (1961–2)] was called to the Scottish Bar, 1985. He became Sheriff of North Strathclyde 1995. He was President of the High School Club, 1993–4 and has been a Governor of the School since 1999; and Chairman, SRU Championship Appeals Panel, 2000.

John Harkness (b. 1944)[197] [1952–62; journalist] became senior legal assistant to the Secretary of State for Scotland, 1971–9; Assistant, then Depute Scottish Parliamentary Counsel, 1979–2000; Assistant Legal Secretary to the Lord Advocate, 1979–99; and First Scottish Parliamentary Counsel to the UK, 2000–2.

Douglas McKerrell (1944–2007)[198] [1958–61 electricity official] became a partner in Maclay, Murray and Spens, 1976–92. He was senior Tutor, Diploma in Legal Practice, Glasgow University, 1980–9, and joined Kidstons & Co. (1992). He was a founding member of the Scottish International Piano Competition.

Brian Adair (b. 1945)[199] [1955–64; potato merchant] became senior partner of his own firm, 1973–2005. He was President, Law Society of Scotland, 1992–93; temporary Sheriff, 1995–9; part-time Sheriff since 2000; a High School Governor since 1992, and Chairman since 2006.

Hector Cameron (b. 1947)[200] [1956–61; transport superintendent] became Chairman, Glasgow Junior Chamber of Commerce; Director, Merchants House, Glasgow; Director, Glasgow of Commerce; and partner, Abercrombie Capital Partners LLP, 2005.

George Moore (b. 1947)[201] [1957–65; PR officer] became a solicitor/advocate. He was joint senior partner, HBM Sayers; Reporter to the Scottish Legal Aid Board; and Chairman of Industrial Tribunals, Scotland.

Kenneth Mure (b. 1947)[202] [1959–64; reading room assistant] became a

Scottish advocate, 1975; and a barrister, Grays Inn, 1990. He was made a Fellow, Chartered Institute of Taxation, 1991.

Alan Gamble (b. 1951)[203] [1963–8; typewriter mechanic] became an advocate, 1978; senior lecturer in Law, Glasgow University, 1976–93; District Chairman, Tribunals Service, Glasgow, 1993; and Convener, Mental Health Tribunal for Scotland, 2005.

Colin Wilson (b. 1952)[204] [1961–9; Headmaster] became assistant legal secretary to Lord Advocate, 1979–99; and until 1993 Assistant, then Depute, Parliamentary Draftsman for Scotland. He was Scottish Parliamentary Counsel, 1993–2006, and First Scottish Parliamentary Counsel, 2006.

Alasdair MacFadyen (b. 1955)[205] [1967–72; BBC producer] worked in private legal practice, 1978–2001. He became a temporary sheriff, 1995–2000; and Sheriff, Grampian, Highland and Islands, 2002.

Seith Ireland (b. 1956)[206] [1965–74; master baker]; was Principal, Ireland & Co., 1986–2003. He was President, Glasgow Bar Association, 1993–94; and Sheriff at Kilmarnock, 2003.

Colin Pettigrew (b. 1957)[207] [1966–74; scientist] was a litigation partner, 1982–2002; and floating Sheriff of North Strathclyde, 2002.

(Prof.) Gavin Little[208] (b. 1964) lecturer in Law, Dundee University; and Professor of Public Law, University of Stirling, since 2004.

Academic

Michael Lessnoff (b. 1940) [1945–58; doctor] attended Balliol College, Oxford. He became Assistant Principal, Department of Education and Science; and Reader, Department of Politics, Glasgow University.

(Prof.) John MacBeath (b. 1940) [1954–9] was a member of the Government Task Force on Standards in Education, 1999–2001; Director of Quality in Education Centre, Strathclyde University; Professor Emeritus at Cambridge University; Director of Leadership for Learning, and Project Director for Centre of Commonwealth Education.

Alastair McLachlan (1940–2007) [1945–58; CA] held senior posts at Knightswood Secondary and King's Park before becoming Rector of Lornshill, 1988–2003.

(Prof. Sir) (Donald) Neil MacCormick[209] (1941–2009) [1946–59; solicitor; School Captain and Dux] took a First Class degree in Philosophy/English at Glasgow, and was a Snell Exhibitioner at Balliol. He became President, Oxford Union, 1965; Fellow, Balliol College, Oxford, 1967–72; tutor, Oxford University, 1968–71; English barrister, 1971; Regius

Professor of Public Law, Edinburgh University, 1972–2008; Vice-Principal, Edinburgh University, 1997–9; SNP member of European Parliament, 1999–2004; Vice-President SNP, 1999–2004. He was awarded the Gold Medal of the RSE, 2004; and was Special Adviser to the Scottish First Minister on Europe and External Affairs, 2007. He is regarded as probably the most distinguished Former Pupil of the second half of the twentieth century.

(Prof.) Hugh Begg (b.1941)[210] [1948–60; haulage contractor; School Captain 1959–60, captain of rugby and athletics] gained degrees from St Andrews, British Columbia and Dundee Universities. He lectured at St Andrews and Dundee Universities; was Assistant Director of Planning, Tayside Region; Head, School of Town and Regional Planning and Dean of the Faculty of Environmental Studies, Dundee University; Ombudsman with Scottish Enterprise; Convenor, Standards Commission for Scotland; member of Local Government Boundary Commission; and Reporter, Directorate for Environmental and Planning Appeals.

(Prof.) James Maxwell (b. 1941)[211] [1953–59; horticulturist] became Professor of Organic Geochemistry (1990–9), and Senior Research Fellow (1999) at Bristol University.

Michael Goodwin (b. 1945) [1958–64; BBC sound director] was a teacher of Physics in Uganda and Mathematics in Glasgow, before becoming Rector, Carrick Academy, 1990.

(Prof.) James Hough (b. 1945)[212] [1957–63; railway clerk] became Professor of Experimental Physics, Glasgow University, 1996; and Director, Institute for Gravitational Research, 2000.

Rob Gibson (b. 1945)[213] [1950–64; police constable] was a teacher of Guidance, 1974–95. Since 1995 he has been a writer and musician, and in 2003 he was elected MSP (SNP), Highland and Islands.

(Prof.) Donald Macleod (b. 1945) [1950–63; commercial traveller] became Professor of Psychology, Scrippes Institute, San Diego.

Graham Donaldson (b. 1946)[214] [1956–65; exhibition manager] taught and lectured before joining HMI. He was HM Depute Senior Chief Inspector of Education, 1996–2002; and Senior Chief Inspector of Education, 2002–9.

(Prof.) Gordon Plotkin (b. 1946) [1955–63; manufacturing furrier] became Director, Laboratory for Foundation of Computer Science; and Professor in Computing Science at Edinburgh University. He was made a Fellow of the Royal Society, 1992.

James Aitchison (b. 1947)[215] [1956–65; clerk] became Headteacher, Gleniffer High School, Paisley, 1984–91; and Headteacher, Boclair Academy,

1991–2002. He was adviser to Schools Inspectorate, Uganda, 2003–5; and Director, Scotland–Malawi School Improvement Programme, 2005.

(Prof.) Michael Stubbs (b. 1947)[216] [1952–65; sales rep.] attended Cambridge University. He became Professor of English, London University 1985–90; and Professor of English Linguistics, University of Trier, Germany, 1990.

Michael Doig (b. 1948)[217] [1953–66; saleswoman] became Headteacher, Cumbernauld High School, 1992–2000; Headteacher, Bearsden Academy, from 2001; and President, Headteachers' Association of Scotland, 2003–4.

(Prof.) David Stone (b. 1949)[218] [1958–66; doctor] was senior lecturer, Epidemiology, Ben Gurion University, 1985–2000; and founding Director, Paediatric Epidemiology and Community Health Unit, Department of Child Health, Glasgow University, 2000.

Brian Miller (b. 1951)[219] [1963–9; insurance agent] was appointed Rector, Dalziel High School, Motherwell, 1990.

Douglas Whitelaw (b. 1952)[220] [1961–70; production manager] worked as a senior scientist on Animal Diseases, Nairobi 1980–8; and was the British Council scientific officer, Australia and New Zealand 1990–3, Depute Director Nigeria 1993–5, and Korea 1996–2000.

Graeme Hyslop (b. 1953)[221] [1965–71; civil engineer] became Further Education Officer, Strathclyde Regional Council; and Principal, Langside College, 1999.

(Prof.) Colin McCaig (b. 1953)[222] [1962–71; manufacturer's agent] was Regius Professor of Physiology, Aberdeen University 2002; and Head of School of Medical Sciences, 2003.

Romilly Squire (b. 1953)[223] [1962–70; lecturer in Art] was a Heraldic artist and Quondam Herald painter in the Court of the Lord Lyon, Edinburgh, and the office of the Chief Herald of Ireland, Dublin, 1983.

(Prof.) Ross Anderson (b. 1956)[224] [1965–73; university lecturer] attended Cambridge University. He became Professor of Security Engineering, 2003.

Gordon Miller (b. 1957)[225] [1970–6; insurance rep.] became Rector, Mearns Academy, 1999–2007; Council Member, HAS, 2000–6 (Treasurer 2003–6); and Rector, Blairgowrie High School, 2007.

(Prof.) Anton Muscatelli (b. 1962), son of head of a shipping firm, joined Drewsteignton at Transitus, and after schooling at the High School gained the Logan prize for Best Graduate in the Faculty of Arts at Glasgow University (1984). At Glasgow he became Chair of Economics, 1992; Head of Department 1994; and Dean of Faculty of Social Sciences 2000–4; before moving on to be Principal and Vice-Chancellor of Heriot-Watt University 2007–9; and Principal and Vice-Chancellor of Glasgow University in 2009.

Melvyn Shanks (b. 1962)[226] [1971–4, going on to Drewsteignton; Approved School investigator] was a High School staff member, 1985–90, teaching Mathematics and Physics. He moved to Belmont House School, where he was promoted internally and became Principal, 2006.

Financial

Ronnie Hanna (b. 1942) [1954–60], a CA, he was Chief Executive of house builders and property developers Bett Brothers plc. He is currently Chairman of A.G. Barr plc (Irn Bru) and Chairman of Glasgow Income Trust plc.

Douglas Dewar (b. 1947)[227] [1952–65; CA] became Finance Director, Scottish Airports Ltd, 1992.

Leon Marshall (b. 1950)[228] [1955–67; meat depot manager] became a CA and senior partner, Stevenson & Kyles CA, 1995. He was Convener, Church of Scotland Central Services Committee, 2001–5.

Douglas Flint (b. 1955) [1964–73] is Finance Director of HSBC plc.

Douglas Griffin (b. 1956)[229] [1965–73; shop manager] became a CA and joined Peat, Marwick, Mitchell & Co. He worked for Barr & Stroud Ltd/Pilkington Optronics; and became Director of Finance, Greater Glasgow and Clyde NHS Board.

Mark Cohen (b. 1959) [1968–76; teacher] became a director of a merchant bank and a writer of comic novels.

Administrators (Politicians)

Peter Mackay (b. 1940)[230] [1949–58; surgeon] attended St Andrews University. He was Private Secretary to Secretaries of State for Scotland, 1973–5; Director for Scotland, Manpower Services Commission, 1983–5; Under-Secretary, Scottish Education Department, 1987–97; Secretary and Chief Executive, Scottish Office Industry Department, 1990–5; member of Napier University Court, 1995–2004; and Chairman, Local Government Boundary Commission for Scotland, 2007.

James Sewell (b. 1944)[231] [1953–62; solicitor] became Assistant Archivist, Durham County Record Office; Assistant Deputy Keeper, Corporation of London Records Office; and City Archivist, Corporation of London, 1984–2003.

John Liddell (b. 1946) [1958–63; minister] was Assistant Director of

Administration, Borders Region; Depute Director, Law and Administration, Grampian Region; and Depute Chief Executive, Grampian Regional Council, 1979.

George Brechin (b. 1949)[232] [1954–66; butcher] became Chief Executive, East and Midlothian NHS Trust, 1994–6; Fife Healthcare NHS Trust, 1996–9; Fife Primary Care Trust, 1999–2004; and NHS Fife, 2002.

Trevor Muir (b. 1949)[233] [1961–5; librarian] worked for the Scottish Special Housing Association, and for the City of Glasgow District Council. He became Director of Housing, City of Aberdeen District Council; Chief Executive, Midlothian District Council; and Chief Executive, Midlothian Council, 1995.

(Sir) (Alastair) Muir Russell (b. 1949)[234] [1954–66; chartered surveyor; Modern Dux] joined the Scottish Office, and became Assistant Secretary, 1981; Principal Private Secretary to Secretary of State for Scotland, 1981–3; Under-Secretary, Deputy Secretary, Secretary and Head of Office, Scottish Agriculture, Environment and Fisheries; Permanent Under-Secretary and Permanent Secretary, Scottish Executive, 1999–2003. He was Principal and Vice-Chancellor, Glasgow University; and was made a Freeman of the City of London, 2006.

Charles Gray (b. 1953)[235] [1964–70; minister] joined the Diplomatic Service and served in West Africa, East Europe and the Soviet Department. He became First Secretary, UK delegation, OECD, Paris 1983–7; joined the Cabinet Office 1987–9; moved to the Foreign and Commonwealth Office (FCO); became Head, Eastern Adriatic Department; Head of Chancery, Jakarta; Counsellor, Washington DC; Head, Middle East Department (FCO); Iran Co-ordinator (FCO); Ambassador to Morocco; and HM Marshal of the Diplomatic Corps, 2008.

James Gray (b. 1954)[236] [1966–71; minister] attended Glasgow and Oxford Universities. He became a shipbroker; Managing Director, GNI Freight Futures; Freeman, City of London 1982; Special Adviser to the Secretary of Environment, 1992–5; Conservative MP for Wiltshire North since 1997; and held various Opposition posts, 2000–5.

(Hon.) Stephen Rodan (b. 1954) [1963–72; banker] was a pharmacist in Scotland, Bermuda and the Isle of Man. He became a member of the House of Keys, Garff, 1995; Minister of Education, Isle of Man 1999–2004; Minister for Health and Social Security, 2004–6; and Speaker, House of Keys, 2006.

Writers (Artists, Architects, Poets, Journalists)

Murray Ritchie (b. 1941)[237] [1947–57; journalist] became a journalist with the *Dumfries and Galloway Standard*, *Scottish Daily Record*, *East African Standard*, and *Glasgow Herald*, 1971. He was named Journalist of the Year at the Fraser Press awards, 1980.

Ronald Neil (b. 1942)[238] [1947–61; solicitor; School Captain] became a reporter, *Daily Express*, BBC 1967–8 (*Reporting Scotland*, *Nationwide*, *24 Hours*); Deputy Editor, *Newsnight*, 1979; Editor, *That's Life*, *Newsnight*, *Breakfast Time*, *Six O'Clock News* and TV News; Director, News and Current Affairs, 1987–9; and Chief Executive, BBC Production, 1996–8.

(Prof.) Gordon Benson (b. 1944)[239] [1949–62; widow] was employed in Camden housing projects before becoming a partner in private architectural practice. Took the chair of Architecture, Strathclyde University, 1986–90; and was Visiting Professor, Edinburgh University, 1991.

Quintin Jardine (b. 1945) [1956–62; teacher] journalist and media relations consultant who published his first novel in 1983. He has since published a further twenty-seven.

(Prof.) Raymond Young (b. 1946) [1955–63; sales manager] became project architect, Strathclyde University; Director, Scottish Housing Corporation; Director, Research and Innovation, Scottish Homes; Senior Research Fellow, Urban Studies, Glasgow University; Chairman, Architecture and Design Scotland; and Visiting Professor, Architecture, Strathclyde University, 2006.

Chick Young (b. 1951)[240] [1963–7; hospital engineer] worked on national daily and evening newspapers, 1969–88; and on Radio Clyde, 1977–85. He wrote for Sunday newspapers; and was a columnist with the *Daily Star* and the *Daily Express*. He has been football correspondent on BBC Television and radio since 1988.

Ronald Frame (b. 1953)[241] [1962–71; advertising agent] attended Oxford University. He became a full-time author in 1981, with work that has included television films and radio drama. His thirteen books include *The Lantern Bearers*, which won the Saltire Scottish Book of the Year Award in 2000. Recently labelled 'Scotland's finest contemporary writer'.[242]

John McLellan (b. 1962) [1971–4; grocer] went on to Hutchesons' GS and Stirling University before becoming editor of the *Evening Times* (1997), *Scotland on Sunday* (2002) and the *Scotsman* (2009).

Sport, Culture, Entertainment

David Morrison (b. 1941)[243] [1953–5; teacher] became Librarian, Lanark County, Edinburgh College of Art, and Caithness. He founded and ran Scotia Review, Wick Folk Club, and the Wick Festival of Poetry, Folk and Jazz.

(Dr) James Murphy (b. 1942) [1951–9; hotelier] became a consultant psychiatrist, Paisley; and Medical Director, Greater Glasgow Community Mental Health Services, NHS Trust.

Richard Camber (b. 1944)[244] [1957–62; retail draper] became Assistant Keeper of Medieval and Later Antiquities, British Museum; Director, Sotheby's London 1983–7; and a consultant for Sotheby's on European Works of Art, 1988.

Bobby Clark (b. 1945) [1957–63; company director] signed for Queen's Park while still at school and played for the successful Aberdeen FC. He enjoyed a good club and international career. He became Head Coach, University of Notre Dame, Indiana.

Eric Woolfson (1945–2009) [1955–63; company director], a successful songwriter in 1960s, his songs were recorded by over 100 artists in Europe and America. He was co-founder, main lyricist and often vocalist of the Alan Parsons Project, a progressive rock band which enjoyed huge success from the mid-1970s until the late 1980s. He wrote five highly successful stage musicals.

Stephen Morrison (b. 1947)[245] [1956–65; master grocer] worked with BBC Scotland (radio and TV). He became a Granada TV producer, Head of Arts and Features, Director of Programmes 1987–92, and Managing Director, 1992–4; LWT Managing Director, 1994–6; Chief Executive, Granada Media Group, 1996–2002; and Chief Executive, All3Media, 2003.

Iain Carslaw (b. 1949) [1954–66; CA], a CA who became a Scottish golf international and won the Scottish Amateur Championship at Downfield in 1978. He was a member of the 1979 Walker Cup team.

Henry Eagles (b. 1949)[246] [1961–7; confectioner] worked at the *Scotsman*, 1975–80, and Scottish Television, 1981–91. He became a freelance television producer; Head of News and Current Affairs, Grampian Television, 2000–4; and Executive Producer, Sport, Scottish TV, 2004.

Keith Macintosh (b. 1949) [1961–7; lawyer; Classical Dux] was a partner in a solicitor's firm. He won the Scottish Amateur Golf Championship in 1979 and was Company Secretary, Clydesdale Bank PLC, 1987.

Graeme Kelling (1957–2004) [1966–75; university lecturer] was a member of Deacon Blue between 1986 and 1994.

TEN

A New Beginning

This chapter centres round the dramatic story of the birth of the new High School, and it highlights the leading part played in this delicate process by Norrie Thomson. The roles of the High School Club, Drewsteignton School under Mrs Baker, the senior teaching staff led by Eric Harle, and the new governing body led by Norrie Macfarlane, who took over its chairmanship in 1979, are also examined.

DREWSTEIGNTON

Although the closing of the High School had been feared for some considerable time, the more optimistic never really believed that it would actually happen. Nonetheless, and fortunately as it turned out, some precautions had been taken. Having been lukewarm about the School in its early days, the Former Pupil Club in the 1920s bought land at Old Anniesland. Despite being intended for use of both the Club and the School, it was legally safeguarded by being kept in the name of the Club. The local authority could close the School and keep the buildings in Elmbank Street, but Old Anniesland would remain as a valuable asset to be used by the Club in any future plan for the continuation of the School.

Supporters of the School had other advantages, which suggested a rescue of the School was worth investigating further. Specifically, the decision to end a School with a great tradition and history, which was much respected in Glasgow and beyond, was deemed to be a step too far. There was evidence of a body of public opinion that seemed to favour some sort of compromise which would allow the High School to survive. Any appeal for help, therefore, was liable to prove fruitful. Moreover, the decision of Gordon Campbell did allow the continuation of the School until it was no longer a viable institution. This 'run-down' ensured more than three years of further existence, keeping the issue alive and topical, before final closure in June 1976 in a blaze of further publicity.[1]

Although a number of options were investigated,[2] the most promising involved coming to an arrangement with Drewsteignton School in Bearsden. It had been founded in 1922 by Mrs Spencer Ponsford and named after a small village near Exeter, with which her family had been traditionally associated. The school, originally a boarding primary school for girls and boys whose parents were abroad, opened in Collylinn Road, Bearsden, to the north-west of Glasgow, but two years later moved to purpose-built premises in Upper Glenburn Road, Bearsden.

Mrs Ponsford died in 1958 and her daughter, Mrs Thora Henderson, who had been teaching at the school, took over the headship but decided to sell up. For a time it appeared that the school might close; however, it was bought by an experienced teacher, Mrs Honor V. Baker,[3] who became its principal, and she reopened it with fifteen pupils in September 1962. Its aims were to be an excellent school with high academic achievement and to build character on Christian principles. But at this stage the school was still seen mainly as a preparatory establishment, preparing children for entry for the selective schools of the area at age nine and at the first year secondary stage (age 11/12). Expansion led in 1968 to the formation of an Educational Trust with nine directors and her husband, Andrew Baker, as its chairman. Kay Holland was in charge of finances. By 1969 the roll had reached 160 and, following market research, the decision was taken to open an independent secondary day school. Successful fund-raising led in September 1971 to the appointment of Eric A. Harle as head of a new senior school, which opened with seventy pupils, from Primary 5 to Secondary 2, at 27 Ledcameroch Road,[4] also in Bearsden.

Moving the school into the Scottish secondary sector was courageous and, equally, a somewhat brave and risky move for Harle. Born in February 1923, his education and teaching experience had been entirely in independent schools (apart from a state elementary school up to the age of eleven): he studied at Portsmouth Grammar School, Winchester College,[5] and Clare College, Cambridge;[6] and he taught for three years at Monmouth School before serving twenty-one years as Head of Mathematics at Wycliffe College. While at the latter, he had been in charge of the Boat Club (which tripled in membership), built a new boat-house, and moved from fours to eights (including Henley). His independent school experience helped secure him the post, but as an Englishman without Scottish experience he appreciated the need to tread warily![7] Nonetheless, within eighteen months a new wing, financed by the proceeds of an enthusiastic fund-raising effort by parents and friends,[8] ensured that the senior school was well established.[9] In April 1973, when the High School Club made an approach to its Board,[10] Drewsteignton was looking for property or land with the aim of further expansion.

By early June 1973 a sub-committee of Drewsteignton directors reported on the advantages of a joint venture with the High School. In a competitive market with rising costs and fees, and the need for capital for investment and development, they wisely appreciated the positive benefit of being part of an arrangement with a School with a long-established tradition and significant assets.[11] For supporters of a new High School, it seemed that the way forward was clear, now that a nucleus of pupils[12] had been provided by the decision of the Drewsteignton Board. Following further 'optimistic discussions',[13] on 27 June 1973 an application for outline planning permission was submitted by the Club Limited to Glasgow Corporation, as the planning authority, for the proposed erection of a secondary school by 1977 on the west side of Crow Road, south of Anniesland Road.[14]

Without delay, the Sub-Committee on Development Applications recommended the granting of outline permission, subject to a number of conditions which were unremarkable given the need for a change of use of some of the land at Old Anniesland from private open use (playing fields) to what was being proposed.[15] Things stalled, however, when the matter reached the Corporation Planning Committee on 4 September. In his report to Committee, the Director of Planning, Robert Mansley, advised that there appeared to be no planning grounds on which to refuse the application.[16] However, the Labour members on the Committee clearly recognised the political ramifications for the Labour-controlled Council[17] and, in particular, for their evolving educational policy. Despite the requirement that their decision should be made on planning grounds alone, by 15 votes to 8 the issue was given over to the Policy Committee, in effect the Executive of the Labour administration. Its Chair, Geoff Shaw,[18] appreciating the sensitivity of the issue, gathered his Committee Conveners on 6 September and asked them to seek information from their departments on the future need for land. He argued that, because in its application the Club had indicated that it did not require the full area of the playing fields as open space (hence the application for re-zoning for building), the Corporation had a locus in ensuring the best use of land within the city. In this scenario the Club could be forced to sell their surplus playing fields to the Corporation, thus ending the building of an independent school.[19] However, although there was evidence of a lack of open spaces in Glasgow,[20] only the Parks Department seemed interested in the land as additional public space for football pitches. Nonetheless, this material consideration was judged to carry enough weight for the Policy Committee to recommend the refusal of outline planning permission, and on 30 October 1973 the Planning Committee turned down the Club's application.[21] However, by this time the Club had already appealed to the Secretary of State because of the failure of the planning authority to determine the application within the statutory time period.

Meantime, the plans to establish a new independent co-educational school at Old Anniesland made progress on other fronts. Drewsteignton was growing, not just in terms of numbers,[22] but also in beginning to be more selective, aiming for academically promising pupils. From 1973 on, the demand for places far exceeded the number of places available,[23] and the scholastic attainment of the intake began to improve.[24] From August 1971, the Upper Glenburn Road premises housed Kindergarten to Junior 4 with Mrs Baker as headmistress, but in summer 1973 she was replaced by Miss Eileen Robertson,[25] who was 'head-hunted' by the Bakers. Although the manner of the appointment was unusual, it was to prove a great success, particularly as, similar to her predecessor, she attended directors' meetings and reported directly to them, which ensured that a voice for the Junior School could be heard at every meeting.

Paradoxically, the growing strength of Drewsteignton made its directors, and Mrs Baker in particular, increasingly fearful of being swallowed up by the High School. The main sticking point was the name for the new school, with Mrs Baker supporting 'Drewsteignton High School'.[26] However, the High School side refused to concede, and on 14 September 1973 the Club registered a new company – 'The High School of Glasgow Limited' – to preserve the name of the High School and establish a High School of Glasgow Education Trust as the fund-raising branch of the new organisation.

Both parties agreed that the number on the Board of Directors for the merged schools should be increased to represent both interests equally.[27] At this stage another important hurdle had to be overcome, as practically all of the Drewsteignton side deemed a distinctly Christian ethos for the new school as being of vital importance. To this end, when the High School produced a list of nominees for co-option onto the Board, Andrew Baker enquired about their 'suitability' to ensure they were in clear or full sympathy with the Christian aims of Drewsteignton.[28] In the event, the nine High School nominees were accepted unanimously,[29] Norrie Thomson's confirmation of the need to safeguard Christian traditions being enough of a guarantee. He understood, and the High School side generally accepted, how important this issue was in securing further progress towards the ultimate objective of the continuation of the High School in some form.

There was optimism that 12,000 Former Pupils, and networking in the west of Scotland, would finance the project conveniently located in the north-west of the city, although the economic climate could hardly have been less propitious.[30] Expectations remained unrealistically high that generous funding of scholarships would ensure children of all backgrounds could attend: the *Glasgow Herald* had even reported earlier hopes from Club spokesmen that perhaps a majority of places might be funded by scholarships.[31] It also reported a determination not to seek grant aid[32] but to go for full independent status, with fees set at around £200 to £300 a year. Nonetheless, a very positive pilot survey carried out by Craigmyle, a fundraising company,[33] suggested it was realistic to aim to build a School of 750 pupils, costing an estimated £1 million, in three phases. It was at this stage, in January 1974, that Drewsteignton Limited formally amalgamated its interests with the High School Limited; in the process, the Drewsteignton Company ceased to exist and was subsumed into the High School of Glasgow Limited.

THE HIGH SCHOOL CLUB

All now centred on the issue of Old Anniesland. On 19 September 1973 the Club had lodged an appeal with the Secretary of State for Scotland, indicating that no notice of approval or rejection had been received from the Glasgow Planning Committee within the legal period of two months for such decisions. Once the appeal had been made, the Secretary of State was statutorily bound to determine it – unless the Corporation changed its mind and granted permission. On 13 December, Gordon Campbell announced that he had appointed Alexander G. Bell[34] as Reporter for an Inquiry to be held in Glasgow's City Chambers on 22/23 January 1974. The speed in setting up the Inquiry, and the appointment of Bell to deal with this case, was no doubt a reflection of Scottish Office ministers' concern to get the matter resolved quickly.

At the Inquiry, the Corporation put its case in writing and Geoff Shaw[35] appeared to give oral evidence. In its view there were already adequate facilities in Glasgow for primary and secondary education,[36] and if any change of use was to be made it should be to re-zone the application site as public open space, which the city lacked.[37] Given that the Corporation had no policy on the matter, nor had it advanced the case for more open spaces before, this line of argument proved unconvincing to the Reporter, who preferred the evidence of the Chairman of the High School Development Committee, Norrie Thomson.[38] Perhaps most telling was the precedent set by the Corporation itself in the previous year, when local authority permission had been given to build the new Whitehill School on land zoned for playing fields on Onslow Drive. The Reporter, therefore, recommended that the Secretary of State sustain the appeal and grant outline planning permission for the development proposed by the High School Club.

The Inquiry went ahead as planned and was completed within one day, but when the Reporter submitted his recommendation on 13 March he did so to a new Secretary of State, William Ross. Following a snap General Election, the Conservative Party had lost power and Labour returned to Government on 5 March.

The civil servants at the Scottish Development Department responsible for planning rapidly consulted their counterparts at the SED.[39] However, given the policy of the new Labour Government towards independent schools,[40] its officials wished to play down the dangerous implication in the Corporation's position that, since there was adequate provision for secondary schooling, permission to build a new independent school should be refused.[41] The corollary of this proposition would be the unacceptable idea that the existence of such schools meant that an authority was failing in its duty to provide adequate education.[42] As Glasgow Corporation had emphasised that refusing planning permission was not on educational grounds, other than saying that a new school was not needed at that location there were no convincing educational arguments to be put forward against the proposal.[43]

When Ross asked the advice of the Lord Advocate,[44] he could not have gained a clearer legal response: 'There is no room in this case for general policy considerations to affect the Secretary of State's judgement on the planning appeal. It is plain on the evidence, which is virtually undisputed, that there are no proper planning grounds on which the appeal could be refused.'[45] The Secretary of State's Principal Private Secretary, Peter Mackay,[46] recorded that Ross 'reluctantly' agreed,[47] despite the opposition of the junior Minister of State, Robert Hughes.[48] The SDD wrote to the Club's agents on 5 June 1974, informing them that the Secretary of State had sustained the Club's appeal and that he had granted outline planning permission for the erection of a secondary school in accordance with the layout shown in the application, and subject to a number of standard and uncontroversial conditions.

With that hurdle cleared, the Rector, David Lees, and the Head of Drewsteignton, Eric Harle, produced a paper on the projected school population and structure from August 1977, the planned first year of operation. It was thought that by then the High School roll at Elmbank Street would no longer be viable and that the Secretary of State would allow the Corporation to close it. The total number of secondary pupils for the new school for session 1977–8 was estimated at 300, forming a total of twelve classes made up of three First Year classes, two classes for each of the Second to the Fifth Years, and one Sixth Year class. It was hoped that by session 1979–80 the roll would reach 425. The structure of promoted posts would follow the Scottish pattern of departmental Heads of subject, with a House system for pastoral, social and sports purposes. As the roll increased, it was expected that the staff complement would rise from twenty-one to twenty-nine in the same period. With regard to accommodation, the detailed plans for the first phase included fifteen classrooms, an Assembly Hall and a library, and these were duly granted detailed planning permission by the planning sub-committee of the Corporation on 23 January 1975. With costs for this part of the programme being estimated at £600,000, the estimated level of fees to be charged rose to £360 per annum, which was in line with charges at Glasgow Academy.

On 22 February 1975 the Director of Education, John Bain, reported that the High School at Elmbank Street would no longer be viable at the end of session 1975–6, and he proposed its closure in June 1976. By then there would be 100 Fifth and 50 Sixth Year pupils left, who would transfer elsewhere to complete their education. There was no open discussion of the future use of the buildings, although Conservative councillors pointed out the shortage of school accommodation and the request of Glasgow Corporation that the Secretary of State provide an additional increase of £2.2 million for school-building in 1975–7. It was generally envisaged that the buildings would be used as a 'library' of technical aids for teachers. On 31 March 1975 Ross gave his approval for the High School to be closed in June 1976. Within a year it was reported that the Elmbank Street building was to become the headquarters of Strathclyde Regional Council[49] at a conversion cost of £3.4 million. It would take twenty-seven months to complete, for the five separate buildings were all to be linked, with the Assembly Hall becoming the Council Chamber.[50]

THE APPEAL

Norrie Thomson ran a very efficient Appeal. He had been President of the Glasgow High School Club when the Secretary of State sealed the fate of the School, but when he retired from this in October 1973 he accepted the invitation to become chairman of the Appeal, working from an office in the Pavilion at Old Anniesland. After about six months it was realised that the job had to be on a full-time basis, and by November 1975 Thomson had given up his job to become Appeal Director and School Bursar.[51] Meantime, the former School Registrar, Miss Catherine McLaren, compiled lists of all boys enrolled in the School between 1920 and 1960, and she spent twelve months tracing addresses where these were unknown to the Club. This work was continued by Dick Rose. As a result, seventy-five areas of Former Pupils were formed, and a small group in each undertook to visit the others and encourage their support. Visits began in November 1974. Former pupils outside these areas, or those overseas, were approached by letter. The parents of both High School and Drewsteignton held meetings and made a significant financial contribution. Plans were then made to approach industry and commerce, trusts, institutions and other outside bodies.

The Appeal for funds proved remarkably successful, showing the widespread goodwill for Glasgow's Town School despite the ferocious economic difficulties of the time. About 80 per cent of the target figure of £600,000 had been achieved when, in May 1976, the lowest of the building tenders was accepted.[52] Work on building the main teaching block at Old Anniesland, designed by Messrs Keppie, Henderson and Partners,[53] got underway.

The old High School closed on 30 June 1976. The following day, Drewsteignton School assumed its name and Eric Harle took on the title of Rector of the High School. By a happy coincidence, 1 July was the annual prizegiving at Drewsteignton and Harle had arranged for a supply of High School badges, which parents were asked to sew onto blazer pockets overnight.[54] The guest of honour was the High School's Professor David Walker, and all present were reminded that the ethos of the merged schools were inseparable. To achieve the High School's 'Sursum semper' one must first employ Drewsteignton's 'Do justly, love mercy and walk humbly with thy God'.

With the concentration of expenditure on Anniesland, spending on Drewsteignton's Bearsden sites was kept to a minimum. However, accommodation there was only sufficient until June 1975, when the Bakers had to move out of 14 Upper Glenburn Road to provide more space. This was packed when session 1975–6 opened with 250 pupils from Kindergarten to P4 inclusive, while Ledcameroch Road housed 380 pupils from P5 to S6. A debate ensued as concern grew over the implications of opening the third site. Eileen Robertson argued persuasively for the need to concentrate the younger pupils on one site in Bearsden and the secondary pupils at Anniesland.[55] In January 1977 the directors decided to site Kindergarten to P6 at Ledcameroch, but with no further room there for Transitus (the school's name for P7), they determined that the rest of the School should be at Anniesland.[56] Although this separation was to become educationally significant, at the time accommodation drove decision-making.[57]

A Schools Liaison Committee (under Norman Macfarlane) had been set up[58] to make recommendations to the governing body. Practically all were accepted without amendment. These included accepting the historical title 'Rector' in place of 'headmaster'; using the Drewsteignton House names (lifeboats) in primary and the High School House names in secondary; favouring a Head Boy and Head Girl in place of Captain and Lieutenant; and using the Scottish terminology 'Junior School' instead of the English 'Preparatory School'. On uniform, Mrs Audrey Whitefield organised a mannequin parade and analysed parental opinions. Staff and pupil opinion had also been sought. On the question of blazer colour, the choice narrowed itself down to blue or grey. The committee studied various shades of blue, including those of Kelvinside Academy, the High School FP blazer, the Drewsteignton blue cap, and a specially prepared blue blazer. The unanimous recommendation, on 21 October 1976, was for the last of these. The new uniform was composed of a blue blazer with blue, brown and gold striped tie, but the badge remained the unchanged High School crest.

For the most part the merger of the schools went smoothly. However, tensions did on occasions come to the surface. One example of this led to a special meeting of the directors on 2 June 1977, held to discuss a letter sent out by Rector Harle to S4 parents. In it he had asserted that the Advanced Level Examinations (of England) were 'more demanding intellectually' and 'opened more doors' than the Higher Grade Examinations (of Scotland). A number of directors objected to what they deemed an unacceptable statement of educational policy for a Scottish school. Leonard Aitkenhead produced a seven-page rebuttal. Harle was to pay a high price for an under-standable judgment but an avoidable mistake. Specifically, Harle accepted that his parental letters would be forwarded to the Board seven days before the intended date of issue to allow representation to be made if deemed appropriate. Generally, his every action in future would be scrutinised. Threatened involvement in operational matters did not bode well for future relations between the school staff managers and the school directors.

OLD ANNIESLAND

In September 1977 the senior school was transplanted to Anniesland, with the main contractors, William Gordon & Co. Ltd, completing the construction on time and within budget. Shortly after the beginning of session, on 28 September Lord Home of the Hirsel, the former Conservative premier, officially opened the new High School. The building was dedicated by the Rt Rev. John R. Gray, Moderator of the Church of Scotland, previously School Chaplain when the School was situated in Elmbank Street, in his parish. As a Former Pupil he had another good reason to be involved that day. The astonishing rescue was complete. Norrie Thomson had remarkably raised £635,000, some £35,000 over target, and in the process he proved so many sceptics wrong.[59] The challenge was now to discover whether the new independent High School could produce an ethos to rival its predecessor.

The new School at Anniesland opened session 1977–8 with 340 pupils in a Transitus (Primary 7) class and six secondary years. The great majority had transferred from the school's temporary home in Ledcameroch Road, Bearsden, which became the Junior School. Fees ranged from £185 a term in Transitus to £220 a term from Third Year on, but Norrie Thomson had been able to introduce seven bursars, while eight more pupils whose parents were under financial strain received some assistance. These awards were made on the basis of both academic ability and need. The directors' aim was that the School should not be confined only to those whose parents could afford the fees. At the same time, it had been decided that nothing should be completely free. The top bursary award was £600, which left the parents £20 a term to pay. Each year would see an annual review of each bursar's situation, ensuring that awards were kept in line with need. There were no bursaries for places in the junior school, where fees ranged from £90 a term to £175.

Fees were necessary for running costs; the initial appeal had paid for the building, which was a single-storey structure, though the gymnasium in the centre rose above the rest. It was set well back from Crow Road in an open situation at the south end of the Old Anniesland playing fields. Its outer walls were of rust-coloured brick topped with a deep band of dark-grey tiles.

Inside, the finishes were simple: some were plastered, while others were exposed, painted block-work. The building was almost square and enclosed a central courtyard, with a pond, beside the gymnasium. There were eight general classrooms; specialist rooms for Home Economics, Art and Music; and a Science department with laboratories for Biology, Physics, Chemistry and General Science. It was all designed by Keppie, Henderson & Partners with flexibility in mind, so that the use of rooms could be changed as later phases of the School were completed.

With an increase in staffing some issues arose. In particular, Drewsteignton had strong links with two inter-denominational Christian organisations, the Scripture Union and the Universities and Colleges Christian Fellowship. As a committed Baptist, Harle's personal leanings were certainly in the same direction and this probably led to the appointment of a number of staff chosen more for their commitment to their religious beliefs than to education. However, several were impressive teachers, and most were well-qualified and dedicated, some having just returned from work in missionary schools overseas. Those who stand out for their quality and for the years of dedicated service they gave to the School include Ron Hockey (Head of Science), Bill Seaman (Head of English), Bob Metcalfe (a geographer who was appointed Deputy Rector from a field of five in January 1974),[60] Audrey Whitefield (Senior Mistress until 1983 when she became Assistant Rector), Sylvia Gardner (Head of Modern Languages and the person most responsible for the development of the careers' department),[61] and Colin Mair.[62]

Norrie Thomson was determined to press on with the next phase of building. The school roll in September 1978 stood at 736 (with 344 in Junior School and 392 in Senior School), but all available accommodation on the site was being fully utilised, including the Tea Room, the George Pate Room[63] and the upstairs Committee Room in the Pavilion. These areas were forecast to be lost in the proposed Crow Road development, which was scheduled for 1980. The other factor was Thomson's extraordinary fund-raising success: at a meeting on 12 September 1978 he announced that he had already raised £115,000 for the next phase and had promises of a further £26,000. It took only a week for the directors to commit themselves to the building of an Assembly Hall with three classrooms attached, at an estimated cost of about £200,000. The project began two months later and was completed and formally opened on 9 November 1979 by Hon. Dr George Weir.[64]

At this stage in the building programme, the directors took stock and determined on the 'consolidation' of a three-stream school.[65] This suggested an emphasis on quality and giving value for money, but the strategy was somewhat overtaken by positive and encouraging signs: examination results (except in Mathematics) were improving,[66] and the roll had increased again to 769 for session 1979–80,[67] despite information that the intake had declined in some independent schools. Talk began of another building, which would be primarily aimed at replacing temporary buildings.

In October 1979 Andrew Baker resigned the chairmanship after fourteen years and, significantly, he was replaced by Norman Macfarlane, thereby ensuring a reinforcement of traditional High School values. A Chairman's Committee was formed: it met more often than the previous, somewhat anonymous, Executive Committee and was more wide-ranging in its discussions. Strategically, it took a positive line over the new Conservative Government's Consultative Paper on 'grant aid', although there was a desire not to become too dependent financially on the scheme.[68] On the school roll, the group proved cautious, at least in the short term, and produced no plans to increase numbers. On staffing, there was some concern that around a quarter of the staff came from outwith Scotland. Operationally, the Committee accepted that corporal punishment could be inflicted by Harle, Metcalfe and Mrs Whitefield (girls).[69] On the presentation of pupils for examinations, the Committee agreed that the final decision should lie with the Rector, but he should 'if possible put the decision on the parent', and the directors wanted a more liberal policy, even though this might produce less favourable examination results.

By late 1980 it was apparent that new building was only just keeping pace with increasing numbers. With Norrie Thomson optimistic as usual, a sub-committee, with the architects from Keppie Henderson and Partners, was set up to plan the future physical development of the school. It envisaged a total spend of £1.6 million, of which Thomson thought a reasonable Appeal target would be £900,000. The first stage would be building an extension to the Assembly block, consisting of a lecture theatre, three classrooms and a teachers' base (for English); an upgrade and relocation of Music and Art (and Technical Drawing); and the beginnings of new Science laboratories in a separate Science block to the south of the existing Assembly building. The Science block was to include seven laboratories, a technicians' room, storage and various smaller specialist areas, and a Science teachers' base. Although designed to cater for the eventual science needs of the School, the laboratories were designed to be phased over several years, with the spaces being used as general teaching areas until conversion

to lab use. In the event of the Appeal not reaching its full target, it was anticipated that the Assembly Hall extension and approximately half of the
proposed lab block would be completed. The reduced lab block would
include pupil toilets, two new labs, a technicians' room and a classroom. A
result of these building developments – Phases III and IV – would allow the
conversion of the old Music room to a new main staff room, the existing
labs to be used as classrooms, and the old staff room to make space for the
Assistant Rector and the Prefects.

Clearly the planned building programme was dependent on the success
of the Appeal. The directors, therefore, decided to appeal first to parents
during the first half of 1981 and, providing the response was good, only then
would they consider going to tender, with the aim of having at least part of
the accommodation ready for the beginning of session 1982–3. Thomson
believed the projected target was realistic in light of the first Appeal, which
had a target of £600,000 and had raised £636,000, and because, since 1975,
the Educational Trust had raised some £950,000, which had included
£150,000 for bursaries.

Two other significant developments date from this period. First,
investment in the House system began in May 1980, when the Chairman's
Committee agreed to pay the four secondary House staff 25 per cent of the
responsibility allowance of Heads of Department; two assistants were also
recruited and were to be paid 8.5 per cent of a Head of Department's salary.
At a Board meeting, Dr Lees held that too many staff were involved in
Guidance for the size of staff. Fortunately the other directors backed the
proposals,[70] and this enabled Audrey Whitefield to create the successful
House system, which was to play such a crucial part in developing the
special ethos of the new High School.

Second, Deputy Rector Robert Metcalfe resigned[71] to become Director
of YMCA National Centre at Lakeside in the Lake District. The directors
advertised only in Scotland, resulting in twenty-nine candidates. On 20
December a long-leet of ten, including three internal candidates, were interviewed, and on 13 January 1981 a shortlist of four candidates (including Mrs
Whitefield) were re-interviewed by the Board. Brian Lockhart was
appointed Deputy Rector. Since 1972 he had been Principal Teacher of
History and Economic History at George Heriot's School in Edinburgh. He
had developed his department considerably and was praised by the HMI,
who were impressed with the popularity of his subjects, especially at Sixth
Year level. During the absence of a senior colleague, he had also taken over
some of the remit of an Assistant Head. His background and experience in

the Scottish grant-aided school system was crucial for the High School directors, whose vision was increasingly crystallising around the creation of a School with an ethos similar to that of schools such as Heriot's. In line with this, the Board determined to follow the SED guidelines for a school the size of the High School and introduced an Assistant Rector (Mrs Whitefield), who joined the management team of Harle and Lockhart.

In February 1981, appreciating Harle's disappointment not to be more involved in the appointment of his deputy, the Chairman's Committee nonetheless determined that senior teaching and non-teaching staff would remain Board appointments. These were spelled out: Rector, Deputy Rector, Assistant Rector, Head of Junior School, Bursar, Assistant Bursar, Company Secretary and Chaplain. The Board also wished to be involved in the appointment of Heads of Department: the Rector would prepare a shortlist and give his recommendation, which would require the ratification of the directors. Within a couple of months the directors were suggesting introducing a retirement age of sixty for all promoted staff but, following 'considerable discussion' at the Chairman's Committee, this retiring age was to be introduced only for Rector, Deputy Rector and Assistant Rector posts.[72] The financial implications for the incumbent Rector, who would be sixty in February 1983, needed to be considered carefully, but the decision brought the High School into line with other independent schools.

Another issue tackled by the Chairman's Committee was the structure and level of fees. Given the competition from the excellent state schools in Bearsden and Milngavie, it decided to keep fees at the Junior School particularly low. Junior 1 fees were set at £194 per term, gradually rising over the six years to £307 in Transitus. Another factor was a determination to be competitive with its traditional rival, Glasgow Academy, whose fees ranged from £255 to £345 at Junior School. Consideration was also paid to class sizes; fortunately, here too the High School claimed an advantage: its classrooms could only accommodate between twenty-four and twenty-eight pupils, while at the Academy Junior School classes were usually thirty-two in number.[73]

Norrie Thomson had good cause for being pleased at the way things were going at the beginning of session 1981–2. The Appeal was progressing satisfactorily, with over £200,000 pledged, enabling the directors to invite tenders to ensure that the original timescale of occupation of the new buildings by September 1982 could be achieved. The school roll continued to rise, and in September 1981 stood at 855 (369+486). Day by day it seemed that the new school was becoming what Thomson had dreamed of: a reborn

High School of Glasgow. The Board overturned the previous Drewsteignton decisions of having a Head Prefect and Speech Day, and instead introduced the Scottish terminology of School Captain and Prizegiving. More significant was the level of bursaries introduced: for session 1981–2 some thirty-nine bursaries were granted by the Educational Trust at a cost of £20,193, plus four from independent trusts at £2,952; five special cases of hardship were also taken on at £2,590. Added to these forty-eight, some seventeen assisted places, with income of £16,307, was forthcoming from the SED.

On a personal front, Thomson had determined to give up his post in early 1983, and the directors had advertised for a Bursar designate. A sub-committee of Macfarlane, Thomson and R.P. McEwan was appointed as Selection Committee, but they failed to find an outstanding candidate despite interviewing eight of the candidates in March 1981. A change of tactics was necessary, and Mrs Kay Holland was promoted internally to the new post of Assistant Bursar in June, while in September J. Ritchie Wilkie was appointed as Deputy Bursar. This was the situation when Norrie Thomson, widely regarded as 'Mr High School', died suddenly and unexpectedly. The whole High School community was stunned.

Chairman Macfarlane, at the directors' meeting on 20 October 1981, held that Thomson 'more than anyone else, had been responsible for the re-establishment of the High School at Old Anniesland and the construction of the new buildings'. A special memorial service at the School was organised for 4 December. The directors determined that a more permanent memorial would be the completion of the new Science block, which would be named 'The Norrie Thomson Building'. It was also agreed that at an appropriate time the directors would seek the continued assistance of Norrie's widow, Elizabeth, in the fund-raising effort, with which she had helped her husband.

It soon became apparent, if it had not been apparent before, how significant, even indispensable, Thomson had been in the task of recreating the High School. His extensive job specification was redistributed to others: Ritchie Wilkie took over the Appeal; Kay Holland[74] took on the other bursarial duties; Sandy Maclaurin became Treasurer of the High School Educational Trust; and Brian Lockhart joined the Club Committee as staff representative.[75] Moreover, on the Board, Thomson's powerful presence was immediately missed, and it was deemed necessary to strengthen High School representation. Jimmy Highgate (Norrie's brother-in-law), Ian Docherty[76] and George Dewar were all recruited. Despite the quality of this new 'team', the loss of Thomson was palpable and his unique contribution was missed in many important decisions at such a vital time. The Club commissioned a bust from James Barclay, and the entrance hall of the School was chosen for its location.

In January 1982 Farrans began work on their £522,739 contract, which included some £75,000 for equipping the new labs. The work progressed well, and the Muirhead Moffat legacy[77] boosted the Appeal. On 30 April the directors unanimously decided to go ahead with the Arts block. In September the Science labs were opened, and the new session found another increased roll of 879 (515 + 364). The Arts block opened to classes in January 1983 and was formally opened by the Countess of Mansfield.[78]

As well as important building works, there were significant academic developments in 1981–3. Macfarlane believed that the curriculum on offer was too firmly centred on traditional subjects, with university entrance the aim.[79] He wished to encourage more diversity. It was agreed to set up an Academic Committee to look at this and other such issues. With Macfarlane as chair, the senior management team of Harle, Lockhart and Whitefield were joined in regular meetings from November 1981 by directors with educational experience: Professor Walker, Dr Lees and Peter Kimber. On the original topic, there was little sympathy for criticism of schools by industrialists, and the educationists emphasised education for living rather than working. Nonetheless, it was agreed that a rounded education would need to include more stress on subjects such as Information and Communications Technology, Modern Languages and Electronics. The quality of examination results was an on-going matter of concern, and the Rector outlined the plans for improvement, which involved strategies to minimise disruption to teaching time, and making departmental heads more accountable for their staff.[80] This led to discussions on the quality of individual staff members, and Lockhart's suggestion that paying above the national scale would help attract and retain teachers.

A particularly important area for the School was its Sixth Year, which was problematic generally in Scotland and especially in the west of Scotland, where significant numbers of talented pupils with good Higher Grade results left school at the end of their Fifth Year. In an effort to combat this trend, the directors had introduced a lowering of the fees for Sixth Year,[81] and on his arrival in April 1981 Lockhart had been given the remit to build up the numbers in Sixth Year, which then stood at only twenty. Related to that, the staff were encouraged to treat all senior pupils in a more adult fashion, and facilities were improved and the curriculum widened. Already apparent was a move toward the Scottish Certificate of Sixth Year Studies (CSYS) instead of the English Advanced Level ('A' Levels). In 1982–3 a 'mixed' system still operated, with English, History, Latin, Physics and Chemistry opting for CSYS, while French, German and Mathematics taught to the 'A' Level syllabus. In November 1982, the High School committed itself to CSYS, with 'A' Level being attempted only for special reasons. This fitted well with the nature of and growth in university applications, for in February 1983 the school's UCCA[82] entry stood at forty-three, of which only four placed an English university as their first choice. It also did not hold back those students who set their target at Oxbridge or elsewhere, following in the footsteps of Lesley Riddoch, who left in 1978 and was elected the first woman President of the Oxford Students' Union in March 1980. Sarah Hook gained a place in 1982 to read Chemistry at Somerville College, Oxford.

Another encouraging aspect of this period was the growth in the quantity and quality of extra-curricular activities on offer. Harle was particularly supportive of Colin Mair, who had responsibility for rugby as well as Latin. He established annual pre-season rugby camps from 1977, and foreign tours in the 1980s. David Hogg played for Scottish Schoolboys in 1979, and David Halliday followed three years later. In October 1980 there was a resumption of the traditional match between the School's First XV and the First XV of Glasgow Academy,[83] while during season 1981–2 the First Rugby XV won twenty-two of its twenty-four fixtures, with a points margin of 640 to 79, taking the scalps of Merchiston, Dollar and the Academy. The directors agreed that the rugby boys could go on an end-of-season tour. Such successes, however, highlighted two problems. The first was the imbalance between boys' and girls' facilities, for the girls had only one grass pitch at Anniesland, leading to a dialogue with Strathclyde Region about the former Girls' High grounds at Kirklee. The second was the determination of the FP Rugby Club to have first call on Anniesland, and to prevent the School First XV from playing on the main pitch on a Saturday morning when the FPs had an afternoon fixture. This issue was complicated, as the High School Club owned the ground while, based on usage, the School paid two thirds of its annual running costs, which reached £32,000 in 1982–3.[84]

During the first half of 1982, Macfarlane and Rector Harle had agreed the terms of the latter's retiring package, and it was decided that it would be best for a new Rector to take up post on 1 August 1983. It was decided, however, to delay the beginning of the procedure as both Glasgow Academy and George Heriot's were both advertising their own vacancies. In October

1982, from over fifty applications a long-leet of nine was drawn up by the Selection Committee of Macfarlane (Convener), Walker, McEwan, Macmillan, Kimber and Nancy Davidson. Following interviews, the committee produced its short-leet of three: Frank Gerstenberg, Head of Oswestry School since 1974; Robin Easton, Head of Modern Languages at Watson's College; and Brian Lockhart, the internal candidate. They were interviewed by the whole Board of twenty members on 16 November 1982 and, after voting by paper ballot, Robin Easton was appointed.[85]

In an awkward transitional period from the old to the new High School, Eric Harle can be credited with producing a sound base for the developing new School. He was always supported in this objective and achievement by his loyal wife, Ruth. He was at his best when planning complicated possible future building arrangements, for then his rigorous mathematical training came into its own. In this regard he had one final and important contribution to make. He had produced detailed plans for future development on 23 November 1979, which he updated on 28 April 1980. The latter spelled out the needs of the School: the extensions on the north and east wings of the Assembly Hall; the new buildings for Science and a games hall and gymnasium. At the directors' meeting of 18 May 1983, and with the Appeal continuing, over £840,000 raised, and the encouragement of Ian Docherty, Harle produced updated, revised plans for the future. His 'Games Hall Plus' paper postulated four options, from what he termed the optimum Option A[86] through to the minimum Option D. Following his presentation the Board decided to keep the Appeal going, and Harle's blueprint opened the way for further building. This was to be his lasting contribution and legacy. He had also played an important part in his years as Rector (1976–83) in bringing together two very different traditions. On his retirement he had achieved a balance of the caring Christian ethos of Drewsteignton with the corporate character of the High School. As time went on, it began to be appreciated how he had laid the important foundation for the development of a special school.

ELEVEN

The High School under Easton,
          1983–2004

This chapter traces the advance of the new High School under the leadership of Robin Easton. In particular, progress is achieved academically and financially. The former led to an increased demand for places and the recruitment and retention of a quality staff; the latter led to a remarkable increase in the buildings at Old Anniesland, improved resources, and the growth in the number of bursaries available. The chapter ends with an analysis of the formula which 're-lit the beacon' and which, within a generation, turned the new High School into one of Scotland's leading schools.

ROBIN EASTON

Robin Gardner Easton was born in Glasgow in October 1943. He was educated at Kelvinside Academy and Sedbergh School, and at Christ's College, Cambridge and Wadham College, Oxford. He joined the Modern Languages department at Melville College in 1966, before proceeding six years' later to Housemaster and Deputy Head of the French department at the combined Stewart's/Melville College, a post he held for another six years. Between 1979 and 1983 he was Head of the Modern Languages department at George Watson's College, and this experience converted him to the merits of co-education.

Easton had an impressive curriculum vitae. As well as a successful academic and teaching career, and a reputation for very hard work in and out of the classroom, he was a Glaswegian with parents who had been well-known in the area; he was a strong advocate of the Scottish educational system and, indeed, of things Scottish in general; and he was a committed Christian. His leadership of the largest Modern Languages department in Scotland at Watson's was also an excellent preparation for the challenges presented at the High School.

Easton took over a School which had come a long way in a short time. However, there were still many who were sceptical about setting up a new independent school and, despite progress, the academic results of its pupils were below the levels being achieved at other local schools, state as well as independent. In 1982 the directors had decided to postpone Harle's application to HMC,[1] fearing a rejection. In short, in August 1983 the High School was viewed in some quarters as a poor relation of the long-established independent schools in the Glasgow area, many of which were single-sex.

Nonetheless, Easton was very fortunate in one particular regard in that he inherited strong senior management in both secondary and primary departments: Brian Lockhart and Audrey Whitefield; and Eileen Robertson and Elizabeth Burnett. They worked well together as a tight-knit team, recognised as such by the school community, directly involved in all aspects of the School.[2]

EARLY CHANGES

Sir Norman Macfarlane[3] believed that, having chosen 'the right man', he would let Easton 'get on with the job', but he also advised him that the directors were keen that the issue of poorly performing staff should be tackled. Taking a measured but sensitive approach, Easton was able to make some early staff changes, encouraging some to move on or retire early. However, the emphasis was on rewarding staff for loyalty and commitment. Encouraged particularly by Lockhart, who was in charge of the extensive extra-curricular programme, Easton persuaded the directors to pay all teaching staff 1 per cent above the national teaching scales, thereby recognising their 'increased workload and loyalty'. At the same time in December 1984, they also agreed to introduce one and a half extra staff in-service days in the session, to push forward 'curriculum preparation'. The enhancement was increased over the next decade, reaching 6 per cent and, in time, the salaries of administrative staff were also augmented in similar fashion. These measures helped to insulate the School from the impact of the national teachers' strike in 1985.

Easton took on a system which restricted the use of the belt to the secondary management team and four House staff. However, following a landmark ruling of the European Court of Human Rights, corporal punishment was ruled out for all state pupils, and for all pupils receiving government financial help to attend independent schools. Easton baulked at imposing different punishments on pupils for the same offences, and the directors agreed. The discipline code was revised to take account of the end of corporal punishment, but Easton was given the power, denied to Harle, to suspend pupils without prior consultation with the chairman or the Board; and he introduced lunchtime detention as an extra sanction for minor misdemeanours.

A further early change was to do away with form classes in Transitus, S1 and S2 based on streaming by perceived ability. The pupils in the lower streams, and their parents, considered themselves to be 'second-class citizens', and there was some evidence to suggest that once placed in a particular stream it was difficult for them to move into the higher classes. It took some time, however, for parents of 'high fliers', as well as for some staff, to be convinced of the benefits of the new system. Nonetheless, the mixing of abilities within form classes made the secondary department a happier place, and the pupils moving from the junior department could feel more confident about the transition.

INCREASE IN PUPIL NUMBERS

From 1984 onwards, the number of pupils applying annually for places increased steadily until a very healthy plateau was reached. Leaving aside periods of industrial action, when applications reached record heights, Secondary 1 applications were between seventy and ninety, and the usual intake was twenty-six. At Transitus level around thirty to forty children applied for the two or three places available. This encouraged Easton to create a third class at the Primary 7 stage, which led in turn, when accommodation was available, to a fourth class in Secondary 1. There was, of course, a temptation to keep increasing the intake, but it was felt that keeping the secondary to a size where all pupils could meet daily in the Assembly Hall was important, and that something would be lost in community spirit if the School grew much beyond that. Therefore, a cap of 100 in a year-group from Secondary 1 upwards was introduced (four form classes of twenty-five), with a maximum class size of twenty-six.

The expansion of Transitus was a great success. Being able to select more pupils for the Senior School was an important element in raising standards both academically and in the extra-curricular areas. Prior to these changes, about two thirds of the secondary department were former Junior School pupils while, subsequently, about half the secondary was composed of new pupils. Parents became aware that similar numbers were joining Transitus and First Year, and applications for the former increased accordingly.

At Kindergarten, there were usually some eighty applicants for the fifty places. Easton was committed to taking siblings and children of active Former Pupils, and this left very few places for new families. It was also frustrating, and indeed damaging to other objectives, that there were normally more than twenty applicants for the one or two places available at Junior 1. Unless a family had to withdraw a pupil, there were usually no places further up the Primary School, and applicants went elsewhere or, in some cases, awaited Transitus. While it was disappointing to lose worthwhile applicants for lack of places, it was reassuring that Easton could count on having all available places in the Junior department taken up and pupils receiving a quality education, thanks to the sterling work of Eileen Robertson and her staff.

By increasing the number of entrants to the Senior School, it was easier to find places for siblings and others with connections to the School. From conversations with prospective parents, Easton came to realise the importance of building a reputation for leading a 'family school'. His decision to take most siblings regardless of perceived academic promise ran contrary to the general approach of other independent schools in Glasgow, most of which gave priority to children who were considered as showing academic ability. Easton's decision does not appear to have adversely affected examination results.

The other growth area was the Sixth Year. Despite the west of Scotland tradition of leaving at the end of S5, it became increasingly common for pupils at the School to stay on for S6. With lower fees than the rest of the secondary years, an extended academic offering and improved facilities, its numbers increased fivefold in a decade. By the end of Easton's tenure, very few pupils left School without completing six years of broad-based secondary education.

A large Sixth Year, however, meant there was a need to develop the curriculum, improve social facilities, balance freedom with responsibility, and offer opportunities to develop leadership qualities. It was in this context that Easton decided to extend the role of prefect to all Sixth Year pupils, and in so doing he helped diminish the tensions created annually when many worthy individuals were not selected as prefects. Not all were won over by this change, but the benefits of such inclusion at a personal and school level sat comfortably with the new ethos being promoted.

PROMOTING THE SCHOOL

Easton and his senior colleagues were very conscious that the High School was a new independent school in an area that contained a considerable number of long-established and highly regarded competitors for pupils. Until the beginning of the 1990s, Glasgow had twelve schools listed by the Scottish Council of Independent Schools (SCIS) as 'all-through and independent schools', and there were four more in Ayr, Dumbarton, Helensburgh and Kilmacolm. There were also three 'Junior and Preparatory Schools' on the Glasgow list, and two more in Ayr and Helensburgh. Parents considering independent education, therefore, had a wide choice, and a number were Former Pupils of other independent schools or had family links with them.[4]

Easton believed that it was of considerable importance that he and his staff convey to prospective parents, and others, that the High School was an efficient, effective and caring institution. Any contact with the school by telephone or letter received a prompt response and, whenever possible, a same-day reply with personal touches added to all standard communications. Like Eileen Robertson in the Junior School, Easton tried to meet and personally show round the School all visiting parents and prospective parents. Open Evenings played a vital role in promoting the School, and Easton made the Rector's talk more of a focal point. A key to success were the Third Year pupil guides,[5] ably supported by the Sixth Year, as were the lengths to which staff went to show the School in its very best light.

In 1983 the only literature for prospective parents was an A5 folder containing loose sheets of paper with information about the School. Whilst the material was well written, there were no illustrations or photographs. It was clear that a more professional production was required, and Easton produced an attractive prospectus. Only two further new prospectuses (both produced by a parent's Glasgow firm) were required in his time, and the second of these survived well into the tenure of his successor. Expenditure on school promotion remained modest but well focused, and Easton confined advertising to specific times when the School wished to publicise entrance tests or invitations to visit the School.

For a number of years, Easton had no professional advice on public relations. Fortunately, negative press stories were infrequent, and there was some success in highlighting pupil achievements, with particularly good publicity resulting from HM inspections. Thereafter, Tony Meehan[6] was able to provide professional support with School promotion in the media and PR matters. The crucial factor in developing the School's reputation was

ABOVE. The Science laboratories were opened at Elmbank Street in 1887.

LEFT. The Officers' Training Corps gained official recognition from the War Office in 1909.

The Assembly Hall at Elmbank Street opened in 1905.

Science laboratory in the Girls' High, 1955. (Reproduced by permission of Getty Images)

Nina Logan was the legendary Kindergarten Mistress from 1916 until 1953.

David Lees was the last Rector of the old High School from 1950 until 1976.

Prof. Sir Neil MacCormick (1941–2009) was arguably 'the most distinguished Former Pupil of the High School of the second half of the twentieth century'. (Reproduced by permission of the University of Edinburgh)

Norman S.S. Thomson (1917–81) is regarded as 'Mr High School'.

Baron Macfarlane of Bearsden was the influential Chairman of Directors of the High School from 1979 until 1992 and since then has been its Honorary President.

Honor Baker was the refounder of Drewsteignton School in 1962 and Principal until 1973. Her husband, Andrew Baker, was Chair of Drewsteignton and then, between 1976 and 1979, of the High School.

A Junior School Event with Miss Eileen Robertson and Lord and Lady Macfarlane.

Eric Harle was Rector of the High School from 1976 until 1983.

Dr Robin Easton was Rector of the High School from 1983 until 2004.

The Jimmie Ireland Stand is one of the most recent additions at Old Anniesland.

ABOVE. The James Highgate (Art)
Building was named after a significant
Former Pupil and benefactor.

RIGHT. Gordon Anderson, a pupil from
1937 to 1949, was Chairman of
Directors between 1992 and 2001.

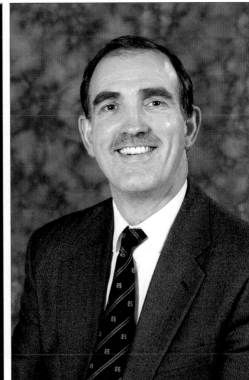

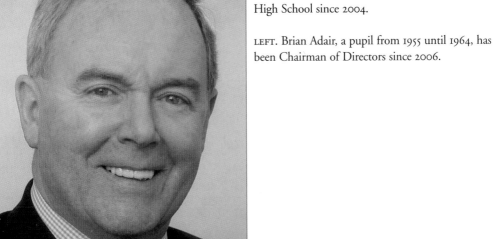

ABOVE LEFT. Professor Sir Michael Bond was Chairman of Directors from 2001 until 2006.

ABOVE RIGHT. Colin Mair has been Rector of the High School since 2004.

LEFT. Brian Adair, a pupil from 1955 until 1964, has been Chairman of Directors since 2006.

RIGHT. Alison Sheppard left the High School in 1989. She swam in five Olympics.

BELOW. Commemoration Day at Glasgow Cathedral, now celebrated annually in late September.

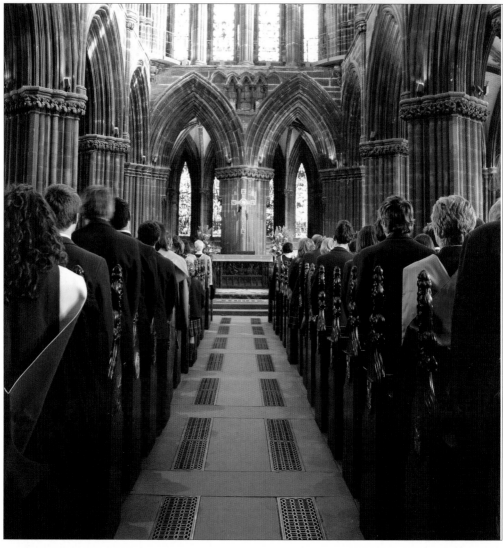

that there were good stories to tell and that the parents spread very positive messages by word of mouth. When the decision was taken to publish examination results achieved within all Scottish schools in the early 1990s, the High School was producing results which compared well with others year after year. Any lingering sense that the School was less distinguished than the other independent schools in the area vanished altogether.

ACADEMIC PROGRESS

Easton was delighted that the High School under Harle had expanded CSYS,[7] as he was convinced that the Scottish education system had a good diet of examinations to offer Sixth Year pupils.[8] Moreover, in seeking to offer the best of Scottish day school education, Easton was conscious of the High School's long history. Any parent who suggested going down the 'A' Level route was given short shrift: Easton would point out that English universities welcomed pupils with Scottish qualifications, and that attempts to marry examinations which were not designed to fit together could put pupils at a disadvantage. The success of High School applications to Oxbridge was an important factor in proving the force of Easton's argument to parents.[9] One pupil gained entry in 1984,[10] but within a decade the average number gaining places reached seven, and in the best years double figures were achieved.[11]

The progress of the School academically was a source of great satisfaction. From appearing below both local independent and state schools in results in the early 1980s, it was soon the case that only Hutchesons' Grammar School was ahead. Moreover, from 1992 onwards the High School was frequently singled out for particular praise. Arguably, the most important statistic is the average number of Highers gained by each Fifth Year pupil, which for some years has ranged around 4.8. This suggests that High School pupils achieved considerable success, and that even less able pupils achieved their full potential.

In 1992 the Scottish Office examination tables showed the High School and Hutchesons' Grammar School sharing first place. The following year the *Scotsman* wrote of the High School's 'spectacular success', and the year after that the results were again among the best. In 1995 five pupils went to Oxbridge, and by 1997 this had reached eight in number. For the next two years the High School topped all the main categories of the Scottish Office statistics, and in 1998 nine pupils went on to Oxford and Cambridge.

FUNDRAISING AND BUILDING IN THE 1980S

Easton little realised on his arrival how much fund-raising and building would dominate his time as Rector. He had scarcely arrived when meetings began with Ian Docherty,[12] from the FP Club, and Ritchie Wilkie,[13] supported by Eileen Robertson and Brian Lockhart, to talk about the needs of the School, in particular the proposed sports complex. Although others took the lead in this Appeal, Easton was soon convinced that the Rector had to be totally committed and involved if it was to be successful. This was his first encounter with architects, and he clearly relished his dealings with Kim Selwood of Keppie Henderson. The first plans, based on Harle's 'Games Hall Plus' were costed at £597,500. By May 1984 the directors had determined on a £300,000 budget, and this could fund only a games hall with changing accommodation.

There was, however, advance on another building front. Belatedly, on 1 September 1984, Strathclyde Regional Council determined to go ahead with the widening and upgrading of Crow Road. This ended vehicular access to the School from Crow Road, and The High School Club was awarded £97,000 in compensation. The Club re-sited the groundsman's house, and the George Pate Room and Tea Room were refurbished in time for the Centenary Year of the Rugby Club.[14]

On 26 September 1984 the directors examined the tenders for the games hall with the addition of two more classrooms, a Sixth Year recreation room and improved staff facilities. The lowest was from Farrans Construction at £412,000 (excluding fees). It was well over budget, and the first thought was to request another estimate for a games hall alone, but at their next meeting on 4 December even that was deemed a step too far. Until the financial shortfall could be bridged, the directors would not proceed with the project. Easton was very disappointed, and he campaigned for a reversal of the decision. By May 1985 he had produced a paper entitled 'The Need for A Games Hall', in which he held that it 'was not a luxury but a necessary addition'. He believed the 'well-being' of the School was at stake and, fortunately, more funding became available. The 1981 Appeal, which had set a target of £900,000 for the 1983 buildings, had been allowed to run on and, with a significant pledge from the Hugh Fraser Foundation, had reached £1.2 million.[15] The new Acting Bursar, Gerry Simonis, was optimistic about future operational surpluses,[16] and the directors agreed to a scheme which, according to Easton, was 'the minimal acceptable project'. For Sir Norman Macfarlane and his directors, however, it was 'another historic decision in the history of the new High School'.

Easton always accepted invitations to speak at the dinners and reunions of Former Pupils. He was often joined by his wife, Eleanor, and together they enjoyed some happy days and evenings in such company, and good relationships were formed. Sir Norman Macfarlane had put him in touch with a Former Pupil in Erskine Hospital, Major-General Jock Macfie, and Easton used to visit him there from time to time (where he was interrogated about the First XV's losses!). In late 1985, just when the directors had accepted a tender of £285,131 from J.H. Gray Ltd for constructing the games hall,[17] the General died, leaving £80,000 to the School. The chairman readily agreed to Easton's suggestion that a gymnasium be added to the games hall. On 8 January 1986, the architects were instructed to complete the work within a budget of £80,000, with a completion date of 22 August. This was to be the final building phase (Phase V), which had begun with the opening of Phase I in 1977. At the official opening of the new block on 27 October 1986 by John J. MacKay, Minister of Education, Agriculture and Fisheries, even Easton stuck to the script that this was the last major phase of the building of the new High School. He soon appreciated, however, that other major phases would be required if the School was to continue its remarkable progress.

Eileen Robertson felt, quite rightly, that the Junior School at Bearsden had been neglected over the years because of the need to create the Senior School at Anniesland. Accordingly, plans were drawn up to replace the Larches with new classrooms for Junior 6, to add a proper entrance to the School and to provide a stage and hall other than the gym. There had been major changes in personnel at Keppie Henderson, including the departure of Kim Selwood, so it was agreed that the project would be opened up to competition. A small committee interviewed five firms before choosing the firm of Wylie Shanks as the School's architects. The directors agreed to fund the project from the School's own resources, a reflection of the School's increasingly healthy financial situation in 1987.[18] In the event, the project cost £446,955. It was opened by Lady Macfarlane on 11 May 1990.

HM INSPECTIONS 1989 AND 1990

How far the High School, both Junior and Senior departments, had travelled was clear in the HMI Reports issued after full inspections, which took place in February 1989 in the case of the former, and February 1990 in the case of the latter.

The Junior school was in good repair, well furbished, imaginatively exploited, and supplemented by the use of off-site facilities . . . The strong, sympathetic leadership [of Miss Robertson] was founded on a coherent philosophy of primary education which focused firmly on the child and was informed by an awareness of recent developments. With the able support of the deputy head [Mrs Elizabeth Burnett], she ensured that organisation and administration were efficient, the articulation of policies clear, the management and evaluation of the curriculum shrewd, and the identification of priorities systematic and appropriate . . . A wide and well balanced curriculum was delivered through suitably varied approaches to teaching and learning which included class, group and individual methods. There were notable strengths in the programmes for language development, mathematics, art and craft and physical education . . .

The junior department of the High School of Glasgow provided primary education of exceptionally high quality. The mutual respect between teachers and pupils was underpinned by teachers' careful planning and preparation and by their concern for their pupils as individuals. Excellent rapport was reflected in the courtesy, co-operation and diligence of the pupils; it resulted in keenly motivated children, most of whom achieved very creditable levels of attainment.

With regard to the Senior department, the HMI stated that

the new High School of Glasgow has as yet a relatively brief history. Already, however, it has formed a strong sense of its own identity. In developing its own traditions it has drawn on much that is best in contemporary educational precept and practice, and many of the learning experiences offered to its pupils bear the hallmarks of excellence. The inspection showed that the school's daily business was conducted in an atmosphere of good order, settled purpose, and concern for others. Relationships were marked by warmth as well as mutual respect, and pupils showed keen application, a lively spirit of enquiry, and an obvious relish for the various facets of school life . . . The educational philosophy which underpinned this exceptionally good ethos gave primacy to the development of the whole pupil: academic attainment and personal growth were seen as interdependent and complementary . . . The tone of the School emerged from a consensus among teachers on educational priorities which was made possible by the establishment of a style of management responsive to the needs of pupils and staff and receptive to new ideas . . . The overall quality of teaching was high: teachers' presentations were well prepared and thought-provoking: a balanced repertoire of strategies engaged the pupils at class, group and individual levels.

The report continued:

Within its short life-span the High School already had a record of substantial achievement, both in its adaptation to changing educational needs and in its preparation of pupils for adulthood. As measured by successful performance in external examinations its accomplishments were considerable. This academic success, however, was seen to be part of an all-round education in which social, sporting and cultural activities and the exercise of responsibility were also important. The educational experience was therefore one of commendable breadth and high quality. Given the leadership of the headteacher, the calibre of the staff and the commitment of senior management to improvement, the school may confidently anticipate a successful future.

The directors were delighted, but if they expected a period of quiet consolidation they had reckoned without Easton, who used the inspection reports as the basis for further development, particularly in the areas of staffing and accommodation.

FUND-RAISING AND BUILDING IN THE 1990S

Easton gained a reputation with the directors as being always eager to move to the next building project. Although he was quite proud of this, one chairman went as far as to comment that an important part of his role was 'to hold Robin in check'.[19] Even before the Senior School inspectors had reported, he had worked with Wylie Shanks to draw up plans for an extensive building project at Anniesland, which included Computing suites, an Art area, new Geography and Modern Studies, Home Economics, History, Classics, Business Studies and Religious Education departments, and a Sixth Form common room. This project was to link the main school building to the sports complex. Astute observers suspected that all this was in anticipation of adding an extra class in each secondary year-group. On 14 June 1990, when Easton placed his 'shopping list' before the Board, it had been costed at £1.2 million. Sir Norman Macfarlane agreed to proceed, provided half the cost was raised by Appeal, with the other half coming from the School's coffers.

With changes in the Appeal Office following the retirement of Mina Malarkey, Easton pressed for a fresh approach to fund-raising. Ian Docherty and Easton opted to work with the small Scottish firm Mulholland. The firm's strategy was to recruit two parents from every class in the School, and include leaders for each year-group, and overall leaders for the Senior and Junior School parent teams. It was the Rector's job to phone the chosen parents, explain what was required of them and invite them to participate. They were to be told that a condition of being part of the parents' teams was that they should agree to give to the Appeal. A similar approach was adopted with Former Pupils, and teams were recruited for all age groups. The directors were targeted, too, as were the staff, to whom Brian Lockhart made an appeal.

Against a target of £600,000, a total of £810,577 was raised, and that enabled Easton to persuade the directors to add two much-needed Science laboratories to the project. Easton was indefatigable in moving the Appeal forward, and the parent team leaders lived up to expectations (one became chairman of directors).[20] The result justified all the effort and strengthened ties between parents, Former Pupils and the School in general, and with Easton in particular.

Six companies tendered in a very competitive process during April 1991, and the J.H. Gray Ltd tender of £706,000 proved the lowest.[21] The work was begun during that summer and, although at one stage it looked as if it would not be completed in time, the School opened on 26 August 1992 as planned, despite the absence of new laboratories, and work still underway on the glazed passageway, the courtyard and the new entrance hall, which created accommodation and circulation problems. Lord Macfarlane[22] opened the buildings three weeks later, on 18 September 1992.

By May 1994 Easton had formulated his detailed plans for the High School 'to maintain its place in the forefront of Scottish education'. With regard to the Junior School, the excellent 1990 extensions, including the impressive rooms for Junior 6, had highlighted the inadequacies of the older parts of its buildings. The modern primary curriculum required the children to work in groups, move around from activity to activity, and have access to equipment such as computers and listening posts. The rooms in the Junior School were not designed for such purposes, and more space was urgently required. Some areas, such as the Kindergarten, were not only cramped but also old-fashioned and in need of refurbishment. Easton was also aware that several competitors had made dramatic improvements: Glasgow Academy had refurbished and produced new nursery facilities; Craigholme had also built a nursery; and Hutchesons' GS had built a new block for Junior 1–3 (Infants).

The first phase for Easton was a new Kindergarten area positioned on the paved area at the rear of the Junior School. This was particularly important, because the Kindergarten was the main entry point to, and first impression of, the High School. He then planned for a new purpose-built block for Junior 1 and 2, to be built at the rear of the 1973 extension and linked to the new Kindergarten. Finally, he hoped for a re-design of the rooms in the main building, creating extra space for Junior 3, 4 and 5. Easton hoped that progress could be made with the Kindergarten in 1995.

This was the first project involving Iain MacLaren of Wylie Shanks, and it was to set a standard for future school buildings. However, there were initial difficulties to overcome in achieving planning permission for what was proposed. Pre-application discussion with the Planning Department of the Bearsden and Milngavie District Council began in November 1994. Although no objections were raised to the proposals for the Kindergarten,[23] the preference for the new Junior 1 and 2 block to be built on the playground delayed the project for a year.

During that time, Easton produced plans for the conversion of the second floor of the former Rector's flat at Drewsteignton into four Music practice rooms, and part of the first floor into a spacious new Music room, replacing the confined space on the ground floor, which would become the Junior School Office. Plans drawn up by Robin Hagart[24] were agreed by the Board, and the conversion took place at a cost of £70,000. For Anniesland, Easton produced his blueprint for a suite of six Music practice rooms.[25] His original plans for building on the Crow Road car park, however, were rejected by the High School Club, so he adopted the more expensive option of building above the existing Music department.[26] He won over the directors by persuading Sir Robert Maclean to agree that the £50,000 which he was donating should be used for this purpose; a further £30,000 was forthcoming from the Educational Trust, and the residue of the Muirhead Moffat estate produced £25,774. This project was also completed in summer 1995.

Meantime, it was clear that the Bowie Library, which had been created from the former gymnasium, was too small. Easton had plans to create a mezzanine floor and, with typical generosity, Former Pupil Ian Bowie immediately (April 1994) agreed to fund half the cost up to £50,000. Following this work the staff room and reception areas for visitors was refurbished at the Senior School, and the bust of Rector Chrystal was removed from Elmbank Street and placed in the entrance hall.[27]

In February 1996 the Junior School development was approved by the Bearsden District Council, and in the following month the directors accepted the lowest tender from Melville Dundas (Glasgow) of £367,853 excluding VAT and professional fees. The total cost of around half a million was to be financed from the School's own resources. On 9 April the Kindergarten extension work began and was completed by early September, in time for the new session. The way was now open to advance plans for the Junior 1 to 5 classrooms.

Throughout his period of office, Easton had been concerned at the rising annual contribution that the School needed to make toward the upkeep of the playing fields. By 1992–3 the sum reached £66,986 and yet, during the winter months, the hockey pitches were frequently unplayable, and in summer the school had to hire tennis courts from other schools or from local clubs. The School required an artificial surface, which would provide a full-sized hockey pitch during the autumn and spring terms, and twelve tennis courts in summer. A sand-filled grass surface could also be used for rugby training and a variety of other sporting activities. Easton took this request to the Board in June 1992, appreciating that the cost would be around £250,000. He hoped that any surplus funds could be earmarked for this project, as well as funds that would become available when the Old Girls' sold their playing fields at Kirklee.[28] Given the other ongoing building projects this was not possible, but Easton returned to the matter when Glasgow Academy constructed an artificial pitch, and Laurel Bank was heard to be drawing up its own plans.

In September 1996 the High School Club formed a committee under its architect, Neil Maxwell, to co-ordinate plans for an ambitious, extensive and expensive refurbishment of the Pavilion. Ian Docherty, representing the Club, approached Easton to seek his support, which he agreed to give provided an artificial pitch was included in the package of improvements. Docherty agreed, and the directors committed £50,000 per year to the project for six years. The Club adopted a development plan, which included an artificial grass pitch, flood-lighting of the main rugby pitch, changing rooms for females and a refectory in the Pavilion. The Club managed to obtain almost £400,000 in lottery funding, and the pitch was completed by September 1997.

The next few years saw the completion of several exciting projects. The Senior School needed a Drama facility and extra space for the English Department; the Club pressed for a proper multi-gym fitness centre; and the Junior School needed the long-awaited modernisation of its classrooms to be completed. Meanwhile, the old stand looking out onto the First XV pitch was declared unsafe, but the Club did not have the finance to replace it. Plans were drawn up by the School and the Club, with a total cost of £4 million.[29] Fortunately, in January 1998, the School was left the residue of the estate of a Former Pupil, Edith Macmillan, in memory of her grandfather, who had taught at the School for some forty years and been Rector early in the twentieth century.[30] Her trustees decided there should be a building named in her honour. Accordingly, Easton was able to progress with a new Junior School building to house Junior 1 and 2, at a cost of £1.3 million.[31]

The directors agreed to go ahead with all the projects if the School launched an Appeal to help with costs. It was called the 875 Campaign, since its launch in 1999 was 875 years since the School's claimed foundation in 1124. Once again Easton was heavily involved, but the burden was eased on this occasion thanks to the help of Katie Keenan, who was employed on a part-time basis to liaise with FPs and to do some initial development work as campaign administrator. The campaign depended on various teams, as in the past. The parents' team of eighty-six parents was chaired by David Maclay, and assisted by Professor Anton Muscatelli in charge of the Junior School team. An innovation was the young FP team of twenty-seven school leavers from 1997–8, who participated in a successful telephone campaign. The result was that, by December 2000, the Appeal had surpassed its target of £1.2 million by some way.

In October 1999 the Macmillan building opened, and in the following year the new stand was opened by Ian Laughland, then President of the Scottish Rugby Union, and the new Drama Studio by Lord Puttnam, both on time and on budget.

Once the funding of these projects was complete, Easton had three other priorities: a new Science building; refurbishment of the Junior 2, 4 and 5 classrooms; and a second artificial pitch. However, the need to upgrade the School's IT facilities was impressed upon him. Iain MacLaren was instructed to draw up plans for the Science and Junior School developments. It was at this point that Easton was contacted by Dr Alistair Ramsay, a Former Pupil living in America:[32] he and his wife[33] wished to give £500,000 to the School for a building connected with Science. Appreciating that the School could not at that time find the rest of the money to fund the Science building, which was expected to cost in the region of £3 million, Easton asked the directors to match Ramsay's funding and construct a new IT building. This was agreed, and it was completed in October 2003.

The final project in Easton's time was the creation of a proper main entrance at the Senior School, with appropriate reception and waiting areas. It proved possible to add a seminar room thanks to the generosity of another Former Pupil and former governor, George Arthur.[34] Easton's successor, Colin Mair, completed the planned programme with a significant improvement to the Norrie Thomson Science block.[35]

STAFFING

At the Senior School, Easton inherited a core of dedicated staff. With morale high, there was little incentive to move, and many PTs in particular stayed a considerable time in post. In English, Bill Seaman led a strong team well, contributing also, along with his experienced colleague David Williams,[36] to the amateur dramatics within the School. Seaman continued in post until October 1996, when another talented member of his department, Jennifer King, took over.[37] In Mathematics, the popular Brian Walker went home to Aberdeen in 1985 and the new PT, Peter Edmond, soon made his mark with his commitment to School life within and without the classroom. In Careers and Modern Languages, Sylvia Gardner left to become Assistant Head at Morrison's, leaving a gap which Sue Cowling filled in Careers,[38] while Fiona Slavin took over the Language department, completing four years before in 1992 handing over as PT to the very able and meticulous Martin Bennie.[39] In Science, conscientious and hard-working Ron Hockey gave up overseeing the different sciences in 1993 to concentrate on Chemistry. His successor, Elizabeth Murray, stayed until 1999, when Gillian Stobo took over. She was promoted internally, and when she left to become Principal of Craigholme School she was replaced by Kenneth Robertson, who has become director of School shows and is currently Scout HQ Commissioner for Scotland.[40] In Physics, John Sharkey left in 1990 to become Science Adviser to the Western Isles, and Arthur Baillie[41] arrived.[42] The academic David Williams was in charge of Biology, and on his retirement in 2003 Martin Dougal took over.[43] In Classics, Kate Thomson, who had taught in Elmbank Street, was a stalwart member of staff from 1980 to 2003, and the outstanding success of the School's debating and public speaking owed everything to her; Alan Milligan from St Columba's, Kilmacolm took over when she retired. In History, Bill Maynard, a laid-back American, left in 1987, and Kelvin Sinclair replaced him, impressing HMI with his leadership of the department.[44] He was supported by the loyal Robin Broadbent, who in recent times has taken on and developed the Careers Department. In Geography, Iain Currie ran a tight ship from 1976 to 2002, and during a large part of this period he promoted rugby and the House system; his successor was Dr Mark Davies.[45] In Business Studies, Adrienne Girvan gave way to Elsie Bouffler, with Tony Jensen taking over in 1997. Successes in Young Enterprise were followed by the School team's 1998 win in the Global Investment Challenge. In PE, Ian Gibb resigned in late 1992 after two decades' service, and his successor, David Barrett, proved himself a most effective PT. Girls' sport was a success story, but unfortunately Marjorie Macpherson had to give up the headship of girls' PE following back problems; she was replaced by Alison Denholm, a former Bannerman House Captain. In Music, Alastair Massey retired early in 1989, and Peter Douglas opened a new era in High School Music. He oversaw the introduction of first-class full-time tutors and specialists: Mark Duncan (Strings), Raymond McKeown (Wind) and Neil McFarlane (Accompanist). In Art, John Wilmington retired after a heart attack in 1986, and Peter Gilchrist took over the reins, overseeing the creation of a new Art building. In RE, Michael Hurn was replaced in 1989 by Colin Price, who introduced Philosophy. In Home Economics, Heather Burnet retired in 2002 after twenty-six years in charge of the subject, being replaced by Sheila Slatford. Computing was developed by David MacCorkindale. Other important staffing developments saw the introduction of Louise Howie as School Nurse in 1994,[46] and the death of the dedicated Anniesland School janitor, Alex Armstrong.[47]

In the Junior School, Eileen Robertson saw regular depletions of her teaching team. In 1987, Margaret Donald was given a retirement dinner; the same year, Seonaid Vickerman gained promotion to Hutchesons' GS. In 1993, Fiona Macphail became Head of the Junior School at Park. In order not to lose such talent to competitors, in 1993 two Senior Teacher posts were created. Isa McManus retired after twenty-three years in 1995; Ann Robinson retired early after twenty-five years' service in 1997; and Sylvia Clarke also departed that year. In 2001 Aileen Lamont retired after twenty years. In 2004 Margaret Scott, who had delivered excellence in Music for twenty-eight years, retired.

In senior management, in 1985 the directors decided to add another member to the senior school team, and Colin Mair was appointed as an additional Assistant Head. Audrey Whitefield retired in late 1993, and from the fifty-four applicants Lesley Douglas[48] joined the School. Brian Lockhart left to become Head at Robert Gordon's College in Aberdeen in 1996. From the forty-six applicants, Colin Mair was chosen as Deputy, while Magnus Brown (from Hutchesons') took Colin's former post. When Robin Easton retired, Colin Mair was chosen as his successor, and John O'Neill of Merchiston was made Deputy, with Maggie Price arriving from Glasgow Academy to join the team.

At the Junior School, Elizabeth Burnett retired after twenty-one years in 1992, to be replaced by Davida Grant as Deputy. When she left to become Head of the Junior School at St Columba's, Jeanette Smart became Deputy. Following a very successful Kindergarten report, she in turn left to become Head of the Junior School at Craigholme and Alison Brown was appointed in her place. In 2001 on the retiral of Eileen Robertson, Karen Waugh, Head of Mearns Primary, became Head of the Junior School, bringing with her invaluable experience of the state sector.

RE-LIGHTING THE BEACON

Easton was much concerned about the ethos of the School and its particular emphasis on high expectations. He and his management team took pride in what they were determined to create: a happy and lively place, with a satisfactory balance between formality and informality, academic excellence and extra-curricular activity. There was mutual respect between staff and students, and an acceptance that happy pupils working hard were the recipe for getting the best from the academic offer and extra-curricular activities. Disciplinary problems were few and far between and remarkably, when any criticism was voiced, it tended to be about the need to tighten up procedures. However, when this happened it was usually countered by colleagues who had taught elsewhere putting 'indiscipline' into context. The School came to pride itself on giving a fair hearing to pupils, and on being proportionate and reasonable in its punishments.

Assemblies of the whole Senior School at the start of each day were significant in establishing community spirit and in fostering shared values. For Easton, as a Christian, assemblies meant that the community entered into God's presence and committed its life and work for that day to Him.[49]

Easton had one of his biggest challenges in his first year when the whole school community was stunned by the sudden death of a Sixth Year pupil. The deaths of some ten young Former Pupils during his twenty-year tenure, and that of Lloyd King,[50] showed the strength of the bonds uniting the High School.

Why was there such remarkable academic progress? Easton would be the first to admit that the progress of the School would not have been so smooth, especially in the 1980s, had other schools not gone through various difficulties. However, it was the 'secret' of the High School that all parts of its community had to play their part if the new School was to become very special. The pupils always gave of their best; the parents supported the school financially and in all other regards; the staff went the extra mile; the senior management teams gave 'thoughtful and energetic support',[51] and the various chairmen and their directors allowed significant freedom but gave sound and cautious advice when necessary.[52] The bonds between School and Club were also strengthened. Eric Harle handed over a School in good heart and going in the right direction. Eileen Robertson's great achievement was to build a flourishing modern primary. She attracted and retained dedicated and highly professional staff, provided a rich and varied curriculum, and improved buildings and resources. Most important of all, she created a unique ethos and environment in which the children in her charge enjoyed learning, developed their skills and talents to the full and grew in thoughtfulness and concern for others.

One could cite excellent teaching, motivated pupils and supportive parents, but these are common to many schools. Undoubtedly the increasing popularity of the School and the healthy competition for places brought in talented children, although Easton believed that the School's commitment to siblings and FP families,[53] and the fact that half the school population joined at Kindergarten, meant that the result was a mixed community academically. How special then was the ethos and its particular emphasis on aiming high? Certainly, the commitment to constant improvement at departmental and classroom levels led to the strategy of encouraging all students to study five Highers. In this way, most pupils were challenged to do their best and, on occasions when it did not result in success, the situation was usually retrieved in Sixth Year, thanks to the experience of having followed the course before, and to increased maturity.

Easton inherited a system of S1 selection by entrance tests, the raw scores of which were added together, with VRQ (intelligence) tests to measure potential. It was a process Harle, as a mathematician, was comfortable with. It seemed to work. He did ask Heads of primary schools to supply references for their children, but a number did not do so. Early on, Easton decided to interview all those doing well enough in the testing to warrant further consideration. It was also an opportunity for children and their parents to see more of the School and be persuaded of its merits. Prospective entrants had not just to do well in the entrance tests, but also to impress the senior member of staff interviewing them; the child's parents also had to prove to Easton that they were 'on side'. The comment that selective schools usually meet, that they cream off the best pupils and the most supportive parents, was true in the case of the High School. Indeed, it was the vital ingredient in explaining the School's success.

The interviews ensured that the School learned much about the strengths and skills of children both in and out of the classroom. Breadth of interest and participation in diverse activities were attributes welcomed in the School and go some way to explaining why progress in one area of School life was often accompanied by progress in another. Once a break-through came in one activity, then self-belief led to more success. In rugby, athletics, hockey, tennis, swimming, skiing and badminton, success came to be expected at local, then district, then national level. Music was another area in which, after disappointments in the early years, there was a marked increase in the standards of performance and in participation, accompanied by considerable expansion. Professional musicians who attended perform-ances compared pupils' standards very favourably with those at specialist music schools. Both Music and Sport became reasons for parents and pupils opting to attend the School.

Easton's acceptance into HMC in 1985 was recognition in the eyes of the independent school world that the School had come of age and was a kite-mark which gave the High School a wider recognition and a new standing. His OBE in 1994 and his doctorate from the University of Glasgow in 2001 were also recognition of the School's status and achievements. No other individual school representative was recognised by Glasgow University when celebrating its 550th anniversary, the only other person from primary or secondary education being the Director of Education.[54] As Rector, he 'led by example: his commitment to the School, his clear perception of the direction in which it should move, his tireless industry[55] and his accessibility set benchmarks for all staff'.[56] In a real sense, the buildings of the High School owe everything to Robin Easton, who in twenty-one years more than doubled the physical size of the School. Yet by far and away his greatest achievement was to re-light the beacon of the old High School. In doing so, he moved the new School significantly in the direction of becoming the 'Town School' again, so fulfilling the vision of Norrie Thomson and Norrie Macfarlane.

CLUB

The High School Club continued to foster relationships between Former Pupils and the School, and in particular managed the grounds at Old Anniesland. When the Rugby Club went open and thereafter merged with Kelvinside, the cricket and hockey sections did likewise, and the result was a considerable increase in the membership of the sports sections. It was important to offer activities for females, and Suzanne Williamson (née Morris) was instrumental in setting up a Ladies' Hockey Club. Lacrosse, Golf (ladies and gents), Hockey (gents) and Triathlon have also been introduced.

With financial support from the Lottery and the Sports Ground Initiative, an artificial pitch was created, flood-lights were installed, the Pavilion was refurbished and the Jimmy Ireland Grandstand was partially funded. Such improved facilities and the increased sporting options have increased associate membership (i.e., members of the sports section who are not Former Pupils). However, School leavers have automatic Club membership for the first five years after leaving School, and are encouraged to continue their membership after this period.

The Club has had a series of first-class office bearers in recent times, and particular mention should be made of Club Presidents William Gardiner (1990–1),[57] Glen Docherty (2005–6) and Gordon Grant (2006–7), as well as Norman Alexander (Secretary since 1988)[58] and Treasurer Eric Hugh.[59] The commitment of such Former Pupils has driven forward the modernisation of the Pavilion and playing fields.

The London Club continues, and between 2003 and 2005 elected its first woman President, Fiona Sanson.[60] (In 2007–9 Jennifer Cameron[61] held the post). Overseas clubs still exist in South Africa and Hong Kong.

REUNIONS OF PUPILS

Many year groups have met regularly in recent years, including the thirteen members of the 1951–2 Sixth Year – the 652 Club (Sixth Year in 1952, and 6

+ 5 + 2 = 13)^{62} – and twenty-two (from twenty-six) members of Class VS1 of 1957–8, who met up for a sixth time in 2008. Also in that year, Lewis Pate arranged for seven members of his VS1 class to meet for lunch sixty-six years after leaving school. Similarly, Margaret Lindsay (née Fingland) and Prof. Shand Anderson arranged 60th reunions for their 1948 and 1949 groups respectively. There have been several 50-year, 40-year and 30-year celebrations, and more recent leavers have started to hold events too, usually with 10-year reunions. It is clear that many FPs enjoy visiting Anniesland and seeing the changes which have taken place since their time at School.

PUPILS[63]

Military

Irvine Lindsay (left 1983) became the naval submarine commander of HMS *Vanguard*, Faslane.

Duncan Tough (SC 1996) became a decorated RAF pilot.

Medicine

(Dr) Gillian MacDougall, first Girls' SC in 1981–2 (when there was only one Captain), has become a doctor in Edinburgh.

Dr Ricky Sharma (SC 1989) studied medicine at Downing, Cambridge and is now a scientist and physicist, and an honorary Consultant in Clinical Oncology, University of Oxford.

Legal

Eoghainn MacLean (left 1984) and Roddy Dunlop (left 1988) became advocates.

Fiona (left 1991) and Rosalind Drysdale (left 1994) are sisters, both appointed School Captains and both studied Law: Fiona at Edinburgh and Rosalind at Jesus, Cambridge.

Fiona Murdoch (SC 1995) studied at Oxford, after which she trained as a solicitor in an international law firm; she is now a professional support lawyer in corporate business.

Christopher Stothers (left 1995) gained distinguished Law qualifications from Cambridge in 1998 and Oxford in 2000. He worked in an international law firm before becoming an Associate in an Intellectual Property Group in London. He also teaches Law at Cambridge and University College London. He published a textbook in 2007.

Ewan Smith (SC 1998) studied at the universities of Oxford, Paris and Harvard Law. He worked for Debevoise and Plimpton LLP (2003–5), before joining the Foreign and Commonwealth Office as part of the Arabian Peninsula group.

Academic

(Dr) Graeme Paton (left 1987) became a soil toxicologist and has published over forty-five papers relating to environmental pollution. He is Professor of Soil Science at Aberdeen University.

(Dr) John Maclennan (left 1993) was School Captain. He studied at Emmanuel College, and became a lecturer in Earth Sciences at Cambridge University.

Financial

Heather Harpur (née Winning) (left 1984) completed a degree in Mathematics at St Andrews University before becoming the youngest female branch manager at Lloyds in 1993.

Alastair Borthwick (left 1985) became an international banker. He had a leadership role in Goldman Sachs for twelve years before joining the Bank of America (2005). He has recently been appointed co-head of their global capital markets.

Kirsty Brown (left 1990) studied accountancy and became Bursar at Trinity GS, Melbourne.

Victoria Frame (SC 1990) took a degree in PPE at Oxford, where she was Secretary of the Union. She made a career in corporate finance, and after attending Harvard Business School worked in New York in retail strategy consulting.

Neil Dryden (SC 1991) achieved an FCH in PPE at Oxford. He became a Senior Manager for Arthur Andersen's Economic and Financial Consulting Team in London before becoming an Assistant Director for Deloitte and Touche. He then became Associate Director in NERA's European Policy Practice.

Administration (Politicians)

Kirsty McNeill (left 1997) gained a degree in PPE at Balliol, Oxford; and Stuart Hudson (SC 2000) gained a degree in History/Politics at Jesus, Oxford. Both were special advisers to prime minister Gordon Brown in the Research and Information Unit of No. 10 Downing Street.

Ruth Curtice (SC 2002) entered into the fast track of the Civil Service.

Culture

David McGuinness (left 1983) graduated from York and Glasgow Universities. He has played as a soloist with all Scottish orchestras (harmonium and melodic) and teaches harpsichord.

Louise Vickerman (left 1989) became principal harpist to Utah Symphony and Opera, and in 2005–6 was Interim Director of Harp Studies at Brigham Young University.

Iain Paterson (left 1991) studied at the RSAMD and confirmed his status as one of Europe's leading young bass-baritones as Fasolt in *Das Rheingold* at the 2007 Salzburg Easter Festival under Sir Simon Rattle.

Marianne Rawles (left 1997) studied at the RNCM, where she won the Sydney Fell Clarinet Prize. She has performed with prominent orchestras, and has broadcast live with her wind quintet, the Langdale Ensemble.

(Dr) Diana Simpson (left 2000) became lecturer in Music Technology, Kingston University. She is an acousmatic composer of international renown.

Nadine Livingstone (left 2002) became a Scottish Opera singer.

Writers

Lesley Riddoch (left 1978) attended Drewsteignton and the High School from 1973 to 1978. She was the first woman sabbatical President of Oxford University Students' Union in 1980 She became a reporter, BBC Radio Scotland, 1985–8; presenter of programmes from 1988, including the *Lesley Riddoch Programme*, 1999–2005; assistant then associate editor of the *Scotsman*, 1994–7.[64]

David Dinsmore (left 1981) became editor of the *Scottish Sun*.

Denise Mina (left 1982) studied at Glasgow and Strathclyde Universities. Her first book, *Garnethill* (1998), won an award for best first crime novel and formed the start of a trilogy. In recent times she has proved a prolific producer of further novels, short stories, comics and plays.

Carlos Alba (left 1983) became a journalist and wrote *Kane's Ladder* (2008).

Libby Brooks (left 1992) became Women's Editor of the *Guardian* (1998) and Young Journalist of the Year at the British Press Awards in the same year.

Sport

In recent years the School has produced many internationalists. The most capped were Greig Williamson (left 1986), who played in 153 cricket matches for Scotland, and Alison Cox (née Denholm) (left 1987), who gained seventy-five outdoor and twenty-one indoor hockey caps for Scotland. She became Head of Girls' PE at the School in 2004.

Alison Sheppard[65] (left 1989) competed in five Olympic meetings, the first of which was at Seoul in 1988, when she was only fifteen and still at the School. She won sixteen medals in Commonwealth, European and World swimming competitions. She was the first Scotswoman since 1954 to win a Commonwealth Gold in swimming.

Kristina Semple (left 1989) was a Triathlon athlete who gained an International Age Group World Championship (female 30–34) in 2003.

Kathryn Gray (left 1994) was in the 2002 Commonwealth Games Ladies' Hockey squad. She has won seventy-three Scottish caps and played four times for Great Britain.

(Dr) Abigail Walker (left 1999) has gained eleven Great Britain hockey caps and thirty-one Scottish caps.

Ailsa Young (left 1999) has gained thirty Scottish hockey caps, and she played in the World Cup in 2002.

TWELVE   The End of the New Beginning

COLIN MAIR, RECTOR FROM 2004

The decision of the School directors to appoint Colin Mair as Rector with effect from August 2004 was a strong vote of confidence in the record of the new independent School. However, it was far more than recognition of past achievements and a green light for 'more of the same'. No one else in the School had Mair's credentials: originally a teacher of Latin (1976–9), he became Head of Rugby (1977–88), Head of Latin (1979–85), Housemaster of Bannerman (1982–5), Assistant Rector (1985–96), and Deputy Rector (1996–2004). He was promoted through the ranks in his thirty-year career in the same school. This was very unusual in Scotland, but it meant that he knew, and had contributed to, every aspect of the life of the School.

Mair was acutely aware that the School's remarkable success reflected certain key strengths: consistently outstanding examination results; high levels of attainment in cultural and extra-curricular activities; a purposeful atmosphere allied to a positive, caring ethos; excellent relationships between all sectors of the School community; and the provision of modern, purpose-built facilities and accommodation. He also had a keen understanding of the factors underpinning past success: attracting and maintaining staff, pupils, parents and directors who were all enthusiastic about and dedicated to the quality of education on offer.

In going forward, the new Rector also appreciated how essential it was to maintain and enhance the School's ambition for excellence. Resting on laurels was not an option given that, after some troublesome times, traditional rivals in educational provision were making progress, defining their own particular styles, presenting these to the public, and even adopting some of the successful High School initiatives. The development of Mair's vision for the future and his priorities for its achievement were influenced by a whole-School inspection in October 2005, the results of which were published on 14 March 2006.

At the time of the inspection the School was full, with the roll standing at 1,056.[1] The particular strengths identified by the Inspectors included the strong sense of identity and pride in the school amongst pupils, staff, parents and directors; the high standard of attainment especially in national examinations; an impressive choice of extra-curricular activities; the care and concern of staff for pupils' well-being; aspects of accommodation; and the positive and productive partnerships with parents and the wider School community.

In the curriculum, pupils from Junior 4 onwards learned French with a specialist teacher. Latin was introduced as a second language for all in First Year, and German was added for all in Second Year. In Senior 3/4 most pupils studied a wide range of courses at Standard Grade, while in S5/6 further courses in Human Biology, Business Management, Classical Studies and Philosophy were offered. Most pupils extended their interests through membership of the School's many clubs and societies. A diverse range of extra-curricular activities enabled pupils to extend their achievements in sport, music and drama, many were involved in the Duke of Edinburgh Award Scheme, and a notable number raised money for charities and other good causes.

The inspection confirmed that the leadership of Mair and his senior colleagues was a major strength. The Rector himself was 'approachable and supportive' and 'had won the strong support of pupils and parents', while the Head of the Junior School, Karen Waugh, was 'highly respected by staff, pupils and parents' and 'provided strong and purposeful leadership'.[2] The Deputies had made a notable impact in their respective areas of responsibility and were all praised: John O'Neill, Magnus Brown[3] and Maggie Price,[4] and Alison Brown (Deputy in junior school). The discussions during an inspection are often more enlightening than the final written report, and this appears to have been the case in this instance. It was no coincidence that a number of changes soon followed. Enhancement of the role of House staff strengthened the already strong pastoral system, but just as important was its release of senior management to enable a focus on strategic matters. There was a move to eight subjects at S3/4 level, and Spanish was introduced as a third Modern Language option for S3 pupils.

Early attention was given to two other areas. First, Mair readily understood the potential benefits of ICT for learning and teaching. He was supported in this by his new Deputy from Merchiston Castle School, John

O'Neill, who brought his expertise to the subject and had a hand in the appointment of the School's first ICT manager in August 2007.[5] In this way, the key vision of improved communication, through the development of regular links between home and School by means of email, came closer. Second, during his first year as Rector, Mair had sought, and acted upon, the 'wish-lists' of staff. These confirmed the widespread desire for a Science extension, a second artificial games pitch and more space for Junior 4 and 5.

With his 'honeymoon' period over and the inspection behind him, Mair began to refine his vision for the School's future. He was aided in this by a number of factors, especially his own background. His father, Colin J.R. Mair, had just been appointed Rector of Kelvinside Academy in 1958 when Colin junior, aged five, began his own schooling there. He was at Kelvinside for all of his schooldays, and the only Rector he knew was his own father. Yet there seemed to be no major problems for either of them: Colin Mair junior was successful academically, Captain of rugby and cricket[6] and, as a first-class all-rounder, became School Captain in his final year. He knew at first hand what the role of a Rector involved and, through personal experience, understood the great benefits to be gained by developing the individual pupil's confidence. Fortunately, he also inherited his father's 'knack' of spotting individuals with talent and challenging them to aspire to higher levels of attainment.

Mair was attracted to the teaching profession as a result of a desire to give pupils opportunities to achieve their potential. Early in his career, he found success in coaching rugby and in helping to redesign an almost moribund House system under the astute leadership of Audrey Whitefield. Few day schools were able to achieve what the High School accomplished in balancing the aspects of pastoral care integral to the emerging state sector Guidance system with enhancement of, and extension from, traditional inter-House competitions.

Taking over the role of the School's SQA Co-ordinator in the mid-1990s, Mair became acutely aware of the increasing number of pupils who required special examination provisions. This led him to question the rationale of Learning Support (LS) that was widespread in the independent sector, which tended to give extra help to pupils at Primary level in order to deal with short-term difficulties. He appreciated the need to take Learning Support to a new level: May Adams had done an excellent job in its early development, and the appointment of Ruth Hamilton as PT of LS from August 2006 soon became a major success story.

Having previously been in charge of the Sixth Form, Mair wished to develop further the opportunities for responsibility and community service. Significant advances were made in these areas that were progressed by John O'Neill, ably assisted by the four senior House staff and Fiona Slavin in her new post of Sixth Year Assistant.

These different strands came together to form a coherent School strategy and stimulated his staff to new initiatives and challenges. The appointment of Melissa Sabba as full-time teacher of Drama, following the previous work of Jenny Ogston, was important in this regard. Mair then went on to encourage staff in more traditional areas, and new levels of achievement and commitment were seen in Music, Art, Sport and Debating, which all continued to thrive under Peter Douglas, Peter Gilchrist, David Barrett and Paul Toner.

In his first five years in post, Colin Mair repaid the faith shown in him by the directors. He had kept the beacon burning brightly.

'TO THOSE WHO FOLLOW AFTER, TO FILL THE PLACE WE FILL . . .'

In pursuit of the High School cause, in December 1972 Leonard Turpie produced a memorandum defending the system of Corporation selective schools. For him they were the way that traditionally Scottish burghs had enabled ambitious lads o' pairts to go to university from the poorest homes, unhindered, because low fees were charged. He thought it illogical that such schools were to be abolished while selection still seemed to be an integral part of any comprehensive school in the guise of streaming, setting, banding or grouping. He questioned why it was acceptable to make special provision for those of lower ability but not for the more able. In 1971–2 some 6 per cent of pupils in Glasgow were being educated in Corporation selective schools (and some 4 per cent more in non-Corporation selective schools). Turpie held that if all of the former were equally divided among the other Corporation schools, it would mean ten more pupils in each School. He suggested that the 'creaming-off' effect of the more academically talented had been exaggerated. He feared that entry by way of place of residence would soon replace selection by merit, while many others would flee toward the then grant-aided and independent fee-paying sector.

Turpie's arguments went unheeded by Glasgow Corporation. By 1982 all selection in the public sector had been ended, and the small amount of single-sex secondary schooling had almost disappeared.[7] Moreover, there was a move away from the grouping of pupils by ability, a practice that had been common in most schools until 1965. Mixed-ability classes came to be regarded as an integral part of a truly comprehensive school, in contrast to traditional internal differentiation.[8]

There were disadvantages inherent in ending selection. Thus, for instance, teachers needed support in dealing with a much broader range of abilities in the classes, and running parallel to that was the growing problem of indiscipline. Moreover, the policy was undermined by 'residential segregation', as parents who could afford to do so purchased homes within the catchment areas of 'good' schools. The situation was complicated further by successive Conservative governments giving parents the legal right to choose the schools their children would attend; although, by the 1990s, only one in eight did so.

Turpie was also correct in prophesising a continuation, indeed strengthening, of the private sector. Some two dozen secondary endowed schools survived outwith Education Authority management, although they received aid from them and the (then) Scottish Education Department. After 1965, one in eight of all Scottish secondary schools remained outside the public sector. They were made up of fully independent and grant-aided schools, all but two of which chose to become independent. The Labour governments of 1974–9 determined to end these grants, which amounted to 54 per cent of their income in 1964.[9] By 1979, the grant had declined to under 10 per cent of their income and, as a consequence, some schools were forced to close or amalgamate with neighbours. The Conservative administration in 1979 slightly increased the grant, but later replaced it with the Assisted Places Scheme, which introduced bursaries to encourage entry to the schools by children whose parents could not afford the fees; the annual total received from this source was much the same as the grant aid had been in the early 1980s. However, that scheme was withdrawn in 1997 when the government changed again. Most recently (2009–10) the charitable status of these schools was under review.

Despite these financial cut-backs the proportion of secondary pupils in the private sector changed little in the first decade of the twenty-first century, remaining at around one in twenty nationally. However, the character of individual schools continued to evolve. In most instances pupils were drawn from a wider range of social classes than formerly. When the new High School joined the independent sector there were few bursaries available, and this meant that a considerable proportion of the pupils came from homes with parents in the upper income groups. This increased the disaffection, even alienation, of a number of staff and Former Pupils who were uncomfortable with the new venture. Recognising the difficulty, many of the new School's supporters were anxious that those who wanted to attend but could not afford the fees would in some way be aided. The directors determined that, as far as possible, the emerging School would offer an education not only to those whose parents were in the upper income groups, but also to those from less well-off households who could benefit from what could be put on offer. With that in mind, in 1976, the directors created the High School of Glasgow Educational Trust to monitor investments and provide bursaries. In 1977–8 some eight pupils received £3,430. By 2009–10 this had risen to thirty-five pupils receiving £230,000, and the directors remained committed to increasing the Bursary Fund still further in the future. This is a 'work in progress'.[10]

•   •   •

THE TOWN SCHOOL

Thanks to its venerable origins, the High School has a unique position in the history of the City of Glasgow. Alone of its public schools, it offered 'higher class' education at the time of the Education Act in 1872. As the custodian of 'secondary' education, the High School sustained its role until a new structure of schools had evolved around it, the School Board having other priorities. These other selective schools – Hillhead High School, The High School for Girls, Allan Glen's School and Notre Dame – helped create a new tradition. This was based on their considerable achievements, moderated by the evolving policy of the Education Authority. Over the next 100 years, the educational system in Glasgow developed within a policy context based on neighbourhood education. Several milestones were passed, including the centralisation of advanced instruction in special subjects in territorial schools; the extension of a network of higher grade schools across the territories of the Boards that made up the Authority area; the abolition of fees in them; and, finally, their absorption into the comprehensive system. At all of these points, this small group of five selective schools was excluded, and left to forge their own distinctive characteristics. This historical separation, and their growing preoccupation with academic achievement, was the character which many sought to change in the 1970s.

However, the pursuit of excellence in these five selective schools was no different from the original purposes of the territorial selective schools in

Glasgow such as Whitehill or Hyndland. These schools also pursued 'secondary education' to the point at which tertiary education or the professions took over. In earlier times, the relatively low demand determined the need to select from a very wide area. As demand grew, competition for places intensified, and only the ablest pupils in the city were successful candidates. Over time, the breadth of their educational aims narrowed and the attainment of academic excellence was made easier by their pupils' abilities. It was also assumed that the schools attracted the kind of staff most likely to achieve their aims.

In judging the five selective schools during the debates of the 1970s, officials of the Scottish Education Department chose to overlook their history, downplay their unique character, disparage their good examination results as no more than should be expected, and marginalise their voice in educational debate. In short, they failed to recognise the contribution of the five schools to regional and national education. The traditional advantages of selective schools in buildings and staffing, both in quality and number, were now to be reassessed, with priority given to pupils in three-year junior secondaries. No longer would the High School be allowed to enjoy the 'special opportunities and conditions for teachers to make the most of their pupils'.[11] In the same vein, many in Glasgow Corporation were convinced that equality of opportunity implied the imposition of uniformity of structures. After eight centuries it seemed that the Town no longer had use for its 'Town School'.

Ultimately the traditional role of selective schools was rejected because their values were no longer deemed appropriate for the late twentieth century: they were criticised for being authoritarian and overly disciplined, for being obsessed with the most able pupils and neglecting the majority, for defining merit in terms of academic performance, for cultivating an ethic of individual achievement through hard work, and for the centrality of external examinations and access to tertiary education. Yet Scottish society viewed secondary schools as a mechanism for promoting the able to higher education and the professions. Even after comprehensive schools were introduced, there remained a lingering acceptance of the innate values of the old system. This is not surprising, because most of those who made the key decisions were the successful products of the previous system, and many may well have been 'ideological prisoners of their own educational background'.[12]

It was an abiding irony that, in the medium term, the comprehensive system brought only cosmetic change. The emphasis in schools throughout Scotland remained on the academically able, with the continuing dominance of external exams and access to higher and further education and the professions. In practice, many comprehensives reflected the characteristics of the schools they replaced. Once single secondary units had been established, there was no overall requirement to introduce the essential elements advocated by proponents of the reformed system, including mixed-ability teaching, a common course of subjects and new forms of assessment. There was opposition to these within the SED and little enthusiasm from teachers. It seems unfortunate, to say the least, that such a high price was paid for the introduction of comprehensive schools in Glasgow. Had 'The Town School' been retained as a centre of excellence, it could have been the role model, and hence a catalyst, for what could be achieved within a local authority-dominated system. That opportunity was lost.

At the final Commemoration Service in April 1976 of the old High School in Glasgow Cathedral, where it all began, the Rev. William J. Morris, the School Chaplain, took as his text Matthew 3:16: 'Do not fear those who kill the body but cannot kill the soul.' It seemed to him then that 'we are surely seeing not just the end of an institution but the end of a symbol of a way of life, perhaps even the symbol of a civilisation'. The closing of the old High School he saw as accepting mediocrity instead of acclaiming those who achieved standards beyond the common reach, for the High School 'represented a society which sought leadership in excellence, sought people of outstanding personality and ability to be its leaders, and sought to create through education a supply of excellence to give leadership in the future'. Yet Morris was far from despondent, believing that the traditions and spirit of the School would rise again.

In 1976, too, Harry Ashmall wrote his book on the School, in which he spelled out the values it stood for:[13] academic excellence and an emphasis on social service, on loyalty to the Crown, on patriotism, on international understanding, on sportsmanship and fair play, on firm discipline, on breadth of extra-curricular activities, on leadership opportunities, on competitive rivalry and on pride in the School.[14] In tune with this catalogue, many of those who had the benefit of an education at the High School believed that they had experienced something distinctive and something worth preserving.

The new High School was created to carry on these traditions. It took a little time to prove itself. However, today, even the most sceptical of former pupils recognise the new School's outstanding reputation. The suspicions about the merger with the 'Anglified Prep School', which were rife in the late 1970s and early 1980s, have vanished.[15] Likewise, the academic deficit at the top end of the ability range[16] has gone and the School has reached the top rung of achievement. The introduction of girls has also been a remarkable success story.[17] If there is work still to do, then it is in developing equal opportunities further for children from lower-income families and for ethnic minorities.[18]

Can the vision of Norrie Thomson, for the new School to be again the Town School of Glasgow, ever be fulfilled? Will this ever be on the political agenda? Without minimising the hurdles to be overcome,[19] there are signs of policy consensus in terms of governance and values. There are also individuals from very different political positions who are sympathetic to increased collaboration between the private and maintained sectors of schooling. They see merit in viewing schooling as more a part of society and less a part of the state. Critical to all this has to be a thorough examination of the role of selection in the educational process. There is a difficult balance to be struck between the alienation of parents able and willing to pay for the best of education for their children and the exclusion of children of ability who are unable to fulfil their potential because their parents are unable to afford the best available education. Equally clearly, an integrated system of schooling cannot be achieved by denying a very important part of our educational heritage: fee-paying schools cannot be wished out of existence, and legislation to do so has been tried and has failed.[20]

On 9 October 2009 the *Times Educational Supplement* reported that 'in a move which would have been unthinkable a few years ago, Glasgow City Council is pushing for a closer partnership with independent schools'. The, at that time, Labour Council leader Steven Purcell was encouraging heads of such schools to become part of what he called 'Team Glasgow'. Just over two months later, on 16 December 2009, the *Scotsman* reported that two Glasgow schools led the academic league tables in Scotland: the High School of Glasgow from the independent sector, and Jordanhill School, the only state-funded school in the country free of local authority control.

From these beginnings, if Scotland's new education minister, Mike Russell, has the courage and wisdom to take forward some of the ideas he put forward in 2006,[21] it does not seem beyond the bounds of possibility that the next historian of the High School some years on will write about the remarkable, even dramatic, changes in the character of schools and the revival of a special relationship of the School with the City of Glasgow.[22] If so, this would be a fitting next stage in the history of a distinguished School whose educational credentials – based on the dedication of its staff, the talents of its pupils and the achievements of its Former Pupils – are respected nation-wide.

NOTES

ACKNOWLEDGEMENTS

1 Harry A. Ashmall, *The High School of Glasgow* (Edinburgh 1976) p. 161.
2 I also decided to include The Glasgow High School for Girls.
3 Provided their schooling at the High School was confirmed. For example in the case of the 100 Glasgow Men (of 1886), articles on 26 of them did so, although probably many more attended the High School but the author did not mention, or know about, their schooling details.

CHAPTER ONE

1 The first documentary mention was in December 1458, when six scholars of the GS witnessed a foundation by the Cathedral Chancellor. John Durkan and James Kirk: *The University of Glasgow, 1451–1577* (Glasgow 1977) p. 25.
2 Ashmall, *High School* pp. 1 and 5.
3 James Grant: *The History of the Burgh Schools of Scotland* (London 1876) p. 2; John Edgar: *History of Early Scottish Education* (Edinburgh 1893) pp. 8–9; John Strong: *A History of Secondary Education in Scotland: An Account of Scottish Secondary Education from Early Times to the Education Act of 1908*, (Oxford 1909) pp. 1–9; John Kerr: *Scottish Education: Schools and University from Early Times to 1908* (Cambridge 1910) ch. 1; Alexander Morgan: *Rise and Progress of Scottish Education* (Edinburgh 1927) pp. 2–8; James Scotland: *The History of Scottish Education, Vol. 1: From the Beginning to 1872* (London 1969) pp. 3–5.
4 The historical existence of St Ninian has been thrown into doubt by Thomas O. Clancy in 'The Real St Ninian', *Innes Review* vol. 52 (2001) pp. 1–28. See also James E. Fraser: *From Caledonia to Pictland: Scotland to 795* (Edinburgh 2009) p.71.
5 P. Hill: 'Whithorn' in M. Lynch (ed.) *The Oxford Companion to Scottish History* (Oxford 2007) pp. 643–4.
6 Mosa Anderson: *St. Ninian: Light of the Celtic North* (London 1964) p. 76.
7 St Kentigern had been educated and trained as a priest of the monastery of St Serf in Culross, Fife. The name 'Kentigern' means 'Chief Lord' but St Serf called him 'Mungo' meaning 'dearest friend'. 'The Life of S. Kentigern by Jocelinus, a monk of Furness' in Alexander Penrose Forbes (ed.): *The Historians of Scotland: Lives of S. Ninian and S. Kentigern* vol. 5 (Edinburgh 1874) pp. 27–119. This

biography was commissioned after 1180 by Bishop Jocelin. Few details can be taken as accurate. Alan O. Anderson: *Early Sources of Scottish History A.D. 500 to 1286* (Edinburgh 1922) vol. 1 pp. 130–1; Geoff Holder: *The Guide to Mysterious Glasgow* (Stroud 2009) pp. 1–15.

8 The term 'cathedral' is from the Latin 'cathedra', meaning seat or throne. A cathedral is, therefore, the location of the bishop's seat and the principal church of a diocese or district.

9 Edgar: *History of Early Scottish Education*, pp. 19–21.

10 Morgan, *Rise and Progress*, p. 10.

11 Richard Fawcett: *Scottish Cathedrals* (London 1997) p. 16. England had two archbishops: Canterbury and York.

12 He ruled Scotland from 1124 to 1153.

13 Henry had married Edith, David's elder sister in November 1100. She took the name of Matilda of Scotland after her marriage. Richard Oram: *David I: The King Who Made Scotland* (Stroud 2004) pp. 49–50.

14 He was to remain bishop until his death in 1147. John Dowden: *The Bishops of Scotland, Being Notes on the Lives of all the Bishops, Under Each of the Sees, Prior to the Reformation*, ed. J. Maitland Thomson (Glasgow 1912).

15 In this period Cumbria was the Scottish name, Strathclyde the English name, for this kingdom.

16 Norman F. Shead: 'Glasgow: An Ecclesiastical Burgh' in Michael Lynch, Michael Spearman and Geoffrey Stell: *The Scottish Medieval Town* (Edinburgh 1988) pp. 116–32.

17 He was ultimately unsuccessful in this.

18 Fawcett, *Scottish Cathedrals*, p. 20. This strongly suggests that 1124 was not the date of the foundation of a school, as no elaborate services would have been possible before the 1136 consecration. However, for a recent endorsement of 1124 see Rab Houston: *Scotland: A Very Short Introduction* (Oxford 2008) p. 61.

19 Nicholas Orme: *Medieval Schools: From Roman Britain to Renaissance England* (New Haven 2006) pp. 47–8.

20 Nine cathedrals in medieval England (including York and Salisbury) were secular, and ten (including Canterbury and Durham) were monastic. There was tension between these two models of religious life: a tension between engagement and exclusion; practicality and idealism. Jon Cannon: *Cathedral: The Great English Cathedrals and the World That Made Them 600–1540* (London 2007) pp. 20–2.

21 No Scottish municipal records exist for this early period. They begin at the end of the fourteenth and beginning of the fifteenth century.

22 D.E. Easson: 'The Medieval Church in Scotland and Education' in *Records of the Scottish Church History Society* no. 6 (1938) p. 14, following the shorter list in Grant, *History of the Burgh Schools*, pp. 3–5.

23 Overlooking Salisbury there stood the cathedral of Old Sarum. Its bishop, Osmund, simultaneously founded a song school and a grammar school before his death in 1099. The former taught the 'three Rs', while the latter taught Latin. In 1220 the foundations of a new cathedral were laid in Salisbury.

24 G.W.S. Barrow: 'David I and Glasgow' in G.W.S. Barrow (ed.), *The Kingdom of the Scots* (2nd edn, Edinburgh 2003) pp. 211–12.

25 Norman F. Shead: 'Greater Glasgow' in Neil Baxter (ed.): *A Tale of Two Towns: A History of Medieval Glasgow* (Glasgow 2008) p. 24.

26 These officials were common to almost all Scottish secular cathedrals. Ian B. Cowan: *The Medieval Church in Scotland* ed. James Kirk (Edinburgh 1995) pp. 78–79.

27 Norman F. Shead: 'Medieval Glasgow: Problems of Evidence', *Innes Review* vol. 55 no. 1 (Spring 2004) pp. 36–7. Ian B. Cowan: 'The Organisation of Secular Cathedral Chapters' in *The Medieval Church in Scotland* ed. James Kirk (Edinburgh 1995) p. 84.

28 *Fasti Ecclesie Scoticanae Medii Aevi ad Annum 1638* ed. D.E.R. Watt and A.L. Murray (Edinburgh 2003) p. 197.

29 Certainly the letter in which this reference appears must be post-1179, but it could be as late as 1221.

30 The description from a charter of William the Lion, quoted in G.W.S. Barrow, *Kingdom*, p. 213.

31 Stephen T. Driscoll: *Excavations at Glasgow Cathedral 1988–1997* (Leeds 2002) p. 5.

32 'Special daughter of the Roman church, no-one in between.' *ODNB*: A.M.M. Duncan (all *ODNB* references from 2004 edition unless otherwise specified).

33 Mentioned in a royal charter, which can only be dated to the period between 1189 and 1195. Norman F. Shead: 'Jocelin, Abbot of Melrose and Bishop of Glasgow', *Innes Review*, vol. 54, no. 1 (Spring 2003) p. 1.

34 J.N. Graham Ritchie, Gordon S. Maxwell and Alistair Gordon: 'Prehistoric, Roman and Early Historical Glasgow' in Elizabeth Williamson, Anne Riches and Malcolm Higgs: *Glasgow* (London 1990) p. 37.

35 Strong, *History of Secondary Education*, pp. 19–20.

36 Alan Mould: *The English Chorister: A History* (London 2007) p. 24.

37 The Sprouston Breviary can be found in the National Library of Scotland. MS Edinburgh NLS Adv. 18.2.13B. They are generally dated at around 1300.

38 Shead, 'Medieval Glasgow', p. 37. Numbers of choristers were all small. In England numbers ranged from fourteen in Exeter and Salisbury to five for Hereford. Mould, *English Chorister*, p. 25.

39 Those vicars responsible for providing music at services in the cathedral.

40 Music in more than one part.

41 Orme, *Medieval Schools*, pp. 64–66.

42 Building work slowed down during the Wars of Independence. As a patron and friend of both Wallace and Bruce, Bishop Robert Wishart (1271–1316) was an important figure in the struggle and diverted timber intended for the cathedral to make siege engines to fight the English army of Edward I. G.W.S. Barrow: *Robert Bruce and the Community of the Realm of Scotland* (Edinburgh, 4th edn, 2005) p. 197.

43 Dowden, *Bishops of Scotland*. The post involved keeping the King's seal and becoming one of his personal advisers.

44 Richard D. Oram: 'Prelatical Builders: A Preliminary Study *c.*1124–*c.*1500' in Richard D. Oram and Geoffrey P. Stell (ed.): *Lordship and Architecture in Medieval and Renaissance Scotland* (Edinburgh 2005) p. 4.

45 Confirmed by the St Andrews Book (W1), the only significant body of polyphony extant from medieval Scotland.

46 Warwick Edwards: 'Polyphony in Thirteenth-Century Scotland' in Isobel Woods
    Preece: *Our Awin Scottis Use: Music in the Scottish Church up to 1603* ed. Sally
    Harper (Glasgow 2000) pp. 226–28 and 252.

47 This is the first documentary reference to choristers. Shead, 'Medieval Glasgow',
    p. 37.

48 Archbishop Eyre: 'The Hall of the Vicars Choral' in George Eyre-Todd: *The
    Book of Glasgow Cathedral* (Glasgow 1898) pp. 292–302. Vicars' Alley, or Close,
    the passage between the Royal Infirmary and the graveyard of the Cathedral,
    is still named after the Hall.

49 John Durkan: 'Education in the Century of the Reformation' in David
    McRoberts: *Essays on the Scottish Reformation 1513–1625* (Glasgow 1962) p. 147.

50 Cowan, *Medieval Church*, p. 180.

51 HSGM (December 1947) p. 25.

52 Scotland, *History of Scottish Education*, p. 16; Durkan, 'Education', p. 168; J.
    Durkan 'Early Song Schools in Scotland' in Gordon Munro et al. (ed.): *Notis
    Musycall: Essays in Honour of Kenneth Elliott* [Musica Scotica Trust] (Glasgow
    2005) pp. 125–32; and G. Munro: 'Scottish Church Music and Musicians
    1500–1700' (University of Glasgow PhD Thesis 1999).

53 Sir James Marwick (ed.): *Charters and Documents Relating to the City of Glasgow
    1175–1649*, Preface to Volume on Charters and Documents
    (Glasgow 1897) pp. 5–6, 44, 66 and 524.

54 However, when the next General Council of the Church took place in Rome
    in 1215, the Fourth Lateran Council, its members noticed that the decree of 1179
    was 'very little observed in many churches'. The Council therefore repeated what
    had been ordered and amplified it. Orme, *Medieval Schools*, p. 202.

55 Shead, 'Medieval Glasgow', p. 36.

56 Cannon, *Cathedral*, p. 416.

57 This happened again in 1264.

58 Jo Ann H. Morgan Cruz: 'England: Education and Society' in S.H. Rigby (ed.):
    A Companion to Britain in the Later Middle Ages (Malden MA 2003) pp. 451–71.

59 Cannon, *Cathedral*, p. 179.

60 Several cathedrals had choristers: usually about six in number. Fawcett, *Scottish
    Cathedrals*, p. 80.

61 A chancellor and precentor appeared in Aberdeen in 1240. Its statutes made
    provision for four boy choristers. Cowan, *Medieval Church*, pp. 86, 102 and
    112. Possibly Bondington knew of the statutes of Aberdeen Cathedral, dating
    from 1256, which spelled out the role of its chancellor, who was to supply a
    suitable teacher to direct its school and instruct the boys in grammar and logic.

62 Dowden, *Bishops of Scotland*, p. 303.

63 John Dowden: *The Medieval Church in Scotland: Its Constitution,
    Organisation and Law* (Glasgow 1910) p. 82. The fragmentary remains of
    choirbooks of Glasgow cathedral displayed how closely the Use of Salisbury
    was followed. Preece, *Our Awin Scottis Use*, p. 28.

64 D.E.R. Watt: 'Scotland: Religion and Piety' in Rigby, *Companion to Britain*,
    pp. 396–410.

65 Brian M. Halloran: *The Scots College Paris 1603–1792* (Edinburgh 1997) p. 177.

66 *Ibid.* p. 184.

67 *Ibid.* p. 189. The Red Book of Glasgow included the burgh records dating from the reign of Robert III.

68 It began in 1411 but the papal bull of authorisation was dated 1413, so the 600th anniversary celebrations are being spread over three years: 2011, 2012 and 2013.

69 The 165 books in the catalogue were deemed a large library given the labour involved in transcription and the expense of the vellum on which they were written. Grant, *History of the Burgh Schools*, pp. 44–5.

70 During the Middle Ages, like other countries in Western Europe, Scotland had neglected the study of Greek. Strong, *History of Secondary Education*, p. 47.

71 Durkan and Kirk, *University*, p. 5. It was modelled on the University of Bologna, with faculties of arts, divinity, law and medicine.

72 Edgar, *History of Early Scottish Education*, p. 94; Grant, *History of the Burgh Schools*, pp. 15–16.

73 Durkan and Kirk, *University*, pp. 11–12 and 22.

74 *Ibid.* p. 25.

75 Called Meikle Wynd in the Deed.

76 The area of the weekly market-place at the meeting of the Trongate, High Street, Saltmarket and Gallowgate.

77 Later Grammar School Wynd, subsequently part of Ingram Street.

78 James D. Marwick: *Extracts from Records of Burgh of Glasgow* Volume of Charters and Documents relating to the City of Glasgow, vol. I (1175–1649) Part 2 (Edinburgh 1894) no. 28 p. 436. As the term 'Rector' was increasingly used in place of 'Master' I use the former even when other sources continue to use the latter. My use of 'master' is synonymous with 'schoolmaster', while 'Master' prefixed to a name is the equivalent of the modern MA.

79 Blackadder was appointed bishop of Glasgow in 1483 and became Glasgow's first archbishop in January 1492. He died on a voyage of pilgrimage from Venice to the Holy Land in July 1508. Robert Renwick (ed.): [Sir James D. Marwick's] *Early Glasgow: A History of Glasgow from Earliest Times to 1611* (Glasgow 1911) p. 60.

80 Grant, *History of the Burgh Schools*, p. 19.

81 C. Innes: *Registrum Episcopatus Glasguensis* (Bannatyne Club 1843) No. 470.

82 While the Church was able to keep its right of patronage in Stirling, Perth and Dunfermline until after the Reformation.

83 Ashmall, *High School*, p. 6.

84 Having taken control of the GS, gradually the TC asserted its rights over other schools in the burgh. James D. Marwick: *Extracts from the Records of the Burgh of Glasgow* vol. I (1573–1642) (Glasgow 1876) p. 397; and Marwick: *Extracts*, vol. II (1630–62) (Glasgow 1881) pp. 96, 167, 212, 284, 374, 413 and 448–9.

85 Shead, 'Glasgow', p. 127.

86 Grammar School Wynd in official language, but in ordinary conversation Schoolhouse Wynd.

87 This was made possible by the decision of Mary, Queen of Scots, to give over all the old church lands in Glasgow to the Council.

88 Marwick, *Extracts*, Charters and other Documents (1894) Charters LIX, pp. 131–7, and LXIII, pp. 149–62.

89 By James Fleming, master of works (12 May 1578).

90 Grant, *History of the Burgh Schools*, p. 9.
91 Durkan and Kirk, *University*, p. 181 footnote.
92 Grant, *History of the Burgh Schools*, pp. 11–12.
93 Durkan and Kirk, *University*, p. 411
94 Durkan, 'Education', pp. 162 and 165.
95 These included Robert Henryson (d. *c.*1490) at Dunfermline GS around 1468 and Ninian Winzet at Linlithgow GS, 1551–61.
96 Leprosy was still an active disease and no respecter of persons.
97 Durkan, 'Education', pp. 158–9.
98 After the Reformation it became St Ninian's Kirk beyond the Brig. In 1585 its rentals came from twelve properties giving income of £6 4s Scots. HSGM (January 1949) p. 52.
99 The Altar of All Saints was sited at the fifth pillar (out from the north-west) in the nave of Glasgow Cathedral. It was supported by lands in Glasgow and Dumbarton.
100 Its altar was at the south door of the Cathedral and was maintained by lands in the Drygate, Rottenrow and Provanside.
101 'Bleis' being the Scottish word for blaze.
102 This practice also occurred at the High School in Edinburgh. James Grant: *Cassell's Old and New Edinburgh. Its History, its People and its Places* (London 1882) vol. 2 p. 290. John Murray: *A History of The Royal High School* (Edinburgh 1997) p. 12.
103 He appears to have been Master at Cambuslang GS before the Reformation.
104 Described as 'a charming interview' by Robert H. Small: 'The High School of Glasgow', *Scottish Field* (December 1963) p. 70.
105 *Onomasticon poeticum, sive, Propriorum quibus in suis Monumentis usi sunt Veteres Poetae, Brevis Descriptio Poetica* (Edinburgh 1592). A copy can still be found in the University of Glasgow Library.
106 *ODNB*: Ronald Bayne.
107 Marwick, *Extracts*, vol. I (1876), p. 30 (29 October 1574).
108 Relations deteriorated later when Sharp was deemed to be a turncoat and King's man.
109 J.D. Mackie: *The University of Glasgow 1451–1951: A Short History* (Glasgow 1954) p. 80. See also James Coutts: *A History of the University of Glasgow: From Its Foundation in 1451 to 1909* (Glasgow 1909) p. 80; and H.M.B. Reid: *Divinity Principals of the University of Glasgow, 1545–1654* (Glasgow 1917).
110 Dated 23 May 1592.
111 The letter is still extant. Boyd had also been a pupil of Thomas Jack. He was a handful at school and university. He fought as a soldier in the religious wars of France. Although he published verse and prose in Latin he is best remembered for his poem on the blindness of love.
112 Sasine was the registration of a deed transferring ownership of property.
113 Sir James Marwick and Robert Renwick: *Extracts from Records of Burgh of Glasgow* Charters and Documents, vol. II (1547–1638) (Glasgow 1906), XL pp. 557–8.
114 Durkan and Kirk, *University*, p. 336.
115 Michael Lynch: *Scotland: A New History* (London 1992) p. 229.

116 College was the more common name for the university in this period.

117 Thomas Dempster (d. 1625), Scottish scholar and historian, wrote of him *vir eruditus Graece et Latine*.

118 In Glasgow University Library.

119 Sharp believed Glasgow University was saved by the King's generosity and he himself owed his life and position to the King's preference.

120 *ODNB*: E.I. Carlyle.

121 Marwick, *Extracts*, vol. I (1876), p. 99.

122 An assessor appointed in 1595.

123 Kerr, *Scottish Education*, ch. 1.

124 Marwick, *Extracts*, vol. I (1876), pp. 192–3 [14 April 1599].

125 His acceptance of this post led to his resignation from his Mastership. Blackburn died in May 1623.

126 The TC agreed on 22 December 1600 to an increase to 6s 8d (Scots) (a quarter of which, 1s 8d, was to go to the doctor) in fees.

127 However, the rental of those lands in the precincts of the School were being lost as the TC took possession. Such quiet spoliation forced Blackburn to look for personal compensation. In March 1596 he accepted a solatium of 210 merks and an annual feu duty of 5 merks for renouncing his claim to the fore schoolhouse and its backyard, a property which was auctioned to Bailie Hector Stewart for 490 merks.

128 Following the order of the kirk session in November 1595 that a 'commodious place to be looked out' for them. James Cleland *The Historical Account of the Grammar School* (Glasgow 1825) p. 1, in the larger volume by James Cleland Burns (ed.): *The History of the High School of Glasgow* (Glasgow 1878).

129 Clearly the GS accepted Irish scholars, and probably accepted Gaelic-speaking Highlanders as well.

130 Edinburgh became Scotland's fourth university when founded by its Council in 1582, on the model of Calvin's Academy in Geneva.

131 The first use of the term 'grammar school' in Scotland appears to have been in Aberdeen in 1418, but its usage became common by the end of the fifteenth century. A.F. Hutchison: *History of the High School of Stirling* (Stirling 1904) p. 9; Scotland, *History of Scottish Education*, p. 17.

132 It was held that logic involved intense intellectual effort and, as its method was common to all branches of knowledge, it came to dominate the university medieval curriculum. Durkan and Kirk, *University*, pp. 85–6.

133 Norman Macdougall: *James IV* (Edinburgh 1989) p. 175.

134 Although in rural areas it was most likely that education was affected by boarding pupils in burgh grammar schools.

135 The Glasgow GS curriculum was mirrored closely by that of the High School of Edinburgh in the same period. Grant, *History of the Burgh Schools*, p. 339ff.

136 Durkan and Kirk, *University*, p. 312.

137 Compared with the three classes a day of two hours in length in French provincial schools.

138 John Hill Burton (ed.): *Register of the Privy Council of Scotland* vol. 2 [1569–78] (Edinburgh 1878) p. 478.

139 The *Rudimenta* of Andrew Symson, schoolmaster at Dunbar, was published

in Edinburgh. The *Liber Secundus* of James Carmichael, schoolmaster at Haddington, was published in Cambridge (both in 1587). David Masson (ed.): *Register of the Privy Council of Scotland* vol. 5 [1592–9] (Edinburgh 1882) p. 112.

140 Masson, *Register of the Privy Council*, pp. 110–12.

141 1580–1646.

142 Entitled *Short Introduction to Grammar. ODNB*: A.S. Wayne Pearce.

143 Durkan: 'Schools and schooling to 1696' in Michael Lynch (ed.): *Oxford Companion to Scottish History* (Oxford 2001) p. 562.

144 G.C. Coulton: *Scottish Abbeys and Social Life* (Edinburgh 1933) p. 186. Coulton seems to take opportunities to attack the medieval Western Church in the belief that by doing so he is attacking the Roman Catholic Church of his own day.

145 Grant, *History of the Burgh Schools*, p. 73 gave far too favourable an account of the position of the schoolmaster.

146 Usually the salary of a master of a burgh school was between 100 and 300 merks and the fees collected. Normally the TC fixed the fees for 'tounis bairnes'; while fees from 'outten tounis bairnes' were left to the discretion of the master, it being understood that these would be charged at a much higher rate.

147 HSGM (January 1951) p. 30.

148 Durkan and Kirk, *University*, p. 354, quoting *The First Book of Discipline*.

149   James McGrath: 'The Medieval and Early Modern Burgh' in T.M. Devine and Gordon Jackson: *Glasgow* vol. 1: *Beginnings to 1830* (Manchester 1995) p. 38.

150 *Ibid.* p. 358.

151 The Act of 1567 was the first in a series issued at regular intervals by the Scottish Parliament over the next 140 years. Scotland, *History of Scottish Education*, p. 51.

152 Durkan, 'Education', p. 165.

153 Lynch, *Scotland*, p. 257.

154 Durkan, 'Education', p. 165.

155 An exception was when John Reid fell foul of the relatives of a boy for 'cruelly wounding him'. Durkan, 'Education', p. 159. Discipline was harsh at this time.

156 As late as 1905 J.O. Mitchell, in *Old Glasgow Essays* (Glasgow 1905), could claim: 'No Glasgow Grammar schoolboy has ever risen so high.'

157 *ODNB*: Leslie J. Macfarlane.

158 David Laing (ed.): *The Letters and Journals of Robert Baillie* (Edinburgh 1841–2) vol. 3 p. 402. Baillie was himself a GS pupil.

159 *ODNB*: D.M. Abbott.

160 I.D. McFarlane: *Buchanan* (Bristol 1981) p. 19.

161 *ODNB*: James Kirk.

162 J. Spottiswoode: *History of the Church of Scotland* ed. M. Napier and M. Russell 3 vols (Spottiswoode Society, 1851) vol. 2 p. 336.

163 *ODNB*: Rob Macpherson. David Masson: *Register of Privy Council Series*, (PCS) 1st series vol. 6 [1599–1604] (Edinburgh 1884) p. 605.

164 *ODNB*: Alan R. MacDonald.

165 C.V. Wedgwood: *Montrose* (Stroud 1952) p. 2. She refers to it as 'the High School', and in the Index (*Ibid.* p. 166) suggests that it was synonymous with the university.

166 *ODNB*: David Stevenson; confirmed by John Buchan: *Montrose* (London 1928) and Edward J. Cowan: *Montrose: For Covenant and King* (London 1977).

167 Max Hastings: *Montrose: The King's Champion* (London 1979) pp. 30–3 describes James Graham's early education in Glasgow from 'one day in 1624' until 'on or about November 10th, 1626' although he does not specifically mention the GS. Given the detailed knowledge we have on Graham's education, it seems likely that had he attended the School we would know about it.

168 Keith M. Brown: *Noble Society in Scotland: Wealth, Family and Culture, from Reformation to Revolution* (Edinburgh 2004) pp. 184–5.

CHAPTER TWO

1 Marwick, *Extracts*, 1876, p. 210.

2 *Ibid.* p. 216. Meaning as cheaply as they can.

3 *Ibid.* p. 218. Some taxation money was also used. Robert Renwick (ed.): *Extracts from Glasgow Burgh Council* vol. VI (Glasgow 1911) p. 273.

4 The link with Blackfriars' Church continued, and on 23 December 1648 the scholars of the GS were allowed to sit every Sabbath in the university seats there. Marwick, *Extracts*, 1881, p. 156.

5 Translated: 'The GS, built by the TC and Citizens of Glasgow, Patrons of Sound Learning.'

6 Marwick, *Extracts*, 1881, pp. 329, 331 and 339.

7 *Ibid.* p. 340.

8 *Ibid.* pp. 348 and 351.

9 Renwick, *Extracts*, vol. VI (1911), p. 273.

10 Scotland, *History of Scottish Education*, p. 78. Kerr, *Scottish Education*, ch. 6. French kylis was a form of skittles or nine-pins. Glaikis involved a puzzle with some notched pieces of wood which was difficult to undo and replace in their former position.

11 Marwick, *Extracts*, 1876, pp. 311–2.

12 Hutchison, *History*, p. 22.

13 Thomas McCrie (ed.): *The Life of Mr Robert Blair Containing his Autobiography from 1593 to 1636* (Edinburgh, Wodrow Society, 1848) p. 9.

14 *Ibid.*

15 He was much involved with national affairs and remained stubborn and consistent in his opposition to episcopacy, campaigning against the changes in worship embodied in Charles I's new Scottish Prayer Book. He assisted in the prosecution of the Royalist leaders captured at the battle of Philiphaugh (1645), principally Sir Robert Spottiswood, who had been a pupil at the GS. He was elected Moderator of the GA of the Church of Scotland in June 1646. *ODNB*: David Stevenson.

16 Laing (ed.), *Letters and Journals*, vol. 1, p. 174. He was 'a man of great piety, ability and high experience' according to Rev. James Kirkton: *The Secret and True History of the Church of Scotland* (Edinburgh 1817) p. 22. He was also hailed as 'one of the brightest lights in his day' by R. Wodrow: *Collections upon the Lives* (Glasgow, 1845) vol. 2 part 1 p. 126.

17 The book is in fine condition and can still be found in the Department of Special Collections in Glasgow University Library.

18 Marwick, *Extracts*, 1881, pp. 9, 14 and 19.

19 The TC gave him £100 Scots for the upkeep of his wife and four children in June 1655.

20 He was to become the minister of Dalry, Galloway (1635–7) and then Kilmaurs (1637–8). When he died in Ireland in 1642, according to his testament, he left no goods except his household furniture, which was valued at less than 25s sterling.

21 The quality of his scholarship in this piece was later complimented by Dr Samuel Johnson.

22 A famous Covenanting divine.

23 Hutchison, *History*, p. 49.

24 'A Brief Historical Relation of the Life of Mr John Livingston, Minister of the Gospel, written by himself, during his banishment in Holland, for the cause of Christ' in *Select Biographies* (Edinburgh 1845) vol. 1 p. 130. After one incident in which he was beaten 'with a stick in the cheek so as my face swelled', his father reprimanded Wallace, who promised 'to forbear beating of me and after that I profited a great deal more in my learning'.

25 David Masson (ed.): *Register of the Privy Council of Scotland* vol. 13 [1622–5] p. 318.

26 The TC ordered the Treasurer to give Wallace 20 merks for riding to Edinburgh 'about the grammer to be imposiet upoun the countrie', 17 July 1630.

27 The principle had been accepted nationally before the end of the 16th century, following the proposal set out in The First Book of Discipline (of 1560). It had proposed quarterly visitations. Grant, *History of the Burgh Schools*, p. 143.

28 Marwick, *Extracts*, 1881, p. 43.

29 GTCAB series 1, vol.8 (4 March 1623).

30 Durante bene placito.

31 By the 18th century some appointments were made *ad vitam aut culpam*, a Latin phrase used in Scots law to indicate the legal permanency of an appointment, unless forfeited by misconduct.

32 Marwick, *Extracts*, 1876, p. 376.

33 He was learned in Greek as well as Latin.

34 They had particular knowledge of Rutherford, who 'demonstrated to them his eminent abilities of mind, and vertuous [sic] disposition'. Thomas Craufurd: *History of the University of Edinburgh from 1580–1646* (Edinburgh 1808) pp. 96–7. However, Rutherford, in 1625, 'having given some scandal in his marriage, was forced to dimit [sic] his charge'. *Ibid.* p. 104.

35 Glasgow TC sent John Anderson by horse to Stirling on 12 February 1642 to tempt Will to Glasgow. He accepted the offer and on 1 March 1642 Will was made a burgess of Glasgow, gratis.

36 Marwick, *Extracts*, 1881, pp. 116 and 126.

37 *Ibid.* p. 127.

38 *Ibid.* p. 161. On appointment Will received an immediate payment of £20 Scots and on taking office he received a further £100 Scots. His annual salary was fixed at 400 merks. Marwick, *Extracts*, 1876, p. 438.

39 On 24 September 1674 his salary was fixed at £120 Scots (i.e., 180 merks).

40 Strong, *History of Secondary Education*, pp. 145–6. Will's salary was the same as in Glasgow, but Stirling provided a free house. Although he obtained an eleven-year contract he died in June 1652. Hutchison, *History*, pp. 64–73.

41 Marwick, *Extracts*, 1881, p. 239.

42 Robert Wodrow: *Life of James Wodrow. Professor of Divinity in the University of Glasgow* (Edinburgh 1828).

43 He had been first doctor 1679–81 and was to become Rector of Paisley GS between 1703 and 1713.

44 James D. Marwick and Robert Renwick (ed.): *Extracts from Glasgow Burgh Council* (Glasgow 1905) vol. III (1663–90) p. 303.

45 Wodrow, *Life*.

46 By 22 November 1690 the magistrates were so disenchanted that they refused Glen permission to keep any school in Glasgow and made it clear that any attempt on his part to ignore the warning would lead to imprisonment.

47 He had been appointed second doctor by a plurality of votes on 23 October 1676. Marwick and Renwick, *Extracts*, vol. III (1905), p. 227. He was second doctor from 1676–81, then eldest doctor 1681–8.

48 GTCAB, vol. 17 (21 May 1688).

49 Marwick and Renwick, *Extracts*, vol. III (1905), pp. 411–12.

50 Grant, *History of the Burgh Schools*, p. 280.

51 Before the end of 1688 the Roman Catholic James VII and II had been deposed in favour of the Protestant William and Mary.

52 The Westminster Confession of Faith of 1647 remains to this day the basic confessional stance of the Church of Scotland. Michael Lynch, *Scotland*, p. 280.

53 Skirven, former master at Hamilton GS, had graduated from Edinburgh University in 1662.

54 James D. Marwick and Robert Renwick (eds): Extracts from Glasgow Burgh Council vol. IV (1691–1717) (Glasgow 1908) p. 132. Walker was previously Rector of the GS at Dumbarton (1690–5).

55 *Ibid.* p. 167.

56 *Ibid.* p. 242.

57 *Ibid.* p. 275.

58 He was then elected master of Hutchesons' Hospital School, a post he held between 1708 and 1710, thereafter being a pensioner in the Hospital.

59 Appointed a doctor on 1 October 1698. Marwick and Renwick, *Extracts*, vol. IV (1908), p. 275.

60 *Ibid.* pp. 414–5 and 417.

61 South-west Scotland was a latecomer to witch-hunting, hence this extraordinarily late date. After the last great outbreak of persecution in 1661–2, witch-hunting went into sharp decline generally in Scotland. Lizanne Henderson: 'The Survival of Witchcraft Persecutions and Witch Belief in South-West Scotland', *Scottish Historical Review* vol. 85 no. 1 (219) (April 2006) pp. 52–74.

62 J. Maxwell Wood and John Copland: *Witchcraft and Superstitious Record in Southwest Scotland* (Edinburgh 1911) pp. 97–8 and 245–8.

63 Visitations had begun again in September 1697 with emphasis on government and management as well as the proficiency of the scholars. Marwick and Renwick, *Extracts*, vol. IV (1908), p. 255.

64 'The status of the Scottish Rector seems to have been saved from the comparative degradation which fell to the lot of the proctor or rector in Oxford or Cambridge.' Kerr, *Scottish Education*, ch. 1.

65 Murray, *History of Royal High*, pp. 12–13. Crauford, *History, University of Edinburgh*, pp. 64 and 117.

66 Skene had previously been master at Haddington GS with a salary of 400 merks. However, 50 merks of this total had to be given over to a doctor employed by him. The salary at Haddington had not changed in two centuries, 'evidence of the early respectability of that seminary'. James Miller: *The Lamp of Lothian, Or, The History of Haddington in Connection with the Public Affairs of East Lothian and of Scotland from the Earliest Records to the Present Period* (Haddington 1844) p. 449.

67 A Royal Commission set up to establish the value of ecclesiastical lands and to settle the stipends of ministers.

68 Scotland, *History of Scottish Education*, p. 123.

69 David Murray: 'Some Early Grammars and Other School Books in Use in Scotland' in *Proceedings of the Royal Philosophical Society of Glasgow, 1905–1906* vol. 37 (Glasgow 1906) p. 148.

70 The TC of Aberdeen was compelled nearly every Christmas to take measures against their disorderly GS boys, who persisted in seizing the building and holding it against all comers. In Edinburgh, the schoolmaster was sued for furniture smashed and windows broken; and there was at least one barring-out, in September 1595, which led the Edinburgh magistrates to order the battering down of the door of their HS. In this process Bailie MacMoran was shot dead. Murray, *History of Royal High*, p. 8.

71 Strong, *History of Secondary Education*, p. 138.

72 This was true also of the universities. In 1664 several lecturers appointed 'clandestine censors' and in 1705 they were employed again to observe the students so that any speaking English could be censured. Strong, *History of Secondary Education*, footnote p. 152.

73 The universities were influential in ensuring that schools in their immediate vicinity remained strictly grammar or Latin schools.

74 The university authorities also recognised this problem and in 1706 held that 'no grammar be taught by the professor of humanity, that being proper and peculiar to a grammar school'. Ashmall, *High School*, p. 129.

75 The document on which the succeeding paragraphs are based can be found in the *Munimenta* of the University of Glasgow (1854) vol. 2 pp. 307–10. Grant, *History of the Burgh Schools*, pp. 336–8 wrongly dated the document because it appeared to have 'been written in the same hand as an act book of the TC in 1573'.

76 This would have taken place in separate English schools in the Town; and such schools were fairly numerous, for in 1639 the TC had thought fit to limit their number to four.

77 John Despauter (1460–1520) was a Flemish grammarian. His works were brought together as 'Commentarii grammatici' in a 1537 Paris edition. It was regarded as the standard grammar text of the time. The other was the work of Aelius Donatus, whose fourth-century grammar was still being used.

78 The purpose of the *Colloquia* was to enable boys to speak Latin by providing them with examples of conversation upon the common life of the day as it presented itself to the young. They were produced by Mathurin Cordier (*c*.1480–1564), a French schoolmaster who taught John Calvin in Paris, and went on to teach at Geneva and Bordeaux. His work went through numerous editions and was in use for three centuries. James Colville: *Some Old-fashioned Educationists* (Edinburgh 1907) pp. 54–77.

79 Marcus Tullius Cicero (106–43 BC) is widely regarded as one of Rome's greatest orators, lawyers and statesmen. His prose writing is held to be as the paragon of Classical Latin.

80 Desiderius Erasmus (*c*.1466–1536), Dutch scholar and humanist, paved the way for the Reformation with his satires on the RC Church, including the *Colloquia Familiaria* (1518).

81 Sebastian Castellion (1515–1563), French preacher and theologian, who, seeing the burning of heretics, turned Protestant. However, he split from Calvin insisting on the need for toleration. He produced 'Four Books of Sacred Dialogues' in 1542 in Latin and French. All his subjects were from Scripture and his work represented scripture history in the form of dialogues.

82 Publius Terentius Afer (*c*.190–159 BC), Roman comic dramatist, whose surviving six comedies were based on the New Greek Comedy.

83 Publius Ovidius Naso (43 BC–*c*.17 AD), Roman poet, known best for his elegiac love poems and the *Metamorphoses,* a hexametric epic which retells Greek and Roman myths.

84 Quintus Horatius Flaccus (65–8 BC), Roman poet, notable satirist and literary critic, who is best known for his Odes.

85 Strong, *History of Secondary Education*, pp. 76–7; Scotland, *History of Scottish Education*, p. 82.

86 *Common Activities.*

87 It was found in the clerk's office in the City Chambers in 1794, and the writing was very similar to other papers in the same parcel, dated 1660. Cleland (ed. Burns), *Historical Account*, pp. 1–2. The view of Cleland appeared in his *Historical Account of the Grammar School* written in 1825, and modified his original suggestion in his 'Annals of Glasgow' written in 1816 when he dated the document as 1620. James Cleland: *Annals of Glasgow. Comprising an Account of the Public Buildings, Charities, and the Rise and Progress of the City* (Edinburgh 1829) p. 281. HSGM (December 1949) pp. 23–5 dates the document at 1650.

88 Time was also found on a Monday morning to examine the boys' knowledge of the Sunday sermon.

89 Time was found on a Friday morning by the Rector to deal with those censured during the week, in order to maintain discipline and restrain the scholars from 'loosnes and disorder'.

90 *GHerald*, 15 August 1907. On 14 December 1699 Haddington's TC ordained 'for the health of the children' that from Hallowmas to Candlemas (31 October to 2 February) its GS would begin classes at 9 a.m. (instead of 6 a.m.). Miller, *Lamp of Lothian*, p. 450.

91 Cleland, *Historical Account*, 1825, pp. 4–6.

92 Alone among the leading Scottish burghs, Glasgow could not choose its

magistrates but instead remained subject to its archbishops. This changed in 1690, enabling Glasgow to challenge the economic position of Edinburgh. McGrath, 'Medieval and Early Modern Burgh', p. 57.

93 Kerr, *Scottish Education*, ch. 12.

94 McGrath, 'Medieval and Early Modern Burgh', p. 39.

95 Donald Withrington: 'Schools and Schooling 1696–1872' in Michael Lynch (ed.), *Oxford Companion*, p. 563.

96 See Chapter 4.

97 Grant, *History of the Burgh Schools*, p. 330.

98 *ODNB*: David Stevenson.

99 See earlier in chapter. In 1646 Baillie dedicated to Blair his *An Historical Vindication of the Government of the Church of Scotland*.

100 Laing (ed.), *Letters and Journals*, vol. 1, p. xxiii.

101 'The little monk of Kilwinning' was bookish and retiring, wanting the quiet life he did not get.

102 *Ibid.* vol. 3 p. 105.

103 His outstanding depth of learning is seen in his knowledge of thirteen languages.

104 *ODNB*: Terry Clavin.

105 *Selections from the Registers of the Presbytery of Lanark, 1623–1709* (Edinburgh, 1839) pp. 42–102.

106 He was created Duke of Hamilton in 1660, thereby giving him parity of social standing with his wife, who was third Duchess of Hamilton in her own right from 1651.

107 *ODNB*: Rosalind K. Marshall.

108 Wodrow, *Life*, p. 27.

109 *ODNB*: L.A. Yeoman.

110 *Ibid.*

111 In 1698 James became fourth Duke of Hamilton and was to continue to prove a great disappointment in later life, particularly in his inconsistent actions at the time of the proposed Act of Union in 1707. He was killed in a duel in 1712. *ODNB*: Rosalind K. Marshall.

112 Also 1st Marquess.

113 Sir William Fraser: *The Annandale Family Book of the Johnstones* (Edinburgh 1894) (2 vols) vol. 1 p. ccliii.

114 He became President of the Privy Council (1694); President of the Scottish Parliament (1695); High Commissioner to the General Assembly (1701, 1705 and 1711); Lord Privy Seal (1702); Scottish Secretary of State and President of the Privy Council (1705).

CHAPTER THREE

1 Marwick and Renwick, *Extracts*, vol. IV (1908), p. 550.

2 *Ibid.* p. 606.

3 It was not forthcoming until December 1721, but despite the delay the scheme was approved then.

4 Cleland, *Historical Account*, 1825, p. 7.

5 The Rector received a fourth part of the fees of the doctors' classes but took all of the 2s 6d from his own class. Robert Renwick (ed.), *Extracts*, vol. V (1718–38) (Glasgow 1909) p. 286.

6 *Ibid.* p. 104.

7 James Arbuckle and Thomas Griffith: *Prologue and Epilogue of Tamarlane* (Glasgow 1721).

8 One of his pupils there was (later Sir) James Steuart (1713–1780), son of Sir James Steuart, Solicitor-General for Scotland under Anne and George I, later called the 'father of political economy in Britain'.

9 Cleland, *Historical Account*, 1825, p. 7.

10 Renwick, *Extracts*, vol. V (1909), pp. 429–30.

11 Clearly Maltman was successful, but the experiment seems to have ended in October 1740 when Maltman became a doctor. He remained on the staff until his death in October 1760. James Renwick (ed): *Extracts* vol. VII (1760–80) (Glasgow 1912) p. 47.

12 Appointed a doctor in December 1734.

13 Cleland, *Historical Account*, 1825, p. 7.

14 Renwick, *Extracts*, vol. V (1909), p. 499.

15 Renwick, *Extracts*, vol. VI (1911), p. 466.

16 Before then Writing was restricted to boys of 14 or 15 years old.

17 Renwick, *Extracts*, vol. V (1909), p. 503. The High School in Edinburgh introduced Writing as an extra in 1704. Alexander Law: *Education in Edinburgh in the Eighteenth Century* (London 1965) p. 75.

18 A dancing school had already been set up in September 1734 by Daniel Barrell with strict regulations to ensure that neighbours were not disturbed. Burgh scholars paid 30s for lessons from 1 October to 1 May. Barrell agreed to go every four years to London or Paris to update his knowledge. Renwick, *Extracts*, vol. V (1909), p. 426.

19 Cleland, *Historical Account*, 1825, p. 9.

20 *Ibid.* p. 8.

21 He was later to become minister of Inveresk for 57 years.

22 John Hill Burton (ed.): *Autobiography of the Rev. Dr. Alexander Carlyle 1722–1805* containing memorials (originally published in Edinburgh 1860; London 1910).

23 *Ibid.* p. 81.

24 *Ibid.* pp. 101.

25 *Ibid.* pp. 102–4.

26 *Glasgow Journal* 2 April 1753.

27 Renwick, *Extracts*, vol. VI (1911), pp. 463–4.

28 *Ibid.* p. 504.

29 Barr had graduated MA in 1735 and been parish schoolmaster in Rutherglen (1738–40).

30 Cleland, *Historical Account*, 1825, p. 9.

31 In 1759 George Lesly, formerly Rector of Bo'ness GS attempted, in spite of the opposition from the magistrates, to set up as a private teacher. He advertised in the *Glasgow Journal* of 11 September 1760, which was perhaps an attempt at kite-flying, for within a couple of months he was appointed a doctor in the GS. He died the following spring.

32 Renwick, *Extracts*, vol. VII (1912), pp. 246–7 and 250.

33 Following a petition, Barr's salary was increased from £40 to £55 per annum, while each of the three doctors had their salaries raised from £15 to £20. This took effect in December 1765. Renwick, *Extracts*, vol. VII (1912), pp. 212–3 and 219. The fees of pupils also went up from 4s to 5s a quarter.

34 David Allison, schoolmaster in the then prosperous suburb of Gorbals, succeeded Bald as a master on 26 March 1783.

35 Bradfute was made a burgess, without fee, of Glasgow on 18 April 1775, following his care and education of youth under his charge. GTCAB series 1 vol. 35. Bradfute resigned his post on 17 August 1787, to be replaced the following month by John Wilson, Rector of the GS in South Leith.

36 James Gibson succeeded Dow, on the latter's death, on 15 January 1794. He had entered Bald's class in 1766, and was the only teacher in the GS for over a century who had been a scholar in it. He was a qualified Church of Scotland minister.

37 Ashmall, *High School*, pp, 66–7.

38 This can be contrasted with the situation in the HS in Edinburgh. When Rector Adam in 1772 decided to introduce his own grammar textbook instead of Ruddiman's, the TC prevented him from doing so. Law, *Education in Edinburgh*, p. 77.

39 *Edinburgh's English Schoolmaster* (Edinburgh 1706).

40 Dividing words into their constituent syllables.

41 Ruddiman (1674–1757) went on to confirm his reputation as Scotland's foremost Latinist with his *Grammaticae Latinea Institutiones* (2 vols, 1725, 1731). *ODNB*: A.P. Woolrich.

42 Sir Graham Moore.

43 Rev. G.R. Gleig: *The Life of Major-General Sir Thomas Munro* (London 1830) 3 vols, vol. 3 p. 422.

44 He wrote under the name Senex and entered Macarthur's class in 1782. His books were written late in life and may have been subject to an old man's imperfect recollection. He was in his 92nd year when his *Glasgow and its Environs: Historical and Topographical* (London 1864) was published.

45 In Edinburgh its HS was assigned to a specific committee of its TC in 1771.

46 On his death in 1791 he bequeathed books, property and money to the city to establish a public library.

47 In the 1780s the four classes at the GS were, in order of seniority, known to the boys as cocks, hens, earocks (= pullets) and chickens. Senex, *Glasgow and its Environs*, p. 405. By 1839 the first-year boys were known as 'tewkies' (another word for chickens).

48 Robert Renwick (ed.), *Extracts*, vol. VIII 1718–95 (Glasgow 1913) p. 42.

49 A position which would be reached by each master in rotation.

50 Renwick, *Extracts*, vol. VIII (1913), p. 42.

51 2 February. Candlemas (mid-winter) had traditionally been an important day in the calendar, and almost all grammar schools had their yearly cock-fight immediately following the holiday. Hugh Miller: *An Autobiography: My Schools and Schoolmasters Or The Story of my Education* (Edinburgh 1854) pp. 46–7.

52 1 May – the beginning of summer.

53 George III's birth-date was 4 June.

54 The day in September when the fourteen Incorporated Trades of Glasgow elected their Deacons.

55 Cleland, *Annals of Glasgow*, p. 289. The tradition was abolished by the (Universities) Commission of 1858. The holiday continued at the university into the twentieth century, while the School abolished its holiday in the late nineteenth century.

56 Robert Reid (Senex): *Glasgow, Past and Present* vol. 2 (Glasgow 1851).

57 Renwick, *Extracts*, vol. VIII (1913), p. 169. However, on 28 November 1782 the TC decided to disallow entertainments, including those given to masters. The expenses on the King's birthday were also curtailed. GTCAB vol. 37. The teaching salaries were far short of those the Council paid to its seven ministers: £138 17s 10d annually in January 1781. GTCAB vol. 38.

58 Ashmall, *High School*, p. 52.

59 This proved more difficult than suggested, for as early as January 1794 the GSC recommended a move to a five-year course, but this was not followed up by the Council. Cleland (ed. Burns), *History*, p. 14. Again, in August 1807, the committee argued that four years' study was not long enough to master the Latin language, but the Council let the issue lie on the table 'for further consideration' *Ibid.* p. 16.

60 Renwick, *Extracts*, vol. VIII (1913), pp. 46–7. This took much longer than expected. A site was still being sought in December 1784. *Ibid.* pp. 154–5.

61 *Ibid.* p. 63. Joining Bald, Bradfute and Dow.

62 *Ibid.* pp. 71 and 96.

63 The Old GS was altered to adapt it for dwelling houses, which meant the removal of its steeple. Its dilapidated state was described by Senex in 1849 and it was demolished in 1874. (1871 sketch Canmore I.D. No. 169259); James Cowan: *From Glasgow's Treasure Chest* (Glasgow 1951) p. 277). Its site was occupied partly by Ingram Street and partly by a fire station that still stands but is now used for commercial purposes. Carol Foreman: *Lost Glasgow: Glasgow's Lost Architectural Heritage* (Edinburgh 2002) p. 41.

64 Renwick, *Extracts*, vol. VIII (1913), pp. 209, 213 and 226–7.

65 Between the High Street and George Square.

66 *Glasgow Mercury* 18 July 1787.

67 Craig was involved in designing suburban villas, of which the best surviving example is at 42 Miller Street, and went on in 1791 to design the 'flashy' Surgeon's Hall in St Enoch's Square. Charles McKean: 'Buildings and Cityscape' in *The Glasgow Story 1770s to 1830s*, available online at http://www.theglasgowstory.com/ story.php?id=TGSCF.

68 *Ibid.* probably quoting the (*Old*) *Statistical Account 1791–9* vol. 5, 'Glasgow, County of Lanark' p. 530.

69 Samuel Lewis: *A Topographical Dictionary of Scotland* 2 vols (London 1846) p. 497ff.

70 Foreman, *Lost Glasgow*, p. 104.

71 The surplus of accommodation resulted in two rooms being provided rent-free by the TC on the second floor for the new Anderson's College in March 1796. One was used for apparatus and the other for lectures. J. Butt: *John Anderson's Legacy: The University of Strathclyde and its Antecedents 1796–1996* (East Linton 1996) p. 26.

72 GTCAB vol. 40.

73 Former Rector of Inverary GS.

74 Gibson remained almost twenty-seven years until resigning in September 1820.

75 1751–1809.

76 On 16 November 1778 he preached 'a most inflammatory sermon' against Popery in the Blackfriars' Kirk. It was published the following month in the *Glasgow Mercury* (10 December) in 'The Church of Rome, the Mother of Abominations'.

77 R. Robertson: *The Trial of Thomas Muir* (Edinburgh 1793) pp. 64 and 132. *ODNB*: H.T. Dickinson.

78 Senex, *Glasgow and its Environs*, p. 403.

79 For Scots attending Balliol College, Oxford.

80 His wealthy father speculated in slaves, failed and had to sell Jordanhill estate.

81 Senex, *Glasgow and its Environs*, pp. 405–11.

82 John Colin Dunlop.

83 Andrew Tennent: 'Statistics of a Glasgow Grammar School Class of 115 Boys', *Journal of the Statistical Society of London* vol. 18 no. 4 (December 1855) pp. 364–6. Tennent read this as a paper to the Statistical Section of the British Association in Glasgow in September 1855. He found the following professions were followed: 53 merchants and manufacturers; 7 lawyers; 4 clerks; 3 military officers; 3 clergymen; 3 sailors; 3 weavers; 2 private gentlemen; 2 bankers; 1 professor; 1 artist; 1 exciseman; 1 soldier; 1 surgeon; 1 carter; 1 porter; 1 editor; 27 unknown, a number of whom died young.

84 *Glasgow Courier* 30 September 1802.

85 Ashmall, *High School*, p. 75.

86 The GSC thought otherwise and split the class into two.

87 William Beattie: *Life and Letters of Thomas Campbell* (Glasgow 1849) vol. 1. p. 51.

88 J. Cuthbert Hadden: *Thomas Campbell* (Edinburgh 1899).

89 *Glasgow Courier* 8 January 1811. *GHerald* 11 January 1811.

90 Cleland (ed. Burns), *History*, pp. 50–3.

91 James Gourlay (ed): *The Provosts of Glasgow from 1609 to 1832* (Glasgow 1942) pp. 54ff.

92 Devine and Jackson (eds), *Glasgow, Volume I Beginnings to 1830* (Manchester 1995), p. 161.

93 There they met up with some teachers of international renown, such as Adam Smith and Joseph Black. They seldom stayed to complete their degrees.

94 Richard B. Sher: 'Commerce, Religion and the Enlightenment in Eighteenth Century Glasgow' in Devine and Jackson (eds), *Glasgow, Volume I*, p. 315.

95 *Ibid.* p. 316.

96 *ODNB*: H.C.G. Matthew.

97 Phrenology was emerging as a pseudo-science which sought to relate the activity of the brain, notably character traits and intellectual ability, with the size and shape of the human skull.

98 *ODNB*: A. Ryan.

99 T.A. Lee: *Seekers of Truth: The Scottish Founders of Modern Public Accountancy* (Oxford 2006) pp. 165–6.

100 *ODNB*: Stanley Brice Frost.

101 Stanley Brice Frost: *James McGill of Montreal* (Montreal 1995).

102 Ray McKenzie: *Public Sculpture of Glasgow* (Liverpool 2002) pp. 415–6.

103 *ODNB*: Monica Clough.

104 *MPHGM*.

105 *MPHGM*.

106 With Samuel Cunard and Donald MacIver.

107 *ODNB*: Lucy Kelly Hayden.

108 Irene Sweeney: 'The Municipal Administration of Glasgow, 1833–1912: Public Service and the Scottish Civic Identity' (University of Strathclyde PhD Thesis 1990) p. 882. His brother, John, was Liberal MP for Glasgow, 1837–48.

109 *ODNB*: R.B. Prosser, revised by Geoffrey V. Morson.

110 Sweeney, 'Municipal Administration', p. 943.

111 *ODNB*: Antony Kamm.

112 *ODNB*: J.H. Burns.

113 In 1747 the Church of Scotland split: the Burghers took the Burgess Oath, which the post-Culloden Hanoverian Government demanded all holders of public office do, thus affirming approval of the religion 'presently professed in this kingdom'. The Anti-burghers did not accept civil compulsion in religious affairs. The Burgess Oath was abolished in 1819.

114 *ODNB*: John D. Haigh.

115 McKenzie, *Public Sculpture*, p. 460.

116 Son of Dr John Moore.

117 His brother stated that while at the School he was described as a 'good-looking youth, tall and graceful with regular pleasant features, brown hair and hazel eyes'. James Carrick Moore: *The Life of Sir John Moore* (London 1834) p. 2. For a recent biography see Roger Day: *The Life of Sir John Moore – Not a Drum was Heard* (Barnsley 2001).

118 The pistols and the pocket edition of Horace were presented to the High School by his great grand-niece and handed over to the School by Major-General Baden-Powell on 30 April 1904. They are exhibited in the School Library at Anniesland. HSGM June 1904.

119 *Ibid.*

120 'Sir John Moore's Monument', *GHerald* 20 August 1819. As the first statue erected in George Square, it faced significant resistance from local residents. McKenzie, *Public Sculpture*, pp. 118–22.

121 *ODNB*: John Sweetman.

122 *ODNB*: Andrew Lambert.

123 *ODNB*: Roger T. Stearn.

124 *ODNB*: Douglas Brown.

125 *Various Views of Human Nature, taken from Life and Manners, Foreign and Domestic* 2 vols.

126 *ODNB*: H.L. Fulton. He is mentioned in Tobias Smollett's last novel, *The Expedition of Humphry Clinker*. 'We had the good fortune to be received into the house of Mr Moore, an eminent surgeon . . . Mr Moore is a merry facetious companion, sensible and shrewd, with a considerable fund of humour.' Vol. 3: Roderick Random (London 1771) ed. Jeremy Lewis (2008) p. 264.

127 Thomas Hamilton (1728–82).

128 *ODNB*: Michael Bevan.

129 *ODNB*: Deborah Brunton.

130 Bald died in mid-session 1782–3, and for the next two and a half years the class was Allison's.

131 Later in life he was elected Lord Rector of Glasgow University (1815–17).

132 *ODNB*: Michael Fry.

133 *MPHGM*.

134 *ODNB*: Douglas Brown.

135 *ODNB*: Paul Wood.

136 James MacLehose: *Memoirs and Portraits of One Hundred Glasgow Men [who have died during the last thirty years and in their lives did much to make the city what it now is]* (Glasgow 1886). Sweeney, 'Municipal Administration', p. 917.

137 *Proceedings at the Annual Distribution of Prizes* (1834) pp. 15–6. Lumsden lodged 25 guineas with the Corporation for the medals on 9 October 1834.

138 *ODNB*: Charles W. Munn.

139 James Hedderwick: *Backward Glances* (Edinburgh 1891) pp. 163–4. The statue of Lumsden was the first monument to be erected in the vicinity of the Cathedral. It was moved to its present site a few yards to the north-east in the 1990s when the Cathedral precinct was redesigned. McKenzie, *Public Sculpture*, pp. 61–2.

140 Lee, *Seekers of Truth*, p. 116.

141 *Ibid.* p. 115.

142 *MPHGM*.

143 S. Muthiah: *The Hindu* 4 June 2003.

144 *ODNB*: Martha McLaren; see also her *British India and British Scotland, 1780–1830* (Ohio 2001) pp. 21–6.

145 'The Stirrupless Majesty' sculpted by Francis Legatt Chantrey (1839) has Munro on horseback without saddle and stirrup, presumably because of his affinity for bareback riding.

146 He published an important history of the GS in 1825. His grandson, James Cleland Burns, republished it and had it brought up to 1878 by the Mathematical Master, Thomas Muir.

147 *ODNB*: Stana Nenadic.

148 McKenzie, *Public Sculpture*, p. 46.

149 *ODNB*: T.W. Bayne, revised by Douglas Brown.

150 In 1917, when the house system was established, one of the original names was Campbell, which was changed to Law in 1926–7.

151 Andrew Aird: *Glimpses of Old Glasgow* (Glasgow 1894) p. 34. He was in competition with his friend and admirer Sir Walter Scott.

152 *ODNB*: Geoffrey Carnall.

153 McKenzie, *Public Sculpture*, pp. 143–4.

CHAPTER FOUR

1 Gavin White: *The Scottish Episcopalian Church: A New History* (Glasgow 1998) ch. 7.

2 Robert Renwick (ed.), *Extracts*, vol. IX (1796–1808) (Glasgow 1914), p. 158.

3 Reaching 511 in 1805–6 over the four classes.

4 To 370 in 1809–10.

5 Calendar of High School Papers HS1/6.

6 Robert Renwick, *Extracts*, vol. X (1809–22) (Glasgow 1915), p. 245.

7 *Ibid.* pp. 256 and 264.

8 *Ibid.* pp. 536–7.

9 The basement floor was 15 feet high, and the upper floor 14 feet high.

10 The prizes would be given out in the Justiciary Court Hall.

11 Calendar HS17/1.

12 The TC hoped that the existing GS building could be sold in public roup at an upset of £2,200. Renwick, *Extracts*, vol. IX (1914), pp. 600–2. However, there was no offer forthcoming for the property so the Council rented out some rooms meantime. Renwick, *Extracts*, vol. X, pp. 587 and 590. Eventually in November 1827 an offer was made for the old GS buildings fronting George Street and they were sold to Anderson's College in March 1828 for £3,000. Robert Renwick (ed.), *Extracts*, vol. XI (1823–33) (Glasgow 1916), pp. 272 and 278. Butt, *John Anderson's Legacy*, p. 41.

13 Renwick, *Extracts*, vol. X (1915), pp. 560–1, 565, 569, 587 and 590.

14 Each boy was presented with a card commemorating the laying of the foundation stone by Alston on 16 August 1820 and the opening 'for the purpose of education' on 17 July 1821.

15 *GHerald* 20 July 1821.

16 Renwick, *Extracts*, vol. IX (1914), pp. 162 and 167. *Reports from Committees of Council 1799–1803* p. 197.

17 Renwick, *Extracts*, vol. X (1915), p. 149.

18 *Ibid.* pp. xxi and 228.

19 The Town Council could afford to be generous: it only contributed £10, the remaining £50 was to be paid for by his successor. Renwick, *Extracts*, vol. IX (1914), pp. 463, 465 and 477–8.

20 Calendar HS16/3

21 Some of these were already operating.

22 Cleland, *Historical Account*, 1825, p. 16.

23 Renwick, *Extracts*, vol. IX (1914), pp. 597–8.

24 In correspondence on 2 September 1820 Dymock described himself as 'a hot Tory' who 'abominate[s] the whole Whiggish opinions'. James Wilson from Strathaven, one of the leaders of the 'Radical Rising' of 1820, had been executed at Glasgow three days before and Dymock held that 'hundreds more would be better for undergoing the same process'. Calendar HS15/2.

25 Renwick, *Extracts*, vol. IX (1914), pp. 626, 632–3 and 672. Renwick, *Extracts*, vol. X (1915), p. 1. *Glasgow Courier* 19 January 1809.

26 The last survivor, Edward Alexander (of Messrs. Corbet, Alexander & Co) died in March 1876. James Tassie, glover, presented a Ramshorn snuffbox to the meeting in 1818 on condition it became the property of the last survivor.

27 For an account of the class meetings see Cleland, *Historical Account*, 1825, pp. 53–5; *Journal of the Statistical Society of London* vol. 18 pp. 364–366.

28 Renwick, *Extracts*, vol. X (1915), pp. 172– 3. GTCAB vol. 50 p. 159ff (6 April 1813) and p. 169 (30 April 1813).

29 Detention therefore was not allowed. Minutes of GSC (1812–7) p. 66.

30 Calendar HS16/4; GTCAB vol. 51 p. 64 (4 November 1814).

31 GTCAB vol. 51 p. 107ff (6 December 1814).

32 Renwick, *Extracts*, vol. X (1915), pp. 266 and 274–5.

33 *Ibid.* p. 293.

34 GTCAB vol. 51 p. 193 (4 April 1815).

35 Renwick, *Extracts*, vol. X (1915), p. 299. GTCAB vol. 51 p. 220 (30 May 1815).

36 Renwick, *Extracts*, vol. X (1915), p. 305. GTCAB vol. 51 p. 247 (18 August 1815).
    Lorrain sent his son, Walter, to the GS. Walter was awarded the Corporation
    Silver Medal for the best specimen of penmanship in 1821–2.

37 Renwick, *Extracts*, vol. X (1915), pp. 325–6.

38 *Ibid.* pp. 332–3.

39 Described by Cleland, *Historical Account*, 1825, p. 18 as a 'commodious lodge'.

40 It cost £280 4s 8d to build.

41 He was to be a married man between 30 and 45. His principal duties were to
    preserve order among the boys out of doors and keep the School and
    playground clean. *Glasgow Courier* 5 June 1817. His emoluments depended
    wholly on collecting one shilling from each pupil. With the roll healthy he
    made £27 in his first year. Numbers, however, dropped and in recompense the
    GS Committee in 1828 awarded him a salary of ten guineas and a fee of one
    shilling and six pence per pupil.

42 Renwick, *Extracts*, vol. X (1915), pp. 338, 342, 351, and 398. Allison had
    formerly been a sergeant in the artillery. He retired in June 1842 when he
    could no longer do his job through old age.

43 From 8 to 9 in the morning, 12 to 1 and 3 to 4 in the afternoon.

44 Renwick, *Extracts*, vol. X (1915), p. 352. This arrangement was to result in adverse
    comments as some pupils spent an inordinate amount of time in the Writing class.

45 *Ibid.* p. 571.

46 *GHerald* 9 October 1820.

47 Renwick, *Extracts*, vol. X (1915), pp. 581–2. *Glasgow Courier* 3 October 1820.

48 Renwick, *Extracts*, vol. X (1915), pp. 613, 615–6.

49 William Pyper (1797–1861) had a distinguished university record in Aberdeen
    before becoming parish schoolmaster in Laurencekirk and Maybole. After his
    time at the Grammar School he joined the staff of the High School in
    Edinburgh, a post he retained for twenty two years. Proving himself an
    excellent Latinist and a thorough classical scholar he was a significant loss to
    the GS. In 1844 he was appointed professor of humanity at St. Andrews
    University, gaining a reputation as an admirable professor. *ODNB*: C.A. Creffield.

50 Renwick, *Extracts*, vol. X (1915), p. 653. It took until March 1824 before
    Cowan was completely relieved of the Gibson burden of paying him £100 p.a.
    out of his own pocket. Renwick, *Extracts*, vol. XI (1916), p. 87.

51 Calendar HS6/16 and HS9/1–2.

52 Based again on Edinburgh's HS, which had formed a library in 1801 when
    George Grindlay had left his books and maps to the school.

53 He made his gift when he ceased to be a member of the Council.

54 Renwick, *Extracts*, vol. XI (1916), p. 16. Paul announced at the prize-giving in
    September 1835 that the library had almost doubled to nearly 1000 books.
    The TC agreed on 26 February 1836 to give £150 to the library, the annual

income of which was to go to purchasing books. Despite this there was no sign of a library operating in 1868.

55 Renwick, *Extracts*, vol. X (1915), p. 711 (6 and 26 December 1822).

56 *Ibid.* p. 649.

57 Calendar HS14/6 (22 December 1825).

58 Renwick, *Extracts*, vol. XI (1916), pp. 190–1, 198–9.

59 *Ibid.* p. 241.

60 The study of poetic metre and versification.

61 Cleland, *Historical Account*, 1825, p. 25. These prizes were eventually discontinued as the 'boys used to present themselves muffled up and go back to bed in order to get an attendance recorded, and so not miss the prize.' Calendar HS 2/14, 2/25, 2/35, 2/39, 3/9, 5/22.

62 His brother, Robert, was runner-up in the same classes.

63 Cleland, *Historical Account*, 1825, p. 37. Fourteen boys gained a dux prize in three years and twenty-six in two years.

64 William Arnot: *Memoir of the Late James Halley A.B. Student of Theology* (2nd edn Edinburgh 1842).

65 J. Sheridan Knowles (1784–1862) was a playwright and actor who completed a degree in medicine at Aberdeen University before opening a school in Belfast. He moved to Glasgow in 1816, where he established and ran a school for nearly twelve years. In 1823–4 he conducted the literary department of the *Free Press* which advocated liberal and social reform and it was then he wrote the educational articles. *ODNB:* Peter Thomson.

66 9 April 1823; 16 April 1823; and 7 May 1823.

67 Numbers were to decline from 516 in 1823 to 398 in 1827. According to Cleland this was a result of growing distaste for public education of boys in early youth in so large a school as the GS. Calendar HS1/6 and HS14/1.

68 Calendar HS14/1 (18 January 1825). Thomas Muir: 'Sketch of the History of the Grammar School from 1825 to the Present Time', p. 55 in Cleland (ed. Burns), *History*.

69 1781–1849. McFarlan moved to St Enoch's in November 1825.

70 Calendar HS14/2 (17 August 1825).

71 *Ibid.*

72 Nonetheless, when masters and GSC agreed in November 1825 given the 'thin' numbers attending the eight diets of examinations to reduce them to four the Principal of the University, Duncan Macfarlan (1771–1857), objected. His opposition led to the dropping of the proposal. The annoyance of masters and GSC was heightened by their knowledge of the irregular attendance of University professors at the exams. Calendar HS4/1.

73 Calendar HS1/2.

74 Murray, *History of Royal High*, p. 46.

75 Between 1827 and 1833 its Convener was Donald Cuthbertson.

76 GS Committee Minutes 23 October 1828; 25 November 1828; 1 January 1829; 8 May 1829; 4 August 1829.

77 Renwick, *Extracts*, vol. XI (1916), pp. 344–5.

78 Calendar HS7/8b.

79 1802–71 student of divinity, former dux of the GS, 1816–7. 'Many university

students spent their vacations teaching, and when they were later licensed for the Church, came back to a school while they awaited a charge.' Scotland, *History of Scottish Education*, p. 218.

80 Renwick, *Extracts*, vol. XI (1916), p. 345.

81 *GHerald* 11 June 1830.

82 *Ibid.* 14 June 1830.

83 The work of Angus Fletcher.

84 Of Chrystal's five sons – William, James, Andrew, Alexander and Robert – all but the eldest attended the School, and the four boys were in their father's Fifth Form class. Robert H. Small Papers, box 1.

85 *Scots Times* 8 May 1832 p. 295. In the early years of the 20th century the statue was removed from the Cathedral to the School building in Elmbank Street, leaving a small bronze plaque with inscription on the wall of the North Transept. In August 1996 with the approval of Historic Scotland and Strathclyde Regional Council (and the City of Glasgow Council) the statue and memorial stone were dismantled into fourteen pieces and then reassembled in the Entrance Hall at Anniesland.

86 Declining numbers were again a pressure for change: they dropped from 420 in 1828 to 293 the following year when the reduction to four classes was carried through. They continued to decline reaching 245 in 1831 before beginning to rise again. Calendar HS1/6.

87 Rowlatt proved 'an admirable scholar and teacher' but he had a 'savage temper and powerful physique'. J.O. Mitchell letter to *GHerald* dated 11 January 1902. His 1834 Class was composed of 109 boys and without an assistant 'the constant presence of a nippy little cane, not infrequently applied, helped largely to maintain discipline'. HSGM April 1903 p. 5.

88 Despite the ongoing problems even Rectors of other grammar schools applied, showing how highly a post at *the* GS was prized.

89 Opened following criticism of the Edinburgh High School's large classes and distance from the New Town.

90 Belfast Academy was criticised for not having an extensive curriculum so the new institution was opened.

91 Calendar HS6/13 (4 September 1834). Muir, 'Sketch', p. 58.

92 Calendar HS17/2 Appendix I.

93 With a retiring allowance of £100 per annum.

94 His *Bibliotheca Classica* was especially valued.

95 *Glasgow Courier* 3 October 1826.

96 Altogether throughout the course 155 pupils were enrolled; the average attendance was 132, and the greatest number at any one time was 137.

97 *Sketch and Catalogue of Mr Douie's Second Class, with Added Supplement* (Glasgow 1852).

98 *GHerald* 13 October 1828.

99 Withrington, 'Schools and Schooling', pp. 563–5.

100 H.M. Knox: *Two Hundred and Fifty Years of Scottish Education 1696–1946* (Edinburgh 1953) pp. 13–14.

101 It owed much to the model of the dissenting academies of England. Law, *Education in Edinburgh*, p. 227.

102 John F. McCaffrey: 'Political Issues and Developments' in W. Hamish Fraser and Irene Maver: *Glasgow Vol. II, 1830–1912* (Manchester 1996) p. 191.

103 R.H. Campbell: 'The Making of the Industrial City' in Fraser and Maver, *Glasgow, Vol. II*, pp. 201–2.

104 *Sketch and Catalogue* (1852).

105 *ODNB*: Jane Potter.

106 *ODNB*: J.K. Laughton, revised by Anthony Steven.

107 *MPHGM*.

108 *MPHGM*.

109 *ODNB*: Anita McConnell.

110 *MPHGM*.

111 Richard H. Trainor: 'The Elite', p. 253. Sweeney, 'Municipal Administration', p. 887.

112 Sweeney, 'Municipal Administration', p. 858.

113 The empire ranked second only to the Bairds of Gartsherrie among the coal and iron dynasties of mid–nineteenth century Scotland. *ODNB*: Anthony Slaven.

114 *MPHGM*.

115 Sweeney, 'Municipal Administration', p. 917.

116 For ranking Dux on an average of five years.

117 *MPHGM*.

118 Elder (1824–69) was born in Glasgow and educated at the GS where his delicate constitution prevented him from gaining the full benefit. However, he proved a talented and hard-working pupil especially of Dr Connell, carrying off the principal mathematical prizes. He went on to attend civil engineering classes at Glasgow University. He was the son of David Elder, 'the father of marine engineering on the Clyde'. McKenzie, *Public Sculpture*, p. 97. *MPHGM*.

119 *ODNB*: Michael S. Moss.

120 McKenzie, *Public Sculpture*, pp. 96–100.

121 Sweeney, 'Municipal Administration', p. 957.

122 *MPHGM*.

123 McKenzie, *Public Sculpture*, pp. 64–5.

124 Sweeney, 'Municipal Administration', p. 858.

125 *Ibid.* p. 854.

126 *Ibid.* pp. 875–6.

127 *ODNB*: John Trevitt.

128 McKenzie, *Public Sculpture*, pp. 165–6.

129 Gowans and Gray (Publishers): *The Lord Provosts of Glasgow from 1833 to 1902: Biographical Sketches* (Glasgow 1902). Trainor, 'The Elite', p. 243. Sweeney, 'Municipal Administration', p. 854.

130 Arnot: *Memoir*.

131 *ODNB* (2009): M.C. Curthoys.

132 His father had forfeited the Ardnave estate on Islay following the Jacobite Rebellion of 1745. Lawrence Shadwell: *The Life of Colin Campbell, Lord Clyde* (Edinburgh 1881) p. 2. See also Archibald Forbes: *Colin Campbell. Lord Clyde* (London 1895) p. 4 ff.

133 When the HS introduced a House system in 1917 one of the four houses was called Clyde House.

134 The battalion to which Campbell was attached took no active part in either of

these engagements. However, it seems possible that he was present at the burial of Sir John Moore.

135 *ODNB*: Roger T. Stearn.

136 GTCAB vol. 67 (29 November 1855).

137 He was nicknamed 'Old Careful'.

138 The Glasgow statue, executed by John Harry Foley (1868) is to be found in George Square, where it was deemed a suitable companion to Moore's statue. It shows Clyde as the Indian army commander leaning on the stump of a palm tree. McKenzie, *Public Sculpture*, pp. 136–9.

139 *Ibid.* On 2 June 1981 Sir Robert Maclean donated the cost of purchasing for the School the sword of Lord Clyde. It was an 1831 Mameluke hilt sabre general officer's dress sword, with a magnificent early Indian blade.

140 *MPHGM.*

141 *ODNB*: Anita McConnell.

142 *MPHGM.*

143 *MPHGM.*

144 *ODNB*: Andrew Grout.

145 *MPHGM.*

146 *ODNB*: Michael S. Moss.

147 *ODNB*: Sinead Agnew.

148 *MPHGM.*

149 The Act instituted a system of special courts to review disputes relating to voter qualifications.

150 *WWW* (from 1897 on).

151 It consisted of 145 pupils and included (later professor) John Towers.

152 F.L.M. Pattison: *Granville Sharp Pattison: Anatomist and Antagonist 1791–1851* (Edinburgh 1987) p. 9. His biographer held him to be a slow starter, unwilling to learn what didn't interest him. His only prize at school was in 1803 when he gained one of the 58 attendance prizes awarded in his class. He was always in the bottom half of the class and left in November 1804 when 87th out of 104 boys. *Ibid.* p. 12.

153 On 7 June 1814 in Edinburgh's High Court.

154 His speech impediment and monotonous and screeching delivery did not help matters.

155 *ODNB*: Andrew Hull. F.L.M. Pattison, *Granville Sharp Pattison*, gives a far less flattering appraisal of him.

156 Butt, *John Anderson's Legacy*, p. 57 held him to be an 'inspired' choice, despite Graham being unable to maintain discipline and having expository powers 'not of a high order'. One of his students was David Livingstone (1813–73), medical missionary and explorer.

157 At constant pressure, the rate of diffusion of a gas is inversely proportional to the square root of its density.

158 *ODNB*: Michael Stanley.

159 Butt, *John Anderson's Legacy*, p. 57.

160 Graham is a seated and gowned figure. The statue was by William Brodie (1872). McKenzie, *Public Sculpture*, pp. 139–40.

161 *ODNB*: K.D. Watson.

162 Robert Chambers: *A Biographical Dictionary of Eminent Scotsmen* (Edinburgh 1855) p. 228ff.

163 *ODNB*: Andrew Grout.

164 He supported Darwin's claim to priority when Alfred Russel Wallace published his own theory of the transmutation of species in 1858. This led Darwin to produce a shortened and more accessible version of the *Origin of Species* in 1859.

165 Especially cotton, timber, spices, indigo and other dyes.

166 *ODNB*: Jim Endersby.

167 The list of his publications fills twenty pages; the list of his honours fills ten pages. The Order, which was founded in 1902, had already being awarded to another HS Former Pupil, Viscount Bryce.

168 *ODNB*: Christopher Hamlin.

169 *MPHGM*.

170 He was fifty-third on 11 October 1830 and then fifth in the public examination on 25 November of the same year.

171 *ODNB*: Ben Marsden.

172 *Ibid.*

173 *ODNB*: David W. Savage.

174 *MPHGM*. Lee, *Seekers of Truth*, pp. 208–9.

175 James McClelland.

176 *MPHGM*.

177 *ODNB*: Iain F. Russell.

178 *Australian Dictionary of Biography* (Online).

179 Stone battles with the town boys. Andrew Lang: *Life and Letters of John Gibson Lockhart* (London 1897) 2 vols.

180 *GHerald* 1 December 1854.

181 *ODNB*: Thomas C. Richardson.

182 *MPHGM*.

183 *ODNB*: George Fairfull Smith.

184 McKenzie, *Public Sculpture*, p. 458.

185 He was the third son of James Dennistoun of Golfhill (1752–1835) and brother of Alexander and John.

186 *ODNB*: Christopher Lloyd.

187 This class held its first anniversary dinner in 1829 and its last in 1851. Its total roll was 104.

188 *ODNB*: Dianne King, referring to the opinion of the *Illustrated London News* on 17 August 1855.

189 *WWBMP* vol. 1.

190 *Glasgow Directory* of 1803 p. 13.

191 *Scots Magazine* vol. 2, June 1818, p. 584.

192 *Glasgow Chronicle* Thursday 4 June 1818, p. 2.

CHAPTER FIVE

1 The apostrophe appears to have been added to his name just as he arrived at the HS.

2 Born 1804, Connell was educated at Kilmarnock Academy and St Andrews University.

3 Connell made an arrangement with Adam Stevenson for the Writing master to turn all his Arithmetic teaching over to the Mathematics department. This left Stevenson, who had been teaching Writing to boys learning Latin in the GS since 1817, free to attract to his classes pupils who wished to study Writing on its own.

4 Originally from Geneva.

5 Lorrain claimed that the Latin classes made as much progress in the first year under the three hours of the new system as they had the previous year under the four hours of the old system.

6 On TC 1833–8 and 1846–9.

7 Dean of Guild 1833–4 and Councillor 1834–42.

8 Councillor 1833–9.

9 A lecturer at the Mechanics' Institute.

10 The teaching of Chemistry effectively lapsed from 1842, but Experimental Science became the department of Natural Science under William Keddie between 1867 and 1878.

11 An attempt to reintroduce the languages failed in June 1851 (HSE Minutes March 1844 to May 1873 p. 29). It was decided in 1844 not to offer phonography (a writing system that represents sounds by individual symbols) because it was not considered to be an ordinary branch of education. *Ibid.* p.8.

12 His successor's annual salary of £50 was to be withheld until after the death of one or other of the existing annuitants (Dymock, Douie or Lorrain).

13 1806–67.

14 A.D. Bache: *Report on Education in Europe* (Philadelphia 1839).

15 *Ibid.* p. 375.

16 References in this paragraph *Ibid.* pp. 375–8.

17 M. Odgers: *Alexander Dallas Bache* (Philadelphia 1947) p. 9.

18 Formerly a master at Ayr Academy, Rowlatt was given leave to take a Cambridge degree and left soon after.

19 Known to the boys as 'Bleezer'. He was Vice-President of the EIS.

20 He had joined the staff in 1836 from Dunfermline GS.

21 He was unanimously chosen from a shortlist of eight, which included two Cambridge men, and the Rectors of Paisley GS and Arbroath Academy. HSE p. 9.

22 *GHerald* 10 September 1852.

23 Recommended by the HSC on 23 May 1866. HSE p. 82.

24 Cleland, *Historical Account*, 1825, p. 36. Following this achievement he won fourteen prizes at Glasgow University between 1827 and 1830.

25 Together with Low, in an attempt to increase both their salaries, McKindlay made a vain attempt to take over the teaching of Geography in 1846. HSE pp. 12–15.

26 His public funeral, following his death in 1869, saw 300 of his former pupils walking in front of the hearse all the way to Old Gorbals cemetery. Behind them came the classes he was teaching when he died, the senior boys, a large number of parents and public representatives, the masters of the School and the Lord Provost. Thirty-five years later some former pupils erected over his grave a monument with the inscription: 'Dr McKindlay still lives in the affectionate memory of his scholars – March 1901.'

27 For session 1864–5, 799. Cleland (ed. Burns), *History*, p. 63.

28 HSE p. 91ff.

29 *Ibid.*

30 *Ibid* pp. 102–3. Kemp died early, aged 46, in June 1873.

31 D'Orsey (1812–1894) was the son of a Warwickshire schoolmaster and was educated at London and Glasgow Universities. He taught at Croy Place Academy and Dunlop Street Academy before joining the HS.

32 It was his custom to teach from 9 a.m. until 5 p.m., with no interval for food or relaxation.

33 GTCAB vol. 61 (16 August 1838).

34 His evidence covered Scotland, especially Glasgow. He had previously taught in Mechanics' Institutes and Sunday Schools and thought the standard of education in Glasgow was in decline. At the HS he claimed new methods of education were being attempted, with the boys taught to use their judgement not just their memories. He hoped that classes could be organised on Saturday evenings to provide an alternative to those who frequented public houses.

35 *Glasgow Argus* 4 and 11 November 1839.

36 A quote from D'Orsey's speech given in 1884 at a dinner given by the HS Club to mark his jubilee. This probably explains how he was able to introduce Physiology, which became one of the subjects he taught.

37 HSE p. 3.

38 He produced *A Duodecimo Grammar in Two Parts* (Edinburgh 1842) and *An Introduction to English Grammar* (Edinburgh 1845).

39 In 1845 Bishop Michael Russell of Glasgow and Galloway suggested ordination to D'Orsey, who worked part-time in the slums of Anderston, which had recently become an industrial suburb of Glasgow with significant numbers of Irish and English immigrants.

40 Coughing up blood-streaked mucus.

41 HSE p. 27.

42 *Ibid.* pp. 28–9.

43 GTCAB series 1 vols 66 and 67: 26 February 1852; 3 March 1853; 12 May 1853; 31 August 1854 and 21 September 1854. *GHerald* (same dates). D'Orsey had asked for a retiring allowance of £200 p.a.

44 From 1856–7 he was a chaplain in Madeira; 1860–4 Chaplain and Lecturer in History in Corpus Christi, Cambridge; 1864–84 he was a lecturer in Elocution at King's College School, Canterbury. See Lynda Mugglestone: *Talking Proper: The Rise of Accent as Social Symbol* (Oxford 2003) p. 237. He was then Lecturer of Public Reading and Speaking at King's College, London. He produced a number of books for tourists and visitors to Portuguese-speaking countries, including *Colloquial Portuguese; Or the Words and Phrases of Every-day Life* (London 1868) and other significant works such as *Portuguese Discoveries, Dependencies and Missions in Asia and Africa* (London 1893). He also wrote on religious matters.

45 The Glasgow newspapers, following an article in the *Reformers' Gazette*, all carried the story. Pearson admitted to having doubts about his fitness for duty, claiming his mind had been unhinged by malicious and groundless slanders. HSE pp. 45–7.

46 *Ibid.* pp. 59–60.

47 GTCAB vol. 64 (10 April 1846).

48 Connell also appears to have been respected by the boys and was singled out as 'the best teacher I ever had'. HSGM June 1902 p. 3.

49 HSE 13 March 1844 pp. 2–3.

50 From the twenty-five applicants the HSC at first chose Dr Abraham Hume from the Collegiate Institution, Liverpool. *Ibid.* p. 20.

51 *ODNB*: Anita McConnell.

52 In the spring of 1847 the masters of the HS called a meeting by private circular. Sixteen teachers met thereafter in Carrick's Hotel, and a week later in the HS. Within a month, Edinburgh teachers had been invited to take part and, in September, the EIS was founded.

53 Ashmall, *High School*, p. 88. There is a monument to him in Grange Cemetery, Edinburgh.

54 Report of Examiners, 1874–5 p. 1.

55 Calendar HS 17/2 Appendix 1 (17 and 20 October 1835). Unfortunately all the documents are not extant.

56 Formerly a soldier in the Polish army, he came as a political refugee to Glasgow in the early 1830s. He was a private teacher in a house in John Street, next door to the HS, before joining its staff in 1836.

57 In total, 110 pupils studied French in June 1845.

58 There had been no German classes since 1837. Wolski told Assistant Commissioner Harvey in 1866 that never more than four pupils had enrolled for German, which made running a class uneconomic. Wolski retired in 1872 and M.C.A. Chardenal became the French Master. Some 173 boys took French in 1873, but of these only 35 took the advanced class. Chardenal resigned in 1877 following poor inspections and was succeeded by M. Lacaille.

59 To be replaced by J. Dalziel Maclean of the Edinburgh Academy. He had 452 boys taking Writing and 39 taking Book-keeping in 1873. HSE pp. 135–9.

60 *Testimonials in Favour of Mr J.A. Hutchison for the Situation of Drawing Master* (Glasgow 1843).

61 To Assistant Commissioner Harvey. Ashmall, *High School*, p. 131.

62 HSGM June 1948 p. 121. Although he described himself as a portrait painter, Hutchison exhibited in a wide range of subjects.

63 *Greenock Advertiser*, 16 May 1828 p. 3.

64 Ashmall, *High School*, p. 22.

65 Minute Book: HSE March 1844 to May 1873; 13 March 1844 .

66 The gymnasium was opened on 23 February 1868. It was designed by architect Carrick, and measured 33 feet square and 15 feet high. It cost under £500 to construct.

67 Minute Book: HSE March 1844 to May 1873 pp. 146–7.

68 *Ibid.* pp. 26 and 78.

69 Calendar HS11/1–15.

70 Leaving Latin to the GS/HS.

71 Cumming was one of the Classical masters at the new Edinburgh Academy from 1826. He was of some standing, becoming President of the EIS in 1849 and receiving an LLD, conferred by Glasgow University the following year.

He left the Academy to become an HMI in 1851.

72 Ian MacLeod: *The Glasgow Academy* (Glasgow 1997) pp. 1–10.

73 This had been suggested by Wolski in March 1851 as a practice common in Prussia instead of class prizes. However, it had been rejected. HSE p. 28.

74 *Ibid.* pp. 120–1.

75 Bell, Bryce, Hutchison (Art), Macnab and Wolski petitioned the Council on 7 March 1867.

76 GTCAB vol. 69 [1867] p. 63.

77 Hence the lack of salary for Macnab in 1841.

78 R.D. Anderson: *Education and Opportunity in Victorian Scotland: Schools and Universities* (Oxford 1983) pp. 103ff; R.D. Anderson: *Education and the Scottish People, 1750–1918* (Oxford 1995) pp. 50ff.

79 Marjorie Cruickshank: 'The Argyll Commission Report 1865–8: A Landmark in Scottish Education', *British Journal of Educational Studies* 15 no. 2 (June 1967) pp. 133–47.

80 An FP and a future Rector of Edinburgh Academy.

81 *Third Report of HM Commissioners Appointed to Inquire into the Schools in Scotland: Burgh and Middle-Class Schools*, no. 16 vol. I (Edinburgh 1868).

82 Appendix following the Second Report of the Argyll Commission on Elementary Schools (Edinburgh 1867) in British Parliamentary Papers (1867) vol. 14 Scotland Part 2 pp. 420–3.

83 *Ibid.* p. 420.

84 *Ibid.* p. 421.

85 In the High School in Edinburgh entry was determined by performance in Classics.

86 British Parliamentary Papers (1867) vol. 14 p. 422.

87 *Third Report* in British Parliamentary Papers (C.4011) (Edinburgh 1868) vol. II, The Special Reports: no. 53 Glasgow High School pp. 304–12.

88 *Third Report*, vol. I, p. 61. There was a complete absence of endowments or bursaries.

89 *Ibid.* p. 75. In fact, the comparison between costs at Glasgow High and Edinburgh High Schools were not so favourable to Glasgow when costs of the full curriculum were compared. *Ibid.* vol. II p. 309. Anderson, *Education and Opportunity*, p. 143.

90 *Third Report*, vol. II p. 306.

91 At this time Scotland was also visited by an English school inspector, D.R. Fearon, who reported on secondary schools to the Schools Inquiry (Taunton) Commission for England. He visited only sixteen leading schools and from these collected information about the social background of the pupils. Taunton vol. VI: Burgh Schools in Scotland (1868) P.P. 1867/8, xxviii, part 5. It was clear that by the late 1860s the upper class had long since ceased to use the burgh schools and the wealthier professional and business classes were already attracted to the English public schools. Argyll Commission *Third Report* vol. I pp. 26–7; Anderson, *Education and Opportunity*, pp. 134–9.

92 The numbers enrolled were Classics 271; English 478; Mathematics (Commercial) 528; French 152; Writing/Book-keeping 460 and Drawing/Painting 90.

93 *Third Report*, vol. II, p. 309. Low (Classics), Bryce (Mathematics), Bell (English) and Macnab (Writing) were all particularly praised.

94 *Ibid.* p. 312.

95 Named as Old and New Grammar Schools of Aberdeen; the Academy and HS in Edinburgh; Glenalmond College and the Aberdeen Gymnasium.

96 Knox, *Two Hundred and Fifty Years*, p. 70.

97 Sir Henry Craik later wrote critically of his time at the HS (1857–60), claiming that most of its best features had been lost and it had declined into humdrum routine. HSGM December 1916 pp. 3–5.

98 Cruickshank, 'Argyll Commission Report', p. 147.

99 He quoted the *Evening Citizen* of 1845.

100 Including the trial of the City of Glasgow Directors, the Sandyford Place murder case, and the famous Yelverton case.

101 HSGM April 1925 pp. 112–16.

102 HSGM April 1924, pp. 68–70.

103 HSGM December 1913 pp. 32–3.

104 *GHerald* 18 October 1889.

105 HSGM June 1913 pp. 93–7 and 114–15. *Glasgow Evening News* 19 October 1891. HSGM March 1933 pp. 87–9.

106 HSGM January 1925 pp. 16–18.

107 Its first President (1870–2), William Arthur, was Lord Provost of Glasgow, as were the next two (Sir James Watson (1873–5) and Sir John Bain (1876–7)). Its first Senior Vice-President was Robert Dalglish MP and the first Junior Vice-President was Rev. J.W. Borland.

108 Form III (1916–17) held its last dinner in November 1975.

109 According to Asquith, the prime minister, Bryce was the 'best educated' among his generation of politicians.

110 *Taunton Vol. VI*, p. 23.

111 *ODNB*: Monica Clough.

112 Sweeney, 'Municipal Administration', p. 913.

113 *ODNB*: Iain F. Russell.

114 *Ibid.* p. 954.

115 Sweeney, 'Municipal Administration', p. 857.

116 Sweeney, 'Municipal Administration', p. 927.

117 *ODNB*: Keith Grieves.

118 *ODNB*: Francis Goodall.

119 *ODNB*: Bill Gammage.

120 *ODNB*: N.J. Travis.

121 Butt, *John Anderson's Legacy*, p.102. Sweeney, 'Municipal Administration', p. 877.

122 Sweeney, 'Municipal Administration', p. 873.

123 *ODNB* (2010): Christopher Wood.

124 *ODNB*: Michael S. Moss.

125 *ODNB*: D.M. Murray.

126 *ODNB*: Rosemary Chadwick.

127 *ODNB*: H.C.G. Matthew. His son, Dr Adam Rainy, was Liberal MP for Kilmarnock Burghs, 1906–11.

128 He was Convener of the HSC.

129 *ODNB*: Donald C. Smith.

130 *ODNB*: Lionel Alexander Ritchie.

131 Lee, *Seekers of Truth*, p. 318.

132 *ODNB* (2009): Kathleen L. Lodwick.

133 Theologian James Denney.

134 Alison is seen as one of the quartet of soldiers from Glasgow, and the HS, who served the Empire. Sir Thomas Munro helped consolidate the British conquest of India; Sir John Moore was the victor of Corunna; Sir Colin Campbell, Lord Clyde, who may have been part of the party of the ninth Foot detailed to bury Moore, bequeathed on his death-bed direct to Sir Archibald Alison the traditions of Scottish military valour in the form of the sword which had been presented to him by the citizens of Glasgow.

135 *ODNB*: James Lunt.

136 *ODNB*: David M. Fahey.

137 Professing Jews could only obtain university medical degrees in Scotland before 1872 when the University Test Acts were repealed.

138 *ODNB*: Kenneth E. Collins.

139 O*DND*: Edna Robertson.

140 He always took a warm interest in the School and was President of the HS Club. HSGM December 1906 p. 25.

141 *ODNB*: Andrew Hull.

142 Butt, *John Anderson's Legacy*, p. 102.

143 *ODNB*: Gordon F. Millar.

144 *ODNB*: Elspeth Attwooll.

145 *ODNB*: David Weston.

146 *ODNB*: Margaret Deacon.

147 *ODNB*: Richard Smail. *GHerald* 16 August 1907.

148 *ODNB*: M.C. Curthoys.

149 *My Windows on The Street of the World* (London 1922) 2 vols vol. 1 p. 45ff. He endowed the Smart Prize at the HS.

150 *ODNB*: J. Mavor Moore.

151 Lee, *Seekers of Truth*, p. 157.

152 *Ibid.* p. 115.

153 *Ibid.* pp. 156–7.

154 *Ibid.* p. 154. Robert Gourlay's father, James (1804–75), was Convener of the Board of Management of the HS between 1850 and 1852.

155 *ODNB*: Gillian Sutherland.

156 *ODNB*: W. Ross Johnston.

157 *ODNB*: Marc Brodie.

158 Alexander Somerville Waugh: *A Scottish Liberal Perspective: A Centenary Commemoration of Sir Henry Campbell–Bannerman 1836–1908* (2008) privately published.

159 His extra surname was acquired as a condition of inheriting his maternal uncle's estate in 1871.

160 His class (1845–50) had a number of reunions, and he attended these in 1897 and 1898.

161 Although he was proficient in French, German and Italian, he took a Third in

Classics and was classed as a Senior Optime in Mathematics.

162 Bill Inglis holds that C-B 'revived the Liberal Party by his principled
opposition to the War', in 'Sir Henry Campbell-Bannerman and the Boer
War 1899–1902' *History Scotland* vol. 8 no. 4 (July/Aug 2008) pp. 42–8.

163 Before this election there were seven former HS pupils in Parliament (four
Unionists and three Liberals); after this election there were ten in Parliament
(two Unionists and eight Liberals).

164 C-B's statue by Paul Raphael Montford (1868–1938) was unveiled by Asquith
near the Municipal Buildings in Stirling in November 1913. His bronze bust
(also by Montford) is found in Westminster Abbey, and a bronze plaque by
Benno Schotz (1891–1984) is situated in the HS. A bronze plaque was also
erected at 129 Bath Street, the Campbell-Bannerman Glasgow home from
1836 to 1860, and unveiled by David Steel, former leader of the Liberal Party,
in December 2008.

165 *ODNB*: A.J.A. Morris. HSGM C-B Centenary Edition, June 1948.

166 *ODNB*: Christopher Harvie.

167 He was the classmate of Dr Hutchison in Mackindlay's Latin Class of 1855–60.

168 *ODNB*: Gordon F. Millar.

169 He was later critical of his education and suggested that a relatively accurate
picture of life in the HS could be gained from *A Hero* (published in 1852)
written by Dinah Craig (1826–1887) who was an inmate in his father's
household. It was held to be drab and humdrum, and the teaching was
uninspired. Classical Masters were of some calibre, however, and Dr Bryce
had a 'personality of keen and incisive force'.

170 *ODNB*: R.D. Anderson.

171 He gained a French prize and his reports were generally good, although his hand-
writing was said to be atrocious. R.J.Q. Adams: *Bonar Law* (London 1999) p.7.

172 In 1926–7 the High School renamed one of its four Houses 'Law House'.

173 Blackfriars' Division.

174 *ODNB*: E.H.H. Green.

175 *ODNB*: Deborah E.B. Weiner.

176 Regarding Low as 'the kindest of schoolmasters' Harriet Jay: *Robert Buchanan*
(London 1903).

177 *ODNB*: J.P. Whelan.

178 *ODNB*: Rohan McWilliam.

179 *ODNB*: Geoffrey K. Brandwood.

180 Sir James L. Caw: *Sir James Guthrie: A Biography* (London 1932) p. 4.

181 *ODNB*: Tom Normand.

182 *Ibid.*

CHAPTER SIX

1 A large number of the voluntary schools were not state-aided.

2 Withrington, 'Schools and Schooling', pp. 563–5; Robert Anderson: 'The History
of Scottish Education, pre-1980' in T.G.K. Bryce & W.M. Humes (eds): *Scottish
Education: Beyond Devolution* 3rd edition (Edinburgh 2008) pp. 205–14.

3 In England and Wales, the 1870 Education Act inaugurated a rivalry between Board and church schools which required further legislation in 1902 and 1944.

4 Renamed Scottish in 1918.

5 Craik was Secretary 1885–1904; Struthers was Secretary 1904–21.

6 Mary E. Finn: 'Social Efficiency Progressivism and Secondary Education in Scotland, 1885–1905' pp. 175–96; and H.M. Paterson: Incubus and Ideology: The Development of Secondary Schooling in Scotland, 1900–1939' pp. 197–215, both in Walter M. Humes and Hamish M. Paterson (eds): *Scottish Culture and Scottish Education 1800–1980* (Edinburgh 1983).

7 Eleven of Scotland's fifteen burgh schools, including the High School, were transferred. Scotland, *History of Scottish Education,* p. 365.

8 Ten years earlier than in England.

9 Lindsay Paterson: 'Schools and Schooling: Mass Education, 1872 to Present' in M. Lynch (ed.), *Oxford Companion,* pp. 566–9.

10 Anderson, *Education and Opportunity,* pp. 108–9.

11 Sir John N. Cuthbertson: *Secondary Education from the School Board Point of View* (Glasgow 1887).

12 At the Finance Committee of the TC on 17 December 1873 it was intimated that the average annual expenditure on the HS in the last thirty years had been £524 p.a. It was agreed on 26 January 1874 to pay £570 p.a. to the HS annually.

13 Although existing and retired staff were to have rights of usage respected.

14 James M. Roxburgh: *The School Board of Glasgow 1873–1919* (London 1971) p. 56.

15 The most detailed report on the inadequate accommodation was probably that of HSC of 5 May 1869. HSE pp. 141–4.

16 An east wing was added with rooms for English and Classical departments, and a spacious Writing room was built in a corner of the playground separate from the main building. A west wing followed in 1874–5 to provide additional rooms for the Mathematics and Drawing departments.

17 Drill was taken by Sergeant McNeil.

18 Annual Report of University Examiners (1875–6), p. 1, saw this as 'an evil which has assumed gigantic proportions in Glasgow'.

19 HSGP 1874–5 pp. 5–13.

20 MSB vol. 1 pp. 84–85.

21 Colebrooke Commission (Scotland): Appendix to Third Report of Royal Commission into Endowed Schools and Hospitals (1875) Appendix, vol. 1, pp. 327–61.

22 Copper-plate writing.

23 Fifty boys spent seven years with the subject (five hours a week).

24 Colebrooke Commission, Appendix, pp. 327–8.

25 *Ibid.* pp. 328–37.

26 *Ibid.* p. 343.

27 *Ibid.* p. 345.

28 *Ibid.* pp. 346–9.

29 *Ibid.* pp. 350–1.

30 *Ibid.* p. 352.

31 *Ibid.* pp. 353–4.

32 MSB vol. 1 pp. 152–7.

33 See comments in the *Bailie* 14 April 1875 p. 6; 21 April 1875 p. 3; 28 April 1875 p. 6; 12 May 1875 p. 7; and the article 'Pleasures of Hope', 19 May 1875 p. 7. The *Bailie* made a plea to restrict education to elementary branches, seeing anything beyond it as 'utterly superfluous' (14 April 1875). Further comments on 30 June 1875 p. 6.

34 The other being on Holland Street.

35 The 'reasonable' figure suggested was partly to ensure that the SB would take on the Academy staff. In the event this proved unnecessary, as the Academy survived under a new company and a new school was built for it in a central location in Belmont Street.

36 Following the receipt of a valuation figure of £33,000.

37 MSB vol. 1 p. 401.

38 Wilson had been dead for fifteen years by the time the statues were created, so presumably the choice of historical figures was determined by Mossman, in consultation with the SB members.

39 The statues were finally erected on 13 January 1879. MSB vol. 2 p. 12. The four statues are raised on rusticated piers projecting from the centre of the west frontage, occupying the spaces between the first-floor windows. From the left they are: Cicero, first century AD Roman lawyer and orator, shown wearing a toga, with scroll in left hand and right arm extended as if addressing an audience (in 1956 the statue became dangerous and was replaced, somewhat smaller, at a cost of £1,200); Galileo (1564–1642), Italian astronomer and physicist, shown wearing Renaissance tunic and heavy robe, holding a telescope and a globe; James Watt (1736–1819), inventor and engineer, shown in contemporary dress holding a governor mechanism and a pair of dividers; and Homer, ancient blind Greek poet, presumed author of the *Odyssey* and *Iliad*, shown with face upturned and holding a lyre.

40 In the later nineteenth century Mossman's work appeared on almost all public buildings in Glasgow. Elizabeth Williamson, Anne Riches and Malcolm Higgs: *The Buildings of Scotland: Glasgow* (London 1990) pp. 71–2.

41 David Thomson addressing the Glasgow Philosophical Society. McKenzie, *Public Sculpture*, p. 109.

42 Chairman of the School Board between 1876 and 1882.

43 3 September 1878.

44 Annual Report of University Examiners (1878–9) p. 1.

45 MSB vol. 1 p. 409.

46 Hardie served as janitor from 1875 to 1902.

47 Tenth Annual Report of University Examiners (1882) p. 10.

48 Twelfth Annual Report of University Examiners p. 22.

49 Thirteenth Annual Report of University Examiners p. 19.

50 Fourteenth Annual Report of University Examiners (1885–6) p. 20.

51 MSB vol. 3. p. 239. All other school buildings erected in Glasgow in 1887 had a similar tablet.

52 *Ibid.* pp. 263 and 287.

53 Later 'D' Block.

54 Rector's Report to Board in HSGP 1901–2 p. 53. It was confined to room 15 in the beginning.

55 The HSC responded on 22 June 1901 by recommending the addition of an extra storey on the central building for lunches. MSB vol. 5 p. 41.

56 An additional high school came under the Board's authority in 1911 when Allan Glen's was transferred to it on condition that it would have equal status with the HS. The number of Higher Grade Schools increased to seven with the addition of North Kelvinside (for Maryhill) and Albert (for Springburn) also in 1911.

57 MSB vol. 2 pp. 182, 202–3, 333 and 414.

58 *Ibid.* p. 212.

59 The fees in 1892 ranged from £7 to £14 per annum. In 1894 the fees were £6 10s to £8 10s per annum. MSB vol. 4 p. 261.

60 *Ibid.* pp. 269–70.

61 The HS had a roll of 698 in 1893, and the HSfG had 418.

62 Taken at age seventeen with four passes at Higher Grade or three Highers and two Lowers. These had to include Higher English, Higher or Lower Mathematics, and either two languages (one of which had to be Latin) or a science and a language. Henry Philip: *The Higher Tradition* (Dalkeith 1992) p.43. Lindsay Paterson: *Scottish Education in the Twentieth Century* (Edinburgh 2003) p. 55.

63 The SED complained of this as late as 1903. Roxburgh, *School Board*, p. 115.

64 *GHerald* 27 April 1910.

65 £10 per annum.

66 Fourteenth Annual Report of University Examiners p. 15. Before an inspection visit, Paton would select some well-prepared passage and bend the book hard back at the place, so that it might open here, as if by accident, in the inspector's hand.

67 In 1899 he had published *Greek and Roman Heroes: A Selection from 'Plutarch's Lives'. Adapted for Reading in Higher Classes of Schools* (London).

68 HSGM December 1937 pp. 16–18.

69 HSGM December 1903 p. 3.

70 The HS rugby victory, over rivals Glasgow Academy, was held as 'astonishing'. HSGM December 1901 p. 6. The (Rugby) Football Club met at Whiteinch on Wednesdays and its 60 members had increased to 236 on two afternoons. HSGP 1902–3 p. 18.

71 Cricket was played at the West of Scotland ground at Hamilton Crescent.

72 Golf was open to all boys in the Senior School and to former pupils for four years after they had left School. Such measures helped improve relationships between the School and the Old Boys.

73 The School booked exclusive use of the Western Baths, Hillhead, for two afternoons in the week. Membership of the club numbered around 125, with teaching how to swim or play water-polo as priorities.

74 A popular Saturday afternoon activity attracting over 50 boys.

75 For stringed instruments and piano it was under former pupil Carl Gatow. It met on Tuesday afternoons and was also open to former pupils.

76 The oldest of the societies, founded in the 1888–9 session, it met every Friday after school. It numbered about 60 members and promoted an interest in literature and proficiency in public speaking. It established the first School Magazine (for pupils and former pupils) in February 1896. The Sixth Formers

involved were unaided by Master or Censor. This 'old Magazine' was replaced by a 'new magazine' in December 1901. See Bibliography.

77 The Society under Former Pupil Alexander Dykes had over 100 members (including former pupils) and was already giving annual concerts in the Queen's Rooms.

78 One of these was given by his close friend, J.L. Paton, headmaster of University College School, London. HSGP 1902–3 p.21.

79 It is most likely that the emphasis was on caps, for they were the item most affordable to all parents.

80 Nigel Watson: *A Tradition for Freedom: The Story of University College School* (London 2007) p. 39.

81 HSGM June 1910 p. 101.

82 Boys were expected to elect a boy of good sense and reliability, and the form master could reject a boy he deemed unsuitable.

83 Still supported today.

84 The SB summoned him to a meeting to explain his curricular proposals before agreeing to proceed. MSB vol. 5 p. 283.

85 Spenser's Third Report to SB 15 June 1903. HSGP 1903–04 p. 52.

86 To help ensure success Spenser persuaded the SB to pay all Form Teachers an additional £10 p.a. MSB vol. 6 p. 31.

87 Friedrich Froebel (1782–1852) was a German educator and founder of the kindergarten system.

88 English, Latin, Mathematics, Science, Drawing, Gymnastics, Singing and Games.

89 Boys who had no knowledge of Latin or were intending to leave at fourteen after two years in the Senior School were offered a course with French in place of Latin in Form I, and French and German in place of Latin and French in Form II.

90 H.C. Barnard: 'A Great Headmaster: John Lewis Paton (1863–1946)', *British Journal of Educational Studies* vol. 11 no. 1 (November 1962) pp. 5–15.

91 He remained headmaster of UCS until 1916 when, as a result of overwork, he took up a post as an examiner for the Board of Education. In 1920 he was appointed headmaster of High Pavement School in his home town of Nottingham, where he remained until his final retirement.

92 The Dr H.J. Spenser Memorial Plaque, the gift of George Pate and crafted by James Barr, was dedicated on 11 November 1955.

93 MSB vol. 7 pp. 175, 201, 208–9 and 232.

94 Now known as the University of Bangor.

95 J.Gwynn Williams: *The University College of North Wales: Foundations 1884–1927* (Cardiff 1985) p. 91. The French class usually numbered between 60 and 70 students, while the German class was tiny. *Ibid.* p. 137.

96 Miss Barrowman and Miss Guthrie, both Honours graduates of Glasgow University, joined its staff.

97 In the higher forms one period was taken from Latin and one from Greek. MSB vol. 8 p. 107.

98 Four verses were reproduced in the December 1903 Magazine. From an early date, only verses one and four were sung.

99 A bumbee tartan refers to a fabric woven like a tartan but one which is

designed with lack of taste and no sense of history. At the HS the cap consisted of horizontal stripes of navy blue and green, each about three-quarters of an inch wide, and a narrow stripe of white. It was never popular, hence its bumbee tartan name. However, it is now the basis for the FP tie.

100 Lord Londonderry was President of the newly created Board of Education and, after the passage of the English Education Act of 1902, inspection was extended and further inspectors were needed. MSB vol. 8 pp. 11–12. He was a Junior Inspector Class I during Morant's reorganisation of the Inspectorate in early 1905. National Archives: ED23/1/128 p. 20. Spencer died at Hove in April 1941 aged 80.

101 On 25 April and 5 May 1904.

102 MSB vol. 4 pp. 313–4.

103 *Bailie* 27 November 1904.

104 HSGM June 1910 p. 101.

105 Annual Report of Rector, June 1905. HSGP 1905–6 p. 50.

106 In 1908, 102 boys were judged by the HM Inspector fit to pass into secondary. HSGP 1908–9 p. 44.

107 Two additional science teachers were appointed. MSB vol. 11 p. 149.

108 MSB vol. 12 p. 330.

109 The Board had responded by refitting the gym with modern equipment.

110 *Ibid.* p. 423.

111 Minutes of Form Masters' meetings (1903–7).

112 MSB vol. 12 p. 498 and 562.

113 He was to be President of the HS Club between 1912 to 1919.

114 Commemorating the fiftieth anniversary of his appointment as Rector.

115 MSB vol. 13 p. 110.

116 The colours of chocolate and gold were introduced by Goodwin in 1911–12.

117 HSGP 1910–11 p. 16–17. The Corps was disbanded in 1974.

118 The English model.

119 By April 1915 they had become Keen, Chalmers, Taylor and Steel.

120 In 1926 Pinkerton changed Campbell to Law, keeping the others unchanged: Bannerman, Clyde and Moore.

121 The first SC was E.J.B. Lloyd, who was in office 1911–13. Thereafter the post was held for one year. Lloyd's immediate successors were distinguished at rugby: Arthur Browning (SC 1914–15), Russell L.H. Donald (SC 1916–17) and John M. Bannerman (SC 1919–20) were all capped for Scotland.

122 Roger Marjoribanks: *Emanuel at Wandsworth 1883–1983* (London 1983) pp. 16–18; C. Wilfrid Scott-Giles and Bernard V. Slater: *The History of Emanuel School 1594–1964* (London 1966 and 1977) pp. 125–38.

123 His tenure was also linked with Captain Scott's ill-fated British Antarctic Expedition (1910–13). Scott raised funds through a lecture tour and, encouraged by Goodwin, the boys of the School financed the pony sledge (named Glasgow).

124 He obtained a doctorate in 1909 for his thesis on 'The Relation of Geometry to Analysis'. He was joint author of *The Elements of Analytical Geometry*.

125 His salary was set at £650 p.a. NAS file ED18/3532.

126 Dates in brackets after names in this section are those that the individual spent on the staff of the HS.

127 HSGM December 1903 pp. 7–9.
128 Anderson left to become headmaster of Willowbank Public School in 1904.
129 HSGM June 1923 p. 121.
130 Classics was clearly still seen as the premier department in the School.
131 He was headmaster of Kilmarnock Academy.
132 A.D. Dunlop: *Hutchesons' Grammar: The History of a Glasgow School* (Glasgow 1992) pp. 89–99.
133 Murray, *History of Royal High.*
134 An Aberdonian with a broad accent.
135 Including *New Latin Course* (1910); *Something about Education* (1919); and *Latin for Beginners* (1929).
136 Born 1893; HS on bursary, 1904–10; his father was a clergyman.
137 In 1913 J.J. Robertson and, in 1916, H.R. Butters came first in the Competition. Butters was born in 1898, attended the HS 1909–16 and was School Dux, 1915–16; his father was a schoolmaster.
138 Halliday Sutherland: *A Time to Keep* (London 1934) p. 39.
139 Fourteenth Annual Report of University Examiners, p. 32. Barker's discipline was legendary 'yet he never punished a boy except by a look, or by a few words of righteous indignation'. Sutherland, *Time to Keep*, p. 33.
140 James Murray: *The History of Allan Glen's School and School Club 1853–2003* (Glasgow 2003) pp. 46–56.
141 A.J. Belford: *Centenary Handbook of the Educational Institute of Scotland* (Edinburgh 1946) p. 422.
142 (Sir) Thomas Muir (1844–1934) had been Mathematics tutor at St Andrews University (1868–71) and assistant Professor of Mathematics at Glasgow University (1871–4).
143 *Bailie* 13 April 1892.
144 Fifteenth Annual Report of University Examiners, p. 25.
145 *ODNB*: A.J. Crilly.
146 He was Censor of the Magazine for six years; secretary of the Form Masters' meetings; and convener of the Committee which superintended the 'formation of the register of Old Boys'.
147 A little-known H.G. Wells applied unsuccessfully for this post. H.G. Wells: *Experiment in Autobiography* (London 1934) vol. 1 pp. 239 and 292.
148 Where he had introduced Chemistry. Les Howie : *George Watson's College: An Illustrated History* (Edinburgh 2006) p. 54. Barclay was President of the Association of Teachers in Secondary Schools. The complete gentleman, he wore a tall hat and frock coat as his normal attire.
149 Born in British Guiana he gained FCH in Maths and Natural Philosophy (1905) before lecturing at Glasgow University.
150 Amours married the daughter of William Marr, the head of the Mathematics department in Glasgow Academy. He was called 'Mooshie' by the boys, a corruption of Monsieur.
151 He was also conductor of the School orchestra for a decade.
152 Herbert Ellicott came from Merchiston in 1904, and taught French and took rugby until 1920; he returned to the staff between 1926 and 1931.
153 HSGP 1906–7.

154 As a result of increasing deafness. MSB vol.7 p.231. He was author of the grammar the boys used in class.

155 Chalmers' early death in 1921 was put down to this.

156 His first spell at the HS.

157 *Fourteenth Annual Report of University Examiners*, p. 16.

158 Other subjects appeared in the curriculum but failed to establish themselves: Italian and Spanish (1887–8); Phonography (replaced by Shorthand in 1888–9); and Elocution (1890–1).

159 Ashmall, *High School*, pp. 108–9.

160 See chapter 8 for Miss Nina Logan. A third sister, Helen, taught in the School during session 1921–2.

161 *Chocolate and Gold: 100 Years of Rugby 1884–1984* (Glasgow 1984) p. 14.

162 Including H.M. Napier (5 caps, 1877–9) and David S. Morton (8 caps, 1887–90) (the first FP to become President of then Scottish Football Union in 1892–3).

163 He held the post from 1896 to 1939.

164 He attended the HS between 1885 and 1894. The first FP to play rugby for Scotland, he was President of the SRU in 1920–2.

165 Frew won 15 caps in 1906–11 and was the second FP captain of Scotland (against Wales in 1910).

166 Known as Skaterigg.

167 Robert Calder, HMI 1875–1903.

168 One of his sons, E. Martinez Alonso, later wrote an account of his time at the HS before the First World War: *Adventures of a Doctor* (London 1962).

169 *WWBMP* vol. 3.

170 *WWW*, 2009.

171 Square brackets contain material from the School Registers: dates of attendance at High School; father's occupation and any comment from Rector.

172 The largest private locomotive-building concern in Europe.

173 *ODNB*: Richard J. Finlay.

174 *ODNB*: Richard Davenport-Hines.

175 *ODNB*: Ann K. Newmark.

176 *ODNB*: Cindy L. Perry.

177 *ODNB*: T. Jack Thompson.

178 *ODNB*: Mary E. Gibson.

179 Sutherland, *Time to Keep*, p. 31.

180 *ODNB*: Harley Williams.

181 Charles Duguid: *Doctor Goes Walkabout* (Adelaide 1977); Michael Page: *Turning Points in the Making of Australia* (Adelaide 1980).

182 *ODNB*: Martin Gorsky.

183 Sir James Robertson, Chief Constable of Glasgow.

184 *ODNB*: Mark J. Schofield.

185 *ODNB*: K.D. Watson.

186 First bursar in 1913.

187 Lee, *Seekers of Truth*, pp. 238–9.

188 *ODNB*: John Richard Edwards.

189 *ODNB*: Robert M. Shackleton.

190 *ODNB*: John Cameron.

191 Lance Price: *Where Power Lies: Prime Ministers v. The Media* (London 2010) p. 47.
192 *ODNB*: Dilwyn Porter.
193 *ODNB*: George B. Kauffman.
194 *One Way of Living* (London 1939) p. 40.
195 *Ibid.* p. 105.
196 *ODNB* : David Hutchison.
197 *ODNB*: Robin Gibson.
198 *ODNB*: Robert A. Crampsey.
199 *ODNB*: Jeremy Dibble.
200 *ODNB*: Richard J. Finlay.
201 *ODNB*: Anne Pimlott Baker.
202 *Chocolate and Gold*, pp. 72–4.

CHAPTER SEVEN

1 These schools were labelled 'higher grade'.
2 Roxburgh, *School Board*, p. 129.
3 Earning between £120 and £350 a year they could afford and were willing to pay the annual fee set at between £3 and 4 guineas in 1887. This compared with a fee for the newly opened Hillhead Public School of between £5 and £6, and that of the High School at £8. The private Academies – Glasgow and Kelvinside – charged between £12 and £14.
4 Born in 1844, a native of Denny, Stirlingshire, Milligan served a pupil teachership at the parish school of Falkirk before going on to the Established Church Training College in Glasgow, from which he graduated with distinction. His first post was at St Andrew's parish school, before promotion to the headship of Mitchell School in Piccadily Street, Anderston between 1866 and 1875. He gained an MA from Glasgow University in 1875. He then took the post of Head in the difficult school of London Road, where he brought order out of chaos and gained the reputation which led him to become the Head at Garnethill Public School at its opening in August 1878.
5 Roxburgh, *School Board*, p. 134.
6 Letter from Milligan to SB dated 6 March 1884.
7 Roxburgh, *School Board*, p. 137.
8 Failure of the City of Glasgow Bank in 1879 contributed to the troubles of the two Academies.
9 Representatives of the academies bitterly attacked this as unfair, even as 'illegal', competition. The Parker Commission, however, although appreciating that the 1872 Act had not encouraged public schools to enter the secondary field, rejected these complaints. Parker Commission (C.5425) (1888) p. 62.
10 MacLeod, *Glasgow Academy*, p. 50; Colin H. Mackay: *Kelvinside Academy 1878–1978* (Glasgow 1978) p. 41.
11 1869–1947.
12 *ODNB* : Elizabeth Edwards. Other Garnethill pupils who made a mark were William M.R. Pringle (1874–1928), the Asquithian Liberal politician; Sir Muirhead Bone (1876–1953), printmaker and draughtsman, who became

Britian's first war artist in May 1916: Captain Sir David Bone (1873–1959), naval captain, who wrote about the severity of sea life; James Bone (1872–1962), London editor of the *Manchester Guardian* from 1912 until 1945; (Prof.) Archibald Main (1876–1947), professor of Ecclesiastical History at Glasgow University (1922–42); Abraham Levine (1870–1949) Fellow of Jesus College, Cambridge and President of the Institute of Actuaries; (Prof.) Arthur Ballantyne (1876–1954), Professor of Ophthalmic Surgery at Glasgow University (1935–41); and Jane Hamilton Patrick (1884–1971), the anarchist.

13 There were originally three levels awarded in the secondary Leaving Certificate, but the Honours level was dropped in 1906 as a concession to the universities, which believed it was interfering with their bursary competitions. Philip, *Higher Tradition*, pp. 55–6 and 60.

14 Garnethill Log Book 19 December 1898 p. 19. SB of Glasgow 'General Summary of Work, 1873–1903', 1903, p. 35.

15 The tradition in Scotland since the Reformation was co-educational, but from the mid-eighteenth century the growing Scottish middle class was increasingly critical of mixing social classes and genders. By the 1850s, influenced by the English preference for single-sex schools, private middle-class mixed-gender schools often split into two, but they were day as opposed to boarding. Moreover such schools were deemed sound, so reform was not as pressing as in England, where reformers sought education for girls appropriate to their separate spheres and social stations. There remained a pride in the Scottish tradition of universal education, including mixed-sex schooling. In September 1873 Cumnock SB rejected separate schooling for the sexes as being against Scottish custom, although cheaper cost was also a factor.

16 Jane McDermid: *The Schooling of Working-Class Girls in Victorian Scotland: Gender, Education and Identity* (Abingdon 2005) p. 58; John McMath: *Progress of School Building in Glasgow from 1873 to 1892* (Glasgow 1892) pp. 11–12, 17–18.

17 McDermid, *Schooling of Working-Class Girls*, p. 59. Garnethill Log Book, HMI Report 1900, p. 186. Garnethill Letter Book vol. 2 (1894–5) pp. 559, 640–2.

18 Garnethill Log Book, April 1895 pp. 1–4.

19 The boys were transferred to Albany Academy.

20 Again High School figures in brackets.

21 In 1894–5 the girls were taught for a short time by Miss Susan Kennedy, the first woman to take the degree of MA at the University of Edinburgh.

22 Before the hall was built, prizegivings were held in the Queen's Rooms, at the corner of Clifton Street and La Belle Place.

23 Kindergarten, Transition and One Junior.

24 Jubilee Magazine, June 1944 no. 29 p. 9. Although perhaps it should be stated that the writer, Isabel M. Milligan, could not be expected to be totally objective, as she was Dr Milligan's daughter.

25 Before the increase, fees were around 4 guineas per annum.

26 Very few boys were taught Greek.

27 The earliest prospectuses set out four separate courses of instruction: Classical, Modern, Scientific and Commercial.

28 Garnethill Letter Book vol. 3 (1895–98) pp. 910–12. Evidence from the later 1890s suggests that Glasgow University had considerably more women

studying medicine than all the other Scottish universities combined. McDermid, *Schooling of Working-Class Girls*, p. 12.

29 Roxburgh, *School Board*, p. 141.

30 MSB vol. 5 p. 26.

31 MSB vol. 9 p. 101.

32 NAS ED 17/90: Girls' High Reports, 1895–1920.

33 Five were male and five female; five were teaching in Scotland and five in England.

34 On 28 September 1905 at a salary of £400 per annum.

35 The title Principal was deemed more suitable for a female than Rector, and also more appropriate than Headmistress, which was often used locally to denote Infant Mistress.

36 Portrayed as 'the mother of all High Schools'.

37 Frances Mary Buss (1827–1894) opened the North London Collegiate School for Ladies in 1850 with 38 pupils. It became a prototype, being moderate in price, socially inclusive, non-sectarian, with a wide curriculum similar to that given to boys and delivered by well-qualified professional teachers. By 1865 it had 201 pupils.

38 Dorothea Beale (1831–1906) was Head of Cheltenham College for Ladies between 1859 and her death.

39 MSB vol. 10 p. 48.

40 Formed in Garnethill Public School in 1887 to enable Old Girls to keep in touch with each other and with the School. The original constitution said 'that former pupils and those in the highest class in the school should be eligible for membership'.

41 She retired in October 1926 and died in January 1940.

42 She was teaching Classics in Bromley HS for Girls.

43 Or Vice-Principal.

44 'Annie Jane' to the girls.

45 Gold medals were given out from 1893 until 1898.

46 She retired in 1945.

47 Lived 1882–1957. *ODNB*: Joanne Workman.

48 Prospectus 1914–15 p. 40.

49 Under Milligan, French had been taken by all pupils in the qualifying class.

50 Henrik Ling's (1776–1839) Swedish system using science and physiology to better understand the importance of fitness.

51 Anne Bloomfield: 'Martina Bergman-Oesterberg (1849–1915): Creating a Professional Role for Women in Physical Training' *History of Education* vol. 34 no. 5 (September 2005) pp. 517–34.

52 She was Classical Gold Medallist in 1908.

53 A hockey field at Anniesland was secured in 1911.

54 Both hockey and golf were begun under Milligan thanks to the personal generosity of SB chairman, Robert Allan.

55 Its chosen subject being 'Is the strong silent man a figment of the imagination?'

56 Anderson, *Education and Opportunity*, pp. 254–7.

57 Hutchesons' Girls' School had to wait until 1927 for the appointment of their first woman Principal. Dunlop: *Hutchesons' Grammar*, p. 106.

58 She was no believer in long hours, but rather 'in grand moments and time to think'.

59 The HMI Report for 1921–2 had held that Reid's 'estimation of the worth of individual pupils is unusually trustworthy'. NAS file ED18/3533.

60 The playing field (of 11,310 square yards) was bought in 1924 and a Pavilion built and four tennis courts laid out in 1925. It was run by the Girls' High Athletic Club to promote interest in athletics among the School's pupils and to encourage a continuance of that interest after they left school.

61 She retired to Cheltenham, being followed within the year by Miss Wishart. On her death the *Gloucester Echo* (Cheltenham) of 22 June 1950 included an obituary article on 'Pioneer Woman Educationist'.

62 NAS ED 17/90 HSfG Inspection Reports, 1895–1920.

63 MEA 1924–5 p. 598.

64 MEA 1925–6 p. 724. This was confirmed 22 to 17 by the EA. *Ibid.* p. 750.

65 Where she died in November 1944.

66 Mrs Tebb was a prizewinner at university and Secretary of the Liberal Club.

67 MEA 1926–7 pp. 50 and 152.

68 Correspondence (July 2009) with Mrs Elizabeth Copeland, the only grandchild of Dr Flora Tebb and the only child of her daughter, Marion (White). Although Marion started as a pupil at the Girls' High when her mother became headmistress, she moved to Park School. Nonetheless, she was Secretary of the Girls' London Club branch for twenty years. On Marion's death in 1993 her will requested that there be no flowers at her funeral, but donations given to the School instead. The sizeable cheque went to bursary funds.

69 NAS file ED18/3533.

70 *Ibid.*

71 Early membership included Professors Blair and Franks, and Benno Schotz.

72 Adding a further 6,713 square yards to the playing fields.

73 The golden lamp of learning; the oak tree of knowledge; the Cathedral for religion; and Pegasus, the winged horse, representing zeal and inspiration.

74 Margaret Gibson, a former School Captain, played hockey for Scotland between 1945 and 1947.

75 Shona Dobbie, a member of staff who coached the girls' badminton team between 1943 and 1947, played for Scotland against England and Ireland.

76 By 1949 a school yachting team had been formed.

77 Inter-school debates were popular, especially as those with the High School, Glasgow Academy and Allan Glen's concluded with tea and a short dance.

78 Formed in 1947.

79 'We learn not for school but for life.'

80 Its first Glasgow Dinner was held in 1936, and a London Club was inaugurated in 1938.

81 Miss Bate (Mathematics then Science); Miss Duff (French and German); Miss Gorrie (Mathematics); Miss Lawson (English); Miss Robertson (History); Miss Shearer (Junior School); Miss Thomson (German); and Miss Walker (Latin, History).

82 Classical Gold Medallist in 1922.

83 Modern Gold medallist in 1927.

84 Only two hockey teams were fielded.

85 This lasted until 1946.

86 Katharine Whitehorn: *Selective Memory* (London 2007) pp. 23–30.

87 She became President of the Old Girls' in 1953 and remained on the staff until retirement in 1966.

88 Letter to author from Katharine Whitehorn, dated 30 December 2008.

89 The HSfG Jubilee Prize was founded in 1948 and is awarded annually by the Professor of Moral Philosophy at Glasgow University to the most distinguished woman student in his Ordinary class.

90 Unfortunately there was not room for the younger Junior pupils.

91 The words of School Captain, Marjory Swinton, from the 'School Notes' of session 1945–6.

92 A post she held until 1957. She was President of the Old Girls' in 1955.

93 Nicknamed 'Medusa'.

94 For Mary Calder of Geography see p. 212 and p. 250.

95 HMI 1948 Report, ED 18/3533.

96 She was very honoured to be the only woman to attend the Glasgow University Court Centenary Dinner in April 1960.

97 Her granddaughter, Elizabeth, treasures the desk and pair of watercolours that were given to Mrs Tebb when she retired.

98 GCM December 1930–April 1931, p. 224.

99 GCM November 1934–April 1935, pp. 973 and 1488.

100 GCM November 1934–April 1935, p. 1487; and November 1935–April 1936, p. 937.

101 GCM 1946–7, pp. 1301 and 1492.

102 H. Stewart Mackintosh.

103 GCM 1948–9, pp. 2405 and 2492.

104 GCM 1948–9, pp. 2778 and 2788.

105 'Inquiry at Girls' High School', *GHerald* 28 February.

106 GCM 1948–9, pp. 2963 and 2975. 'New Bid for School Harmony', *GHerald* 19 March 1949.

107 'Parents Demand Inquiry', *GHerald* 30 March 1949.

108 'No Progress at Girls' High School Talks', *GHerald* 7 April 1949.

109 'Weekly Visits', *GHerald* 30 April 1949.

110 GCM 1948–9, p. 3255; and 1949–50, p. 462.

111 *GHerald* 25 June 1949.

112 'Woodburn Not to Interfere', *GHerald* 4 July 1949.

113 'Committee's Visits to Continue', *GHerald* 24 December 1949.

114 GCM 1949–50, pp. 1424 and 1945.

115 'Full Harmony Not Yet Restored', *GHerald* 24 June 1949.

116 GCM 1950–1, p. 448.

117 She became President of the Old Girls' in 1958.

118 Until Miss Barker agreed that the School be involved in a Primary pilot.

119 The options for Science were either Physics and Chemistry, or Botany and Chemistry.

120 Fiona Herriot took part in the Commonwealth Games of 1966, and in the 1970 Games Foil, Barbara Lyle (née Williams), Judith Bain (née Herriot) and Susan Youngs won the silver medal.

121 *ODNB*: Virginia Russell.
122 *WWS* (2008) p. 485.
123 *Courier*, 25 September 2009.
124 HSG*M* 2005/06 p. 105.
125 *WWS* (2008) p. 520.
126 *WWS* (2008) pp. 164–5.
127 *WW* (2009) pp. 1465–6.
128 *WW* (2009) p. 134.
129 *WWS* (2008) p. 355.
130 *WWS* (2008) pp. 137–8.
131 *WWS* (2008) p. 110.
132 *WWS* (2008) pp. 55–6.
133 *WWS* (2008) p. 75.
134 *WW* (2009) p. 1506.
135 *WWS* (2008) p. 326.
136 *WW* (2009) p. 1893.
137 *WW* (2009) p. 928.
138 Joan Bridgman: 'At School with Margaret Thatcher', *Contemporary Review* vol. 285, no. 1664 (September 2004) pp. 136–9. See also John Campbell: *Margaret Thatcher, Volume 1: 'The Grocer's Daughter'* (London 2001 edn) pp. 42–3.
139 *WWS* (2008) p. 198.
140 The first reference to the Ladies' Section is made in the 1979 Magazine.
141 She is now a member of the HS Educational Trust.
142 Honorary Vice-President of Club Ltd.
143 Development Director of the High School.

CHAPTER EIGHT

1 Roxburgh, *School Board*, pp. 225–7.
2 *Ibid*. p. 157ff.
3 *Scotsman* 30 October 1885.
4 Free education did not improve attendance rates. Roxburgh, *School Board*, p. 168.
5 Philip, *Higher Tradition*, p. 70.
6 Alasdair F.B. Roberts: 'The Operation of the "Ad Hoc" Education Authority in Dunbartonshire between 1919 and 1930' in T.R. Bone (ed.): *Studies in the History of Scottish Education 1872–1939* (London 1967), p. 243.
7 Leith became part of Edinburgh in 1920.
8 This was based on the belief that education concerned the physical, intellectual and moral sides of child development and as such had to be part of an overall approach to the provision of social services.
9 Although the TC could overturn decisions of the Education Committee.
10 Swingeing cuts in public expenditure, especially in education, were introduced by the Geddes Committee (1922).
11 The name change (Scotch Education Department to Scottish Education Department) also took place in 1918.

12 The raising of the leaving age to fifteen, agreed in principle in 1918, was delayed until 1947.

13 Craik believed that only 10 per cent of children could do so, and Professor Darroch, who had the chair of Education at Edinburgh University, was of a similar opinion. However, these personal views did not become part of legislation.

14 Andrew McPherson and Charles D. Raab: *Governing Education: A Sociology of Policy since 1945* (Edinburgh 1988) p. 248.

15 Paterson, *Scottish Education*, p. 71.

16 Anderson, 'History of Scottish Education', 2008, pp. 219–28.

17 Paterson, 'Schools and Schooling', pp. 566–9.

18 MEA, Burgh of Glasgow (1919–20) p. 93.

19 Maxton explained that Labour's failure to make a serious impression in education elections was the Scots' belief that education should be left to professional people who had a university education. Gordon Brown: *Maxton* (Edinburgh 1986) pp. 86–8.

20 MEA vol. 2 (1920–1) pp. 213–14.

21 Book of Service and Remembrance (1921). A further 145 were mentioned in dispatches, 26 of these twice, two three times, and Colonel John M. Sloan of the Indian Medical Service a remarkable seven times.

22 MEA vol. 2 p. 300. Provided it involved no expense for the local authority.

23 The Memorials were moved to the entrance hall of the new School when it was built.

24 As Secretary of the HS Club between 1919 and 1944 and President of the HS Club between 1944 and 1947, Buchanan can also take credit for the purchase of the playing fields. A memorial plaque to that effect was erected on 26 November 1960.

25 A third floor on the dressing-room wing of the Pavilion was added and opened on Friday 2 June 1961. The George Pate Room – named after the 1949–54 President of the Club – was designed to give extra changing accommodation but also increased the facilities available for social functions.

26 MEA vol. 8 p. 688.

27 MEA vol. 10 pp. 813–14.

28 MEA vol. 11 p. 590.

29 The High School Club vainly attempted to revive the plan to transfer the School to Anniesland under the new Glasgow Corporation. GCM, Dec. 1930–April 1931, p. 818.

30 GCM (April–November 1934) pp. 2220 and 2866.

31 Originally the PE facilities were to be cut back at the expense of developing Music, but Rector Talman persuaded the Council to maintain Gym capacity and instead use the exam hall as a music room when not otherwise in use. GCM (April–November 1933) p. 1616.

32 GCM (April–November 1936) p. 2846.

33 GCM (November 1937–April 1938) p. 1090.

34 GCM (May–November 1940) p. 1674.

35 And continued to do so until 1967.

36 *Chocolate and Gold*, p. 227. He returned to the staff 1926–31 and was interim Rector in 1930 before the arrival of John Talman.

37 *Ibid.* pp. 69–79 and p. 288 gives details of all the internationalists.

38 He won 19 caps between 1934 and 1939.

39 Mackenzie was at the School from 1936 to 1947.

40 John Dougall: 'Peter Pinkerton', *Proceedings of the Edinburgh Mathematical Society* (1930–1) pp. 268–71.

41 Small, 'The High School of Glasgow', p. 74.

42 *Ibid.*

43 Translated as 'Ever upwards'.

44 *NAS* file ED18/3532.

45 He later became Director of Studies (1940–9) at Jordanhill Training College.

46 His grandfather was a miner.

47 Attended 1926–34. His father was a minister, and he studied Classics at university.

48 The various parents' committees showed remarkable resource and initiative in securing premises; a three-teacher cell in the church hall at Langside Hill, another in the Tudor Picture House at Giffnock, a two-teacher cell in Ross's Creameries in Broomhill, a one-teacher cell in the bridal suite of the Great Western Hotel, and another in the nursery of a doctor's house in Lilybank Gardens.

49 James Talman (1918–44) had come with his younger brother, John S.S. Talman, from Allan Glen's in 1932. James had left the High School in 1937, while John left in 1940, being SC in his final year. David Gibson, who had been designated SC, left for service in the forces and John, who had been designated School Lieutenant (Vice-Captain), took his place.

50 In 1948 he was elected as an Assessor of the General Council in the Court of Glasgow University.

51 Small, 'The High School of Glasgow', p. 74.

52 The dates in brackets after names in this section are those that the individual spent on the staff of the HS (unless stated otherwise). Much material comes from a ledger of Staff Appointments and Resignations (Original School No. 04/62/304) which can be found in the School Archives.

53 Having previously served seventeen years at Garnethill.

54 The abbreviation PT for Principal Teacher (or Head of Department) occurs frequently in this section.

55 He was well known as part-author and part-performer in the regular BBC radio programme *Down at the Mains* which had a great following. He penned and scored *Happy Island*, an operetta for the School. His daughter, Eileen, became a famous Scottish actress.

56 He was also Deputy Rector before going to the Headship of Jordanhill College School.

57 He became PT at Pollokshields.

58 Head of Allan Glen's (1917–43) and President of the EIS.

59 He was editor of the Book of Service and Remembrance containing the names of the former pupils who died serving in the First World War. Later he became Rector of Hillhead High School.

60 Elgin Academy, Gordon's College and Watson's College.

61 Gillespie retired as Rector of Forfar Academy and Hutton as a PT in Stewart's College.

62 Jack Webster: *Jack Webster's Aberdeen* (Edinburgh 2007) p. 147.

63 He had previously served in the School between 1904 and 1920. He became Headmaster of Albert Road Academy.

64 He went on to become Head of Hamilton Crescent School.

65 He entered the ministry after retiring.

66 He later took on the headship of Onslow Drive Secondary.

67 Centre 'C' Block was derelict, apart from the war memorial, awaiting reconstruction.

68 She had a range of merit awards given every week, with pride of place going to the 'Manners Medal'.

69 Anon., HSGM (Dec. 1953).

70 These included her sister Sarah who died in 1939; Jessie Wylie (retired in 1937); Elizabeth Calder (1917–40); Jane G. Lawson (1917–41); and Jemina Downie who retired in 1941 to be replaced by Mary Knox (1941–8). An occasional man, including George Marshall (1920–42), inhabited their territory.

71 Miss Ruby Ritchie took Primary 3b in 1942–6 and instilled in the boys a sense of honour and good Christian ethics.

72 Remembered by many boys as a relatively young, kind lady, who sadly died early from a brain tumour.

73 On her death aged ninety-seven in 2004 she stunned friends and family by leaving £2.7 million in her will.

74 She was appointed Depute Head in the Junior School, 1948–50.

75 He followed a line of powerful and respected janitors: James Carson, Alexander Gibbons, Colour Sergeant William Tucker and Sergeant-Major J.T. Bowes (1907–33).

76 The Glasgow Club elected as presidents John Dallas (1926–8); John Richmond (1928–30); H.N. Napier (1932–3); W.F. Robertson (1934–5) ; David Perry (1936–7); Colonel J.G. MacKellar (1947–8); J.F. Lambie (1955); Major E.J. Donaldson (1956–9); and James Hutton (1960–1).

77 As in the previous chapter, within the square brackets can be found: the dates of attendance at the High School; father's occupation (unless the parent was a widow), and any other School information, including quotes from the large Register (1914–76).

78 British Insulated Callender's Cables.

79 *WWS* (2008) p. 253.

80 Debr. (2009) p. 1081; *WW* (2009) p. 1476.

81 *WWS* (2008) p. 211.

82 Debr. (2009) p. 31; *WW* (2009) p. 44.

83 *WWS* (2008) p. 235.

84 *WWS* (2008) p. 469.

85 *Herald*, 21 January 2010.

86 *WWS* (2008) p. 520.

87 *WWS* (2008) p. 541.

88 *WWS* (2008) p. 256.

89 *WWS* (2008) p. 311.

90 *WWS* (2008) p. 195.

91 *WWS* (2004) p. 260.

92 *ODNB*: Philip.
93 *ODNB*: Douglas J. Cusine.
94 *WWS* (2004) p. 217.
95 HSGM 1989 p. 76.
96 *ODNB*: David M. Walker (revised).
97 *ODNB*: A.F. Rodger.
98 *WWS* (2004) p. 234.
99 Debr. (2009) p. 71.
100 *WWS* (2008) p. 195.
101 *WWS* (2008) pp. 194–5.
102 Debr. (2009) p. 1751; WW (2009) p. 2412.
103 *ODNB*: J.D.Y. Peel.
104 *WWS* (2008) p. 269.
105 Debr. (2009) p. 1223.
106 *WWS* (2008) p. 170.
107 *WWS* (2008) p. 492.
108 *ODNB* (2010): Peter Lindstedt.
109 *WWS* (2008) pp. 111–12.
110 *WWS* (2008) p. 332.
111 *WWS* (2008) p. 223.
112 *Debr.* (2009) p. 1657; *WW* (2009) p. 2283.
113 *ODND:* Chris Hall.
114 *WWS* (2008) pp. 394–5.
115 He was the third FP to captain Scotland (1935–9), following G.M. Frew and J.M. Bannerman.
116 He was the fifth FP to captain his country, following W.H. Munro, who captained Scotland when playing his first international, against Ireland, in February 1947.
117 His brother, Donald (HS 1939–45) also collected six Scottish rugby caps.

CHAPTER NINE

1 He also gained a BA Honours from London University in 1945.
2 Minutes of Joint County Council of Moray and Nairn Education Committee, 17 July 1946.
3 He married Olive Willington of Montreal in 1935 and they had one son and two daughters.
4 The same issue had been a problem in Elgin, but following his ultimatum to the Education Committee (Minutes of Joint County Council of Moray and Nairn Education Committee, 2 October 1946 p. 95), the Council asked the SED for permission to proceed with the erection of two houses.
5 The large number was a result of the exceptional status of the post. This was also reflected in the salary, which was 10 per cent greater than the highest Scottish secondary head's salary.
6 GCM (1949–50) p. 1937, 2004 and 2013.
7 The staff photograph of August 1958 included 49 secondary staff (8 Science;

7 Mathematics; 7 Modern Languages; 6 Classics; 6 English; 4 Art; 3
Geography; 3 Music; 3 PE; and 2 History) as well as 13 primary staff; 3 office
staff; 3 Janitors and a lab technician.

8 Compared with schools like Glasgow Academy and Hutchesons' Grammar School.

9 The school team of 1948–9 had also been successful under the leadership of
Jimmy Docherty, who went on to win eight Scottish rugby caps (1955–8). It
also included Hamish Kemp, who won 27 consecutive caps from 1954–60,
and J. Percy Friebe (Club President, 1979–81), who won a cap against England
in 1951–2.

10 Following the Green Paper of 1971.

11 There was no stigma attached to repeating, and at least two School Captains
did so: Andrew Little (SC, 1957–8) and Ronald Neil (SC, 1960–1).

12 An attack on the ethos of the High School in the early 1960s under David
Lees and his then Deputy Peter Whyte can be found in *Education for Losers –
Memoirs of a Dunce* (Bloomington, Indiana 2005) pp. 6–34. Financed by its
author, David Anderson (P1, 1952–3), and written under the nom de plume of
Joe Dullerson, his acknowledged unhappy home life colours his largely
unreliable, though at times rather amusing, memories of the School, its staff
and his fellow pupils. Probably more significant are the criticisms of Prof. Dr
John MacBeath, who arrived at the High School aged fourteen following
education in Canada. In comparison, the High School 'seemed in the dark ages.
The belt was used in every lesson.' Peter Wilby, *The Guardian*, 13 January 2009.

13 D-ED8/1/41/36 (Mitchell). Meantime, the School War Memorial had been
brought up to date, and was officially dedicated on 7 November 1958 and
unveiled by Mrs Talman.

14 NAS file ED48/1921 pp. 15–17.

15 Dr Lees suffered from a coronary attack in 1971–2.

16 *Ibid.*

17 Interview with Mrs Lees, April 2009.

18 HSGM June 1976 p. 5.

19 Having joined the Board in 1955.

20 This involved concern for the expansion of the system and the building of
new colleges at Ayr, Falkirk and Hamilton.

21 The dates in brackets after names in this section are those that the individual
spent on the staff of the High School. The abbreviation PT (Principal Teacher)
occurs frequently.

22 In 1972 the High School had 23 honours graduates on its staff (ratio pupils to
(hon grad.) staff 30:1), with overall pupil–staff ratio 13.5:1; the Girls' High had 18
and the next lowest ratio of 33:1, with an overall pupil–staff ratio of 15.4:1. The
territorial, selective Hyndland had 18 (ratio 49:1) and overall pupil–staff ratio of
15.8:1; and the comprehensive Knightswood had 19 (ratio 63:1) and overall
pupil–staff ratio of 17.7:1.

23 This in itself is a powerful mitigating factor going a long way to negate the
HMI criticisms of the School and its leadership in 1972. Frequent staff
changes ensured a discontinuity in education, which affected adversely
academic results. Of the seventeen teachers who joined the staff in 1968,
thirteen of them left within three years. Of the eighteen new staff arriving in

1972, nine left within a session, and another ten staff joined them in the exodus. Ledger of Staff Appointments and Resignations.

24 Participation was by invitation only, with the Modern Languages staff in charge.

25 She resigned in 1954 after she married.

26 She developed novel approaches for the time, such as having the more able boys assist the others. She was often visited by former pupils, in particular Bill Tennant, the STV news presenter.

27 August 1957 till June 1962.

28 He was previously on the staff between 1952 and 1959.

29 He became head of Possil HS.

30 He left in 1976 to become Deputy Head at Cathkin HS.

31 He was promoted to a deputy headship at Dalkeith HS.

32 Special Assistant between 1963 and 1966, he became PT at Jordanhill College School.

33 Later Head at Colston HS.

34 A former School Captain (1956–7), he organised the charter of PS *Caledonia* on 27 May 1957. He later became a Classics Adviser.

35 Father of Richard.

36 Then Rector of Knightswood School.

37 He became Head of Peebles HS.

38 Donald McCormick left the school in 1968 to join Grampian TV.

39 David Menzies became an adviser in Strathclyde region.

40 He resigned from this post when the Glasgow Corporation determined to pursue comprehensive schooling.

41 He previously had been on the HS staff between 1957 and 1964.

42 He became PT at Shawlands Academy.

43 He became PT at Whitehill Senior Secondary.

44 He went on to be PT at Albert Secondary.

45 From PT post at Adelphi Secondary.

46 He became PT in Kelvinside Academy.

47 He retired in 1964 aged 72.

48 When Mackenzie met Quintin Jardine at a book reading, he suggested to him that 'Bandit' would be a good name for a character in one of his Skinner crime novels. In due course Jardine introduced a young Inspector – who joined the Lothian and Borders from the Strathclyde force – called David 'Bandit' Mackenzie.

49 A native of Alloa he had gained an FCH at Glasgow in 1926.

50 Destroyed by fire in 1962.

51 He died in 2008.

52 Ross Gibbons, John Caldwell, Iain Wotherspoon (recently arrived from Keil School) and Hugh Begg all played for Scottish Schools and, later, Gilmour Greig played for Canada.

53 He went to be Depute Head at Knightswood Secondary when this promotion was still unusual for PE specialists. He became President of GHS Rugby in 1970, and later honorary President of GHK.

54 Known to others as 'Minty' for his reputation for taking 'refreshments' during the school day.

55 Ivy Bell of Mathematics (1953–5) was the first full-time secondary appointment and much admired by her pupils. Previous female appointments had been restricted to part-time or temporary, especially during the war.

56 He became PT History at Lochend and returned as PT at the School 1968–71. He was appointed Rector of Forfar Academy aged thirty-one in 1971, and later became Head at Morrison's Academy, Crieff.

57 Alistair Mack became PT History at Eastbank Academy.

58 He left to lecture at Jordanhill College.

59 Indeed on the demise of the HS, Dr Lees asked Stanley and Joyce Mumford to arrange an annual social meeting of those he called 'The Exiles': teachers in the HS in its last year.

60 When 'Exiles' met their former HS parents, the latter were surprised that they were not part of the new HS. Some even suggested that they would not have donated money had they realised that so few HS teachers had joined the new school.

61 Bellahouston, Garnethill, Our Lady and St Francis', Pollokshields (at the time called Albert Road Academy), Queen's Park, St Mungo's, Whitehill and Woodside.

62 Allan Glen's (boys), High School (boys), High School (girls), Hillhead High (co-educational) and Notre Dame (girls).

63 NAS file ED18/3532.

64 Alastair F.W. Laing: 'Sursum Semper? A Socio-Historical Study of Educational Policy-Making in Glasgow Following the Issue of Circular 600' (Unpublished Thesis, Edinburgh University, 1984) p. 43.

65 Glasgow Director of Education Report D-ED9/1/9/1 (21 June 1943).

66 David Torrance: *The Scottish Secretaries* (Edinburgh 2006) pp. 172–3.

67 NAS file ED48/3 para. 17(d); 16 March 1945.

68 Sir John Mackay Thomson (Secretary, 1940–52) was conservative in outlook and a confirmed Classicist. After an Oxford education he had been Sixth Form Master at Fettes, and then Rector of Aberdeen GS. McPherson and Raab, *Governing Education*, p. 82.

69 The municipal wards of Anderston, Blythswood and Sandyford.

70 NAS file ED118/3532.

71 HSGM June 1945, 'The Future of the High School' pp. 85–90.

72 Given the historical link between Town and School, the Club accepted that the Council should be represented on the Board of Governors if it wished.

73 Most notably George Pate.

74 L.M. Turpie: 'How it All Happened, or "The Convergence of the Twain"' HSGM, May 1977 p. 18.

75 Ken Jones: *Education in Britain: 1944 to the Present* (Cambridge 2003) p. 78.

76 It was also seen as unnecessary. When in 1950 the Scottish Council of the Labour Party wrote to the then Secretary of State, Hector McNeil, with a conference resolution that all fee-paying should be abolished, he pointed out that only 41 of 3,200 schools in Scotland charged fees. Background note on fee-paying policy, 1939–51: NAS file ED48/3.

77 McPherson and Raab, *Governing Education*, p. 367.

78 Note the terminology.

79 John Highet: *A School of One's Choice: A Sociological Study of the Fee-Paying Schools of Scotland* (London 1969) p. 21.

80 Fees were abolished in England because there was an inadequate supply of free places, which did not obtain in Scotland. NAS file ED48/3 para. 17(c), 16 March 1945. With adequate free places Scottish authorities had, until 1965, the discretionary power to charge fees. Glasgow, Edinburgh, Renfrew, Angus, Dumfries, Fife, Inverness and Kincardine did so.

81 On election to Glasgow Council in May 1966, Pat Lally found the campaign against selective and fee-paying schools the main issue. For him 'the crux of the argument against the Corporation's funding of selective schools was that supporting such institutions reinforced divisions in society. Those who attended such schools tended to attract privilege and opportunity at the expense of their peers.' Pat Lally: *Lazarus Only Done it Once* (London 2000) p. 17.

82 Ministerially, the driving force was the Parliamentary Under-Secretary of State, Mrs Judith Hart, who was more left of centre than Ross and was very well connected with the UK Labour party hierarchy.

83 Perth Junior Academy and Rothesay Academy Primary had just ended fees and lowered the figure from 28 to 26. This left 17,000 pupils in state fee-paying schools in Scotland.

84 In the case of the HSfG, an old and cramped building certainly deterred some parents.

85 Highet, *School of One's Choice*, pp. 37–8; although during 1967–8 Glasgow collected £59,185 in fees.

86 In 1964 average annual earnings were around £1,000 per year.

87 These figures applied to Glasgow ratepayers. In the case of pupils whose parents did not reside within Glasgow, an additional fee of £65 p.a. was charged. This 'levy' was customarily waived where parents residing without Glasgow were occupiers of land or premises in the city (normally for business purposes) of a rateable value not less than £75 p.a. This levy was increased from £24 in August 1960: the parents of Bearsden protested but continued to send their sons to the HS. However, it did have an adverse impact on the number attending Jordanhill College School.

88 Its head at this time, Norman Graham, was a distinguished former HS pupil and had a son attending Edinburgh Academy.

89 At this time the Glasgow Labour Group did not agree and set up a sub-committee to examine the future of such schools in a comprehensive system. John Watt: 'The Introduction and Development of the Comprehensive School in the West of Scotland, 1965–80' (PhD Thesis, Glasgow University, 1989).

90 *Glasgow Evening Times* 11 April 1967.

91 The phrase used by Rector David Lees in a speech to the HS London Club Dinner in early March 1967.

92 *GHerald* 7 March 1967.

93 Three Labour councillors were threatened with the withdrawal of the party whip for supporting the immediate abolition of selective schools.

94 The comfortable majority of 25–4 was the result of a Labour split. Edinburgh, also Conservative-dominated, followed a similar course.

95   Wilson had gained a majority of 97 for the Labour Party in the election of 31 March 1966.

96   The *GHerald* editorial of 23 January 1969 deemed this move to be 'misguided action'.

97   Chairman Alasdair Wylie, Councillor Peter Gemmell and J.C. McFarlane, representing the Church of Scotland, were all lawyers.

98   In Edinburgh, its Education Committee decided by 16 votes to 5 to retain selectivity in certain schools even after the end of fee-paying.

99   Laing, 'Sursum Semper', p. 76.

100   The former Labour Lord Provost, Myer Galpern, had sent his son to the HS.

101   Indeed this remained the view of a number of Labour councillors throughout the controversy.

102   At this stage the Labour politicians in Glasgow had different 'solutions' to the issue. One, backed by Roman Catholic representatives, held that, owing to the location of the City's fee-paying schools, it was not possible to make them fully territorial comprehensives, and instead all five should be become non-territorial single-sex schools. Another supported making the schools territorial comprehensives by joining Allan Glen's to the City Public Secondary School; and linking the HSfG and Hillhead HS as two single-sex schools, with Notre Dame becoming a territorial comprehensive for girls. In this latter scenario the High School (boys) would be integrated into the system of territorial comprehensive education, and if this proved impossible the School should be used as a further education college. Laing, 'Sursum Semper', p. 78.

103   This stance had traditionally been accepted by both major political parties. It was deemed to be in accordance with democratic principles to leave discretion to education authorities (rather than to abolish all fees by central direction). NAS file ED48/3 para 17(a); 16 March 1945.

104   Margaret Thatcher became Secretary for Education in England.

105   George Pottinger: *The Secretaries of State for Scotland 1926–1976: Fifty Years of the Scottish Office* (Edinburgh 1979) p. 176. Fees and selectivity were two separate issues. The latter was generally unpopular in Scotland, hence the Conservative emphasis on freedom of choice for all parents to choose the type of secondary school they wished for the children, selective or non-selective. This was the basis of their May 1971 election manifesto in Glasgow. The special circumstances surrounding the Roman Catholic issues are dealt with by Laing, 'Sursum Semper', pp. 81–3.

106   Its fees at this time ranged from £144 to £246 p.a.

107   Educated at the selective grant-aided St Aloysius College.

108   To keep the distinctive character of the former selective schools, pupils would be drawn equally from eleven areas of the city (by ballot if oversubscribed) and, to cater for the less academic, Homecraft and Technical subjects would be offered. However, a bussing, mixed ability, selective comprehensive solution was politically unacceptable.

109   *Ibid.* p. 86.

110   Confirmed by Councillor John Mains, leader of the Labour Group. *GHerald* 24 March 1972.

111   NAS file ED48/1921, SED minute 1 March 1972.

112 Paralleled with the similar debates taking place in Edinburgh at the same time as the Royal High's future was threatened.

113 Stephen Rodan was at the forefront of the pupil campaign, which in only ten days produced a petition of over 38,000 signatures.

114 At the meeting delegations from other bodies supporting the proposals were also heard.

115 *GHerald* 15 March 1972.

116 *GHerald* 9 March 1972.

117 The older pupils would continue until June 1974 at the latest.

118 The primary with effect from August 1972; the secondary by June 1974.

119 Dated 25 February 1972.

120 This study was to include not just the 3,600 pupils in the former fee-paying schools, but also the 8,300 pupils in the selective senior and junior secondaries.

121 SED: 'Secondary School Organisation' – Glasgow: Division One File JAF/A4/7.

122 The selective schools were seen as a 'development backwater'. Watt, 'Introduction and Development', footnote p. 218.

123 The disparity in figures, comparing those who completed a six-year secondary course at selective schools with those doing so at the city's comprehensive schools, led the SED to conclude that the latter 'lost' substantial numbers of pupils able and willing to profit from a full six-year course. Laing, 'Sursum Semper', pp. 101–2.

124 HMI also emphasised that only the HS was of venerable origin, while the others (including the HSfG) were relatively recent creations, helping 'to overcome the pressure that the mystique which appears to surround them might otherwise apply'.

125 Like other RC councillors, Docherty was privately sympathetic to selective schools, believing that they had produced an RC professional class. Watt, 'Introduction and Development', p. 375.

126 Along with David Finlayson, Rector of Allan Glen's, and Sister Mary Julia, Deputy Headmistress of Notre Dame. NAS file ED48/1922 (April 1972).

127 Lees had asked the Secretary of State to issue a default Order requiring the Corporation to adhere to their existing approved scheme and make arrangements for selective admissions in August 1972. He was deemed more culpable for using headed school notepaper for his letter! Lees countered that he was writing in his official capacity with statutory responsibilities. NAS file ED48/1923.

128 Reported in the 4 May edition of both *Scotsman* and *GHerald*. NAS file ED48/1923.

129 In this letter to the PM, Campbell mentioned that the HS, which had 'produced' two prime ministers, was threatened with closure.

130 Norman Wylie, who had been educated at Paisley GS when it had been fee-paying.

131 National Archives. PREM 15/891.

132 At a meeting on 14 April between the Secretary of State and Glasgow's representatives, this was confirmed. NAS file ED48/1922.

133 Under Lord President Emslie, who had been educated at the HS.

134 NAS file ED48/1923.

135 The appeal was finally dealt with by five Law Lords on 15 November 1972.

They unanimously dismissed the appeal with costs. They determined that the Secretary of State had been correctly exercising his statutory powers. In doing so he ensured that the method of introducing selectivity was consistent with continuity of education for the children and involved proper consultation with parents and teachers. The Law Lords rejected the claim that Campbell was merely adopting delaying tactics to save the city's selective schools.

136 The HS Register of pupils gives details of 302 boys who left to go to another school in the last years of the High School's existence. Of these, 190 (63%) went to Corporation schools, including 39 to Hillhead, 37 to Shawlands, 10 to Eastwood, 10 to King's Park, 9 to Penilee, 8 to Hyndland, 7 to Bellahouston, 4 to Cleveden, 2 to Bearsden, and 64 to 29 other corporation schools; 63 (21%) went to grant-aided schools, including 48 to Hutchesons', 9 to Jordanhill, 3 to Morrison's, 2 to Dollar, and 1 to St Aloysius; and 49 (16%) to private schools, including 26 to Drewsteignton, 15 to Kelvinside, 3 to Glasgow Academy, 3 to Keil, 1 to Loretto, and 1 to Fettes.

137 National Archives, PREM 15/891 9.

138 This meant that the Primary 5 intake to Elmbank Street in 1971 was the last such intake.

139 Councillor L.M. Turpie, in a memo of December 1972, argued that these moves occurred almost by default and that parents had to be organised and make a Secretary of State aware of their views emphatically and with supporting detail.

140 *GHerald*.

141 Indeed it was noticed that the quality of applicants for places in the HS secondary had declined, while only 139 sat the entrance test for 120 places at the Girls' High instead of the usual figure of between 300 to 400. NAS file ED48/25 (July 1972–January 1973).

142 Perfunctory in both cases.

143 NAS file ED48/1926; 'Selective Schools in Scotland': JA 703/3 (14 December 1972).

144 *Ibid*. In December 1972 the Education Committee pegged Lees' salary to national scales, ignoring the usual practice of conservation.

145 McPherson and Raab, *Governing Education*, p. 382.

146 Examination performance was seen as creditable, but selective schools 'produce a less balanced education than is desirable and that generally pupils at the lowest end of the ability range – but still able pupils by any standard – in many cases achieve less than might reasonably be expected of them because they tend to be pressed into courses which are not really appropriate for them'. NAS file ED48/1926.

147 *Ibid*. In general terms this might have been true, but there is also evidence that many teachers saw comprehensive schools as an English import which threatened 'good' Scottish schools. Watt, 'Introduction and Development'.

148 Also in 1972–3 he caused a political row by overturning the public inquiry result opposing a new runway at Edinburgh Turnhouse.

149 McPherson and Raab, *Governing Education*, p. 382.

150 Paterson, *Scottish Education*, p. 138.

151 NAS file ED48/1926.

152 Secretary for Education (DES) between 1970 and 1974.

153 Jones, *Education in Britain*, p. 100.
154 Hansard 9 March 1973 vol. 852 col. 228/9.
155 NAS file ED48/1926 (SED file JA/703/3 part VII).
156 Expected in 1976.
157 The last Primary 7 group dispersed in August 1974 to a number of schools: to Hutchesons', Glasgow Academy and Kelvinside, and to local state schools. Four – Melvin Shanks (later Head at Belmont House School), Leslie Milne, Glen Leishman and Ben Cohen – went to Drewsteignton, spending 1974–7 at Ledcameroch Road before transferring to the new High School at Old Anniesland in 1977. Shanks left at the conclusion of Sixth Year in 1980 and was later to join the staff of his old school. The other staff continuities were Frank Bates and Charlie Forsyth.
158 Although it is not clear what promises were broken.
159 The meetings in the six schools began with Councillor Docherty stressing that the divide between the Education Committee and parents was so wide that no amount of consultation would have bridged that divide. He then went on to tell parents and staff what the Education Committee had decided. Watt, 'Introduction and Development', pp. 226–7.
160 Letter from Campbell to PM Heath dated 3 March 1973. National Archives, PREM. 15/91.
161 SED file ED48/1921 puts forward this case in a powerful and convincing manner.
162 As a third of the HS pupils came from without the city, it seemed not unreasonable to wait until after regionalisation before making a final decision.
163 Soon to be headed by Geoff Shaw, who latterly led Glasgow's opposition to selective schools, and the HS in particular.
164 In Kent Road, a mere quarter of a mile west of the HS.
165 *G Herald* 28 April 1973.
166 Watt, 'Introduction and Development', pp. 223–4.
167 *Ibid.* p. 225.
168 Or six schools, including St Mungo's.
169 Turpie's memorandum was the only substantial, and somewhat isolated, intellectual contribution to defending the High School and selective schools generally.
170 Within a decade, this solution would likely have had the same outcome as actually occurred, namely an independent school, although much of Scotland might have warmed to a different model on the lines of Jordanhill College School.
171 Pottinger, *Secretaries of State*, p. 184.
172 Macleod, *Glasgow Academy*, p. 164. This figure reached 548 for 93 places in 1961. *Ibid.* p. 178.
173 *Ibid.* p. 179. And second best in 1966.
174 *WW* (2009) p. 759.
175 *WWS* (2008) p. 233.
176 *WWS* (2008) p. 342.
177 *WW* (2009) p. 1439.
178 *WWS* (2008) p. 170.
179 *WWS* (2008) p. 295.
180 *WW* (2009) p. 2124.

181   *WWS* (2008) p. 464.
182   Debr. (2009) p. 259.
183   *WW* (2009) p. 1484.
184   *WWS* (2008) p. 567.
185   *WWS* (2008) p. 132.
186   *WWS* (2008) p. 258
187   *WW* (2009) p. 1576.
188   *WWS* (2008) p. 294.
189   *WW* (2009) p. 2077.
190   *WWS* (2008) p. 237.
191   *WWS* (2008) pp. 351–2.
192   *WWS* (2008) pp. 235–6.
193   *WWS* (2008) p. 359.
194   *WWS* (2008) p. 431.
195   *WWS* (2008) p. 556.
196   *WWS* (2008) p. 176.
197   *WW* (2009) p. 1008.
198   *WWS* (2004) p. 347.
199   *WW* (2009) p. 7.
200   *WWS* (2008) p. 113.
201   *WWS* (2008) p. 393.
202   *WWS* (2008) p. 403.
203   *WWS* (2008) p. 208; *WW* (2009) p. 839.
204   *WWS* (2008) p. 557.
205   *WWS* (2008) p. 331.
206   *WWS* (2008) p. 267.
207   *WWS* (2008) p. 431.
208   *WWS* (2008) p. 307.
209   *WW* (2009) p. 1462; *WWS* (2008) p. 323; George Reid, *Herald* Obituary 8 April 2009.
210   *WW* (2009) p. 163; *WWS* (2008) p. 74.
211   *WW* (2009) pp. 1582–3.
212   *WWS* (2008) p. 254.
213   *WWS* (2008) p. 213.
214   *WWS* (2008) p. 166.
215   *WWS* (2008) p. 50.
216   *WW* (2009) p. 2249.
217   *WWS* (2008) p. 165.
218   *WWS* (2008) pp. 510–1.
219   *WWS* (2008) p. 385.
220   Debr. (2009) p. 1802.
221   *WWS* (2008) p. 263.
222   *WWS* (2008) p. 318.
223   *WWS* (2008) p. 501.
224   *WW* (2009) p. 46.
225   *WWS* (2008) p. 385.
226   *WWS* (2008) p. 482.

227 *WWS* (2004) p. 166.
228 *WWS* (2008) p. 373–4.
229 *WWS* (2008) p. 229.
230 *WW* (2009) pp. 1491–2; *WWS* (2008) p. 342.
231 *WW* (2009) p. 2098.
232 *WWS* (2008) p. 89.
233 *WWS* (2008) p. 399.
234 *WWS* (2008) p. 468.
235 *WW* (2009) p. 927.
236 *WW* (2009) p. 926.
237 *WWS* (2008) p. 453.
238 *WW* (2009) p. 1703.
239 *WW* (2009) p. 177.
240 *WWS* (2008) p. 567.
241 *WW* (2009) p. 808.
242 By Alexander McCall Smith.
243 *WWS* (2008) p. 397.
244 Debr. (2009) p. 262.
245 *WW* (2009) p.1664.
246 *WWS* (2008) p. 179.

CHAPTER TEN

1 The *GHerald* (2 October 1975) included a picture of the 'Class of '75' on its front page, with the sub-heading 'After 800 years, the end of a proud part of Glasgow's history'. The remaining pupils and staff were 'the last in a long, long line'.

2 These included starting a Preparatory School in Glasgow, which in time would become a full primary and secondary school; starting a Fourth to Sixth Year College; discussions with Glasgow Academy with a view of combining their resources of land (New Anniesland being adjacent to Old Anniesland) and 'erecting a Scottish Eton'. Laing, 'Sursum Semper', p. 106, quoting Leonard Turpie in interview of 26 March 1984.

3 As well as presenting pupils for Music examinations in England and Scotland, her choirs had broadcast in BBC programmes and she had long experience in youth work. *Milngavie and Bearsden Herald* 2 April 1971.

4 Torburn House purchased from Strathclyde University.

5 At the outbreak of war in September 1939, Harle had completed his first Sixth-Form year at Portsmouth and was regarded as a star mathematician. The school was evacuated and all the staff called up. An arrangement was made for him to study at Winchester College (1939–41) under the inspiring C.V. Durell, who was also famous for his textbooks. Harle duly won a Mathematics Scholarship to Clare College, Cambridge.

6 Where he achieved a First Class degree.

7 He had been preceded by Ian Gibb, who trained in PE at Jordanhill and, following three years at Morrison's in Crieff, arrived at Drewsteignton in September 1970 to take over the role of Second Master. By 1974 the situation

had evolved: Bob Metcalfe had been appointed Deputy Rector and Ian took over the burgeoning PE department. Hilary Ganley was appointed Senior Mistress, to be replaced by Audrey Whitefield in 1976.

8   Opened by former Glasgow Director of Education, Dr Stewart Mackintosh.

9   Margaret Donald in GHSM (1977), pp. 21–3. Its fees ranged from £102 to £252 pa.

10 Minute of Directors' Meeting, Drewsteignton School (Bearsden) Ltd, 25 April 1973.

11 *Ibid.*, 3 June 1973.

12 There was no debate about the inclusion of girls, which meant that co-education for the new HS was accepted despite the traditions of the old HS. The advantage was not just a doubling of the potential market, but also meant bringing in the former pupils of the HSfG who, for the most part, had been alienated by the changes in the Girls' High organisation since the advent of the comprehensive system.

13 *GHerald* 27 June 1973.

14 Minute of Sub-Committee on Development Plan, Glasgow Corporation, 25 August 1973, Print no. 9, p. 679.

15 Minute of Sub-Committee on Development Applications, 29 August 1973, Print No. 10, p. 775.

16 Because, in his professional opinion, permission should not be refused on planning grounds, Mansley pointed out, perfectly properly, that he could not appear as a technical witness at any public inquiry into an appeal against refusal of permission by the elected members contrary to his advice.

17 Of 111 Glasgow councillors, some 83 were Labour.

18 Educated at the Edinburgh Academy.

19 *GHerald* 7 September 1973.

20 'Areas of Need', Report by Glasgow Corporation, 1973.

21 Minute of Planning Committee, 30 October 1973 Print No. 14, p. 1131.

22 In September 1971 Harle inherited a total of 245 pupils (including only 70 in senior school); by September 1974 the total was 603 (of whom 348 were in senior school). An HMI report of the time gave a breakdown of Drewsteignton's catchment area: 50% of pupils came from Milngavie and Bearsden; 26% from the North (Bishopbriggs, Kilsyth, Drymen, Strathblane and Helensburgh); 12% from Glasgow (City) and 12% from the South (Airdrie, Hamilton, Strathaven, Johnstone and Kilmacolm).

23 Further buildings were opened by Sir Eric Yarrow, himself a former Drewsteignton pupil, in November 1973.

24 Helped by the merger discussions. Although in 1974 there were 200 applications for 60 places, of the top-placed 40, some 22 declined the offer of a place.

25 Eileen Robertson gained an MA at Edinburgh University and a Dip Ed with Merit from Moray House College, and started her teaching career in 1962 as an English and History teacher in Methven Junior Secondary school. Four years later she moved to Jaffa, Israel, to take up a post at the Tabeetha Church of Scotland School, but she was evacuated at the start of the Six Day War. She taught English, History and Geography at Auchterarder before taking a post in the English School in Cyprus in 1970.

26 The other issues which needed sensitive handling were the composition of the governing body, which was overcome by appointing Andrew Baker as chair with the casting vote; concerns that Harle had not been confirmed as the Head of the merged school (this took place in October 1973); and the desire to keep the school roll below 750. (Although Norrie Thomson accepted this lower figure, the aim of 1,000 pupils was retained for Appeal purposes.)

27 It was made up of nine from Drewsteignton, eight from the GHS FP Club, and one from the Old Girls' Club.

28 Memo dated 16 January 1974.

29 They included Dr H.H. Pinkerton, Norrie Thomson, Gordon Anderson, A.L. Aitkenhead (President of the HS Club), Norman Macfarlane and Mrs Nancy Davidson (representing the Girls' High).

30 The Arab–Israeli Six Day War led to massive increases in oil prices, and the country was heading for a three-day week. The failed showdown with the miners precipitated the fall of the Heath Government.

31 *GHerald* 19 April 1973.

32 Which was unlikely to be forthcoming.

33 Laing, 'Sursum Semper', p. 110.

34 Sandy Bell was the Senior Reporter at the recently formed Scottish Office Reporters' Unit (now Directorate of Planning and Environmental Appeals), to which most, but not all, planning appeals were delegated. Although the planning issues appeared on the face of it to be fairly straightforward, this was set up as a 'report case', in which the Reporter was required to hear the evidence and then submit his findings to the Secretary of State, with a recommendation. The Secretary of State was not bound to follow that recommendation.

35 Significantly, he was the only Corporation policy witness at the Inquiry. None of the heads of the Technical Departments gave evidence to support the case presented as being that of the Corporation by the Leader of the Labour Administration.

36 It held that there were six secondaries and twenty-one primaries located near Old Anniesland.

37 SED, Division One File JAF/A4/1, Report of Inquiry into Planning Appeal by Glasgow High School Club, 22/23 January 1974.

38 *GHerald* 23 January 1974. Thomson, who had been High School Captain in the 1930s, gave details of the plans to charge fees of £300 p.a. and build a bursary programme which would cover 30 per cent of the pupils, who would be given levels of financial help depending on need. Drewsteignton would effectively become a primary department of the High School, and its pupils would form approximately half of the annual intake.

39 SED, Division One File JAF/A4/1, Memo from SDD to SED, 28 March 1974.

40 A policy of opposition, but not to the point of abolishing them.

41 Laing, 'Sursum Semper', p. 112.

42 SED, Division One File JAF/A4/1, Memo from Div. I to Div. II, 29 March 1974.

43 *Ibid.*, Memo from SED to SDD, 1 April 1974. The effect of any 'creaming off' would be limited, given the wide catchment area of the proposed new School.

44 Ronald King Murray, who had been educated at George Watson's College.

45 SED, Division One File JAF/A4/1, Memo from Lord Advocate to Secretary of State, 14 May 1974.

46 Educated at the HS.

47 NAS file DD12/2699.

48 A former pupil of Robert Gordon's College.

49 The new Council had come into being in May 1975 and had replaced Glasgow as the Education Authority. It was temporarily leasing premises.

50 *GHerald* 14 February 1976.

51 Prompted by Harle, by 1973 Drewsteignton had appointed Alistair D. Mathie as its Bursar.

52 *GHerald* (23 October 1976) reported that £516,291 had been raised.

53 The architects who had designed the War Memorial in the 1920s, and who had acted as agents for the planning applications and the planning appeal.

54 *Milngavie and Bearsden Herald* 16 July 1976.

55 Directors' Meeting, 18 November 1975. Her voice was influential because of the impact she had made in her Head of the Preparatory School role. The Bakers remained supportive, while Harle rightly did not interfere in her staffing and curriculum arrangements. The improvements she introduced soon meant that fewer and fewer pupils left to go elsewhere. The days of Drewsteignton as a Prep School, albeit a good one, were numbered. In 1977 she was appointed Head of the High School Junior School.

56 14 Upper Glenburn Road was sold in January 1978 for £51,250 to W.S. Gordon & Co. Ltd.

57 It so happened that the pattern of Transitus being taught by secondary staff was followed by some local independent schools.

58 In 1975.

59 The Former Pupils gave over half the total raised (*GHerald* 28 September 1977).

60 Metcalfe was very much the figure to whom pupils related, perhaps a result of his cheerful and outgoing personality. His expedition experience assisted planning for the move to Anniesland, and his versatility ranged from 'A' Level Geography teaching to Transitus rugby coaching.

61 She went on to join the management team at Morrison's Academy, Crieff, as Assistant Rector.

62 Other long-serving staff included Betty Little (Harle's secretary) and Dorothy MacBean (girls' PE).

63 Named after the benefactor who was President of the Club, 1949–54.

64 This event was combined with the re-dedication of the War Memorials, which had been moved from Elmbank Street, by Very Rev. John R. Gray. The Book of Remembrance, with a page turned every day, was also put in place.

65 Directors' Meeting, 19 September 1979.

66 One of the Directors, Peter Kimber, who also held a senior post in the Scottish Exam Board, analysed the School's 1980 results: the Ordinary Grade results were improving, and the Higher results did not signify a weak department. (Thanks to Ed Martin, the Mathematics department was producing satisfactory results.) He concluded that the School was doing well for the average and weaker pupils, and the priority now was to produce a steady flow of top-quality pupils.

67 And to 805 (365 + 440) in September 1980.

68 In the event, the school received £18,000 from the SED for assisted places in their first year of operation, 1981–2.

69 Analysing the figures for 1978–9, Harle had used the tawse on 45 boys; Metcalfe had punished 56 boys; and Mrs Whitefield had used the strap twice.

70 28 May 1980.

71 In June 1980, to take effect on 31 December of that year.

72 Chairman's Committee, 8 April 1981.

73 The other advantage of the HS was the benefit of being co-educational before other independent schools.

74 She was to leave in December 1982 to go south with her husband after 'unique and valuable service to the School over the years'. The directors, at that time, reorganised the Bursar's department, introducing Norman C.B. Wright as Executive Director, with Gerry Simonis being appointed Assistant Bursar.

75 Robin Easton joined him in 1983. Club presidents in the period included Stewart Cooper (1987–9); Kenneth Wallace (1989–90); Stanley Butler (1992–3); Basil Shearer (1995–6); Roy Hepburn (1997–8); David Kerr (1998–9); Ian Litster (1999–2000); and Robert McPhail; (2000–1).

76 He accepted the post of Chair of the Appeal in February 1982, and became President of the Club in 1994–5.

77 When the sum involved went over £200,000 and the Trustees agreed to finance the Arts block, it was decided to call that section of the School 'The Muirhead Moffat Building'.

78 This occurred on 10 June 1983. It had been delayed by the General Election.

79 Directors' Meeting 21 September 1981.

80 This led in November 1982 to the production of a paper on 'Responsibilities of Heads of Department'.

81 By session 1982–3 the Sixth Year fees were £300 a term, compared with Fifth Year fees of £450.

82 The university and college application body.

83 The series was restored, with both sides having won 59 times.

84 The merger of Kelvinside and High School FP teams in December 1982 enabled the use of twenty acres at Auchenhowie, but its lack of changing accommodation and distance from the High School restricted its use.

85 Frank Gerstenberg was appointed in 1985 to head Watson's College, while Brian Lockhart remained Deputy Rector of the HS until appointed Head of Robert Gordon's College in Aberdeen in 1996.

86 Option A entailed building a games hall and gym, replacing temporary buildings (The Cedars), building additional accommodation for Business Studies and Computing Studies, and modifying use of the 1977 building (gym becoming library). Option D entailed building a games hall only.

CHAPTER ELEVEN

1 HMC: The Headmasters' Conference, the prestigious body representing independent schools, set a high academic standard for its member schools. It

later became the Headmasters' and Headmistresses' Conference.

2 This is evidenced by the fact that in just over twelve years, four members of the Senior Management Team became Heads of leading Scottish independent schools, and two became Heads of the Junior Schools of independent schools.

3 He was awarded a knighthood in the New Year's Honours List in January 1983.

4 By 2004 there were just eight 'all-through and independent schools' and one 'Junior and Preparatory School' in Glasgow, and three more of the former category in Ayr, Helensburgh and Kilmacolm, a reduction from twenty-one to twelve.

5 Prospective parents were impressed by their maturity and loyalty to the School.

6 An HS parent himself.

7 The Certificate of Sixth Year Studies was the Scottish equivalent of the English Advanced Level.

8 He had worked under Sir Roger Young, Principal of Watson's College, who campaigned for the CSYS.

9 The final nail in the coffin of the 'A' Level lobby came with the introduction of Advanced Highers in Scotland, and the subsequent evidence that they were at least as demanding as 'A' Levels and that it was statistically harder to get A passes in Advanced Highers.

10 Bruce Normand went to Churchill College, Cambridge: he was to gain a first in Natural Science and a scholarship to MIT. In 1985 Sarah Money went to Brasenose College, Oxford, while Rahul Rohatgi studied Engineering at St John's, Oxford. In 1987 Charlotte Behan went to Newnham College, Cambridge to read Medical Sciences; Fiona Murdoch (SC) gained an Exhibition to New College, Oxford to read Jurisprudence, while Jennifer Young went to St Hilda's, Oxford to read Physics.

11 In 2006 the HS provided nine of the ninety-four Scottish school entrants to Cambridge (two others deferred entry until 2007).

12 Supported by Ian Templeton, President of the Club, 1985–7. He is presently a member of the Educational Trust.

13 He died tragically in the summer of 1984.

14 At a cost of £228,000.

15 The £900,000 had been spent on the Arts and Science blocks, leaving £300,000 for the games hall.

16 The fee increase at this meeting was set at 9 per cent for 1985–6.

17 With architects Keppie Henderson agreeing to limit their professional fees to £65,000 plus VAT.

18 The school roll had increased steadily: 1985–6: 368 + 530 = 898; 1986–7: 369 + 565 = 934.

19 Professor Sir Michael Bond in conversation (8 April 2009).

20 Brian Adair.

21 Gray had been the contractor for the games hall complex, and the total cost had come in at £968,168 – lower than expected, given the recession in the building trade. It was probably this that led to the decision to complete the original extension plan with two additional classrooms at the end of the science block (within the original budget of £1.24 million, including fees and VAT).

22 He had been created Baron Macfarlane of Bearsden in 1991 (Life Peer).

23 Indeed, it discovered that planning permission had been given in 1973 for a Kindergarten extension, on the precise area where it was now proposed.

24 Robin Hagart played a significant role in the buildings and their maintenance over an eighteen-year period. He became Club President, 1996–7. His family connections with the School span four generations of Former Pupils.

25 Prompted in part by the new Music facilities recently completed by Glasgow Academy, which included a dozen music practice rooms, and similar schemes at Dollar Academy, St George's School and St Leonard's School.

26 Estimated costs rose from £150,000 to £220,000.

27 Strathclyde Regional Council and Historic Monuments agreed to its removal, but the cost of £5,027 was an issue until in February 1996 the Environmental Department of Glasgow Development Agency agreed to fund 50 per cent of the removal costs.

28 In fact, Kirklee was not sold on the open market, because planning permission was not forthcoming for developers. As the title deeds had been lost, the Council claimed it was theirs and enforced a Compulsory Purchase Order. The compensation awarded to the Old Girls' was donated to the Bursary Fund (the hockey pitch having been already constructed).

29 Refurbishment and alterations to the existing Pavilion: £380,000; the new Jimmie Ireland Stand (for 550), refectory and multi-gym fitness area: £1.1 million; Junior School extension at Bearsden: £1.2 million; Crow Road (Drama Studio) development: £850,000.

30 Hutchison.

31 At a later date, the School received an additional £200,000 for its Bursary Fund and £100,000 to support Former Pupils at university.

32 He had first contacted Easton in 1997, fifty years after he had been School sports champion.

33 Dr Anne Barlow Ramsay.

34 He was Club President 1981–3.

35 Following another successful Appeal, which raised £960,000.

36 He retired in 1992.

37 She retired in 2000. She married Lloyd King, Geography/Modern Studies teacher 1979–2002. She was succeeded by Rachel Elstone and then, in 2006, Paul Toner became PT.

38 Before being promoted to senior management at Hutchesons' GS. Robin Broadbent has been Head of Careers since 1995.

39 The French assistant, Mme Paulette Kennedy, who had worked in both Junior and Senior Schools, retired in 1993.

40 Frank Bates from the Chemistry staff of the HS left in 1984 to join Balfron High School.

41 He became much involved nationally with Examination Board (SQA) work.

42 Melvyn Shanks, a pupil at the High School, was a member of the Physics staff (1985–1990).

43 He took a HS trip to the Azores (2008) and also runs School football.

44 In 2002, Sinclair became President of Euroclio, the European Standing Conference of History Teachers' Associations.

45 Geography flourished under Davies. He left in 2009 to go to Fettes.

46 She was recently succeeded by Jane Sim.

47 Head Janitor (1979–96). The Class of 1995–6 presented a flag to the School in his memory. He was replaced by the reliable Ian Harper. The new HS has been well served by its janitorial staff, which follows a long line of respected and committed predecessors.

48 She went on to be Deputy Head at Mary Erskine's School and the first female Rector of Kelvinside Academy.

49 This was the most overt way in which Easton ensured the continuation of the Christian values and ethos of Drewsteignton.

50 Lloyd King had been responsible for the success of the school's impressive Outdoor Education programme. He retired early and tragically died suddenly within a year, in May 2003, aged 51.

51 February 1989 HMI Report.

52 Lord Macfarlane set the style for chairmanship, and the success of the School during his period of office ensured that his successors – Gordon Anderson, Professor Sir Michael Bond (the first non-FP to hold the office since Andrew Baker) and Brian Adair – worked closely with the Rector, who was regarded as Chief Executive.

53 This policy was criticised as a form of elitism, especially as every year there appeared to be an increasing number of disappointed children who did not gain places.

54 Other FP doctorates that year were Alan S. Brown; Professor Robert Jack; Professor Ross Lorimer; Professor David Flint; (Sir) Muir Russell; Sir Neil McCormick; and the Chair of Governors, Professor Sir Michael Bond.

55 Fortunately his incredibly understanding wife, Eleanor, who sometimes baulked at Easton's exceptionally long and hard working weeks, was a wonderful support.

56 February 1989 HMI Report.

57 A director of the School for a number of years. He remains a Trustee of the Educational Trust.

58 Born in 1948, he attended the School 1958–67, studied Law at Glasgow and became a partner in Bird Semple. He took over as Secretary in 1988.

59 He has recently become a director of the School and was President of the Club (2008–9).

60 Now Fiona Bellinger.

61 Née Faultless.

62 As a group staying on an extra year beyond Highers, all thirteen went to university.

63 A cross-section of recent leavers, showing the variety of careers they have embarked on. A number were elected School Captain (SC).

64 *WWS* (2008) p. 451.

65 Now Alison van der Meulen.

CHAPTER TWELVE

1 There were 49 in nursery, 316 in Junior School and 691 in Senior School.

2 The respect she achieved amongst educational circles was reflected in her appointment as an HMI Associate Assessor in 2007.

3 Amongst his duties are the House and Guidance systems.

4 Amongst her duties are the curriculum and helping young new pupils to settle into the Senior School.

5 Karen Waugh, being knowledgable about ICT issues, had a major role in prompting this appointment.

6 In time he went on to gain Scottish 'B' caps in both sports.

7 By the 1980s, there remained only one, girls-only, secondary: Notre Dame Catholic School in Glasgow.

8 Paterson, *Scottish Education*, pp. 137–8.

9 Having reached as high as 63 per cent in 1955.

10 The Educational Trust is chaired by James Miller (President of Club, 1991–2) and has David Newton (President, 2001–2) as its Secretary and Peter Taylor (President, 1983–5) as its Treasurer.

11 SED File ED48/1921 p. 8.

12 Watt, 'Introduction and Development', p. 406.

13 These values could equally well apply to the HSfG.

14 Ashmall, *High School*, pp. 143–8. Note how different this list is from that of its critics.

15 Indeed relations between the Club, under its President Gordon Wishart, and the School, are at a historic high.

16 Which was the 'complaint' levelled against the old HS by HMI in the early 1970s.

17 Helped greatly by the loyalty and support of the Old Girls of the Girls' High.

18 The new School has nothing to equate with the significant contribution of the Jewish contingent to Elmbank Street.

19 Gary McCulloch: 'From Incorporation to Privatisation: Public and Private Secondary Education in Twentieth-Century England' in Richard Aldrich (ed.): *Public or Private Education? Lessons from History* (London 2004) pp. 53–74.

20 Ted Tapper: *Fee-Paying Schools and Educational Change in Britain: Between the State and the Market-Place* (London, 1997) pp. 170–200.

21 Dennis MacLeod and Michael Russell: *Grasping the Thistle* (Argyll 2006), esp. pp. 160–5. Happily, in February 2010, he supported the 'radical' plans of East Lothian Council.

22 A new relationship with Glasgow Cathedral was begun in session 2007–8 when the newly appointed minister, Rev. Dr Laurence Whitley, accepted the position of the High School Chaplain.

BIBLIOGRAPHY

PRIMARY SOURCES

The Mitchell Library houses major sources of material indispensable to any research on the history of the School:

Following the advent of the Grammar School Committee (GSC) in October 1786 (renamed the High School Committee – HSC – in 1834) the practice grew up of each Convener collecting and keeping custody of its records and minutes during his term of office and then, when appropriate, handing them on to his successor. This seemed to work reasonably well until Henry Paul (1791–1860) was Convener between 1833 and 1839. When he left the Council it seems that he (and later his heirs) kept the documentation. This probably explains why it was not used in the 1878 history of the School. However, at some point, we know not when, it arrived in the Mitchell, and in 1972 it was organised for use by researchers by Hamish B. Whyte. The Calendar of High School Papers, 1790–1840 (typescript, Glasgow 1972) was available to Harry Ashmall when he was writing his 1976 history.

The bulk of papers cover the years 1820–40, and within that span about half the total cover the period 1834–40. They consist mainly of personal letters, joint letters (from schoolmasters) and reports: the transactions of the committee and their dealings with the schoolmasters. There are also Class Books covering 1790–1835, giving names of pupils in each class, examination marks, and a note of prizes. They can be found in the strong room in two boxes: MS140/1-15 and MS140/16 and 17, and are referenced in the footnotes as HS. Of especial use were HS1/2; HS1/6; HS2/14; HS2/25; HS2/35; HS2/39; HS3/9; HS4/1; HS5/22; HS6/13; HS6/16; HS7/8b; HS9/1-2; HS11/1-15; HS14/1; HS14/2; HS14/6; HS15/2; HS16/3; HS16/4; HS17/1; and HS 17/2 Appendix.

The Robert H. Small Papers were collected by the former Head of Classics at the High School for a projected history of the School. They can be found in four boxes: TD 408, boxes 1–4. Box 1 has significant material on Rectors of Glasgow Grammar School; Box 2 has a great wealth of information on Glasgow Council Committees and Minutes; Boxes 3 and 4 have press material, most of little relevance to the School. This material was also available to Harry Ashmall.

Minutes of the sub-committee of the Town Council which dealt with educational matters – High School and Education (HSE) Minutes, March 1844–May 1873 – can be found at C2/17.

Material on Macarthur's Fourth and Fifth Classes are stored at MS147, while material on his Sixth Class can be found at MS146.

The Mitchell also houses:
Glasgow Town Council Act Books (GTCAB), Series 1, especially:
Vol. 17 May 1683– July 1689
Vol. 35 March 1772–September 1777
Vol. 37 December 1781–March 1786
Vol. 38 March 1786–October 1789
Vol. 40 November 1791–October 1793
Vol. 50 October 1812–September 1814
Vol. 51 October 1814–April 1817
Vol. 61 February 1837–December 1838
Vol. 64 May 1845–August 1847
Vol. 66 July 1850–October 1853
Vol. 67 November 1853–July 1858
Vol. 69 November 1864–November 1871

Minutes of Glasgow Corporation (GCM): Twenty volumes from December 1930 until
    1950.

Extracts from Records of Burgh of Glasgow:
Sir James Marwick:
Volume I, 1573–1642 (Glasgow 1876)
Volume II, 1630–1662 (Glasgow 1881)
Volume of Charters and Documents I: Relating to Glasgow 1175–1649 (Glasgow 1894)
Preface to Volume on Charters and Documents (Glasgow 1897)

Sir James Marwick and Robert Renwick:
Volume III 1663–1690 (Glasgow 1905)
Volume of Charters and Documents II (1547–1638) (Glasgow 1906)
Volume IV 1691–1717 (Glasgow 1908)

Robert Renwick:
Volume V 1718–1738 (Glasgow 1909)
Volume VI 1739–1759 (Glasgow 1911)
Volume VII 1760–1780 (Glasgow 1912)
Volume VIII 1781–1795 (Glasgow 1913)
Volume IX 1796–1808 (Glasgow 1914)
Volume X 1809–1822 (Glasgow 1915)
Volume XI 1823–33 (Glasgow 1916)
Abstract of Charters and Documents 1833–1872 (Glasgow 1917)

Register of Privy Council of Scotland (PCS)
John Hill Burton (ed.): Register of PCS 1st series vol. 2 1569–78 (Edinburgh 1878)
David Masson (ed.): Register of PCS 1st series vol. 5 1592–9 (Edinburgh 1882)
David Masson (ed.): Register of PCS 1st series vol. 6 1599–1604 (Edinburgh 1884)
David Masson (ed.): Register of PCS 1st series vol. 13 1622–5 (Edinburgh 1897)

Church Records
C. Innes (ed.): *Registrum Episcopatus Glasguensis* (Bannatyne Club, 1843)
Register of Presbytery of Glasgow, October 1592–February 1608
Register of the Presbytery of Lanark, 1623–1709 (Edinburgh, Abbotsford Club, 1839)

Minutes of School Board (1873–1919) (MSB)
Vol. 1 (1873–8) D-ED1/1/1/1 (Mitchell catalogue) to D-ED1/1/1/22 (1918–19)
Vol. 2 (1879–84) D-ED1/1/1/2
Vol. 3 (1884–90) D-ED1/1/1/3
Vol. 4 (1891–6) D-ED1/1/1/4
Vol. 5 (1901–2) D-ED1/1/1/5
Then annually from 1902–03 (Vol. 6) until 1918–19 (Vol. 22)

General Summary of Board Work 1873–1903, Glasgow 1903, D-ED7/96/2

Minutes of the Education Authority for the Burgh of Glasgow (MEA): Eleven
    volumes from 1919 until 1930. D-ED2/1/1 (1919–20) to D-ED2/1/11 (1929–30)

Newspapers

Bailie: 14, 21 and 28 April 1875; 12 May 1875; 19 May 1875; 30 June 1875; 25 April 1877;
    13 April 1892; 27 November 1904
Glasgow Argus: 4 and 11 November 1839
Glasgow Courant: 27 September 1756
Glasgow Courier: 30 September 1802; 19 January 1809; 8 January 1811; 13 March 1813; 5
    June 1817; 23 September 1819; 3 October 1820; 3 October 1826
Glasgow Evening News: 19 October 1891
Glasgow Evening Times: 11 April 1967
Glasgow Free Press: 9 and 16 April; 7 May, 1823
Glasgow Herald (*GHerald*): 11 January 1811; 20 August 1819; 9 October 1820; 20 July
    1821; 13 October 1828; 11 and 14 June 1830; 5 May 1837; 2 and 6 October 1837; 26
    February 1852; 10 September 1852; 3 March 1853; 12 May 1853; 31 August 1854; 21
    September 1854; 1 December 1854; 11 January 1902; 16 August 1907; 27 April 1910;
    4 December 1920; 16 June 1944; 28 February 1949; 30 March 1949; 7 April 1949;
    30 April 1949; 25 June 1949; 4 July 1949; 24 December 1949; 24 June 1950; 7
    March 1967; 23 January 1969; 9, 15 and 24 March 1972; 4 May 1972; 9 August
    1972; 28 April 1973; *Herald*: 8 April 2009
Glasgow Journal: 9 November 1741; 2 April 1753; 27 September 1756; 15 July 1762
Glasgow Mercury: 10 December 1778; 18 July 1787
Literary Register: 8 February, 15 March and 22 March, 1823
Scots Times: 6 October 1827; 8 May 1832

Reports

(Old) Statistical Account 1791–1799, Vol. 5: Glasgow, County of Lanark.
Education Commission (Scotland): Second Report of Argyll Commission on
    Elementary Schools (Edinburgh 1867), Vol. 14: Scotland Part II.

Education Commission (Scotland): *Third Report on Burgh and Middle-Class Schools* (Edinburgh 1868), Vols I and II special reports.
Schools Inquiry (Taunton) Commission, Vol. VI: Burgh Schools in Scotland (1868)
Colebrooke Commission (Scotland): Appendix to Third Report of Royal Commission into Endowed Schools and Hospitals (1875) Vol. I pp. 327–61

Miscellaneous

Garnethill School for Girls' Log Book (D-ED7/96/2)
Garnethill Public School Letter Book Vol. 2 (1894–5); Vol. 3 (1895–8) (E-ED7/96/6)
Minutes of Form Masters' meetings (6 October 1903–10 October 1907)

Primary Sources, High School

The other major source of primary material is the High School itself. Louis de Banzie began to organise the historical material, and he made a considerable contribution, particularly with his Inventory, Scrapbook and Chronology. With the writing of this book, it was important to build on his work, and Audrey Mackie itemised and catalogued material which had found its way to the archive room in recent years. The Development Office, in the person of Katie Keenan, has been the other invaluable source of information and help, particularly with the FP profiles and the history of the Glasgow High School for Girls.

The following material, found at the School, has been of particular importance:
High School for Girls' Prospectuses (GHSGP) 1907–1916
High School for Girls' Magazines (GHSGM) from No. 7 issued in December 1922 until no. 54 issued in 1969 (no. 1 issued in January 1920)
High School of Glasgow Prospectuses (HSGP) from 1874–5 to 1910–11
High School of Glasgow Magazines:
The original magazine was the magazine of the Literary Society, 1896–7 (produced by Alexander Montgomerie in eight double-columned pages), but no copies are extant.
From December 1901 it was issued three times a year (December; March/April, and June) until 1943, when it became twice a year (December and June). From 1956, it was published annually, in June, until 1976. The new High School has produced an annual Magazine since then.
Reports of the University Examiners
Under the School Board, annual inspections took place, recorded in: the First Report (1873–4) to the Fifteenth Report (1887–8)
Annual Prospectus:
The High School also produced a Prospectus from 1874–5 until 1910–11
High School of Glasgow Registers:
The School has two Registers: the small Register from 1 September 1902 to 2 September 1908; and the large Register from 1909 to 1972.
High School Ledger of Staff Appointments and Registers (Ref. 04/62/304)

SECONDARY SOURCES

Early Printed Sources (before 1900, in chronological order)

James Arbuckle and Thomas Griffith: *Prologue and Epilogue of Tamarlane* (Glasgow 1721)

Tobias Smollett: *The Expedition of Humphry Clinker* (London 1771)

R. Roberston: *The Trial of Thomas Muir* (Edinburgh 1793)

Thomas Crauford: *History of the University of Edinburgh from 1580–1646* (Edinburgh 1808)

Rev. James Kirkton: *The Secret and True History of the Church of Scotland* (Edinburgh 1817)

James Cleland: *Historical Account of The Grammar School of Glasgow* (Glasgow 1825), which was incorporated along with Thomas Muir: *A Sketch of the History from 1825 to 1877* into *The History of The High School of Glasgow* (Glasgow 1878) edited, with a memoir of Dr Cleland, by James Cleland Burns

Robert Wodrow: *Life of James Wodrow, Professor of Divinity in the University of Glasgow* (Edinburgh 1828)

James Cleland: *Annals of Glasgow, Comprising an Account of the Public Buildings, Charities, and the Rise and Progress of the City* (Edinburgh 1829)

Rev. G. R. Gleig: *The Life of Major-General Sir Thomas Munro* (London 1830) 3 vols

Donald Cuthbertson: *Addresses Delivered at the Annual Distribution of Prizes to the Pupils of Glasgow Grammar School from 1828 to 1833* (Glasgow 1833)

James Carrick Moore *The Life of Sir John Moore* (London 1834)

High School of Glasgow, *Proceedings at Annual Distribution of Prizes*: October 3, 1834 (Glasgow 1834); 1836 (Glasgow 1836); September 26, 1838 (Glasgow 1838) and 26 September 1839 (Glasgow 1839)

A.D. Bache: *Report on Education in Europe* (Philadelphia 1839)

Report by a Committee on the High School, as to the Future Constitution and Government of the School (Glasgow n.d.)

David Laing (ed.): *The Letters and Journals of Robert Baillie* (Edinburgh 1841–2) vol. 3

William Arnot: *Memoir of James Halley* (2nd edn Edinburgh 1842)

Testimonials in Favour of Mr J.A. Hutchison for the Situation of Drawing Master (Glasgow 1843)

James Miller: *The Lamp of Lothian, Or, The History of Haddington in Connection with the Public Affairs of East Lothian and of Scotland from the Earliest Records to the Present Period* (Haddington 1844)

Robert Wodrow: *Collections upon the Lives . . .* (Glasgow, Maitland Club 1845) vol. 2 part 1

A Brief Historical Relation . . . of Mr. John Livingston . . . in *Select Biographies* (Wodrow Society, Edinburgh 1845) vol. 1

Samuel Lewis: *A Topographical Dictionary of Scotland* (London 1846) 2 vols

Thomas McCrie (ed.): *The Life of Mr. Robert Blair, Containing his Autobiography from 1593 to 1636* (Edinburgh, Wodrow Society 1848) vols 1 and 2

William Beattie: *Life and Letters of Thomas Campbell* (Glasgow 1849) 3 vols

Robert Reid (Senex): *Glasgow, Past and Present* (Glasgow 1851) 3 vols

J. Spottiswoode: *History of the Church of Scotland* (ed. M. Napier and M. Russell) 3 vols Spottiswoode Society (1851)

Sketch and Catalogue of Mr. Douie's Second Class, with Added Supplement (Glasgow 1852)

Hugh Miller: *An Autobiography: My Schools and Schoolmasters; Or, The Story of My Education* (Edinburgh 1854)

Robert Chambers: *A Biographical Dictionary of Eminent Scotsmen* (Edinburgh 1855)

John Hill Burton (ed.): *Autobiography of the Rev. Dr. Alexander Carlyle 1722–1805 Containing Memorials* (Edinburgh 1860; London 1910)

Robert Reid (Senex) *Glasgow and its Environs: Historical and Topographical* (London 1864)

Alexander Penrose Forbes (ed.): *The Historians of Scotland: Lives of S. Ninian and S. Kentigern* vol. 5 (Edinburgh 1874)

James Grant: *The History of the Burgh Schools of Scotland* (London 1876)

Lawrence Shadwell: *The Life of Colin Campbell, Lord Clyde* (Edinburgh 1881)

James Grant: *Cassell's Old and New Edinburgh: Its History, its People and its Places* (London 1882)

James MacLehose: *Memoirs and Portraits of One Hundred Glasgow Men* (Glasgow 1886)

Sir John N. Cuthbertson: *Secondary Education from the School Board Point of View* (Glasgow 1887)

James Hedderwick: *Backward Glances* (Edinburgh 1891)

John McMath: *Progress of School Building in Glasgow from 1873 to 1892* (Glasgow 1892)

John Edgar: *History of Early Scottish Education* (Edinburgh 1893)

Sir William Fraser: *The Annandale Family Book of the Johnstones* (Edinburgh 1894) vol. 1

Andrew Aird: *Glimpses of Old Glasgow* (Glasgow 1894)

Archibald Forbes: *Colin Campbell, Lord Clyde* (London 1895)

Andrew Lang: *Life and Letters of John Gibson Lockhart* (London 1897) 2 vols

George Eyre-Todd: *The Book of Glasgow Cathedral* (Glasgow 1898)

J. Cuthbert Hadden: *Thomas Campbell* (Edinburgh 1899)

Modern Printed Sources (after 1900, in alphabetical order)

R.J.Q. Adams: *Bonar Law* (London 1999)

Alan O. Anderson: *Early Sources of Scottish History A.D. 500 to 1286* vol. 1 (Edinburgh 1922)

Mosa Anderson: *St. Ninian: Light of the Celtic North* (London 1964).

R.D. Anderson: *Education and Opportunity in Victorian Scotland: Schools and Universities* (Oxford 1983)

R.D. Anderson: *Education and the Scottish People, 1750–1918* (Oxford 1995)

Harry A. Ashmall: *The High School of Glasgow* (Edinburgh 1976)

G.W.S. Barrow: *Robert Bruce and the Community of the Realm of Scotland* (4th edn Edinburgh 2008).

Neil Baxter (ed.): *A Tale of Two Towns: A History of Medieval Glasgow* (Glasgow 2008)

A.J. Belford: *Centenary Handbook of the Educational Institute of Scotland* (Edinburgh 1946)

James Bridie: *One Way of Living* (London 1939)

Gordon Brown: *Maxton* (Edinburgh 1986)

Keith M. Brown: *Noble Society in Scotland: Wealth, Family and Culture, from Reformation to Revolution* (Edinburgh 2004)

Stanley Brown: *Memoirs of a Secondary School Teacher* (privately published, 2000)

T.G.K. Bryce and W.M. Humes (eds): *Scottish Education: Beyond Devolution* (3rd edn Edinburgh 2008)

John Buchan: *Montrose* (London 1928)

J. Butt: *John Anderson's Legacy: The University of Strathclyde and its Antecedents 1796– 1996* (East Linton 1996)

John Campbell: *Margaret Thatcher, Vol. 1: The Grocer's Daughter* (London 2001 edn)

Jon Cannon: *Cathedral: The Great English Cathedrals and the World That Made Them* (London 2007)

Sir James L. Caw: *Sir James Guthrie: A Biography* (London 1932)

Chocolate and Gold: 100 years of Rugby, 1884–1984 (Glasgow, 1984)

James Colville: *Some Old-Fashioned Educationists* (Edinburgh 1907)

G.C. Coulton: *Scottish Abbeys and Social Life* (Edinburgh 1933)

James Coutts: *A History of the University of Glasgow, from its Foundation in 1451 to 1909* (Glasgow 1909)

Edward J. Cowan: *Montrose: For Covenant and King* (London 1977)

Ian B. Cowan: *The Medieval Church in Scotland* (ed. James Kirk) (Edinburgh 1995)

James Cowan: *From Glasgow's Treasure Chest* (Glasgow 1951)

Roger Day: *The Life of Sir John Moore: Not a Drum was Heard* (Barnsley 2001)

T.M. Devine and Gordon Jackson (eds): *Glasgow, Volume I: Beginnings to 1830* (Manchester 1995)

David Dobson *Scottish Schoolmasters of the Seventeenth Century* (St Andrews 1995)

John Dowden: *The Medieval Church in Scotland: Its Constitution, Organisation and Law* (Glasgow 1910)

John Dowden: *The Bishops of Scotland, Being Notes on the Lives of All the Bishops, under Each of the Sees, prior to the Reformation* (Glasgow 1912) (ed. J. Maitland Thomson)

Stephen T. Driscoll: *Excavations at Glasgow Cathedral 1988–1997* (Leeds 2002)

Charles Duguid: *Doctor Goes Walkabout* (Adelaide 1977)

Joe Dullerson: *Education for Losers – Memoirs of a Dunce* (Author House 2005)

A.D. Dunlop: *Hutchesons' Grammar: The History of a Glasgow School* (Glasgow 1992)

John Durkan and James Kirk: *The University of Glasgow, 1451–1577* (Glasgow 1977)

George Eyre-Todd: *Who's Who in Glasgow* (Glasgow 1909 and 1929)

Richard Fawcett: *Scottish Cathedrals* (London 1997)

Ian Flett: *The Association of Directors of Education in Scotland: The Years of Growth, 1945–75* (ADES 1989)

Carol Foreman: *Lost Glasgow: Glasgow's Lost Architectural Heritage* (Edinburgh 2002)

W. Hamish Fraser and Irene Maver (eds): *Glasgow Volume II: 1830–1912* (Manchester 1996)

James E. Fraser: *From Caledonia to Pictland: Scotland to 795* (Edinburgh 2009)

Stanley Brice Frost: *James McGill of Montreal* (Montreal 1995)

James Gourlay (ed.): *The Provosts of Glasgow from 1609 to 1832* (Glasgow 1942)

Gowans and Gray (publishers): *The Lord Provosts of Glasgow from 1833 to 1902: Biographical Sketches* (Glasgow 1912)

Brian M. Halloran: *The Scots College Paris, 1603–1792* (Edinburgh 1997)

Max Hastings: *Montrose: The King's Champion* (London 1979)

John Highet: *A School of One's Choice: A Sociological Study of the Fee-Paying Schools of Scotland* (London 1969)

Geoff Holder: *The Guide to Mysterious Glasgow* (Stroud, 2009)

Rab Houston: *Scotland: A Very Short Introduction* (Oxford 2008)

Les Howie et al.: *George Watson's College: An Illustrated History* (Edinburgh 2006)

Walter M. Humes and Hamish M. Paterson: *Scottish Culture and Scottish Education, 1800–1980* (Edinburgh 1983)

A.F. Hutchison: *History of the High School of Stirling* (Stirling 1904)

Harriet Jay: *Robert Buchanan* (London 1903)

Ken Jones: *Education in Britain 1944 to the Present* (Cambridge 2003)

John Kerr: *Scottish Education: Schools and University from Early Times to 1908* (Cambridge 1910)

H.M. Knox: *Two Hundred and Fifty Years of Scottish Education, 1696–1946* (Edinburgh 1953)

Pat Lally: *Lazarus Only Done it Once* (London 2002)

Alexander Law: *Education in Edinburgh in the Eighteenth Century* (London 1965)

A.F. Leach: *The Schools of Medieval England* (2nd edn London 1916)

T.A. Lee: *Seekers of Truth: The Scottish Founders of Modern Public Accountancy* (Oxford 2006)

Michael Lynch: *Scotland: A New History* (London 1992)

M. Lynch (ed.) *The Oxford Companion to Scottish History* (Oxford 2007)

Jane McDermid: *The Schooling of Working-Class Girls in Victorian Scotland: Gender, Education and Identity* (Abingdon 2005)

Norman Macdougall: *James IV* (Edinburgh 1989)

I.D.McFarlane: *Buchanan* (Bristol 1981)

Colin H. Mackay: *Kelvinside Academy 1878–1978* (Glasgow 1978)

Ray McKenzie: *Public Sculpture of Glasgow* (Liverpool 2002)

J.D. Mackie: *The University of Glasgow, 1451–1951: A Short History* (Glasgow 1954)

Martha McLaren: *British India and British Scotland, 1780–1830* (Akron, Ohio 2001)

Dennis MacLeod and Michael Russell: *Grasping the Nettle* (Argyll 2006)

Iain MacLeod: *The Glasgow Academy* (Glasgow 1997)

Andrew McPherson and Charles D. Raab: *Governing Education: A Sociology of Policy since 1945* (Edinburgh 1988)

Roger Marjoribanks: *Emanuel at Wandsworth 1883–1983* (London 1983)

James Mavor *My Windows on the Street of the World* (London 1992)

J.O. Mitchell: *Old Glasgow Essays* (Glasgow 1905)

Alexander Morgan: *Rise and Progress of Scottish Education* (Edinburgh 1927)

Alan Mould: *The English Chorister: A History* (London 2007)

Lynda Mugglestone: *Talking Proper: The Rise of Accent as Social Symbol* (Oxford 2003)

James Murray: *The History of Allan Glen's School and School Club 1853–2003* (Glasgow 2003)

John Murray: *A History of The Royal High School* (Edinburgh 1997)

M. Odgers: *Alexander Dallas Bache* (Philadelphia 1947)

Richard Oram: *David I: The King who Made Scotland* (Stroud 2004)

Nicholas Orme: *Medieval Schools: From Roman Britain to Renaissance England* (New Haven 2006)

Michael Page: *Turning Points in the Making of Australia* (Adelaide 1980)

Lindsay Paterson: *Scottish Education in the Twentieth Century* (Edinburgh 2003)

F.L.M. Pattison: *Granville Sharp Pattison: Anatomist and Antagonist, 1791–1851* (Edinburgh 1987)

Henry Philip: *The Higher Tradition: A History of the Public Examinations in Scottish Schools and How They Influenced the Development of Secondary Education* (Dalkeith 1992)

George Pottinger: *The Secretaries of State for Scotland 1926–76: Fifty Years of the Scottish Office* (Edinburgh 1979)

Lance Price: *Where Power Lies: Prime Ministers and the Media* (London 2010)

H.M.B. Reid: *Divinity Principals of the University of Glasgow, 1545–1654* (Glasgow 1917)

Robert Renwick (ed.) [Sir James D. Marwick's] *Early Glasgow: A History of Glasgow from Earliest Times to 1611* (Glasgow 1911)

James M. Roxburgh: *The School Board of Glasgow 1873–1919* (London 1971)

James Scotland: *The History of Scottish Education, Vol. 1: From the Beginning to 1872* (London 1969)

Ronnie Scott *Death by Design: The True Story of the Glasgow Necropolis* (Edinburgh 2005)

C. Wilfrid Scott-Giles and Bernard V. Slater: *The History of Emanuel School, 1594–1964* (London 1966 and 1977)

John Strong: *A History of Secondary Education in Scotland: An Account of Scottish Secondary Education from Early Times to the Education Act of 1908* (Oxford 1909)

Halliday Sutherland: *A Time to Keep* (London 1934)

Ted Tapper: *Fee-Paying Schools and Educational Change in Britain: Between the State and the Market Place* (London 1997)

David Torrance: *The Scottish Secretaries* (Edinburgh 2006)

Nigel Watson: *A Tradition for Freedom: The Story of University College School* (London 2007)

D.E.R. Watt and A.L. Murray (eds): *Fasti Ecclesie Scoticanae Medii Aevi Ad Annum 1638* (Edinburgh 2003)

Alexander S. Waugh: *A Scottish Liberal Perspective: A Centenary Commemoration of Sir Henry Campbell-Bannerman 1836–1908* (privately published 2008)

Jack Webster: *Jack Webster's Aberdeen* (Edinburgh 2007)

C.V. Wedgwood: *Montrose* (Stroud 1952)

H.G. Wells: *Experiment in Autibiography, Vol. 1* (London 1934)

Gavin White: *The Scottish Episcopalian Church: A New History* (Glasgow 1998)

Katharine Whitehorn: *Selective Memory* (London 2007)

Elizabeth Williamson, Anne Riches and Malcolm Higgs: *The Buildings of Scotland: Glasgow* (London 1990)

J. Gwynn Williams: *The University College of North Wales: Foundations 1884–1927* (Cardiff 1985)

J. Maxwell Wood and John Copland: *Witchcraft and Superstitious Record in South-West Scotland* (Edinburgh 1911)

Articles

Robert Anderson: 'The History of Scottish Education, pre-1980' in T.G.K. Bryce and W.M. Humes (eds): *Scottish Education: Post Devolution* (3rd edn Edinburgh 2008)

H.C. Barnard: 'A Great Headmaster: John Lewis Paton (1863–1946)', *British Journal of Educational Studies* vol. 11 no. 1 (November 1962)

G.W.S. Barrow: 'David I and Glasgow' in G.W.S. Barrow (ed.): *The Kingdom of Scots* (2nd edn Edinburgh 2003)

Anne Bloomfield: 'Martina Bergman-Oesterberg (1849–1915): Creating a Professional Role for Women in Physical Training', *History of Education* vol. 34 no. 5 (September 2005)

Joan Bridgman: 'At School with Margaret Thatcher', *Contemporary Review* vol. 285, no. 1664 (September 2004)

R.H. Campbell; 'The Making of the Industrial City' in W.H. Fraser and Irene Maver: *Glasgow, Vol. II: 1830–1912* (Manchester 1996)

Thomas O. Clancy: 'The Real St Ninian', *Innes Review* vol. 52 (2001)

Thomas Clancy: 'Church Institutions' in M. Lynch (ed.) *The Oxford Companion to Scottish History* (Oxford 2007)

Ian B. Cowan: 'The Organisation of Secular Cathedral Chapters' in *The Medieval Church in Scotland* (ed. James Kirk) (Edinburgh 1995)

Marjorie Cruickshank: 'The Argyll Commission Report 1865–8: A Landmark in Scottish Education', *British Journal of Educational Studies* 15, no. 2 (June 1967)

Jo Ann H. Morgan Cruz: 'England: Education and Society' in S.H. Rigby (ed.): *A Companion to Britain in the Later Middle Ages* (Malden MA 2003)

T.M. Devine: 'The Golden Age of Tobacco' in T.M. Devine and Gordon Jackson (eds): *Glasgow: Vol. I* (Manchester 1996)

John Dougall: 'Peter Pinkerton' in *Proceedings of the Edinburgh Mathematical Society* (1930–1)

John Durkan: 'Education in the Century of the Reformation' in David McRoberts: *Essays on the Scottish Reformation 1513–1625* (Glasgow 1962)

John Durkan: 'Schools and schooling to 1696' in M. Lynch (ed.) *The Oxford Companion to Scottish History* (Oxford 2007)

John Durkan: 'Early Song Schools in Scotland' in *Notis Musycall: Essays in Honour of Kenneth Elliott* (eds Gordon Munro et al.) (Glasgow 2005)

D.E. Easson: 'The Medieval Church in Scotland and Education', *Records of the Scottish Church History Society*, 6 (1938)

Warwick Edwards: 'Polyphony in Thirteenth-Century Scotland' in Isobel Woods Preece: *Our Awin Scottis Use: Music in the Scottish Church up to 1603* (Glasgow 2000)

Mary E. Finn: 'Social Efficiency, Progressivism and Secondary Education in Scotland, 1885–1905' in Walter M. Humes and Hamish M. Paterson: *Scottish Culture and Scottish Education 1800–1980* (Edinburgh 1983)

Louise O. Fradenburg: 'Scotland: Culture and Society' in S.H. Rigby (ed.): *A Companion to Britain in the Later Middle Ages* (Malden MA 2003)

Lizanne Henderson: 'The Survival of Witchcraft Persecutions and Superstitious Record in South-West Scotland', *Scottish Historical Review*, vol. 85 no. 1 (April 2006)

P. Hill: 'Whithorn' in M. Lynch (ed.) *The Oxford Companion to Scottish History* (Oxford 2007)

Bill Inglis: 'Sir Henry Campbell-Bannerman and the Boer War 1899–1902', *History Scotland* vol. 8 no. 4 (July/August 2008)

John McCaffrey: 'Political Issues and Developments' in W. Hamish Fraser and Irene Maver (eds): *Glasgow Volume II: 1830–1912* (Manchester 1996)

Gary McCulloch: 'From Incorporation to Privitisation: Public and Private Secondary Education in Twentieth Century England' in Richard Aldrich (ed.): *Public or Private Education? Lessons for History* (London 2004)

James McGrath: 'The Medieval and Early Modern Burgh' in T.M. Devine and Gordon Jackson (eds): *Glasgow, Volume I: Beginnings to 1830* (Manchester 1995)

Charles McKean: 'Buildings and Cityscape', *The Glasgow Story 1770s to 1830s*, available online at http://www.theglasgowstory.com/story.php?id=TGSCF

David Murray: 'Some Early Grammars and Other School Books in Use in Scotland' in *Proceedings of the Royal Philosophical Society of Glasgow, 1905–1906* vol. 37 (Glasgow 1906)

Richard D. Oram: 'Prelatical Builders: A Preliminary Study *c*1124–*c*1500' in Richard D. Oram and Geoffrey P. Stell (eds): *Lordship and Architecture in Medieval and Renaissance Scotland* (Edinburgh 2005)

H.M. Paterson: 'Incubus and Ideology: The Development of Secondary Schooling in Scotland, 1900–1939' in Walter M. Humes and Hamish M. Paterson: *Scottish Culture and Scottish Education, 1800–1980* (Edinburgh 1983)

Lindsay Paterson: 'Schools and Schooling: Mass Education, 1872 to Present' in M. Lynch (ed.) *The Oxford Companion to Scottish History* (Oxford 2007)

J.N. Graham Ritchie, Gordon S. Maxwell and Alistair Gordon: 'Prehistoric, Roman and Early Historical Glasgow' in Elizabeth Williamson, Anne Riches and Malcolm Higgs: *Glasgow* (London 1990)

Alasdair F.B. Roberts: 'The Operation of the "Ad Hoc" Education Authority in Dunbartonshire between 1919 and 1930' in T.R. Bone (ed.): *Studies in the History of Scottish Education 1872–1939* (London 1967)

Norman F. Shead: 'Glasgow: An Ecclesiatical Burgh' in Michael Lynch, Michael Spearman and Geoffrey Stell (eds): *The Scottish Medieval Town* (Edinburgh 1988)

Norman F. Shead: 'Jocelin, Abbot of Melrose and Bishop of Glasgow', *Innes Review*, vol. 54 no. 1 (Spring 2003)

Norman F. Shead: 'Medieval Glasgow: Problems of Evidence', *Innes Review* vol. 55 no. 1 (Spring 2004)

Norman F. Shead: 'Greater Glasgow' in Neil Baxter (ed.): *A Tale of Two Towns: A History of Medieval Glasgow* (Glasgow 2008)

Richard B. Sher: 'Commerce, Religion and the Enlightenment in Eighteenth Century Glasgow' in T.M. Devine and Gordon Jackson (eds): *Glasgow, Volume I: Beginnings to 1830* (Manchester 1995)

Robert H. Small: 'The High School of Glasgow', *Scottish Field*, vol. III no. 732 (December 1963) pp. 70–5

Andrew Tennent: 'Statistics of a Glasgow Grammar School Class of 115 Boys', *Journal of the Statistical Society of London* vol. 18 no. 4 (Dec. 1855)

Richard Trainor: 'The Elite' in W. Hamish Fraser and Irene Maver (eds): *Glasgow Volume II: 1830–1912* (Manchester 1996)

D.E.R. Watt: 'Scotland: Religion and Piety' in S.H. Rigby (ed.): *A Companion to Britain in the Later Middle Ages* (Malden MA 2003)

Donald Withrington: 'Schools and Schooling, 1696–1872' in M. Lynch (ed.) *The Oxford Companion to Scottish History* (Oxford 2007)

Theses

Alastair F.W. Laing: '"Sursum Semper?" A Socio-historical Study of Educational Policy-making in Glasgow Following the Issue of Circular 600' (PhD Thesis, University of Edinburgh, 1984)

Gordon Munro: 'Scottish Church Music and Musicians, 1500–1700' (PhD Thesis, University of Glasgow, 1999)

Irene Sweeney: 'The Municipal Administration of Glasgow, 1833–1912: Public Service and the Scottish Civic Identity' (PhD Thesis, University of Strathclyde, 1990)

John Watt: 'The Introduction and Development of the Comprehensive School in the West of Scotland, 1965–80' (PhD Thesis, University of Glasgow, 1989)

INDEX

Notes

1. Sub-entries are arranged alphabetically, except where *chronological* order is more significant
2. The following abbreviations are used:
   FP former pupil; GGS Glasgow Grammar School; GHS Glasgow High School; HS New High School; HSfG High School for Girls; OG Old Girls; PT principal teacher/head of department; SB School Board; SC School Captain
3. Most references are to Glasgow, except where otherwise indicated.
4. Dates supplied with entries for people are *generally* those of their time at the school
5. Chapter extents are indicated by **bold** numbers

principals
  Alice Reid (1905–26) 171–5
  Flora Tebb (1926–47) 175–82
  Frances Barker (1947–69) 182–8
  Helen Jamieson (1970–6) 189–90
  pupils, significant 190–6, 203, 254–5,
    260, 264
  renamed Cleveden Secondary School
    264–5
Gleg, James 23
Gleig, Rev. G.R. 402
Glen, George (GGS Rector 1681–9) 25–6,
  31, 35
Glen, Thomas W. (1940–54) 211, 247
Glenorchy, Lady 110
Goldie, Alexander (1933–46) 210
Goodfellow, Jessie 175
Goodwin, Alfred 143
Goodwin, (Fritz) Shirley (GHS Rector
  1909–13) 143–5, 150
  House system instituted by (1910) 144
  portrayed *Plate 25*
Goodwin, Michael (1958–64) 272
Gordon, 'Greasy Mac' R. (classics master
  1928–49) 209
Gordon, Patrick (Dux 1880) 69
Gorrie, Margaret (maths mistress
  1938–70) 177
Goskirk, Donald (1947–60) 249
Gourlay, Robert (1841–1916) 116
Gow, Annie Scott (later Mrs King-Gillies,
  maths mistress 1913–39) 176
Gowans, Robert A. (1934–9) 212
Goyder, George (1826–98) 107
Graham, James Angus 1907–90) 7th
  Duke of Montrose 166
Graham, John (1573–1626) 4th Earl of
  Montrose 19, 33, 34
Graham, John (1612–59) 1st Marquess of
  Montrose (1612–50) 19
Graham, John (1828–1904) 116
Graham, John (1861–1943) and Katie
  153
Graham, Samuel (1972–6) 247
Graham Sir Norman (Scottish Education
  Department Secretary, 1973) 232, 259,
  262–3

Graham, Thomas (1805–69)/Graham's
  Law 82–3
Graham, William (1838–1909) 116
Graham-Gilbert, John (1794–1866) 86
Graham(e), James (1765–1811) 59
Grant, Alastair (science master 1955–65)
  213, 248
Grant, Davida (Junior School Deputy
  Head 1992) 312
Grant, Gordon (HS Club President
  2006–7) 315
Grant, James (1876/1882) 403
Grant, Michael (PT and history 1974–6)
  251
Grant, Vince (1962–73) 248
Grassom, Bob ('Shiny Bub', 1963–70) 246
Gray, Charles (1964–70) 275
Gray, James (1966–71) 275
Gray, J.H., Ltd 306
Gray, Very Rev. John (1913–84) 218, 287
Gray, Kathryn (left 1994, hockey
  international) 319
Gray, Mark (PT, art 1967–74) 250
Gray, Robert, Jr 49
Greek language 170, 173
  early 19th century 65, 68–9, 71, 75
  Gold Medal 113
  Greek Testament 68
  and School Board (1872–1918) 126, 128,
    129, 130, 137, 140, 142
Green, Margaret (Brunton Medal winner
  1934) 177
Gregory, W. Macdonald (science master
  1915–35) 211
Greig, James (Elementary Schools Report
  1867) 100
Griffin, Douglas (1965–73) 274
Griffith, Thomas 402
Grindlay, George (library bequest 1801)
  350
Grindlay (HSfG Janitor) 175
grocers, parents as 151
Gunn, Sir James (1893–1964) 165
Gunn, Parry (English master 1926–45)
  210
Guthrie, Isobel (early 20th century) 177
Guthrie, Sir James (1859–1930) 123

Mackie, Audrey xvii, 401

McKindlay, John 91

McKindlay, Patrick (Peter, classics master 1844–69) 90, 91, 102–3, 356
pupils of 110, 112, 113

McKinnon (*later* Donald), Dorothy 197

MacKinnon, Margaret 197

Mackinnon, Thomas (1912–81) 235

Mackintosh, Charles Rennie 191

Mackintosh, H. Stewart (Director of Education) 184, 187–8

Mackintosh, James (1891–1966) 157

Mackintosh, Rebecca (SC 2008) 231

McLachlan, Alastair (1940–2007) 271

Maclachlan, George (rugby coach 1949–61) 250

McLaren, Rev Alexander (1826–1910, pupil 1835) 109

McLaren, Catherine (Registrar 1940–68) 242, 285

McLaren, Hugh (1922–31) 221

MacLaren, Iain (architect) 307, 309

McLaren High School 249

Maclaurin, A.D. (Sandy) (1931–9) 231, 292

Maclay, David 309

Maclay, Sir Joseph, 1st Baron (1857–1951) 107

MacLean, Eoghainn (left 1984) 316

Maclean, Hector (1940–9) 227

Maclean, J. Dalziel (book-keeping, retired 1903) 149

Maclean, John (1771–1814) 57

McLean, Mary (HSfG mistress c.1927–50) 184

McLean, Robert (19th century advocate) 103

Maclean, Sir Robert (1920–5) 216, 307

McLean, Sheila (b.1951) 195

McLean, Sir William (1910–19) 158

MacLehose, James (1886) 403

McLellan, Douglas (1967–72) 269

McLellan, John (1971–4) 276

McLellan, Robert (art master 1957–67) 250

Maclennan, Alexander (1872–1953) 155

MacLennan, Sir Hector (1918–23) 220

Maclennan, John (SC, left 1993) 317

McLennan, Marcella (née Mackay: OG's President 1996) 197

McLennan, Sheila (OG's secretary 1931–3) 196

Macleod, Dennis 397

Macleod, Donald (1950–63) 272

Macleod, Sir Frederick (1858–1936): Macleod & Co. 108

McLeod, Walter (1915–2008) 235

McLintock, Sir William, 1st Baronet (1873–1947) 161

Macliver, Colin *see* Campbell, Colin

Macliver, Peter (1822–91) 86

MacMahon (née Gallacher), Rev. Janet 194

McManus, Isa (Junior School teacher 1972–95) 311

McMath, John 403

Macmillan, Edith (grand-daughter of Rector Hutchison: bequest 1998) 309

MacMillan, Heather (née Kelly, Old Girls' President 1990) 197

Macmillan, Hector (English master 1949–62) 246

McMillan, John (classics master 1837–44) 88, 90, 116

Macmillan, Peter (maths master 1973–4) 247

Macmillan (in Selection Committee 1982) 295

Macmillan Building (1999) 309

Macnab, Allan (writing and book-keeping teacher) 95

McNab, Donald (maths master 1958–65) 247

McNabb, Elizabeth (PT classics from 1926) 177

Macnair, Terence (b.1942) 269

McNeil, Hector (Secretary of State) 382

McNeil, Sergeant (PE assistant) 149

McNeill, Major-General Alistair (1884–1971) 154

McNeill, Kirsty (left 1997) 318

McNicol, Cameron 249

MacNicol, Rev. Nicol (1870–1952) 153

music
 careers of former pupils 165, 249, 318
 and School Board (1872–1918) 135, 140,
   146, 149
 twentieth century and new beginnings
   170, 186, 212, 249, 288, 289, 311
 practice rooms created 307
 twenty-first century 314, 321, 323
Mythology lessons 74

Natural Philosophy 75, 95
Natural Science/Natural History 97, 172
 and School Board (1872–1918) 126, 128,
   129, 148
Navigation as subject 75
needlework 172
Neil, Ronald (1947–61) 276
Neilson, Peter (1795–1861) 76
new beginning (1977) 251, **278–95**, 296,
   389–93
 Appeal 285–7
 Drewsteignton School 249, 251,
   278–82
 High School Club 282–4
 Old Anniesland 287–94
'New Building' (1934) 203
New Curriculum/Optional Curriculum
   (1874) 128–9, 142
new Grammar School on George Street
   (1789–1820) 46–7
 Class Meetings (reunions of old
   pupils) 49
 masters and classes 47–9
new Grammar School on John Street
   (1820) 61–86
 class meetings 64
 masters 63–4
 rector (1815–30) *see* Chrystal
New Zealand, ex-pupils in (1871) 103
Newton, Miss (welfare) 245
Newton, David 397
Nicholas V, Pope 8
Nicholson, Hon. John (1868–1941) 158
Nicol, Norman L. (science master
   1935–47) 211
Nicolson, Robert A. (1865–1923, FP and
   science master from 1887) 148

Nimmo, John (Dux prizes won 1790–3)
   69
Nina, Miss *see* Logan, (Agnes) Nina
Ninian, Saint 1–2, 329n
Niven, Janet (Brunton Medal winner
   1926) 177
Norman (née Love), Margaret (OG's
   President 1994) 197
Normand, Bruce 394
Normand, Hulbert C. (history master)
   140
Normanton, Helena (HSfG mistress
   1913–15) 172
Norrie Thomson Science block 292, 310
Northcliffe, Lord 164

Ogston, Jenny (drama mistress) 323
Old Anniesland: Plate 53
Old Anniesland 235
Old High School closed (1976) 285
Old Pedagogy (house in Rottenrow) 8
O'Neill, Arthur ('Paddy', Deputy Rector
   1966–73) 247–8
O'Neill, John (Deputy Rector 1996) 312,
   321–2, 323
Optional Curriculum (New Curriculum
   of 1874) 128–9, 142
Orr, Jack ('Daddy', PT and English
   1951–62) 246
Orr, Richard (classics 1965–9) 246
OTC (Officers' Training Corps) 144, 146,
   149, 209, 246
Ovid 29

Paddock (PT/drawing 1902–4) 149
Paisley, James (PT/music 1955–9) 249
Paisley, Robert (Dux prizes won 1818–21)
   69
Panvinius, Onuphrius 22
parents
 co-operation with 137, 289
 and fund-raising 306
 occupations of 151
 Parent–Teacher Association 176, 241
Park, Sir Maitland (1862–1921) 163
Park, Patric (1820–4) 86
Parker, Sir James (1811–12) 82